WIDNES

CLIFF HAYES

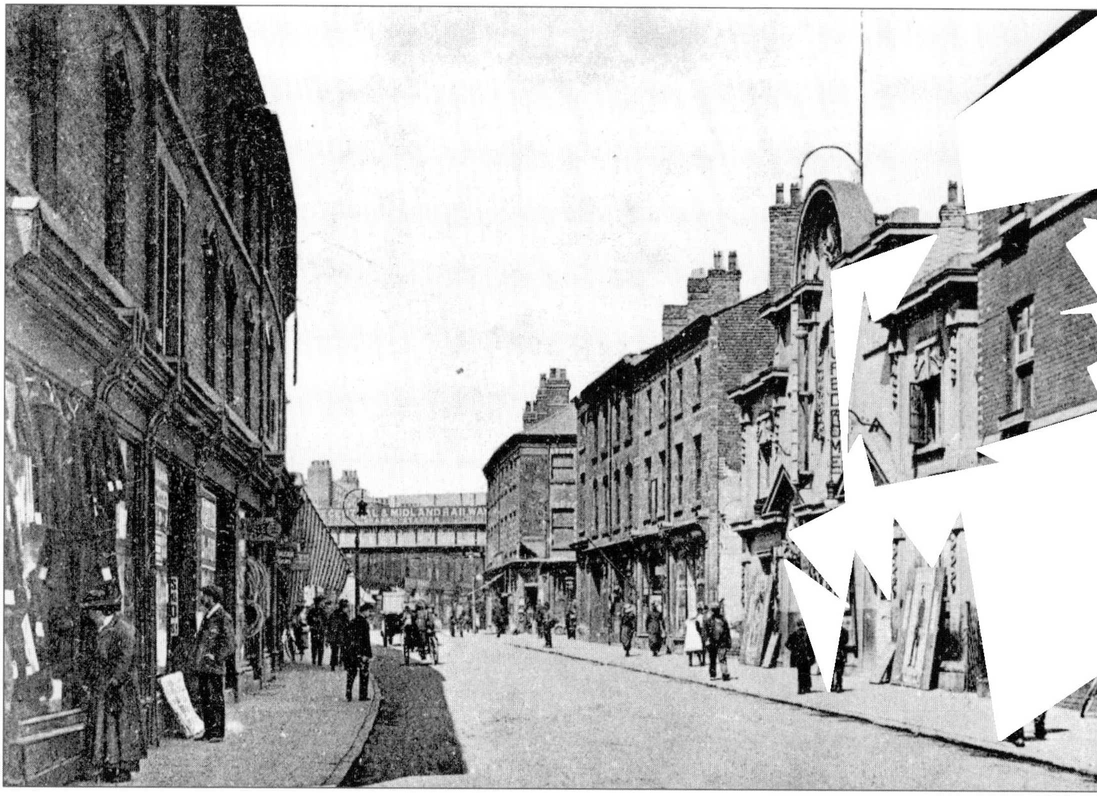

Victoria Road below Ditton Road, looking back into the town centre. The Picturedrome on the right was Widnes' fourth cinema; it opened on 17 December 1910 and closed in 1959. It was described in its opening publicity as 'the most luxurious and handsome building in Lancashire'. Admission was 2*d*, 4*d*, 6*d*, and 1*s* for a deluxe seat.

This book is very fondly dedicated to my parents May (née Barrow) and Alf Hayes who gave me a good start in life and a warm and happy home to remember, in the Ball O' Ditton.

BRITAIN IN OLD PHOTOGRAPHS

WIDNES

CLIFF HAYES

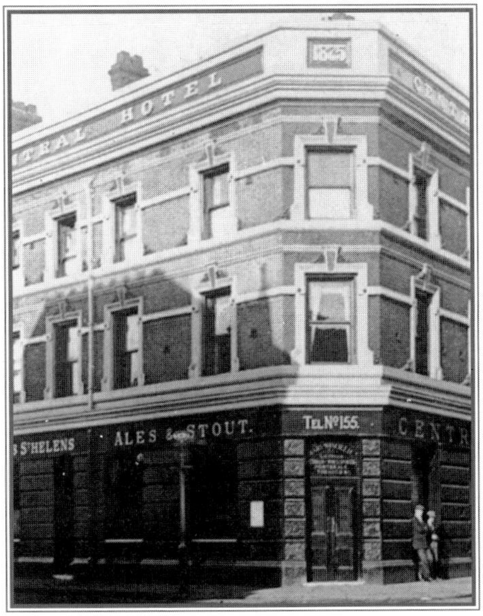

SUTTON PUBLISHING LIMITED

Sutton Publishing Limited
Phoenix Mill · Thrupp · Stroud
Gloucestershire · GL5 2BU

First published 1998

Title page photograph: The Central Hotel on the corner of Victoria Road and Ditton Road, 1930s. The doorway to the left was the snug and off-sales entrance, the one on the corner the public bar. I worked here as barman (midweek) for a couple of years in the early 1960s. Tuesday night would see me and six regulars in the bar, and half a dozen in the 'best' side. Mild was 1*s* 2*d* in the bar and 1*s* 4*d* in the best, while bitter was 2*d* dearer.

British Library Cataloguing in Publication Data
A catalogue record for this book is available from the British Library.

ISBN 0-7509-1691-5

Typeset in 10/12 Perpetua.
Typesetting and origination by
Sutton Publishing Limited.
Printed in Great Britain by
Ebenezer Baylis, Worcester.

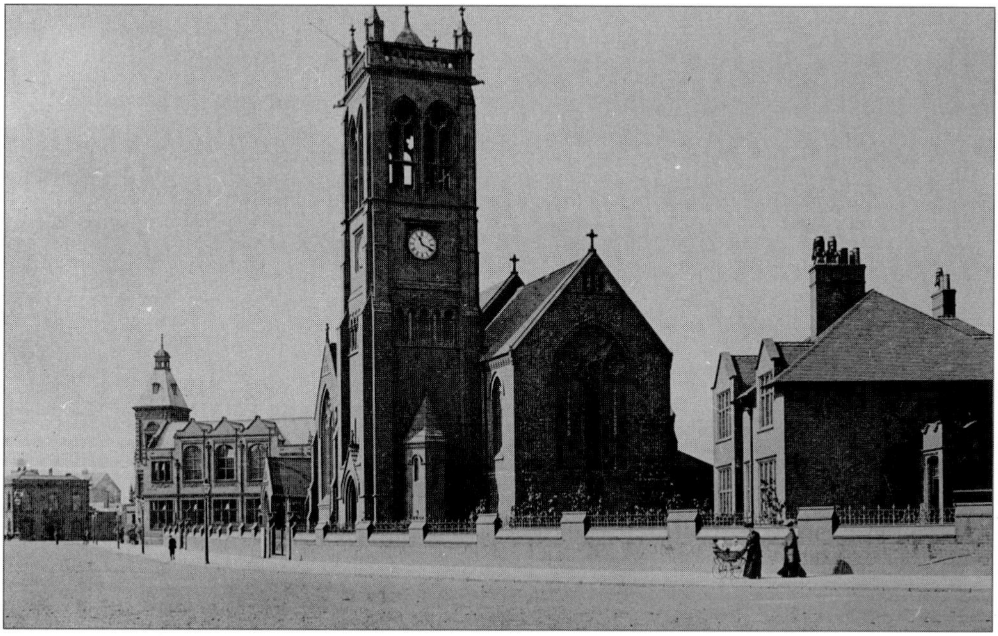

St Paul's Church in Victoria Square, Widnes, 1910. Here we see the church with its new tower and clock, added when St Paul's became independent from St Mary's West Bank, the mother church. The Bishop of Liverpool dedicated the new tower and clock on 20 September 1906.

Contents

ACKNOWLEDGEMENTS

Many of the photographs that I have used in this book come from the collection of Bob Martindale. Without his co-operation, the book would lack some unique and very interesting photographs. Bob is one of life's real gentlemen, one of those you only too rarely come across. Thanks also to the Ditton Dodger – Alan Potter the barber, or gentlemen's hairdresser, as they are known these days – for his football photographs, to Neville Conroy for permission to reproduce his photographs, and to Gordon Coltas for his great Locofotos. Thanks must also go to Kay Marshall and the staff at Widnes Library, always helpful and always supportive. Last but definitely not least, I should mention my relatives in Widnes, Olive and Harry Jones at Hough Green, Roy and Rita Jacks at Halton View, Keith Helsby (for his bridge photographs), Maureen of Ditton, Irene, Dave and the boys at Crow Wood, and many more (we're a big family the Hayes and the Barrows).

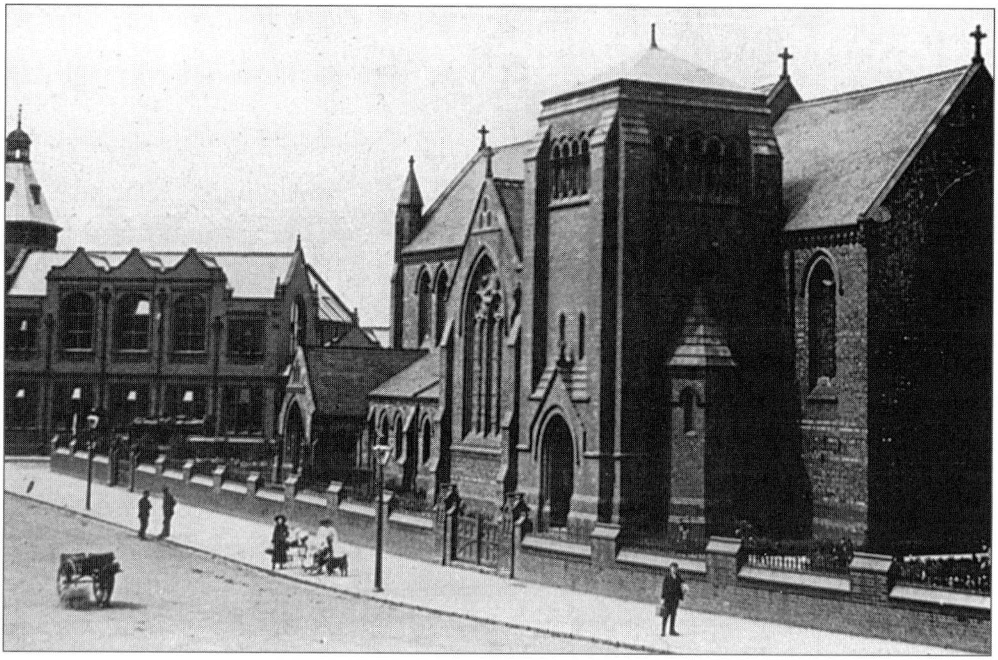

St Paul's Church, Victoria Square,1900. This is how the church looked when it was opened on 18 November 1884. The opening service was led by the Bishop of Liverpool, Revd Dr John Charles Ryle.

INTRODUCTION

The making of Widnes is not a complicated story. The town was formed out of the strong will and moral feelings of a group of men who came here in search of a future in chemicals.

Before 1820 the area was just a collection of villages. We can reliably say that the town of Widnes is made up from Hough Green, Ditton, Wood End, Appleton, Simms Cross, Farnworth and Cronton. These seven villages were agricultural. Hough Green, Ditton and Cronton were for a time under the control of West Derby, and later Childwall Abbey. Cuerdley came under the control of Warrington for a while.

After the Norman Conquest, Lancashire was put under the control of Roger de Poictou who parcelled it out between his men, and some who already lived here. The Barony of Widnes was created and included the areas of Huyton, Tarbock and Rainhill, as well as Appleton and Wood End. The first (and last) Baron de Widnes was one Yorfrid, although there were several variants on the name, such as Yardfrid. He did not think much of his grant and only came to Widnes when he was called for his final ruling on a court matter. In 1133 Yorfrid died, and as he had no male heir the land was split between his two daughters' husbands: William FitzNigel, the 2nd Baron of Halton, added Widnes to his title and became Baron of Halton and Widnes; Albert de Guella, 3rd Baron of Manchester, inherited the eastern edge of the area (Cuerdley, etc).

Widnes became a Crown possession under Halton and when Thomas Earl of Lancaster was beheaded for treason in the twelfth century the running of the area passed back to the north of the river. Courts were held in Farnworth for ownership, dues and the other disputes of the time, though guilty parties usually went to Halton Castle, and anyone demanding a re-trial or appeal had to make the journey to Halton. This was the reason for the granting of the first charter for a ferry.

In 1350 Henry, Duke of Lancaster, gave Widnes men (villeins) the right to become freemen, enabling them to choose their own bailiffs and later their own court officials. Strong and powerful families were settling the area. Hale and Cuerdley came under the Ireland family. Bold had long been the property of the Bold family, who also owned Farnworth; the Ditchfield family lived at Ditchfield Hall and owned Ditton and Hough Green. Part of Appleton came under the Harwarden family who lived at Upper House and the now forgotten hall called Fenilstreet. The area north of Appleton and Appleton village itself was controlled by the Appleton family who had given their name to the district. The giving of land as dowries altered the picture very little over the next 300 years.

The Reformation brought these families into prominence as they stuck firmly to the 'old' faith. In 1639 the area was noted for secret masses, houses with priests' holes and refusals to pay church rates. Blessed Ambrose Barlow (now a saint) was connected strongly with the area for about twenty years and he is recorded sneaking into Ditton Hall for a mass and lying low for weeks at Fenilstreet, Appleton, while the King's men searched for him. Blessed Edmund Arrowsmith also preached in the area, and in fact Widnes can boast a Catholic martyr, one Lawrence Hill who left Widnes and ended up in the service of Dr Thomas Godden, chaplain to Catholic Queen Catherine at Somerset House. He was hanged at Tyburn on 21 February 1679 after Titus Oates declared him a religious traitor in one of his purges.

Farnworth Wakes came in 1714, a 'mock' mayor was elected and the area began to put together the basis of self-government. The local lords of the manors and the Duchy of Lancaster let Farnworth make many of the decisions relating to the running of their village and the other villages in the area. The court was a rural court, and from Hough Green right down to Wood End was an agricultural area. This is how it entered the nineteenth century.

By the mid-1830s plans were well in hand for the St Helens Railway to extend to Widnes Dock. The canal was bringing in raw materials for the chemical industry, and the area was set to change dramatically for ever. It was said that a manufacturer could set up a factory and turn out chemicals more cheaply in Widnes than anywhere else in England.

The factories needed workers and it was obvious from the start that the villages could not supply enough hands. Word went out that there was work in Widnes and the employers set about putting up cheap quickly built houses for the influx of labourers. The Welsh settled in the West Bank area and found jobs in the new factories down there. The building of the railways brought the navvies into West Bank, and some of them decided to settle down there and send for their families. The Irish potato famine brought even more workers who settled in the Simms Cross area and around Victoria Road, where the factories had now spread. The building of the new railway bridge over the River Mersey, which started in 1864, provided work for thousands more.

All this was in place for the massive expansion that went into the making of Widnes.

CHAPTER ONE

THE TOWN

Widnes received its Charter of Incorporation which made it a town on 26 May 1892. The townsfolk had been trying for fifteen years to get the status of Municipal Borough, and the people felt that they and the town had worked hard and deserved it. The Local Board formed in the 1860s had looked after the town before that, but the astonishing rate of growth in the population of Widnes had pushed things forward.

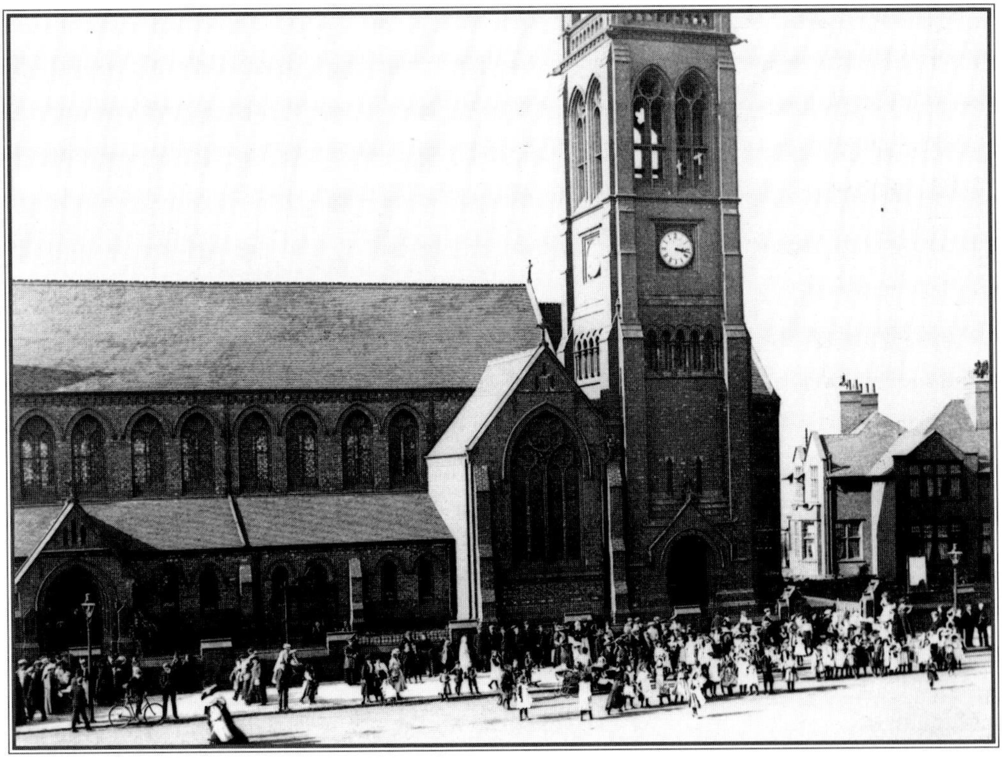

Victoria Square and St Paul's Church just after the dedication of the bells, 1907. When on 12 November 1910 the popular Bishop of Liverpool, Dr Chavasse, had led the opening of the church of St Mary at West Bank, these bells rang a peal of 'Bob Major'. It was rung by the Lancashire Association of Bellringers and contained 5,376 changes, lasting more than three hours.

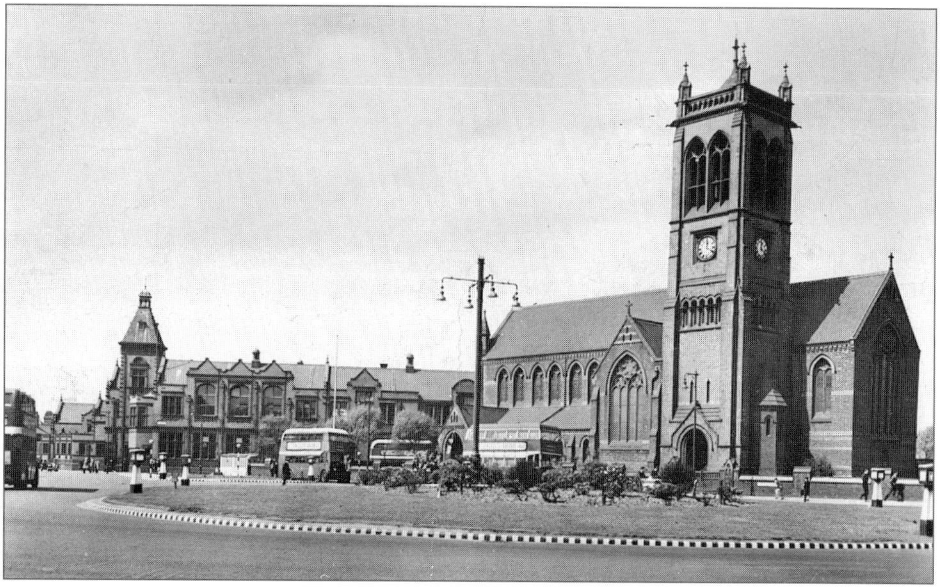

Victoria Square, early 1950s. The town hall area, Victoria Square and its buildings were created out of open fields, where Snig Lane met Moor Lane. The church opened in 1884, built on land that had been given in 1878 by the estate of John Gerard Leigh.

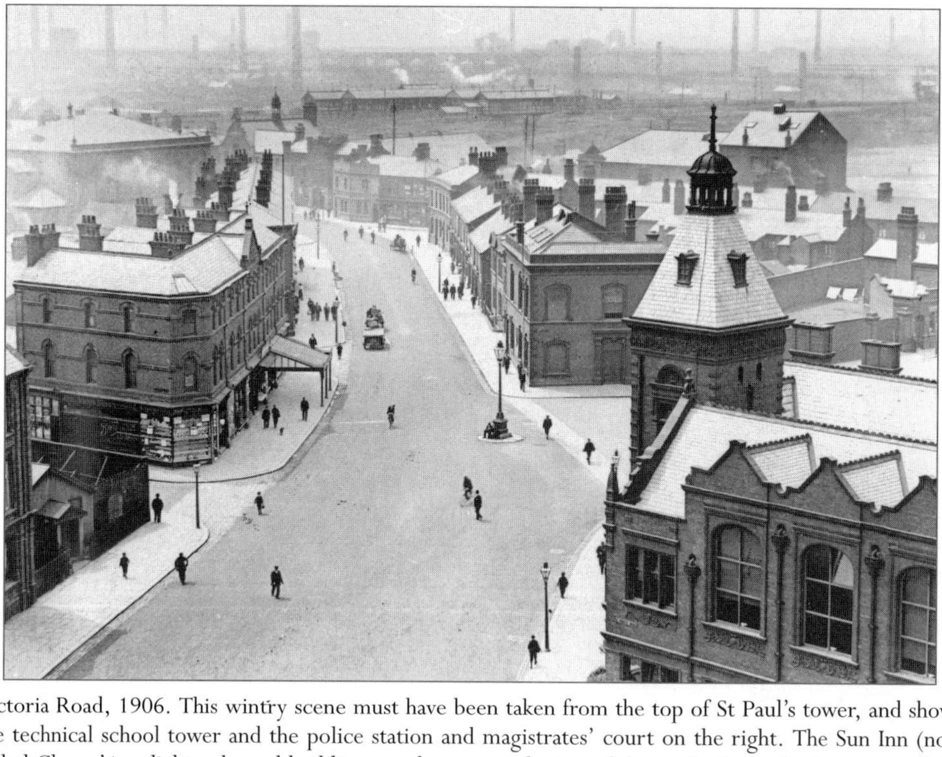

Victoria Road, 1906. This wintry scene must have been taken from the top of St Paul's tower, and shows the technical school tower and the police station and magistrates' court on the right. The Sun Inn (now called Clancy's), a light-coloured building, can be seen at the top of the road, almost in the centre of the picture, and the tall apex-roofed building at the right back was the Alexandra Theatre in Alexandra Street. Widnes Central station is the long low building in the centre back of the picture. You will have worked out by now where Victoria Road Methodist Chapel (now the Queen's Hall) stands.

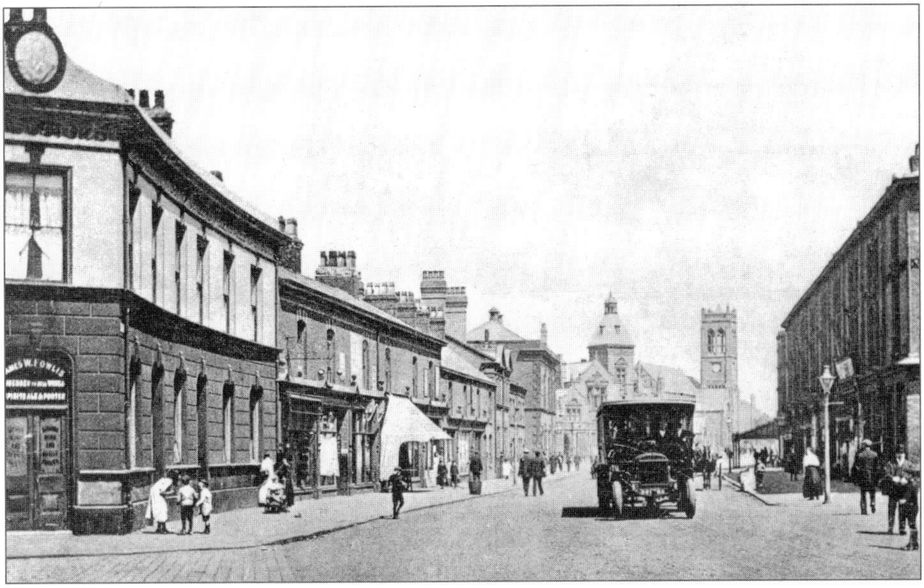

Victoria Road, looking from the corner of Alexandra Road/Whitt Road up to Victoria Square. The public house on the left had a proper name, the Alexandra Hotel, but it was always known as the Doctor's, after a certain Doctor Gerrard who kept the pub at the turn of the century. Even on this photograph from about 1912 the word Doctor's is painted on the narrow corner, above the name of James W. Fowlis, licensee, and the doctor's likeness is visible at the top of that corner. There was a great second-hand shop further up on the left, run by a Mr Jones: it was a mecca to the youngsters in Widnes in the 1950s. They would go there with objects they had found or junk that was being thrown out – and Mr Jones would buy. The shop was crammed full of surprises; you could rummage through the stacks of unwanted furniture, war paraphernalia, stuffed birds, old coins and medals – you name it, he had it!

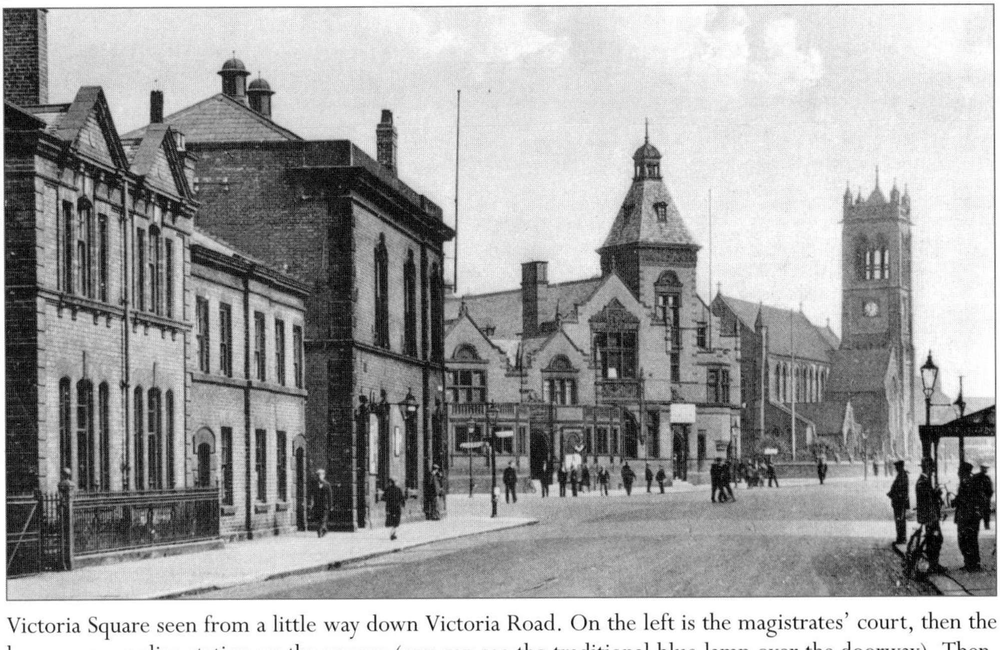

Victoria Square seen from a little way down Victoria Road. On the left is the magistrates' court, then the large square police station on the corner (you can see the traditional blue lamp over the doorway). Then, from left to right, the library, the technical school and St Paul's Church.

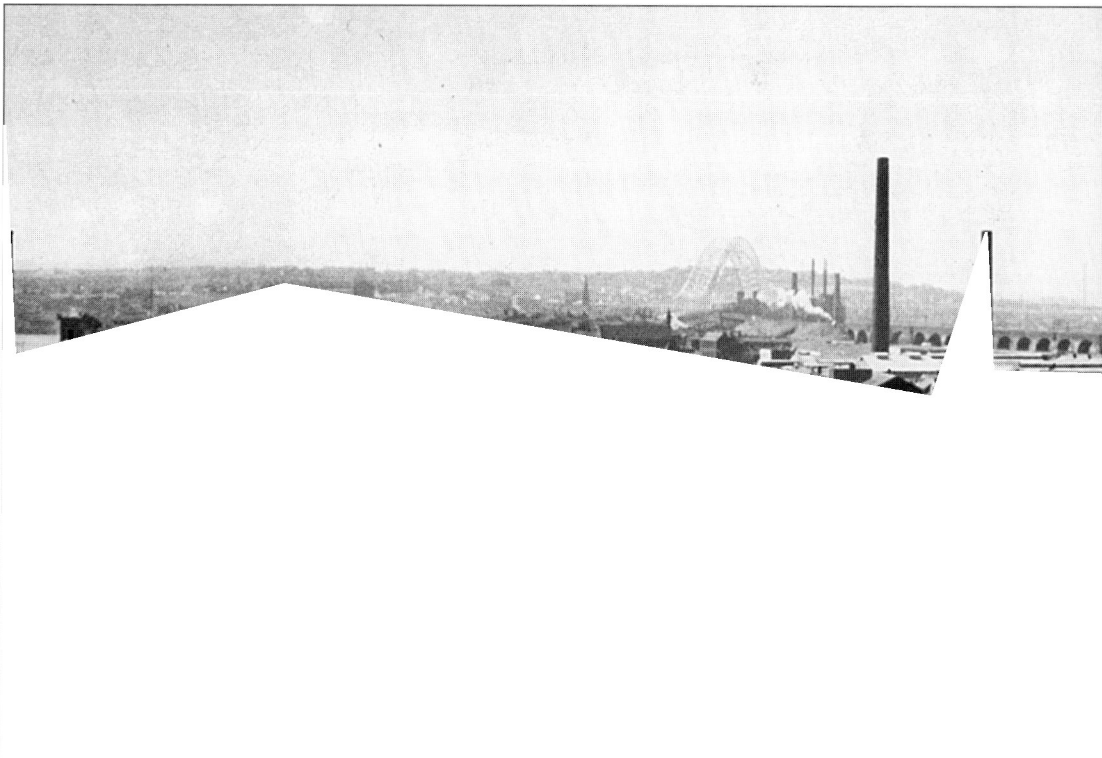

Looking south from the new town hall, June 1968. The rubble in the left foreground is the remains of the police station and magistrates' court in the course of demolition to make Moor Lane a dual carriageway. The row of shops on Victoria Road seen behind the rubble probably holds many fond memories for anyone who was a teenager in the 1960s. Among them was the Brazilian, the first coffee bar in Widnes and the height of sophistication, with its dark interior, 'mod' furniture, cappuccino, juke box and even a small wooden floor downstairs where you could jive away the lunchtime. Oh, it was all fab, gear and groovy in those heady days! Now it forms part of the Kingsway Hotel.

There is far too much to point it all out on this picture, but can you make out the Queen's Hall and the new extension nearest the camera? The three extra floors built above the *Weekly News* building further down Victoria Road on the right can also be seen; these were used by Swales as a general printers. Witt Road is on the bottom right and the newsagent's shop on the corner of Alexandra Street is just visible. It was one of those shops that sold everything, including imported American records and ex-juke box singles. The long low building behind was the infamous Black Cat billiard hall.

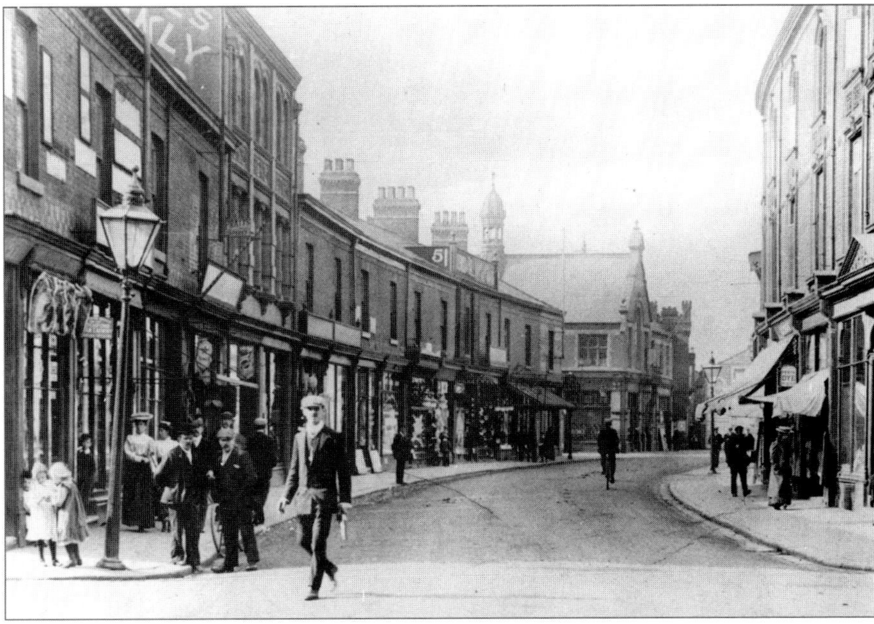

Victoria Road, caught some time around the turn of the century, from a spot almost under the railway bridge running into Widnes Central station. The *Weekly News* offices are on the left. This was a three-storey building, whereas the others in the row were only two. This third floor held the composing room where the *Widnes Weekly News*, *Runcorn Weekly News* and for a time the *South Liverpool* edition were put together. The large building further down the road is the Widnes Conservative Club.

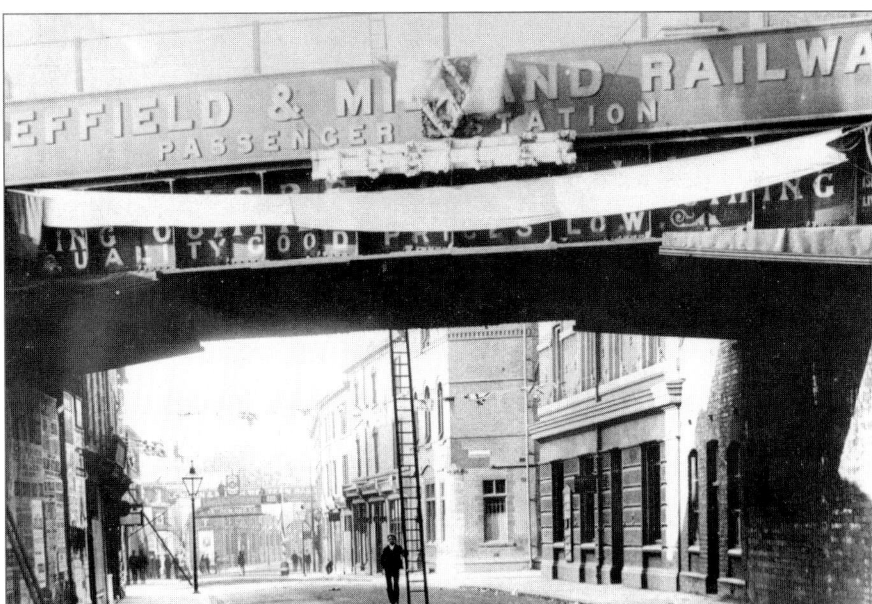

This 1897 photograph is what you would have seen if you had turned round from where the photograph above was taken. Widnes was *en fête* for Queen Victoria's Diamond Jubilee and even the Victoria Road railway bridge received the treatment. The Central Hotel is on the right just under the bridge and Ditton Road corner is beyond it.

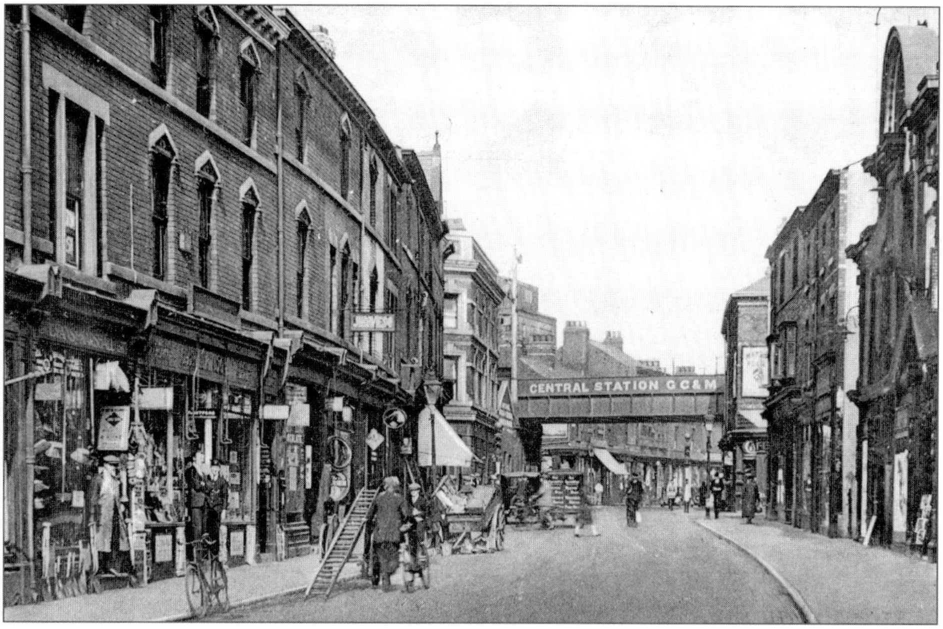

This is the very bottom of Victoria Road, early 1930s. This part, up to Ditton Road, is sometimes referred to as Waterloo Road. The Picturedrome is on the right, with its advertising bills outside, and the Central Hotel can be seen on the left up near the bridge. This was once a busy part of Widnes with plenty of shops. I can remember as a teenager taking my bike for repairs to Charlie Bingham's cycle shop along this busy and bustling row, which also contained a hardware shop, a stationers and a radio and gramophone record shop.

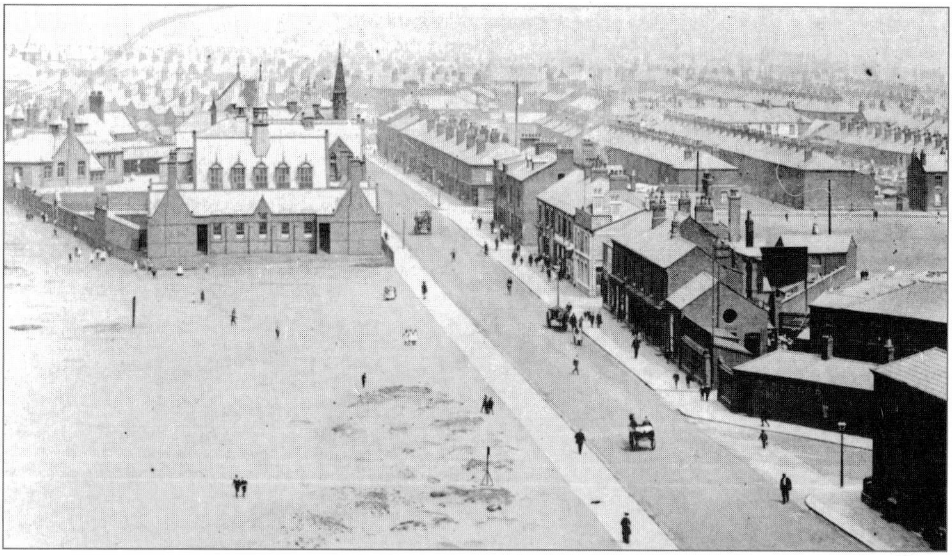

Widnes Road, Widnes. This picture can only have been taken from the top of St Paul's new tower so it must date from 1906 or later. The open space nearest the camera was later the Labour Exchange, and next to it the Empire Cinema, opened in May 1937. The buildings on the left belong to Simms Cross Infant and Primary School, one of my old schools. The block of buildings on the right, next to the Grapes inn, with the horse and cart outside, housed Edwards the printers and a dairy which kept cows in a shed at the back. Today it is still a dairy belonging to Dale Farms.

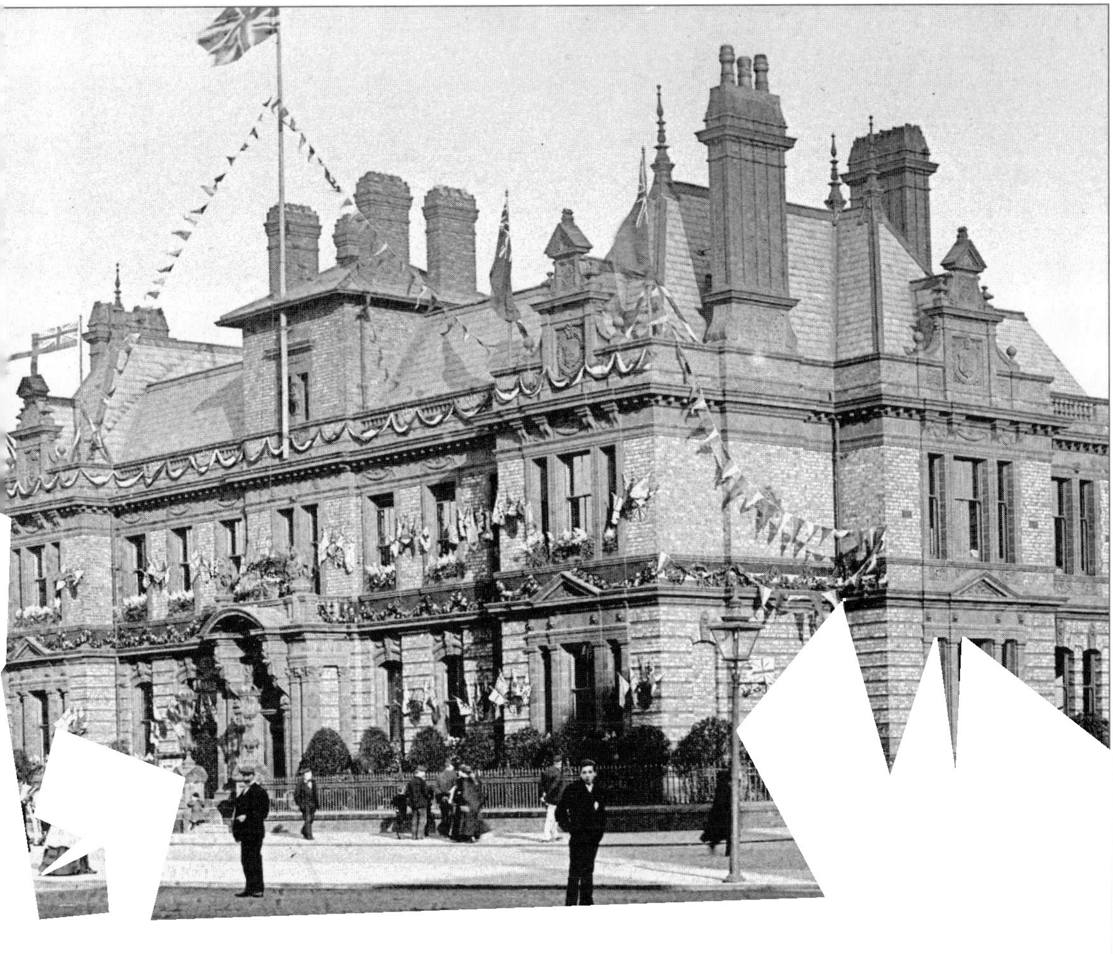

Widnes Town Hall, 1913. It is bedecked in flags and bunting in honour of the royal visit of King George V and Queen Mary on 7 July. When Parliament passed the Widnes Improvement Act in 1867 this allowed the Widnes Local Board to borrow the money to set Widnes on the path to Incorporation. The board were lucky: because of the high land prices that the Leigh family, who owned much of the area, were asking, their chosen centre still consisted of open fields and there was a blank canvas with which to work; though they were in no great hurry to complete their great plan for Victoria Square. The town hall, whose design was the result of a competition, was not started until Widnes was granted its Charter of Incorporation, and technically it is true to say it was never finished: the winning design included a tower and a clock but when the councillors saw the building, as it is above, they decided to save the town's money as it was grand enough already! The town hall was finally opened in 1896 and was the centre of civic life and important occasions until the new civic buildings were constructed on Kingsway in the 1960s.

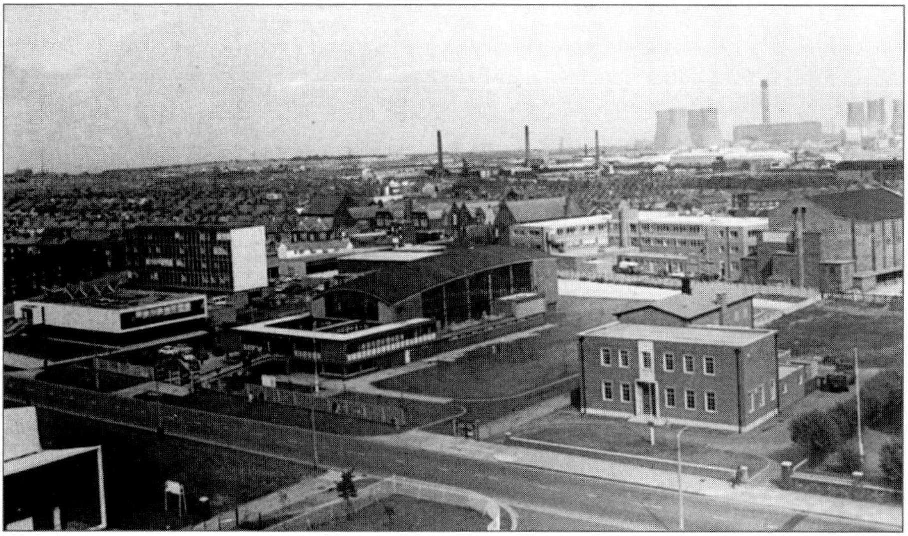

Looking across Kingsway from the new civic buildings, September 1968. From left to right the buildings are the magistrates' court, with police station behind, the swimming baths and the Masonic Hall. The back of the Empire Cinema can be seen behind the Masonic Hall and Simms Cross School can just be seen behind the curved roof of the baths.

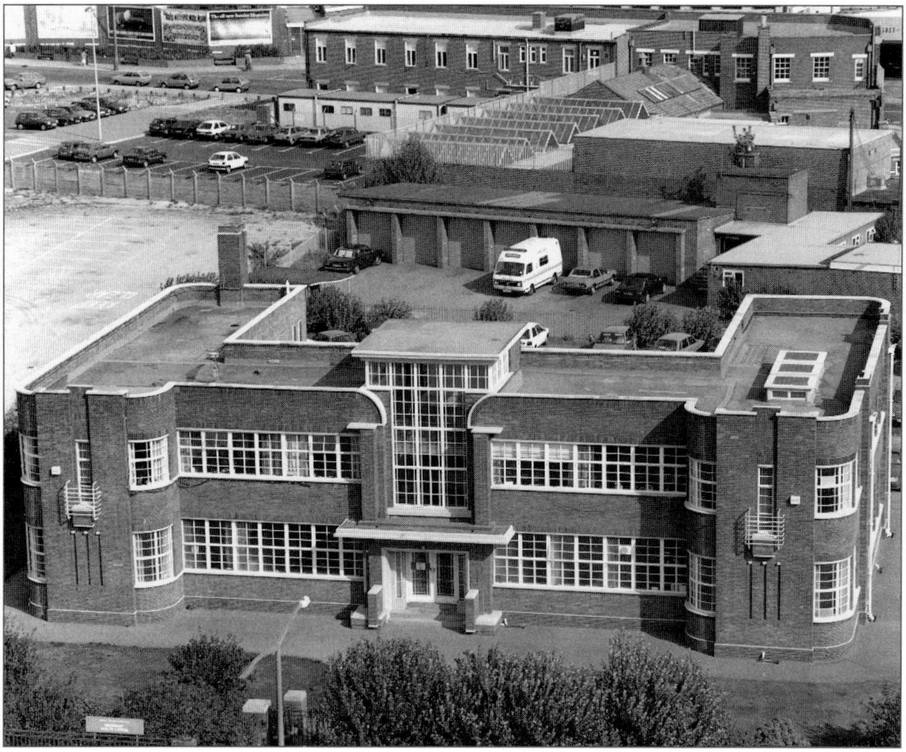

The health centre on Kingsway was built in 1937 as the Widnes Clinic. I can never look at this place without tasting the concentrated orange juice that was given out in the late 1940s to all tender infants such as I. I had my first tooth taken out at the dentist there, and can still smell the gas. This picture is from the early 1970s and the empty space that was the Empire Cinema is at the top left.

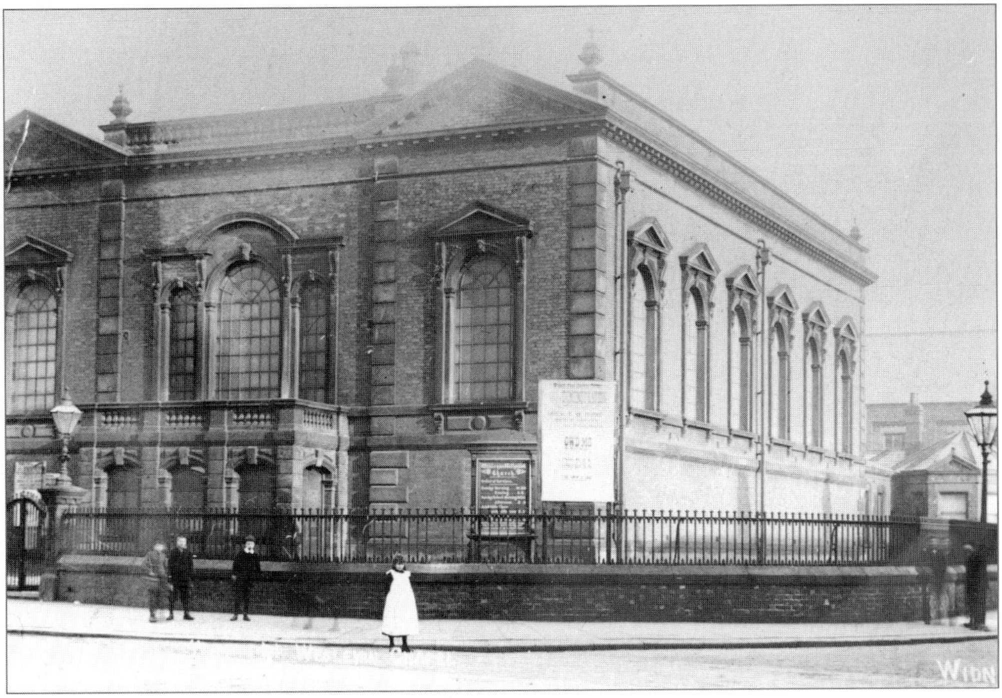

The Victoria Road Wesleyan Methodist Chapel, *c.* 1906. This hall was opened in July 1864 and was the largest and grandest of all the Wesleyan chapels in the area. Farnworth, Cronton, Hale Bank, Hough Green and Moss Bank all had small meeting houses that came under this chapel. On the opening day, over 300 people came from Runcorn to be at the service, and it is recorded that it took more than two hours for the ferry boat to complete over thirty crossings and return the visitors to the Cheshire side.

This Methodist chapel closed down in the 1950s and on 1 May 1957 the building re-opened as the Queen's Hall. The fact that the hall had once been a Wesleyan chapel and had been consecrated raised many problems for people holding events there in the early years, as alcohol could not be sold in the building. It was not until an extension was added along the left-hand side of the hall that a bar was built.

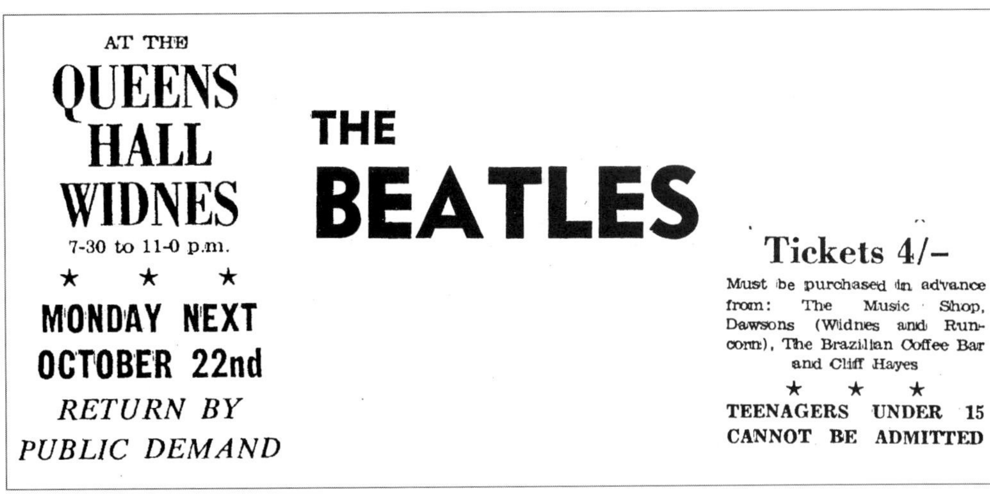

An advertisement for a dance at the Queen's Hall in 1962 featuring an up-and-coming group – The Beatles, tickets 2*s* 6*d*. And as you will note from the end of the cutting I was one of the people selling the tickets.

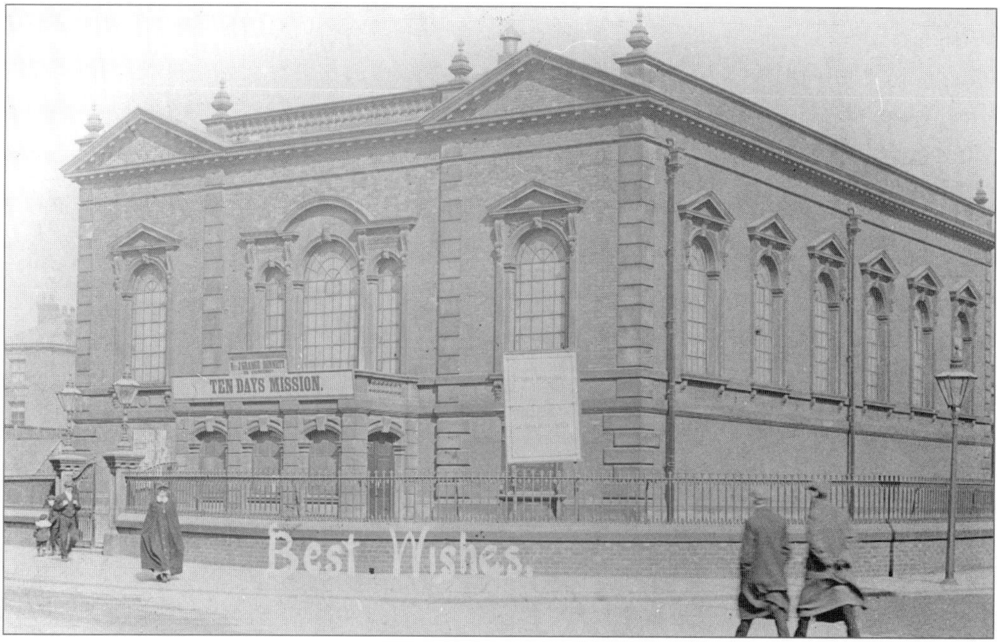

Another view of the Wesleyan Methodist chapel in Victoria Road. This is from 1908 when a ten-day mission brought thousands flocking to the building. This image was used as a card to send best wishes for Christmas 1908. Many of the great names in Widnes' past and most of the philanthropists of Widnes were connected with this or other Methodist chapels.

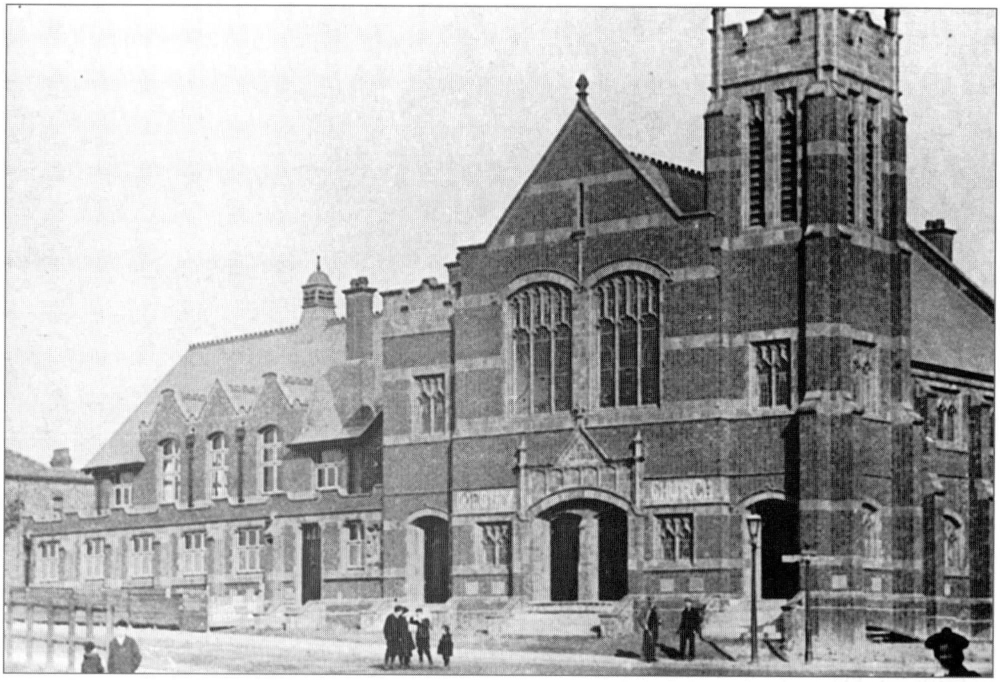

The new Wesleyan church at Widnes, *c.* 1908. It stood at the bottom of Peel House Lane. The church was complete with day schools and Sunday schools, and was opened on Tuesday 4 February 1905.

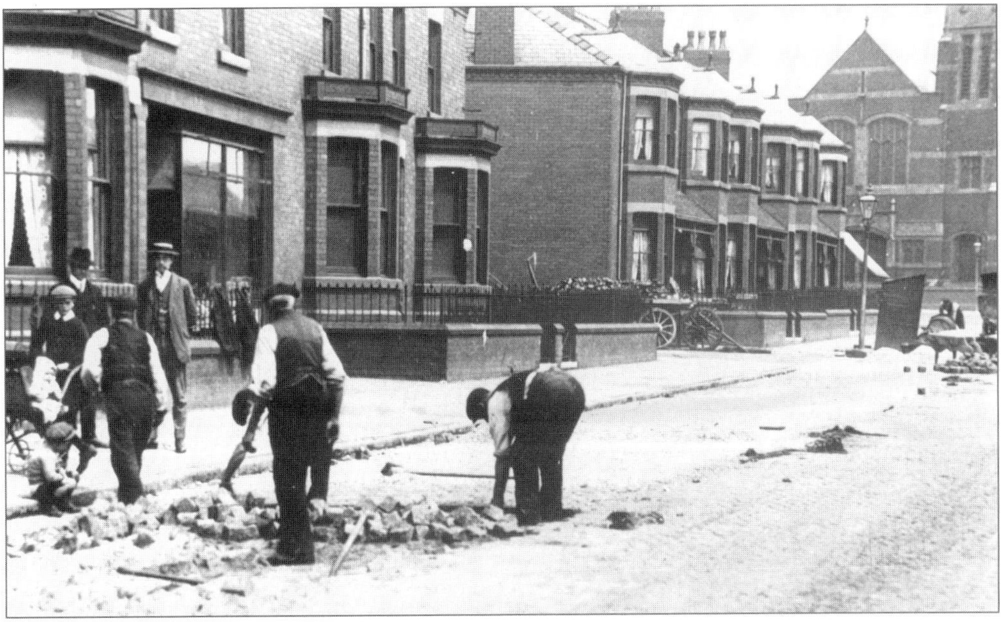

Workmen on Albert Road near the Wesleyan chapel, *c*. 1912. Ossie Lyons' barber's shop is on the left. It is hard to say whether they were laying the setts for the first time or whether they had been doing some repair work or sewer work.

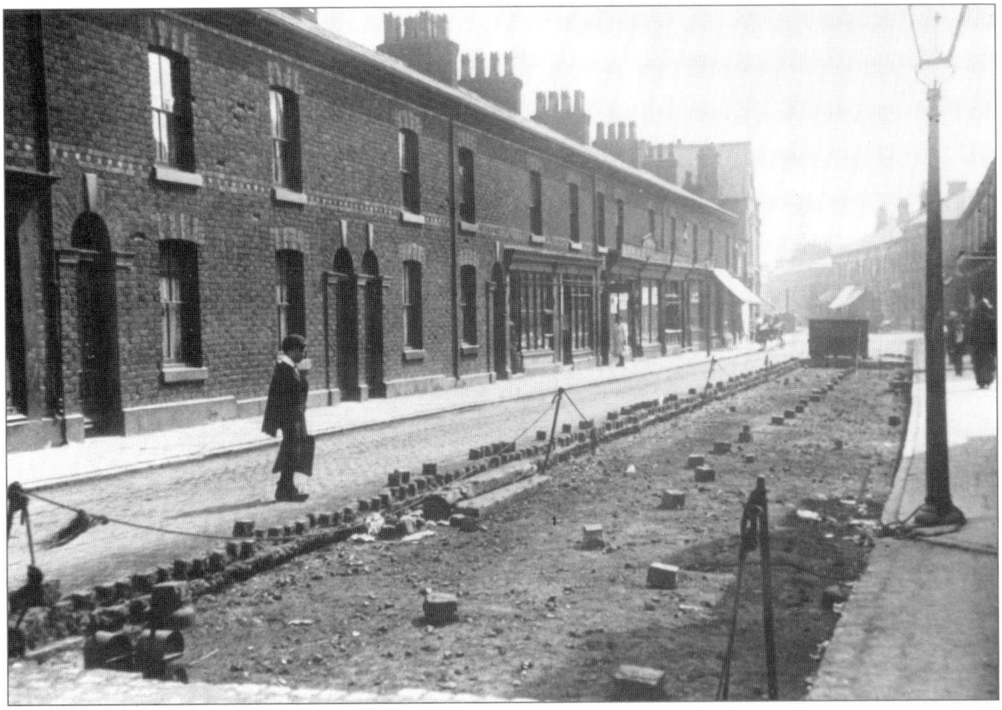

Another view of Albert Road with roadworks in progress, looking towards the Deacon Road junction, *c*. 1912. It is interesting to see that while some of the houses have been converted into shops others are still domestic dwellings. The Bradley Hotel can be clearly seen at the end of the block, and this area became the main shopping area in Widnes in the 1960s.

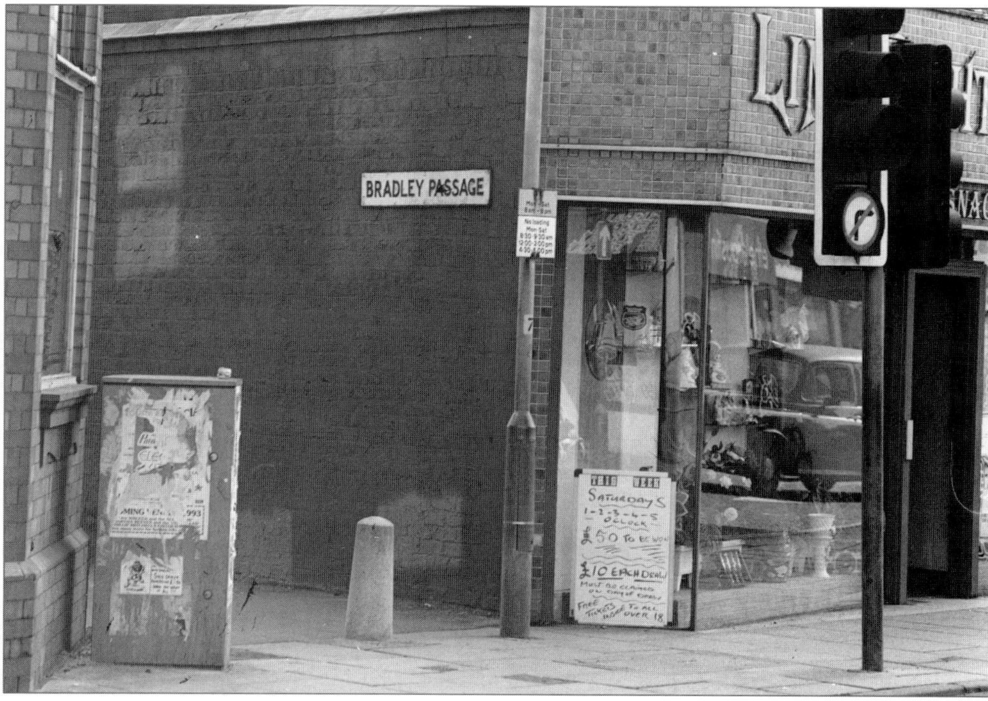

Bradley Passage at the junction of Albert Road and Deacon Road, *c.* 1960. This passageway ran down the side of the Bradley Hotel and was always busy as it led to Southern's Works, Orr Zinc White Works, and many other factories.

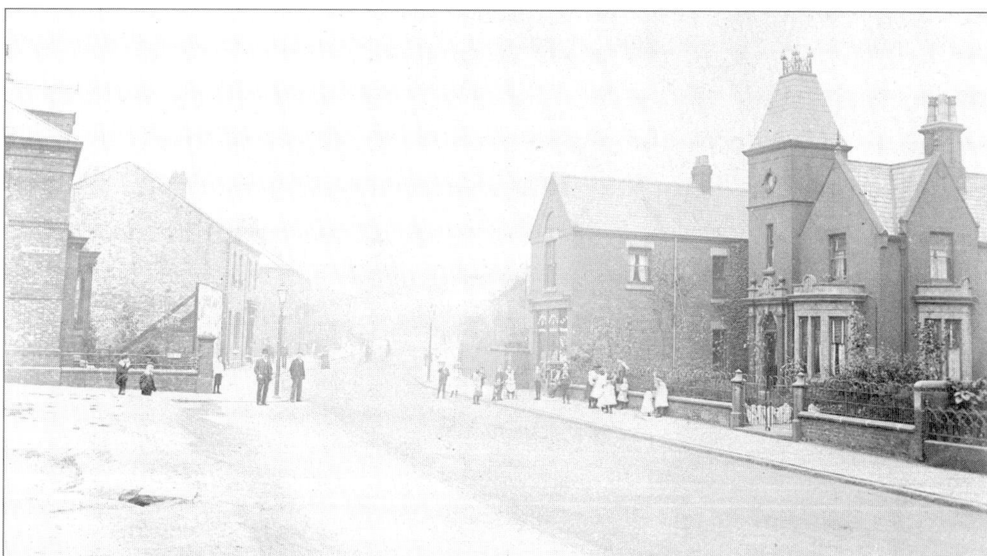

Albert Road at the turn of the century. The building on the right is Appleton Villa which was owned by 'Bozza' Martin (Charles Edward Martin), who later built the Bozzadrome Cinema on the site of the Albert Hall. The Bozzadrome opened on 29 November 1915 with the film *War is Hell*. The Regal Cinema was later constructed on this site. Another of Widnes' cinemas, the Premier, was built on the waste ground on the left of the picture. It was handy to have two cinemas directly opposite each other; if one was full or you did not fancy the film you could nip across the road to the other!

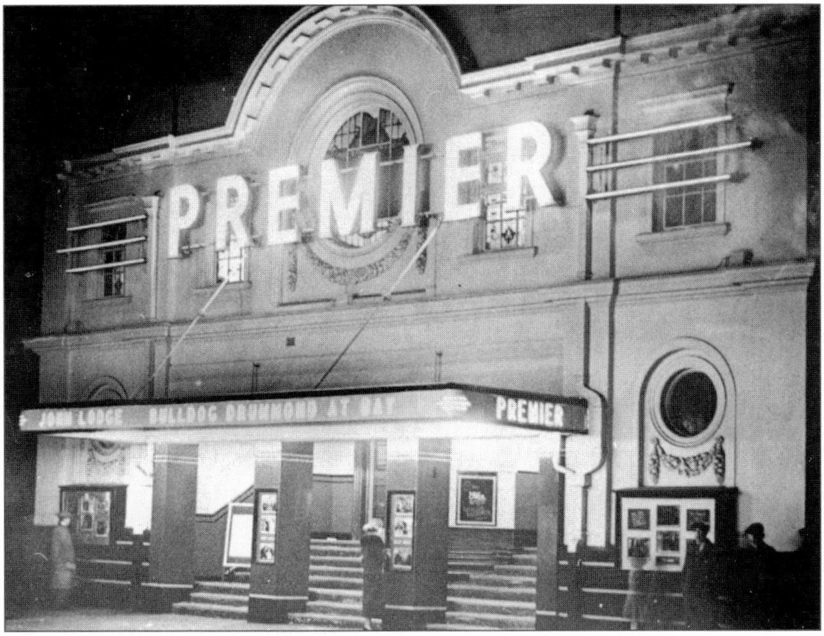

The Premier Cinema, Albert Road, 1930s. The cinema opened in 1915 with *Jewel of Fate* and showed silent films until it became the first cinema in Widnes to show a talkie when on 21 October 1929 *Interference* was screened. The Premier in the 1950s and '60s was always looked upon as the poor relation of Widnes cinemas. It seemed always to be showing war and cowboy films. However, I remember being refused entry to see *Rock Around the Clock* as I was only thirteen years old and it was an 'A' film, which meant you had to be accompanied by an adult if you were under sixteen. As boys we used to hang around the entrance and ask grown-ups to 'take us in' when there was a film about space or a grisly war film we wanted to see.

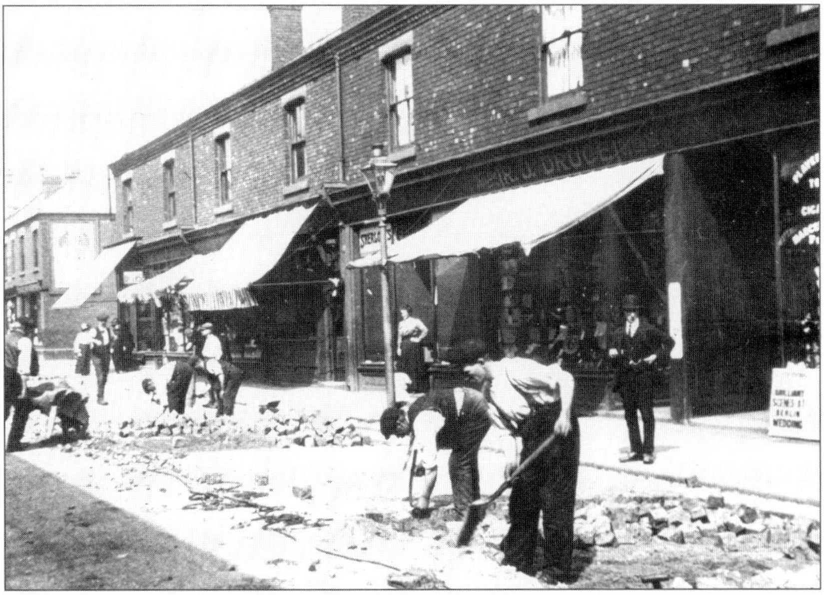

Albert Road, *c.* 1907. Shopkeepers and passers-by watch as the men turn a mud street into a cobbled way. Forshaw's card shop now occupies the premises on the extreme right.

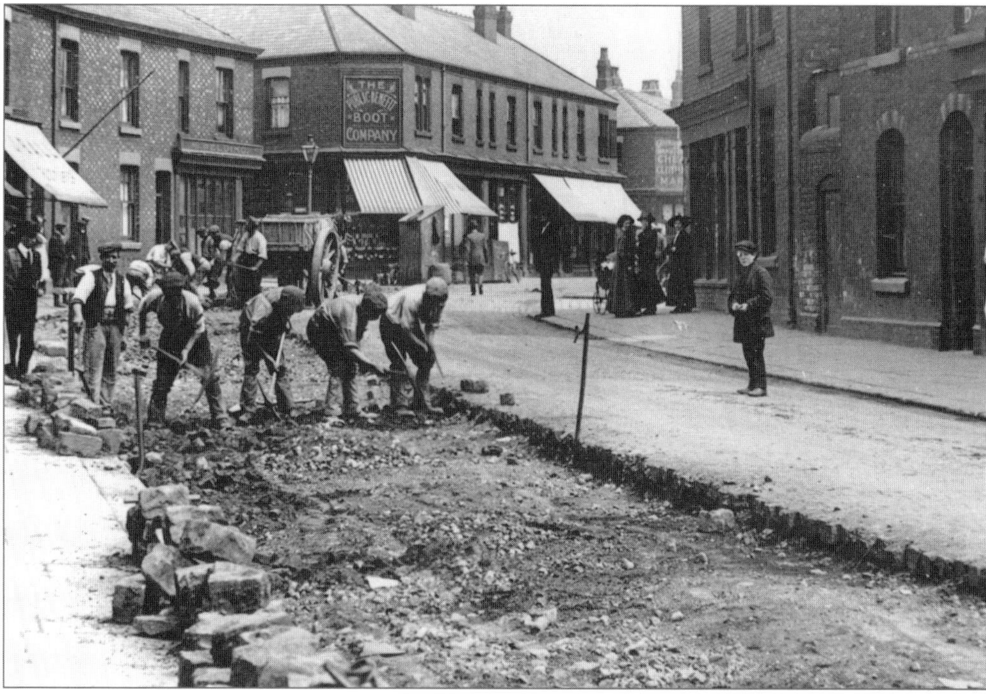

Our sett-layers are seen yet again in this picture; they were busy lads. Here they are working their way down Widnes Road, almost to Simms Cross. The road was then still a mixture of private houses and shops, including The Public Benefit Boot Company in the centre of the picture. The area of Simms Cross took its name from an ancient cross, one of several, set up around Farnworth Church where travellers, processions and funerals would pause, rest and pray on their journey to the parent church.

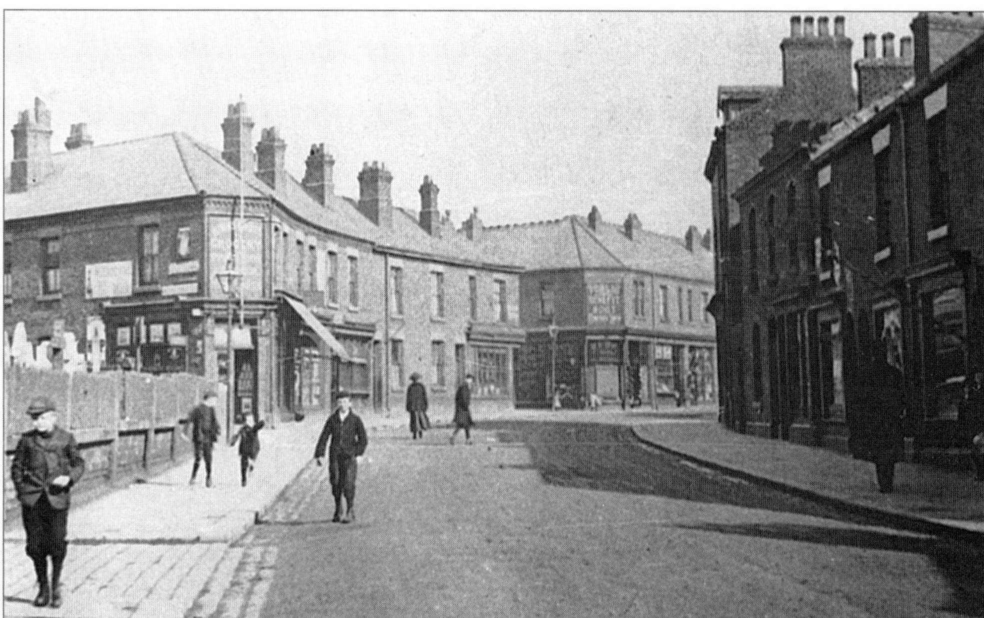

Albert Road, Simms Cross, *c.* 1920. This is just a few yards further down the street from the picture above. On the left you can see the gravestones in the old graveyard.

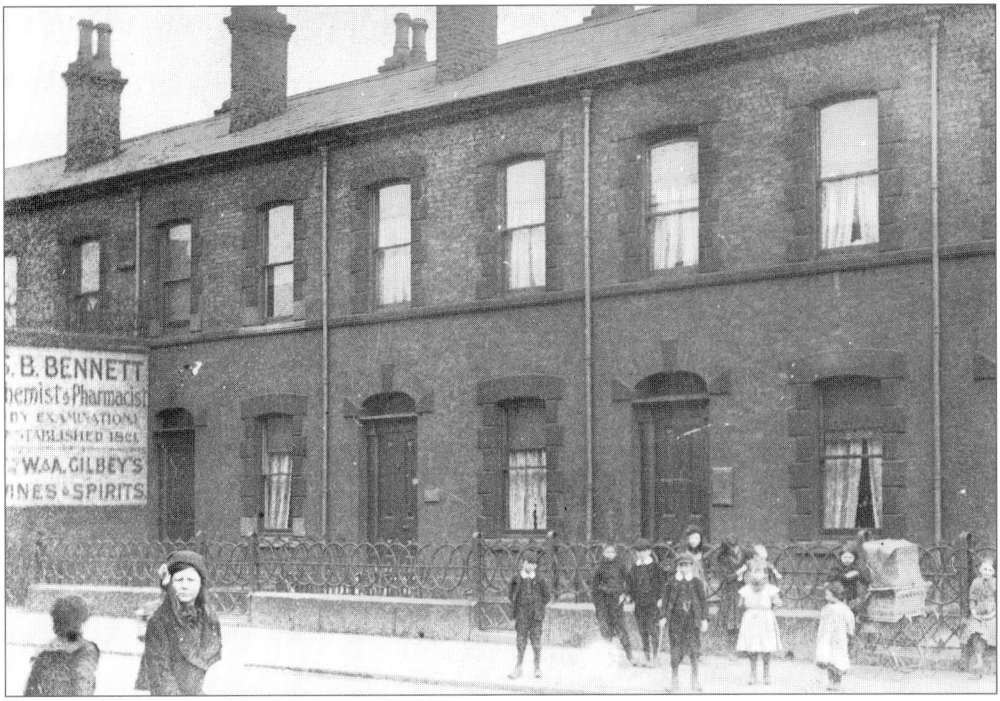

Kaludah Terrace, Albert Road, 1909. These houses stood near the Farrant Street junction and though they look like private houses, you can see that two of them have plaques at the front door indicating that the occupants were using them for business of some sort. My grandfather William (Billy) Hayes had a barber's shop in the next terrace to this one, and my father, Alf, carried on the business with his brother Steve for many years. At the start of this century the Hayes also had a coal yard on Lugsdale Road which was at the back of these houses.

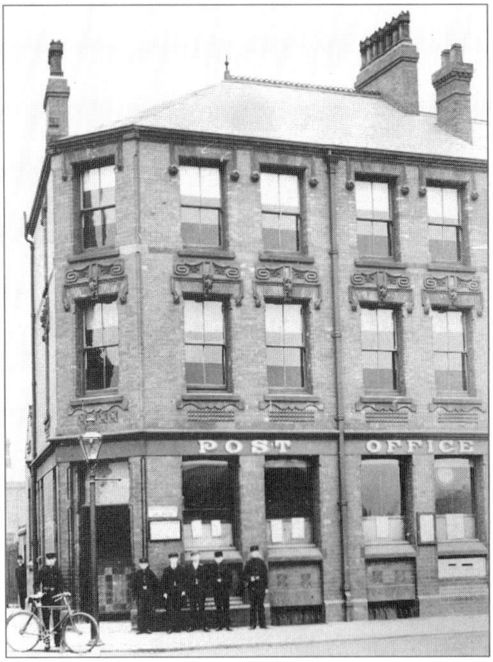

This was Widnes' first purpose-built post office and stood on the corner of Victoria Square and Emily Street. It was open seven days a week from 7.30 a.m. until 8 p.m., and 9 p.m. on Fridays. Most Widnesians will remember this building as the Co-op Café, which is what it became when the post office moved across the road to the corner of Vicarage Road and Widnes Road.

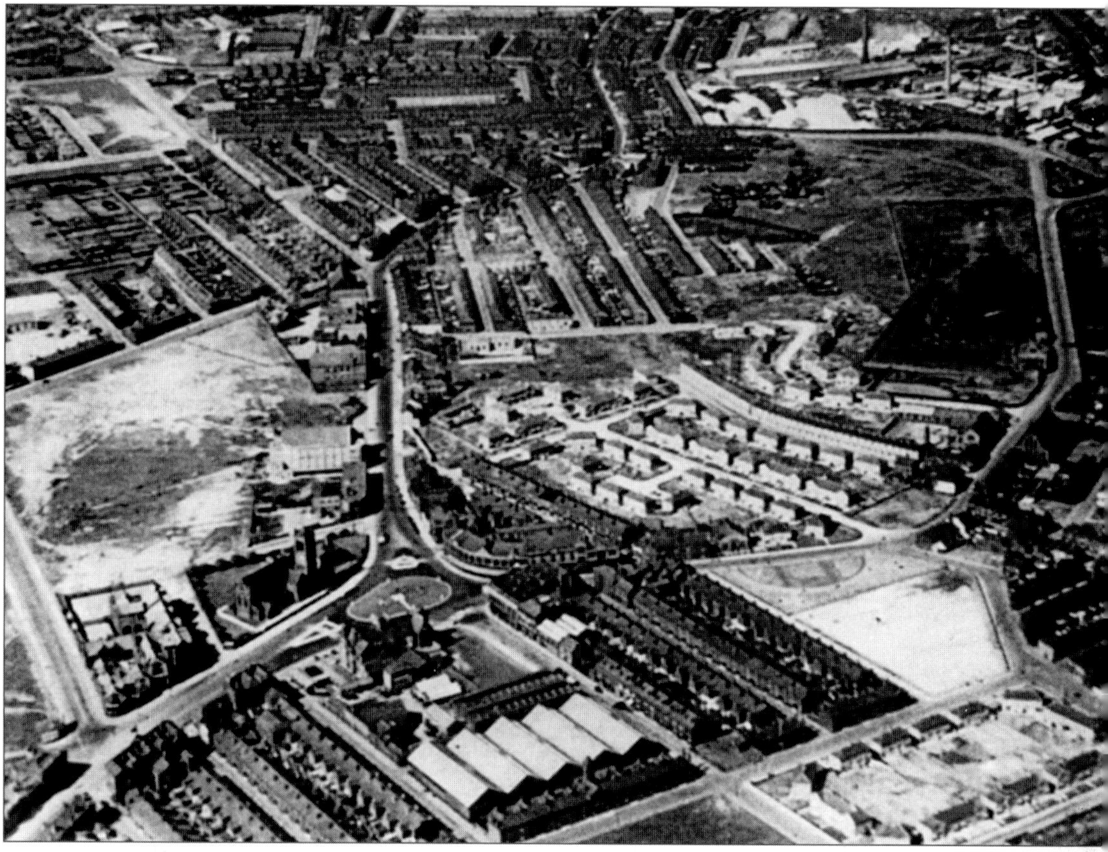

An aerial view of Widnes, 1937. Victoria Square, low on the left, is clearly seen, along with the library, technical college and St Paul's Church. The town hall is across the square from the church and right at the bottom the large roof of Widnes' old covered market is visible; now alas this has been cleared away. At the age of seventeen, for about a year, I had a stall on that market selling household goods. I sold bargain packs that contained a bottle of bleach (hypo as we called it), a bottle of disinfectant and a bottle of liquid soap, all for half a crown, 2*s* 6*d*. Another of my bargains was a Brylcreem-type hair oil, in a plastic pouch, for 1*s* 11½*d*.

Widnes Road is very clear, going away from Victoria Square, and the Empire Cinema and Simms Cross School are on the left. The large field behind these buildings would flood every winter, and sometimes it was under water for two or three weeks at a time. Great for schoolchildren when it froze – we would spend hours making slides. The school also used the field for sports days. Lugsdale Road dominates the right of the picture, and you can see plenty of open spaces among the factories leading up to Warrington Road (top right).

CHAPTER TWO

SPECIAL OCCASIONS

'Work hard, play hard' was a popular expression in Widnes' past. Work hard they certainly did, but when there was something to celebrate Widnesians did it in style. It did not matter what it was – from the Sunday school walks to Lifeboat Days – the people of Widnes knew how to enjoy the occasion. When Queen Victoria held her Jubilee in 1897, Widnes was judged the third best decorated town in England. Triumphal arches were the speciality of the day. Widnes Foundry made one of steel for the King's visit on 7 July 1913, and before that, when Edward was crowned in 1902, there were grand arches in Waterloo Road, West Bank, Victoria Square and Albert Road, as well as at Halton View and Farnworth Street, and again the name of Widnes was up there as one of the best dressed towns in the country.

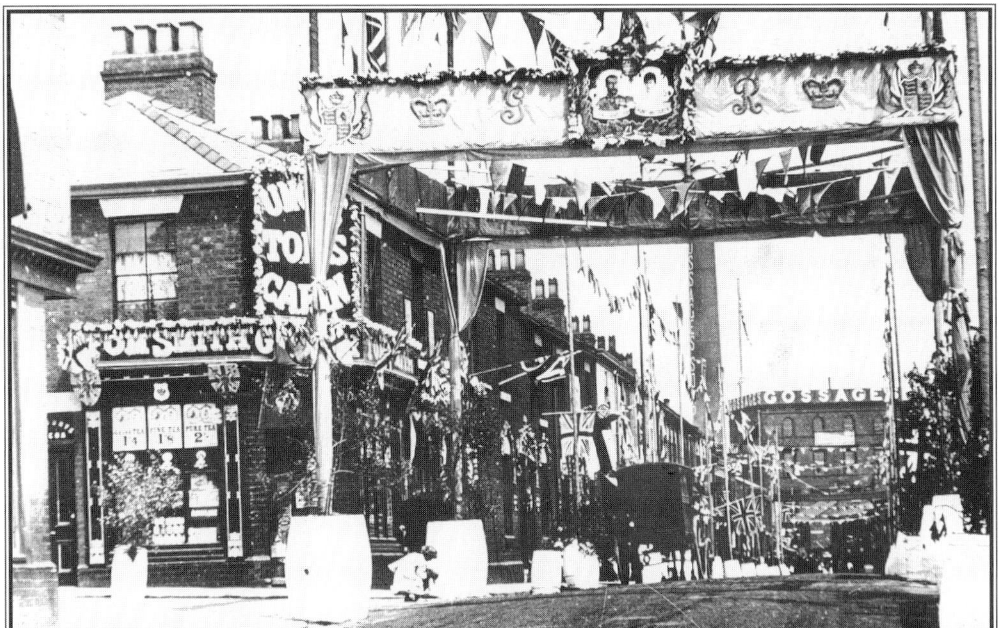

This is one of the arches erected for the royal visit in July 1925 and it shows just how much trouble the people in the area went to for their second royal visitor. The time when King Edward VII drove slowly along the Bold Road in July 1909 could hardly be included, although a crowd did turn out to wave, and technically he did cross the Widnes Borough boundary momentarily! West Bank really hung out the flags as King George V came down Waterloo Road and on to the Transporter Bridge for the journey over to Cheshire.

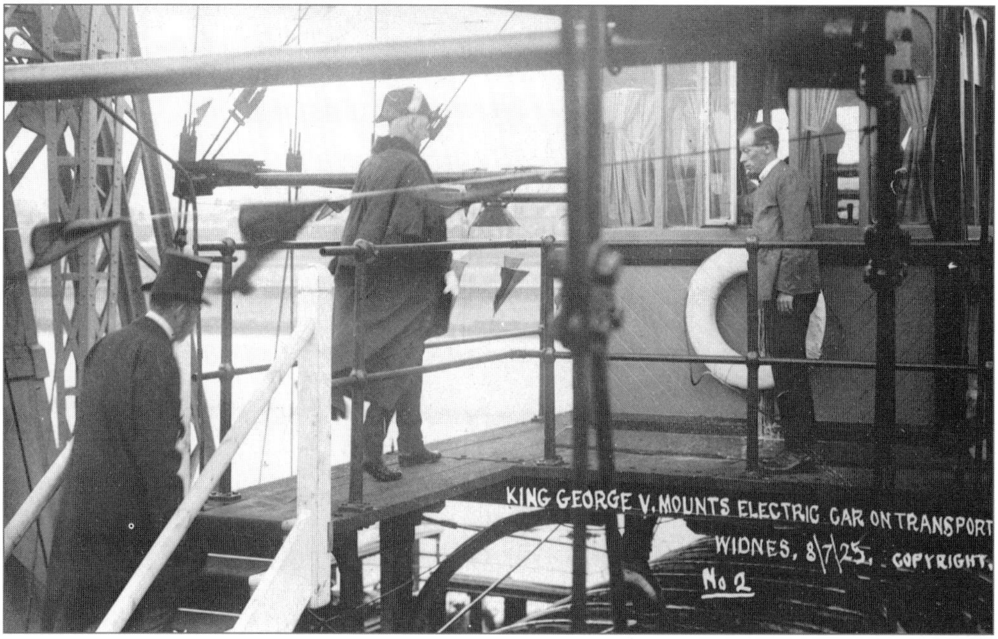

King George V captured on film during the royal visit, 8 July 1925. The control car on the Transporter was specially titivated, and the King is seen here behind the Mayor of Widnes, just about to enter the control cabin. It took 2½ minutes to cross the Mersey and the Ship Canal where it passed just 4½ ft above the wall that separates the two waterways.

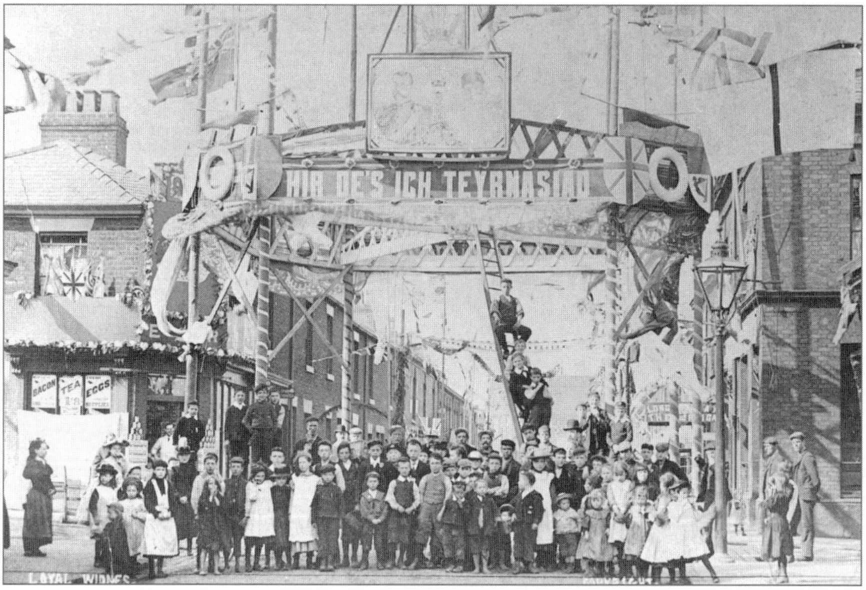

This is the 'loyal arch' erected at the top of Mersey Road in 1913. The King did not pass under this arch; if he had, he might have been puzzled about the message which was in Welsh. This was because there were so many Welsh people living in West Bank at that time, and it was the Welsh Chapel that had put up the arch. This photograph was taken from the exact same spot as the picture on page 25. If you have a keen eye you may have noted that the grocer, Tom Smith, was still selling tea at 1*s* 8*d* (twelve years later). Tom was also a councillor for many years and was Mayor of Widnes in 1908–9.

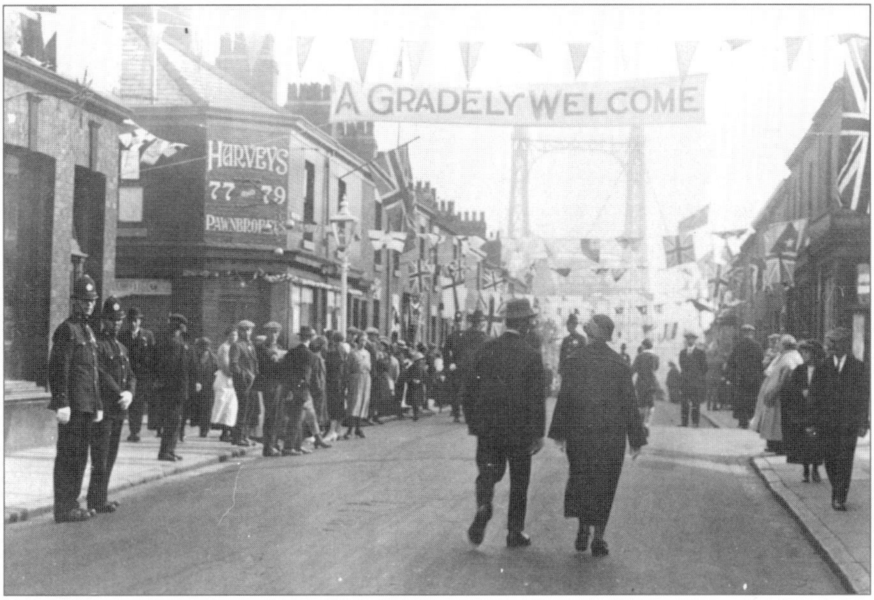

Mersey Road, West Bank, looking down towards the Transporter Bridge. Taken on the morning of the royal visit in July 1925, this picture shows the crowds beginning to gather and take their places for a quick glimpse as the royal couple went past. The banner bears a Lancashire greeting.

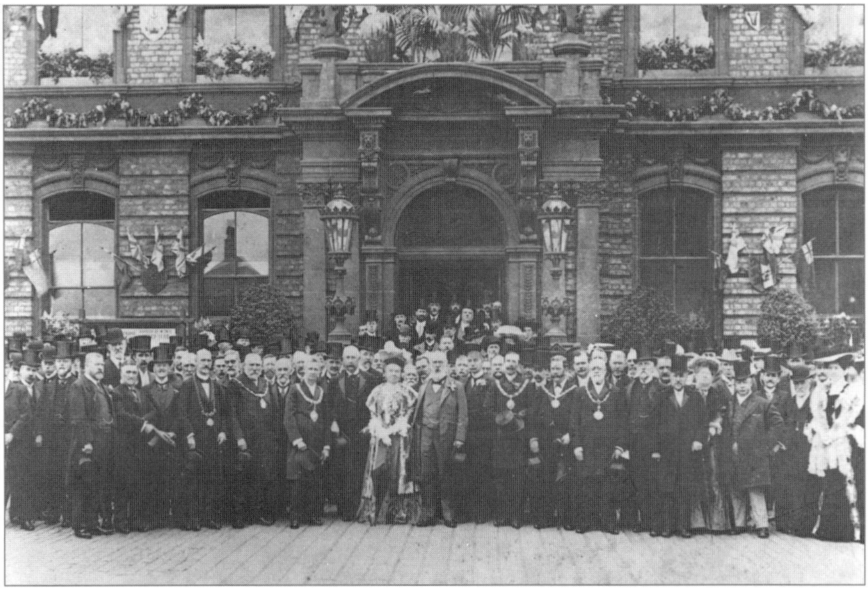

The scene outside Widnes Town Hall when the dignitaries gathered for a photograph before proceeding down Waterloo Road, in their processional carriages, for the official opening of the Transporter Bridge, 29 May 1905. Sir John Brunner, the gentleman with the white beard in the centre, performed the opening ceremony. His wife can be seen standing next to him with the mayors of all the local towns including the Mayor of Widnes and Chairman of Runcorn, all proudly posing in their official regalia. I wonder how the Chairman of Runcorn arrived at this ceremony – did he go in his carriage to cross the Mersey at Warrington, or did he walk over the footbridge with someone carrying his robe and chain of office, or did they cheat and send the Transporter car for him?

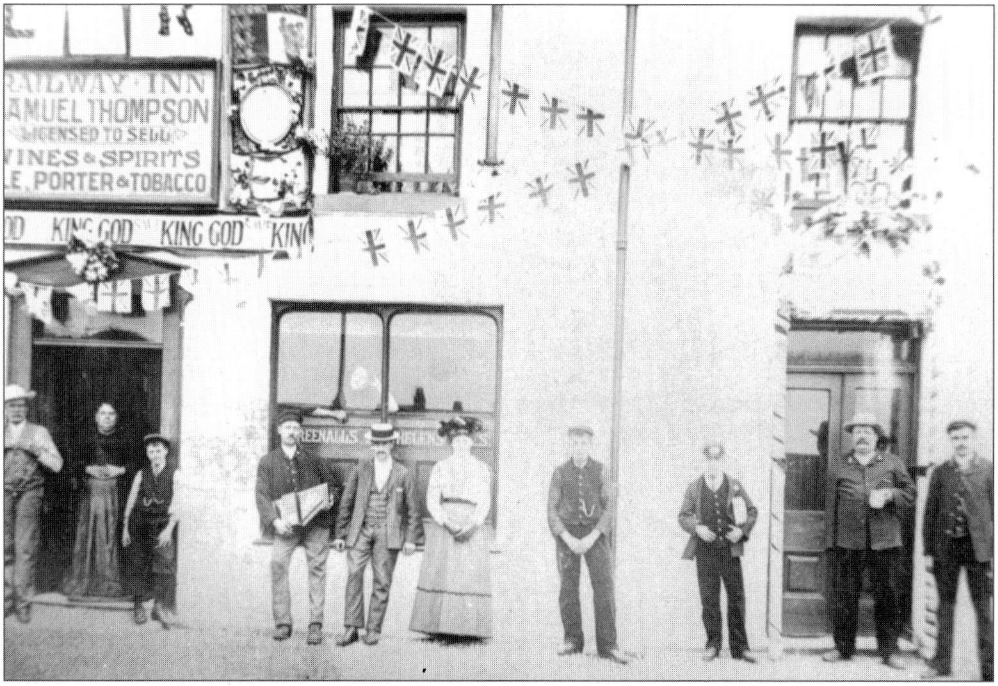

Widnes, like the rest of England, had to put all celebrations on hold in July 1902 when King Edward's coronation had to be delayed because of his ill-health. They held their breath, and prayed hard, the King recovered, and the ceremony finally went ahead in August that year. The Railway Inn was at the bottom of the brow up to Ditton Junction station and was nicknamed the Junction Hotel: here we see their efforts for the King's coronation.

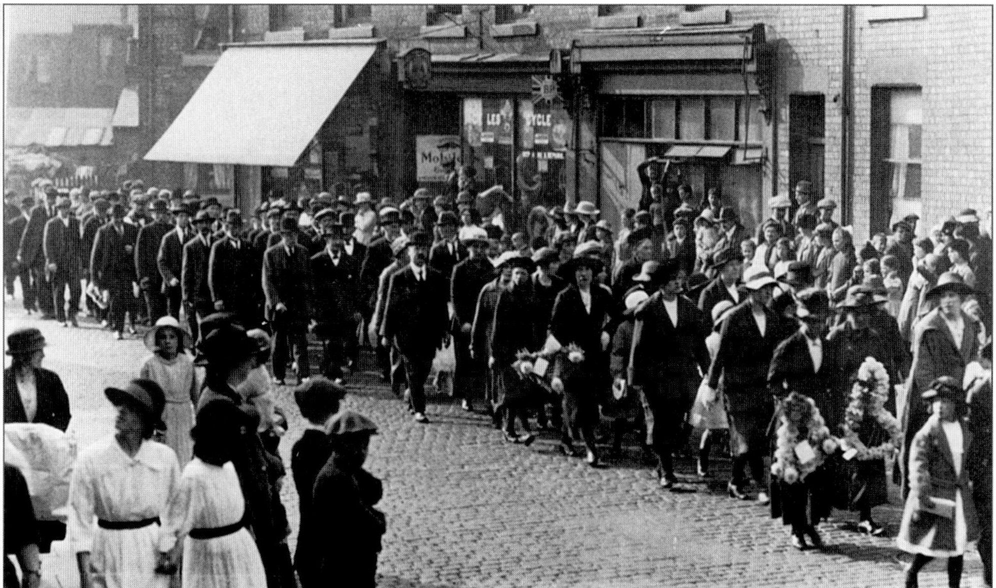

A solemn procession makes its way towards Victoria Square before going on to Victoria Park where Lord Derby was about to unveil the 42 ft high obelisk which bore the names of the 818 men who had 'made the supreme sacrifice' in the First World War, 1914–18. Included in these names is that of Sergeant Thomas Mottershead, who was awarded a posthumous VC.

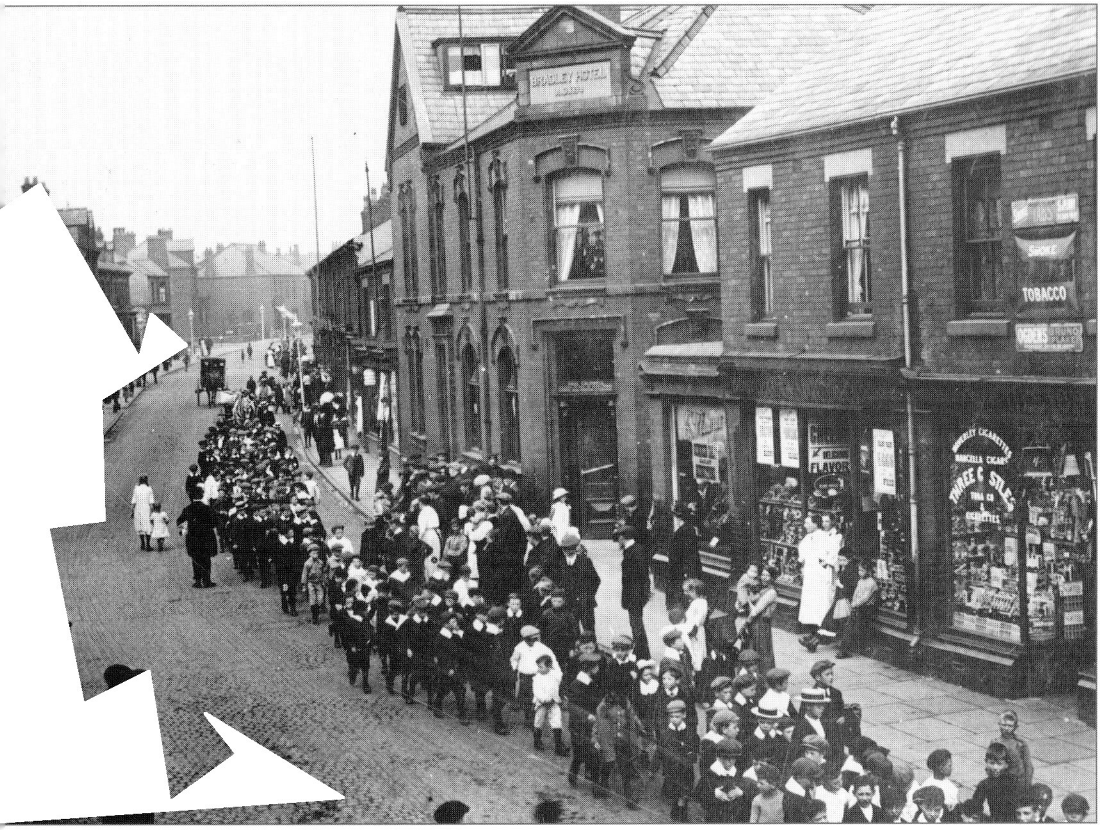

Widnes, like many other Lancashire towns, followed Manchester and had a Whit Walk or rather two Whit Walks, with the Church of England walking on the Bank Holiday Whit Monday and the Roman Catholics the following Friday. Here is the tail end of the procession on Whit Monday 1905 walking down Albert Road and passing the bottom of Deacon Road. Note the date on the Bradley Hotel, 1894, and the grocer's and the tobacconist's shops next door.

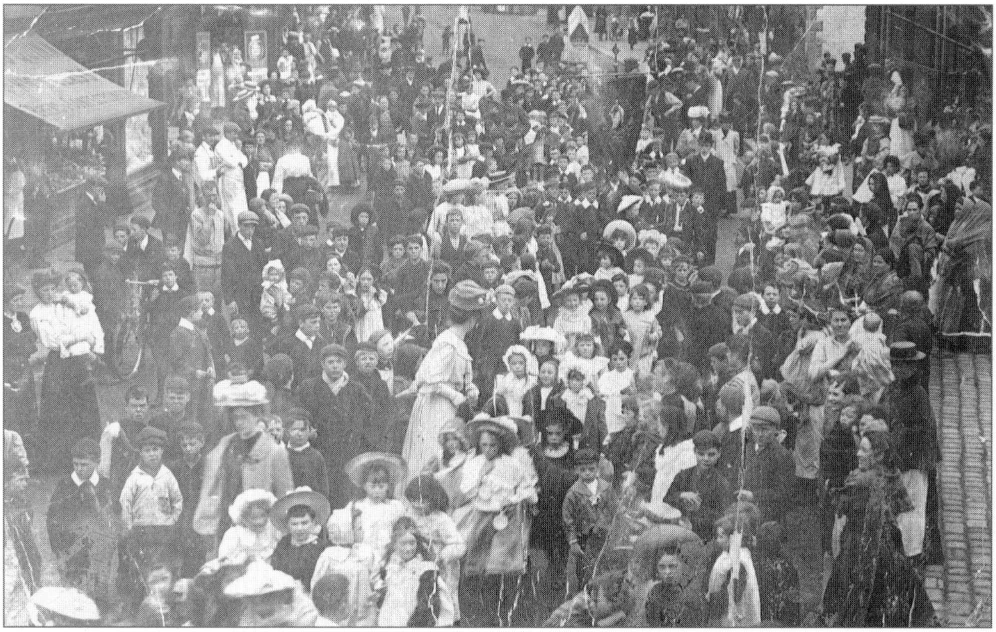

St Bede's Roman Catholic Church at Appleton was a large church and had a large congregation. This is the Sunday school on their Whit Walk or 'Procession of Witness' as it was termed at the time. The Sunday school teachers seem to be keeping everything in order, though I suspect that the Walk hadn't really begun yet, as who was 'walking' and who was watching seems to be a little confused at the front of this picture, from the turn of the century.

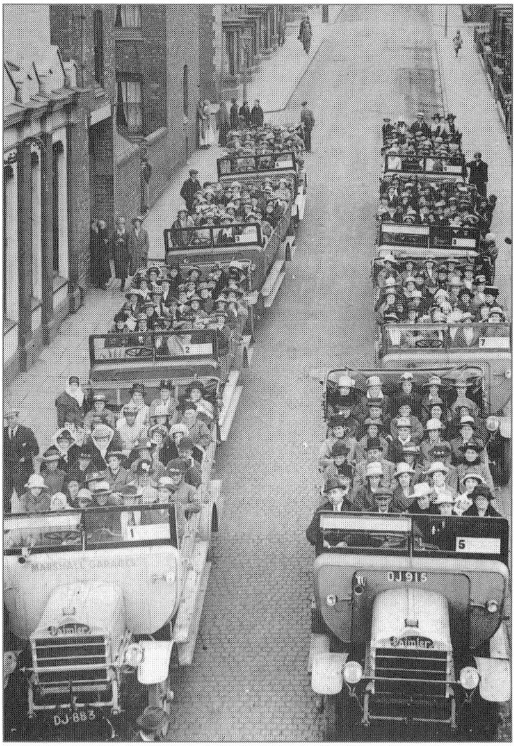

Far better to go by charabanc, which is what these ladies did on an outing organised by the Widnes Conservative Club in 1922. They are pictured here in Mersey Road, waiting to board the transporter to take them over the river. Perhaps they were going to north Wales, or to Chester Races; the Con Club ladies' outing to Chester Races on Ladies' Day was one trip my mother never missed!

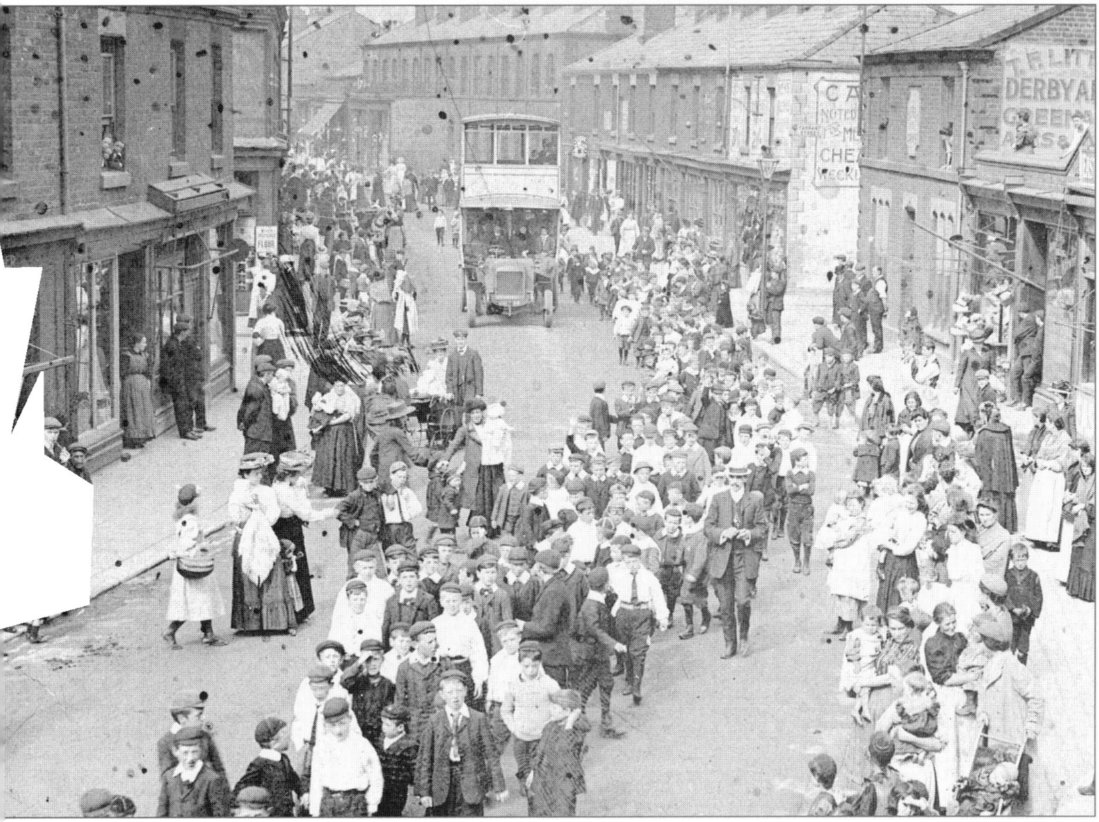

The Co-operative movement also held processions, and here we see one of them in Widnes Road, in 1909. Captured in the picture is one of Widnes' first buses and behind the bus is Kaludah Terrace where Woolworths is today, and has been for many years. The Derby Arms, where T.R. Little was the landlord, is on the very right of the picture. I worked there for quite a few years as barman when Austin and Rose Gilmore, a lovely couple, had the pub. Can you just make out the pole sticking out of the shop just to the right of the bus? That was the barber's shop of my grandfather Billy, and later my father, Alf, and uncle Steve. The shop on the corner, painted in a lighter colour, was a well-known pawnbroker's and shoe shop.

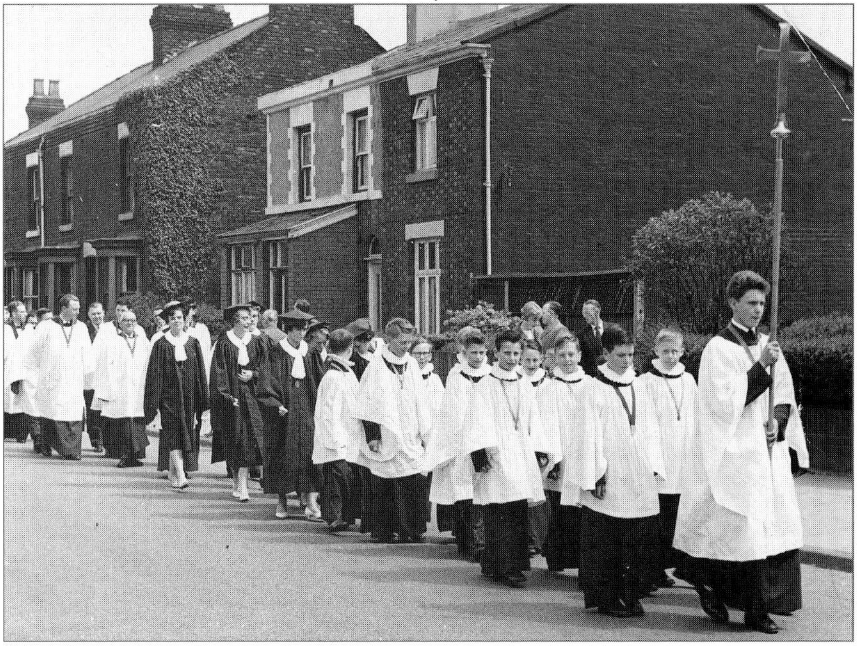

The choir from St Michael's (C of E) Church at Hough Green leads the Procession of Witness that took place on Whit Sunday afternoon, 1960. The procession formed at the Ball O' Ditton and made its way up Liverpool Road to the church at Hough Green. The procession was almost at Chestnut Lodge when captured for posterity. The tall gent at the front of the men is Ernie Osman who went on to take up the ministry, and peeping out over his left shoulder is Mr Walker the organist; Joyce Steadman is just in front of him. She had a beautiful voice and took many of the solos in church. The lad with the cross, well that's me. A devil on a Saturday night, an angel on a Sunday morning.

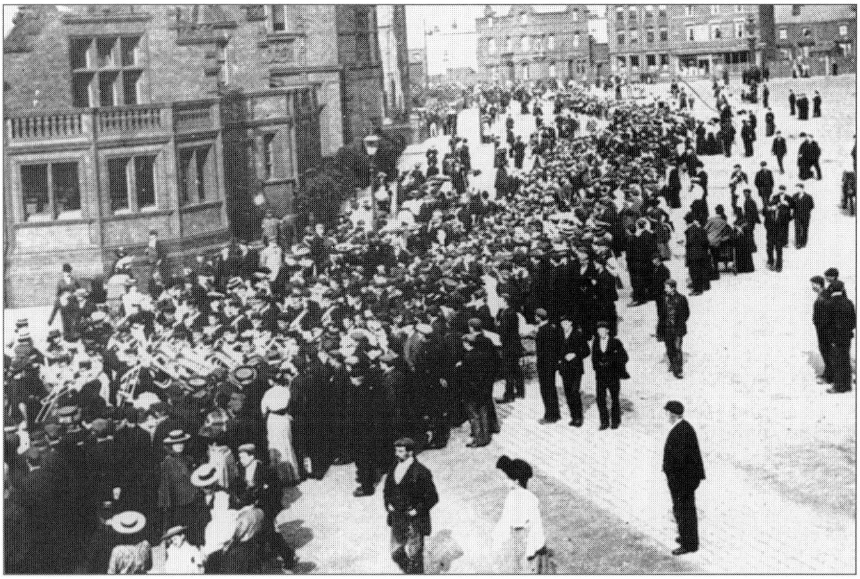

Victoria Square on the Co-op Field Day, 1906. The brass band leads the parade past the library, probably heading for Gossage's recreation ground or a field out that way. The site of the large Co-operative shop and headquarters of the Runcorn and Widnes Co-operative Society is at the top right.

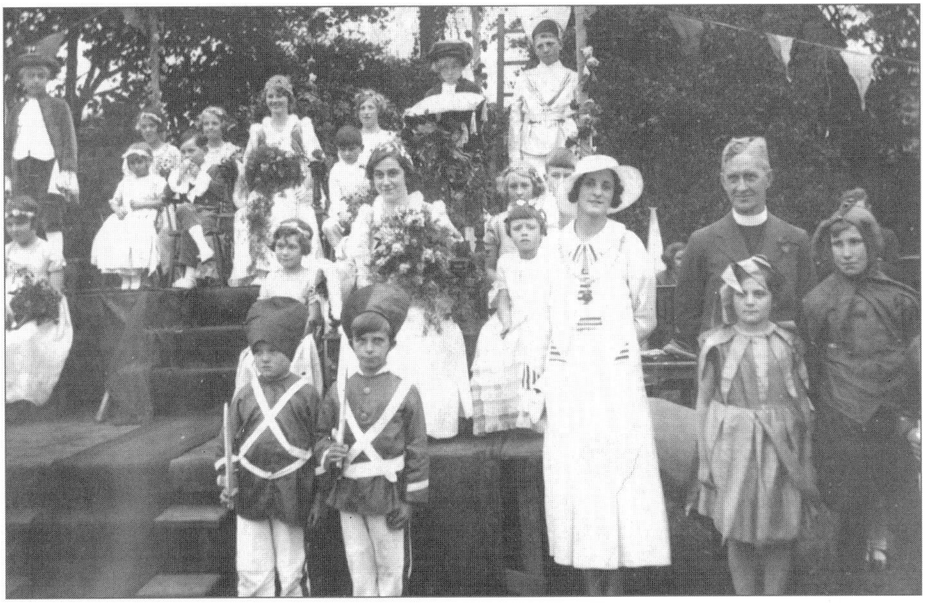

The Hough Green June Fair was *the* big occasion for the Church of St Michael in Hough Green. Here we see the 1937 Fair: the vicar, Mr Carr, and Mrs McCausland are standing on the right of the picture, while Rose Queen, Alice Harrison, and her retinue smile for the camera. The soldiers at the front were from a set piece called 'The Wedding of the Painted Doll'. When I took part in 1952 as a soldier I thought it was really good – and unique. Now I realise the same costumes were worn year after year, and the outfit with the sword, hat and cross belts shown here is probably the very one that I wore fifteen years later.

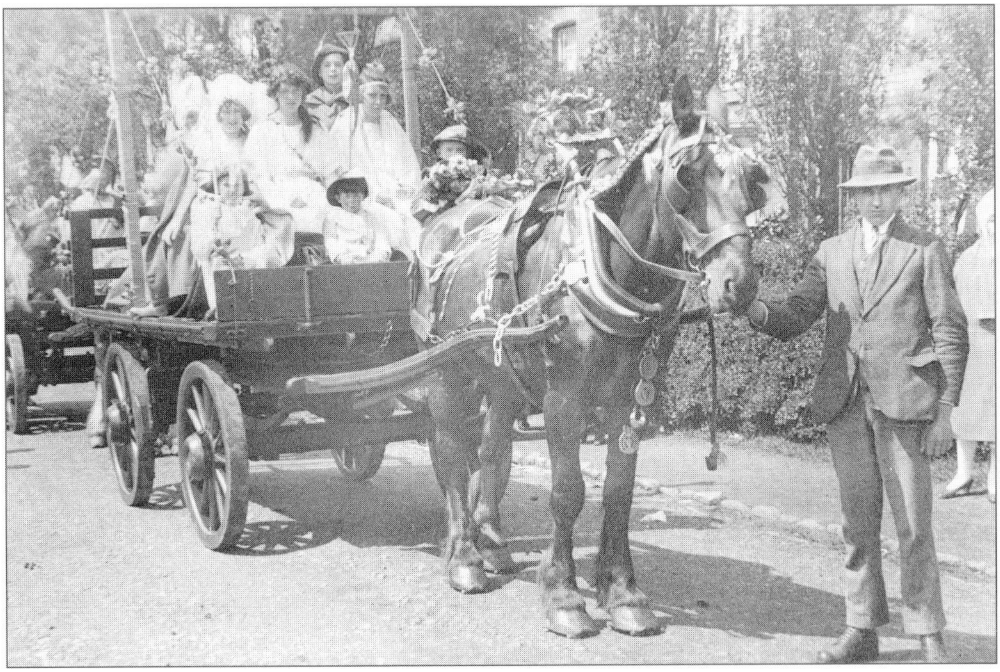

Hough Green and the June Fair, 1923. Here we see the Queen of May, Hilda Kay, and her courtiers, together with retiring Queen, Margaret Lewis, sitting on a decorated cart in Ash Lane, waiting to join the procession up to the church.

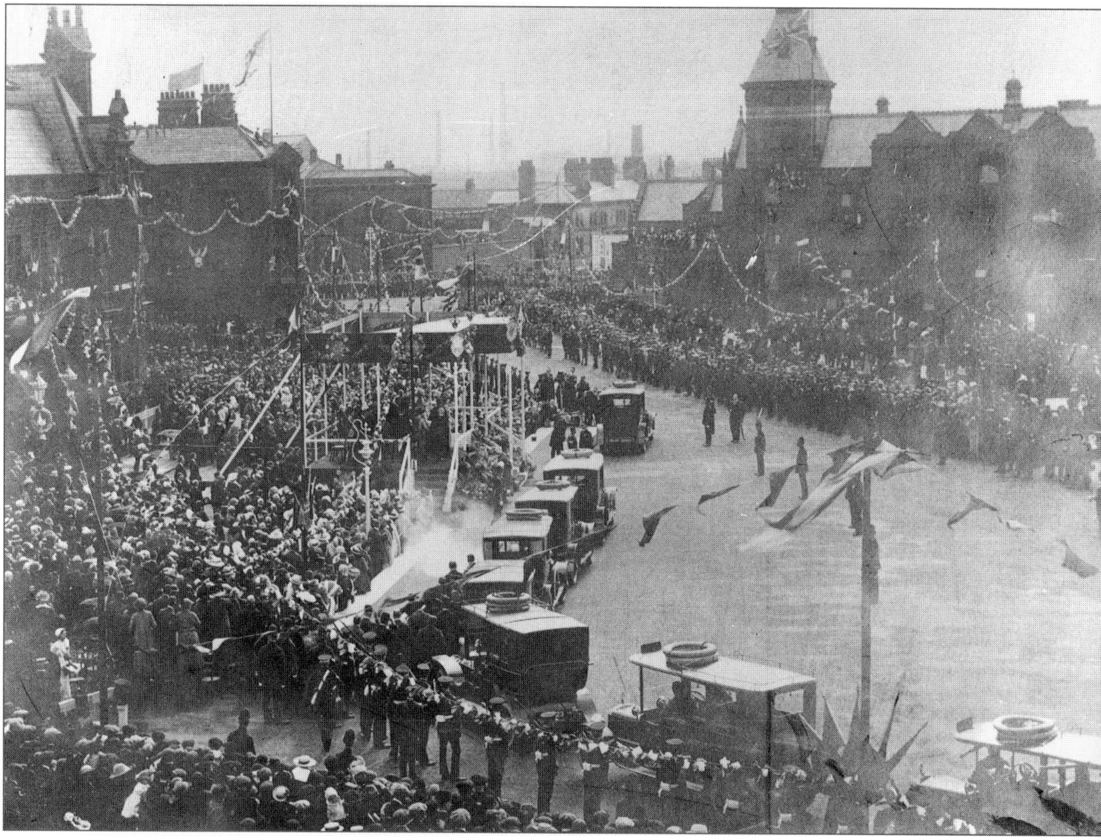

Here we see the royal motor cavalcade, carrying King George V and Queen Mary, drawn up beside the specially erected podium in front of the town hall, July 1925. The royal couple had been staying with Lord Derby at Knowsley and came into Widnes via Norlands Lane. As the King entered Victoria Square, the Nazareth House Boys' Band (Nazareth House was a home for orphans) and the Widnes Musical and Opera Society sang a special version of 'God Save the King', which was somewhat drowned by the bells of St Paul's Church that rang out as the couple entered the square. The King and Queen stopped for about twenty minutes and then drove down Victoria Road, Waterloo Road and Mersey Road, and after inspecting the workings of the Transporter Bridge, crossed over to Cheshire. Now as we tell what happened that day it seems very full and busy, but the actual royal visit only lasted just over an hour. Even the King worked hard when in Widnes.

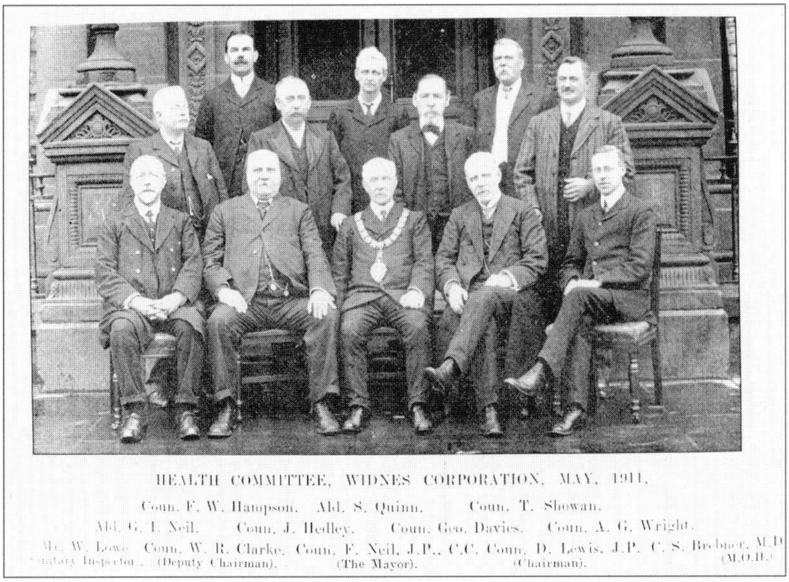

The Widnes Corporation Health Committee, May 1911. May was the month when Widnes elected new civic leaders and the newly elected committees had their photographs taken. Here we see Councillor F. Neil, the Mayor, sitting in the centre, and next to him a rare photograph of Councillor David Lewis, the man who did so much charity work in the Widnes and Liverpool area. These men fought for a better Widnes, and were forthright in their plans for more sewers, better water, and water closets for every house. The year 1911 was a time of great industrial unrest in Widnes, with many strikes and men out of work – another problem the councillors had to face.

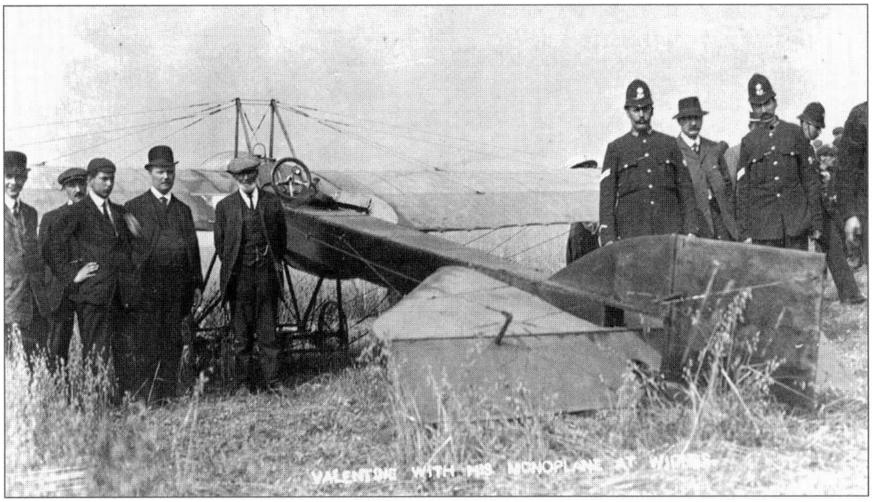

During a 'Round Britain Air Race', sponsored by the *Daily Mail*, with a prize of £10,000, one of the twenty-one contestants made an unexpected visit to Widnes. This was James Valentine of Mottram Hall, Prestbury, in his monoplane. He had been blown off course during bad weather and landed on fields that are now Widnes Golf Course. He stayed the night at Upper House Farm, and during that night word spread; by 3 a.m. a crowd of over 1,000 had arrived to see him take off again. The police had to be called to clear a way through the crowds, and after signing autographs and shaking hands, Valentine finally took off at 8 a.m. on 29 July 1911 with the advice 'Fly south, find the River Mersey and follow the ship canal to the left'. This he did and landed at Trafford Park air receiving station around noon.

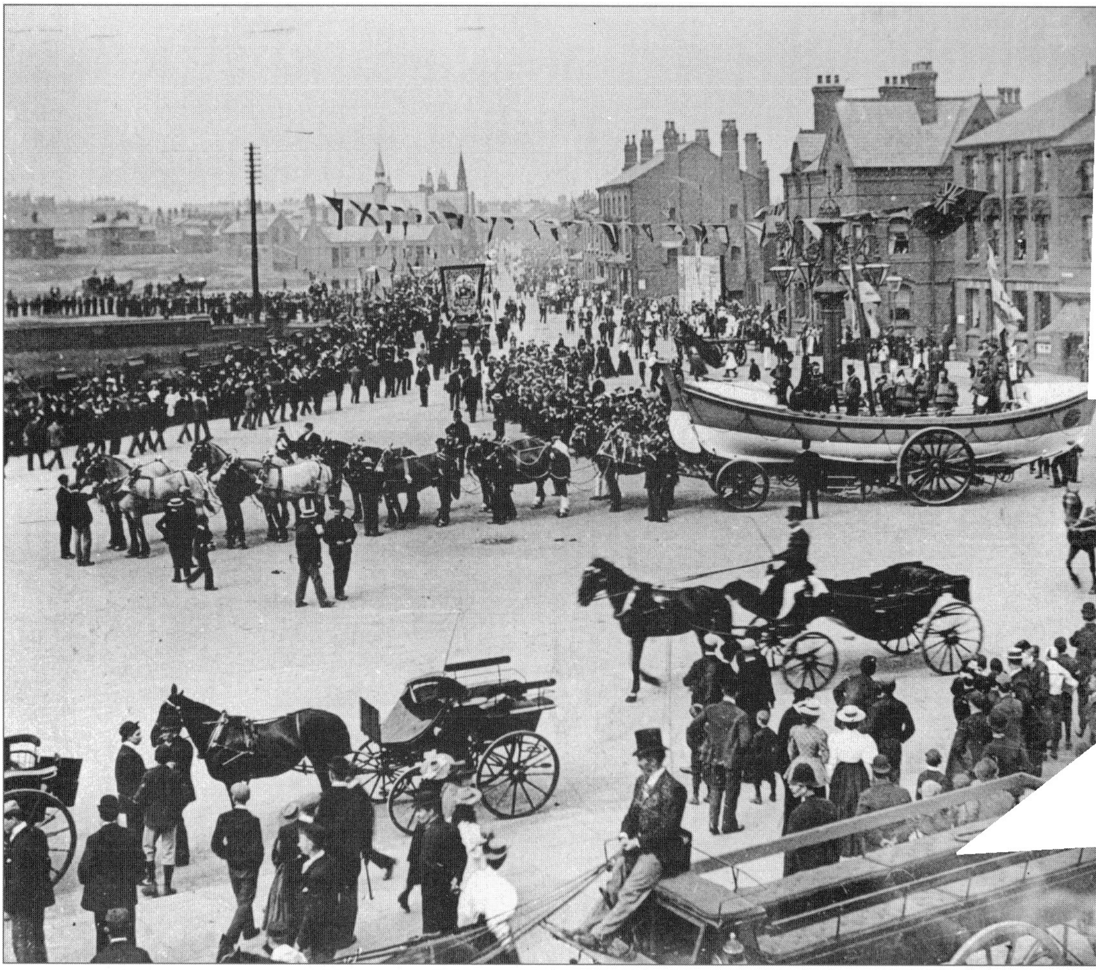

Lifeboat Day in Widnes, *c.* 1880. The exploits of Grace Darling and the bravery of lifeboat men in general made thrilling reading in the magazines and books of late Victorian times. Each town was inspired to do something, and the larger and more prosperous towns bought lifeboats, named them after their town and gave them to the seaside communities. This is Widnes' effort, a grand parade with all the town's dignitaries turned out for the occasion. Because the name Widnes is not on the boat pictured here they may just have borrowed it to raise funds towards their own lifeboat. Of course there was a procession with bands and flags, and here we see men walking away from the square with a banner leading them. The town hall had not yet been built, but across the square land had been given and marked out for St Paul's Church and Vicarage. Simms Cross Junior and Infant School, which had opened in November 1878, can be clearly seen at the centre back of our picture. The second building on the right was the post office at the time; later it became the Co-op Café.

CHAPTER THREE

PEOPLE & PLACES

Widnes can count itself fortunate that the men who started the industrialisation of the area had faith in their ability, and brains to keep inventing and improving the processes needed for the manufacture of chemicals to progress. From 1800, when the villages that now make up the area of Widnes were still easily identifiable, to the turn of the last century, when Widnes Council were fighting hard to keep Widnes going forward and prospering against the tide of mass emigration away from the smells, smoke and dangers at the heart of the chemical industry, the area changed beyond recognition. Names that we now take for granted as road names and the names of buildings in the town once belonged to real people who put their money, energy and time into the building of Widnes, for example Hutchinson and Gossage who were bold leaders in the chemical industry. Behind Orr's zinc white is the story of John Bryson Orr, who, with Thomas Kenyon, set out in the depression years of 1893–5 to make 'zinc white', used in the manufacture of paint, instead of 'lead white' which was poisonous. He ended up taking over the Vine Works and employing over 600 workers, when all around men were being laid off.

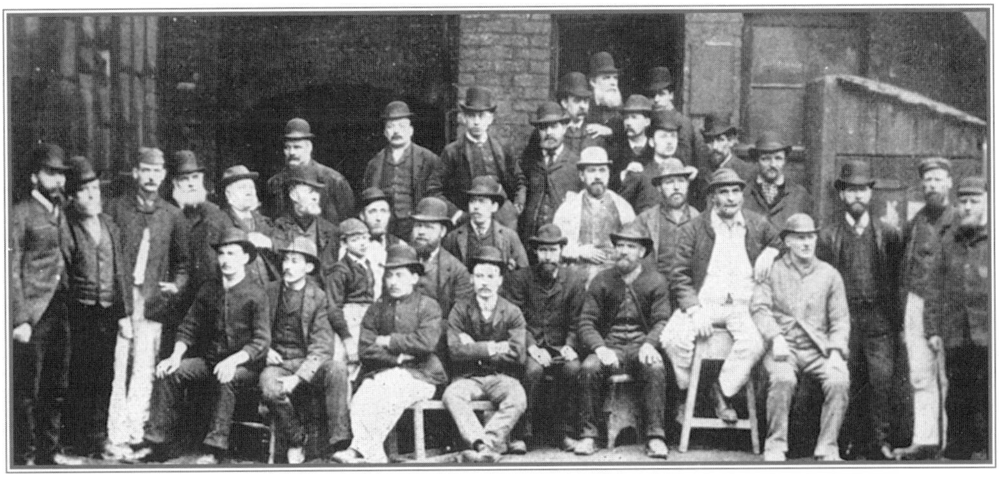

The Gaskell-Deacon Process men and their foremen (sitting) before the big depression and lay-offs in the chemical industry, *c.* 1890. Mr Holbrook Gaskell of Manchester joined Henry Deacon, who had been successful in earlier ventures with John Hutchinson. They made ammonia, soda and sulphuric acid. At the time of this picture the Gaskell-Deacon Works employed nearly 500 men and was the largest single employer in Widnes.

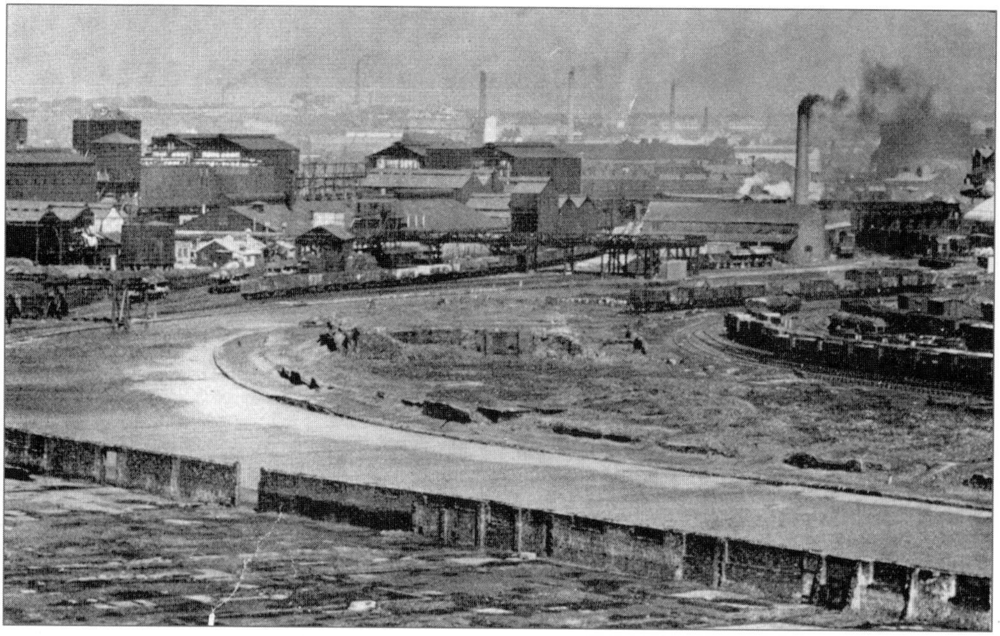

Spike Island and the St Helens Canal, *c.* 1930. The canal, which was known as the Sankey Navigation when it was first cut in 1755, only went as far as Sankey Bridges, where it joined the River Mersey. It was extended to Fiddler's Ferry so that the salt from the Cheshire 'Wiches' – Nantwich, Northwich and Middlewich – could reach St Helens more quickly. Copper ore and coal were also taken up this canal.

The coming of the railway heralded the decline of the canals. The St Helens–Runcorn Gap Railway was the first to be built, and it took trade away from the Sankey Navigation. The railway company even built a dock, now filled in, which meant that they could carry on unloading even at low tide. The Sankey Navigation hit back by reclaiming a dock from the river and extending their canal to Widnes (Wood End) in about 1834. This 'new cut' as it was called is what we see here, and as boats loaded with raw materials were passing up and down it was an ideal place to set up a factory.

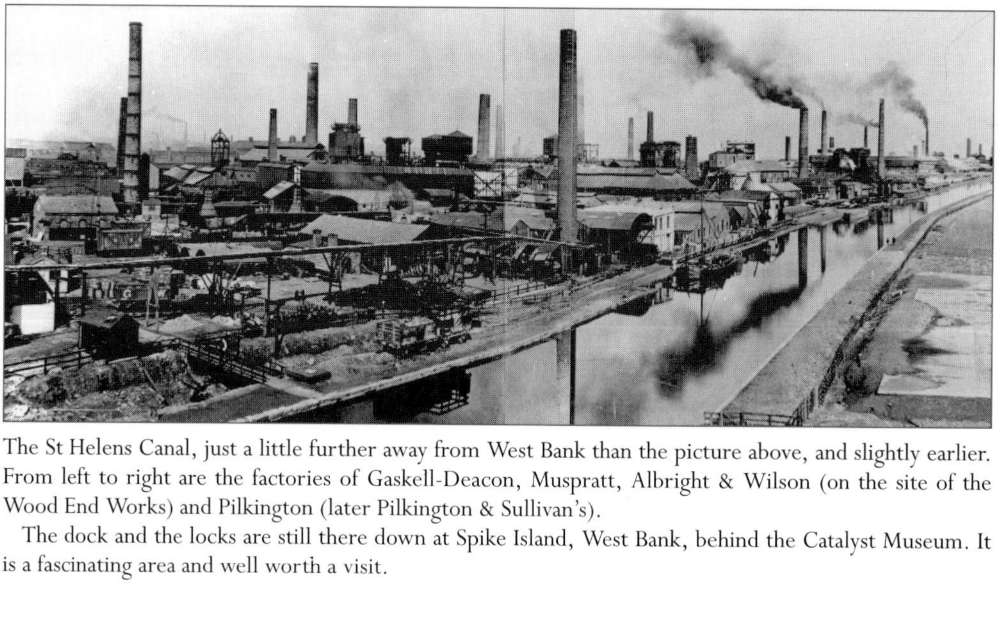

The St Helens Canal, just a little further away from West Bank than the picture above, and slightly earlier. From left to right are the factories of Gaskell-Deacon, Muspratt, Albright & Wilson (on the site of the Wood End Works) and Pilkington (later Pilkington & Sullivan's).

The dock and the locks are still there down at Spike Island, West Bank, behind the Catalyst Museum. It is a fascinating area and well worth a visit.

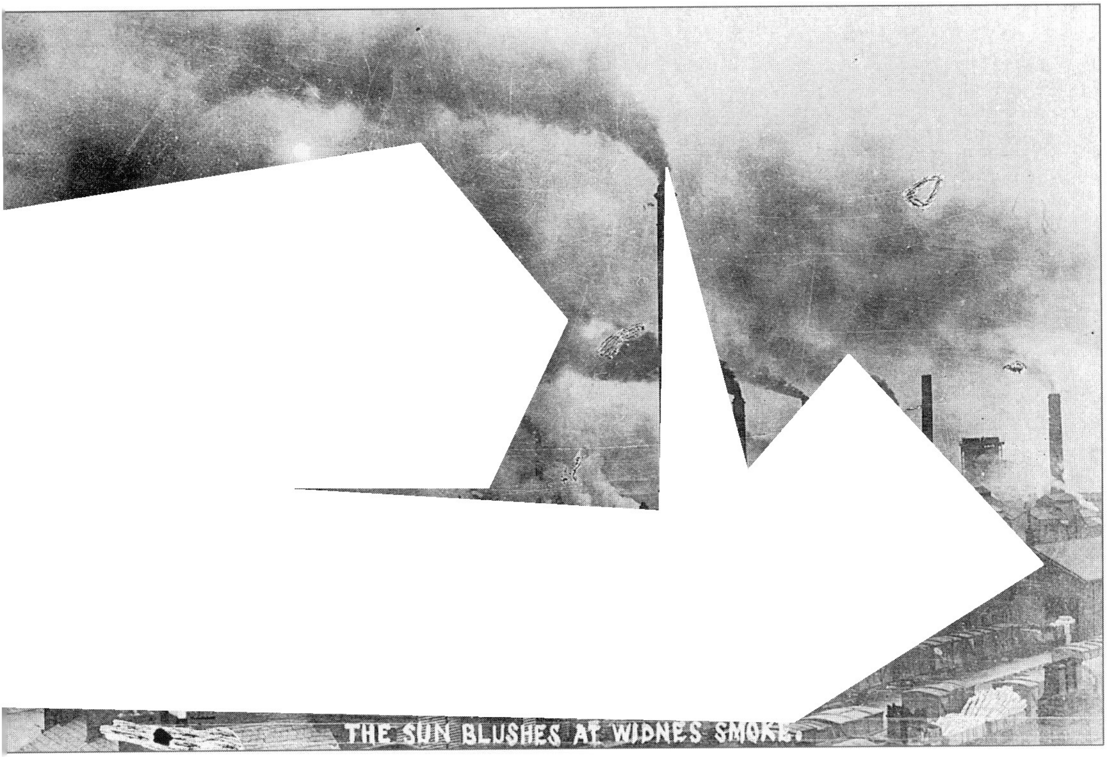

The most famous postcard ever to come out of Widnes. It was produced in 1900 by W. Hall, the man who recorded much of Widnes' past and won several gold medals in photographic competitions. His office was on Christie Street, and historians owe him a large debt for the marvellous collection of photographs he left behind. The tallest of the chimneys in the picture is Bolton's chimney, then the largest in Widnes, built in 1884 for the Mersey Copper Works.

Widnes had to fight for many years against the Obnoxious Vapours Society, and there are over fifty years' worth of letters, complaints and litigation between the men who ran the factories and the men who suffered from the fall-out. There is a very old joke of a farmer at the beautifully named Primrose Valley Farm, just behind the large chemical works off Gorsey Lane, Cuerdley, who when asked what crops he was planting in a certain field replied 'It doesn't really matter – I'm just planting compensation'. He was referring to the fact that the air would kill whatever he planted anyway, and he would sue the large factory owners, and win his compensation! In fact, many chemical manufacturers found it easier to buy out the farmers and put managers on wages in the farms. For every letter bemoaning the lack of greenery in Widnes, one of the town's leaders would produce one saying how nice someone's garden was, only a mile away from Widnes. When Liverpool Corporation claimed that Widnes' air was killing the flowers and trees in Calderstone's Park, the town hit back with photographs of strong young trees, said to be taken on St Bede's Road (later named Kingsway), in Widnes.

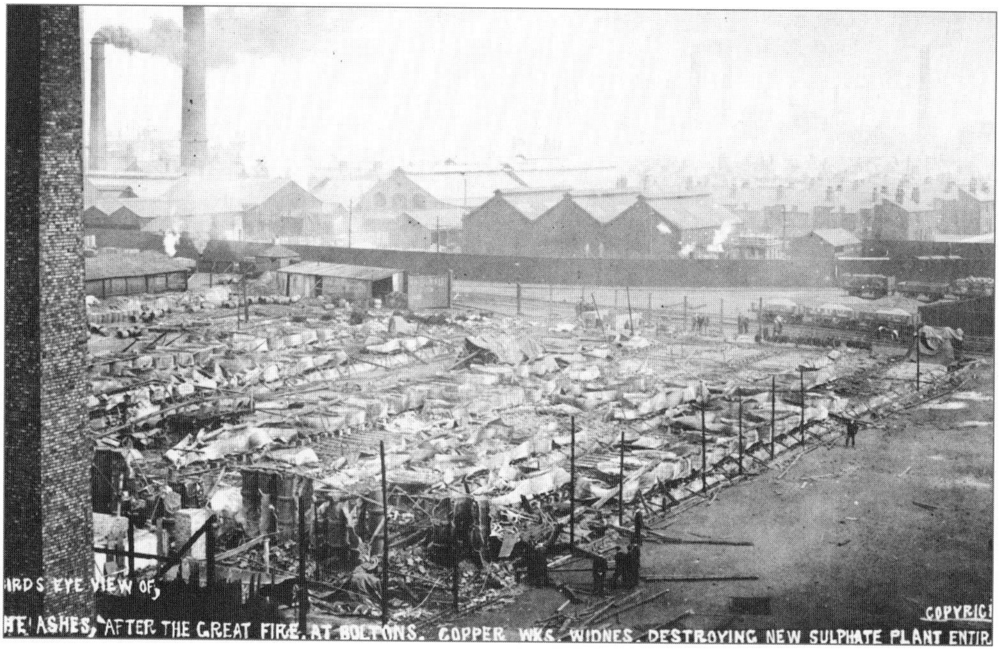

With chemical factories and furnaces so prevalent in Widnes, it is not surprising that there were accidents. This picture shows one of the more spectacular ones, a great fire at Bolton's Copper Works, Hutchinson Street, at the turn of the century. The factory had opened in 1881 as the Mersey Copper Works, and they made copper rods and plates, used mostly for the building of railway engines. They later expanded into manufacturing copper-covered rollers for calico printing.

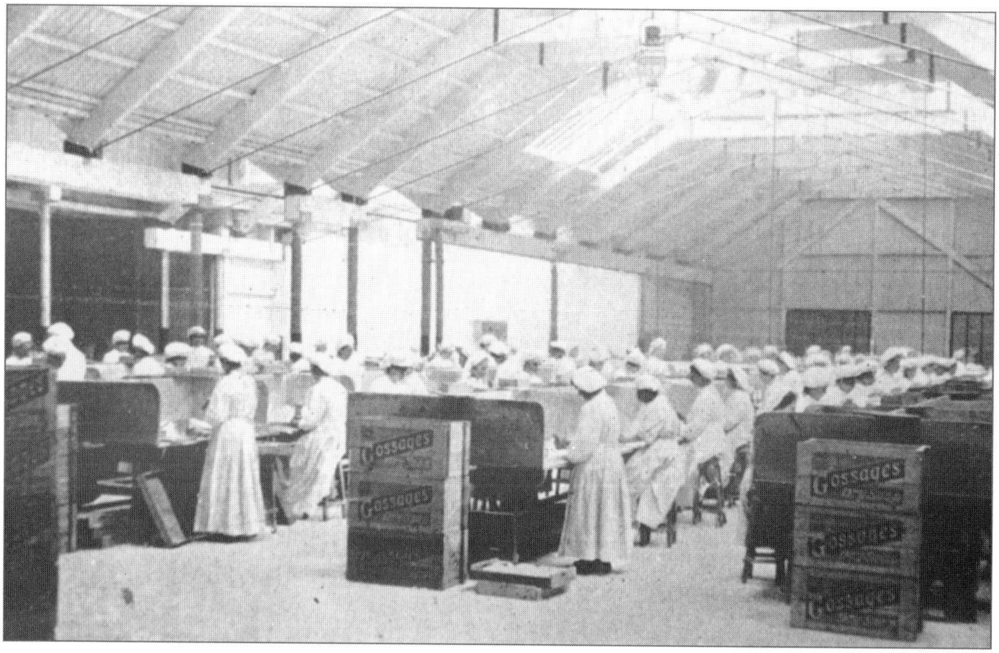

Gossage's made soap, and made soap well. They were among the first to start packaging it to appeal to the middle classes. Here we see their newly opened packing department in about 1912 and some of the hundred girls employed to wrap the new mottled soap that Gossage had invented.

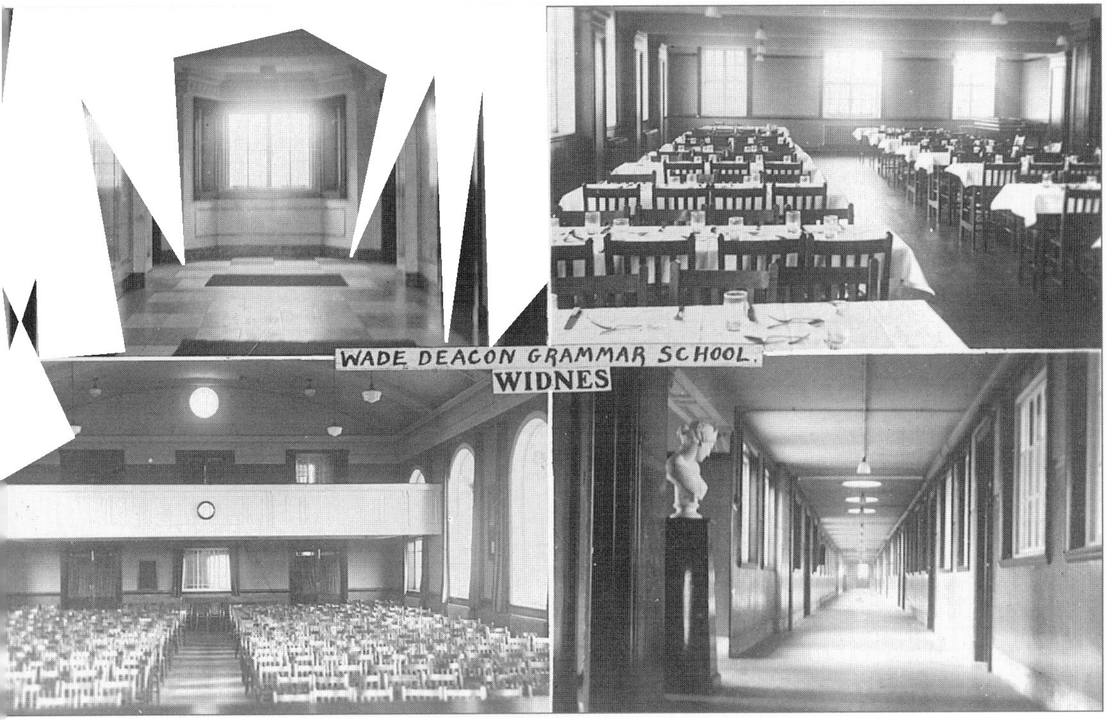

This postcard shows Wade Deacon Grammar School, Widnes, 1935. I attended this school from 1956 and we had four 'houses' named after great industrialists. I wish they had told me who Muspratt was! I spent fours years in Muspratt House (Yellow) without knowing about Frederick Muspratt and his Wood End Chemical Works. His younger brother Edmund Knowles Muspratt took over in 1855 and built up the firm. James Liebig Muspratt fought the Obnoxious Vapours Society, while at the same time doing his best to cut down the emissions from his factory. The Muspratts were strong supporters of the Widnes Workmen's Public House Co. Limited, which provided tea, cocoa and other non-alcoholic drinks from a public house in Anne Street, and 'cocoa rooms' in Hutchinson Street. Anyone who bought tea or cocoa could use the free stove to cook their own food, and the house was open from 5.30 a.m. for the early shift workers. Max Muspratt followed his father and grandfather into the industry; he also showed a lot of compassion for employees. How much more interesting it is to put personalities to the names.

We were never the top house; it was always Red (Deacon House). Henry Deacon, after studying under Faraday and James Nasmyth, the iron founder and engineer, came to Widnes in the early 1840s. He married Emma Wade, and their son was Sir Henry Wade Deacon, a name we know so well.

Gossage's (Green) was of course William Gossage, who they said kept more people clean than any other, whose processes brought the price of soap down from 6*d* to 2*d* per lb. Gossage invented so many processes for newer and cleaner ways of making the chemicals that he is regarded as one of the founders of the chemical industry in Widnes.

Blue (House) was called after John Hutchinson who came to Widnes in 1847. He gave the town the first alkali works, using a process that was to bring Widnes so much wealth, prosperity and work. Unfortunately the other side of the coin was pollution, smoke and smells. Hutchinson gave Widnes the cheapest gas in Britain, and he formed the Widnes Gas and Water Company that struggled to provide drinkable water for the local people. Unfortunately he died young (aged forty) in 1865, with many plans unfinished. The memoriams (obituaries) that followed his death constantly referred to him as 'The Father of the Widnes Chemical Industry'.

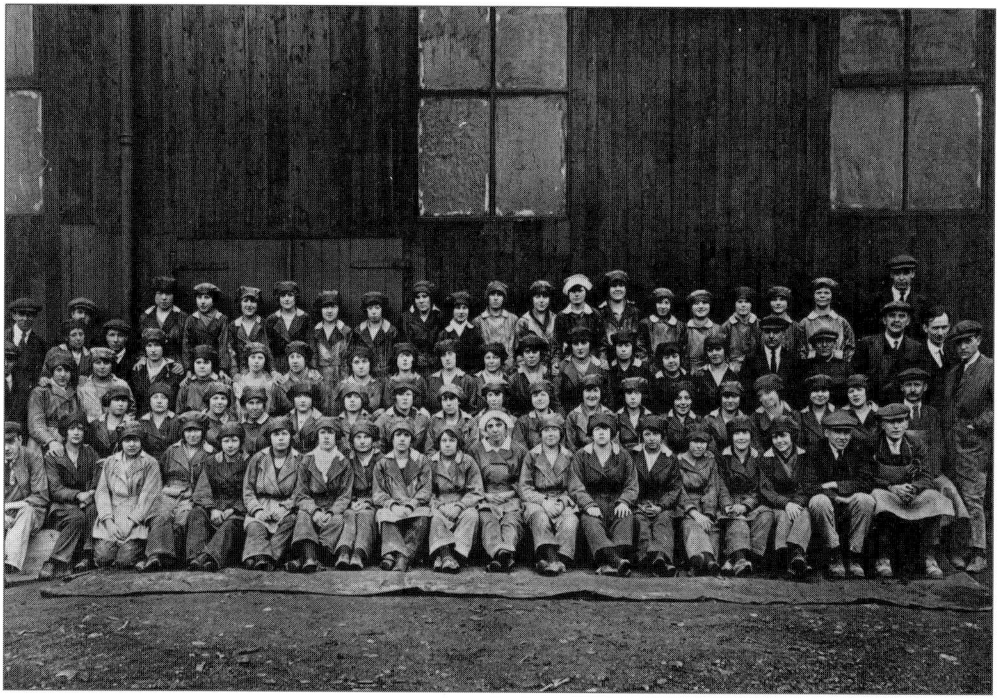

The girl packers, and a few of the men, from the Greenbank Works (Pilkington & Sullivan) at Moss Bank, 1926. This department moved from the St Helens Works in 1921. Their rough working clothes reflect the fact that they were packing tins with bleaching powder and caustic soda known as ‘Red Heart’.

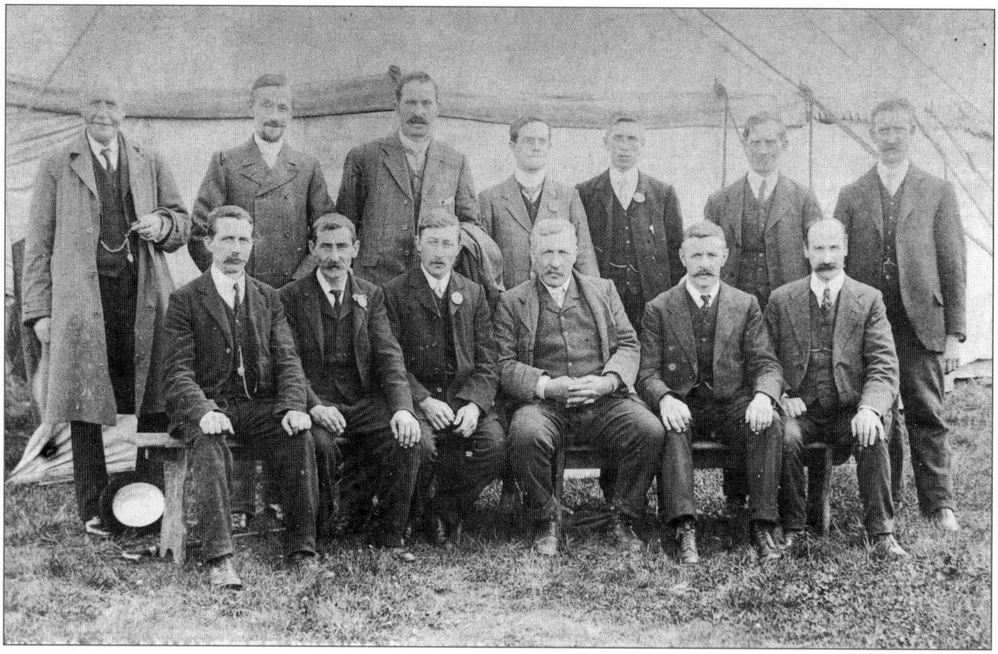

The committee that ran the Widnes Show, which had evolved from the Farnworth Wakes, 1910. The show was held on Dennis Recreation Grounds on Birchfield Road, which is where this photograph was taken, in front of one of the marquees.

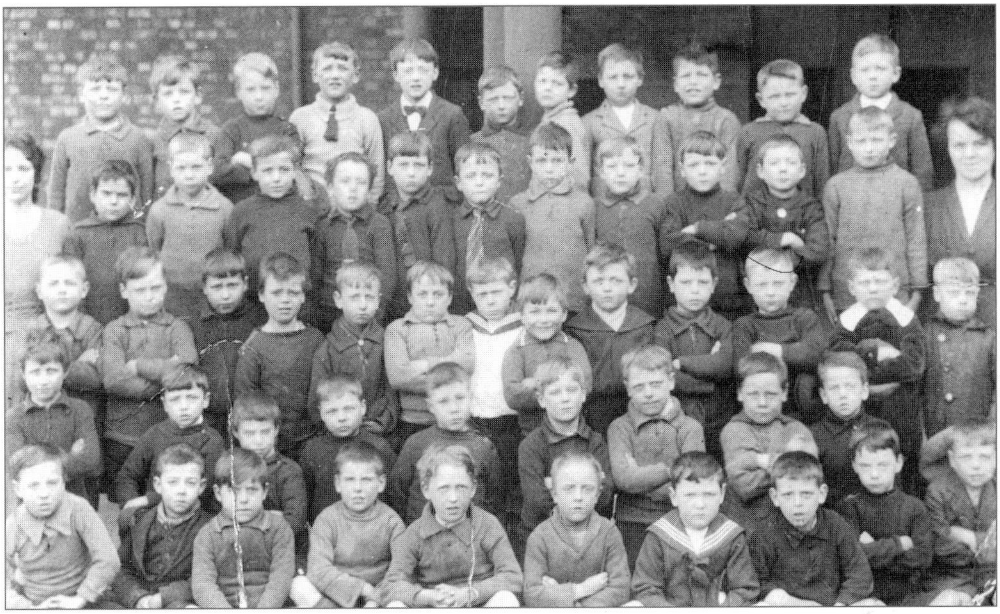

Simms Cross Junior Boys, *c.* 1922. What a lot of characters there are on this picture! I wonder if that is a young Miss Chamberlain on the right; she was still teaching in the 1950s when I went there. This must be two classes as there are two teachers and fifty-four little cherubs in the picture – including the two brave souls whose mums had sent them in sailor suits.

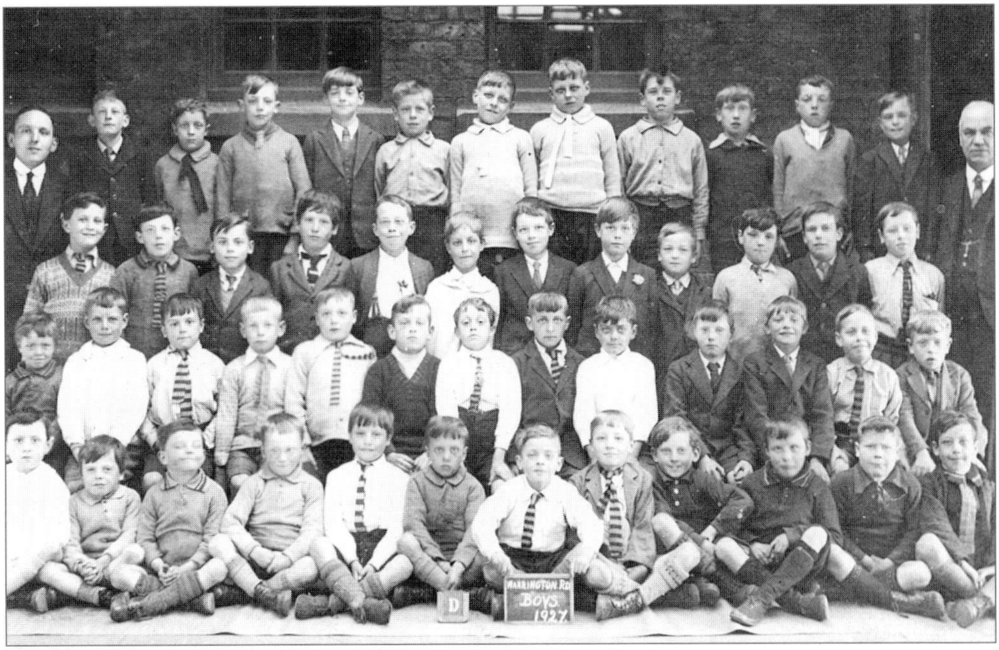

Warrington Road Boys, Class D, and a much more prosperous-looking lot we have here, 1927. Six of them are even in suits or jackets. The school opened in 1877 as a Board School where the children were taught the three R's, plus grammar, geography and literature. In 1911 the children at this school were given bread and butter when they arrived in the morning and a cup of cocoa, donated by Cadburys, before they went home after school, as many of the children were going hungry because their parents were out of work.

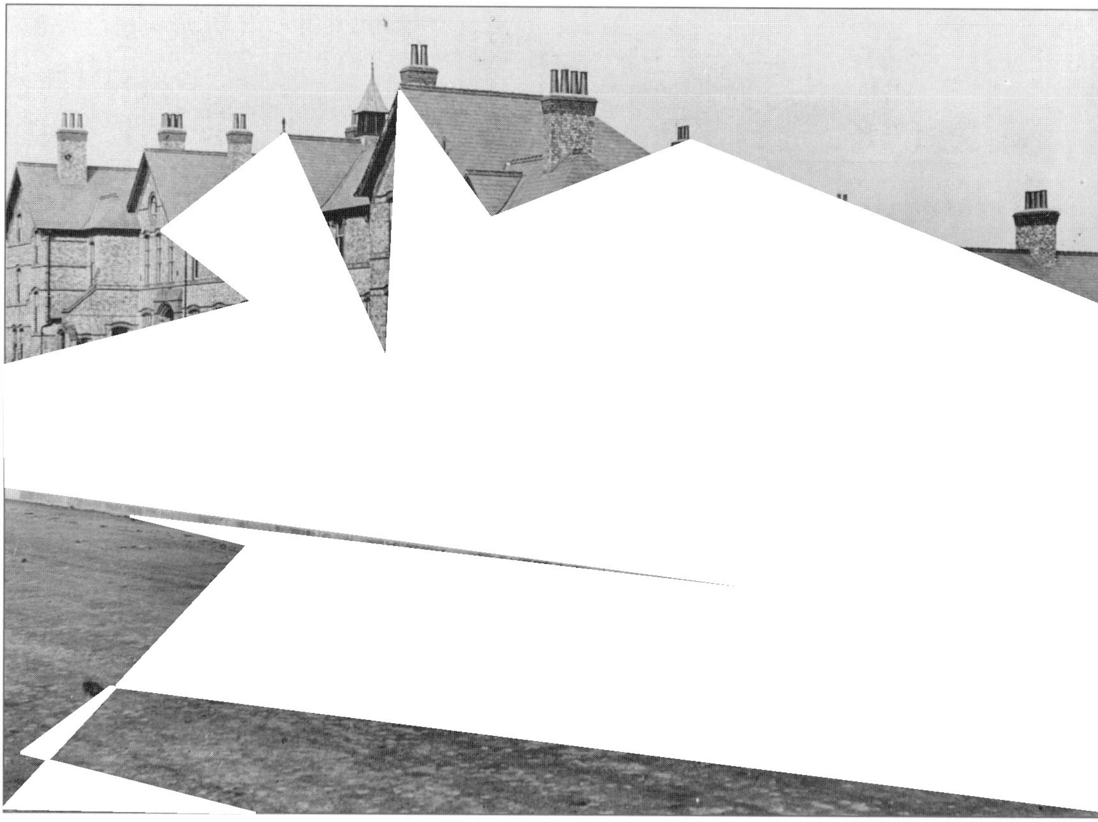

The 'Approved School', Norlands Lane, Farnworth. This dismal-looking building opened in 1877 as the 'Nautical School' which was an Approved School for boys. The seafaring connection could come from the fact that at Liverpool they had set up training ships anchored in the River Mersey, where 'problem' boys and boys on the streets were taken to be given a training for the sea. The Catholic Church also used an old sailing ship as an asylum for orphans and waifs where the boys lived on board and were taught to read and write and learn a trade. These places were hard, and the children lived under a harsh regime.

Walking down Norton Lane and seeing this building was enough of a deterrent to any young lads who might have been thinking of running amok. Just seeing the boys from this school going to the pictures or the swimming baths, with their teachers watching them closely, marching in crocodile lines in their grey uniforms and crewcut hairstyles, would send shivers down my spine. Fortunately, or unfortunately, depending on your personal views, this building is no longer used for this purpose. It was for a time St Aidan's Roman Catholic School, but has been re-vamped and turned into modern offices, with the Norlands Nursing Home at the back.

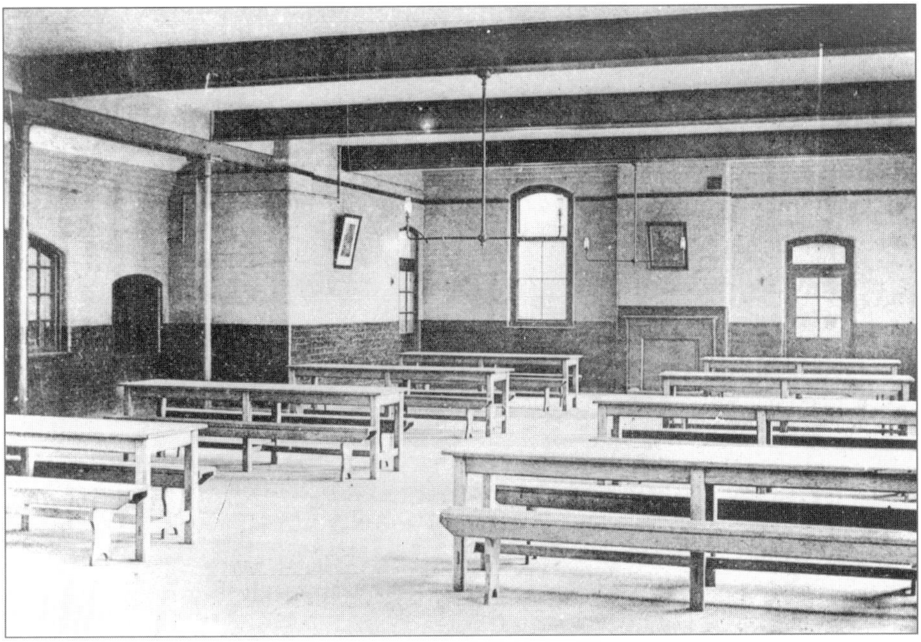

The dining hall of Farnworth Nautical School sometime between the wars. It is hard to date the picture as it was a sparse place and changes and luxuries did not enter the thoughts of the Board of Governors. They were being hard on the boys in their care for their own good. Note the gas pipes and gas lights hanging down in the centre of the room.

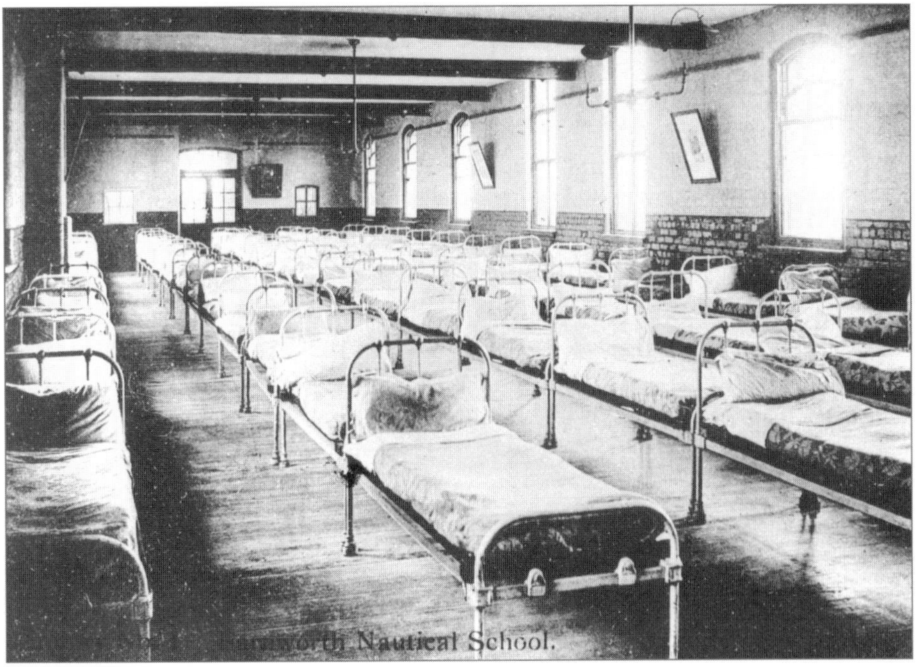

The 'ward' of the Farnworth Nautical School, *c.* 1930. Many a comedian has got a laugh from his audience by telling them how good his school was: everyone thought highly of it; in fact it was 'approved' by the government! The school became known as the Approved School, but our picture shows the harsh reality of life for the boys there: no lockers, no bedside tables, no privacy.

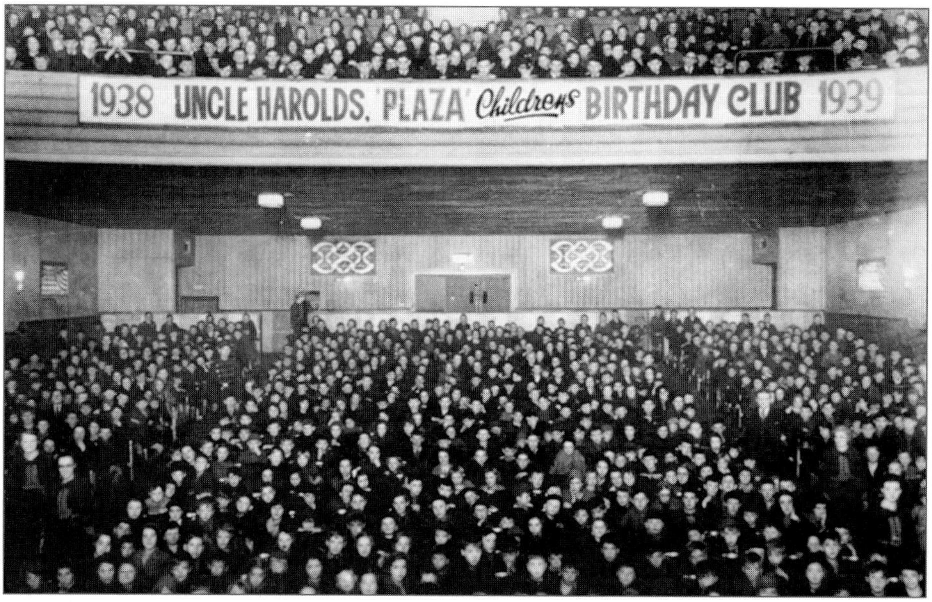

The Plaza Cinema in Peel House Lane, showing 'Uncle Harold's Children's Birthday Club' (Saturday morning), 1939. The cinema opened in 1937 so this was its second birthday celebration. 'Uncle Harold' was Harold Cookson, and he can be seen standing halfway up the aisle on the right. There are six usherettes in the picture too; they were there to keep us in order while Ming the Merciless, Flash Gordon and Robot Robbie kept us enthralled.

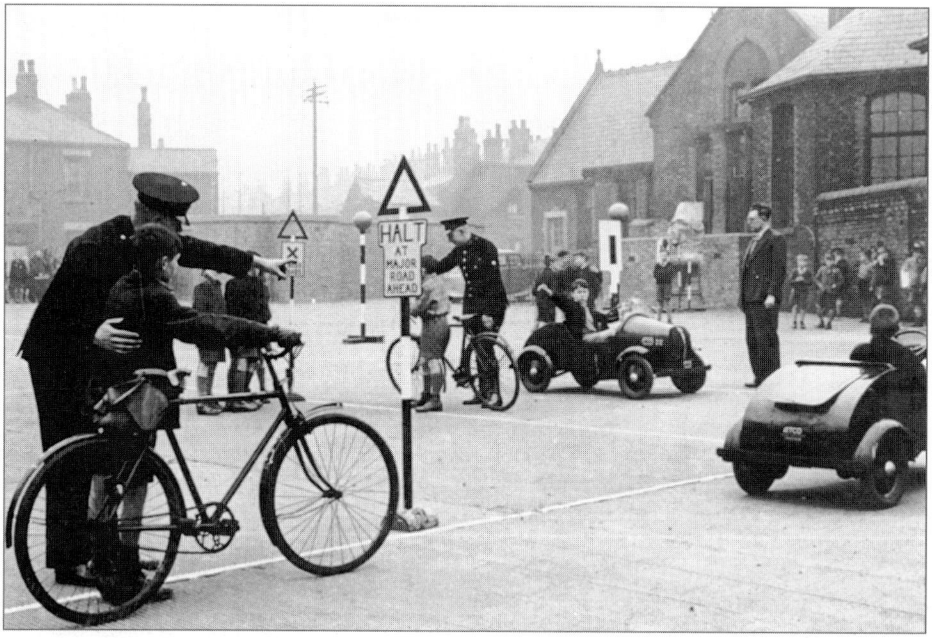

Widnes Constabulary are giving instructions on bicycle proficiency and road safety lessons at Simm's Cross Junior School, 1947. The headmaster, Mr Barton, is looking on. Mr Barton was of the 'old school': stern, but fair. My classmates and I were terrified of him, but looking back now I can see that he was humane, and that he did a very good job. He played a big part in the National Union of Teachers' campaign for better schools and smaller classes (photograph *Daily Post*).

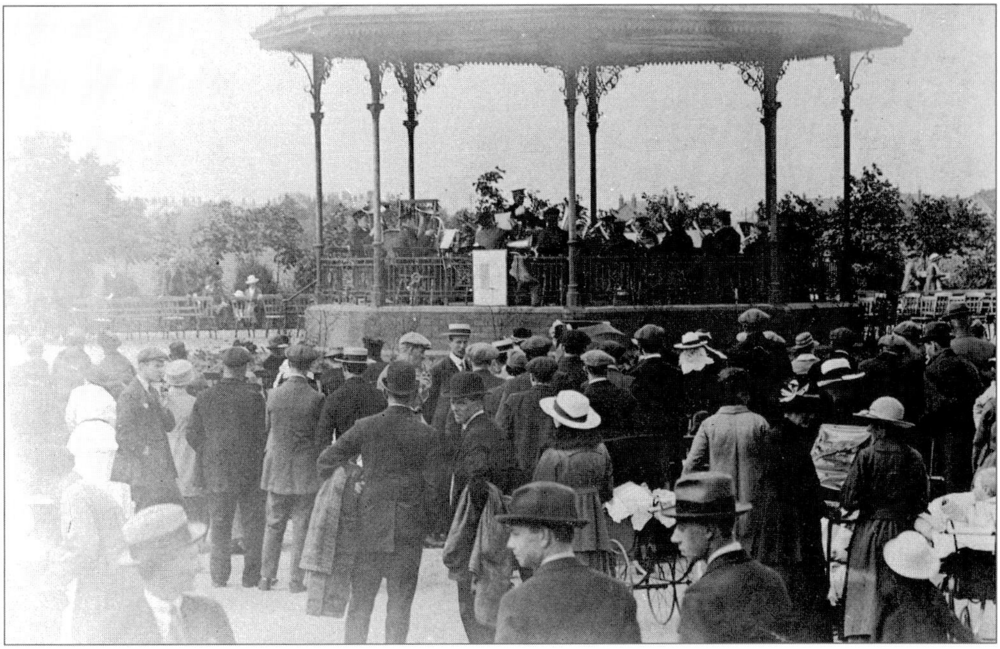

Foden's Works Brass Band playing in Victoria Park, 1925. When Widnes Corporation decided to follow the lead of other large towns and introduce music into the parks on Sundays, they received more than their fair share of opposition from the vicars and religious leaders in Widnes. Although the open-air concerts had been popular for some years the introduction in 1924 of Sunday concerts provoked a letter of opposition signed by the Reverends Mr Baker from Farnworth, Mr Dawson from St Ambrose, Alban Marsh from St Mary's, Mr Storer from St Paul's and Edward Peel, Wesleyan, among others. It was even proposed that ministers should give sermons in Victoria Park on Sunday evenings, but that never materialised. Eventually Sunday concerts were given the go-ahead, but they could not start until 8 p.m. when all church services were over.

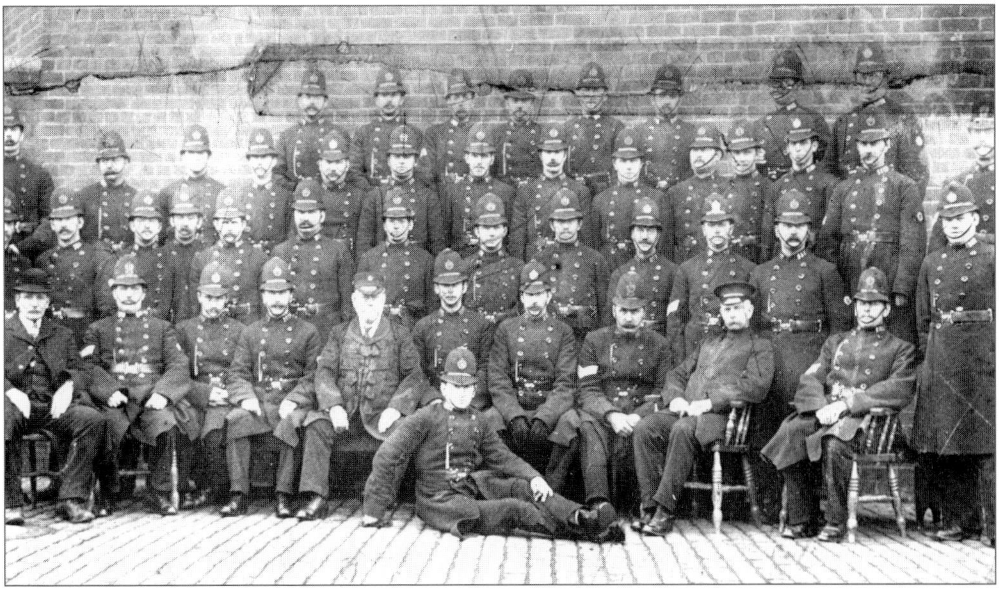

The wonderful Widnes Constabulary, 1904. All seem eager and ready for duty.

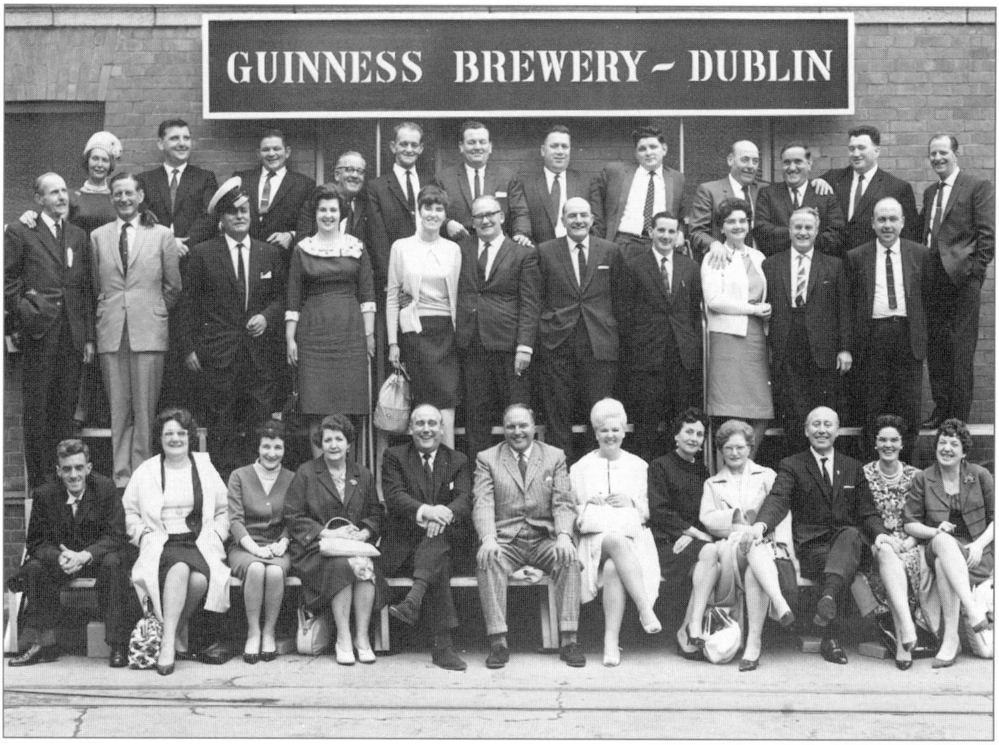

This is an outing from the Widnes Licensed Victuallers, 1959. On behalf of their customers these licencees and their wives spent a hard day inspecting the plant and product of the Guinness Brewery in Dublin. I can make out Austin Gilmore from the Derby, the Shuttleworths from the Sun Inn, and Dave Barrow from Cork Harbour, as well as my own mum in the front row. How many landlords can you name?

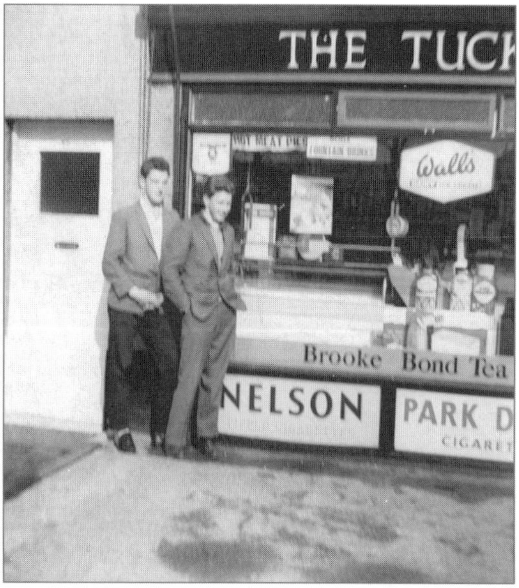

Opposite the Wade Deacon School in the late 1950s was a tuck shop. After school it sold crisps and Wagon Wheels, and it had one of those machines with a big goldfish bowl on top that dispensed carbonated water to be flavoured with raspberry or other syrups. In the winter there was hot Vimto and Oxo – especially welcome on a cold and wet Saturday morning when rugby was being played. That is me on the right outside the tuck shop on a Saturday afternoon in 1958 waiting with my mate Ronnie Shuttleworth to meet two young ladies after football.

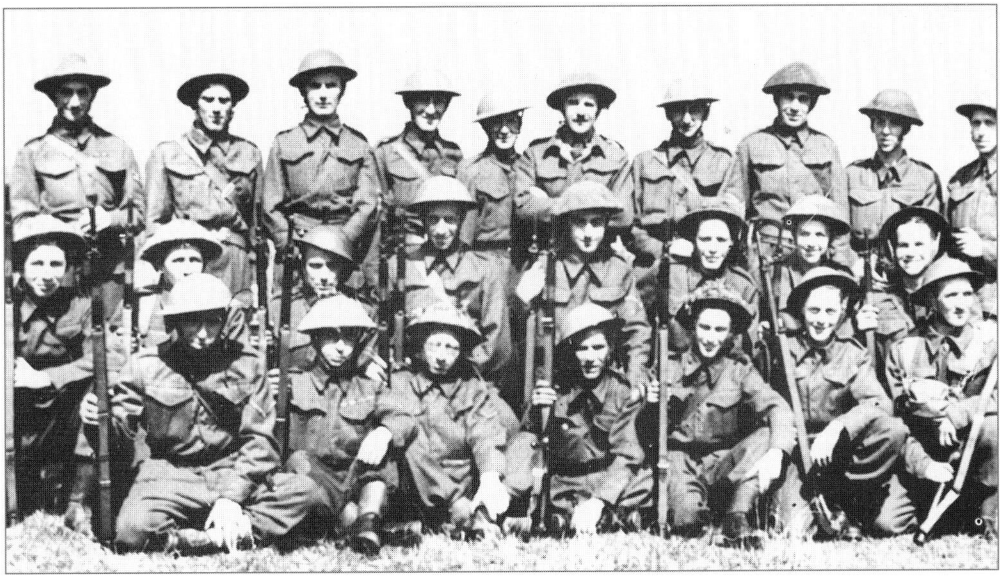

The 2nd Batallion Widnes Home Guard on parade, 1941. When first formed they were called the Local Defence Volunteers (the LDV), but Jimmy Handley's famous radio programme *ITMA* nicknamed them the 'Look, Duck and Vanish boys', much to the government's displeasure – so they were renamed the Home Guard.

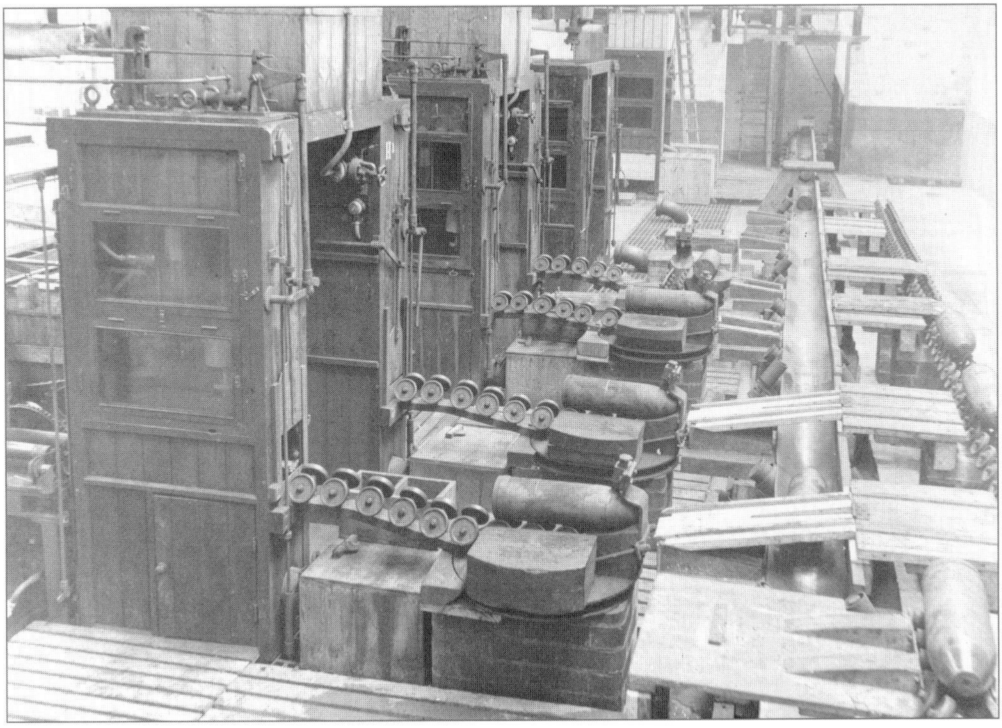

Widnes was very heavily involved in war production in both world wars. During the Second World War it was considered a prime bombing site by the Luftwaffe. The authorities set up an army camp, with anti-aircraft guns, just off Heath Road at Ditton, to guard Widnes and the approaches to Liverpool. Here we see phosgene gas being packed into shells at Pilkington's Works, Widnes, in 1916, as part of the gas warfare of the First World War.

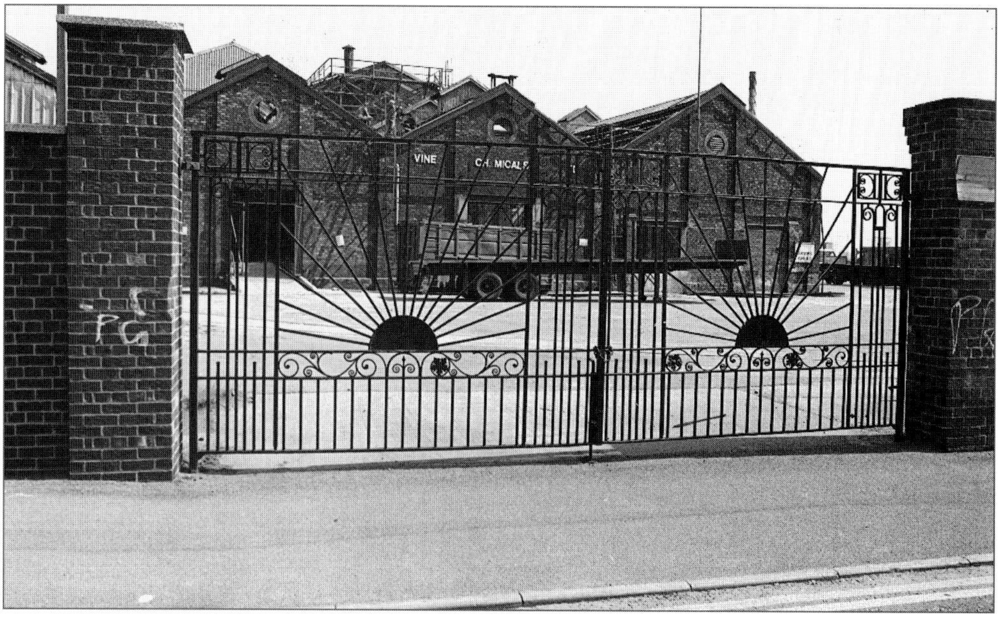

The Vine Works of Orr Zinc White, in Moor Lane, Widnes, *c.* 1970. Zinc white was used for making paint, linoleum and many rubber goods. John Bryson Orr took over the Vine Works, named after Vineyard House which was close to the site, in 1898. Today this is the site of Widnes Market and the new road system, but the gates seen here live on at the entrance to the Catalyst Museum.

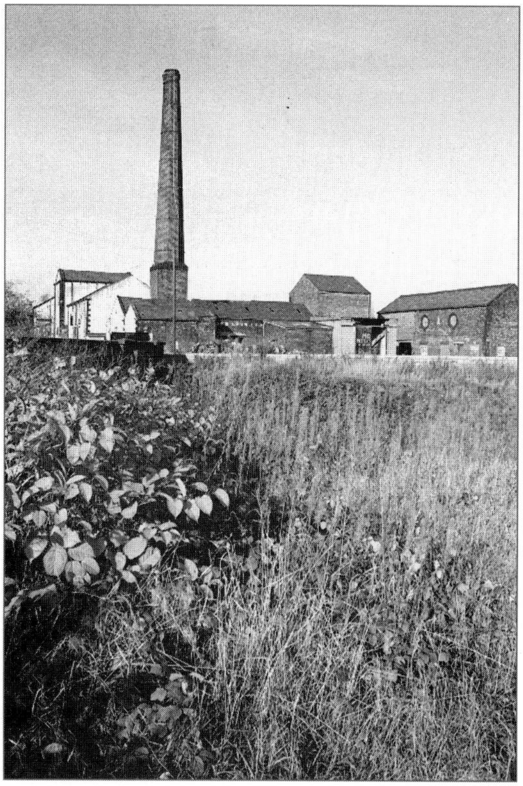

When Gossage's Soap Works closed in 1932 the management were so confident that there was still money to be made in soap manufacture that they purchased the old Pithe and Size Mill off Derby Road, Widnes, which was known locally as the Jute Factory, and set up the Widnes Soap Company Limited. They manufactured soap for the lower end of the market – carbolic soap, household soap – and ran the factory, seen here in the early 1960s, for many years at a profit. This was a successful management buy-out.

Chapter Four

The Original Villages

As the centre of Widnes developed in the 1880s and '90s, so the outlying villages also grew. The industrialists and factory owners moved out to the unspoilt areas like Cronton, Hough Green and Appleton, while West Bank and Simms Cross were turned into tightly packed rows of back-to-back jerry-built houses. In 1906 a house on Brown Street, Simms Cross (papered and painted) would cost 4s per week, and in Ross Street 6s per week. The average wage at the time was 23s per week for industrial workers. When public transport developed around the town it meant that the clerical staff and middle management could move out of the town centre to where the bosses lived, and areas such as Hough Green and Leigh Avenue built middle-class housing. This led to the development of housing estates, and the original villages changed forever.

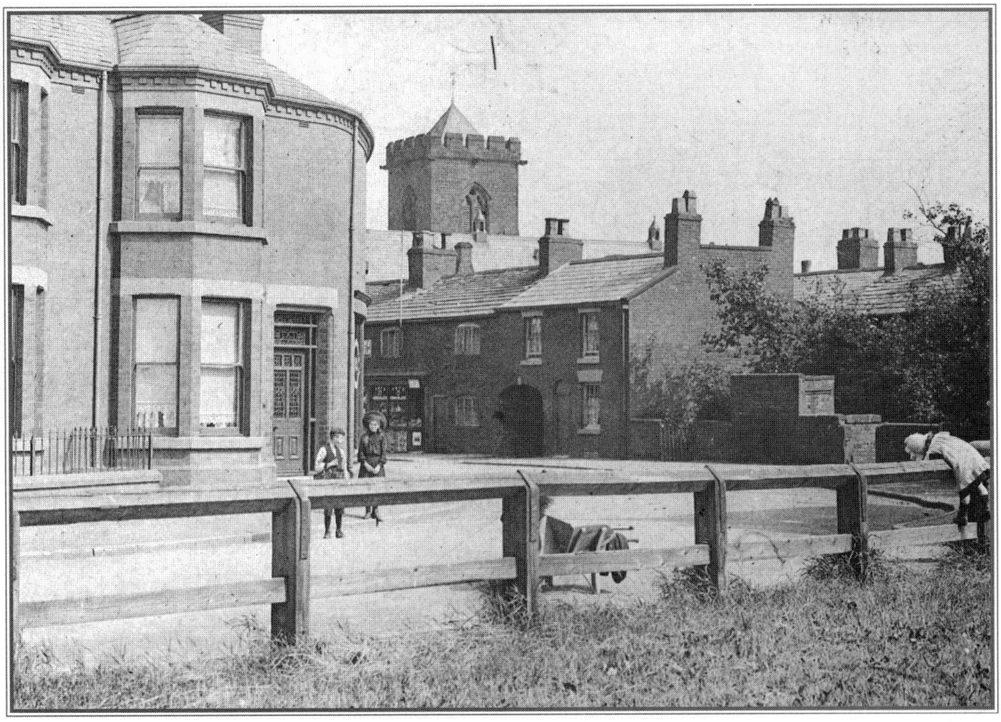

Appleton village, looking across Birchfield Road, at the turn of the century. St Bede's Church tower dominates the skyline, and the passageway between the houses, centre of the picture, is Tithebarn Street, once leading down to where the 'tenths' of all farmers' produce were kept in a barn. The pavement bends east and there is no sign of St Bede's Road (later Kingsway) as yet.

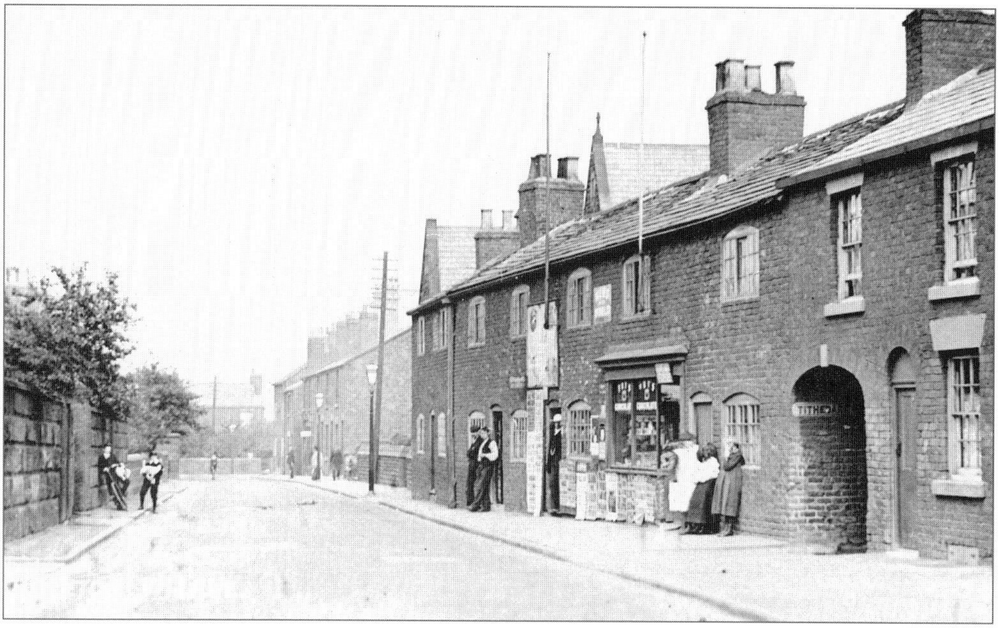

A view of Appleton village, looking down from Birchfield Road, *c.* 1900. Tithebarn Street can be seen on the right. The road is called Appleton Village and bends from the Kingsway/Birchfield junction down to the Leigh Avenue and Deacon Road junction, and this does lead to some confusion. This picture was taken when the area behind the wall on the left was still the Appleton estate (thirty-four acres) which belonged to the family of the late William Henry Deacon, who had died of a fever in 1876, aged fifty-three.

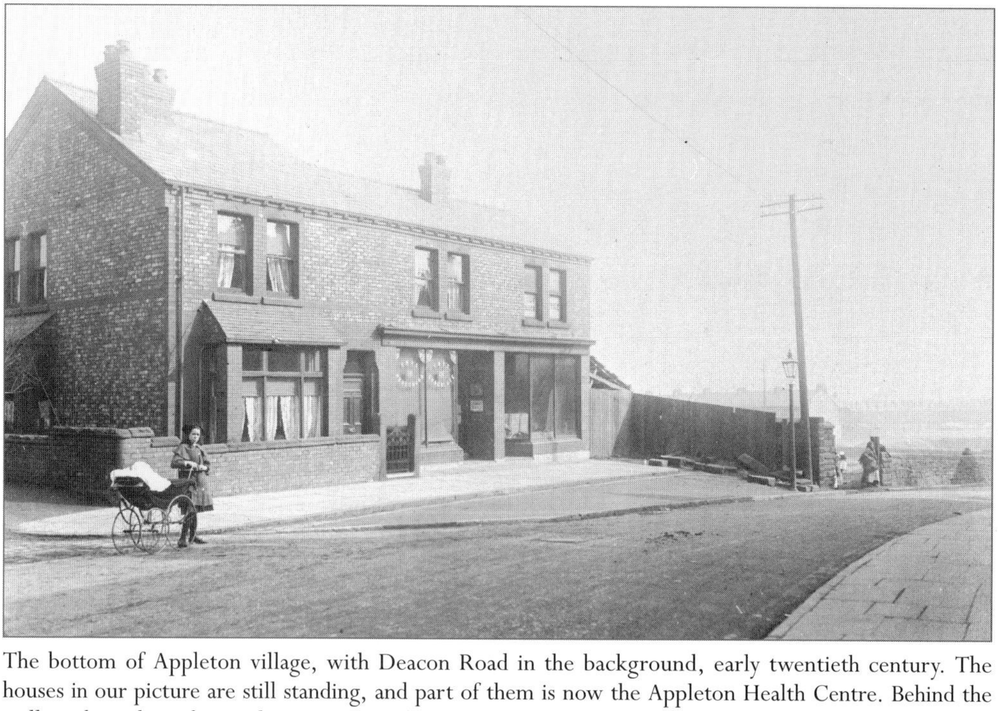

The bottom of Appleton village, with Deacon Road in the background, early twentieth century. The houses in our picture are still standing, and part of them is now the Appleton Health Centre. Behind the wall on the right is the Appleton Quarry which provided much of the stone for local building work in the early 1800s.

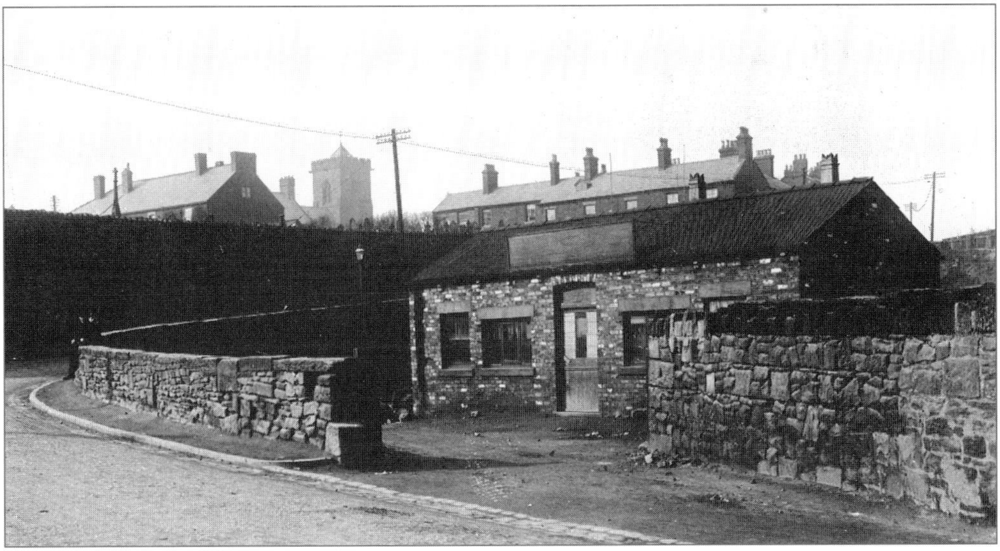

This is a closer view of the quarry which was on the corner of Deacon Road and Appleton Village. It had long ceased to be a working quarry when this picture was taken, *c.* 1910. It looks as though it was being used as a storage area. On the skyline you can see St Bede's Church, built in 1847, and the school beside it. Also visible is Appleton Lodge, with its tall chimneys, to the right of St Bede's tower. Do not confuse the lodge with Appleton House and Hall, which were at the top of Appleton Village. It was at this lodge that John Hutchinson, the founder of the chemical industry in Widnes, lived and died. He said that he was Church of England, but was never seen in a church; however, his wife (née Mary Elizabeth Evelyn Kinsey) was Roman Catholic, so perhaps that is why they lived so near St Bede's.

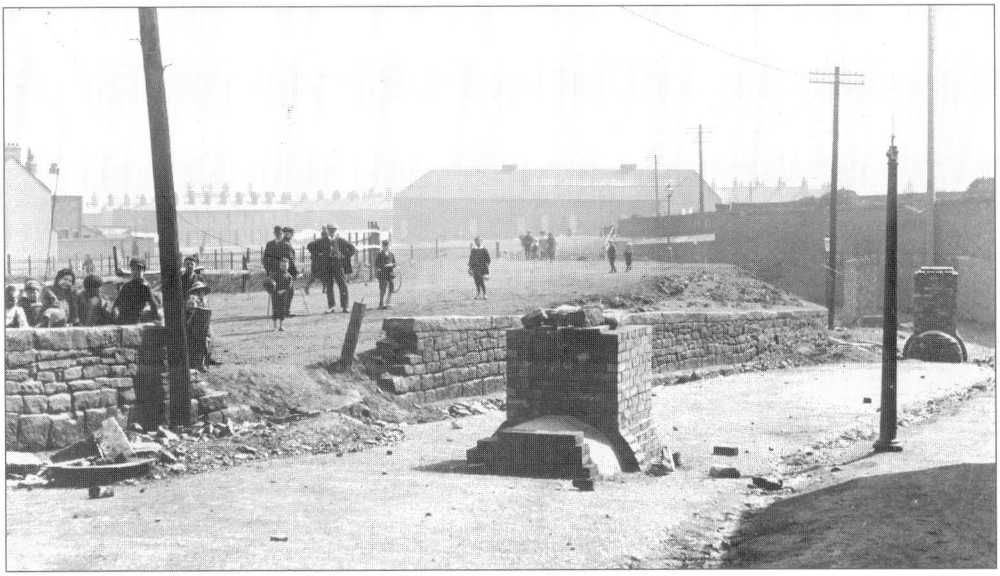

The corner of Deacon Road under construction, looking down from Appleton Village, *c.* 1910. Early omnibuses could not make the steep climb, and passengers were often asked to get out and push. The quarry wall is probably still there under the road, and those brick stacks are to enable the gutters to take the rainwater away from the new road. The large roof in the background belonged to the Empire Skating Rink, built hurriedly in 1909 when a craze for roller skating swept the country. In March 1910 it was converted into a cinema, with admission from 2*d* to 9*d*.

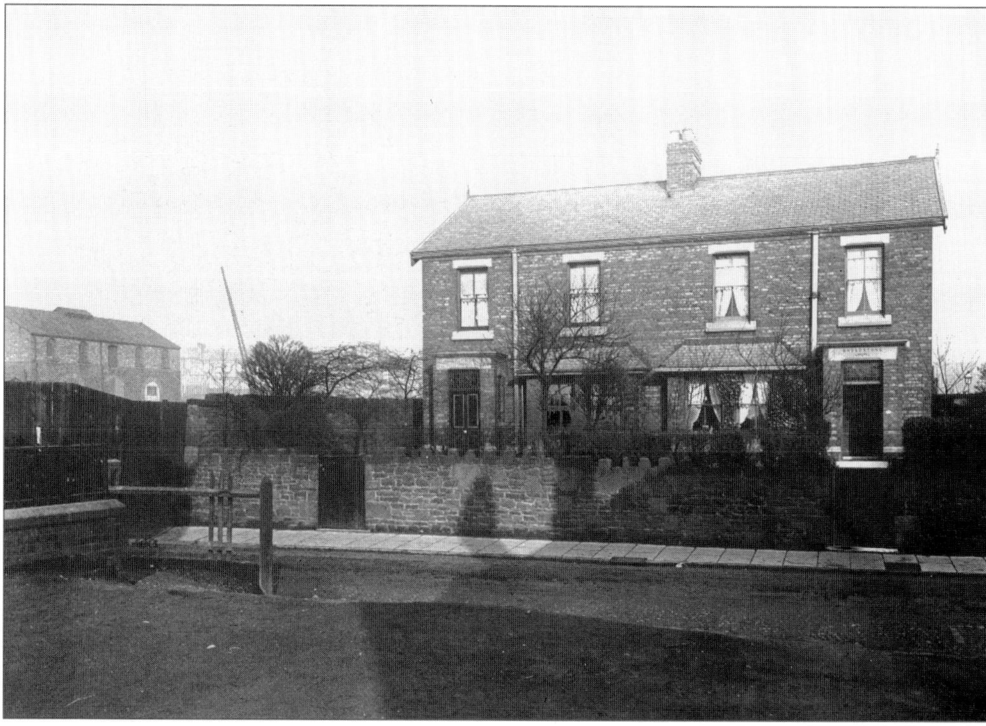

Deacon Road (named after the first Henry Deacon), *c.* 1908. The road looks as though it still needed quite a lot of work on it. The large squarish building on the left was the RAOB Club (the Buffs). The whist drive on a Thursday night was one of the local social highlights. The club is still there but the entrance is from Sayce Street now, not Deacon Road, and the bowling green that was at the front has gone.

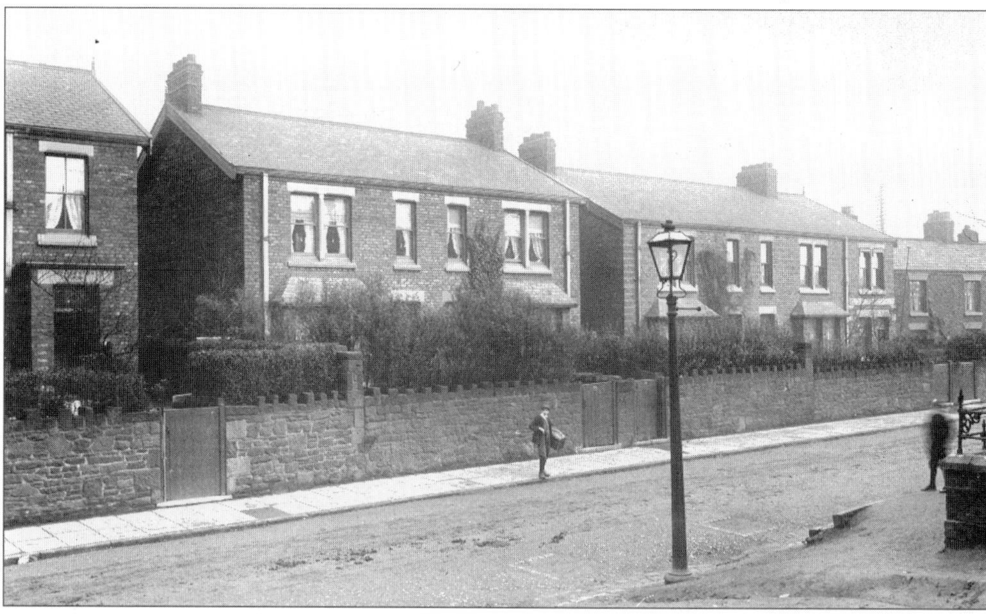

This is looking the other way from the picture above. You can see how much higher one side of the road is than the other. From 1903 until 1912 Widnes spent a lot of money improving the roads and making life better for the new omnibuses that they had introduced.

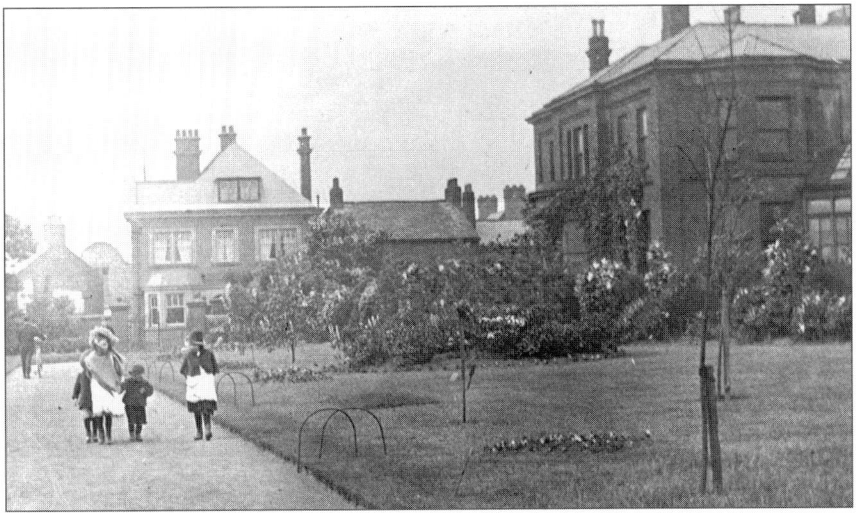

An early picture of Victoria Park just after it was opened on 31 May 1900 by the mayor, Alderman John Whittingham Warcing. At the Birchfield Road entrance there was a plaque bearing the details of that opening day and the name of John S. Sinclair, the borough engineer who oversaw much of the work. At the centre back is a building that was opened as the New Hotel; most people remember it as the Angel and Elephant run by the Stevens family in the 1950s and '60s. It is now called the Appleton Arms. The large house on the right is Appleton House, once the home of the Deacon family who did so much for Widnes and who, between them, gave much of the money to buy the estate and turn it into Victoria Park. Appleton House was built almost on the site of Appleton Hall, which the Appleton family built when they first came to the area in the 1500s. It seems that they brought the name Appleton with them to the Widnes area, not the other way round as is sometimes suggested. On the family crest were three pineapples (often used by wealthy families as a sign of welcome and money), and from these we have Pineapple Terrace and at one time an inn called the Pineapple.

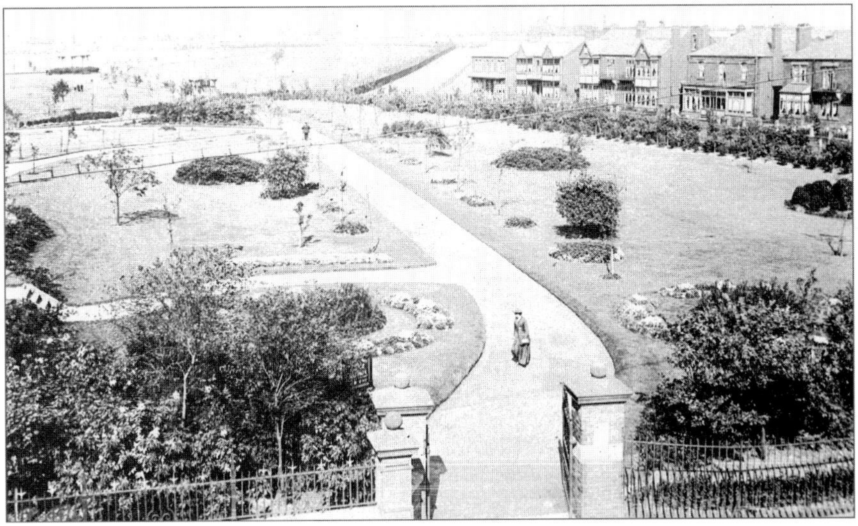

Looking from the upper floors of the Angel and Elephant into Victoria Park, *c.* 1904. The steps up to Appleton House can be seen on the left. Some of the open spaces that the park provided were to give way to the amenities that followed over the years. The ground at the back became the bowling greens and Veterans' Club after the First World War. To the left of the bandstand was where the Cenotaph would be placed, and just above the lodge steps was a well-remembered large aviary, full of finches, budgies and parrots.

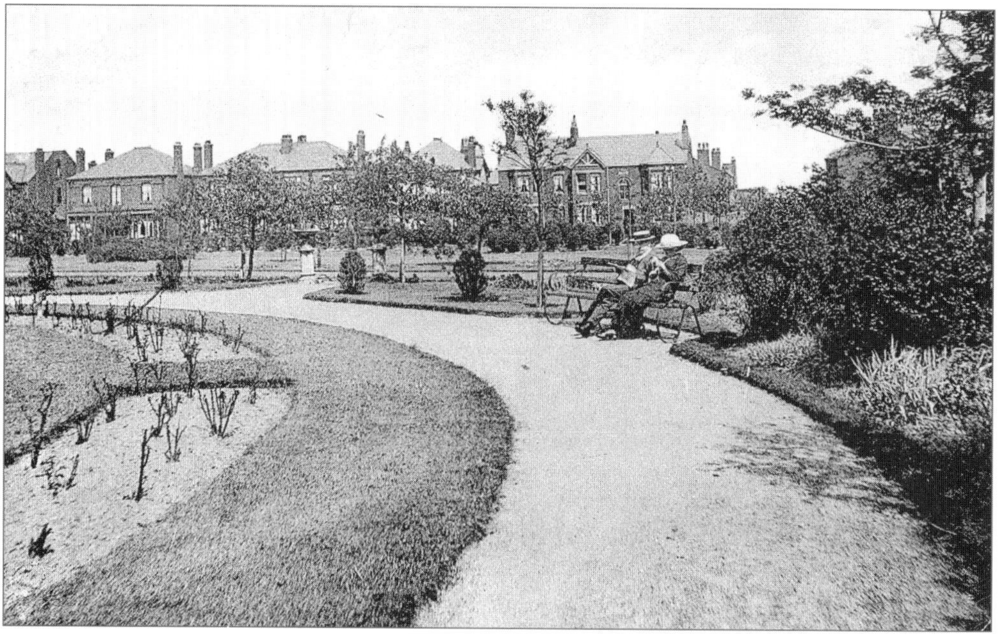

A tranquil view of Victoria Park and the Rose Gardens, March 1913. Fairfield Road can be seen behind, which was part of the newly built Peel House Estate.

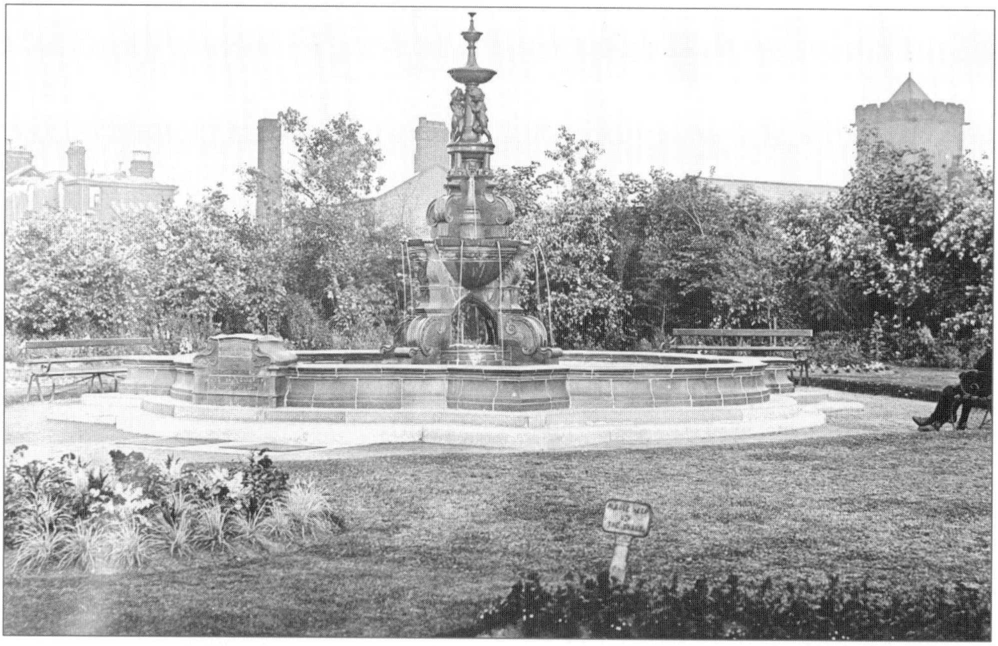

A fine picture of the Gladstone Fountain in Victoria Park, *c.* 1922. The fountain was erected in memory of William Ewart Gladstone PM just a few years after the park opened. King George V commented on the grandeur of the fountain during his visit to Victoria Park in 1925. Plans were put forward in 1990 to remove the fountain to Victoria Square, outside the old town hall, and that is where it can be found today, in wonderful working order. St Bede's Church today houses many treasures from the past, a fifteenth-century chasuble and a sixteenth-century chalice among them. It has a chair probably used by the Blessed Ambrose Barlow, and part of the altar and one stained-glass window came from A.W. Pugin, the famous architect.

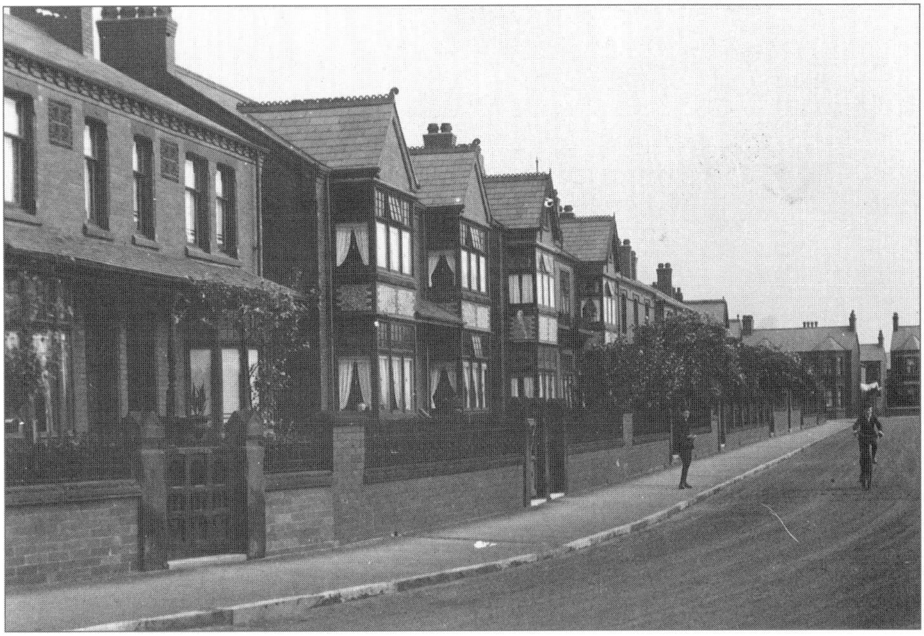

Fairfield Road, Widnes, *c.* 1908. This is typical of the middle-class housing that sprang up at the turn of the century. These houses were built overlooking the newly created Victoria Park and were much sought after. John Steele Swale, the newspaper proprietor, lived in one of these double-bay-windowed ones.

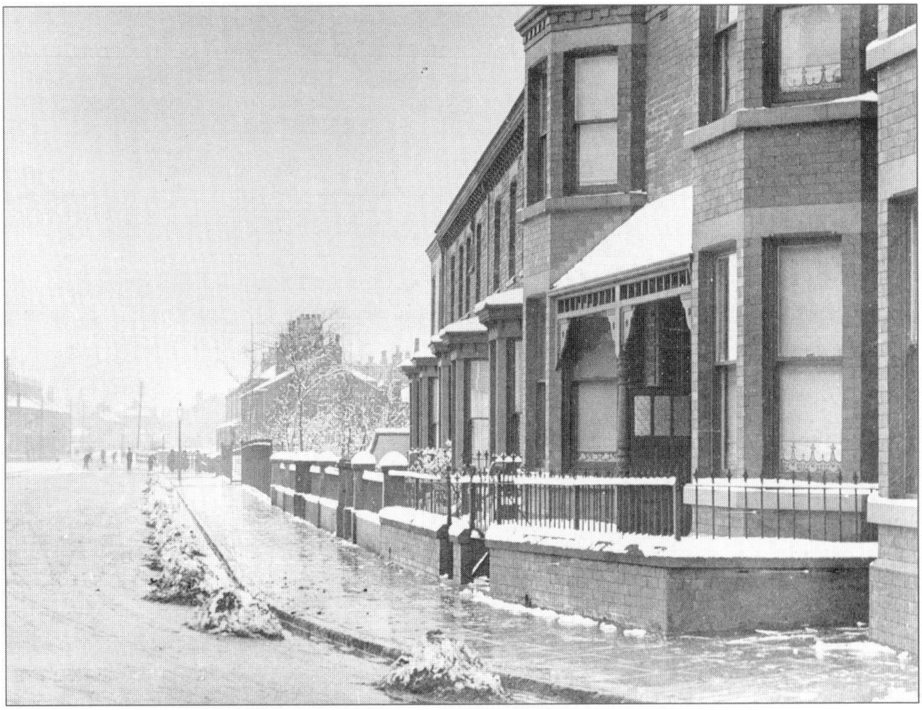

Birchfield Road and a winter scene, early 1920s. Workers can be seen in the distance clearing the roads and leaving the snow in neat piles.

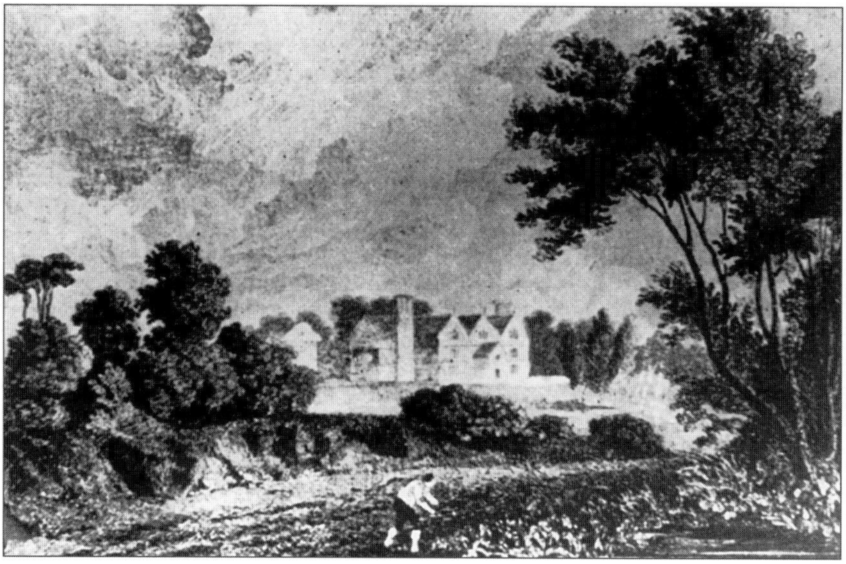

Upper House, Widnes. This was built in about 1670 by the Wright family, and stood where Widnes Golf Club house stands today. This view is an engraving from 1820 by N.G. Philips, showing the hall with its small-paned windows and large decorative chimneys in a very rural setting. The Kelly family lived there for many years during the nineteenth century, and it was taken down in around the mid-1920s. The Golf Club was formed in 1924.

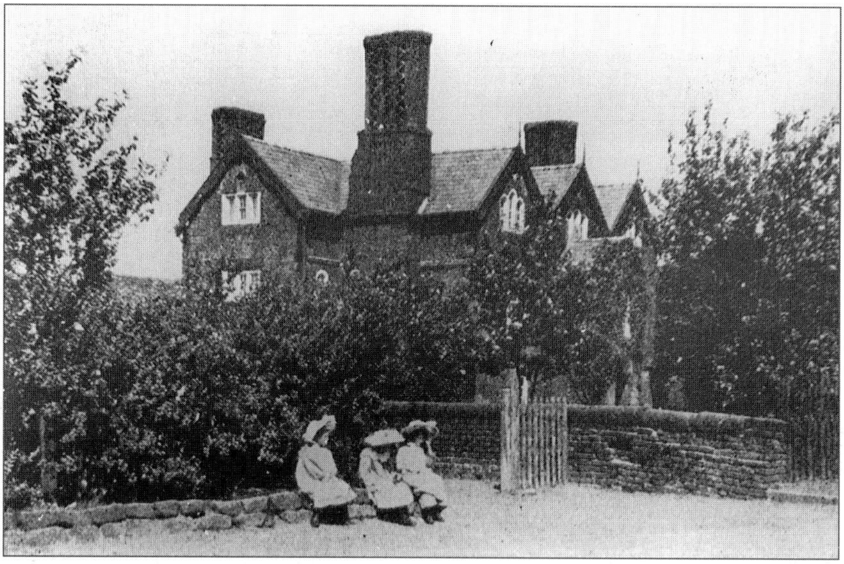

Upper House, 1880s. My grandmother used to tell the story that one day she went down to the house and asked to look around. She used to serve the Kelly family from the small shop she ran in Ditton village. She was taken downstairs to the lower of the cellars where there was an iron door. Behind this was a passage which they said ran all the way to Farnworth Church. Studying the area, it seems rather improbable, as Farnworth Church is over two miles away. The house was built and owned by Catholic families, and in the Townley Papers from 1639, which were written as guides to priests and other Catholics on the run, the house was noted as having 'priests holes, safe hiding and escape'. My gran told the story so convincingly that I can easily believe that there just may be the remains of the door and the passage still there, under the nineteenth hole.

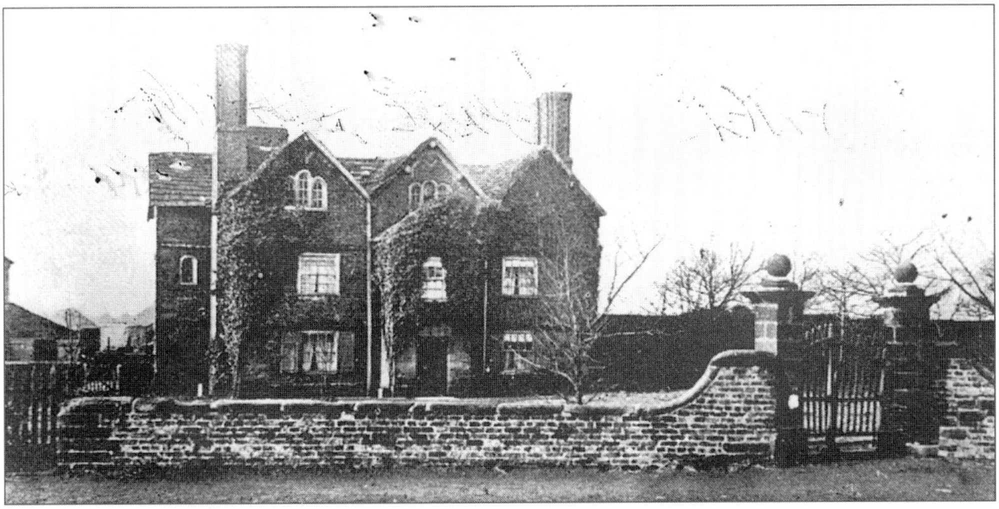

This is a later photograph of Upper House, from off Highfield Road. At one time this place was referred to as Widnes House (or Hall) and is shown as such on a map from 1845. Mr Valentine, the aviator, spent the night here in 1911 (see page 35). The estate covered much of the land behind the house, and was famous for its orchards, which in the mid-1800s sent eight tons of apples a year to the Liverpool markets. The land is now used as Widnes Golf Course, and the building peeping in on the left of the picture was the barn, used today as a changing room and professional's shop at the Golf Club.

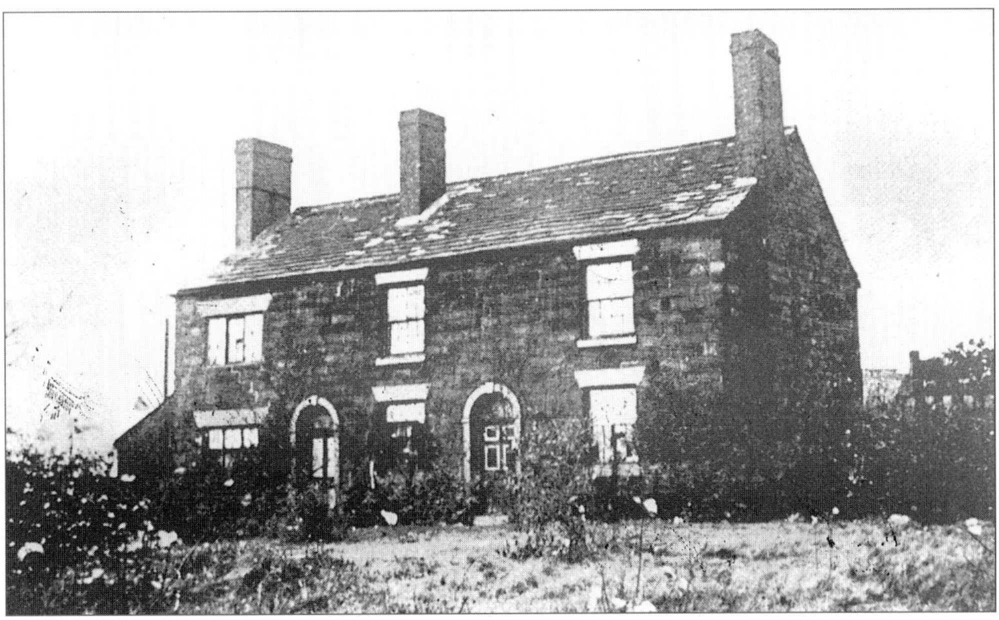

Here we see Lower House – a much smaller and simpler affair than Upper House. It was situated around where the bowling green for the Albion Hotel used to be (now a car park). It was never more than a farmhouse, and was said to have been built by the Houghton family. At the time of the Reformation, the Hawarden family lived there: they were the chief Catholic family in the area. Many of their sons entered the priesthood and we note that Father William Hawarden practised there from 1660 to 1728 when his brother Father Thomas Hawarden took over until his death in 1746. A younger branch of the family lived at the now lost Fenilstreet House which was somewhere around where St Bede's School is today. Lower House was pulled down in a poor state of repair in about 1890, after being the home of the Kelsall family for many years.

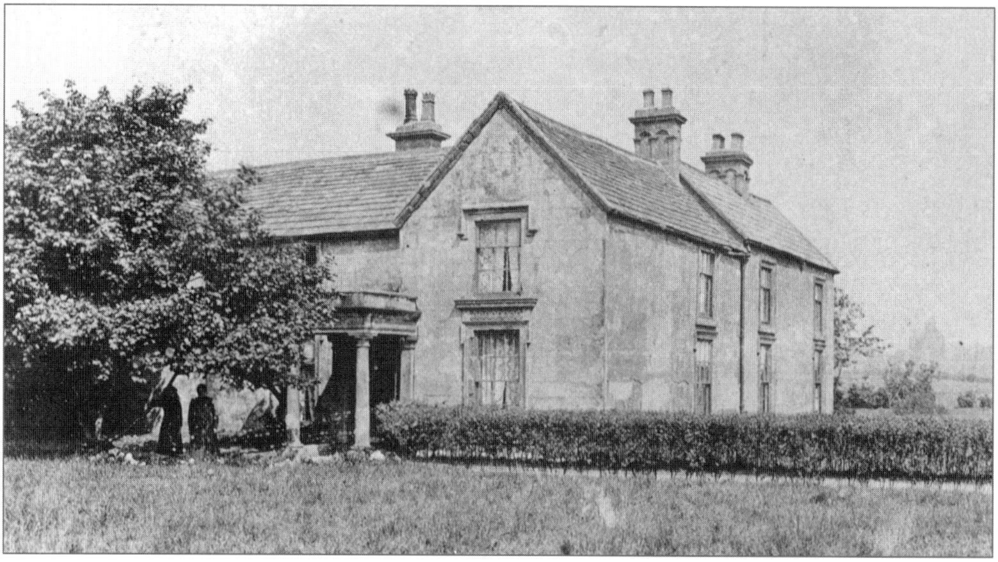

Peel House, captured by local photographer J. Atherton, 1885. The history of this hall is obscured in the mists of time. It is thought that there was a house here as early as 1400. It was then known as Pole House and it was here in 1460 that William Smyth (Smith) was born: 'son of Robert Smyth – a country squire of moderate estate'. William went on to become Bishop of Lincoln and did much for his home area, building a chapel at Cuerdley and in 1507 endowing the school at Farnworth with £10 a year and raising it to grammar school status. It was said that wherever the good bishop went he left behind him the perfume of charity. He died on 2 June 1513.

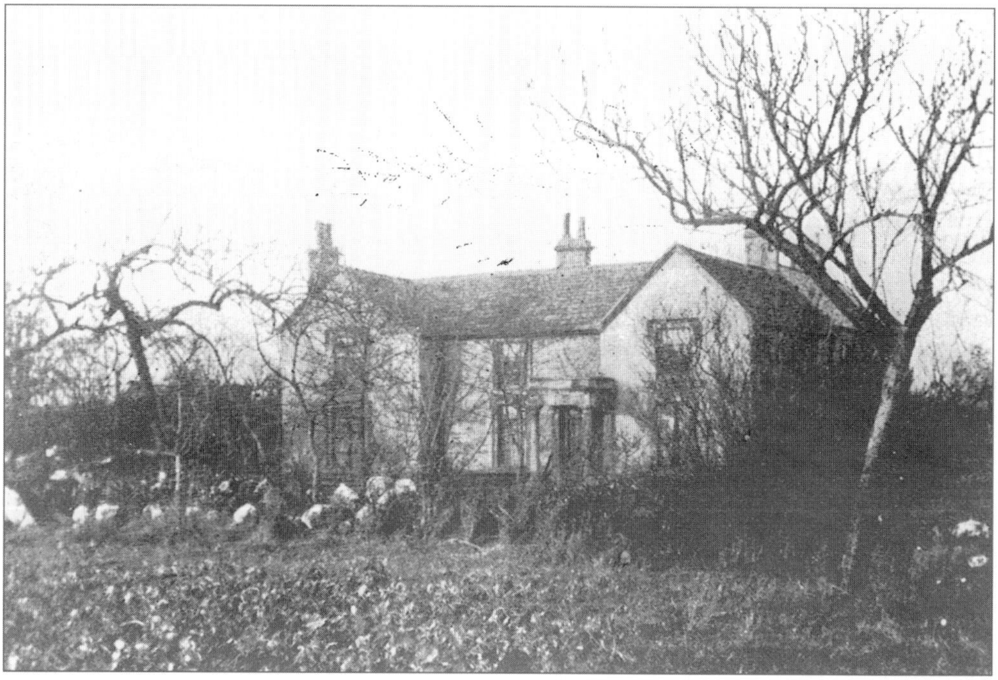

Peel House, 1900. The hall was on the left-hand side going up Peel House Lane, around the Lockett Road area. A company called the Peel House Estate and Development Company was formed in 1890, and started laying out the area for a housing estate. Peel House was pulled down in 1903.

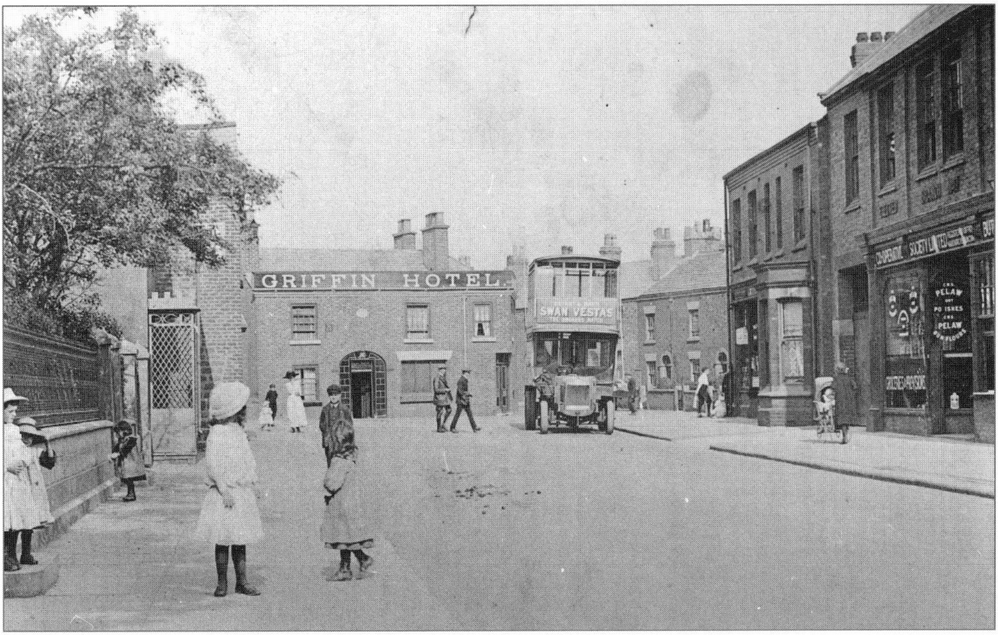

Looking down Derby Road towards the Griffin Hotel on Farnworth Street, 1910. The double-decker bus is waiting to start its journey back to Victoria Square – a much easier trip than the one up Peel House Lane. The Griffin Inn took its name from the family crest of the Bold family, who owned much of the land in this area. The story of the fight with the griffin (or dragon) is told on page 64. The Co-operative store can be seen on the right.

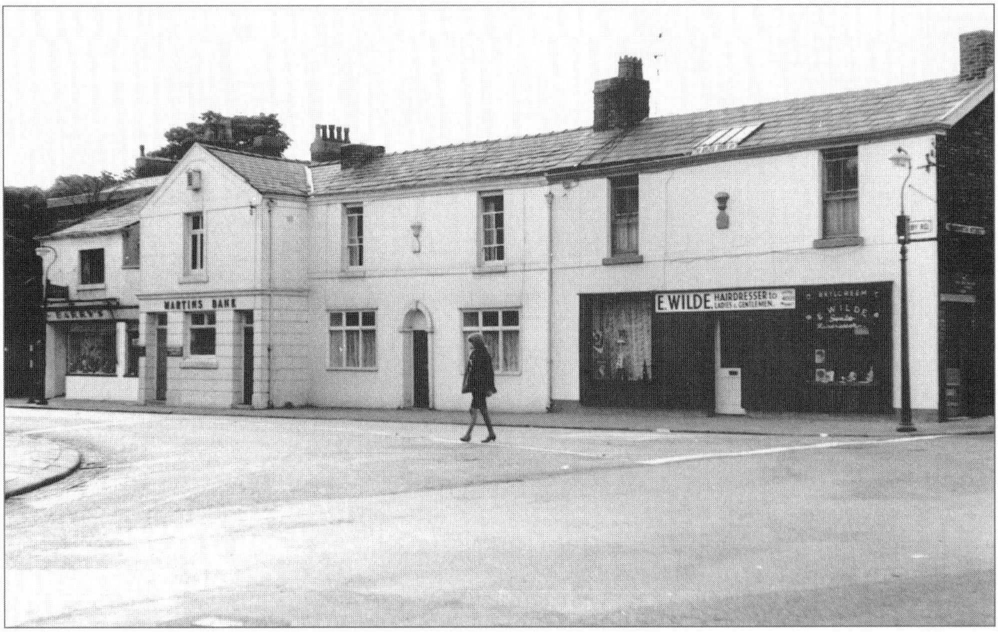

The Derby Road, Farnworth Street corner, mid-1960s. The shops have lost their hustle and bustle. Ernie Wild the barber was a well-liked local character who dispensed haircuts, advice and racing tips from that corner for many years. When it was just a lane, Derby Road had the odd title of Puzzle-Pate, though I have never seen an explanation of this name.

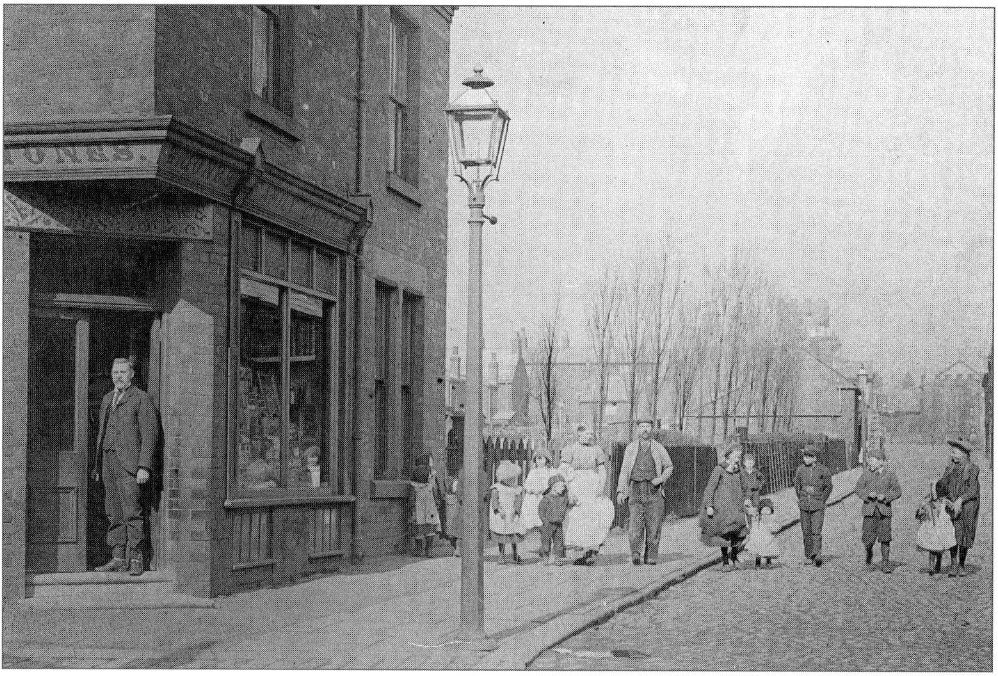

Mr Jones outside his post office/grocer's shop, 1910. The children are posed across Farnworth Street – are they his family, or passers-by?

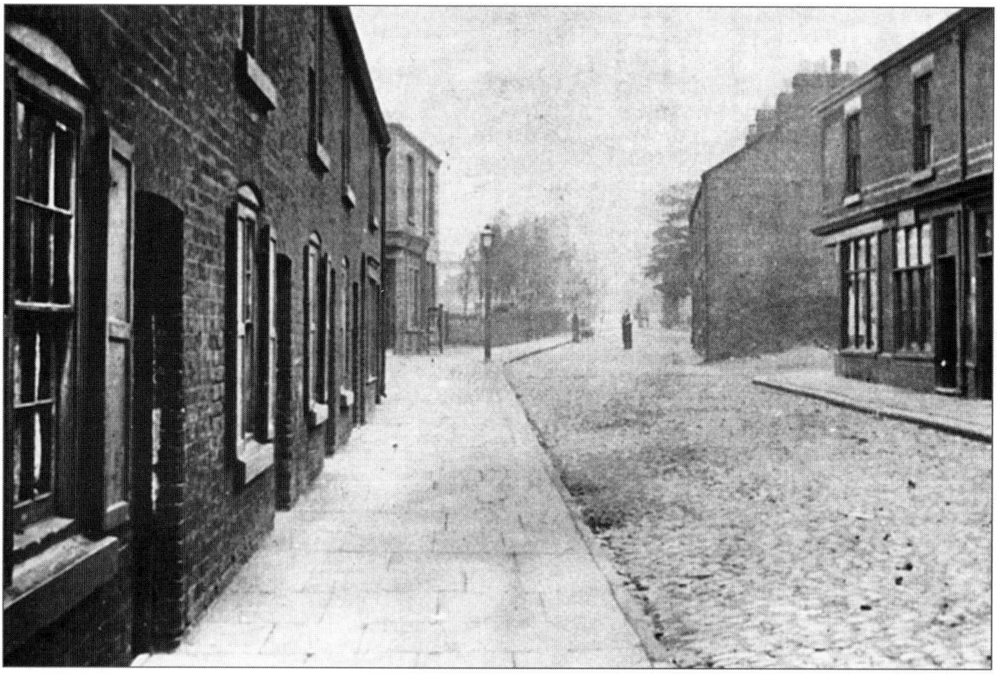

Farnworth Street, looking towards the church, which is lost in the mist at the top of the picture, *c.* 1900. Windermere Street is the gap on the right.

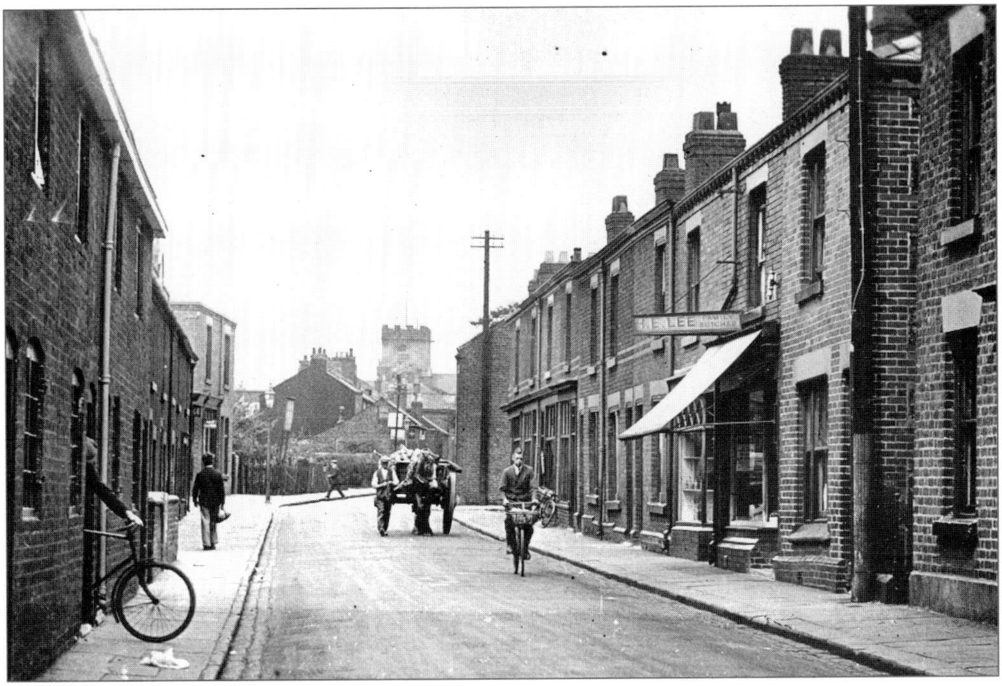

This is the same view as the previous picture, but nearly twenty-five years later. The square building on the left opposite Windermere Street was the post office with a builders' merchants and a DIY shop next door. H.E. Lee's, a family butcher, is on the right.

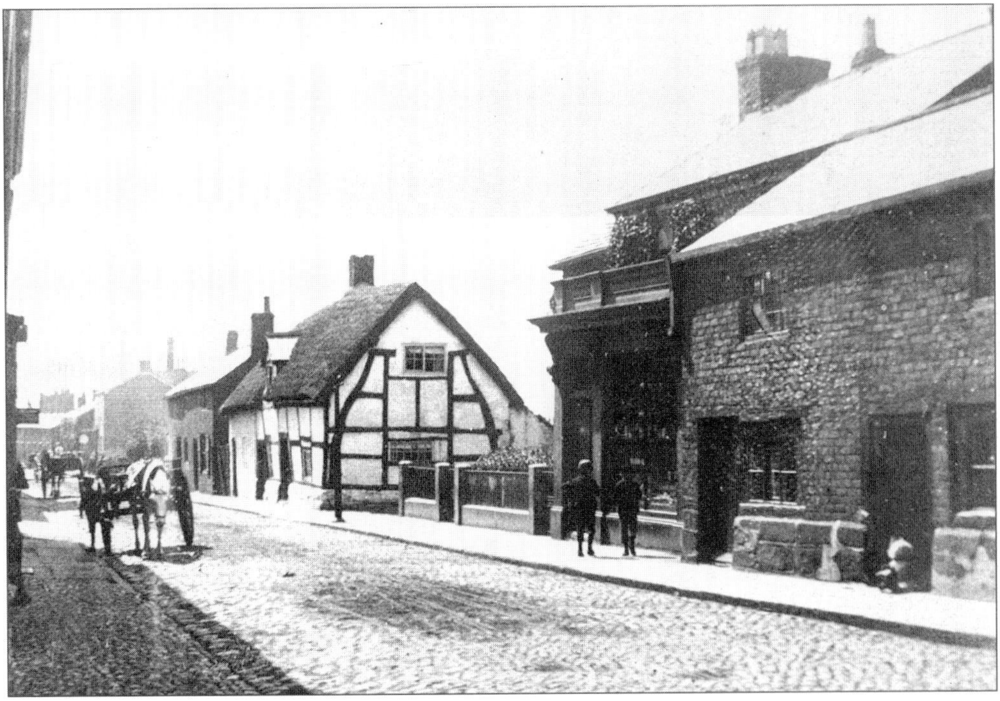

Looking down Church Street (Farnworth Street) about a century ago. The old thatched cottage is a rare sight so it is nice to see it here. Russell Court stands on this spot today.

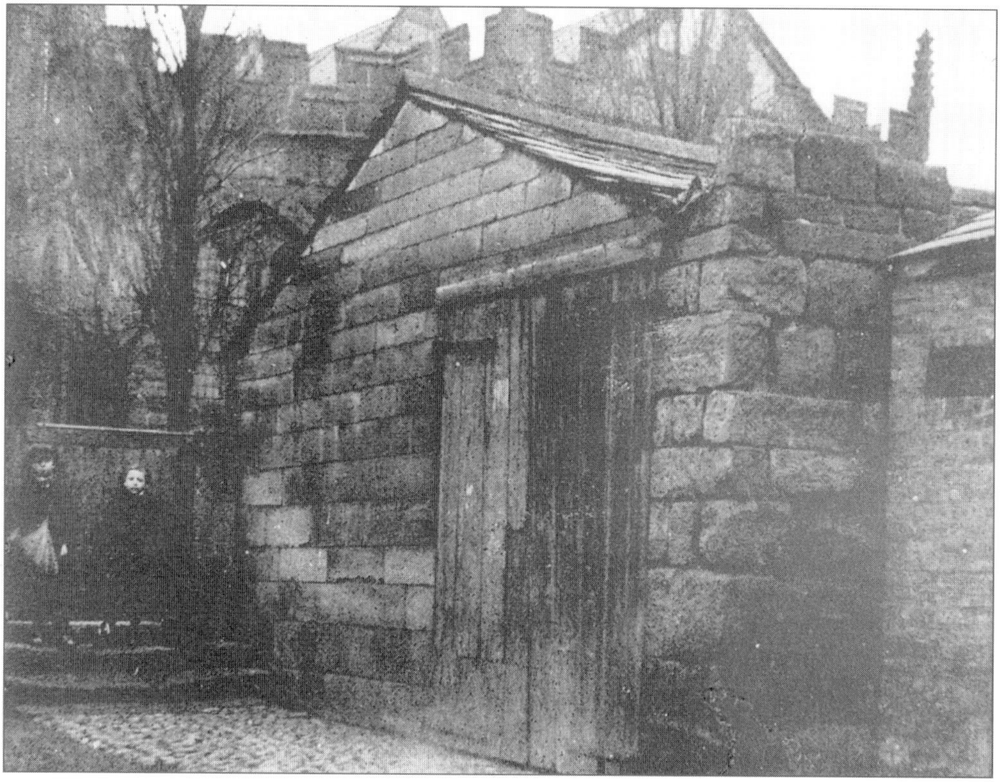

Farnworth Bridewell, or lock-up, 1895. Erected in 1827, the stone-built jig or Bridewell adjoined the churchyard on the eastern side. Lock-ups like this were common in every town and village. They were places where the local constabulary could hold people until they could be put before a magistrate, usually for drunkenness or other minor offences. The name originated from St Bride's Well, a large prison in London. When a local police station was built, this little lock-up was used for many other things, as a depot for gravedigging tools among others.

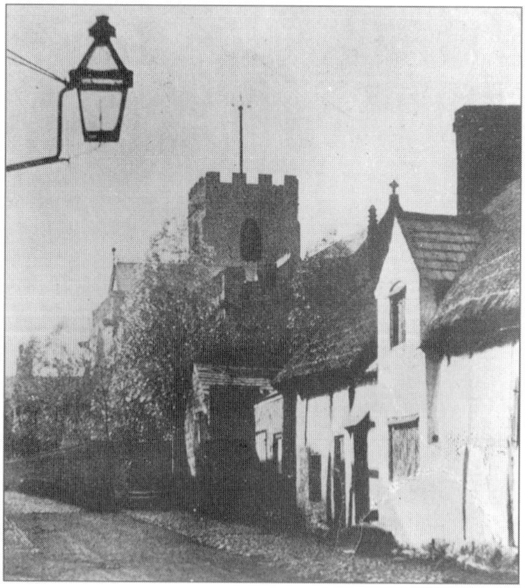

This view is towards Farnworth Church from Dragon Yard. Yes, that really is the name – look in your A–Z! I was told a folk tale of one of the Bold family who, after a winged creature was seen stealing sheep, covered himself in a sheepskin and was carried off by the dragon to its lair, where he drew his sword and slew it. You can just see the Bridewell again in this picture, by the trees. It is still there today, thanks to a preservation order.

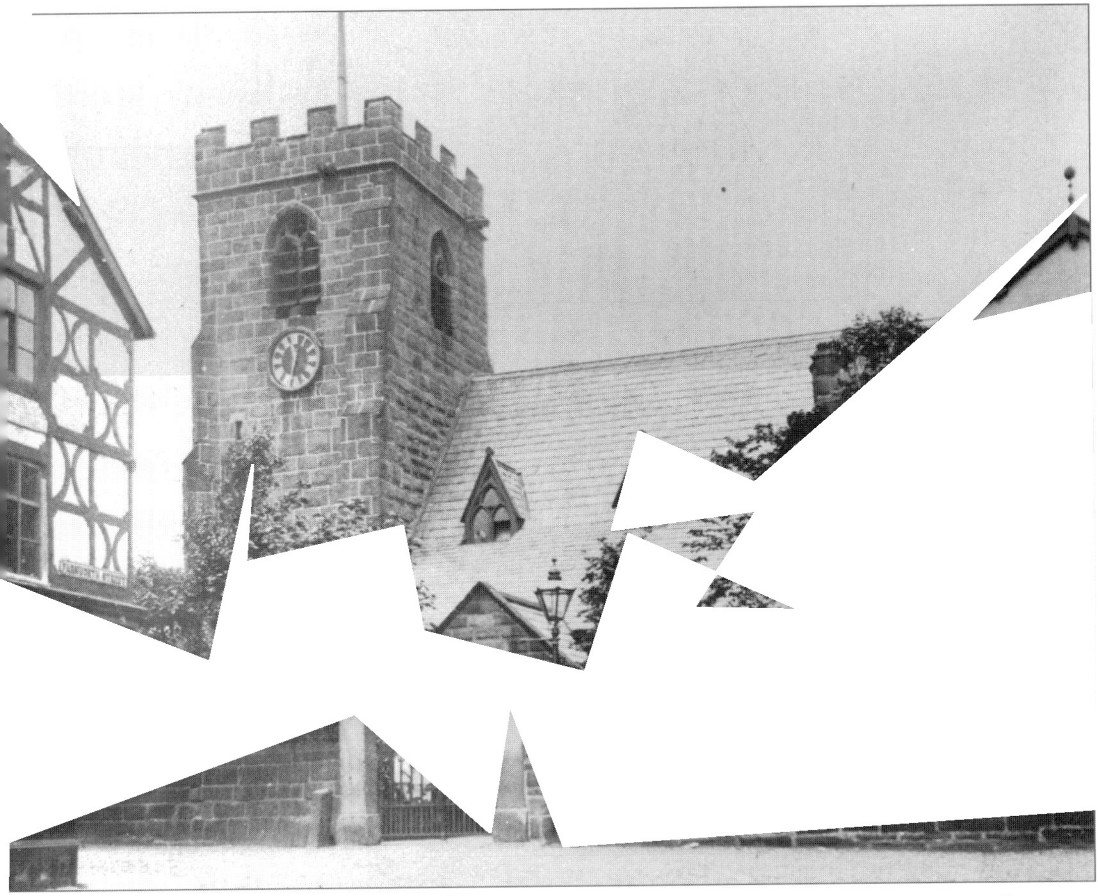

St Luke's Church, Farnworth, 1926. This lovely old church has a fascinating history. It was originally dedicated to St Wilfrid and I could devote a whole book to the church alone. Part of St Luke's is definitely Norman, and it is believed that there could have been a place of worship here even before that. The west wall is late twelfth century, the tower fourteenth century, the piers from the 1300s; the east end late fifteenth century. The timber-framed gables are from around the time of the Civil War. This was a church 400 years before Henry VIII started his Church of England. Reading and writing were practised by candlelight in the corner for 500 years before the discovery of America. I would say that every schoolchild in the area should be taken to St Luke's for a living history lesson: to learn about the bread shelf for the starving poor – 1724; pews that date from 1602; see the secret door from Bold Hall designed as a bookshelf; and the sad story of the daughter of Peter Bold, Mary, who in 1822 married a Polish prince and became Princess Sapeila, and after only two years of marriage died aged twenty-seven and lies buried here. There is also a beautiful window thought to be designed by William Morris himself, and the church register goes back to 1538; only three churches in the whole of Lancashire do that. A lot of good work is going on at the church in preserving history as well as souls, and they have plans for history factsheets and other projects. I wish them well.

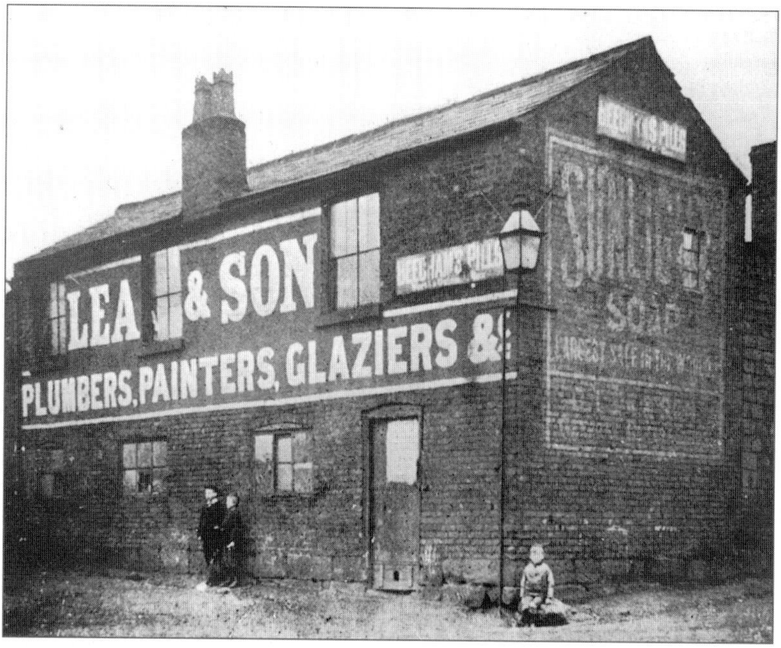

This building once housed the Farnworth Grammar School and its tall barn-like structure rang to Latin grammar and times tables for over 100 years. It was 15*s* extra per quarter for writing and arithmetic. When a new school was erected in Peel House Lane in 1883 this old building was sold to a former pupil, John R. Lea, for £30, and he used it, as you can see, for his painting and glazing business.

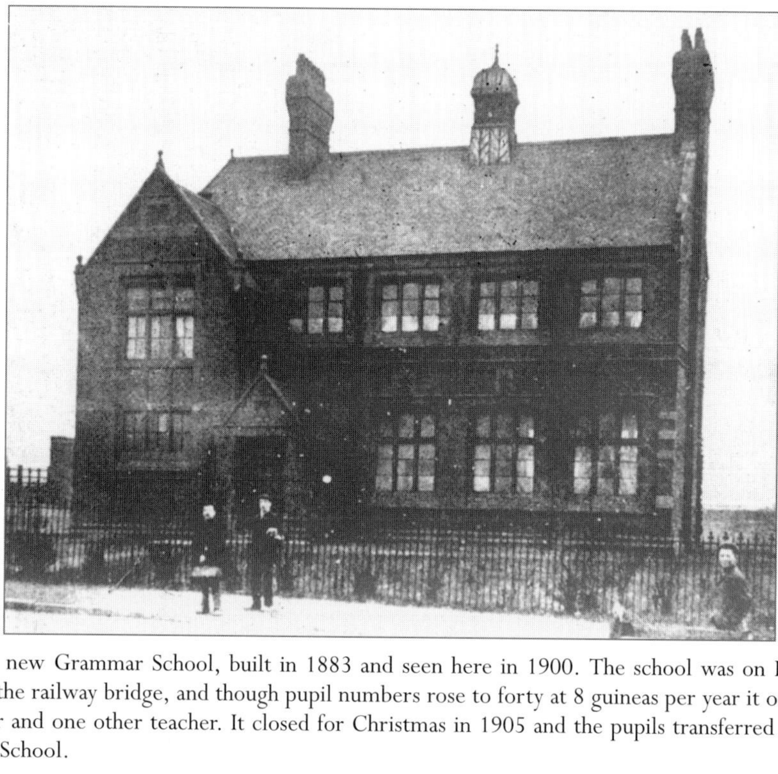

This is the new Grammar School, built in 1883 and seen here in 1900. The school was on Peel House Lane near the railway bridge, and though pupil numbers rose to forty at 8 guineas per year it only had the headmaster and one other teacher. It closed for Christmas in 1905 and the pupils transferred to Widnes Secondary School.

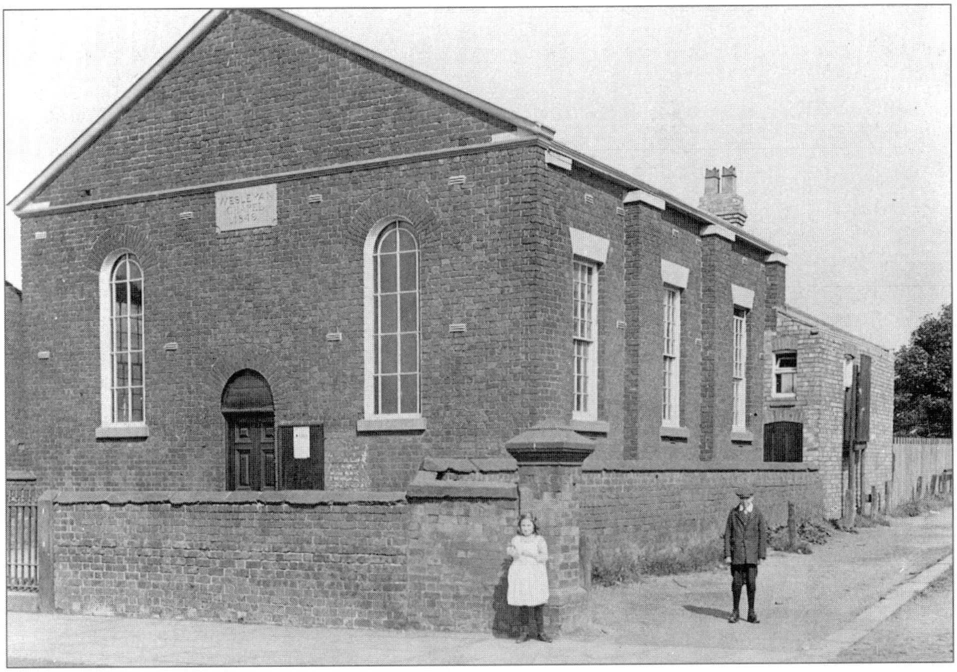

The Wesleyan Methodist chapel that stood on the corner of Beaconsfield Road in Farnworth opened in 1849. This picture is from the turn of the century.

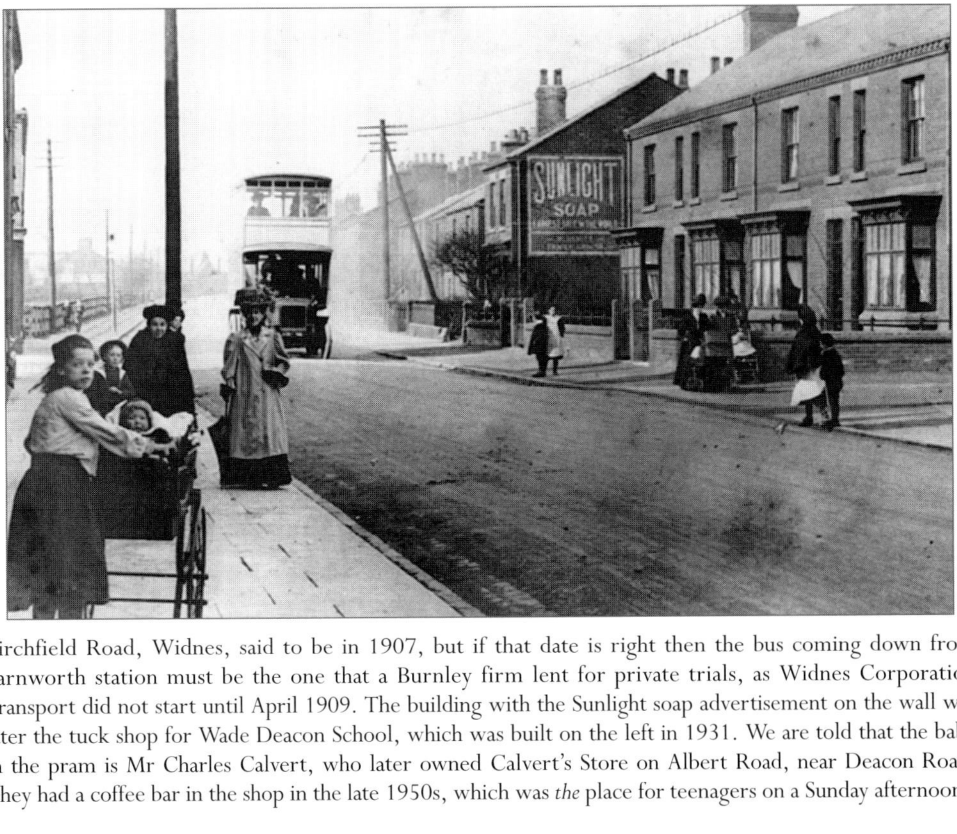

Birchfield Road, Widnes, said to be in 1907, but if that date is right then the bus coming down from Farnworth station must be the one that a Burnley firm lent for private trials, as Widnes Corporation Transport did not start until April 1909. The building with the Sunlight soap advertisement on the wall was later the tuck shop for Wade Deacon School, which was built on the left in 1931. We are told that the baby in the pram is Mr Charles Calvert, who later owned Calvert's Store on Albert Road, near Deacon Road. They had a coffee bar in the shop in the late 1950s, which was *the* place for teenagers on a Sunday afternoon.

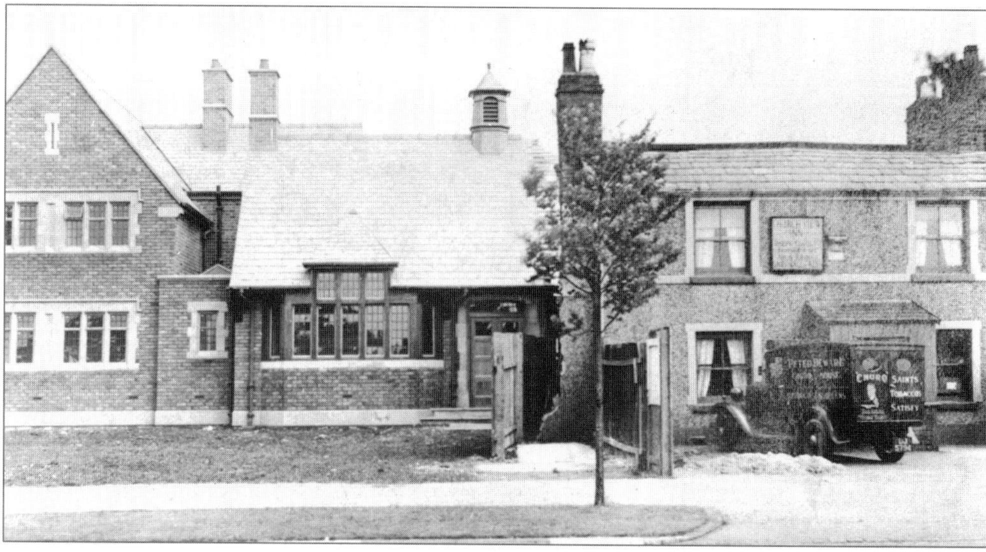

The building on the right with a tobacco delivery van outside is the old Church View Inn on Lunts Heath Road, late 1920s. It does not look like this today. It has moved into the building on the left and been enlarged and modernised. The inn was once a house on the Hunts Heath Farm estate and stood on the footpath that ran from Cuerdley to Farnworth Church, hence its name – Church View.

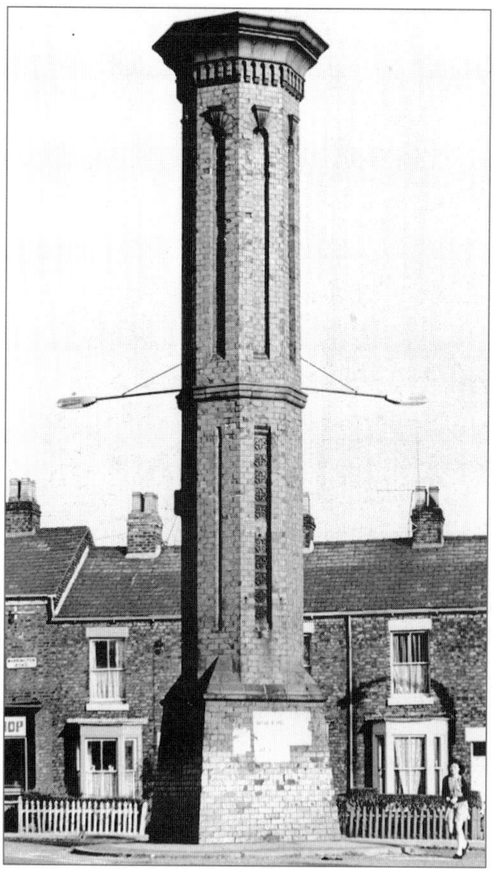

One of the more unusual listed buildings in Widnes is the Victorian sewer vent by the Navy Club on Mill Brow and Albert Road. There were five of these structures in Widnes at one time; now only one survives. They were handy for sticking posters on and attaching lights to. We see here the one that stood on Warrington Road, near St Ambrose Road, at Halton View.

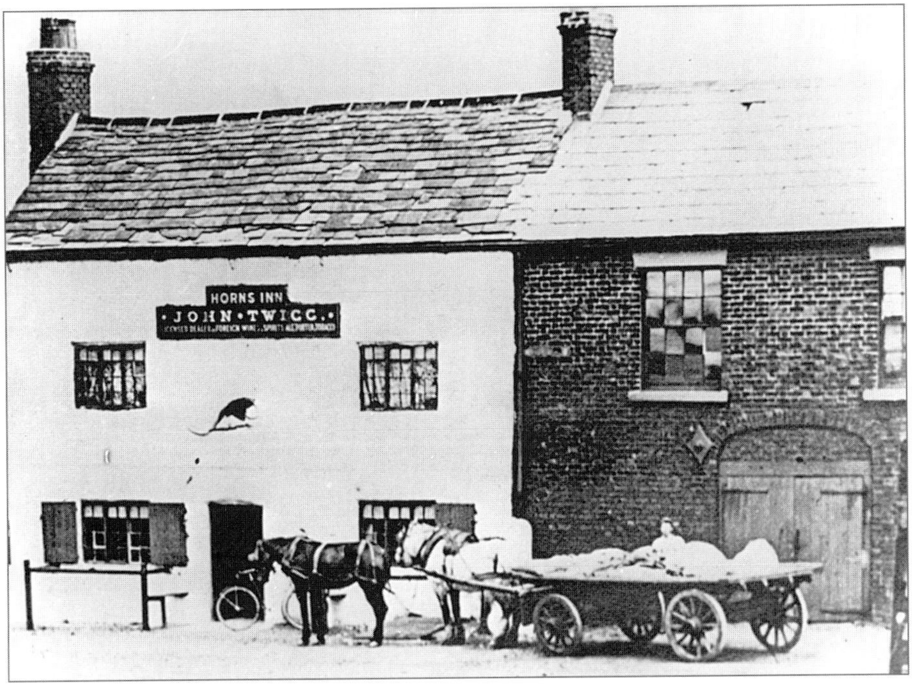

This is the Horns Inn, about a century ago. It stood on Station Road leading down to what was Widnes' first railway station, known as Farnworth & Bold, on the St Helens Railway. The later Farnworth station was on the Warrington–Liverpool railway line.

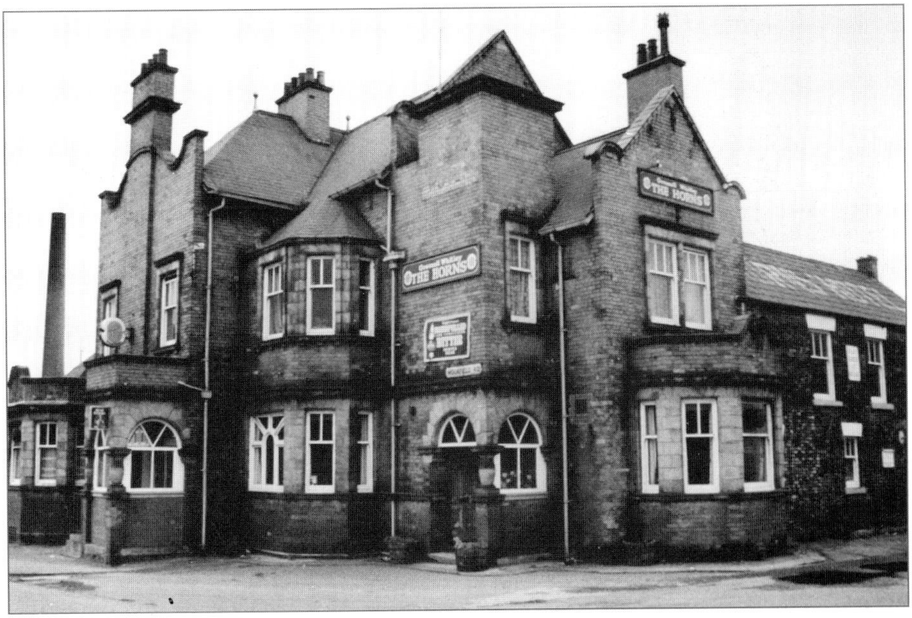

This is the Horns Hotel, as most of us remember it, standing on the corner of Station Road and Moorfield Road. The original old inn, with the hotel name on the roof, is at the side of the large newer building. This photograph was taken in 1990 just before the hotel was demolished. It was used a lot by workers from the Peter Spencer Works nearby. When I was a teenager in the 1960s my aunt Nancy (Barrow) ran a little kiosk on the bridge next to the hotel.

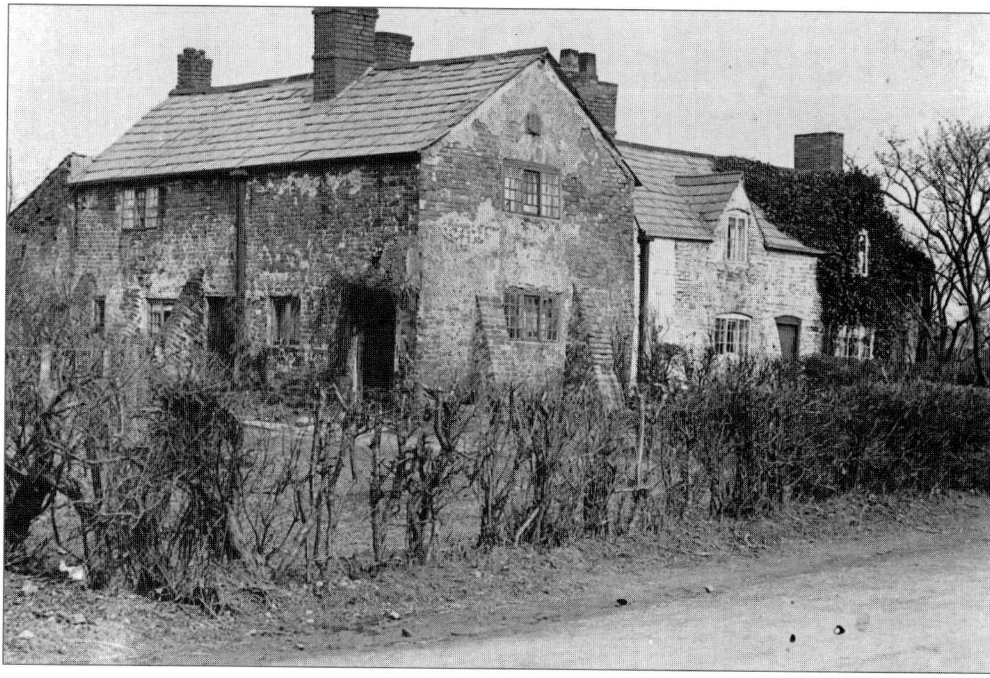

Farnworth House was a large farm on Cronton Lane. Even here, in about 1920, it looks a dilapidated set of buildings! It was once the workhouse for Farnworth; the Hillcrest Hotel is now on this spot.

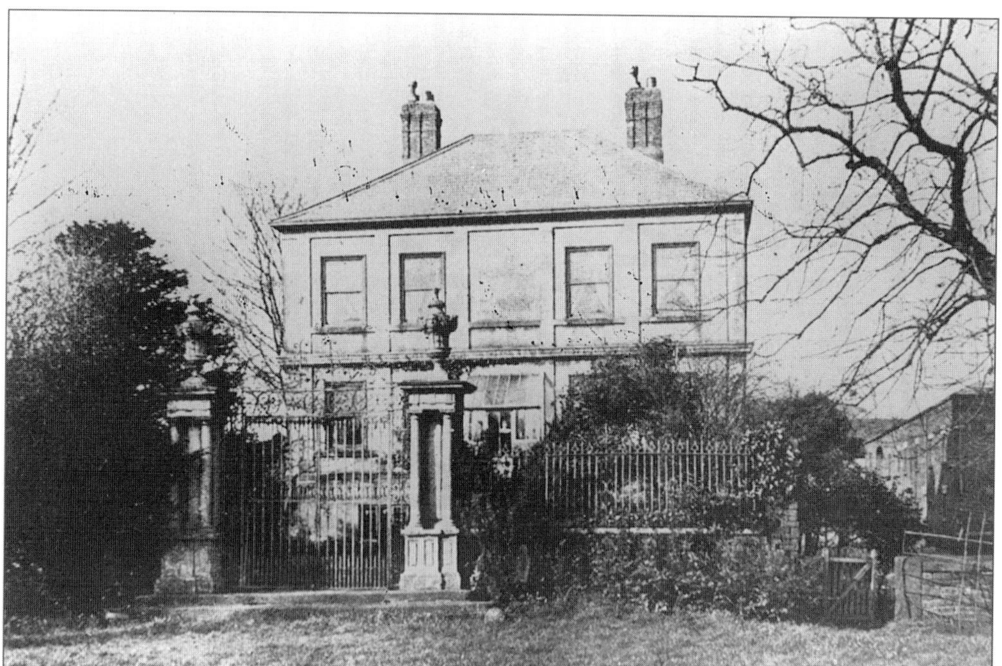

Cronton Hall is seen here, one of the few halls around Widnes and still standing. It is on Cronton Road and has been in the Patton family for many years. This picture is from 1900 but the hall as we see it was rebuilt in 1740 and extended further in 1816.

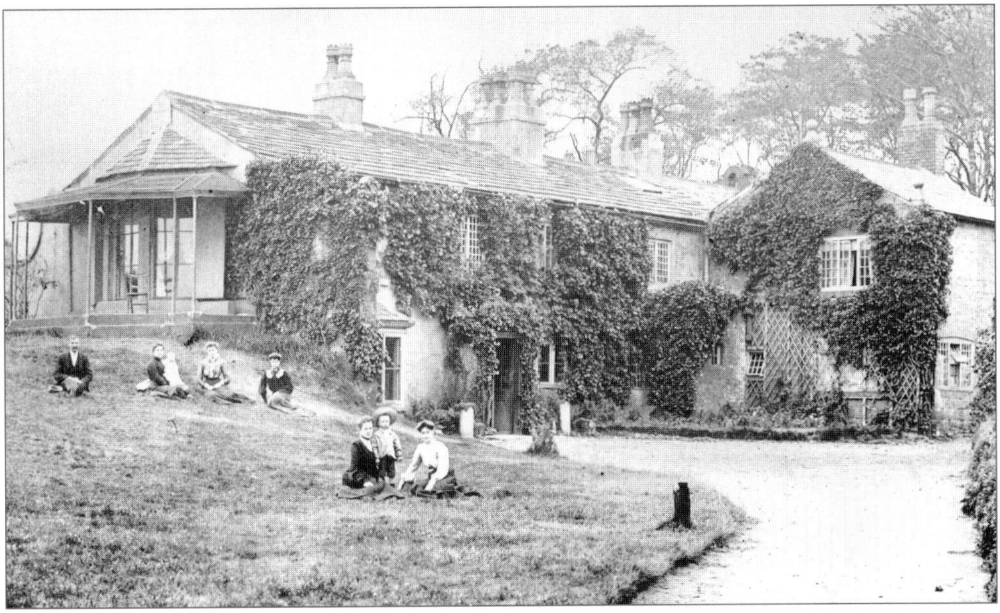

Pex Hill was bought by the Local Board under the Widnes Improvement Act in 1867, which gave the Board authority and money to improve the gas and water supplies. Pex Hill was to be the reservoir and Stocks Well, beyond Hough Green, the pumping station. This picture shows the home known as The Bungalow on Pex Hill near the reservoir, in 1910. Looking from the other side, the main approach, it appeared to have only one storey – you can see the bank on the left. It was in a very poor state of repair and was partially pulled down just before the Second World War. Vince Karalius built his home on the spot where this house stood.

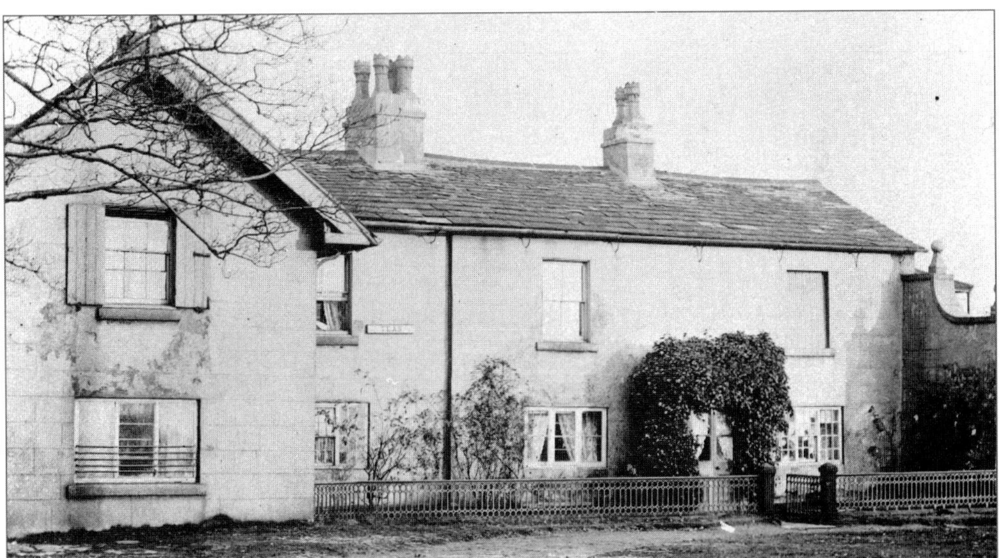

Pex Hill House, thought to be in the 1920s. The 'Teas' sign can be seen on the house wall. Some say the hill's name comes from one Peg Pusey of Bold who threw herself down a steep slope of the hill, when spurned in love; others say she was pushed. There is a small matter of the pixies who live there, and sometimes if you lie quietly in the grass, in twos, you can spot them. Pixies' Hill became Pix Hill, and then Pex Hill. The name Pex Hill is first found in the 1300s and the academic version is that it was probably the hill where the Picts lived – Picts Hill – or possibly a personal name, Pecc's Hill.

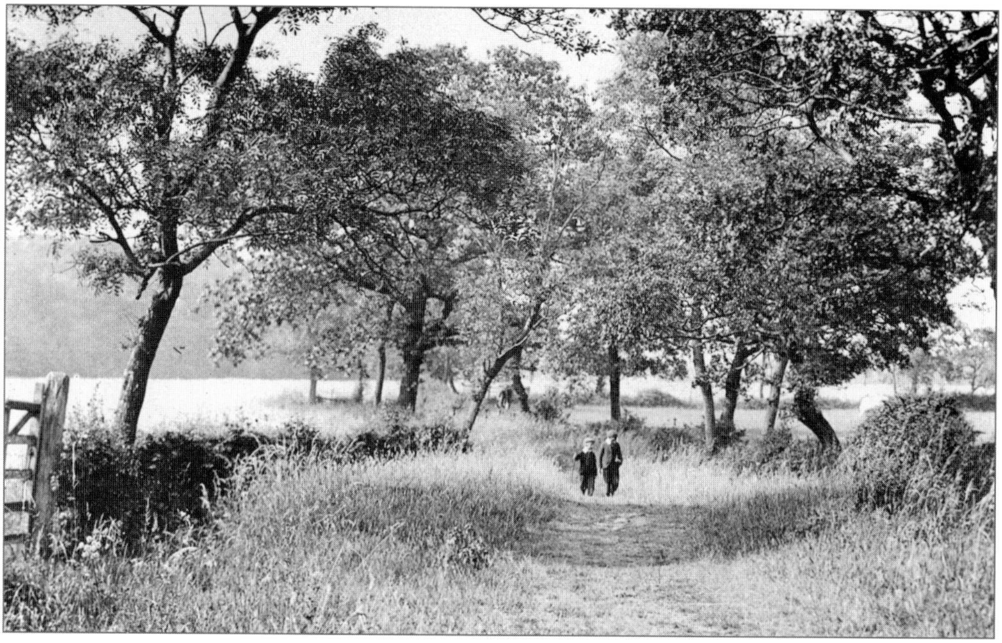

Lover's Lane, Cronton, 1905, says the caption, and I assumed that it was a picture of Sandy Lane, Cronton, taken from Cronton Road and looking down to Upton Lane. Local historian Bob Martindale pointed out the rising ground to the left, and suggested that it is the footpath or lane going round the back of Cronton Hall. Once we started discussing it, the suggestion was made that it could be the footpath from Cronton Lane down to Rock House on the bend of Upton Lane – so we leave it up to you. Our two young gentlemen caught on this turn-of-the-century picture are probably just out for a stroll.

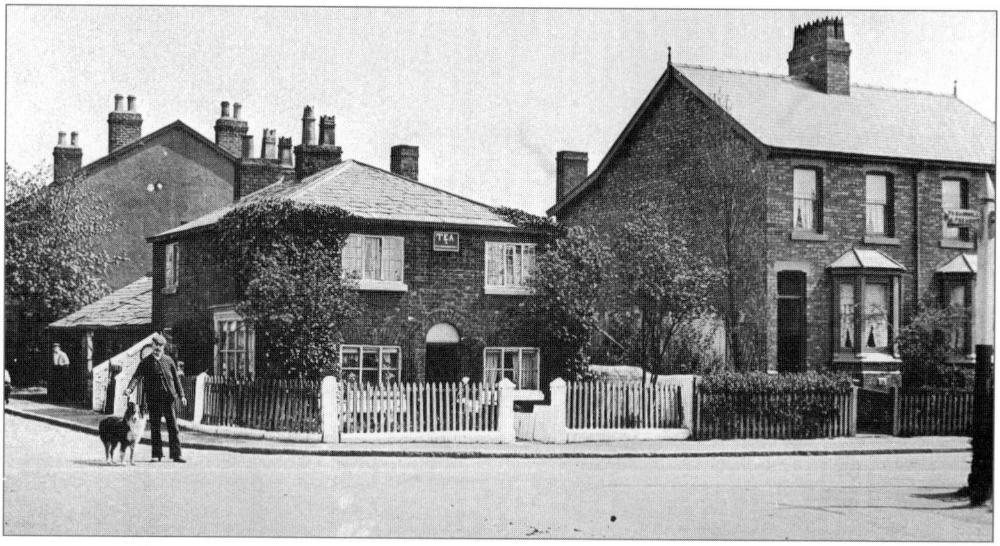

This is the crossroads at the centre of Cronton, *c.* 1908. The photographer was standing on Cronton Lane with Chapel Lane on the right. As long as I can remember there has been a 'chippy' on this corner. Even in the picture we can see that it is a tea rooms and café. The name Cronton comes from Crow-ton, the dwelling or village where the crows nest, though there have been some strange spellings in history, including Growynton in 1248 when first mentioned, and Crouwenton in 1333. Cronton was part of the barony of Halton, and though it has spent the years since 1974 under Merseyside, it is really an outlying part of Widnes.

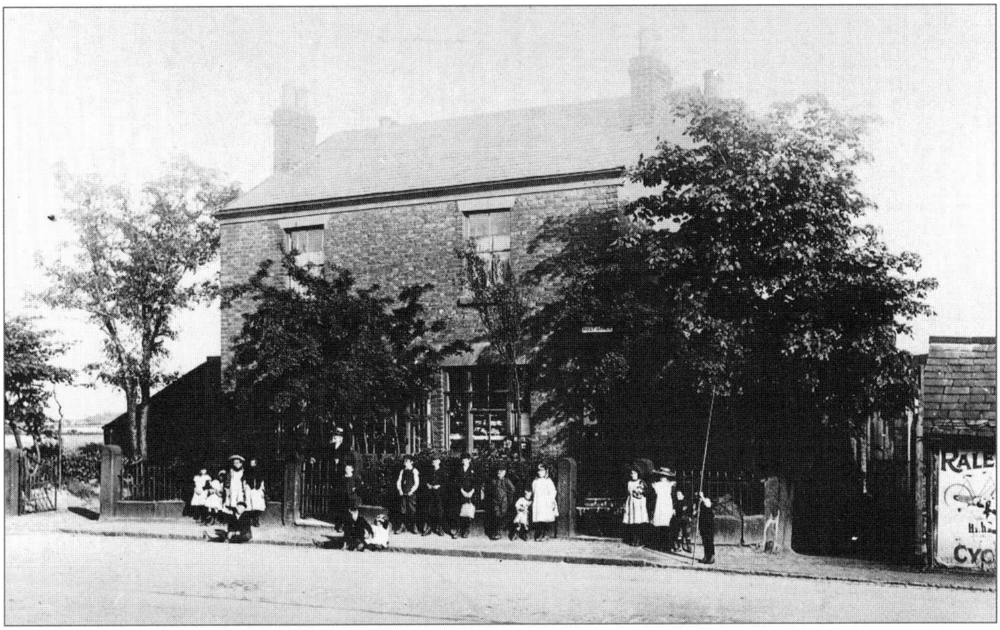

Cronton post office in Cronton Lane, *c.* 1910. The low building on the right was the smithy, but judging by the advertisements on the front the owner was also looking after the modern mode of transport, the bicycle, as well as the traditional one of horses. The post office stood on the opposite side of the road to the Black Horse Hotel.

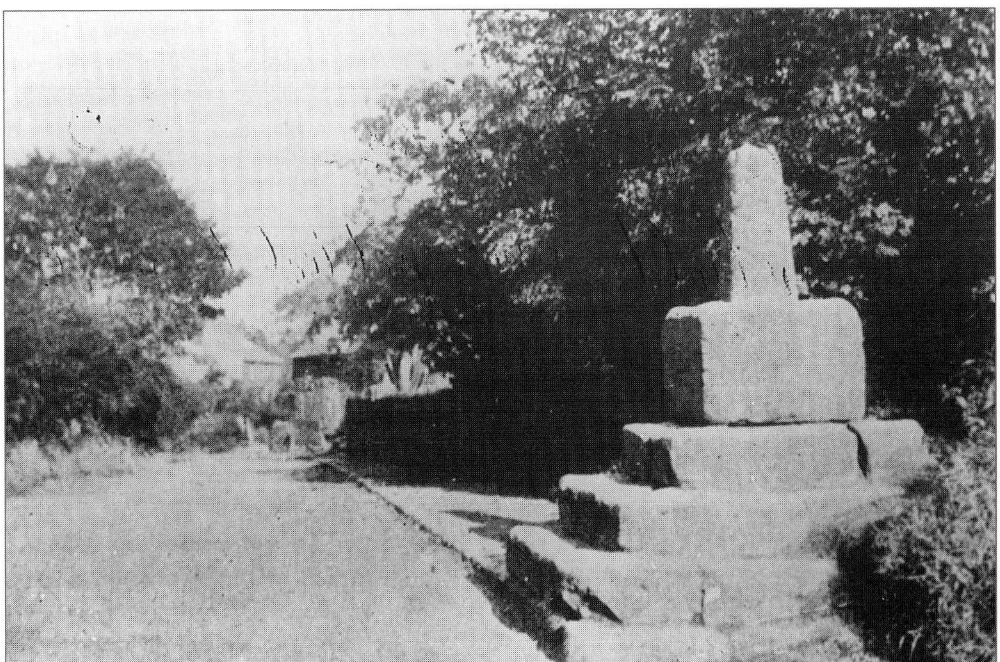

Cronton Cross, or the remains of it, seen over a century ago. The original main street in Cronton was Penny Lane, and Hall Lane and the Cross stood opposite Town End Farm at the crossroads. There were four crosses around the mother church of Farnworth, Pumpton to the north, Cuerdley to the east, Simms to the south and Cronton to the west. Cronton was once quite famous as a centre for watch-making.

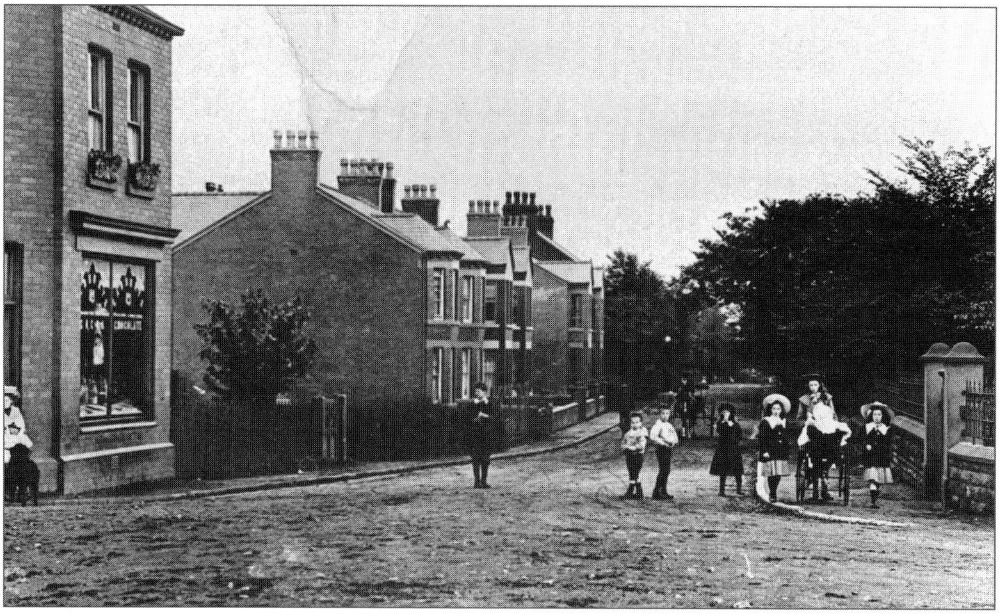

This scene looks down Ditchfield Road from Liverpool Road, 1910. The gate-posts on the right belonged to St Michael's C of E School, next to the church. It is a social club today. My mother was a pupil at this school in around 1919 and never tired of telling me that she used to walk the 1½ miles from Ditton, there and back, every day, and sometimes she even walked home for lunch. This photograph was given by Miss Margaret Lewis, who was the baby in the pram (right).

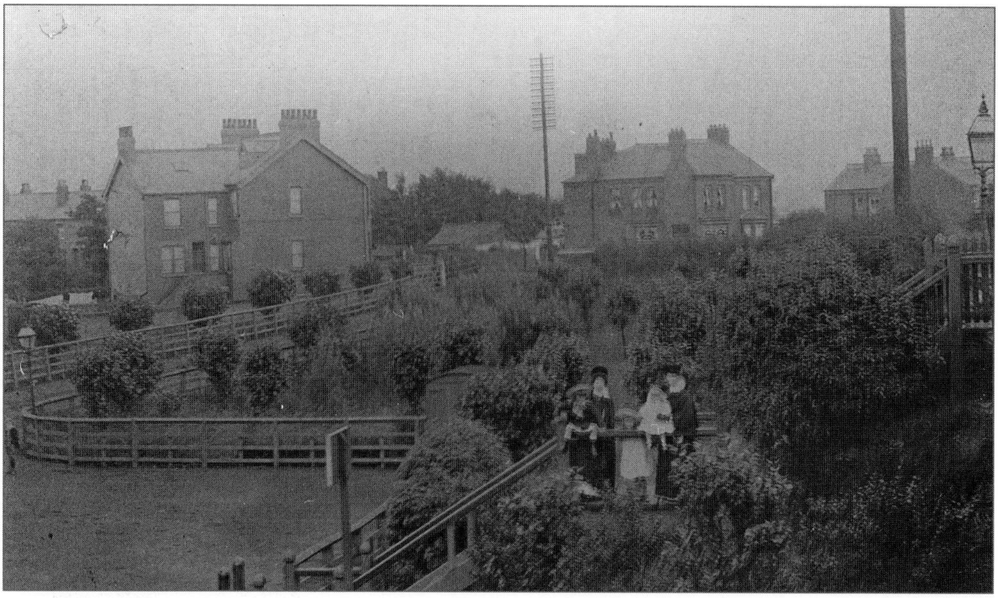

Hough Green from the station, says the caption by photographer Mr W. Hall in 1910. This area was not the original Hough Green (the Green of the Houghton family); that was on Hough Green Road, near where it joins Northern Lane; the road called Becher's is there today. The spot we see here was once called Welshman's House, and the house was pulled down to make way for the railway station, which opened in 1874 as Hough Green (for Ditton). It was after this that people started to refer to the area around Hough Green station as Hough Green, and the name stuck.

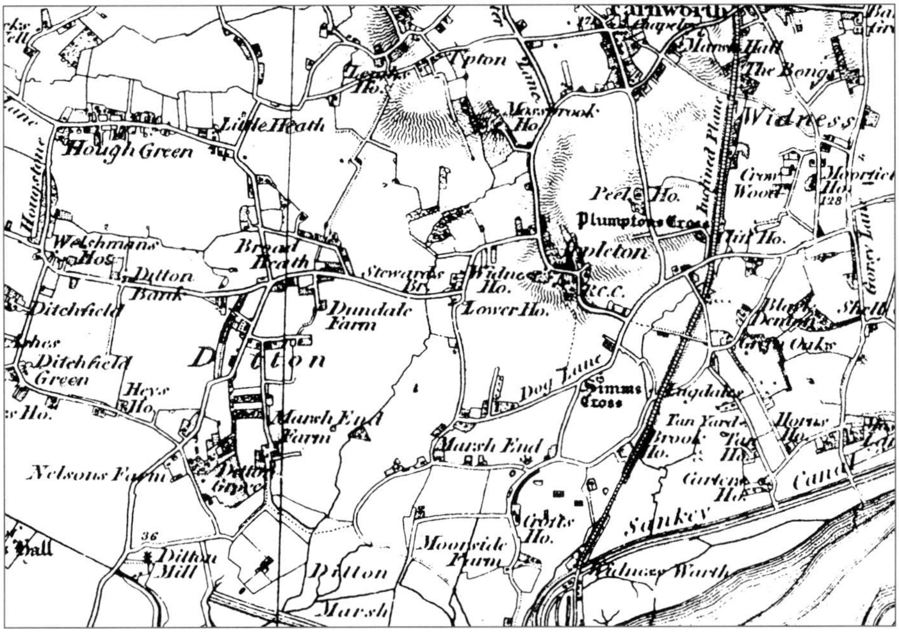

The area of Hough Green, Ditton and Appleton shown on a map from 1845. Welshman's House, later to become the railway station, can be seen, and the word Ditton then applied to an area between Chestnut Lodge and St Michael's Ditton RC Church. What we know as the Ball is Broad Heath on this map, and Stewards Brook marks what was later to become Liverpool Road.

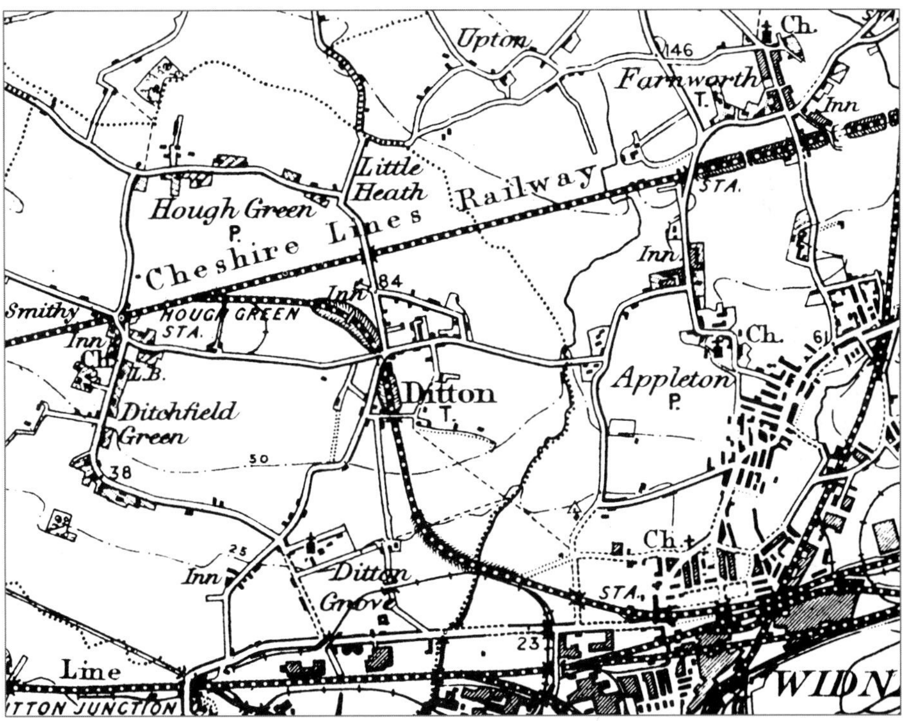

This map dates from fifty years later, and the railway has arrived. Hough Green is still north of the newly opened Hough Green station, and the words Broad Heath have disappeared from Ditton.

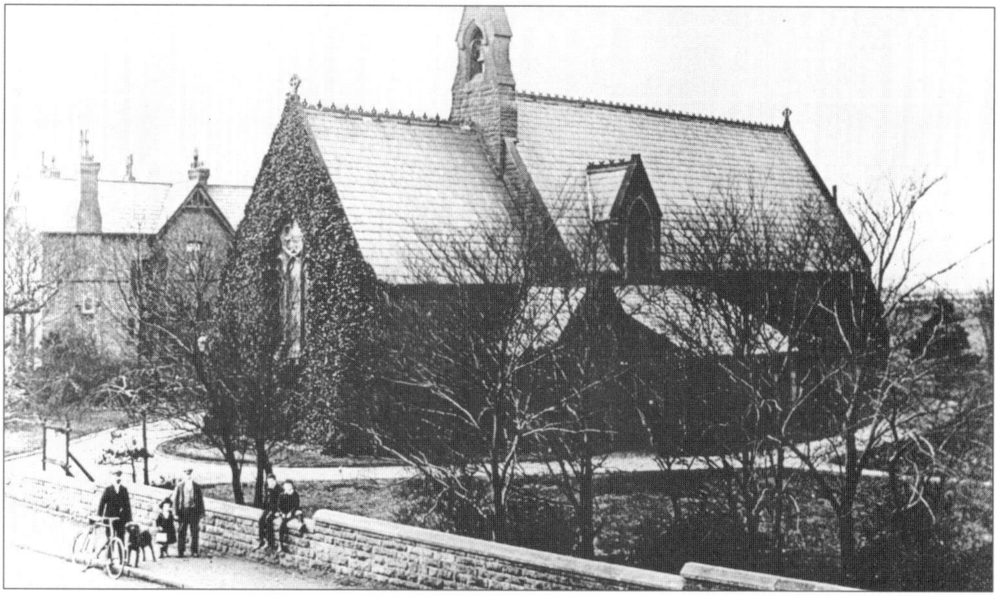

St Michael's Church, Hough Green, standing at the top of Ditchfield Road, *c.* 1910. The church was built in about 1871 at the same time as the railway station. It was consecrated in 1874, ready to serve the expected growing community. I was a choirboy here for about six years, and knew the grounds well, including the large orchard at the back of the vicarage. Can you make out the headstone in the trees in the right foreground of this picture? It was the murder stone of Edward Culshaw, who in 1784 was brutally killed. The stone originally stood on the murder spot, on Liverpool Road, but was moved into the churchyard when Leather's Farm was pulled down.

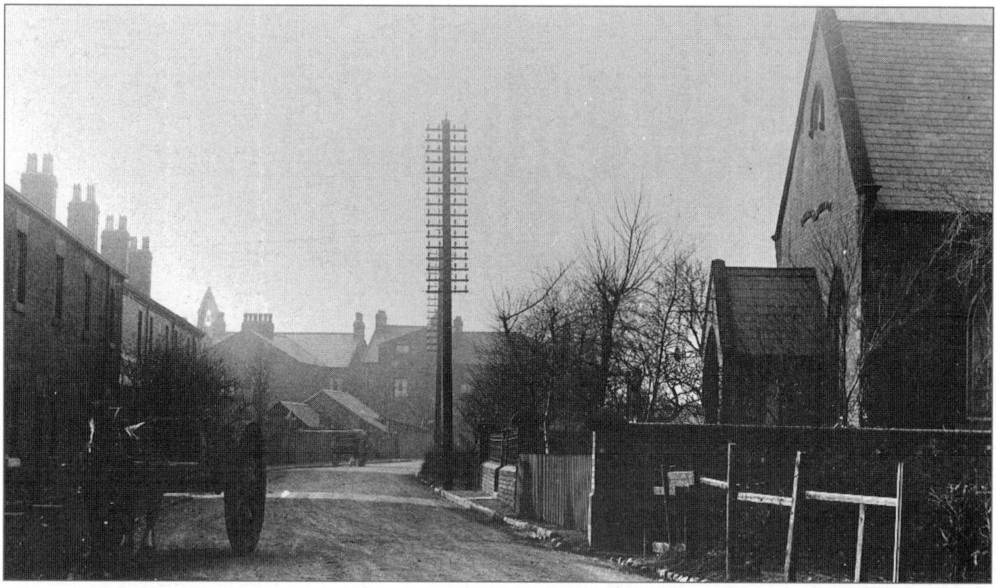

This is the top of Liverpool Road, *c.* 1900. The building on the right was Hough Green Methodist Chapel, and the bell of St Michael's Church is visible above the houses. One of the houses at the side of the horse and cart on the left of the picture was a sweet shop that gained many of my pennies when I walked to church and saved the penny bus fare! The two low huts further up the road are now a vets and 'Presentations', the shop of Fred the florist.

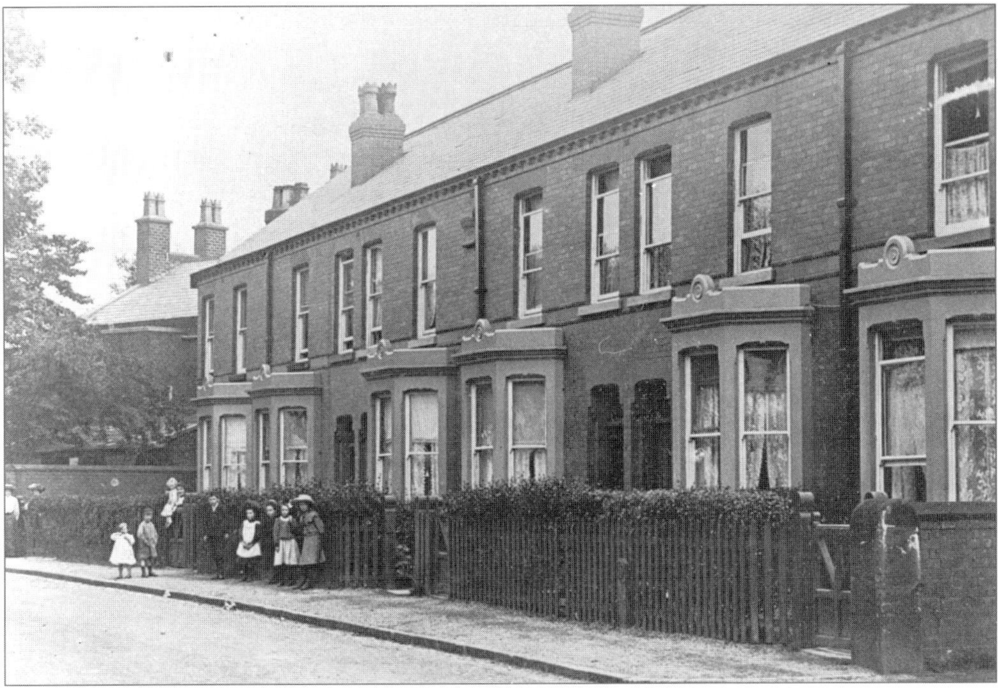

A lovely Edwardian picture of Oakfield Villas, Ditchfield Road, Hough Green. The name Ditchfield comes from the Ditchfield family, who lived at Ditton Hall in the 1600s and provided many of the priests who held secret masses around the Lancashire area. The Ditchfield line died out in 1680 with the death of Father Edward Ditchfield.

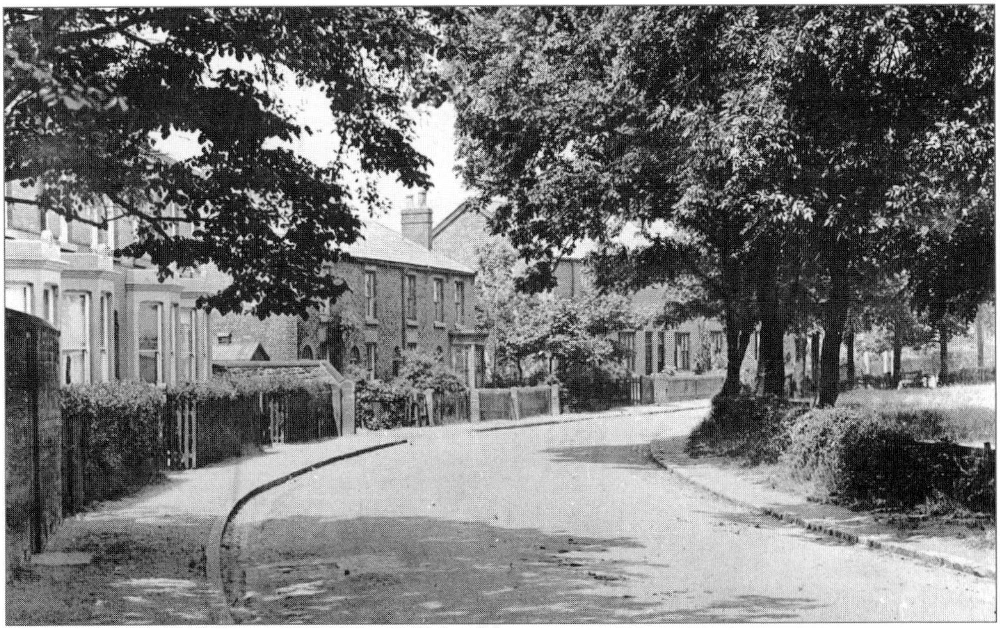

Ditchfield Road by the wall surrounding Oakfield House, looking up towards the railway station, *c.* 1920. The blocks of houses on the left are Oakfield Villas, O'Kel Cottages and Barley Grove. Oakfield Drive is there today.

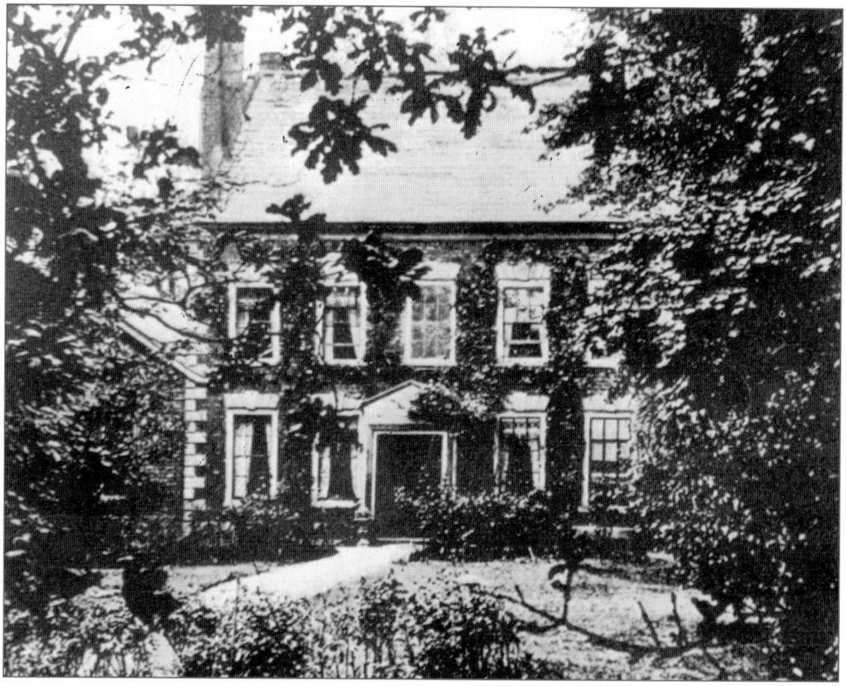

Ditchfield Hall, as it looked in 1880. The hall was built by relations of the Ditchfield family in about 1750 and was for a time the home of the Hawarden family. John Laverick was the last person to live there. He kept his racehorse, Uncle Bones, in this front garden.

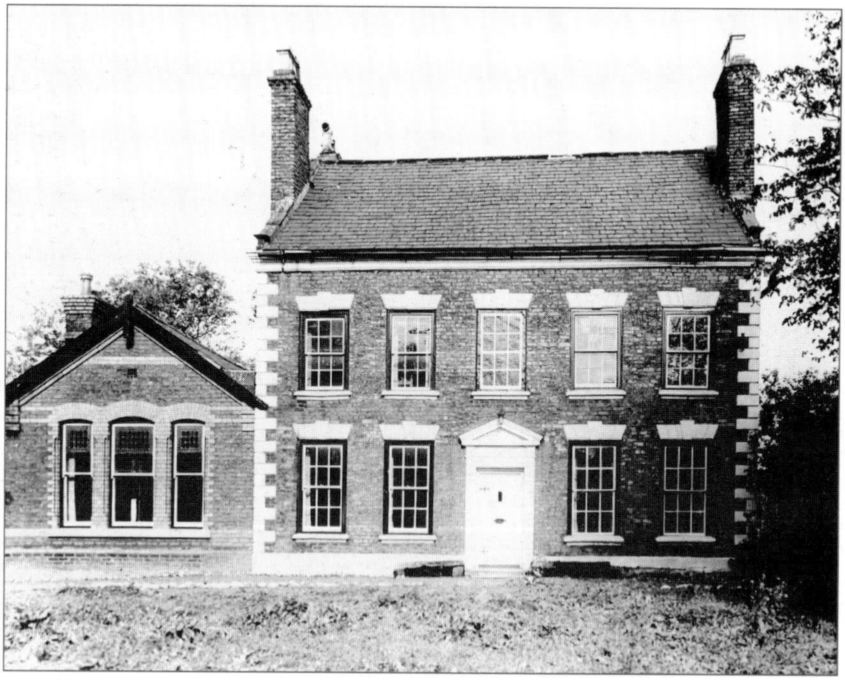

Ditchfield Hall, *c.* 1940. Although the hall had fallen into some disrepair efforts were made to revive its fortunes, and here we see the hall looking quite presentable, with its false window above the door, and its billiard hall to the left. It was pulled down by Wimpy in 1965 to make way for Sandyway Avenue.

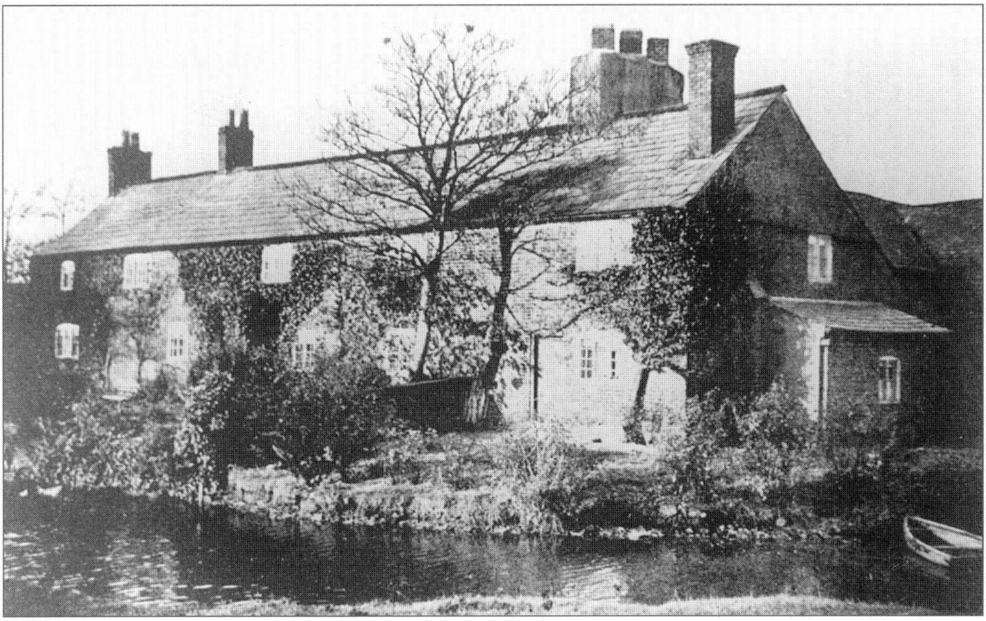

Tarbock Hall, 1900. Like Ditchfield Hall and Appleton Hall this house is strongly linked with the Catholic families in the area. The hall stood in a hollow just west of Hough Green. It had a moat which was kept filled by Ochre Brook, filled in after 1860. The family were always Catholic in their sympathies but seemed to keep their heads down more than their neighbours, the Irelands and the Bolds. Fines and imprisonments reduced the Tarbuck family and they eventually moved to Cartmel in the Lake District.

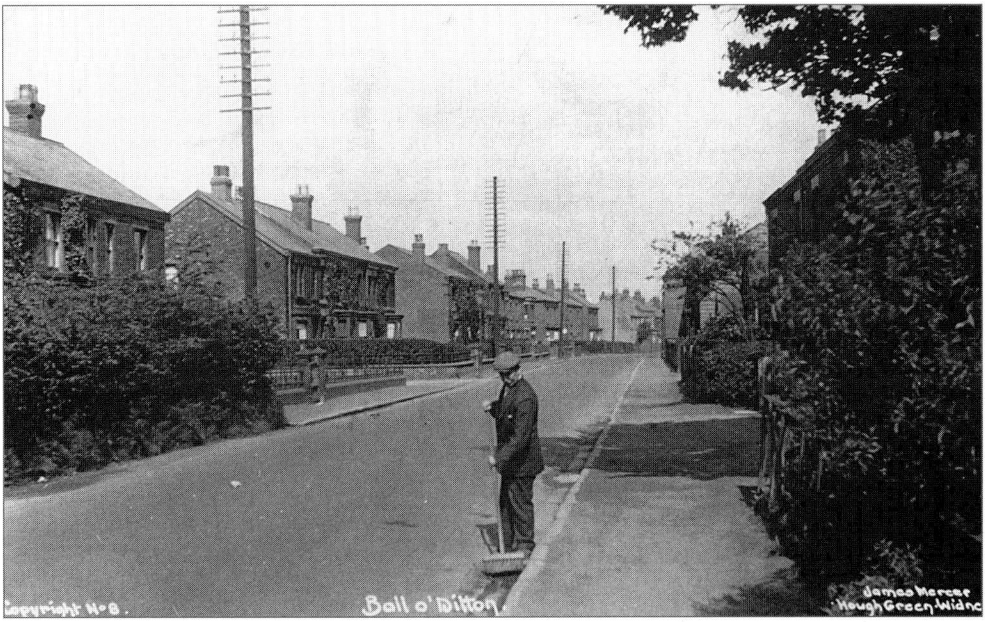

The Ball O' Ditton, looking from Chestnut Lodge towards the Ball itself, *c.* 1907. I was told many years ago that the inn here was originally the Globe and a model of the world hung outside it. From being the Globe to the 'place where a ball hung outside' was not a big step, and it became known as the Ball Inn at Ditton and then the Ball of Ditton. Our photographer was standing opposite the more recent bus stop at Chestnut Lodge, and on the right you can just see what was the tin chapel.

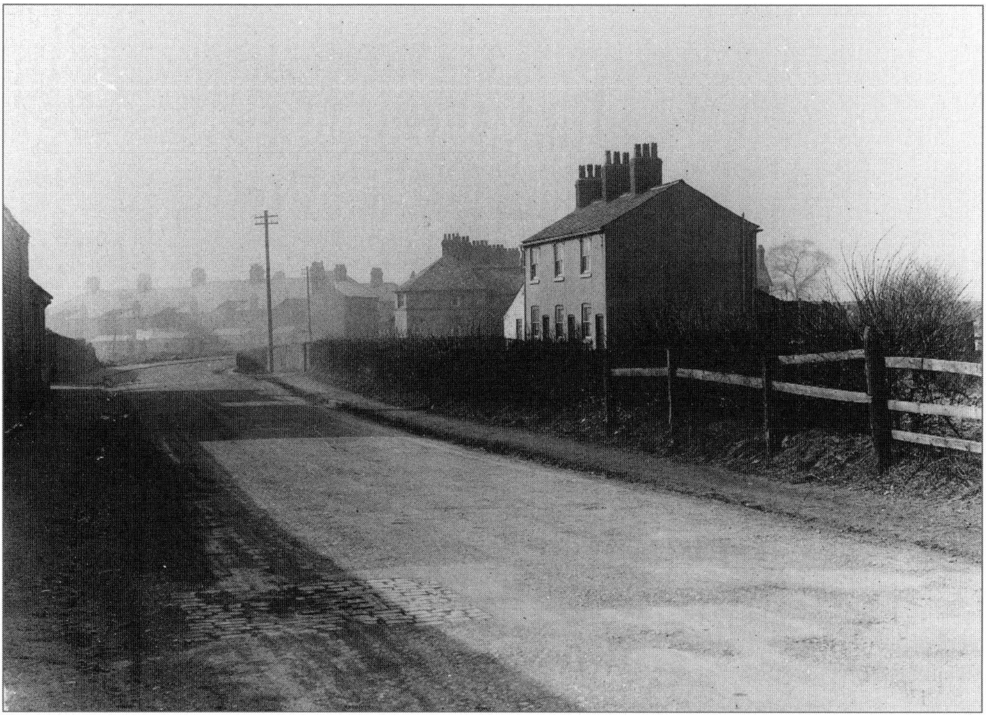

Hale Road, Ditton, *c.* 1900. This is the original Ditton, and today you would find a car showroom and garage on the right of the picture. It was Booth's Garage, run by Lew Booth, for many years. It is now run by his son John. The houses nearest the camera were once St Mary's School.

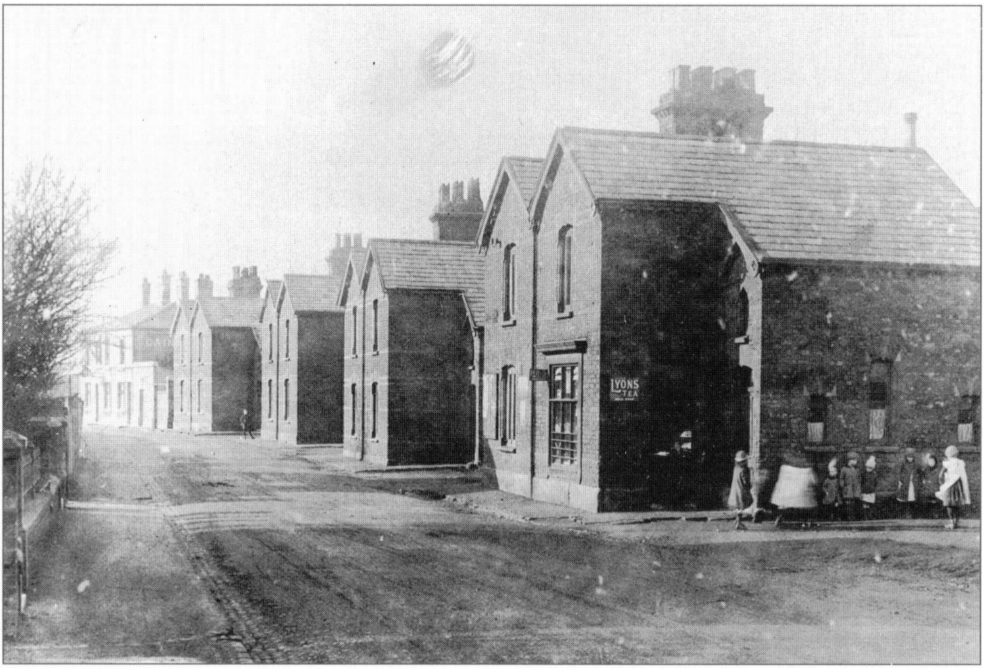

The bottom of Hale Road, and the building furthest from the camera is the New Inn; everything else in the picture has long since gone, replaced by newer housing.

CHAPTER FIVE

WEST BANK & WIDNES DOCKS

West Bank has always been a little cut off from Widnes. History tells us that it started off as Wood End, and in the early years of the last century (1800–1820) people would come from Manchester and Liverpool to bathe in the waters of the Mersey and enjoy the delights of the sands. West Bank always seemed to house a mixture of immigrant families who came to the area for work. In the 1820s and '30s it was the Welsh who came, in the 1860s it was the Irish and in the 1890s it was Poles and other Europeans who settled here. Being so close to the early factories and with so many streets packed closely together it was always considered a poor area. Living in the shadow of the new road bridge has not helped it, and you get a cut-off feeling when visiting there today, though a lot has been done to improve and revitalise the area.

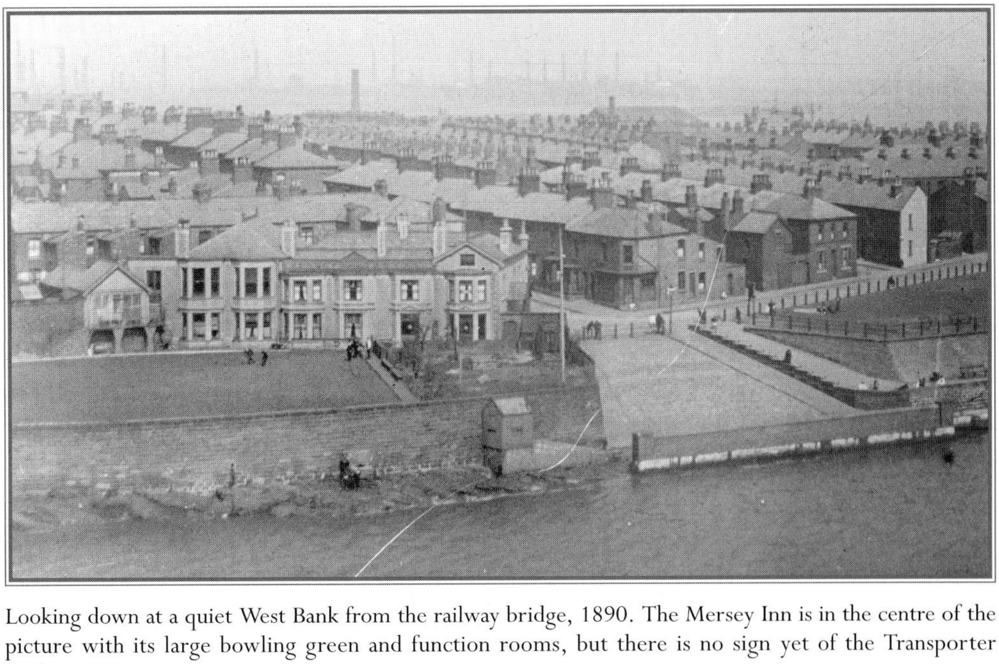

Looking down at a quiet West Bank from the railway bridge, 1890. The Mersey Inn is in the centre of the picture with its large bowling green and function rooms, but there is no sign yet of the Transporter Bridge.

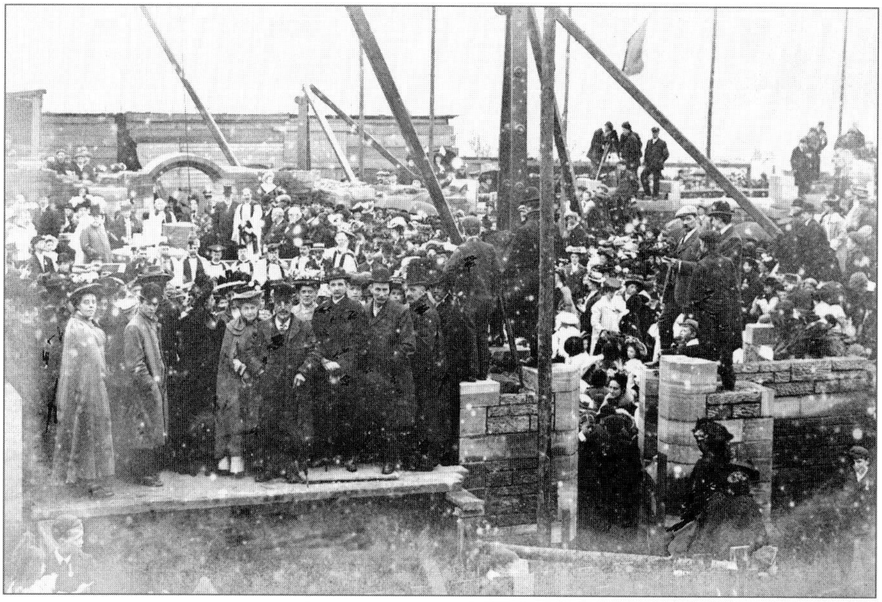

The scene as Mrs Gossage laid the foundation stone of the new St Mary's Church, 14 May 1908. Her husband had been one of the benefactors of the fund for the buying of houses in West Bank and clearing them to build this, the second St Mary's Church. Mr F.H. Gossage gave £1,000 himself and his firm Messrs William Gossage & Sons Ltd gave £3,000.

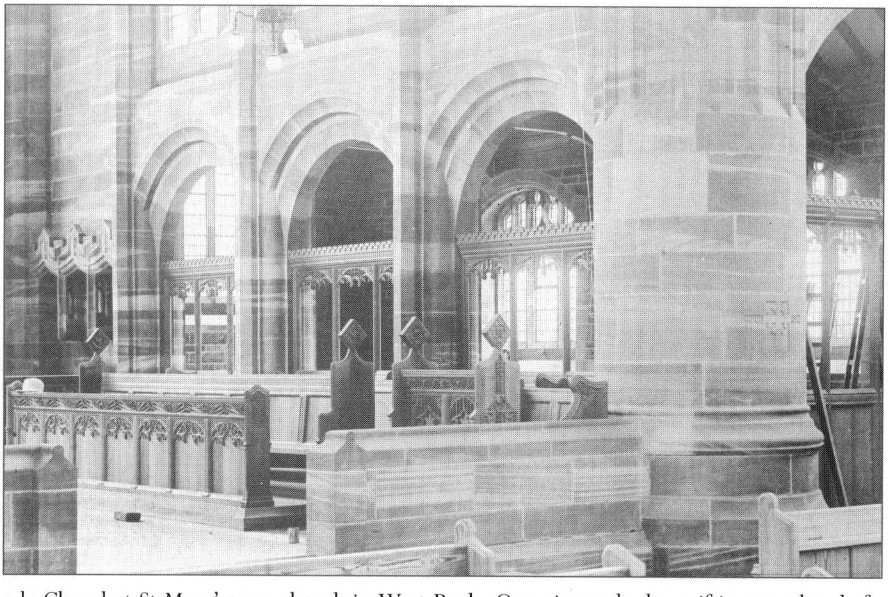

The Lady Chapel at St Mary's new church in West Bank. Our picture looks as if it was taken before the church was quite finished as ladders, poles and bits of wood can be seen. West Bank may have been a poor area, but St Mary's had the finest of everything, and the cost of building the church was £16,669. The church was opened officially on Saturday 12 November 1910, and Bishop Chavasse of Liverpool officiated, calling it one of the finest churches in the whole of the north of England. There were a lot of critics of the church who said it would have been better to spend £8,000 on the church and £8,000 on the poor. But the mayor, Fred Neil, and the bishop both declared that the poor of Widnes were not one whit poorer because this magnificent church had been built with the best of everything.

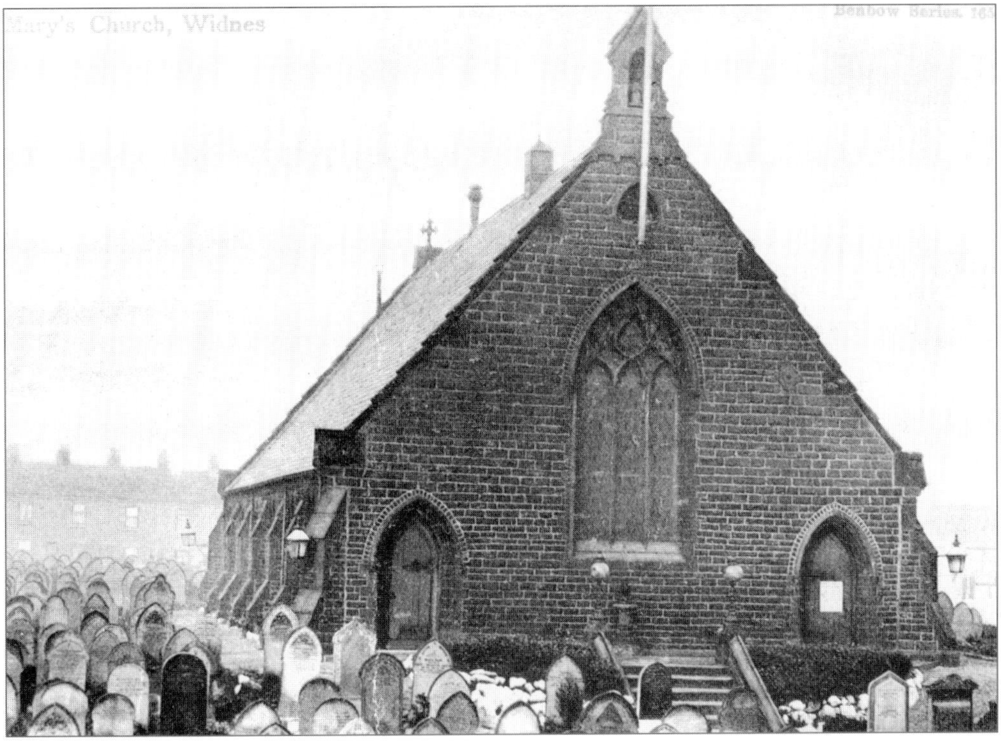

The first St Mary's Church at West Bank. It was opened in 1858 for the growing community around Widnes Docks with money raised from the industrialists who had just moved into the area. The original plans for this church showed a tower and spire, but it was never really completed and spent its life without either of these. The church had been partly built on chemical waste and in 1901 cracks were found in the walls which then began to bulge outwards and the roof beams twisted, making it necessary to build a new church.

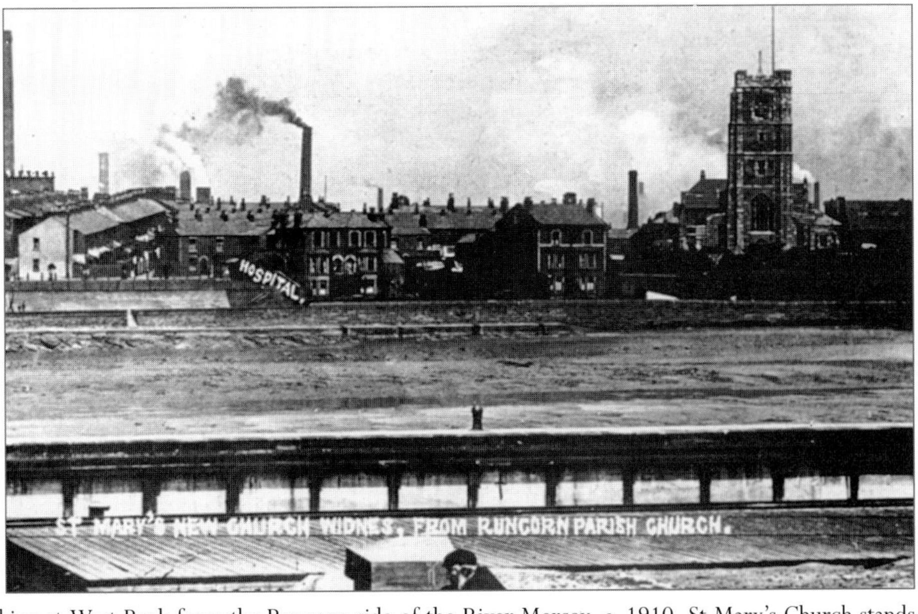

Looking at West Bank from the Runcorn side of the River Mersey, *c.* 1910. St Mary's Church stands out well and the accident hospital is marked on the picture.

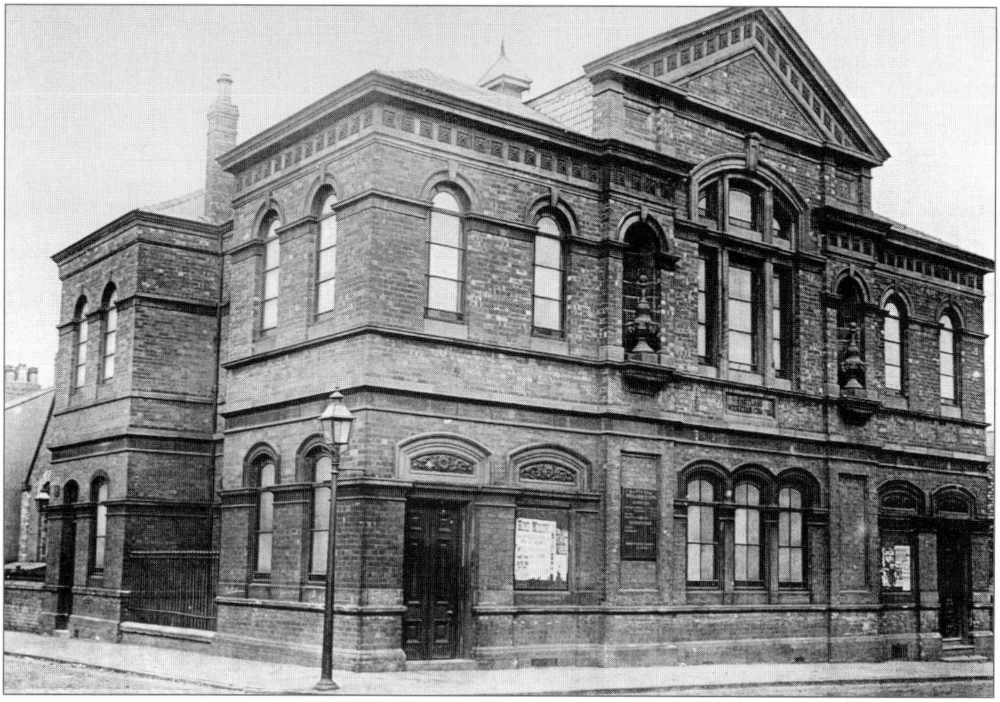

The Hartland Wesleyan Methodist Chapel in West Bank, *c.* 1900. The chapel opened in the mid-1880s and cost under £2,500 to build. Of this cost £1,000 was put up by Mr Gossage and £1,000 by Mr Sutton Timmis, who had suggested the name because of the tremendous amount of work done by William Hartland on the Widnes circuit.

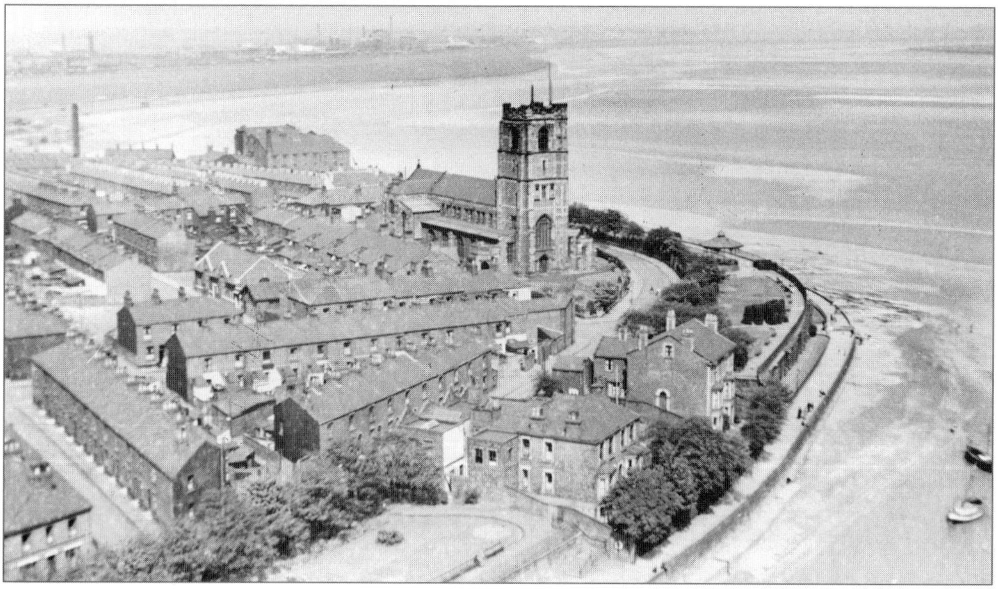

West Bank looking from the Lamp House at the top of the Transporter Bridge, May 1938. The church of St Mary dominates this picture, high up overlooking the rows of houses. The large building at the bottom centre of this photograph was the Accident and Emergency Hospital, which opened in 1878 to deal with the growing number of casualties from the rapidly expanding chemical industry.

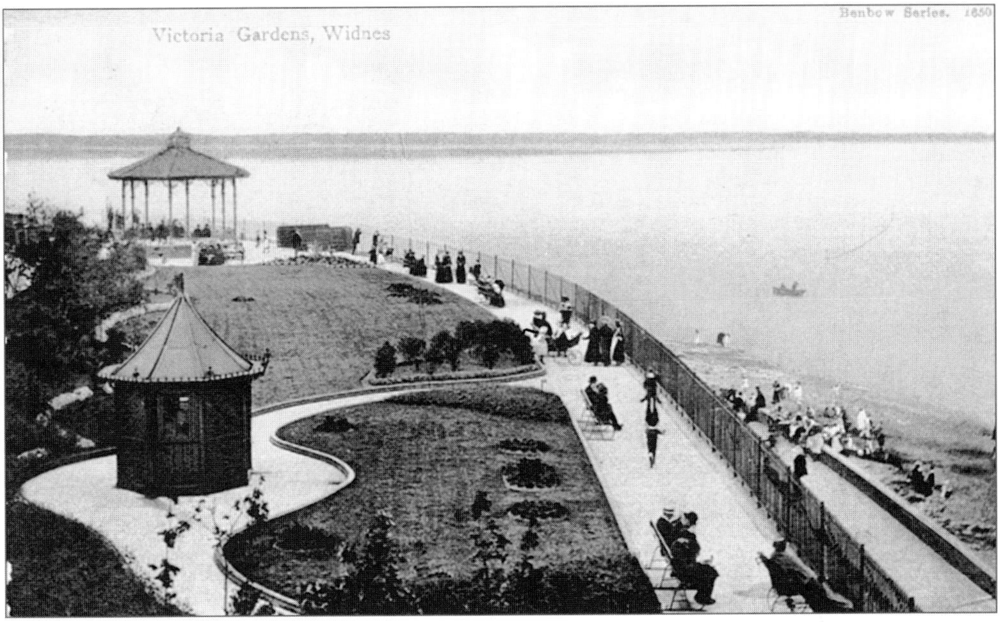

Victoria Gardens and the Promenade, West Bank, from a postcard dated 1904. It shows the lovely blue river, people sitting on the shoreline picnicking and bathing, the lovely green gardens and the feeling of fresh air. It cannot be the West Bank, can it? Widnes was very proud of its Victorian Promenade which is still there today.

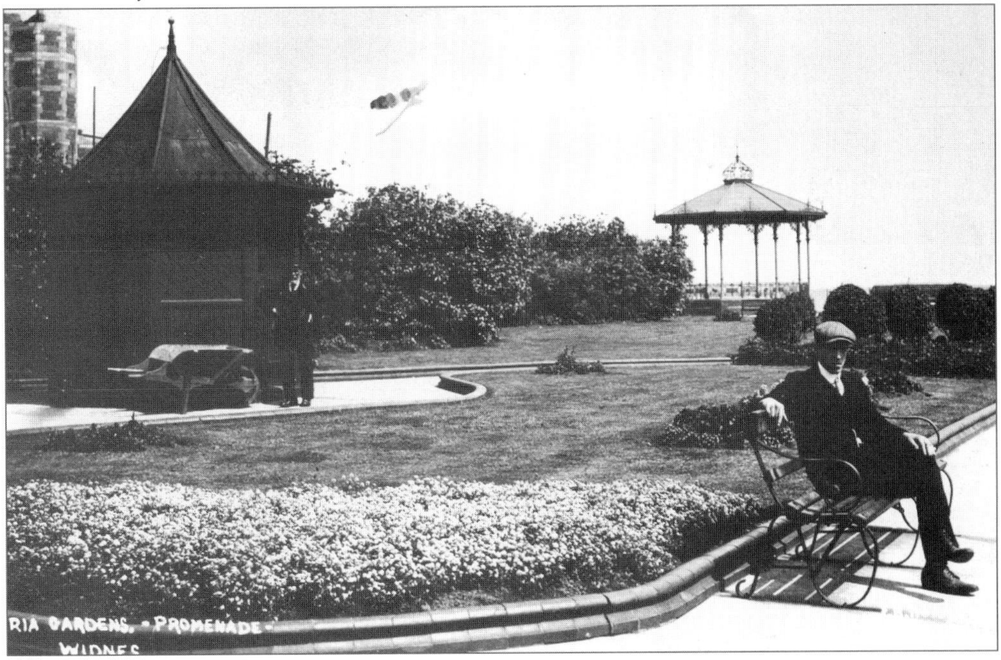

A quiet reflective moment in Victoria Gardens, with only the gardener to keep an eye on things. The gardens were thought out soon after Queen Victoria died, and were opened on 21 May 1903. There was just an open space here before the formal gardens and bowling greens were laid, which made it a much more attractive place to visit. St Mary's Church is on the left of the picture and looks as if it is still under contruction, so I would say the year is 1909.

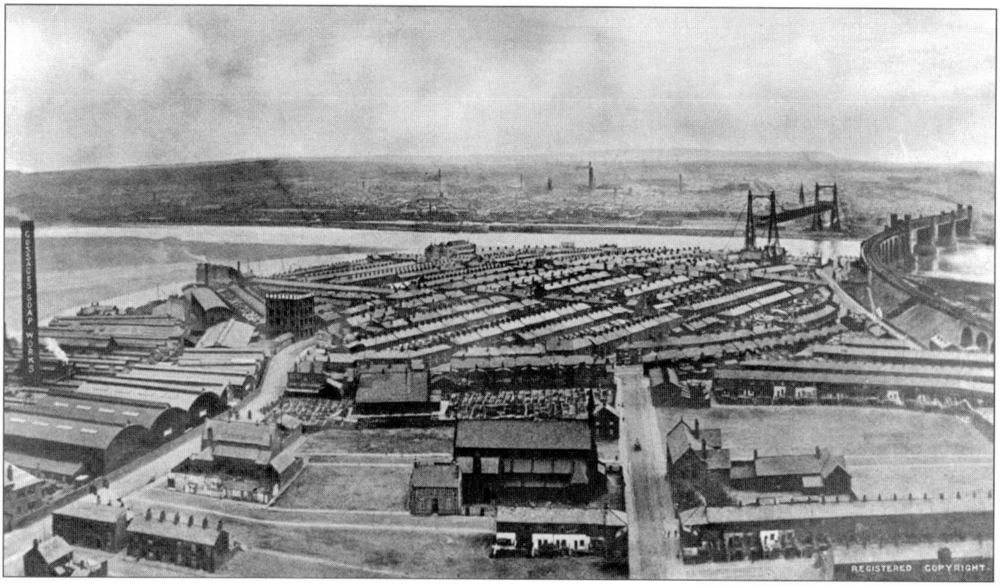

An aerial view of West Bank. Pencilled on the back of this picture is '1930s', but I think it is 1909 because the tower of St Mary's Church cannot be seen. Gossage's chimney and offices are still there, so it is in or before 1932. The road in the centre of the picture, with St Patrick's RC church on the left of it, was Cromwell Road. The original plans were for this to be the main street, north to south in Widnes, away from West Bank.

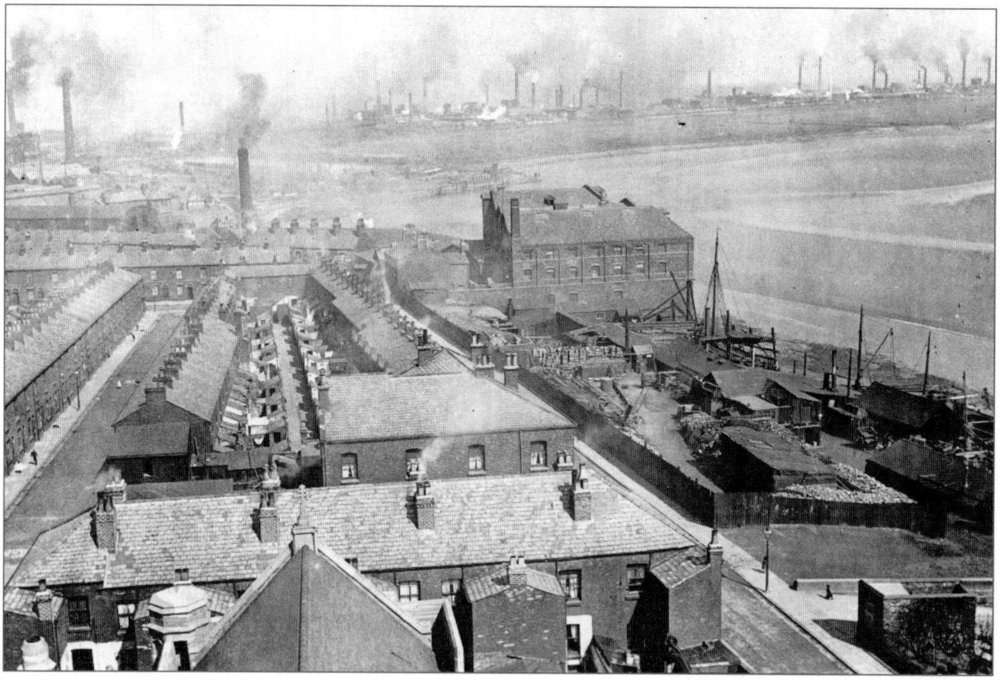

West Bank, and the factories on the banks of the St Helens Canal. This photograph was taken from the tower of St Mary's Church in about 1913. Note the boatyard on the river bank, and the end of the Victoria Promenade which can just be seen in the right-hand corner.

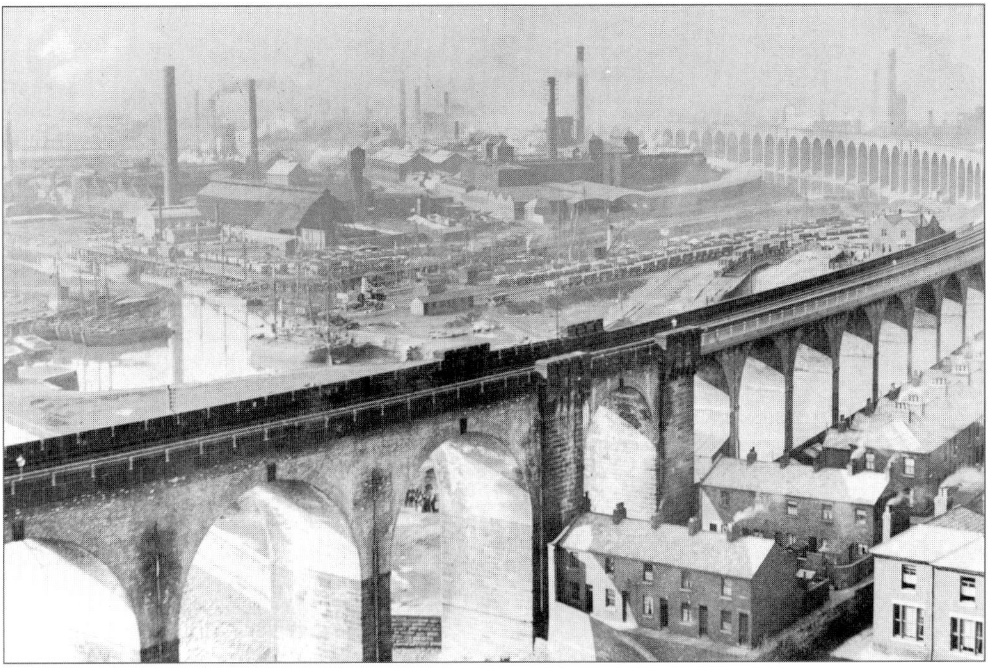

Looking at the land which was once Widnes Marsh, from the top of the Transporter Bridge, *c.* 1920. John Hutchinson had been the first to realise that this boggy land, used only for turf cutting and grazing, might one day be valuable. He acquired the land in the late 1850s and rented it out to be used for dumping chemical waste. You can see Widnes Dock which Hutchinson built in 1884, and every inch of the marsh is covered with factories and railway sidings. It is impossible to ignore the railway viaduct with its sixty-five arches, which lifted the railway line roughly 190 ft from Ditton Junction up to the bridge.

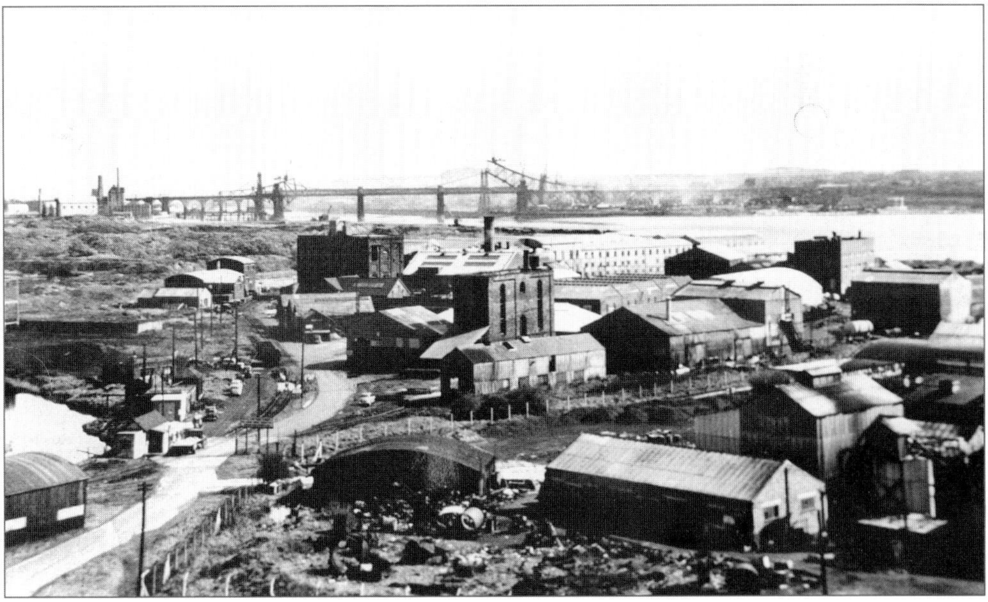

A view across Ditton Marsh and Widnes Marsh towards the bridges and Runcorn in the distance, 1959. The area had a decidedly run-down and tatty air about it, and the Calder and Mersey Canal looks very dilapidated.

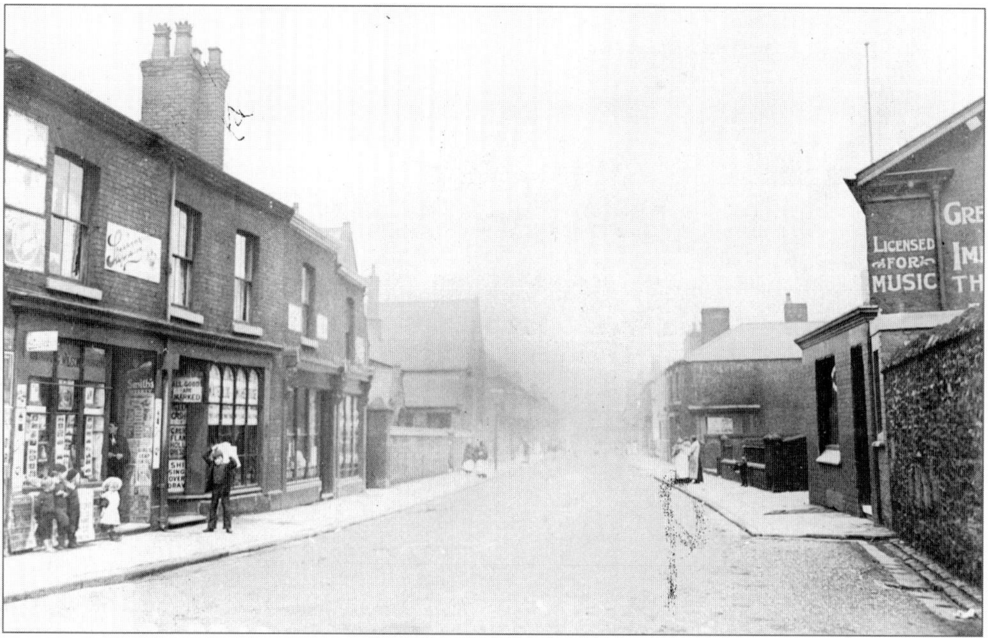

Waterloo Road, looking away from West Bank, in an Edwardian photograph. The youngsters pose outside G. Wilson's newsagent's shop on the left. The inn on the right was the Albion, but not the one that we have now on Liverpool Road.

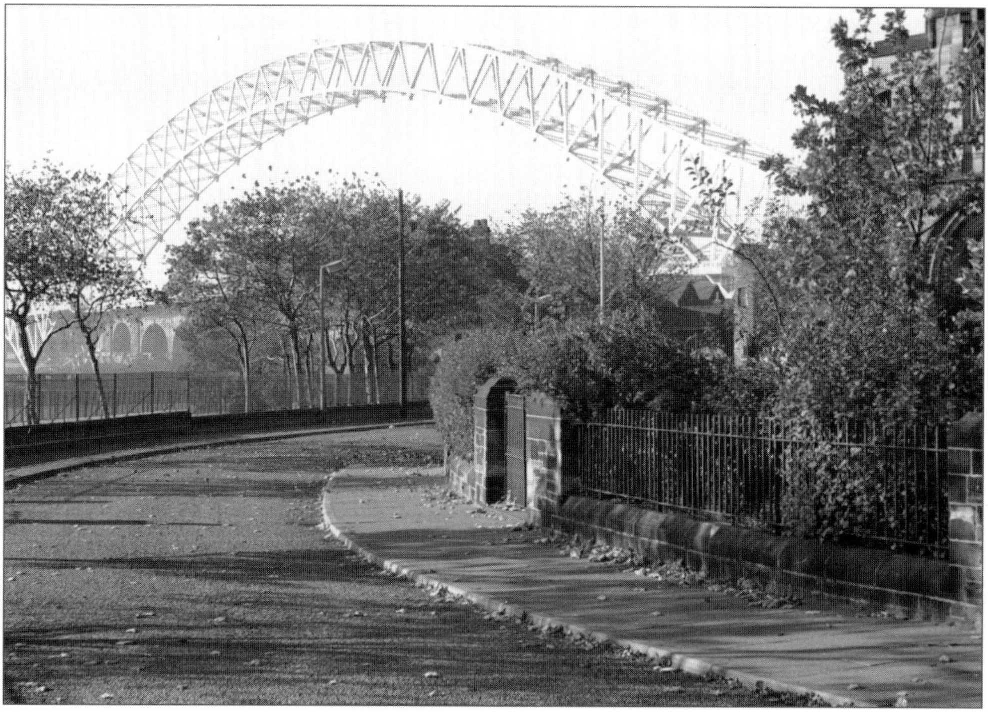

St Mary's Road, West Bank, only a few years ago, and it could almost be West Bank today. The gate to the church of St Mary is on the right. The new road bridge dominates this view as it dominates a lot of West Bank itself.

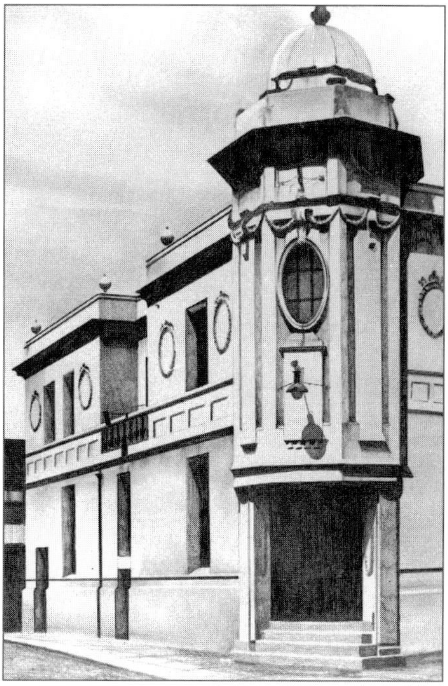

The Alexandra Theatre on Alexandra Street was built in 1887 by Doctor Gerrard, a publican, and two gentlemen, James Kiddie and Mr W. Bray. It was the only purpose-built theatre in Widnes. Before the advent of cinemas, the theatre specialised in the popular melodramas of the time, with pantomimes at Christmas. Unfortunately it burnt down on 29 December 1948, when the fire brigade fought a losing battle to save the building where Stan Laurel and Charlie Chaplin had trod the boards and had sent laughter echoing up to the rafters of what was nicknamed 'The Wooden Shed'.

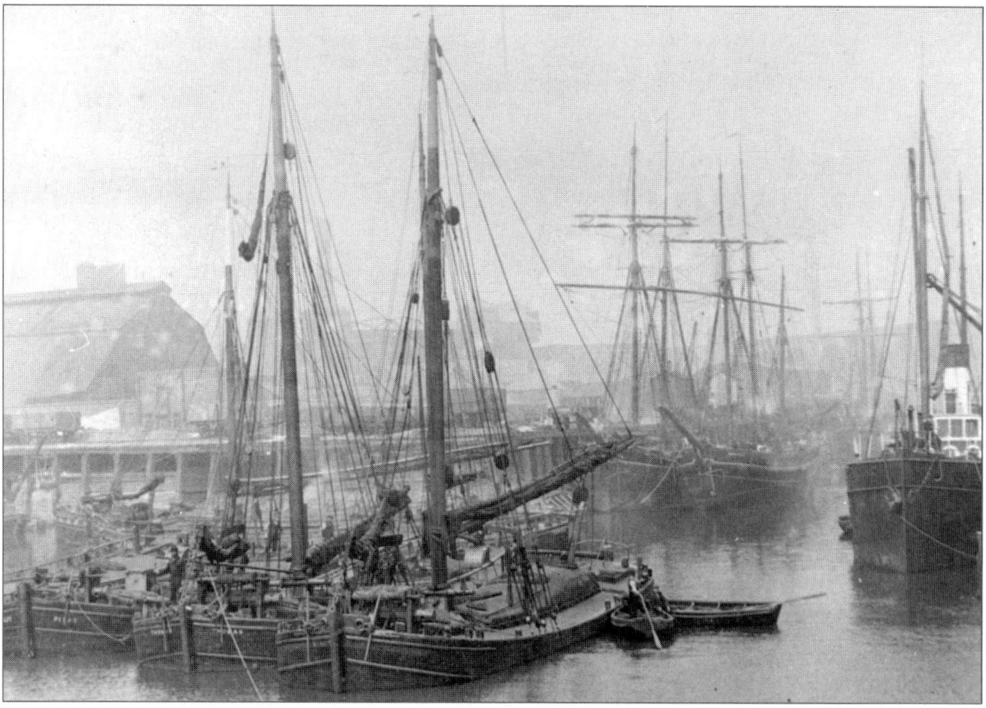

The West Bank Dock, Widnes, as it was known, although technically it was outside West Bank and on Widnes Marsh, *c.* 1902. It was constructed by John Hutchinson in 1864 just two years before he died. Here we see a mixture of Mersey flats (nearest the camera), two-masted schooners (middle) and a coaster (far right). The flats could be pulled up and down the St Helens or the Weaver canals, and then they could use their sails to either cross the river or venture up to Liverpool.

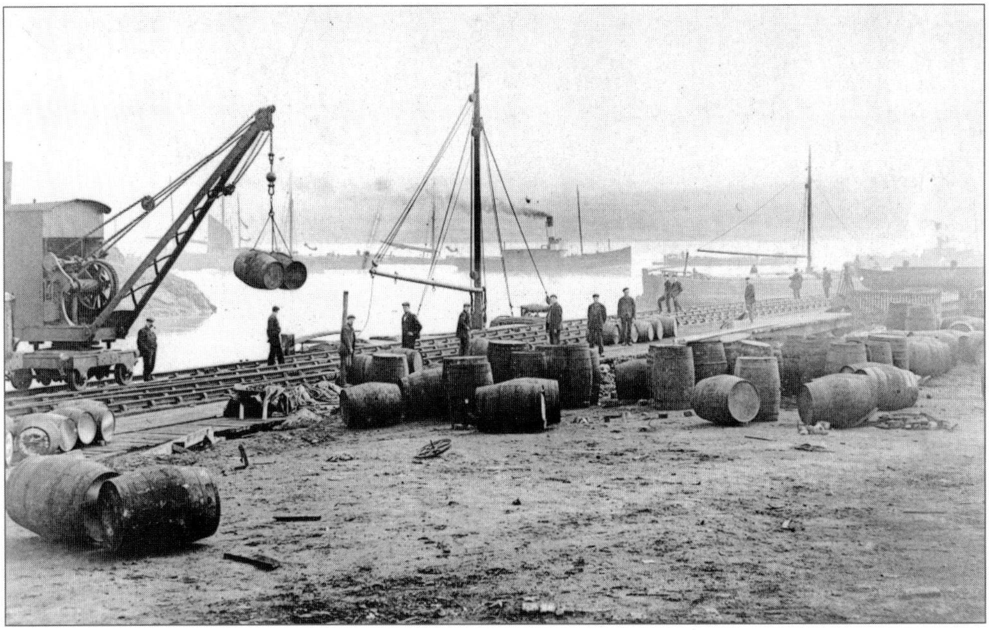

Loading at the Calder & Mersey Extract & Ore Company, 1900. Ditton Marsh and Widnes Marsh were two separate areas along the River Mersey, divided by Ditton Brook which drains the areas of Halewood, Huyton and Speke and then passes through Ditton Junction to join the River Mersey. It was at the meeting of this brook and the river that deepening and straightening took place to make quays for the Calder & Mersey Extract Company. This firm built their large factory there for the production of tanning extracts and oils that were shipped from there to the leather trade not only in Britain but all over the continent.

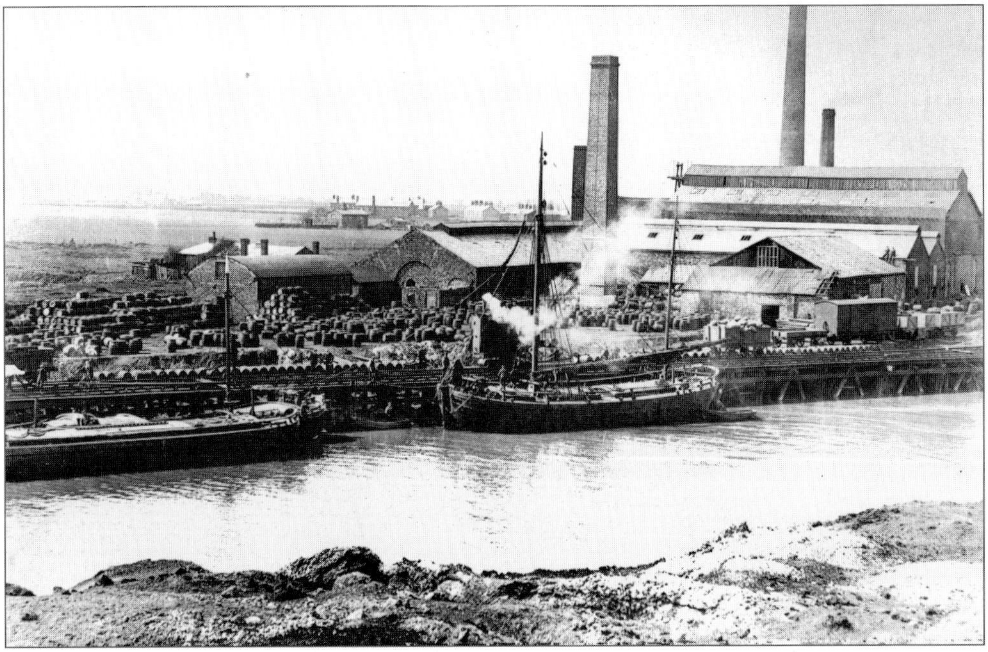

Ditton Brook, and boats loading and unloading at the Calder & Mersey Works, *c.* 1905. This factory was almost entirely destroyed by fire in 1918 but was subsequently rebuilt.

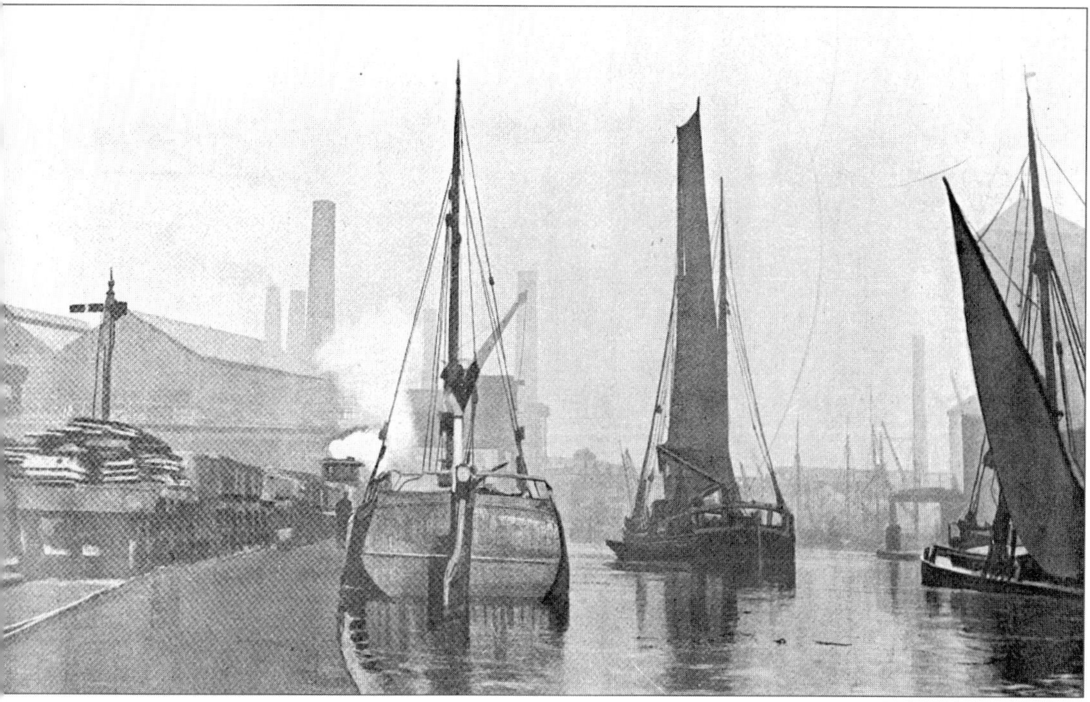

Mersey flats, boats that could use either the canal or the river, are seen here at the end of the St Helens Canal at West Bank, in about the late 1890s.

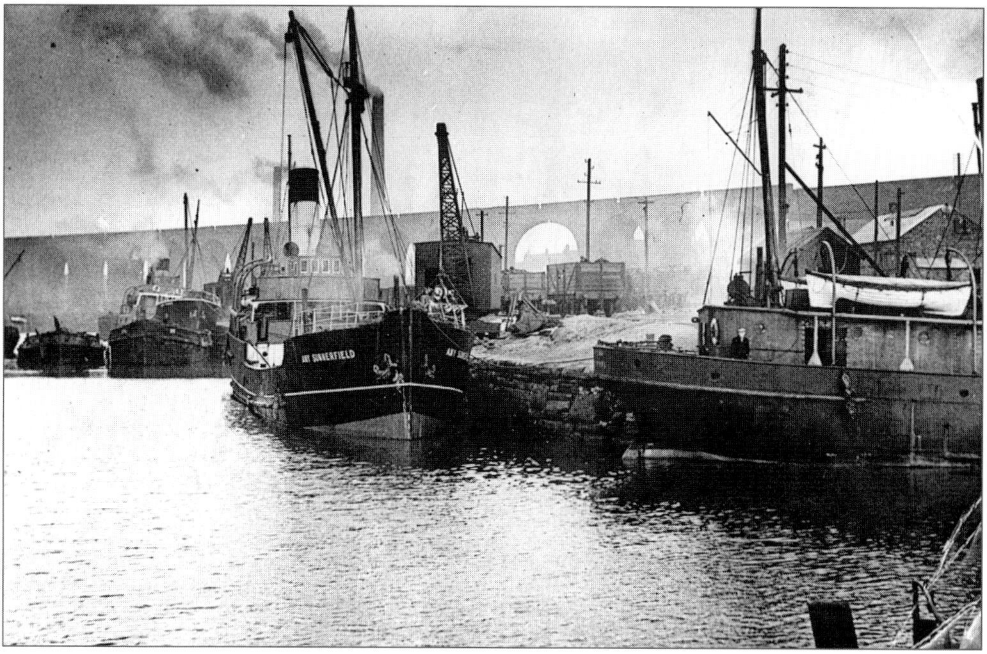

Widnes Docks were fairly busy right up to the late 1950s, and still in use, though infrequently, in the 1960s, as we can see in this picture from about that time.

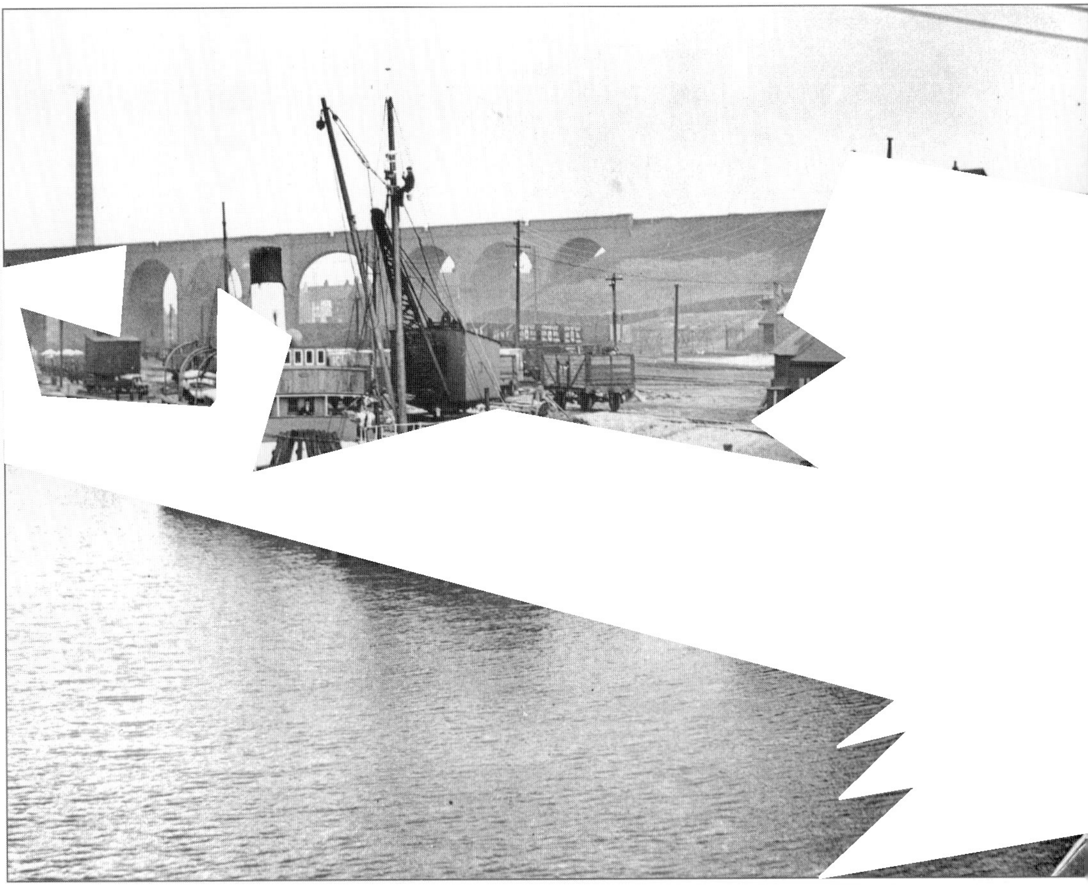

Widnes Docks opened in 1862 and played a large part in the development of West Bank and what was later Ditton Road. The railway came right alongside the loading and unloading wharves and the extensive railway network meant goods could be moved to any of the works along the St Helens Canal without further unloading. Our picture has caught the *Amy Summerfield*, a small coaster, in the docks and in front of her is the *Thelwall* (a Liverpool registered coaster). The whole area has an abandoned look about it.

What our 1930s photographer has also captured is the famous 'skew' arch on the Widnes side of the bridge. Local legend has it that the designer of the bridge could not get the curve of the bridge right and as work progressed from Ditton Junction and also the railway bridge took shape, he and the engineers and contractors were beside themselves with worry about the completion date and the final piece of the curve. Then one of the workmen suggested that one arch should 'skew' the opposite way to all the others and proceeded to build it, to illustrate his point and, abracadabra! the problem was solved. The fourth arch from the right, just above the *Amy Summerfield*'s bridge, is the arch in question and can clearly be seen to bend the opposite way to all the other arches.

CHAPTER SIX

BRIDGING THE MERSEY

The word Mersey means boundary, and up till 1974 it had been just that, way back to the age of the Romans. It was once the border between Northumbria and Mercia; the boundary between Christianity and paganism; and the division between Lancashire and Cheshire. In 1800 it seemed more of a barrier than a boundary, a barrier to the growing expansions in transport and trade. If only the Duke of Bridgewater had found monetary backing in Runcorn, when in 1780 a plan was put forward for a canal bridge to cross the Mersey! If only Widnes Corporation had been a little more ambitious in 1902 and pushed for a government road bridge instead of leaving individuals to form the Transporter Bridge Company! But 'if onlys' do not make history, deeds do – and here we take a look at the three bridges that have been built across the Runcorn Gap.

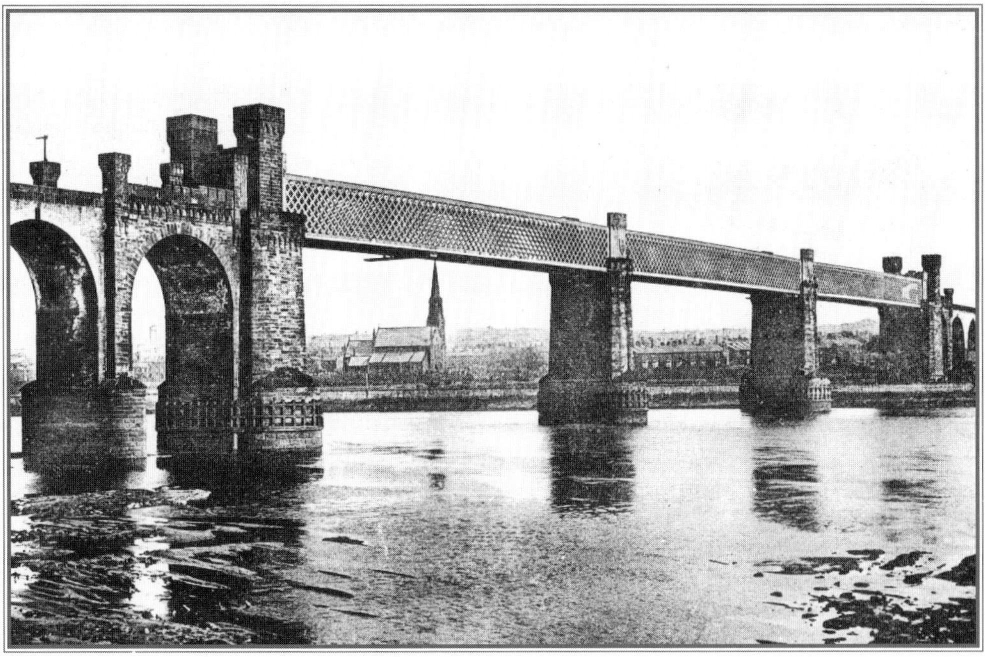

The Runcorn/Widnes Railway Bridge, 1900. The view is taken from the Widnes side and shows the town of Runcorn beyond the bridge.

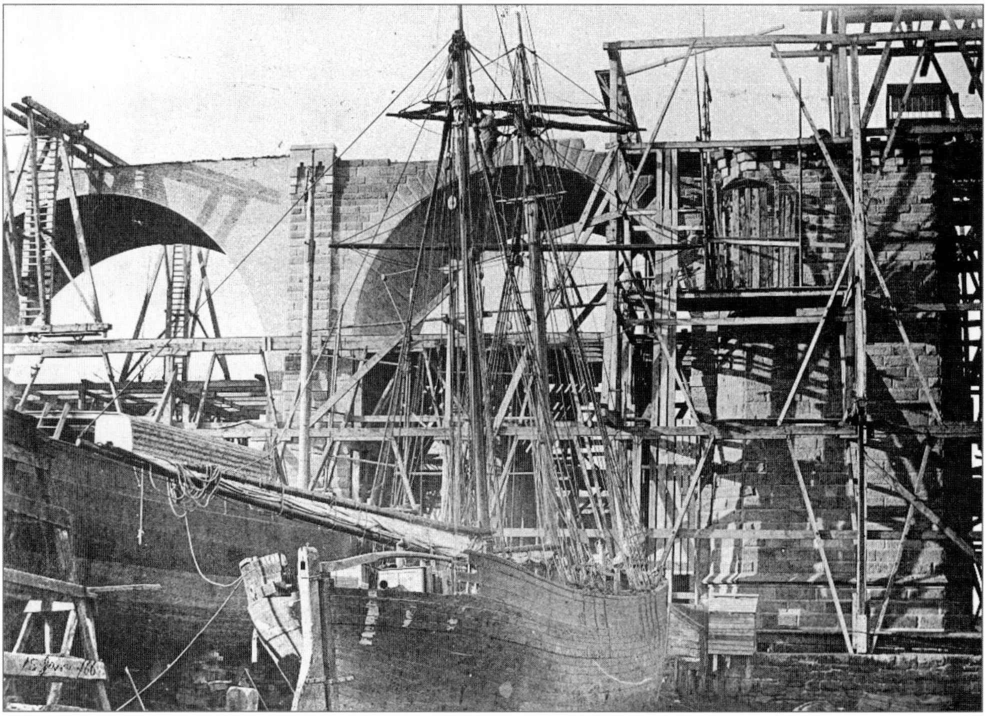

This picture was taken during the construction of the railway bridge. Building work was started in 1863 and took five years to complete. During the work the width of the Nez (the outcrop of rock at West Bank) was much reduced.

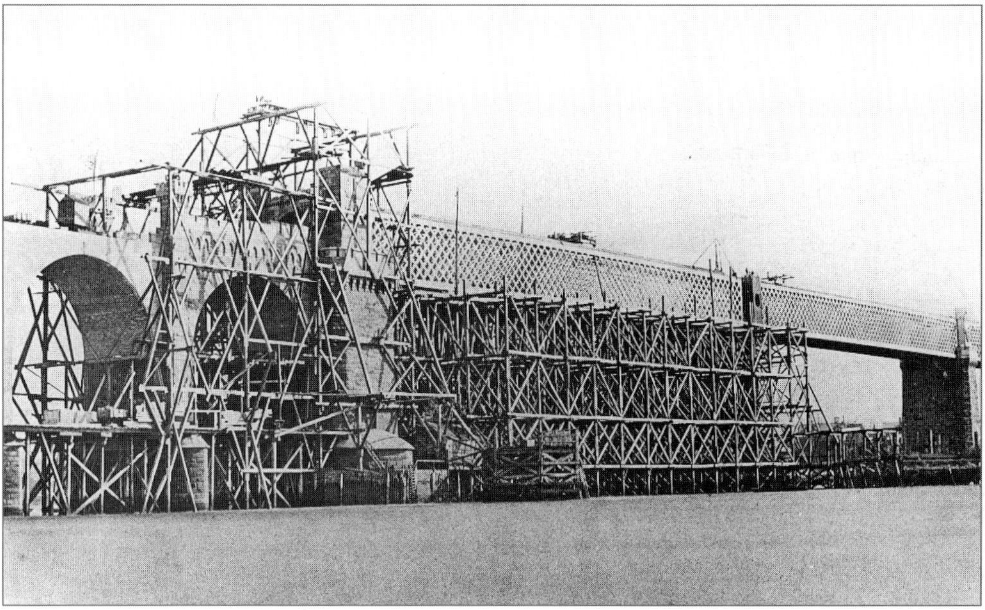

This is a little later in the construction work, 1867. It is taken from the same spot as the picture on page 93. The cast-iron spans over the brickwork weigh an average of 700 tons each, and there are three in all. To take all this weight the foundations of the bridge were driven into the solid rock some 45 ft below the watermark, which in itself was a marvellous feat of engineering.

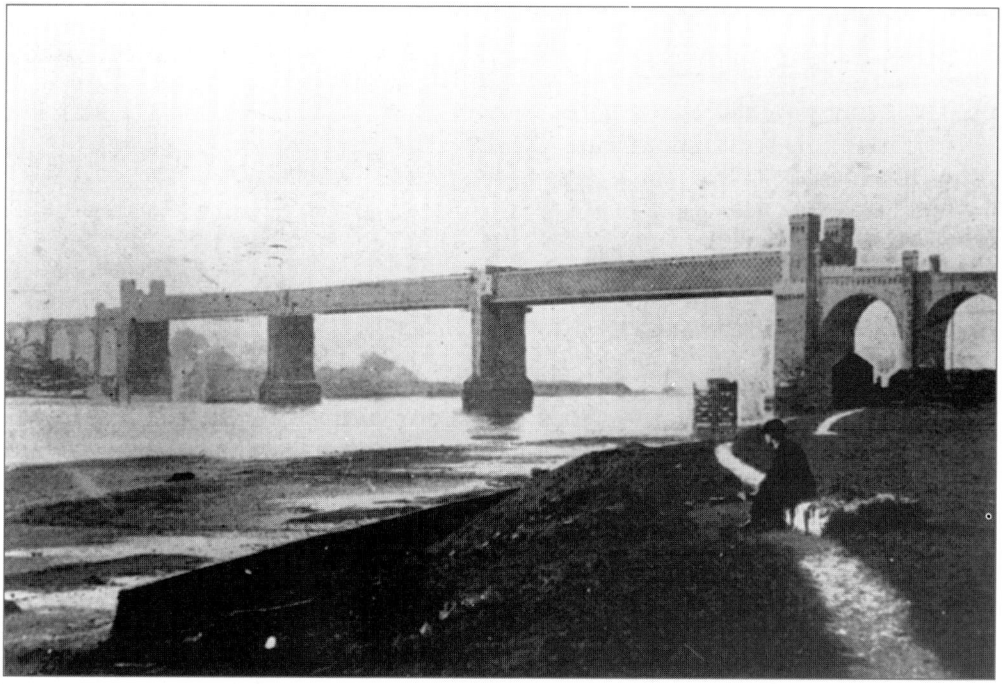

The completed railway bridge, this time from the Runcorn side, 1879. Close study will show you that the towers on the Runcorn side are different from those on the Widnes side. On the Runcorn side the towers are much grander and are castellated, in memory of the fort that was built on this side of the river by Princess Ethelfleda. In fact the bridge received the grand title of the Ethelfleda Bridge on its opening day, 21 May 1868.

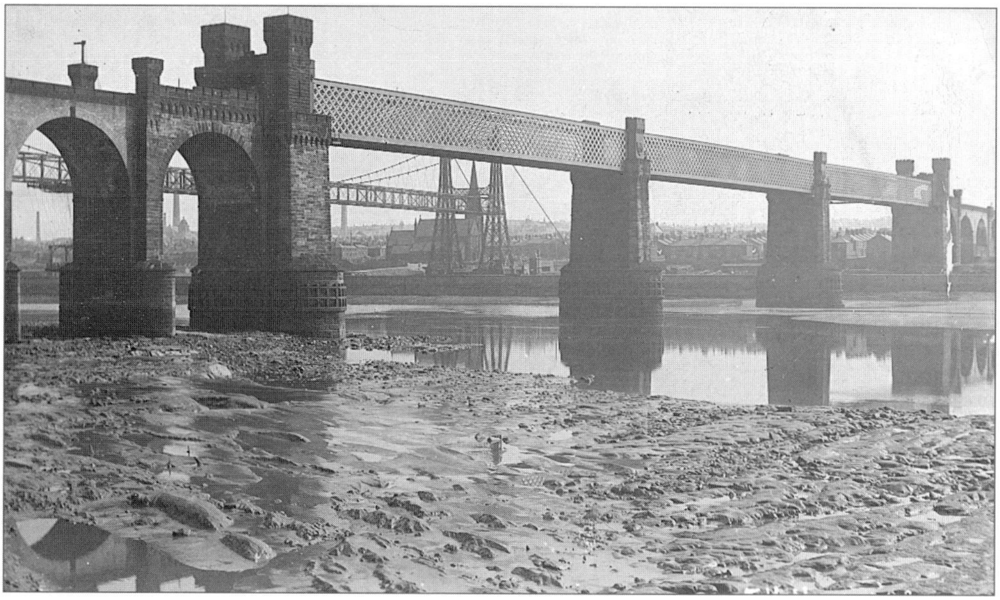

The completed railway bridge and beyond it the newly constructed Transporter Bridge, 1908.

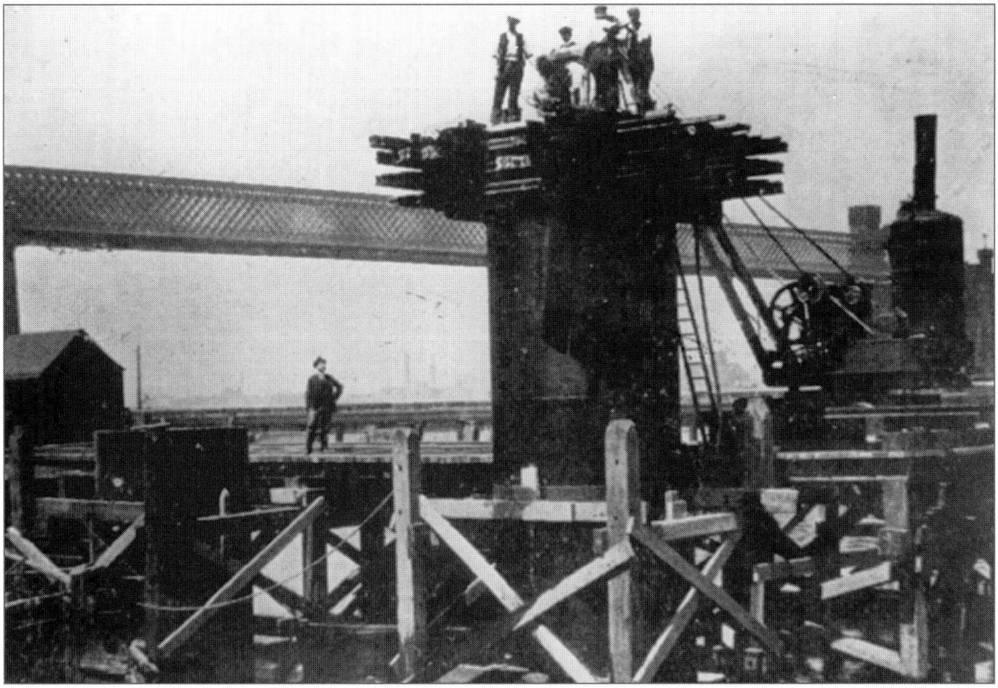

On 10 July 1900 Parliament gave its approval for the construction of a transporter bridge across the River Mersey between Widnes and Runcorn. It was to be built by a private company, the Widnes & Runcorn Bridge Company, which had been set up in 1899 with a share capital of £100,000. Widnes Corporation put up £25,000 and Runcorn £10,000; the rest consisted of private shareholdings including those of the directors, who were Sir John Brunner, Mr H. Wade Deacon, Mr H. Sutton Timmis and Major Wareing. Here our photograph shows workmen sinking one of the cylinders on which the approach was built. It was taken in 1902 by J. Stevens.

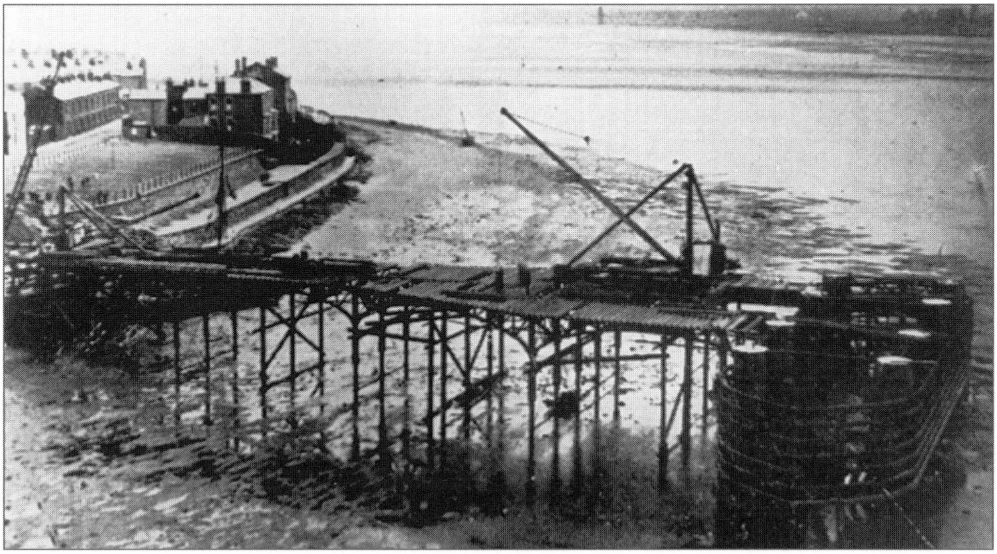

Here we see the Widnes approach being built, 1903. It was much further out into the river than on the Runcorn side. This photograph illustrates how much work had to be done in sinking the foundations into the bedrock of the river before the towers themselves could be started.

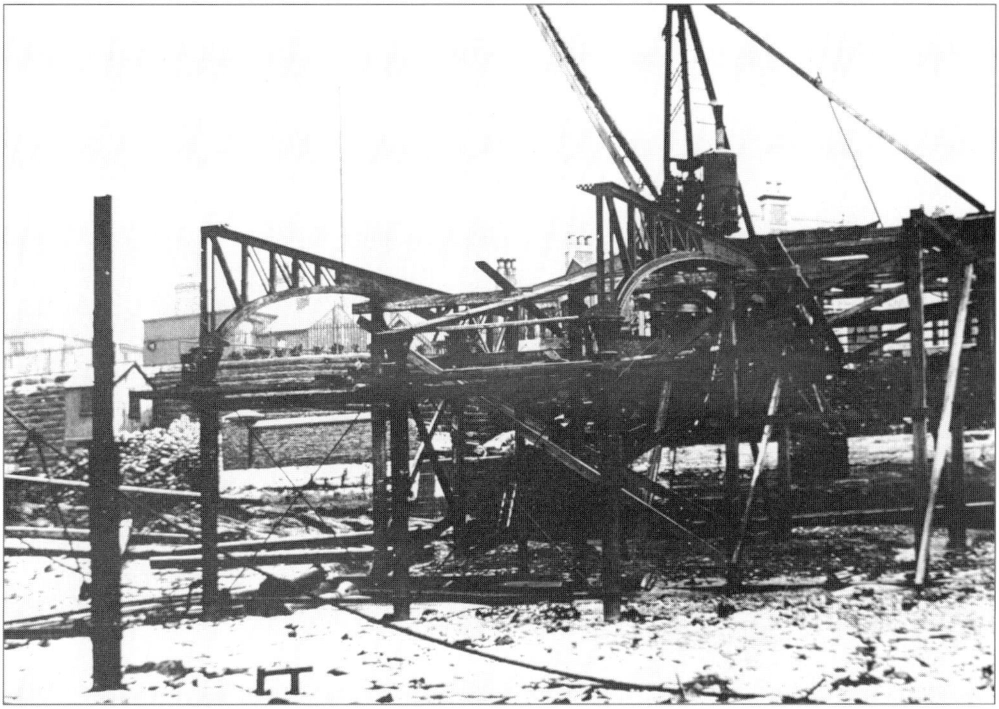

The cast-iron work being put into position on the Widnes side of the bridge. The Arrol Bridge and Roof Company of Glasgow built the bridge.

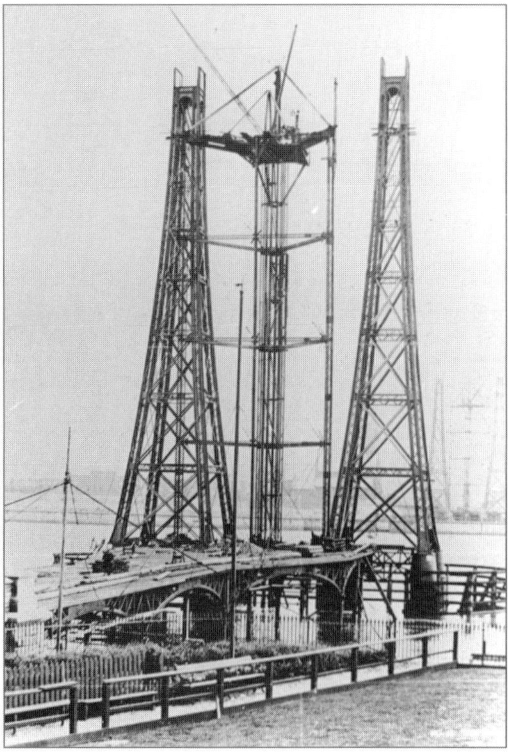

Here are the towers going up on the Widnes side. The finished towers were 190 ft high and 30 ft wide at the base, slimming down to 6 ft 9 in at the top.

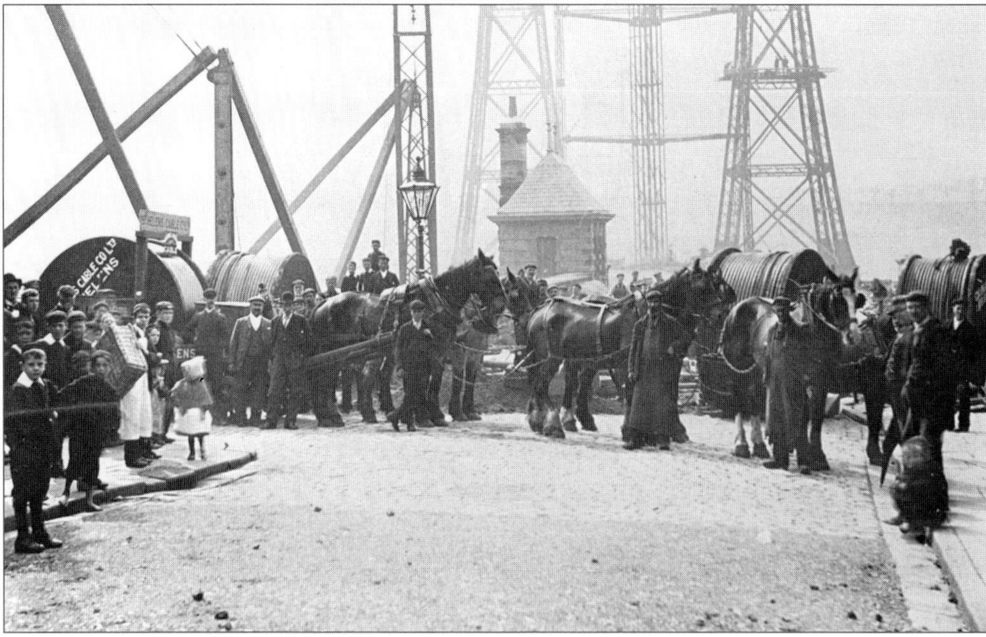

The workforce on the bridge fluctuated considerably as each stage of construction took place. Here we see the cables, which stretched across from tower to tower, being delivered, with the help of six hefty horses, by the St Helens Cable Company Limited.

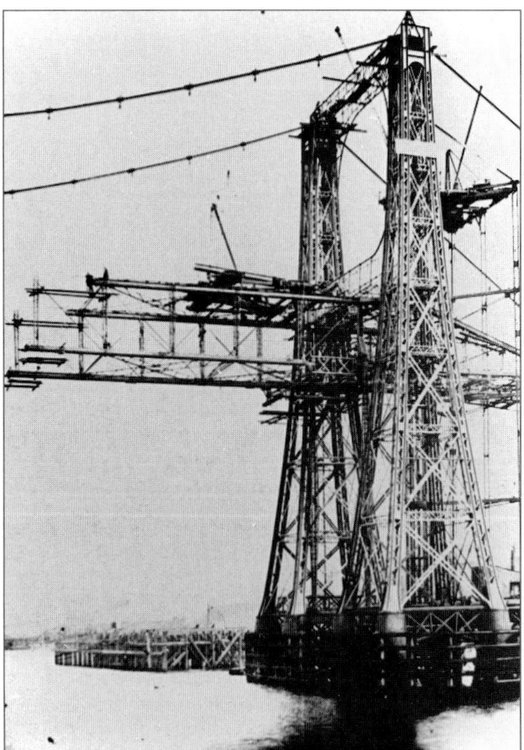

Like a giant Meccano set the piers mounted up, seen here on the Runcorn side, and then the span inched its way the 1,000 ft across the river. The two men working here on the span give an idea of its size. An Act of Parliament stated that the span had to be 77 ft above high water.

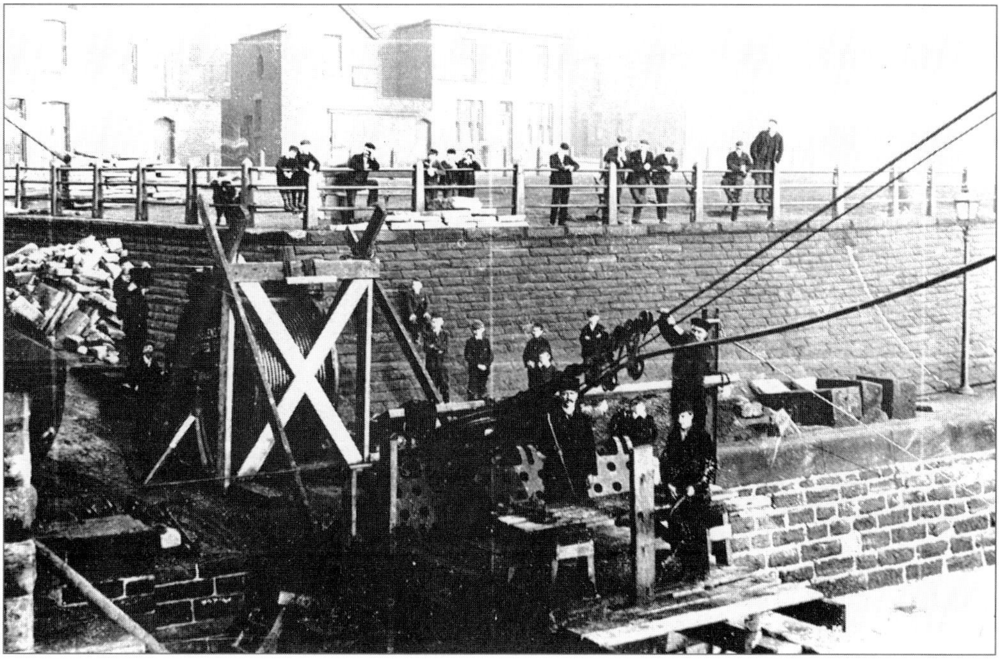

This picture shows the men feeding the cables across the river, and the large bolts which held those cables taut can be seen. It took a lot of manpower and physical hard work to stretch the first two cables across the river.

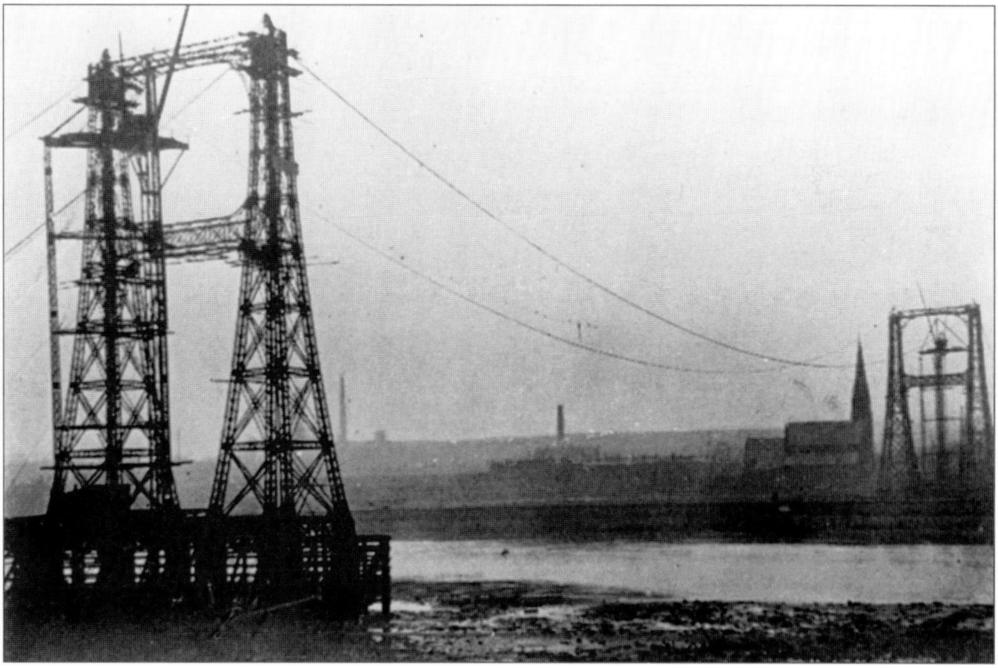

Here the cables are in place, 1904. Each cable was made up of 19 steel ropes bound together, each rope contained 127 wires, so each cable contained 2,413 wires, and was a foot in diameter; they weighed 250 tons each. The metal work for the towers and approaches of the bridge was cast in Widnes by the Widnes Foundry Company.

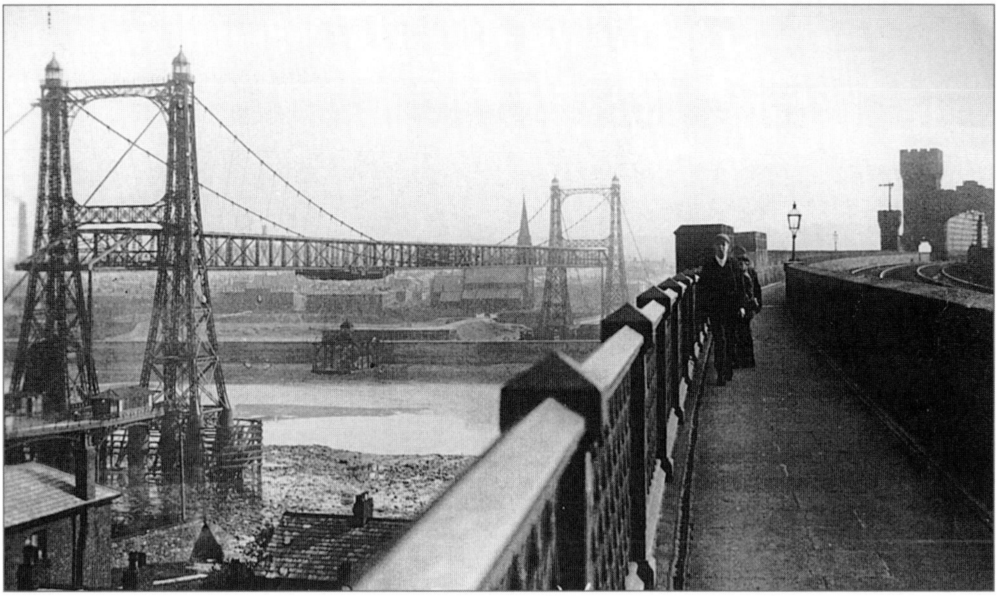

This postcard shows the completed Transporter Bridge from the footpath of the railway bridge, *c.* 1910. Many pictures refer to the railway bridge as the Runcorn Bridge and sometimes the Runcorn/Widnes Bridge. Widnesians know the truth – it is the Widnes/Runcorn Bridge (Ethelfleda). Pictures of this footpath are rare; it was put on to the railway bridge to take the place of the ferry. The London North-Western Railway bought out the rights of the Widnes/Runcorn ferry in 1865 and ran the ferry until the footpath was completed, and the penny that was charged for the ferry became the charge for walking across the bridge.

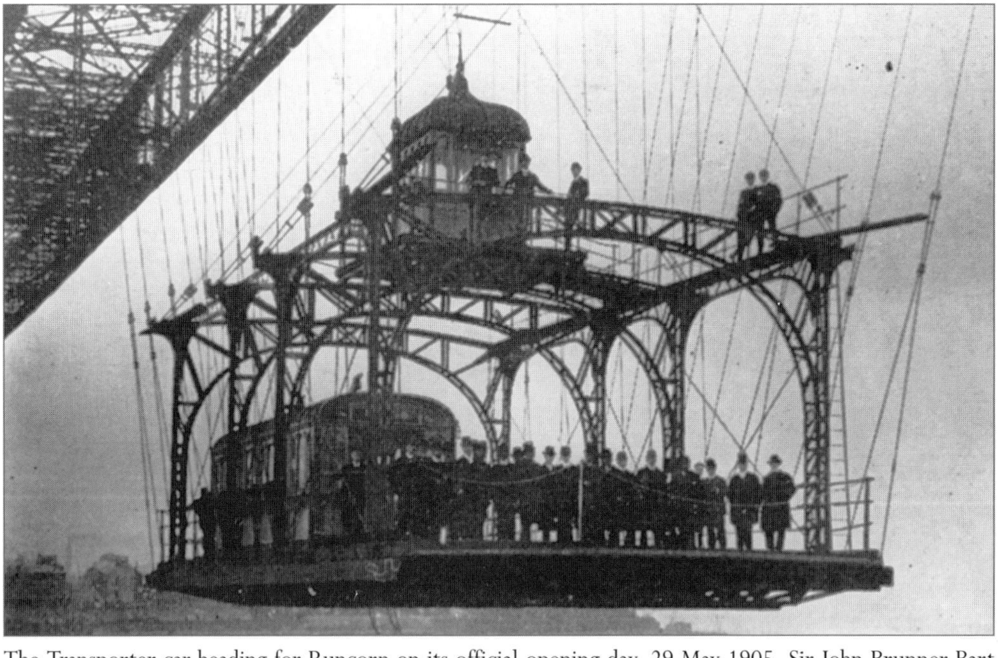

The Transporter car heading for Runcorn on its official opening day, 29 May 1905. Sir John Brunner Bart MP, Chairman of the Transporter Bridge Company, had just officiated at the opening and here we can see the dignitaries enjoying the first official trip across the river. Alderman S. Quinn, the Mayor of Widnes, and Mr Samuel Taylor, Chairman of Runcorn UDC, also made speeches at the opening ceremony.

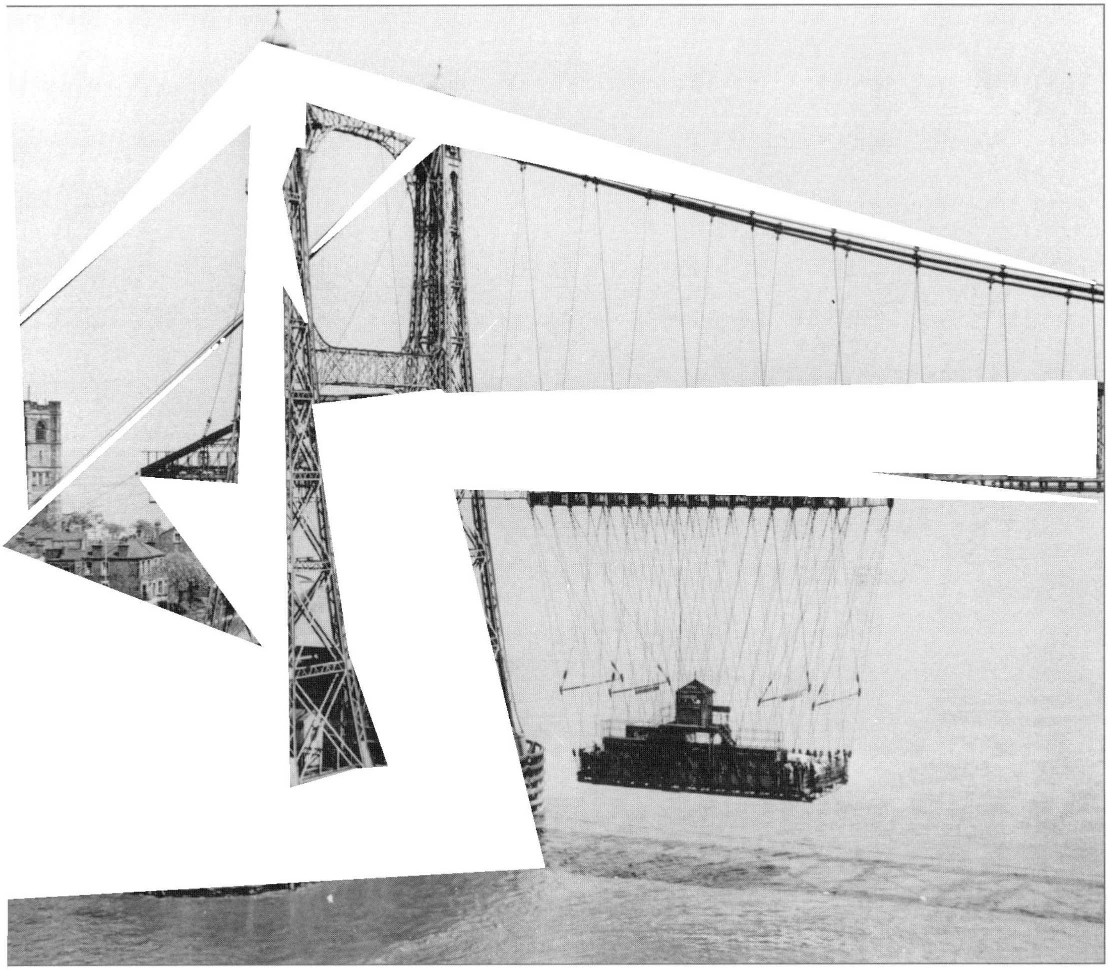

The Widnes end of the Transporter Bridge in the late 1950s. We see here a full Transporter car just about to pull in to the Widnes side. It took, on average, just over two minutes to cross the 1,000 ft span, except when ships were passing along the Ship Canal – then the Transporter car had to stop over the canal wall to let the ships pass in front of it. Sometimes passengers could be stuck there for a good ten minutes while a couple of ships went by. The Transporter cost approximately £135,000 to build, and was one of only four in Britain. In its day it was the largest of its kind in the whole world. I know it has been said before but it is a pity that they could not have left it in position. In the end it cost over £1,000 more to demolish it than to build it.

In 1911 the Widnes & Runcorn Bridge Company transferred the bridge to Widnes Corporation who ran the bridge (and paid the wages) until its closure. The Corporation upgraded the power system of the crossing and it was again Sir John Brunner who re-opened the bridge on 21 May 1913.

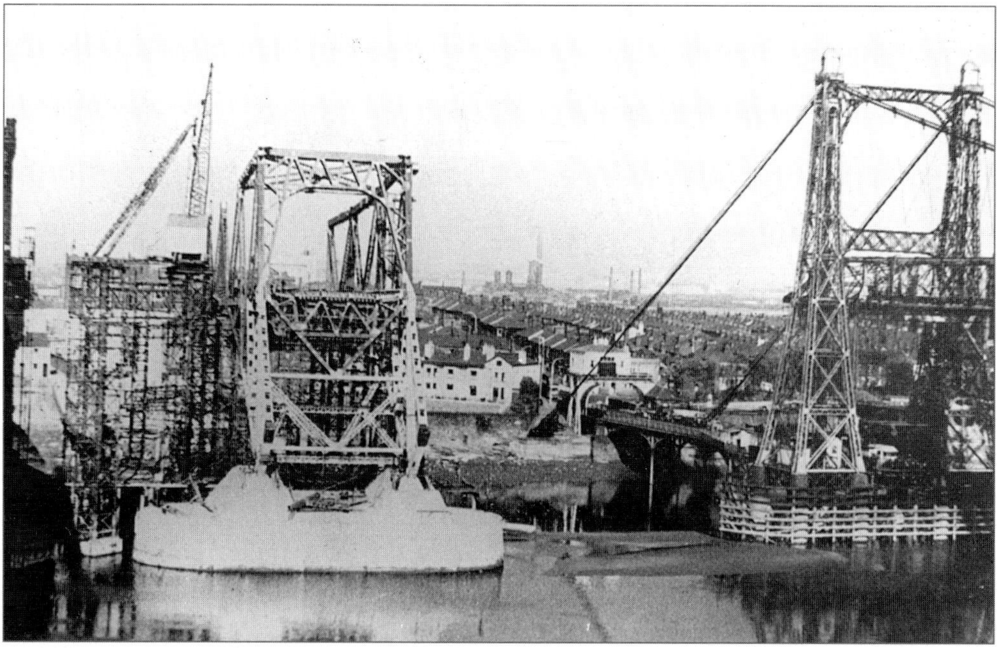

Construction work on the new high-level road bridge that was to take the place of the Transporter is seen here, *c.* 1958. As early as 1947 it was known that the Transporter Bridge could not cope with the increase in road traffic, and various plans were put forward from this date. In the early 1950s it looked as though a suspension bridge would be built at this point, but tests revealed too many difficulties with such a plan, and it was decided to go for a single-span steel arched bridge (photograph Keith Helsby).

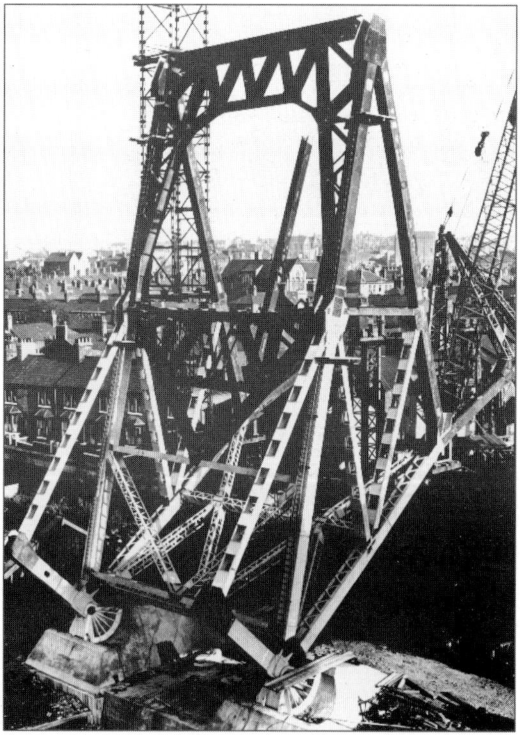

This striking photograph shows construction work inching forward on the road bridge from the Runcorn end, 1958. It took a total of five years to complete the bridge, and many streets and houses on both sides of the river had to be cleared away to make room for the approach roads (photograph Robert Martindale).

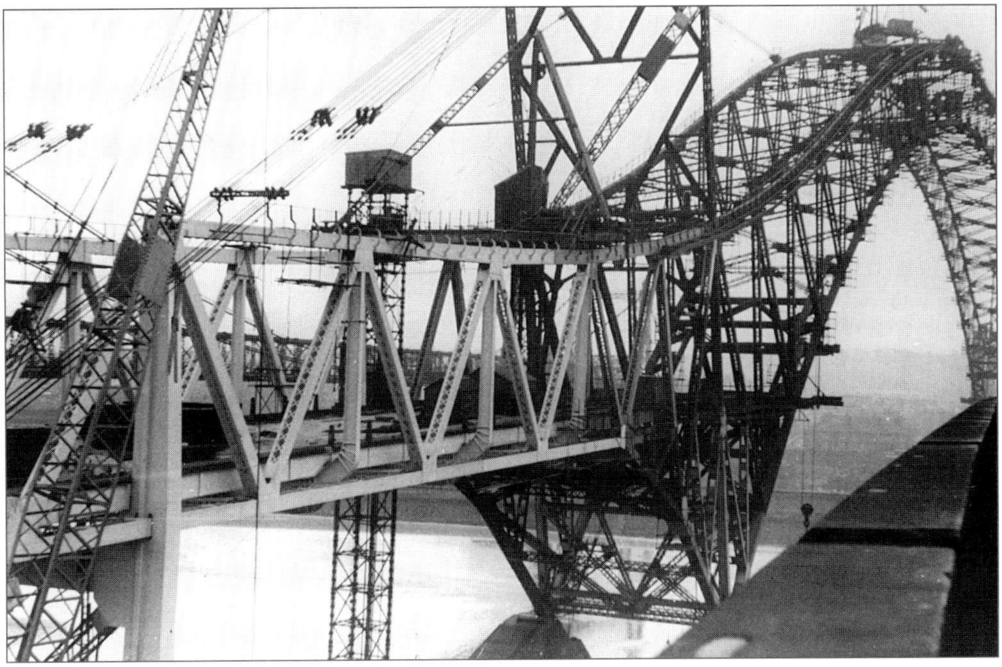

The partially constructed road bridge is seen from the footpath of the railway bridge. The span was completed long before the roadway below it was put in place, and there were many Widnesians who thought they would have to cross the hard way – over the top. When my cousin Norma saw it she said 'I'll never get over that on my bike' (photograph Keith Helsby).

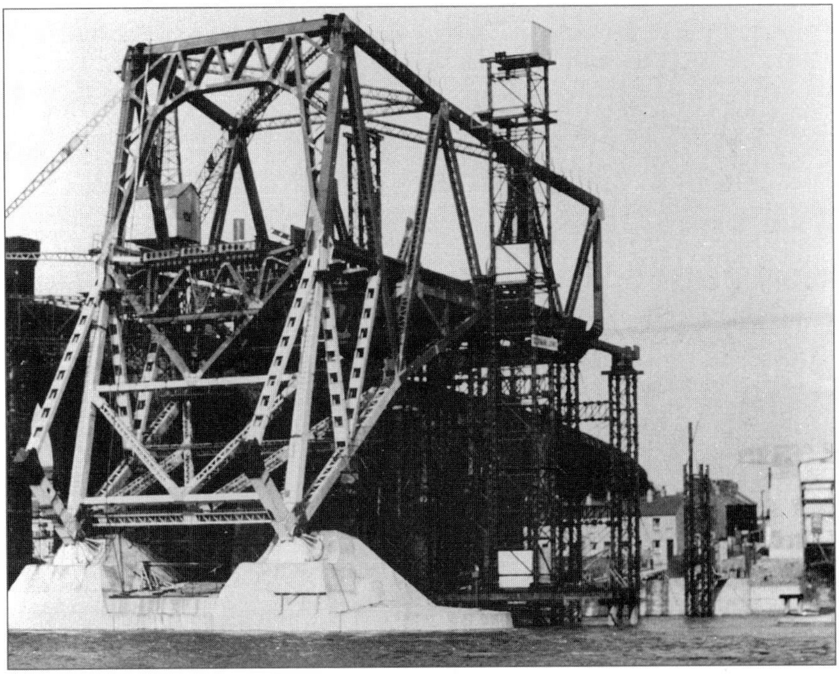

The work to construct the road bridge really did make life hard down in West Bank. Houses that had enjoyed sunshine and fresh air were now overshadowed by this dark giant. Here we see the concrete stanchions to carry the approach road being erected at West Bank (photograph Robert Martindale).

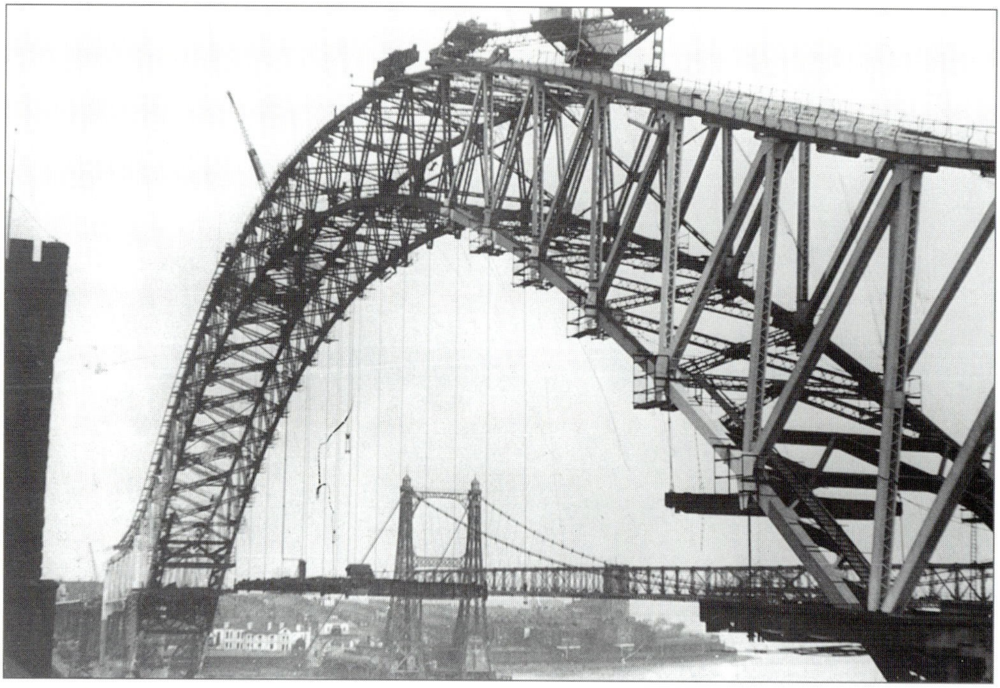

The road bridge, and the roadway is starting to go into place, 1955. The span of the bridge is 1,082 ft and the top of the arch is 306 ft above high-water level. The bridge was built by the same company that built the Sydney Harbour Bridge in Australia, Messrs Mott, Hay & Anderson (photograph Keith Helsby).

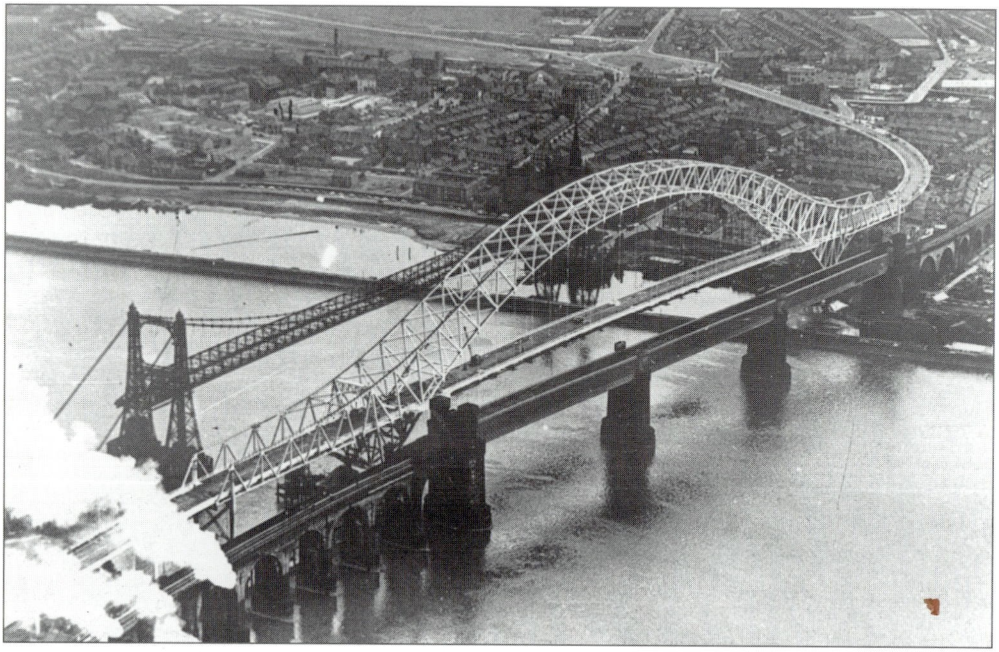

An aerial view showing all three bridges in place, 1961. The Transporter did not stay up long after its closure on Saturday 22 July 1961, the day after Her Royal Highness Princess Alexandra had officially opened the road bridge.

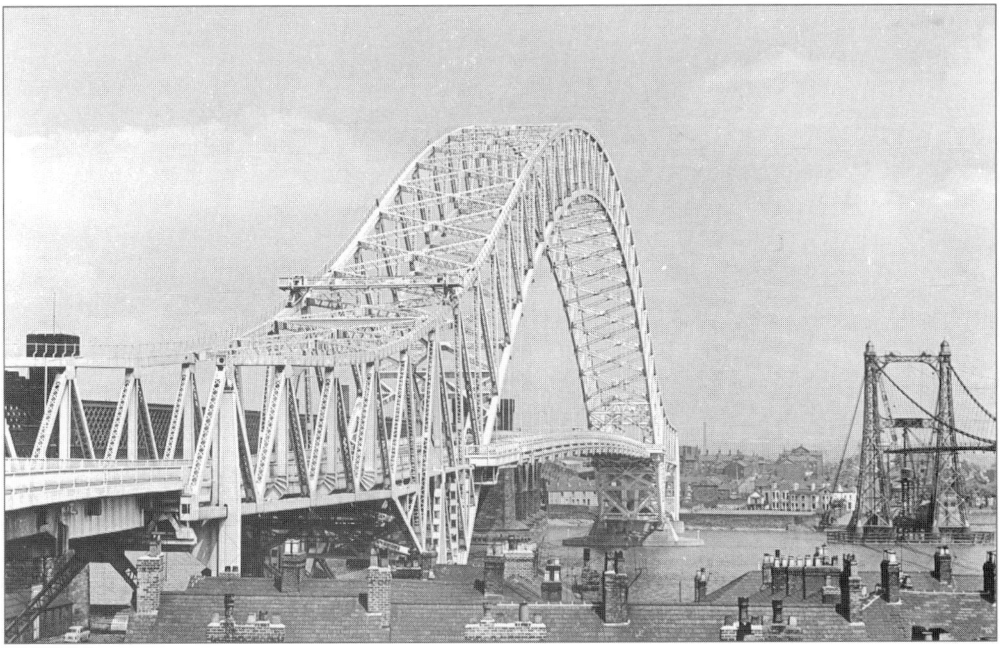

The completed road bridge seen just before its official opening. Including the approach roads, the bridge is 1,628 ft in length, and the approach footpaths run at bedroom-window level for quite some distance on either side, giving people some early morning frights (photograph Keith Helsby).

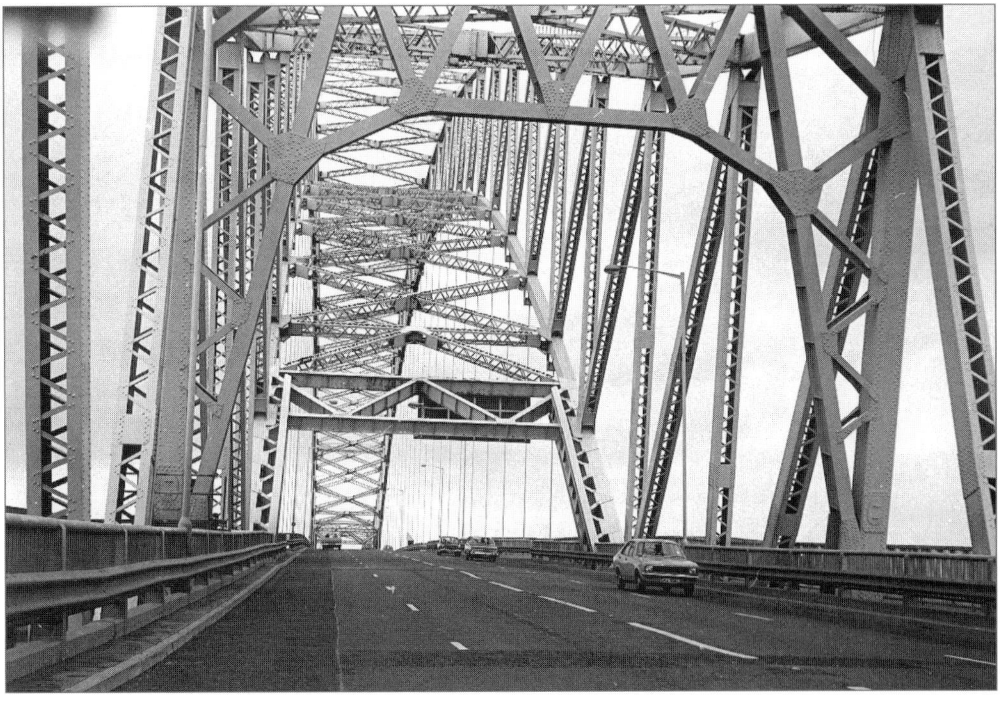

This view was taken on the road itself, looking over towards Widnes, just after the bridge opened. Although it has been widened since, when the bridge opened it had two 6-ft footpaths on either side of the carriageway, which was 33 ft wide.

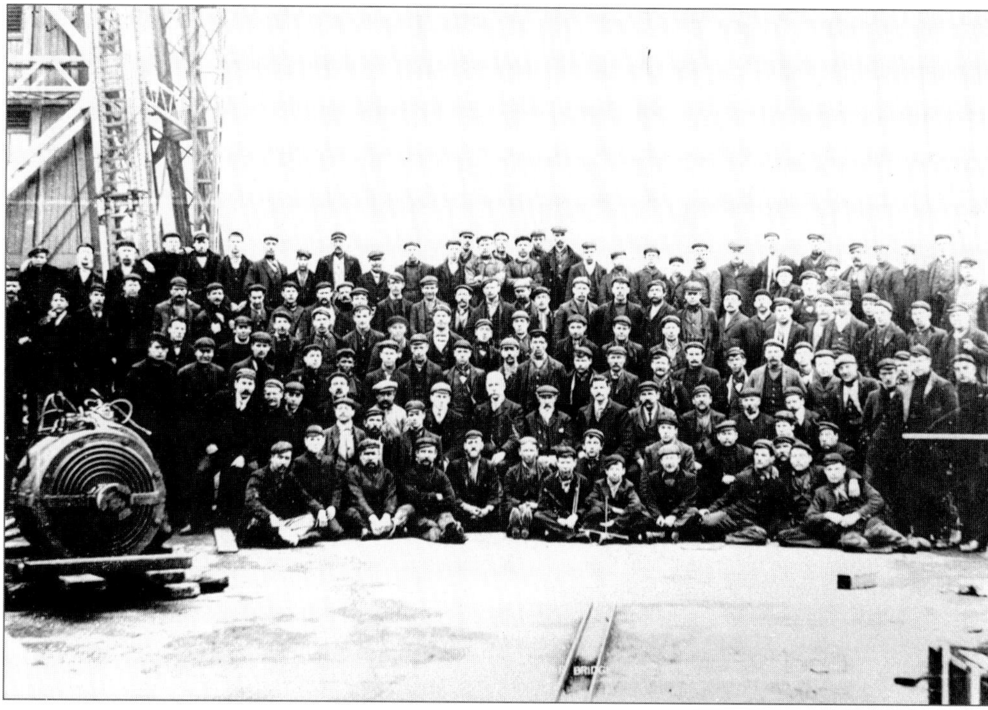

The official workforce who had worked on the construction of the Transporter Bridge on its completion, 1905. The man in the middle, without a cap, is Sir John Brunner, Chairman of the Transporter Bridge Company.

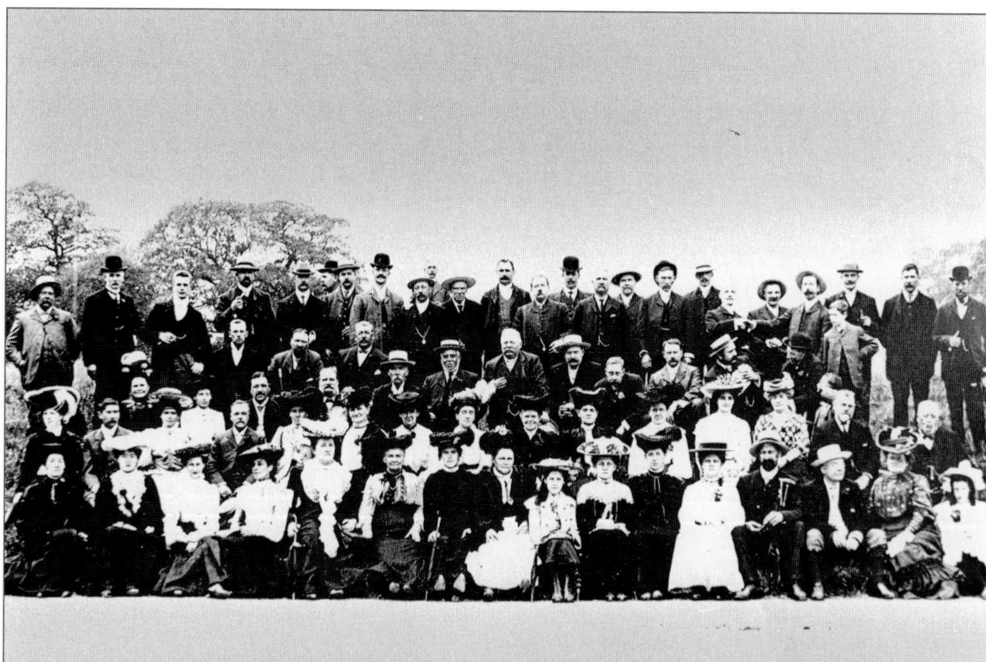

The construction staff were rewarded for their efforts with a day out in the country at Frodsham. All the men and their families set off by train to spend a day deep in the countryside, and here are some of them, all dressed in their best bib and tucker.

CHAPTER SEVEN

SPORT & THE CHEMICS

For a hundred years the name Widnes has been linked with that of Rugby League. The Widnes team, the Chemics, were one of the original teams who resigned from the Union Code and formed the Northern Union in 1895. Over the years the Chemics seem to have stumbled from crisis to crisis, but they were always right at the heart of the Rugby League scene. They can trace their roots back to 1873 as the Farnworth and Appleton Football Club, and every winter the team's progress or lack of it was the main talking point after the weather!

Widnes Rugby Union came back into prominence starting as the 'Wade Deacon Old Boys', and then the 'Old Widnesians', playing from a changing room next to the Scout Hut on Wade Deacon playing fields (now St Joseph's RC School playground). It was a mate from work (Swales), Harry Jones, who persuaded me to turn out for that team, and I remember him taking me to see a farmer's field in Heath Road and proudly saying that they were going to build a club house there with a proper bar, and become a great club. He was right, and he was one of the people who made it happen. I was playing in the Old Widnesian 'B' team with Harry the day he celebrated his fiftieth birthday, and at seventeen I thought 'I hope I can match Harry.' I didn't: I played my last RU game at twenty-six on the ICI Rec. against Wallasey Police, and feeling my years hung up my boots and got married.

The setting up of the new Super League was unsatisfactory for Widnes. After the problems at Oldham, Widnes should learn some of the lessons and although they seem very down and poorly supported at the moment let's keep our fingers crossed that they can rise again, as they have done in the past, and become one of the great teams in the rugby world.

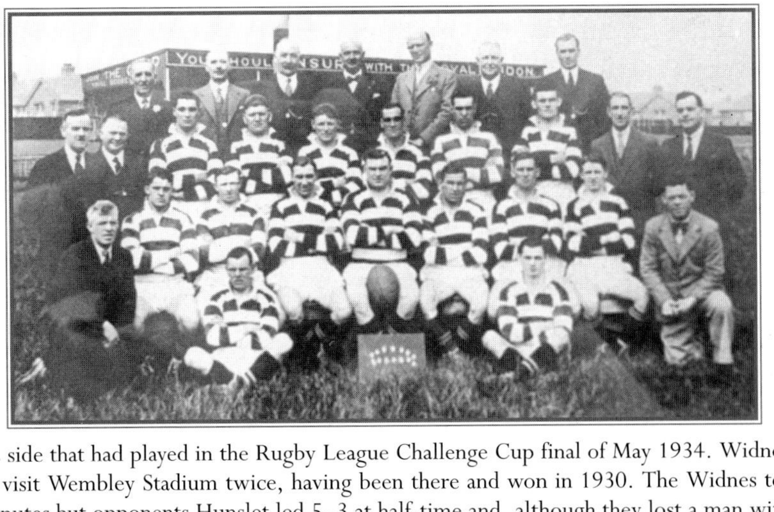

The Widnes side that had played in the Rugby League Challenge Cup final of May 1934. Widnes were the first side to visit Wembley Stadium twice, having been there and won in 1930. The Widnes team scored after five minutes but opponents Hunslet led 5–3 at half-time and, although they lost a man with a broken collar bone, went on to win 11–5. It is strange that this picture records all the players' names but none of the officials. Peter Lyons, the trainer, is sitting front left and Bob Jones, the chairman, is behind him with Tommy Naughton, the club secretary, on his right.

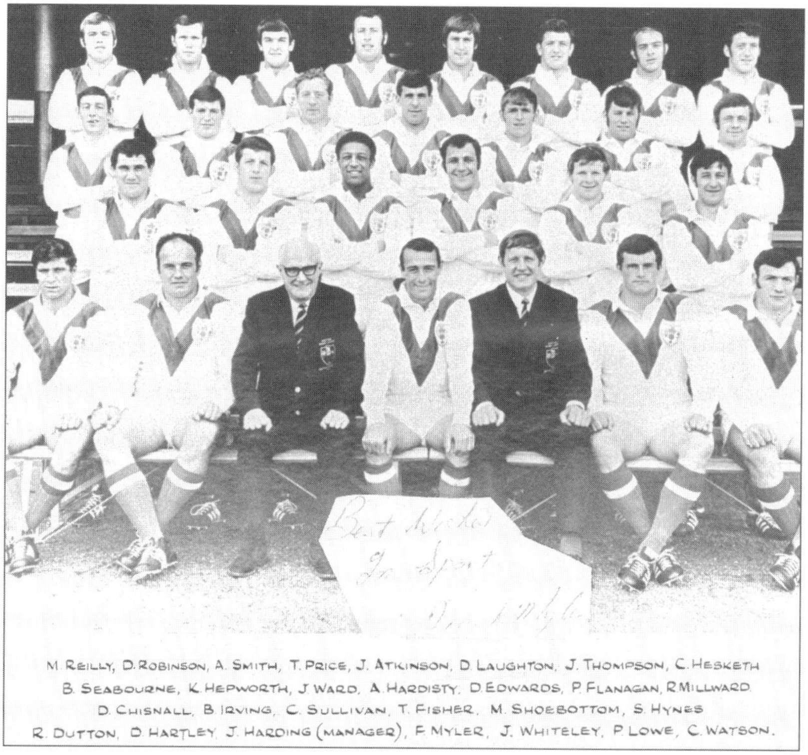

The Great Britain Rugby League touring team of 1970. Widnes is well represented in the team with Ray Dutton, Dougie Laughton and Frank Myler (captain) among them. Widnes provided its first international player in 1908 when Jack Lally turned out for England, and its first tourists in 1914 when Jack O'Garra and Albert Johnson went to Australia.

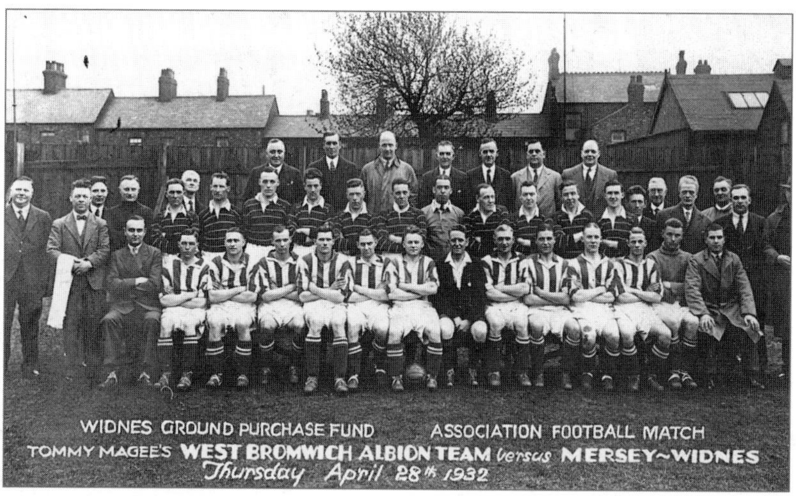

Teams line up for the official photograph to mark a soccer match between Tommy Magee's West Bromwich Albion and a Mersey/Widnes eleven. This was the only time a top-line Association Football match was played at Norton Park. It was organised to raise funds towards the Ground Purchase Fund, and raised over £200 for the cause. The Widnes team had players from Liverpool Football Club, Everton, Runcorn and even one from Bury FC. The club secretary, Tommy Naughton, who did so much to raise the money and after whom the ground is named, is on the far left of the back row.

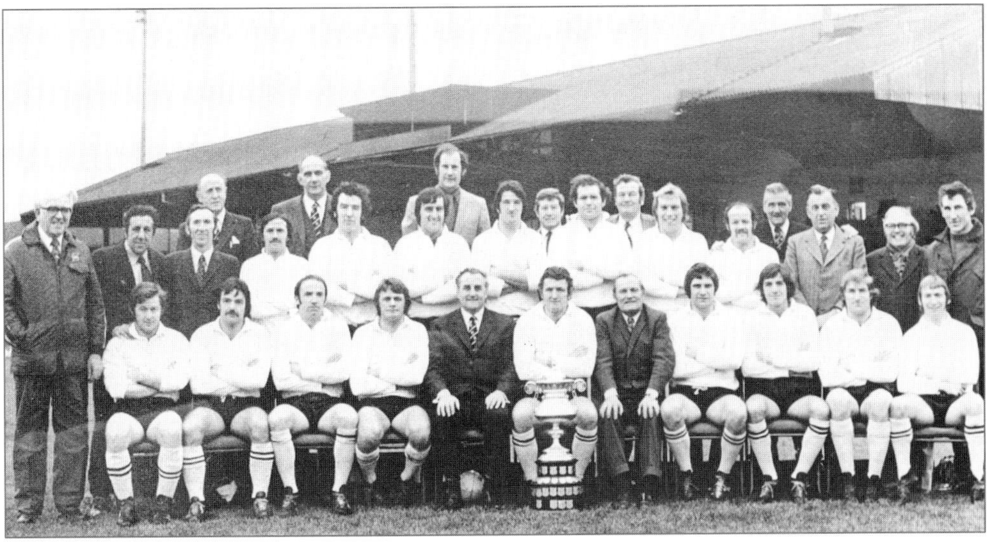

One of the great Widnes teams of the past. This side had just won the Lancashire Cup and is pictured here with it, 1974. They had just lifted the trophy by beating Salford 6–2 in the final, held at Central Park, Wigan. The 'Lancs Cup' was always decided early in the season, and with that under their belt this team went on to beat Warrington 14–7 at Wembley to take the glittering prize of the Rugby League Challenge Cup at the end of the season. They were 'Cup Kings' in the 1970s, winning the Lancashire Cup four more times in the next five years, and the Challenge Cup again in 1979. They also won the BBC Floodlit Trophy in 1979 and the John Player Trophy twice, as well as being Division One Champions in 1977–8. There are some great names on this photograph as well as the players – Vince Karalius, far right, and Frank Tobin (the man with the magic sponge) is far left with Harry Dawson, the great goal kicker, next to him. Ray Owen pops up in the back row just above the cup.

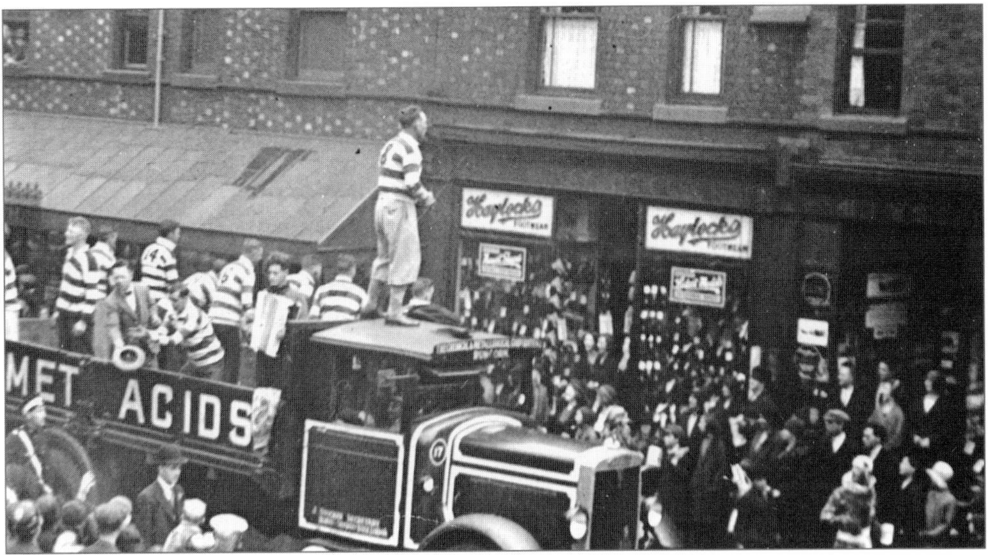

The Widnes Rugby League side on their return from Wembley touring the town on a lap of honour on the back of a lorry, 1934. Although Widnes were beaten 11–5 by Hunslet they still considered it an achievement to get to Wembley. It was their second appearance there, and the crowds turned out to cheer their returning heroes. Nat Silcock was captain and among the team seen here are the two great 'Tommys', McCue and Shannon.

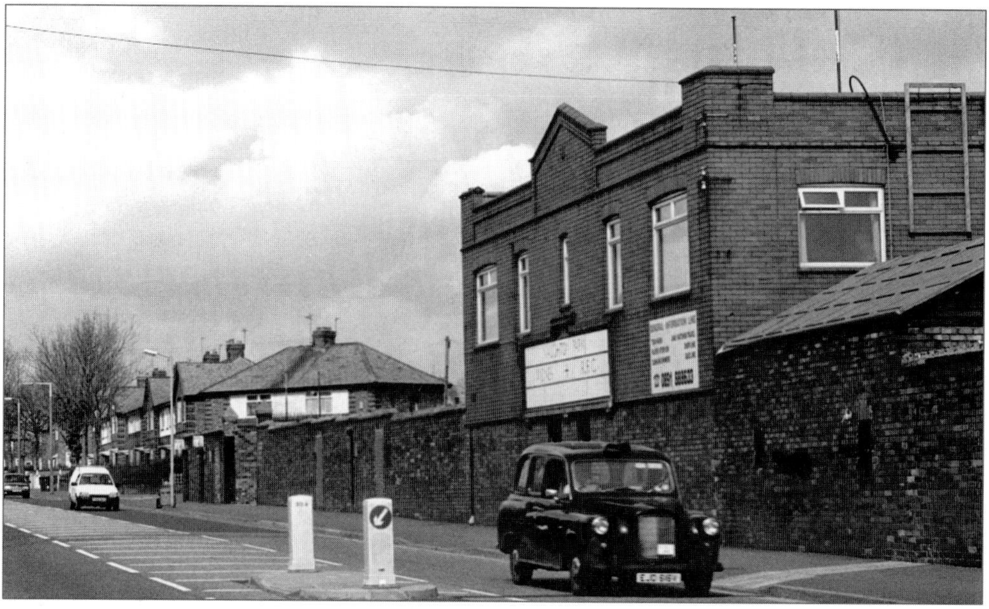

Naughton Park, the home of the Widnes Rugby League Football Club. This is how the club house, on Lowerhouse Lane, looked just a few years ago, at the start of the 1990s. The team moved here over a century ago in 1884 and at the same time adopted their famous black and white colours. Although the first mention of the Widnes Rugby Football Club was in 1878 the team was formed from the Farnworth and Appleton Cricket and Football Club which had been playing rugby since 1873. So it was only right that Widnes RL celebrated its centenary in 1973. The team is now known as the Widnes Vikings.

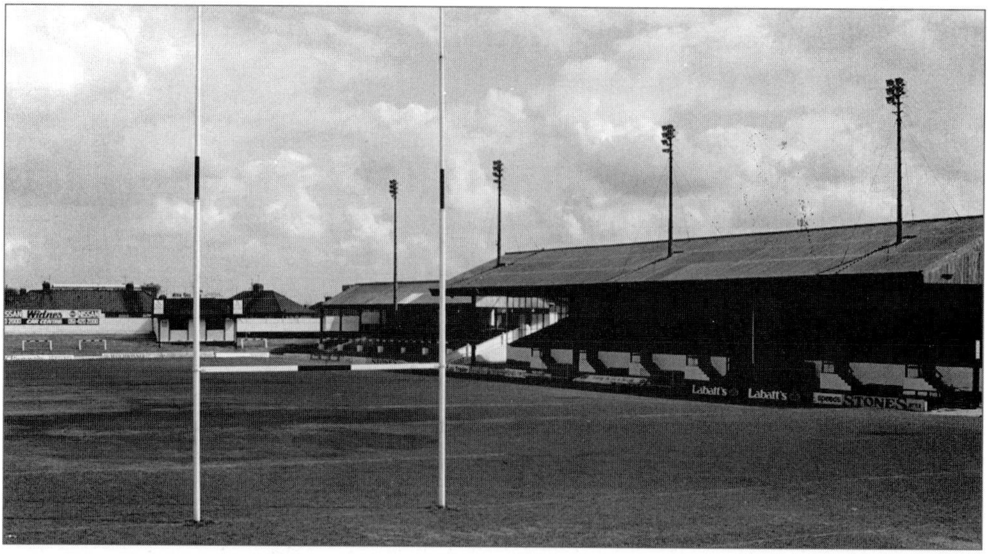

Naughton Park: a view of the ground, 1995. This photograph was taken from the terrace behind the club house and changing rooms. The ground held almost 25,000 people when St Helen's played Widnes in the winter of 1960 for a Challenge Cup match, and the gate receipts were £2,951 11*s* 9*d*. I have played here twice myself in curtain raisers when I was ten and eleven years old, once in a schoolboys' match and once in the final of the Widnes & District Boy Scout Trophy. The picture shows the ground quite compact and rather small, but to me it seemed an enormous stadium, and I can still remember the thrill of running out of the tunnel where my heroes ran. The floodlights were added in the mid-1970s.

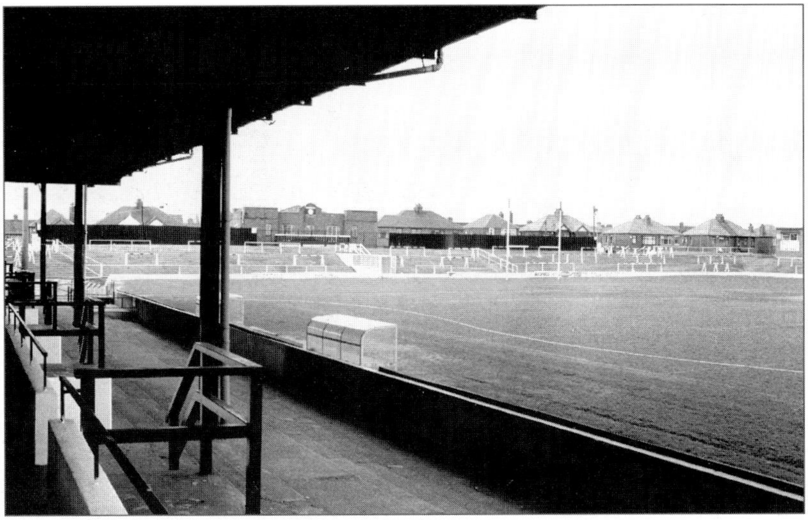

Looking from the stand over to the club house and Lowerhouse Lane, 1995. The ground, which appeared on a map in 1895, built up very slowly, and the stands and terraces were constructed as the years went by. In 1930 the Lowerhouse Lane housing estate was planned, and £3,250 was the agreed purchase price. Mr Tom Naughton, the secretary, led the fund-raising efforts. Thanks to Tommy the money was finally raised, and when he was killed in a road accident in 1932 it was agreed to name the ground in his memory. Next time you pass Lowerhouse Lane, remember it's Tommy Naughton Park. September 1932 saw the Mayor of Widnes declaring the ground officially reopened, and Widnes played and beat Salford in a 'friendly' with gate receipts of £273, a record at the time. It reopened as Halton Stadium in February 1998.

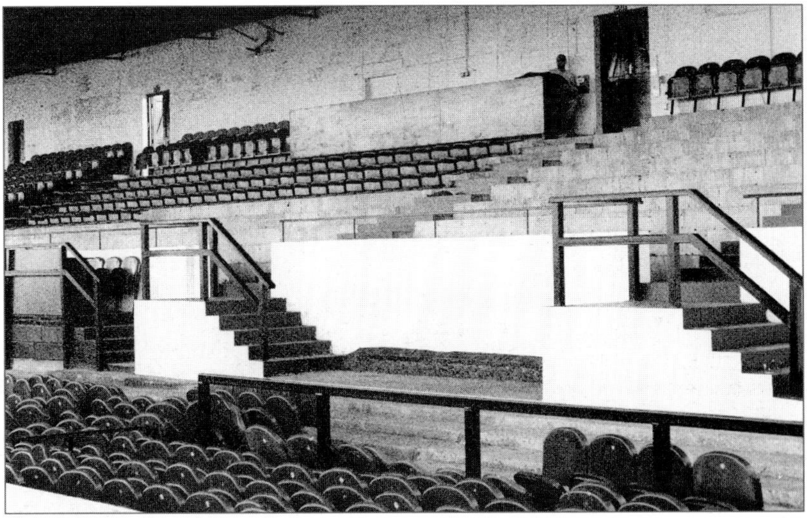

The main stand at Naughton Park, 1995. The seats are being taken away in preparation for its major refit and ground update, which was very costly for the club. Widnes Rugby League have always been strapped for cash; in the 1930s they often had only a few pounds in their bank balance. I was one of the youngsters who sold the 'penny on the ball' tickets and would stand, every home match, just inside the gates selling tickets at 2*d* each, or seven for a shilling. If you were lucky you were chosen to carry the board round at half-time with the winning number on it, and this earned you the princely sum of half-a-crown – which meant untold delights that Saturday night. It was easy work when the weather was fine, but in blustery and windy conditions, which it mostly was, the sight of a twelve-year-old staggering round with a blackboard used to raise many wry comments from the specatators.

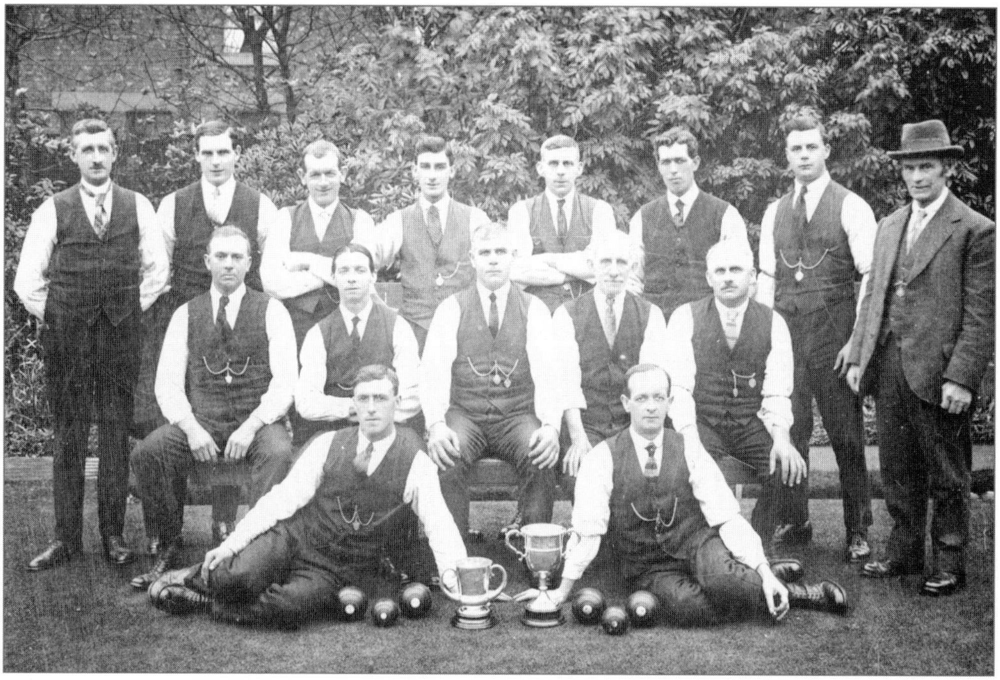

The Ball O' Ditton Crown Bowling Team pictured with their trophies, 1924. The Ball was very proud of its bowling team and had one of the best in the district. They used to say that Ditton was the cleanest of the villages because they had the Broomes to sweep it clean and the Barrows to cart it away, and there are quite a few Broomes and Barrows on our picture including two of my uncles – George and Frank Barrow.

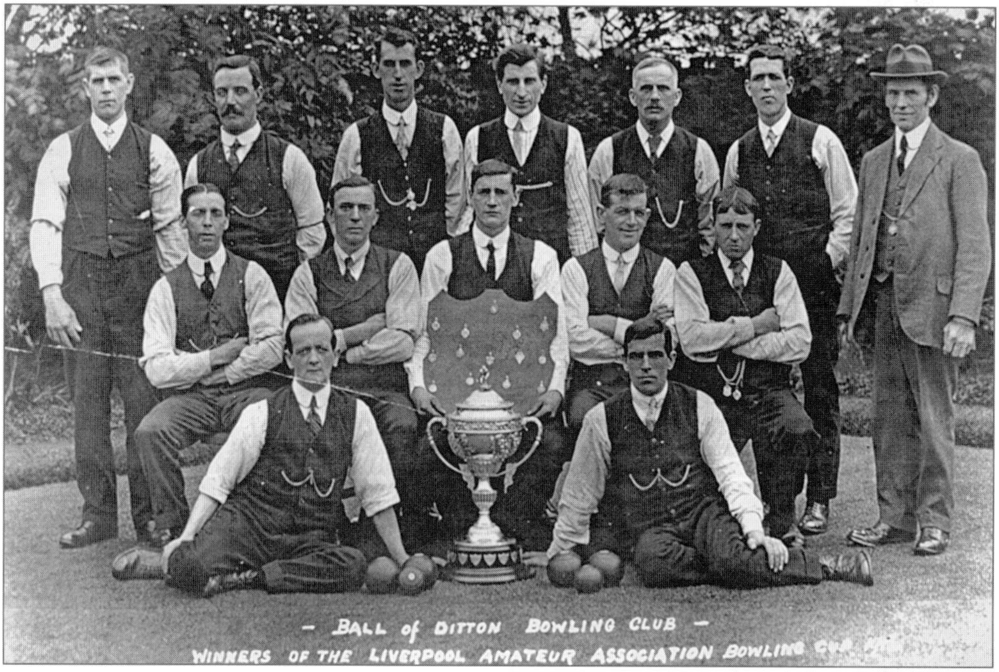

Another winning year for the Ball O' Ditton team as they line up proudly with the Liverpool Amateur Association Bowling Cup, 1932.

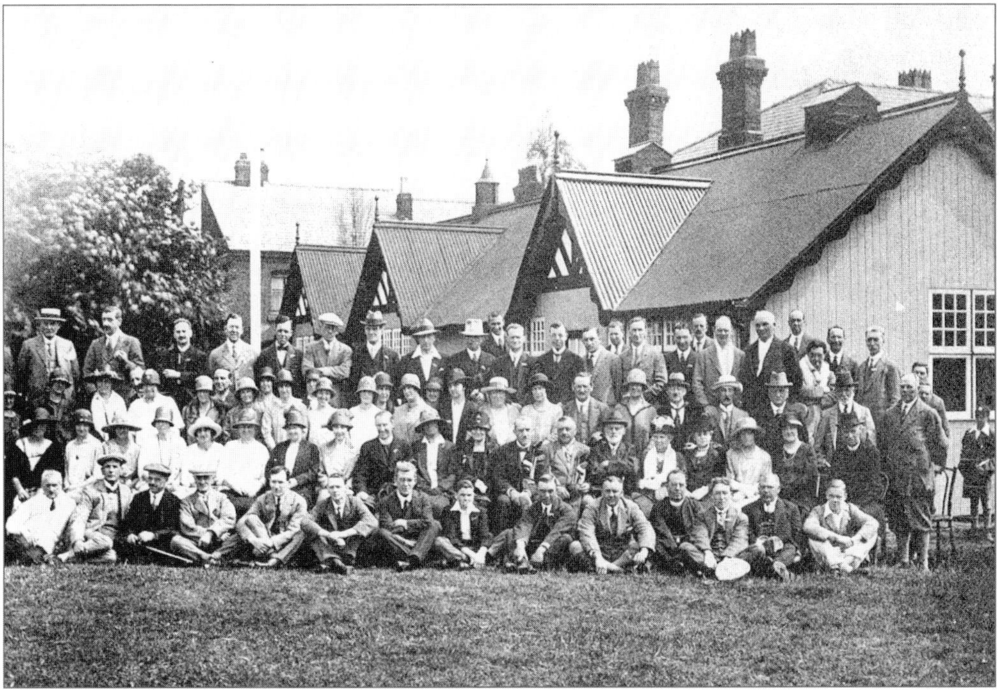

The Hough Green Golf Club, with many ladies prominent in this picture from the 1920s. The vicar of St Michael's is in the centre of the picture; the club house was on Ditchfield Road within his parish.

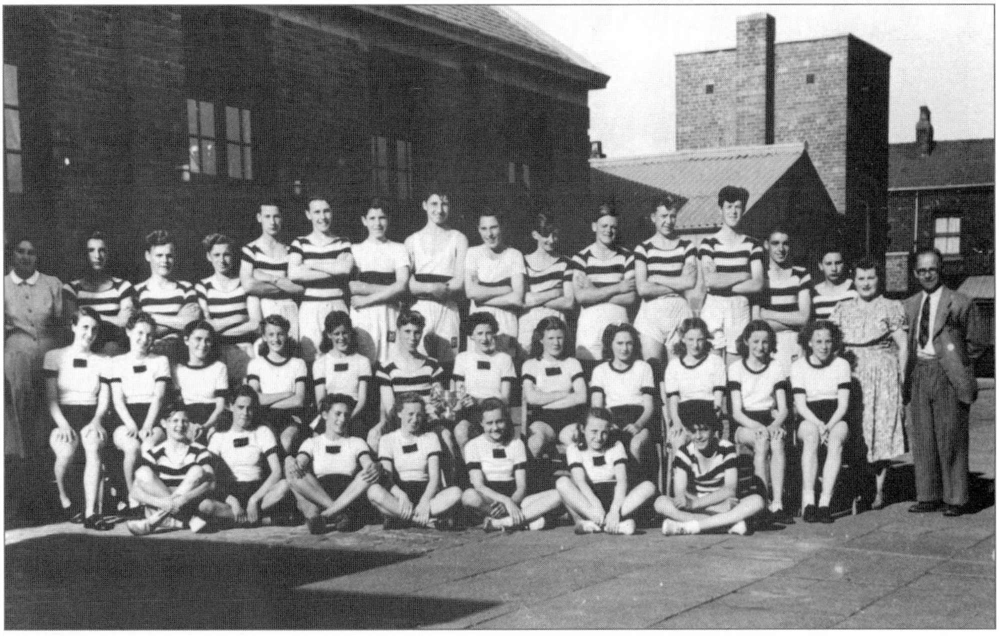

The Widnes Athletics Team that took part in the Lancashire Sports Day, mid-1950s. The team was made up of pupils from all the Widnes schools, and your name was put forward by your sports teacher. Heats were then organised. The teacher on the right of the picture has her name recorded on the back as Dolly Ridyard.

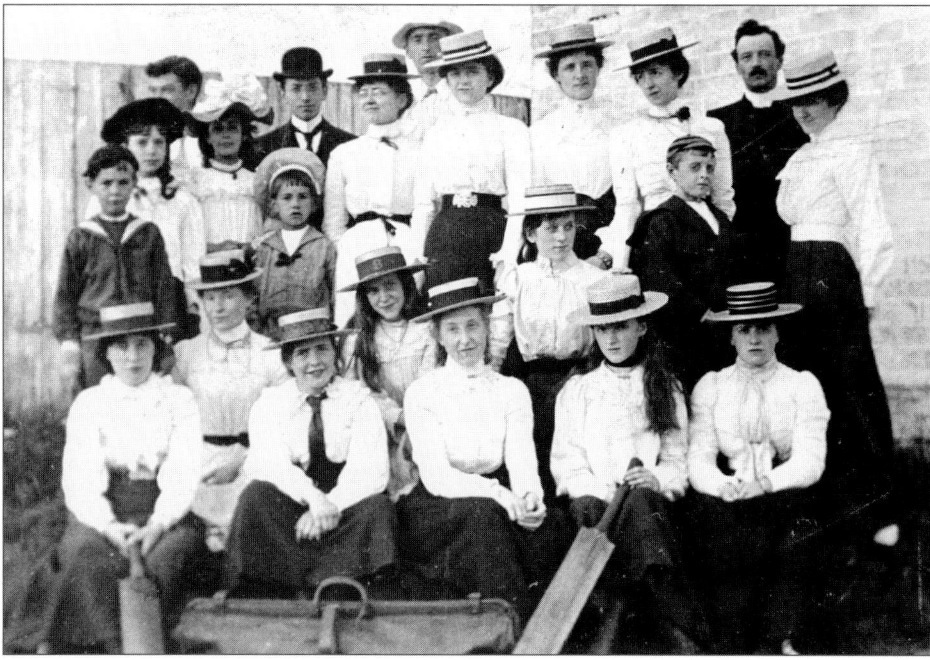

Hough Green Ladies' Cricket Team at the turn of the century: what a proud picture these athletic young ladies make.

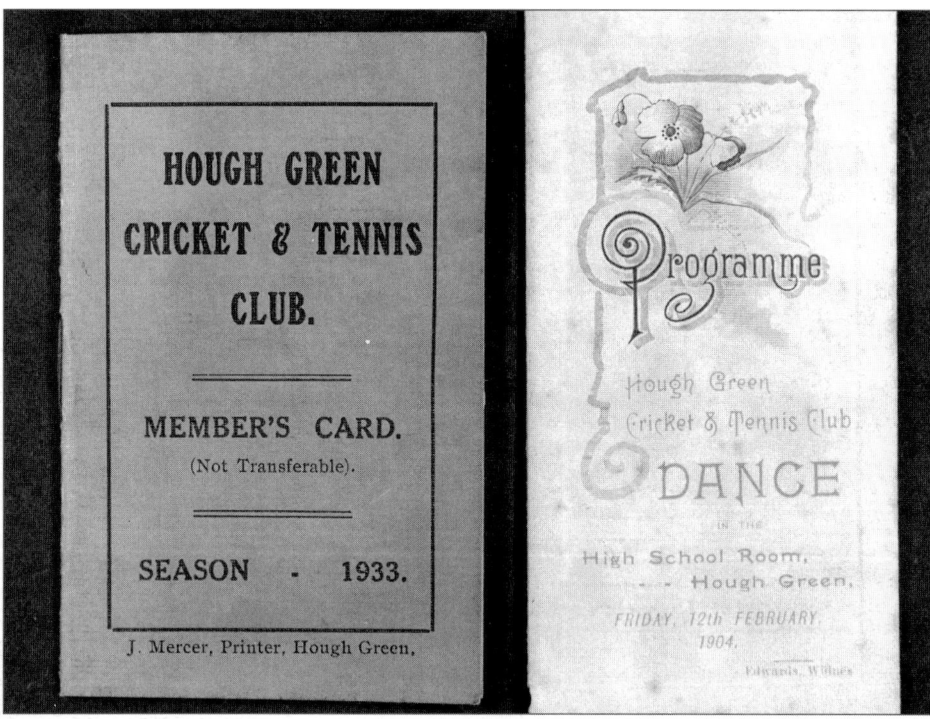

HOUGH GREEN
CRICKET & TENNIS
CLUB.

MEMBER'S CARD.
(Not Transferable).

SEASON - 1933.

J. Mercer, Printer, Hough Green.

Programme

Hough Green
Cricket & Tennis Club
DANCE
IN THE
High School Room,
Hough Green,
FRIDAY, 12th FEBRUARY
1904.

Edwards, Widnes

The Hough Green Cricket & Tennis Club was a very active body. In the summer they were busy on the greens and in the winter they held a full programme of socials and dances. Here we see a member's card from 1933 and a dance programme from Friday 12 February 1904.

Chapter Eight

Transport – Trains & Buses

Widnes saw the coming of the railways much earlier than most other Lancashire towns. The St Helens–Runcorn Gap Railway arrived just after the famous Liverpool–Manchester railway in 1830. It provided a station near the Horns Bridge which was known as Farnworth (for Bold) station. Later the main station for Widnes, which opened in 1872 on the Liverpool Central–Manchester Central line (next to the cemetery), was called Farnworth station, and this has caused much confusion in old photographs. In the heyday of rail travel Widnes was very well served and had seven stations in the 1940s.

Another unique feature of transport in Widnes was the fact that it was one of the few Lancashire towns that did not have trams. They were considered only very briefly in 1890 when a proposal for steam trams was put forward, and again in 1902, but these plans were just not taken forward. I think the steepness of many of the roads in Widnes, including Deacon Road, Peel House Lane, Liverpool Road from Stewards Brook and St Bede's Road (later Kingsway), deterred our would-be transport executives.

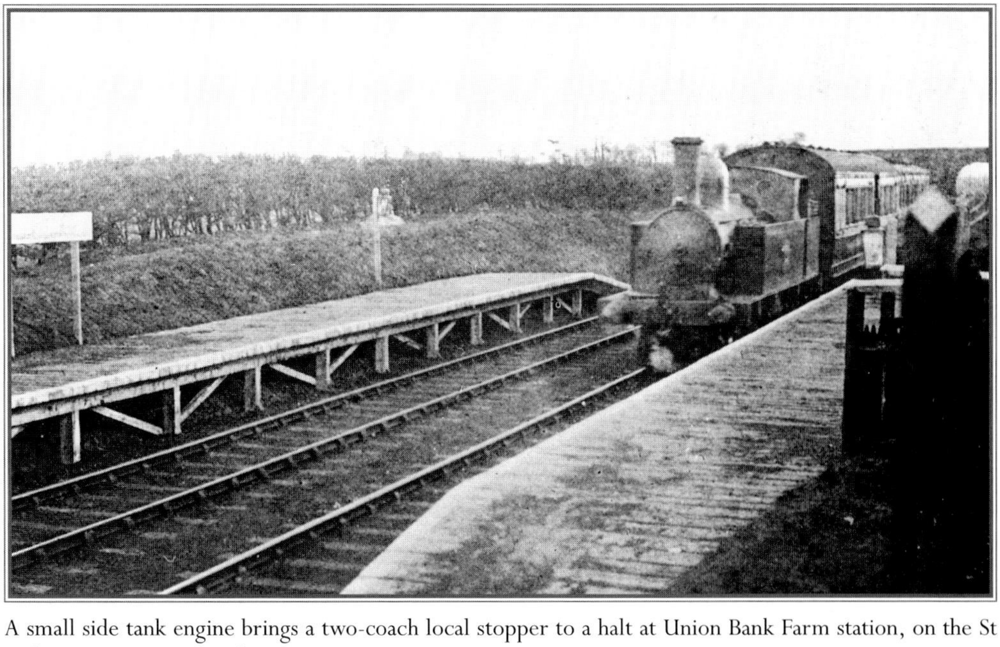

A small side tank engine brings a two-coach local stopper to a halt at Union Bank Farm station, on the St Helens–Runcorn Gap railway, *c.* 1875.

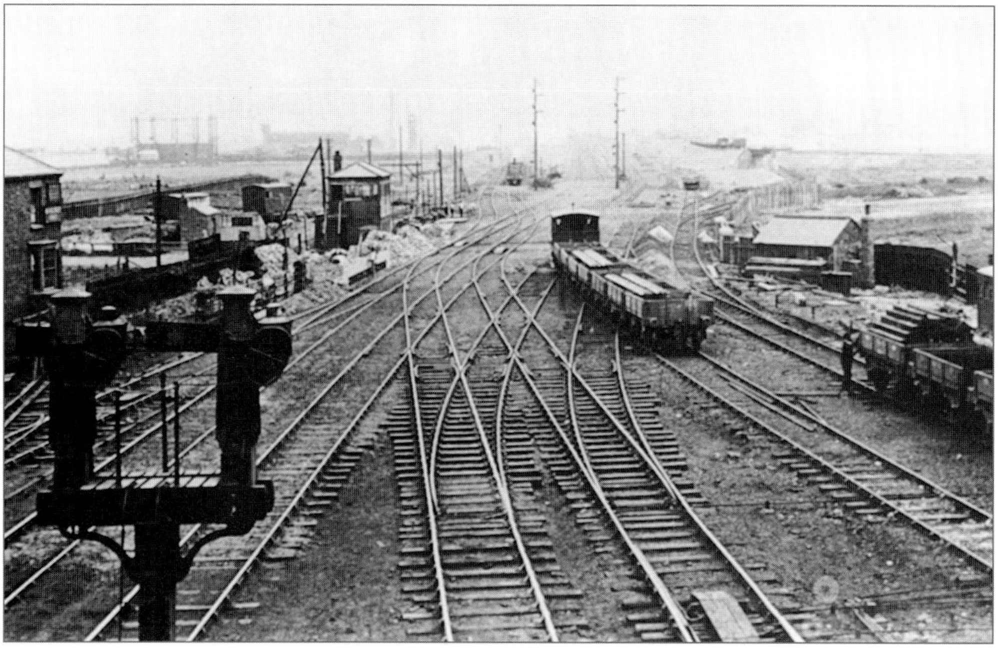

Taken from the road bridge at Ditton Junction across the road from the railway station this picture looks up the incline towards Runcorn, 1884. It shows quite clearly how trains coming down from Runcorn had to traverse two sets of points before continuing on the main line through the station. I am sure this contributed to the tragedy in September 1912 when a train crowded with holidaymakers failed to negotiate the cross-over and crashed head-on into the bridge, killing fifteen people and leaving forty-two very badly injured. The layout and track were changed after that accident.

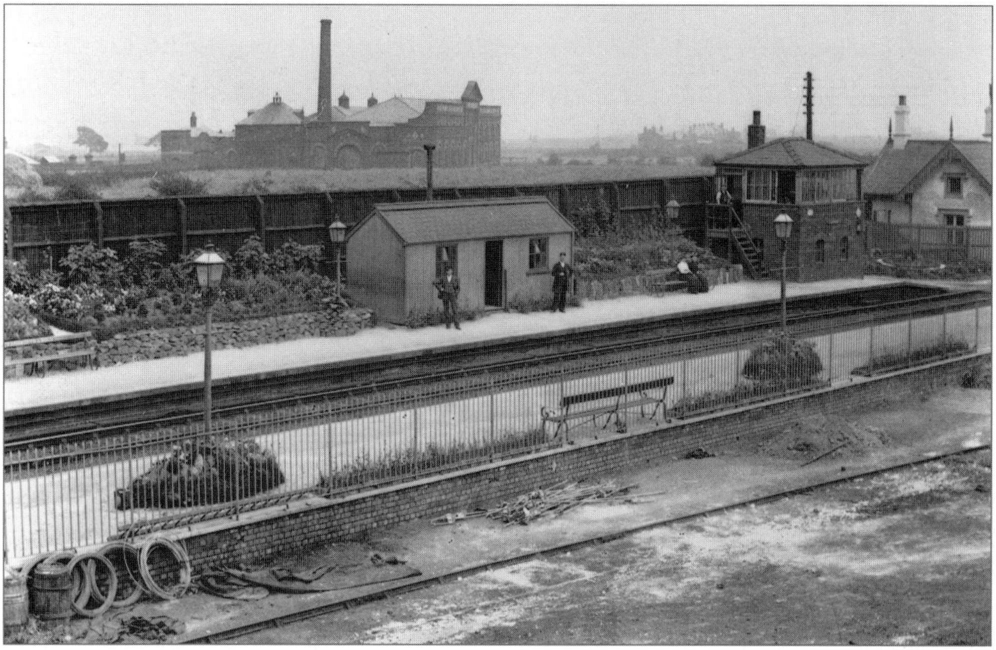

Farnworth (for Bold) station, *c.* 1890. It shows a well-tended station complete with signal-box and passengers' waiting hut. The large building behind the station is the Lancashire Manure Factory.

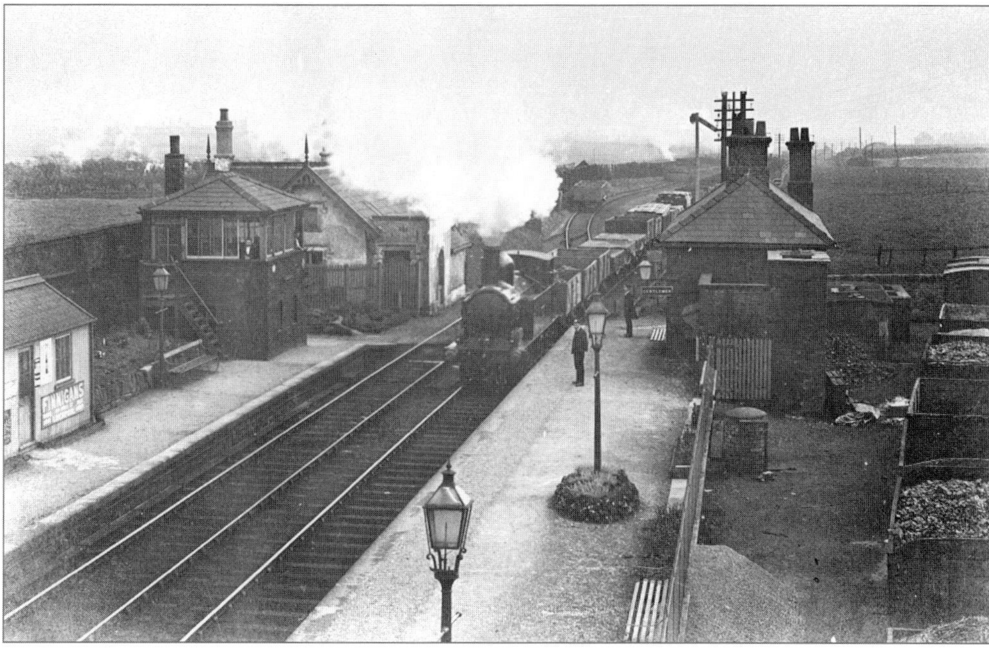

A picture of the same station, and although the caption reads Farnworth station it is Farnworth (for Bold) and our photographer is actually standing on Horns Bridge looking north. A side tank of mixed freight and coal chugs its way south towards the river, and the sidings on the right are full of waggons waiting to be

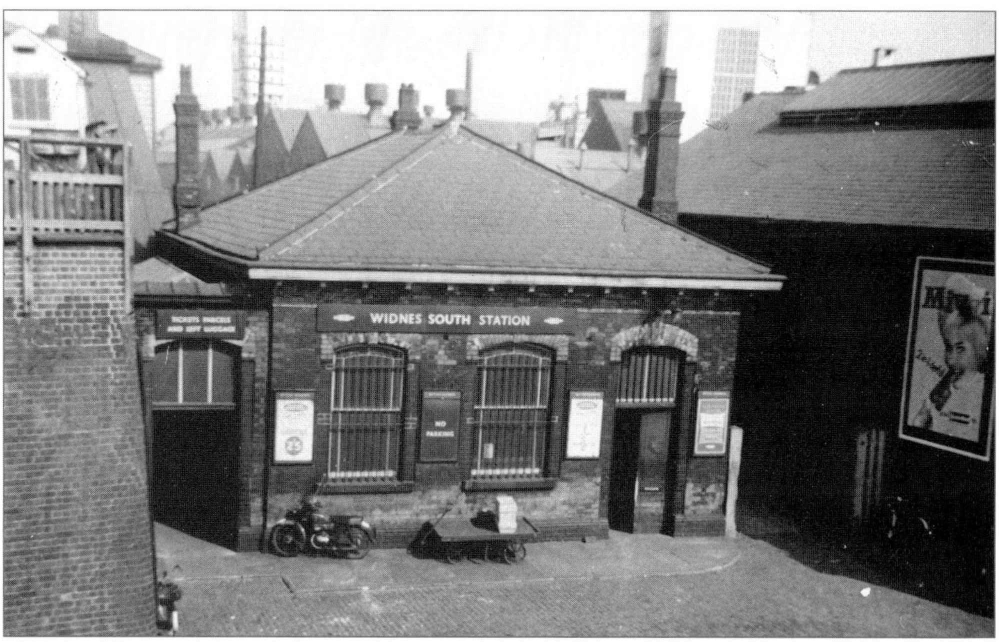

Widnes South station. This station was almost the forgotten station in Widnes, and many people did not know its official name. It was tucked away down by the original swimming baths on Waterloo Road, near Hutchinson Street, and was used almost entirely by goods traffic. The only time that I can remember boarding a train at this station was going to Wembley on a 'special' when Warrington played St Helens in about 1959.

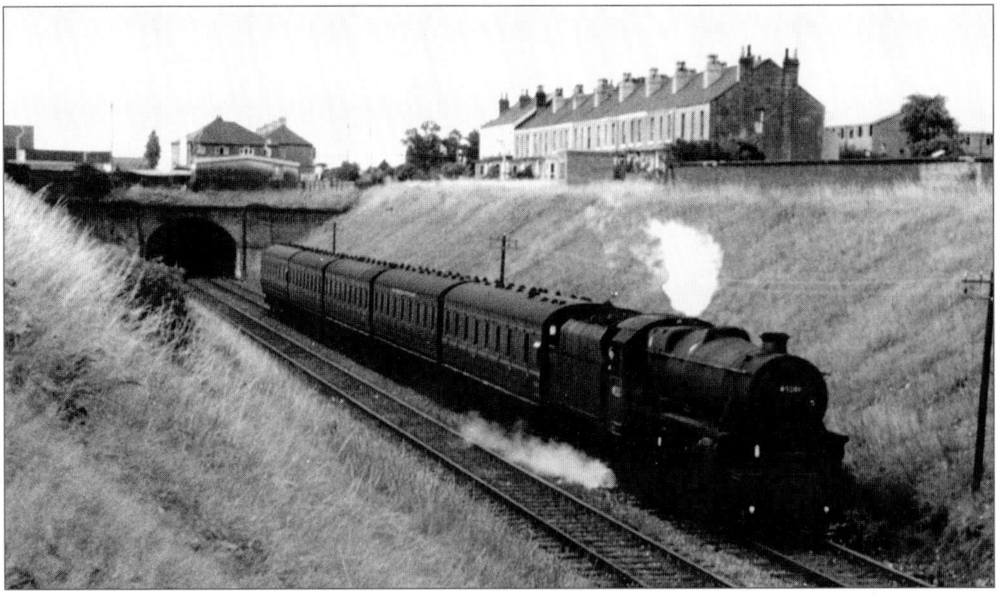

The Widnes loop from Hough Green through Widnes Central station and back on to the Warrington Central line, was opened in 1877. This is thought to be the last passenger train to use this line in 1958, and we see a 'Black 5' with five coaches having just emerged from the tunnel under Chestnut Lodge, heading for Widnes Central.

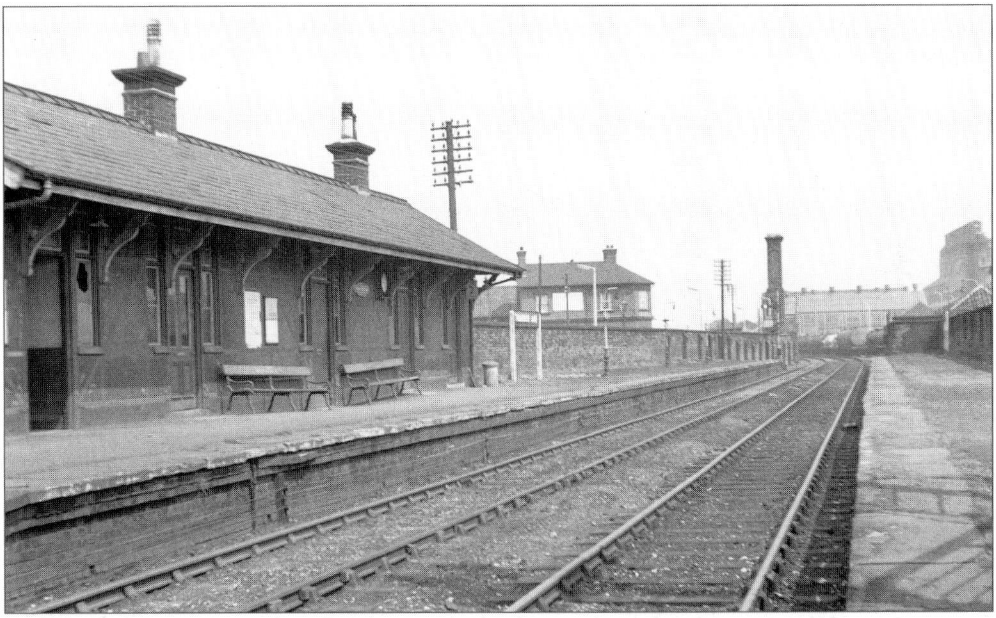

Tan House Lane railway station towards the end of its days. Seedy looking, run down, with an air of neglect, our photograph was taken as Doctor Beeching's axe was in the course of swinging. Never a popular station and in the poorer district of Moss Bank, it was mostly used by workers to and from the factories and for travel to Liverpool or Manchester at weekends. The Golden Bowl public house can be seen in the centre of the picture behind the wall and one of the famous Victorian sewer vents is also visible to the right of it. I was told that the Golden Bowl pub took its name from a trophy it won for bowling, which the landlord exhibited in the window for so many years that the pub changed its name.

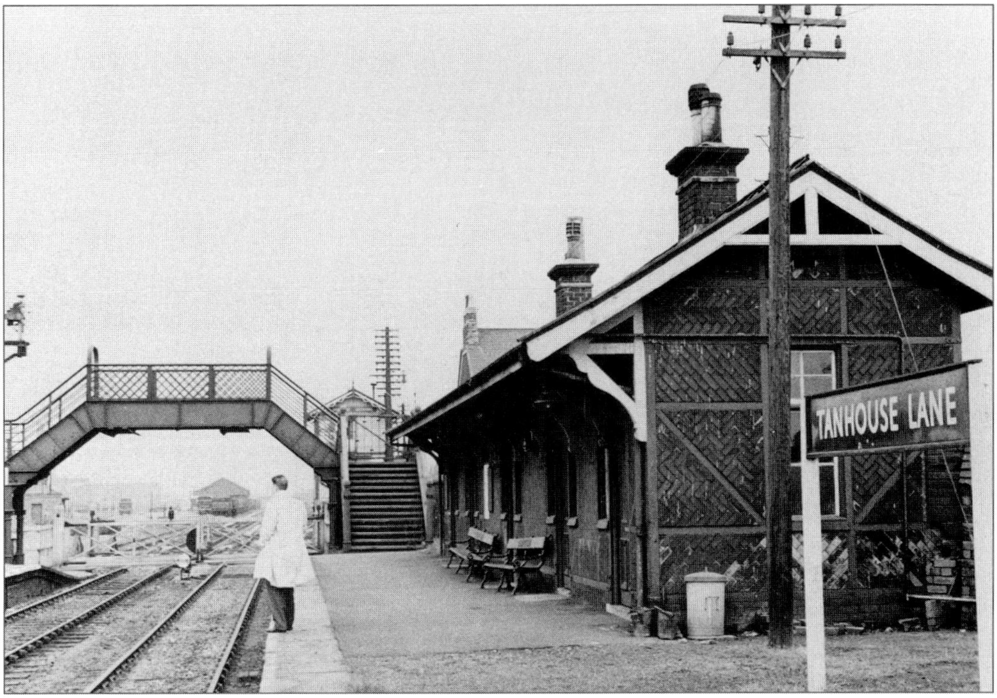

Tan House Lane railway station only days before its closure, 1961. The level-crossing gates which went into the works on the right can be seen, as can the footbridge for anyone in a hurry while the crossing gates were closed.

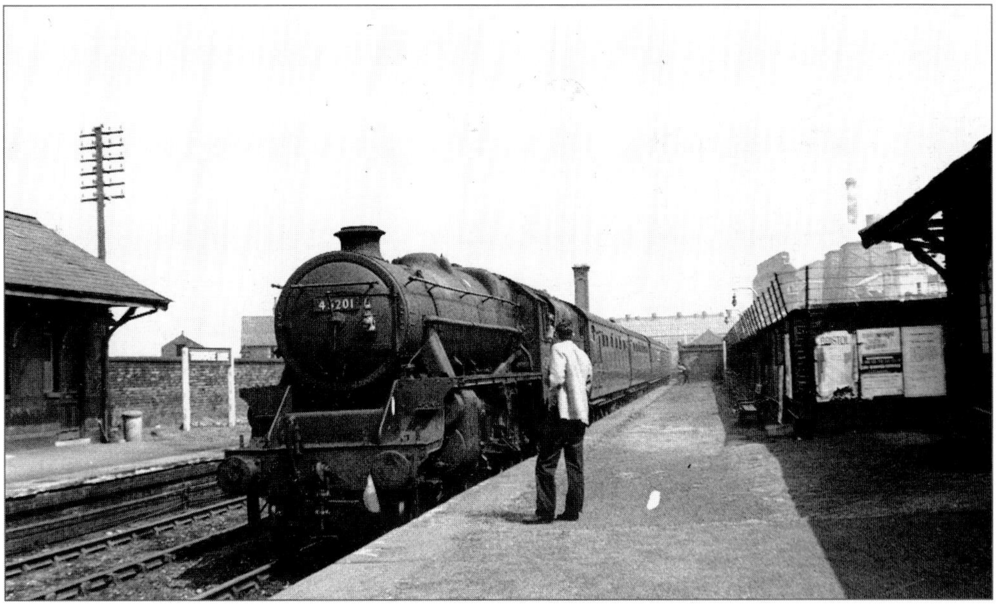

Tan House Lane railway station, looking the other way this time, as a 'Black 5' on a local stopper pulls slowly into the station. Anyone not careful could jump on to the wrong train at Warrington Central and find that instead of heading quickly towards Farnworth, they were crawling slowly through industrial south Widnes with stops everywhere before rejoining the main line at Hough Green.

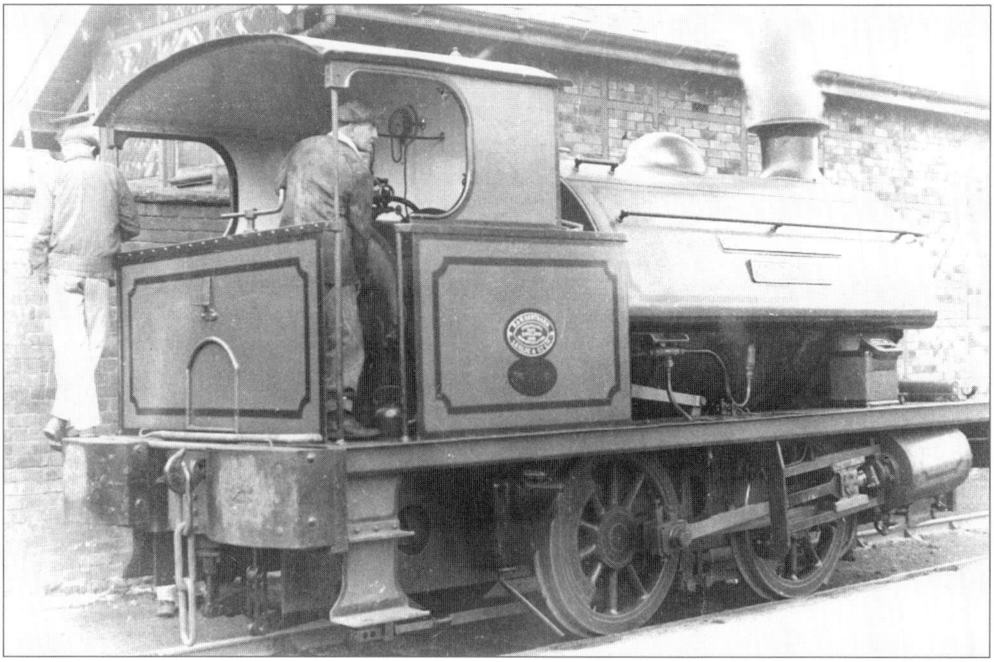

An industrial steam engine, 'Falcon', at the Pilkington-Sullivan's Works in Tan House Lane, Moss Bank. The engine was an 0–4–0, driven here by Freddy Johnson; it was one of hundreds of little shunting engines that busied themselves around the factories in Widnes.

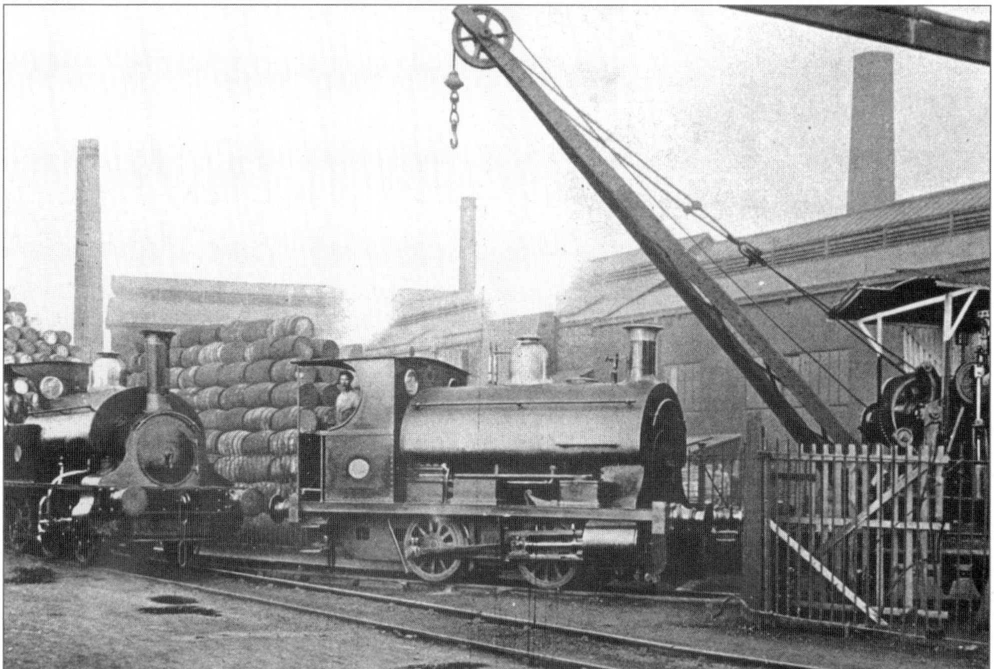

Here we see two more shunting engines; these belong to the factory of William Gossage and appear to date from *c.* 1910. Some of the engines were very basic, and the one in the centre of the picture is only a two-cylinder 0–4–0.

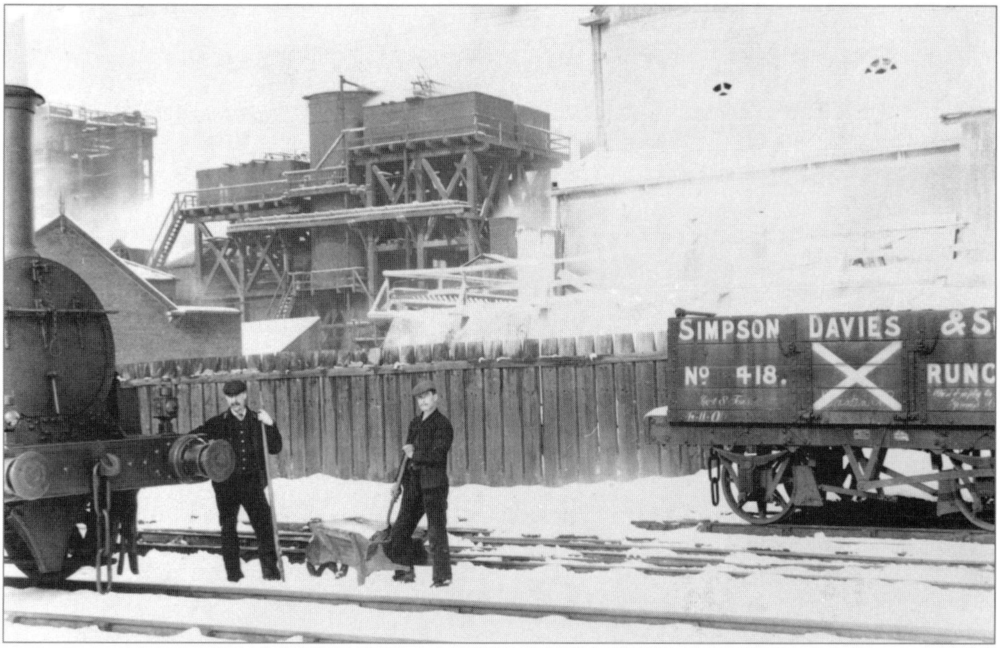

Another industrial scene, this one at Sullivan's Works, 1900. Both driver and fireman would become quite attached to their locomotive and usually tried to stick to the same one each day. Some of the engines were quite temperamental, and drivers tried to avoid these.

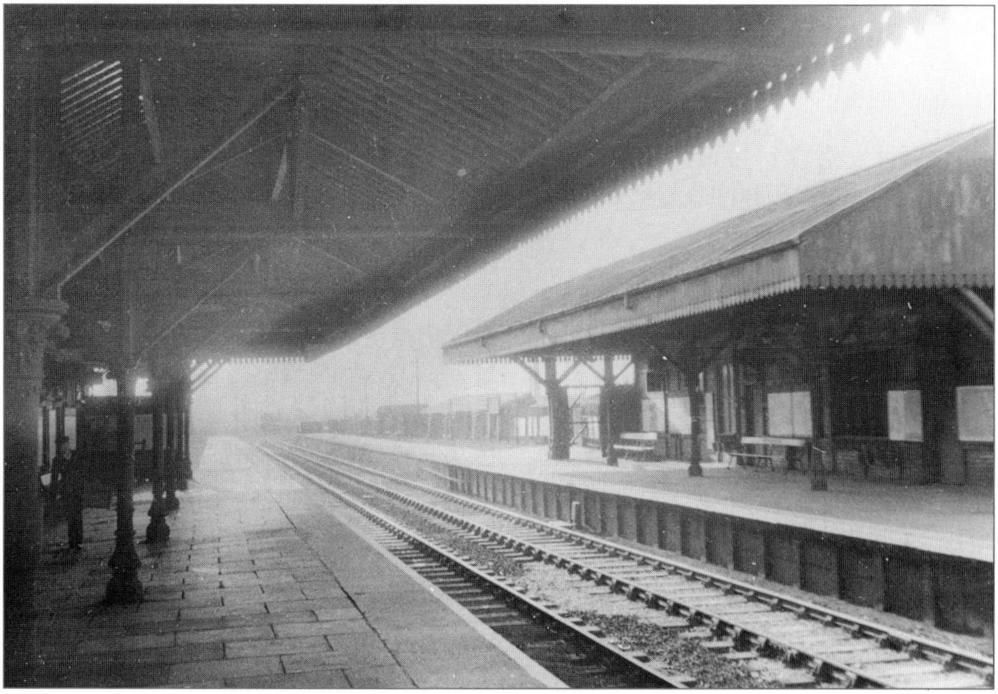

Widnes Central station, May 1956. Central station was behind the Central Hotel and access to the station was via a cobbled ramp up the embankment from Ditton Road. The station opened in 1877 and closed in 1961, and is now under Ashley Way (photograph by kind permission of Neville Conroy).

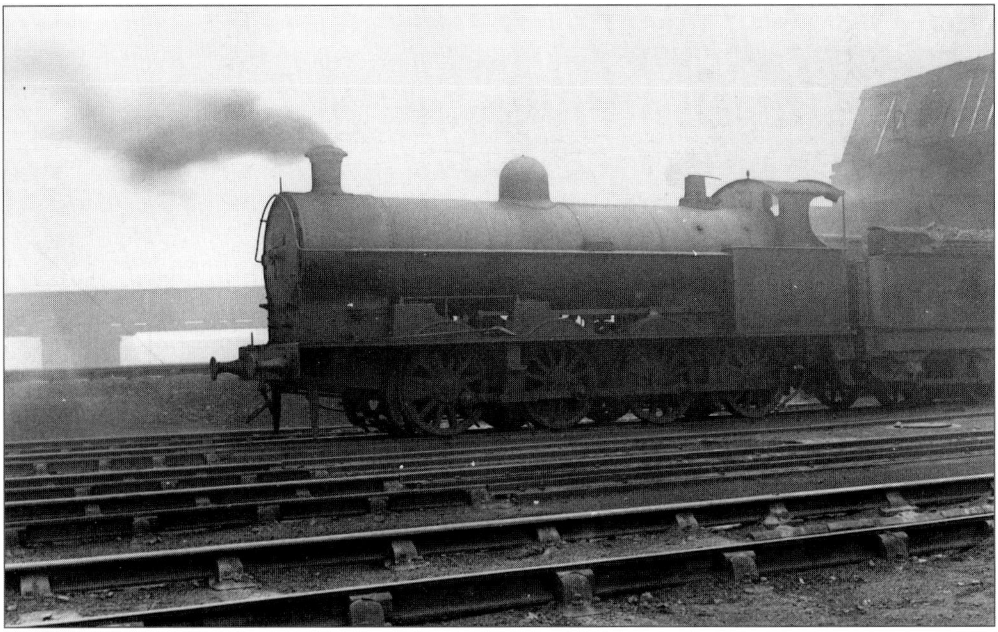

Widnes had its own railway shed, known as the Motive Power Depot (MPD). Shed 8D was under the control of Speke, which was numbered 8A. Here in a photograph from 1931 we see a straight boilered 0–8–0 (coffee pot), no. 9169, outside the shed waiting for its next turn of duty (Locofotos).

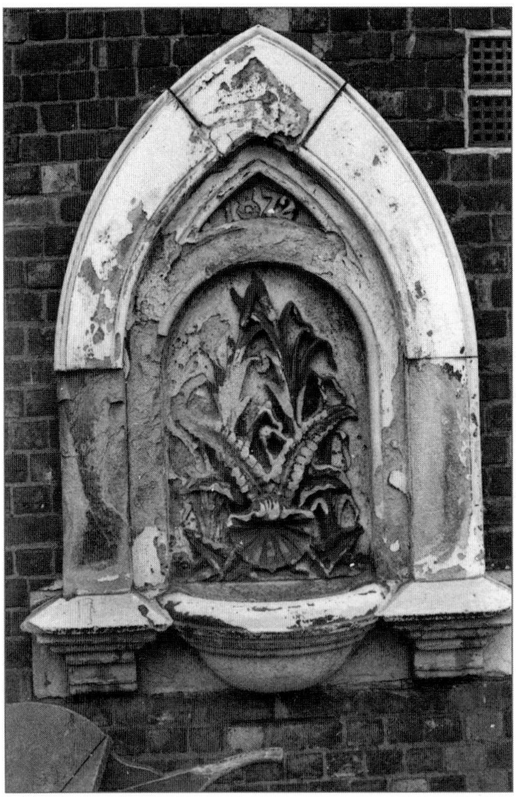

Farnworth station, and a close-up view of the elaborately decorated drinking fountain which graced it, 25 May 1975. The fountain gives the date of the station's opening as 1872, although quite a few references give the date of this station and Hough Green as 1874. This is the station where, in 1964, Paul Simon wrote 'Homeward Bound' (photograph Gordon Coltas).

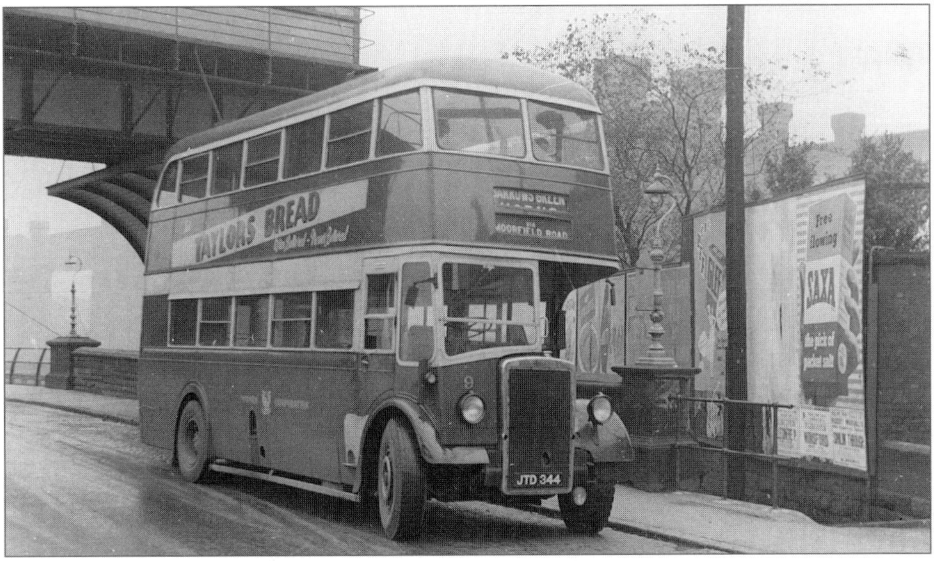

A Widnes Corporation bus waiting for passengers coming off the Transporter Bridge ready for the long journey, for a Widnes bus, right up to the Horns Hotel and Barrows Green, *c.* 1960. At the time there was no direct public transport between Widnes and Runcorn. The journey involved getting off the bus and crossing by the Widnes Corporation Transporter and then getting a Crosville at the other side which took you onwards. The H23 bus for a time followed the route Liverpool–Widnes–Warrington–Chester; but it took an age to complete the journey (an ABCROSS photograph, Alan B. Cross).

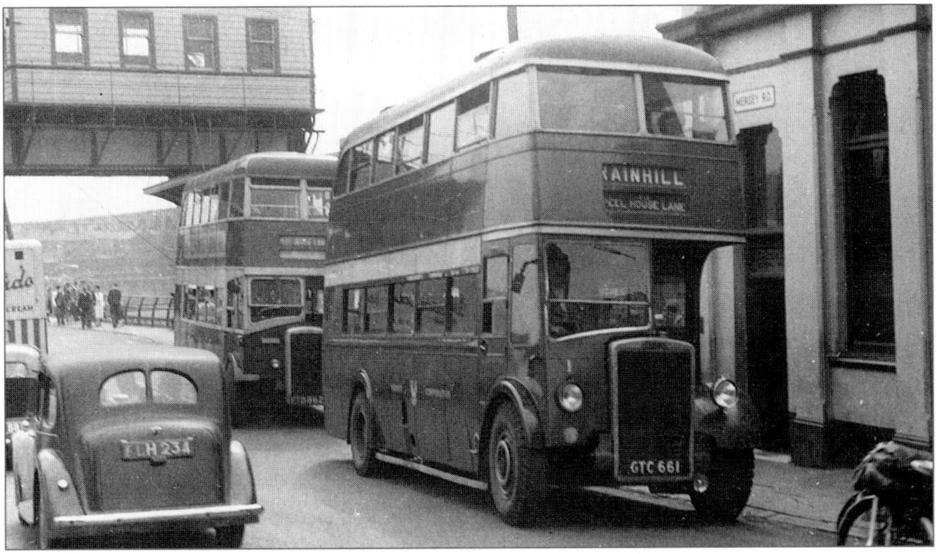

Here we have two buses waiting outside the Mersey Inn, West Bank, 1950s. True to bus tradition the first is for Rainhill via Peel House Lane, and the one behind is for Peel House Lane. It will follow the first bus probably completely empty. The Mersey Inn was noted for its entertainment and would have turns on of a weekend, but even this did not help in those few years at the end of the 1960s when Widnes pubs shut at 10.30 p.m. but the Runcorn ones stayed open until 11 p.m. on a Friday and Saturday night. At 10.25 patrons would pile out of the Mersey Inn and other pubs, still with a pint in their hands, and take the Transporter to Cheshire for another half-hour's drinking. If you missed the 11.15 p.m. car back it meant a long dismal walk over the railway bridge (an ABCROSS photograph).

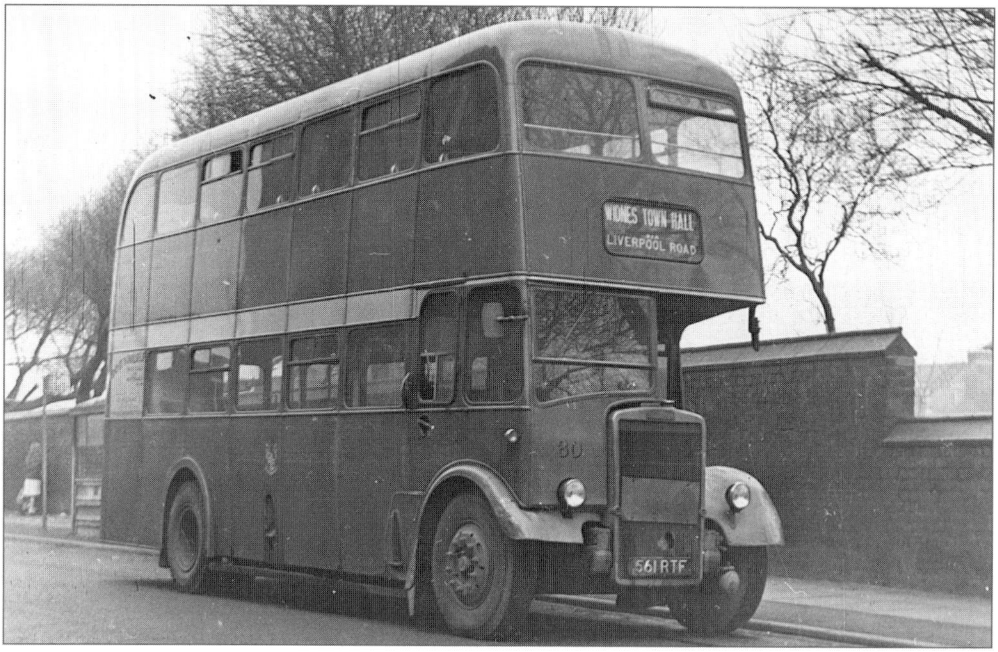

St Paul's Road was where the bus waited for Hough Green and Hough Green Farm. There were four variations on the journey to Hough Green, so it was a great guessing game to deduce which bus would arrive first. Here we see a Leyland bus which has just arrived from Hough Green via Liverpool Road and Deacon Road (photograph Ribble Enthusiasts' Club).

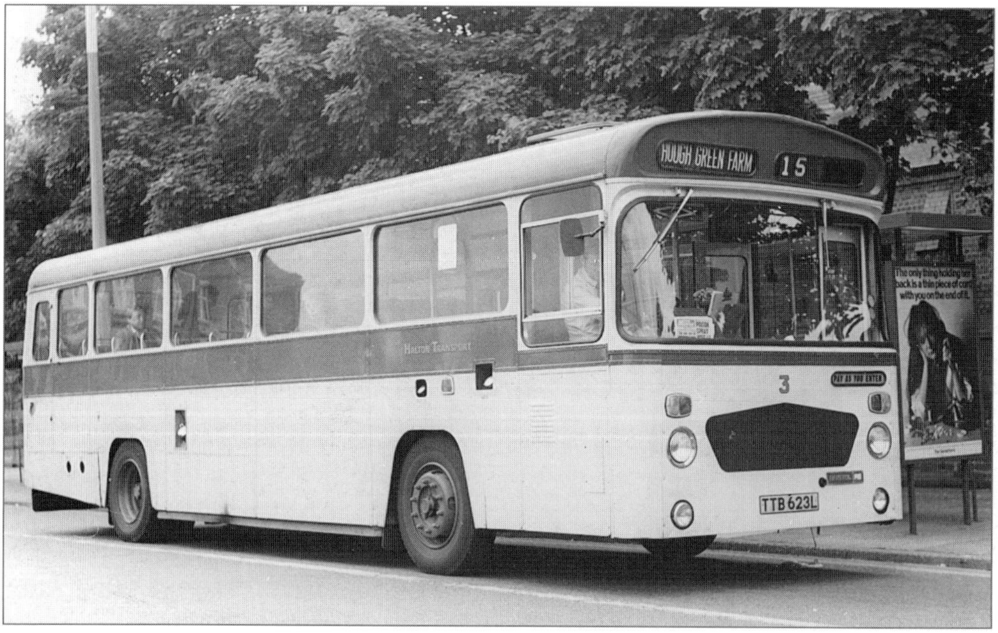

A Halton Transport single-decker bus heading for Hough Green Farm, 1980. This photograph is only seventeen years old, but is consigned to history by the great shake-up in the deregulation of buses.

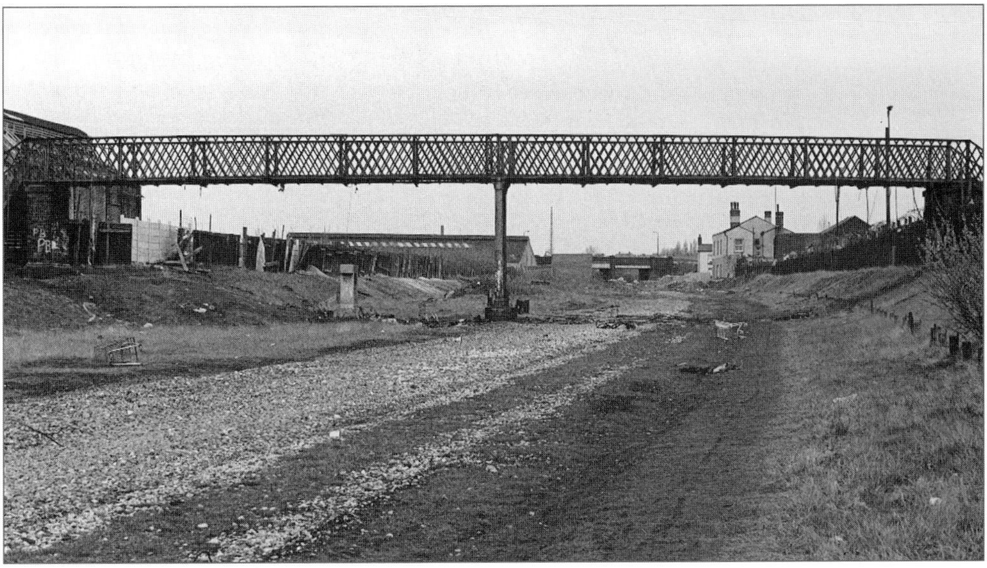

Here is the track-bed that was the St Helens railway, laid down over 150 years before the date of the picture – 1982. The footbridge was the Bradley Passage and was a well-used thoroughfare over to Halton View. The white building on the right was known as Brown's Pub on Page Lane. Of course you know that this track-bed is now covered by the Widnes bypass.

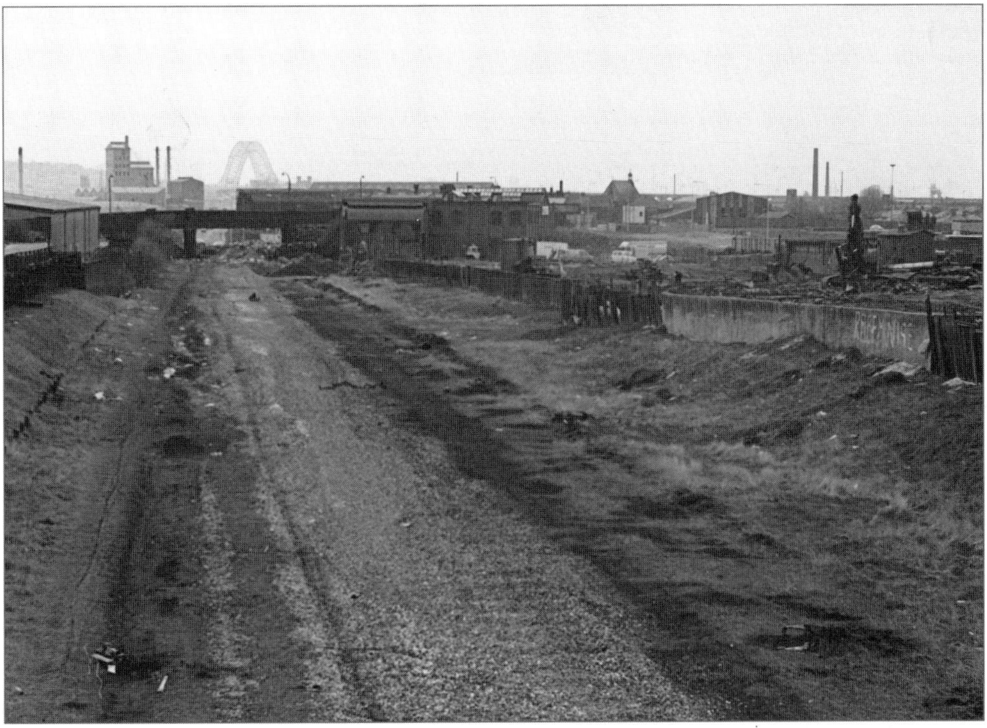

A picture from the pedestrian bridge, Bradley Passage, seen above, looking south towards the River Mersey and the road bridge, 1982. If you can make it out, there is a JCB busy clearing the site of the Vine Works, which was itself built on the site of Vine Yard House. Lugsdale Road bridge can be seen in the distance, and this area is now the site of the new Widnes Market.

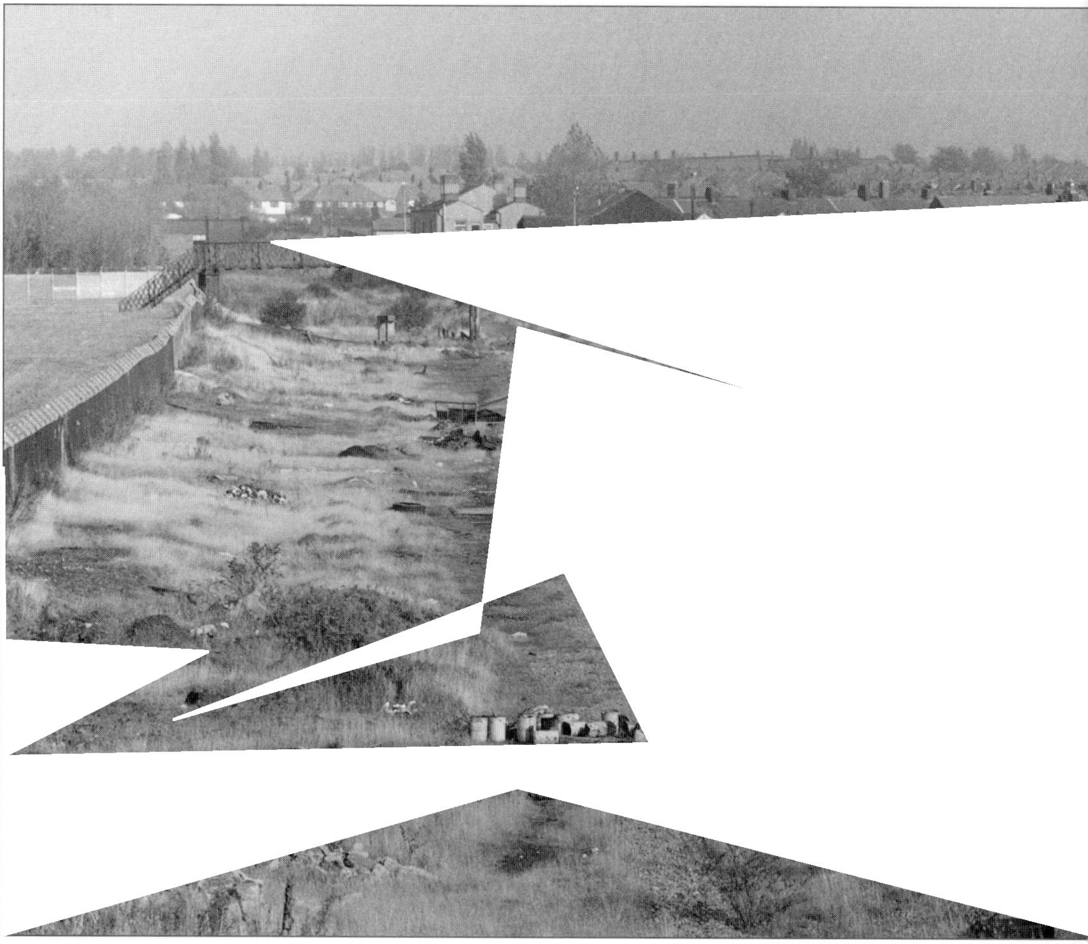

Looking from the Lugsdale Road bridge at the track-bed of the once busy railway that started as the St Helens–Runcorn Gap line in 1832 and was only the third or fourth railway in the whole country. Appleton station once stood here (see page 115). It was this line that pushed the St Helens Canal into extra activity and into building a dock for 24-hour loading and unloading, and the chemical industry in Widnes sprang from that rivalry between rail and water transport. Brown's Pub can be seen just behind the footbridge, and Page Lane and Gregson Street are on the right.

Widnes has done much to clean up its image: golf courses built on the tip, bypasses and dual carriageways on abandoned railway lines, and new and better housing and shopping facilities, but there is still much more to do. I hope they keep in mind the motto put forward a hundred years ago at a meeting to plan the future for Widnes – 'Take Heart, Press Forward, and Always Do it For the People.'

高等学校理工类课

无机化学例题与习题

Wuji Huaxue Liti yu Xiti

（第3版）

吉林大学
徐家宁　井淑波　史苏华　宋天佑　编

高等教育出版社·北京
HIGHER EDUCATION PRESS　BEIJING

内容提要

本书为宋天佑等编写的普通高等教育“十一五”国家级规划教材《无机化学》（第二版）的配套学习辅导书，共 21 章（不设第 1 章），2 ～ 11 章为基础理论部分，12 ～ 22 章为元素部分。各章包括三部分内容：第一部分为典型的例题；第二部分为习题，题型包括选择题、填空题、简答题和计算题；第三部分为习题参考答案，对简答题和计算题都给出了较详尽的解答。本书内容丰富，涉及知识面广，难度较大的题占有一定比例。

本书可作为综合性大学、师范院校及其他理工类院校学生学习无机化学和普通化学课程的配套学习辅导书，还可作为报考研究生的复习参考书。

图书在版编目（CIP）数据

无机化学例题与习题 / 徐家宁等编. -- 3版. -- 北京 ：高等教育出版社，2011.11 （2012.10 重印）

ISBN 978-7-04-033478-4

Ⅰ. ①无… Ⅱ. ①徐… Ⅲ. ①无机化学－高等学校－习题集 Ⅳ. ①061-44

中国版本图书馆CIP数据核字(2011)第211066号

策划编辑 鲍浩波　　责任编辑 鲍浩波　　封面设计 于文燕　　版式设计 王艳红
责任校对 殷 然　　责任印制 张泽业

出版发行 高等教育出版社
社　　址 北京市西城区德外大街4号
邮政编码 100120
印　　刷 北京市四季青双青印刷厂
开　　本 787mm×1092mm　1/16
印　　张 21.75
字　　数 540千字
购书热线 010-58581118
咨询电话 400-810-0598
网　　址 http://www.hep.edu.cn
　　　　 http://www.hep.com.cn
网上订购 http://www.landraco.com
　　　　 http://www.landraco.com.cn
版　　次 2000年7月第1版
　　　　 2011年11月第3版
印　　次 2012年10月第2次印刷
定　　价 31.80元

物 料 号　33478-00

第三版前言

《无机化学例题与习题》(第二版)作为普通高等教育"十五"国家级规划教材《无机化学》的配套学习辅导书,自2007年出版以来,受到广大读者的欢迎。2009年,主教材修订,《无机化学》(第二版)推出。为与主教材保持同步,使兄弟院校师生更好、更方便地使用这套教材,我们决定修订本书。

本次修订的原则,一是保持第一版和第二版的特色:题型全,解答详细,难度较大的综合题占有一定比例;二是与《无机化学》(第二版)的内容相呼应,所选例题主要以该教材各章的习题为素材,本书各章的序号与该教材一致,不设第1章;三是适当压缩篇幅,以求精练。

本书共21章,2～11章为基础理论部分,12～22章为元素部分。

参加本次修订工作的有宋天佑(各章的例题)、史苏华(2～11章习题)、井淑波(12～22章习题)和徐家宁(各章习题参考答案),最后由徐家宁统一修改、定稿。本书在修订过程中得到了无机化学教学组教师张丽荣、于杰辉、范勇、王莉等的大力支持,研究生刘杰、郑薇、宋伟等参与了部分工作,在此一并表示感谢。

由于编者水平所限,错误之处在所难免,诚请广大读者批评指正,使本书在下次修订时进一步完善。

徐家宁
2011年5月
于吉林大学化学学院

目　录

第 2 章

化学基础知识

第一部分　例题

例 2.1　已知 1 dm^3 某气体在标准状况下质量为 2.86 g，试计算该气体的平均相对分子质量，并计算其在 17 ℃和 207 kPa 时的密度。

解：先计算气体的物质的量 n。

由理想气体状态方程

$$pV=nRT$$

得

$$n=\frac{pV}{RT}$$

依题意 $V=1\ dm^3=1\times10^{-3}\ m^3$，$p=101.3\ kPa$，$T=273\ K$，代入求出 n。

$$n=\frac{101.3\ kPa\times1\times10^{-3}\ m^3}{8.314\ J\cdot mol^{-1}\cdot K^{-1}\times273\ K}$$

$$=0.044\ 63\ mol$$

由题设知 0.044 63 mol 气体的质量为 2.86 g，故该气体的摩尔质量为

$$M=\frac{2.86\ g}{0.044\ 63\ mol}=64.1\ g\cdot mol^{-1}$$

即平均相对分子质量为 64.1。

设 17 ℃和 207 kPa 时气体的体积为 V，由理想气体的状态方程知

$$V=\frac{nRT}{p}$$

代入题设条件

$$V=\frac{0.044\ 63\ mol\times8.314\ J\cdot mol^{-1}\cdot K^{-1}\times(273+17)\ K}{207\ 000\ Pa}$$

$$=5.198\times10^{-4}\ m^3$$

即气体的体积为 0.519 8 dm^3。

设气体的密度为 ρ，则

$$\rho=\frac{m}{V}=\frac{2.86\ \text{g}}{0.519\ 8\ \text{dm}^3}$$
$$=5.50\ \text{g}\cdot\text{dm}^{-3}$$

例 2.2 在 300 K，3.00×10^6 Pa 时，某气筒内封有 10 mol 氧气，试求该气筒的容积。将此气筒加热到 373 K，然后开启阀门放出氧气，在保持温度不变的情况下压强降低到 1.00×10^5 Pa，试求放出氧气的质量。

解：理想气体状态方程为

$$pV=nRT$$

将题设的 $T_1=300$ K，$p_1=3.00\times10^6$ Pa，$n_1=10$ mol 及 R 值代入其中，即可求出气筒的体积 V。

$$V=\frac{n_1RT_1}{p_1}$$
$$=\frac{10\ \text{mol}\times8.314\ \text{J}\cdot\text{mol}^{-1}\cdot\text{K}^{-1}\times300\ \text{K}}{3.00\times10^6\ \text{Pa}}$$
$$=8.31\times10^{-3}\ \text{m}^3$$

将题设的 $T_2=373$ K，$p_2=1.00\times10^5$ Pa，求得的 $V=8.31\times10^{-3}\ \text{m}^3$ 以及 R 值代入理想气体状态方程，即可求得气筒中剩余的氧气的物质的量 n_2。

$$n_2=\frac{p_2V}{RT_2}$$
$$=\frac{1.00\times10^5\ \text{Pa}\times8.31\times10^{-3}\ \text{m}^3}{8.314\ \text{J}\cdot\text{mol}^{-1}\cdot\text{K}^{-1}\times373\ \text{K}}$$
$$=0.268\ \text{mol}$$

放出的氧气的物质的量

$$n=n_1-n_2$$
$$=10\ \text{mol}-0.268\ \text{mol}$$
$$=9.732\ \text{mol}$$

放出的氧气的质量

$$m=nM$$
$$=9.732\ \text{mol}\times32\ \text{g}\cdot\text{mol}^{-1}$$
$$=311\ \text{g}$$

例 2.3 410 K 时某容器内装有 0.30 mol N_2，0.10 mol O_2 和 0.10 mol He，当混合气体的总压为 100 kPa 时 He 的分压是多少？N_2 的分体积是多少？

解：先求出组分气体 He 的摩尔分数。

$$n=\sum_i n_i=0.30\ \text{mol}+0.10\ \text{mol}+0.10\ \text{mol}$$

$$=0.50\ \text{mol}$$

$$x(\text{He})=\frac{n(\text{He})}{n}=\frac{0.10\ \text{mol}}{0.50\ \text{mol}}$$

$$=\frac{1}{5}$$

$$p_i=p_{总}\,x_i$$

$$=100\ \text{kPa}\times\frac{1}{5}$$

$$=20\ \text{kPa}$$

即 He 的分压为 $p(\text{He})=20\ \text{kPa}$。

由公式 $p_{总}V_i=n_iRT$ 得

$$V_i=\frac{n_iRT}{p_{总}}$$

将题设条件 $n(N_2)=0.30\ \text{mol}$，$T=410\ \text{K}$ 和 $p_{总}=100\ \text{kPa}$ 代入公式即可求出

$$V(N_2)=\frac{0.30\ \text{mol}\times 8.314\ \text{J}\cdot\text{mol}^{-1}\cdot\text{K}^{-1}\times 410\ \text{K}}{100\,000\ \text{Pa}}$$

$$=10\ \text{dm}^3$$

即 N_2 的分体积为 $10\ \text{dm}^3$。

例 2.4 在一定温度下，将 0.66 kPa 的氮气 $3.0\ \text{dm}^3$ 和 1.00 kPa 的氢气 $1.0\ \text{dm}^3$ 混合在 $2.0\ \text{dm}^3$ 密闭容器中。假定混合前后温度不变，求混合气体的总压。

解: 先求混合气体中氮气组分的分压。

依题意，某温度下 $p_1=0.66\ \text{kPa}$，$V_1=3.0\ \text{dm}^3$，可以求出在该温度下氮气占有混合气体总体积 $V_2=2.0\ \text{dm}^3$ 时所具有的压强 p_2。

根据 Boyle 定律，n，T 一定时

$$V\propto\frac{1}{p}$$

即

$$p_1V_1=p_2V_2$$

故

$$p_2=\frac{p_1V_1}{V_2}=\frac{0.66\ \text{kPa}\times 3.0\ \text{dm}^3}{2.0\ \text{dm}^3}$$

$$=0.99\ \text{kPa}$$

按分压的定义，这就是混合气体中氮气的分压 $p(N_2)$，同理可以求出混合气体中氢气的分压，$p(H_2)=0.50\ \text{kPa}$。由分压定律公式 $p_{总}=\sum p_i$，故

$$p_{总}=p(N_2)+p(H_2)$$

$$=0.99\ \text{kPa}+0.50\ \text{kPa}$$

$$=1.49\ \text{kPa}$$

例 2.5 某温度下一定量的 $PCl_5(g)$ 发生如下反应

$$PCl_5(g) \rightleftharpoons PCl_3(g) + Cl_2(g)$$

当 30% $PCl_5(g)$解离时达到平衡，总压为 1.6×10^5 Pa。求各组分的平衡分压。

解：设起始时有 1.0 mol $PCl_5(g)$。

根据反应式 $PCl_5(g) \rightleftharpoons PCl_3(g) + Cl_2(g)$

依题意达到平衡时

$$\begin{aligned} n(PCl_5,g) &= 1.0\ \text{mol}\times(1-30\%) \\ &= 0.7\ \text{mol} \\ n(PCl_3,g) &= 0.3\ \text{mol} \\ n(Cl_2,g) &= 0.3\ \text{mol} \end{aligned}$$

故平衡时体系中

$$\begin{aligned} n_{总} &= \sum_i n_i \\ &= 0.7\ \text{mol} + 0.3\ \text{mol} + 0.3\ \text{mol} \\ &= 1.3\ \text{mol} \end{aligned}$$

PCl_5 的摩尔分数

$$\begin{aligned} x(PCl_5,g) &= \frac{n(PCl_5,g)}{n_{总}} \\ &= \frac{0.7\ \text{mol}}{1.3\ \text{mol}} \\ &= 0.54 \end{aligned}$$

同理 $x(PCl_3,g)=x(Cl_2,g)=0.23$。

由 $p_i=p_{总}\,x_i$ 得 PCl_5 的平衡分压

$$\begin{aligned} p(PCl_5,g) &= 1.6\times10^5\ \text{Pa}\times0.54 \\ &= 8.6\times10^4\ \text{Pa} \end{aligned}$$

同理 $p(PCl_3,g)=p(Cl_2,g)=3.7\times10^4$ Pa。

例 2.6 在 100 kPa 和 298 K 时，有含饱和水蒸气的空气 3.47 dm^3，如将其中的水除去，则干燥空气的体积为 3.36 dm^3。求在此温度下水的饱和蒸气压。

解：含饱和水蒸气的空气是一种混合气体，它遵循分压定律。

由公式 $p_iV_{总}=n_iRT$ 和 $p_{总}\,V_i=n_iRT$ 联立得

$$p_iV_{总}=p_{总}V_i$$

故

$$p_i=p_{总}\frac{V_i}{V_{总}}$$

将混合气体的总压 $p_{总}=100$ kPa，干燥空气的分体积 $V_i=3.36\ dm^3$ 和混合气体的总体积 $V_{总}=3.47\ dm^3$ 代入，可求出干燥空气的分压 p_i。

$$p_i=100\ \text{kPa}\times\frac{3.36\ dm^3}{3.47\ dm^3}$$

$$=96.83\ \text{kPa}$$

由公式 $p_{总}=\sum_i p_i$，所以水汽的饱和蒸气压即水的分压为

$$p(H_2O)=p_{总}-p_i$$
$$=100\ \text{kPa}-96.83\ \text{kPa}$$
$$=3.17\ \text{kPa}$$

例 2.7　313 K 时将 1 000 cm^3 饱和苯蒸气和空气的混合气体从压强为 9.97×10^4 Pa 压缩到 5.05×10^5 Pa。问在此过程中有多少克苯凝结成液体？已知 313 K 苯的饱和蒸气压为 2.41×10^4 Pa。

解：在压缩前后混合气体中苯的分压均等于苯的饱和蒸气压。则压缩前空气的分压为

$$p_1=9.97\times10^4\ \text{Pa}-2.41\times10^4\ \text{Pa}=7.56\times10^4\ \text{Pa}$$

压缩后空气的分压为

$$p_2=5.05\times10^5\ \text{Pa}-2.41\times10^4\ \text{Pa}=4.81\times10^5\ \text{Pa}$$

压缩前后空气的物质的量、温度均未发生变化，由 $p_1V_1=p_2V_2$ 得压缩后混合气体的体积为

$$V_2=\frac{p_1V_1}{p_2}=\frac{7.56\times10^4\ \text{Pa}\times1\,000\ \text{cm}^3}{4.81\times10^5\ \text{Pa}}=157.2\ \text{cm}^3$$

凝结成液体的苯的物质的量等于压缩前后苯蒸气的物质的量之差

$$n_{凝}=n_1-n_2=\frac{pV_1}{RT}-\frac{pV_2}{RT}=\frac{p}{RT}(V_1-V_2)$$
$$=\frac{2.41\times10^4\ \text{Pa}}{8.314\ \text{Pa}\cdot\text{m}^3\cdot\text{mol}^{-1}\cdot\text{K}^{-1}\times313\ \text{K}}\times(1\,000-157.2)\times10^{-6}\text{m}^3$$
$$=7.8\times10^{-3}\ \text{mol}$$

凝结成液体的苯的质量为

$$7.8\times10^{-3}\ \text{mol}\times78\ \text{g}\cdot\text{mol}^{-1}=0.608\ \text{g}$$

例 2.8　313 K 时 $CHCl_3$ 的饱和蒸气压为 49.3 kPa，于此温度和 98.6 kPa 的压强下，将 4.00 dm^3 空气缓缓通过 $CHCl_3$，致使每个气泡都为 $CHCl_3$ 饱和。求

(1) 通过 $CHCl_3$ 后，空气和 $CHCl_3$ 混合气体的体积；

(2) 被空气带走的 $CHCl_3$ 的质量。

解：(1) 将题设的过程理解为一个 $p_1=98.6$ kPa，$V_1=4.00\ dm^3$ 的空气气泡缓缓通过 $CHCl_3$ 液体，气泡在被 $CHCl_3$ 饱和的过程中体系的总压没变，气泡的体积增大。通过 $CHCl_3$ 后的气泡是个混合气体体系，$V_{总}$ 是其体积，$p_{总}=98.6$ kPa。$CHCl_3$ 的饱和蒸气压 49.3 kPa 是混合气体中该组分的分压 p_2，设另一组分空气的分压为 $p_{空}$，则

$$p_{空}=p_{总}-p_2$$
$$=98.6\ \text{kPa}-49.3\ \text{kPa}$$
$$=49.3\ \text{kPa}$$

对组分气体空气，使用 Boyle 定律，因为 T,n 不变，$p_{空}V_{总}=p_1V_1$，故

$$V_{总}=\frac{p_1V_1}{p_{空}}$$

$$V_{总}=\frac{98.6\ \text{kPa}\times 4.0\ \text{dm}^3}{49.3\ \text{kPa}}$$
$$=8.0\ \text{dm}^3$$

(2) 对组分气体 $CHCl_3$ 使用理想气体状态方程 $p_2V_{总}=nRT$，故混合气体中 $CHCl_3$ 的物质的量为

$$n=\frac{p_2V_{总}}{RT}=\frac{49.3\ \text{kPa}\times 8.0\ \text{dm}^3}{8.314\ \text{J}\cdot\text{mol}^{-1}\cdot\text{K}^{-1}\times 313\ \text{K}}$$
$$=0.152\ \text{mol}$$

因为 $CHCl_3$ 的摩尔质量 $M=119.5\ \text{g}\cdot\text{mol}^{-1}$，故带走的 $CHCl_3$ 的质量为

$$m=Mn=119.5\ \text{g}\cdot\text{mol}^{-1}\times 0.152\ \text{mol}$$
$$=18.16\ \text{g}$$

例 2.9 某氨水的密度为 $0.910\ \text{g}\cdot\text{cm}^{-3}$，其中氨的浓度为 $12.85\ \text{mol}\cdot\text{dm}^{-3}$。求氨的摩尔分数。

解：设有 1 000 cm^3 氨水，其质量

$$m=V\rho$$

将题设数据代入式中

$$m=1\ 000\ \text{cm}^3\times 0.910\ \text{g}\cdot\text{cm}^{-3}$$
$$=910\ \text{g}$$

依题意其中 NH_3 的物质的量

$$n(NH_3)=12.85\ \text{mol}$$

这些溶质 NH_3 的质量为 $m(NH_3)$，则

$$m(NH_3)=n(NH_3)\times M(NH_3)$$
$$=12.85\ \text{mol}\times 17.0\ \text{g}\cdot\text{mol}^{-1}$$
$$=218.5\ \text{g}$$

溶剂水的质量为 $m(H_2O)$，则

$$m(H_2O)=m-m(NH_3)$$
$$=910\ \text{g}-218.5\ \text{g}$$
$$=691.5\ \text{g}$$

溶剂水的物质的量为 $n(H_2O)$，则

$$n(H_2O)=\frac{m(H_2O)}{M(H_2O)}$$
$$=\frac{691.5\ \text{g}}{18\ \text{g}\cdot\text{mol}^{-1}}$$

$$=38.42\ \text{mol}$$

$$x(NH_3)=\frac{x(NH_3)}{x(NH_3)+x(H_2O)}=\frac{12.85\ \text{mol}}{12.85\ \text{mol}+38.42\ \text{mol}}=0.251$$

例 2.10 已知 60 ℃时水的饱和蒸气压为 19.9 kPa，在此温度下将 180 g 葡萄糖溶到 180 g 水中。求此水溶液的蒸气压。

解：溶剂的物质的量

$$n_{剂}=\frac{180\ \text{g}}{18\ \text{g}\cdot\text{mol}^{-1}}=10\ \text{mol}$$

溶质的物质的量

$$n_{质}=\frac{180\ \text{g}}{180\ \text{g}\cdot\text{mol}^{-1}}=1\ \text{mol}$$

故

$$x_{剂}=\frac{n_{剂}}{n_{剂}+n_{质}}=\frac{10\ \text{mol}}{10\ \text{mol}+1\ \text{mol}}=0.909$$

根据 Raoult 定律

$$p=p^{*}x_{剂}$$

故此水溶液的蒸气压为

$$p=19.9\ \text{kPa}\times0.909=18.1\ \text{kPa}$$

例 2.11 300 K 时，4.0 g·dm^{-3}的聚氯乙烯溶液，其渗透压为 65 Pa。计算聚氯乙烯的平均相对分子质量。

解：由渗透压公式 $\Pi=cRT$ 得

$$c=\frac{\Pi}{RT}$$

将题设条件 $\Pi=65$ Pa 和 $T=300$ K 代入，得

$$c=\frac{65\ \text{Pa}}{8.314\ \text{J}\cdot\text{mol}^{-1}\cdot\text{K}^{-1}\times300\ \text{K}}=2.61\times10^{-2}\ \text{mol}\cdot\text{m}^{-3}=2.61\times10^{-5}\ \text{mol}\cdot\text{dm}^{-3}$$

依题设每升溶液中的 2.61×10^{-5} mol 聚氯乙烯的质量为 4.0 g，设聚氯乙烯的摩尔质量为 M，则

$$M=\frac{4.0\ \text{g}}{2.61\times10^{-5}\ \text{mol}}$$

$$=1.5\times10^5\ \text{g}\cdot\text{mol}^{-1}$$

故聚氯乙烯的平均相对分子质量为 1.5×10^5。

例 2.12 测得人体血液的凝固点降低值为 0.56 K，求人体温度为 37 ℃时血液的渗透压。已知 $k_f=1.86\ \text{K}\cdot\text{kg}\cdot\text{mol}^{-1}$。

解： 先求出血液的质量摩尔浓度 b，由公式 $\Delta T_f=k_f b$ 得

$$b=\frac{\Delta T_f}{k_f}$$

由题设知 $\Delta T_f=0.56\ \text{K}$，又已知 $k_f=1.86\ \text{K}\cdot\text{kg}\cdot\text{mol}^{-1}$，故

$$b=\frac{0.56\ \text{K}}{1.86\ \text{K}\cdot\text{kg}\cdot\text{mol}^{-1}}=0.301\ 1\ \text{mol}\cdot\text{kg}^{-1}$$

对于稀溶液，质量摩尔浓度 b 在数值上等于物质的量浓度 c，故知血液的物质的量浓度 $c=0.301\ 1\ \text{mol}\cdot\text{dm}^{-3}$，相当于 $3.011\times10^2\ \text{mol}\cdot\text{m}^{-3}$。

题设温度为 37 ℃，相当于(273＋37)K，即温度 $T=310$ K。

再由公式 $\Pi=cRT$，求出渗透压 Π。

$$\begin{aligned}\Pi&=3.011\times10^2\ \text{mol}\cdot\text{m}^{-3}\times8.314\ \text{J}\cdot\text{mol}^{-1}\cdot\text{K}^{-1}\times310\ \text{K}\\&=776\ \text{kPa}\end{aligned}$$

第二部分　习题

一、选择题

2.1 在一次渗流实验中，一定物质的量的未知气体通过小孔渗向真空，需要的时间为 5 s；在相同条件下相同物质的量的氧气渗流需要 20 s。则未知气体的相对分子质量应是

(A) 2；　(B) 4；　(C) 8；　(D) 16。

2.2 实验测得 H_2 的扩散速率是一未知气体扩散速率的 2.9 倍。则该未知气体的相对分子质量约为

(A) 51；　(B) 34；　(C) 17；　(D) 28。

2.3 常压下将 1 dm^3 气体的温度从 0 ℃升到 273 ℃，其体积将变为

(A) 0.5 dm^3；　(B) 1 dm^3；　(C) 1.5 dm^3；　(D) 2 dm^3。

2.4 在 25 ℃，101.3 kPa 时，下面几种气体的混合气体中分压最大的是

(A) 0.1 g H_2；　(B) 1.0 g He；　(C) 5.0 g N_2；　(D) 10 g CO_2。

2.5 合成氨的原料气中氢气和氮气的体积比为 3∶1，若原料气中含有其他杂质气体的体积分数为 4%，原料气总压为 15 198.75 kPa，则氮气的分压是

(A) 3 799.688 kPa；(B) 10 943.1 kPa；(C) 3 647.7 kPa；(D) 11 399.06 kPa。

2.6 将一定量 $KClO_3$ 加热后，其质量减少 0.48 g。生成的氧气用排水取气法收集。若温度为

21 ℃，压力为 99 591.8 Pa，水的饱和蒸气压为 2 479.8 Pa，氧气的相对分子质量为 32.0，则收集的气体体积为

(A) 188.5 cm^3；　(B) 754 cm^3；　(C) 565.5 cm^3；　(D) 377.6 cm^3。

2.7　由 NH_4NO_2 分解得氮气和水。在 23 ℃，95 549.5 Pa 条件下，用排水取气法收集到 57.5 cm^3 氮气。已知水的饱和蒸气压为 2 813.1 Pa，则干燥后氮气的体积为

(A) 55.8 cm^3；　(B) 27.9 cm^3；　(C) 46.5 cm^3；　(D) 18.6 cm^3。

2.8　1 000 g 水中溶解 0.1 mol 食盐的水溶液与 1 000 g 水中溶解 0.1 mol 葡萄糖的水溶液，在 1.013×10^5 Pa，下列有关沸点的陈述中正确的是

(A) 都高于 100 ℃，但食盐水比葡萄糖水要低；

(B) 都高于 100 ℃，但葡萄糖水比食盐水要低；

(C) 食盐水低于 100 ℃，葡萄糖水高于 100 ℃；

(D) 食盐水高于 100 ℃，葡萄糖水低于 100 ℃。

2.9　若溶液的浓度都为 0.1 $mol\cdot dm^{-3}$，则下列水溶液的沸点由高到低排列，顺序正确的是

(A) Na_2SO_4，NaCl，HAc；　(B) $Al_2(SO_4)_3$，NaCl，Na_2SO_4；

(C) NaAc，K_2CrO_4，NaCl；　(D) NaCl，$K_2Cr_2O_7$，$CaCl_2$。

2.10　如果某水合盐的蒸气压低于相同温度下水的蒸气压，则这种盐可能会发生的现象是

(A) 起泡；　(B) 风化；　(C) 潮解；　(D) 不受大气组成影响。

2.11　在 100 g 水中含 4.5 g 某非电解质的溶液于 −0.465 ℃时结冰，则该非电解质的相对分子质量约为(已知水的 $K_f=1.86\ K\cdot kg\cdot mol^{-1}$)

(A) 90；　(B) 135；　(C) 172；　(D) 180。

2.12　在相同温度下，和 1% 尿素[$CO(NH_2)_2$]水溶液具有相同渗透压的葡萄糖($C_6H_{12}O_6$)溶液的浓度约为

(A) 2%；　(B) 3%；　(C) 4%；　(D) 5%。

2.13　处于恒温条件下的一封闭容器中有两杯液体，A 杯为纯水，B 杯为蔗糖水溶液。放置足够长时间后则发现

(A) A 杯水减少，B 杯水满后不再变化；

(B) B 杯水减少，A 杯水满后不再变化；

(C) A 杯变成空杯，B 杯水满后溢出；

(D) B 杯水干并有蔗糖晶体，A 杯水满后溢出。

2.14　处于室温一密闭容器内有水及与水相平衡的水蒸气。现充入不溶于水也不与水反应的气体，则水蒸气的压力

(A) 增加；　(B) 减少；　(C) 不变；　(D) 不能确定。

2.15　为防止水在仪器内结冰，可在水中加入甘油($C_3H_8O_3$)。欲使其冰点下降至 −2.0 ℃，则应在 100 g 水中加入甘油(水的 $K_f=1.86\ K\cdot kg\cdot mol^{-1}$)

(A) 9.89 g；　(B) 3.30 g；　(C) 1.10 g；　(D) 19.78 g。

2.16　土壤中 NaCl 含量高时植物难以生存，这与下列稀溶液的性质有关的是

(A) 蒸气压下降；(B) 沸点升高；(C) 冰点下降；(D) 渗透压。

二、填空题

2.17 当气体为 1 mol 时，实际气体的状态方程式为__________。

2.18 一定体积的干燥气体从易挥发的三氯甲烷液体中通过后，气体体积变______，气体分压变______。

2.19 某气体在 293 K 和 9.97×10^4 Pa 时占有体积 0.19 dm^3，质量为 0.132 g，则该气体的摩尔质量约等于______，该气体可能是______。

2.20 某理想气体在 273 K 和 101.3 kPa 时的体积为 0.312 m^3，则在 298 K 和 98.66 kPa 时其体积为______m^3。

2.21 将 4.4 g CO_2，14 g N_2 和 12.8 g O_2 盛于一容器中，气体总压为 2.026×10^5 Pa，则混合气体中各组分气体的分压为：CO_2______Pa；N_2______Pa；O_2______Pa。

2.22 在相同的温度和压力下，两个容积相同的烧瓶中分别充满 O_3 气体和 H_2S 气体。已知 H_2S 的质量为 0.34 g，则 O_3 的质量为______g。

2.23 在 300 K，1.013×10^5 Pa 时加热一敞口细颈瓶到 500 K，然后封闭细颈瓶口并冷却到原来的温度，则该瓶内的压强为______。

2.24 有一容积为 30 dm^3 的高压气瓶，可以耐压 2.5×10^4 kPa，则在 298 K 时可装______kg O_2 而不致发生危险。

2.25 10.00 cm^3 NaCl 饱和溶液的质量为 12.003 g，将其蒸干后得 NaCl 3.173 g，则 NaCl 的溶解度为______；溶液的质量分数为______；溶液的物质的量浓度为______；溶液的质量摩尔浓度为______；溶液中盐的摩尔分数和水的摩尔分数分别为______和______。

2.26 在 26.6 g 氯仿($CHCl_3$)中溶解 0.402 g 萘($C_{10}H_8$)，其沸点比氯仿的沸点高 0.455 K，则氯仿的沸点升高常数为______。

2.27 下面几种溶液：① 0.1 $mol\cdot dm^{-3}$ $Al_2(SO_4)_3$；② 0.2 $mol\cdot dm^{-3}$ $CuSO_4$；③ 0.3 $mol\cdot dm^{-3}$ NaCl；④ 0.3 $mol\cdot dm^{-3}$ 尿素。按溶液的凝固点由高到低的顺序是______。

2.28 海水结冰的温度比纯水结冰的温度______，其温度改变值可以用______关系式表示。

三、简答题和计算题

2.29 在体积为 0.50 dm^3 的烧瓶中充满 NO 和 O_2 混合气体，温度为 298 K，压强为 1.23×10^5 Pa。反应一段时间后，瓶内总压变为 8.3×10^4 Pa。求生成 NO_2 的质量。

2.30 将氮气和水蒸气的混合物通入盛有足量固体干燥剂的瓶中。刚通入时，瓶中压强为 101.3 kPa。放置数小时后，压强降到 99.3 kPa 的恒定值。

(1) 求原气体混合物各组分的摩尔分数；

(2) 若温度为 293 K，实验后干燥剂增重 0.150×10^{-3} kg，求瓶的体积。假设干燥剂的体积可忽略且不吸附氮气。

2.31 302 K 时在 3.0 dm^3 的真空容器中装入氮气和一定量的水，测得初压为 1.01×10^5 Pa。

用电解法将容器中的水完全转变为氢气和氧气后，测得最终压强为 1.88×10^5 Pa。求容器中水的质量。已知 302 K 时水的饱和蒸气压为 4.04×10^3 Pa。

2.32 在 303 K，7.97×10^4 Pa 时由排水集气法收集到 1.50 dm^3 氧气。问有多少克氯酸钾按下式发生了分解？

$$2KClO_3 \xrightarrow[\triangle]{MnO_2} 2KCl + 3O_2$$

已知 303 K 时水的饱和蒸气压为 4.23×10^3 Pa。

2.33 由 C_2H_4 和过量 H_2 组成的混合气体的总压为 6 930 Pa。使混合气体通过铂催化剂进行下列反应：

$$C_2H_4(g) + H_2(g) = C_2H_6(g)$$

待完全反应后，在相同温度和体积下，压强降为 4 530 Pa。求原混合气体中 C_2H_4 的摩尔分数。

2.34 某项实验要求缓慢地加入乙醇(C_2H_5OH)，现采用将空气通过液体乙醇带入乙醇气体的方法进行。在 293 K，1.013×10^5 Pa 时，为引入 2.3 g 乙醇，求需空气的体积。已知 293 K 时乙醇的饱和蒸气压为 5 866.2 Pa。

2.35 在 273 K 和 1.013×10^5 Pa 下，将 1.0 dm^3 干燥的空气缓慢通过二甲醚(CH_3OCH_3)液体。在此过程中，液体损失 0.033 5 g。求二甲醚在 273 K 时的饱和蒸气压。

2.36 25 ℃，一个容器中充入等物质的量的 H_2 和 O_2，总压为 100 kPa。混合气体点燃充分反应后，容器中氧的分压是多少？若已知在 25 ℃时水的饱和蒸气压为 3.17 kPa，则容器中气体的总压是多少？

2.37 在 288 K 时，将 NH_3 通入一盛水的玻璃球内至 NH_3 不再溶解为止，已知玻璃球内饱和溶液质量为 3.018 g。再将玻璃球放在 50.0 cm^3，0.50 $mol\cdot dm^{-3}$ 的 H_2SO_4 溶液中，将球击破。剩余的酸需用 10.4 cm^3，1.0 $mol\cdot dm^{-3}$ NaOH 中和。试计算 288 K 时 NH_3 在水中的溶解度。

2.38 在 303 K 时，丙酮(C_3H_6O)的蒸气压是 37 330 Pa，当 6 g 某非挥发性有机物溶于 120 g 丙酮时，其蒸气压下降至 35 570 Pa。试求此有机物的相对分子质量。

2.39 3.24 g 硫溶解于 40 g 苯中，该苯溶液的沸点升高 0.81 K，问此溶液中硫分子是由几个硫原子组成的？已知苯的 $K_b=2.53\ K\cdot kg\cdot mol^{-1}$。

2.40 将 10 g 葡萄糖和甘油分别溶于 100 g 水中，问所得溶液的凝固点各为多少？

2.41 0.570 g $Pb(NO_3)_2$ 溶于 120 g 水中，其凝固点比纯水凝固点降低了 0.08 K，相同质量的 $PbCl_2$ 溶于 100 g 水中，其凝固点比纯水凝固点降低了 0.0381 K，试判断这两种盐在水中的解离情况。已知水的 $K_f=1.86\ K\cdot kg\cdot mol^{-1}$。

2.42 常压下将 2.0 g 尿素(CON_2H_4)溶入 75 g 水中，求该溶液的凝固点。已知水的 $K_f=1.86\ K\cdot kg\cdot mol^{-1}$。

2.43 某化合物的苯溶液，溶质和溶剂的质量比是 15：100。在 293 K，1.013×10^5 Pa 下将 4.0 dm^3 空气缓慢地通过该溶液时，测知损失 1.185 g 苯。假设失去苯后溶液的浓度不变。已知苯的 K_b 为 2.53 $K\cdot kg\cdot mol^{-1}$，K_f 为 5.1 $K\cdot kg\cdot mol^{-1}$。求

(1) 溶质的相对分子质量；

(2) 该溶液的凝固点和沸点(293 K 时，苯的蒸气压为 1×10^4 Pa；1.013×10^5 Pa 时，苯的

沸点为 353.1 K，凝固点为 278.4 K）。

2.44 与人体血液具有相等渗透压的葡萄糖溶液，其凝固点降低值为 0.543 K。求此葡萄糖溶液的质量分数和血液的渗透压？已知葡萄糖的相对分子质量为 180，水的 $K_f = 1.86\ K \cdot kg \cdot mol^{-1}$。

第3章

化学热力学基础

第一部分　例题

例 3.1　油酸甘油酯在人体中代谢时发生下列反应

$$C_{57}H_{104}O_6(s)+80O_2(g) \xlongequal{} 57CO_2(g)+52H_2O(l)$$

$\Delta_r H_m^\ominus=-3.35\times10^4\ kJ\cdot mol^{-1}$，计算消耗这种脂肪 1 kg 时，反应进度是多少？将有多少热量释放出？

解：设油酸甘油酯的摩尔质量为 M，则

$$\begin{aligned} M &= (12\times57+1\times104+16\times6)\ g\cdot mol^{-1} \\ &= 884\ g\cdot mol^{-1} \end{aligned}$$

设消耗这种脂肪 1 kg 时，反应进度为 ξ，则

$$\begin{aligned} \xi &= \frac{1\,000\ g}{884\ g\cdot mol^{-1}} \\ &= 1.13\ mol \end{aligned}$$

根据摩尔反应热的定义式

$$\Delta_r H_m^\ominus=\frac{\Delta_r H^\ominus}{\xi}$$

故

$$\begin{aligned} \Delta_r H^\ominus &= \Delta_r H_m^\ominus\cdot\xi \\ &= -3.35\times10^4\ kJ\cdot mol^{-1}\times1.13\ mol \\ &= -3.79\times10^4\ kJ \end{aligned}$$

即 1 kg 这种脂肪代谢时将有 3.79×10^4 kJ 热量放出。

例 3.2　已知

$C_3H_8(g)+5O_2(g) \xlongequal{} 3CO_2(g)+4H_2O(l)$　　$\Delta_r H_m^\ominus(1)=-2\,220\ kJ\cdot mol^{-1}$

$2H_2O(l) \xlongequal{} 2H_2(g)+O_2(g)$　　$\Delta_r H_m^\ominus(2)=572.0\ kJ\cdot mol^{-1}$

$3C(s)+4H_2(g) \xlongequal{} C_3H_8(g)$　　$\Delta_r H_m^\ominus(3)=-104.5\ kJ\cdot mol^{-1}$

求 $CO_2(g)$ 的 $\Delta_f H_m^\ominus$。

解： 根据物质的标准摩尔生成热的定义，$CO_2(g)$ 的 $\Delta_f H_m^\ominus$ 是指 $CO_2(g)$ 的生成反应

$$C(石墨)+O_2(g) \longrightarrow CO_2(g)$$

的摩尔反应热。

而这一生成反应可由题设给出的反应得到

$$C_3H_8(g)+5O_2(g) \longrightarrow 3CO_2(g)+4H_2O(l) \qquad \times\frac{1}{3}$$

$$2H_2O(l) \longrightarrow 2H_2(g)+O_2(g) \qquad \times\frac{2}{3}$$

$$+)\ 3C(石墨)+4H_2(g) \longrightarrow C_3H_8(g) \qquad \times\frac{1}{3}$$

$$\overline{\qquad C(石墨)+O_2(g) \longrightarrow CO_2(g) \qquad}$$

所以根据 Hess 定律，CO_2 的标准摩尔生成热为

$$\begin{aligned}\Delta_f H_m^\ominus &= \Delta_r H_m^\ominus(1)\times\frac{1}{3}+\Delta_r H_m^\ominus(2)\times\frac{2}{3}+\Delta_r H_m^\ominus(3)\times\frac{1}{3}\\ &=\left[(-2\,220)\times\frac{1}{3}+572.0\times\frac{2}{3}+(-104.5)\times\frac{1}{3}\right]\ \mathrm{kJ\cdot mol^{-1}}\\ &=-393.5\ \mathrm{kJ\cdot mol^{-1}}\end{aligned}$$

例 3.3 已知

$$2MnO_4^-+10Cl^-+16H^+ \longrightarrow 2Mn^{2+}+5Cl_2+8H_2O$$

$$\Delta_r G_m^\ominus(1)=-142.0\ \mathrm{kJ\cdot mol^{-1}}$$

$$Cl_2+2Fe^{2+} \longrightarrow 2Cl^-+2Fe^{3+} \qquad \Delta_r G_m^\ominus(2)=-113.6\ \mathrm{kJ\cdot mol^{-1}}$$

求反应 $MnO_4^-+5Fe^{2+}+8H^+ \longrightarrow Mn^{2+}+5Fe^{3+}+4H_2O$ 的 $\Delta_r G_m^\ominus$。

解： 根据状态函数和状态函数的改变量的性质，由题设

$$2MnO_4^-+10Cl^-+16H^+ \longrightarrow 2Mn^{2+}+5Cl_2+8H_2O$$

$$\Delta_r G_m^\ominus(1)=-142.0\ \mathrm{kJ\cdot mol^{-1}}$$

所以
$$MnO_4^-+5Cl^-+8H^+ \longrightarrow Mn^{2+}+\frac{5}{2}Cl_2+4H_2O$$

$$\Delta_r G_m^\ominus(3)=-71.0\ \mathrm{kJ\cdot mol^{-1}}$$

由题设
$$Cl_2+2Fe^{2+} \longrightarrow 2Cl^-+2Fe^{3+}$$

$$\Delta_r G_m^\ominus(2)=-113.6\ \mathrm{kJ\cdot mol^{-1}}$$

所以
$$\frac{5}{2}Cl_2+5Fe^{2+} \longrightarrow 5Cl^-+5Fe^{3+}$$

$$\Delta_r G_m^\ominus(4)=-284.0\ \mathrm{kJ\cdot mol^{-1}}$$

因为

$$
\begin{array}{rl}
& MnO_4^- + 5Cl^- + 8H^+ \longrightarrow Mn^{2+} + \frac{5}{2}Cl_2 + 4H_2O \\
+) & \frac{5}{2}Cl_2 + 5Fe^{2+} \longrightarrow 5Cl^- + 5Fe^{3+} \\
\hline
& MnO_4^- + 5Fe^{2+} + 8H^+ \longrightarrow Mn^{2+} + 5Fe^{3+} + 4H_2O
\end{array}
$$

所得化学反应的标准摩尔吉布斯自由能改变量为

$$
\begin{aligned}
\Delta_r G_m^\ominus &= \Delta_r G_m^\ominus(3) + \Delta_r G_m^\ominus(4) \\
&= [(-71.0) + (-284.0)]\ \mathrm{kJ\cdot mol^{-1}} \\
&= -355.0\ \mathrm{kJ\cdot mol^{-1}}
\end{aligned}
$$

例 3.4 已知某弹式热量计与其内容物总的热容为 4.633 $\mathrm{kJ\cdot K^{-1}}$，在其中完全燃烧 0.103 g 甲苯 $C_7H_8(l)$ 使热量计升温 0.944 K。求下面恒容反应的热效应 $\Delta_r U_m$。

$$C_7H_8(l) + 9O_2(g) \longrightarrow 7CO_2(g) + 4H_2O(l)$$

解：过程的恒容反应热用 Q_V 表示，热容用 C 表示，依题意 $\Delta T = 0.944$ K，故有

$$
\begin{aligned}
Q_V &= C\Delta T \\
&= 4.633\ \mathrm{kJ\cdot K^{-1}} \times 0.944\ \mathrm{K} \\
&= 4.374\ \mathrm{kJ}
\end{aligned}
$$

即 $\Delta_r U = -4.374$ kJ

根据反应式 $C_7H_8(l) + 9O_2(g) \longrightarrow 7CO_2(g) + 4H_2O(l)$

反应进度

$$
\begin{aligned}
\xi &= \frac{n_0(C_7H_8, l) - n(C_7H_8, l)}{\nu(C_7H_8, l)} \\
&= \frac{\dfrac{m(C_7H_8, l)}{M(C_7H_8, l)}}{\nu(C_7H_8, l)} \\
&= \frac{\dfrac{0.103\ \mathrm{g}}{92\ \mathrm{g\cdot mol^{-1}}}}{1} \\
&= 1.120 \times 10^{-3}\ \mathrm{mol}
\end{aligned}
$$

由 $\Delta_r U_m = \dfrac{\Delta_r U}{\xi}$，将求得的 $\Delta_r U$ 和 ξ 值代入，得

$$
\begin{aligned}
\Delta_r U_m &= \frac{-4.374\ \mathrm{kJ}}{1.120 \times 10^{-3}\ \mathrm{mol}} \\
&= -3\,905.4\ \mathrm{kJ\cdot mol^{-1}}
\end{aligned}
$$

例 3.5 在一弹式热量计中完全燃烧 0.30 mol $H_2(g)$ 生成 $H_2O(l)$，热量计中的水温升高 5.212 K；将 2.345 g 正癸烷 $[C_{10}H_{22}(l)]$ 完全燃烧，使热量计中的水温升高 6.862 K。已知 $H_2O(l)$ 的标准摩尔生成热为 $-285.8\ \mathrm{kJ\cdot mol^{-1}}$，求正癸烷的燃烧热。

解：由题设 $H_2O(l)$ 的标准摩尔生成热为 $-285.8\ \mathrm{kJ\cdot mol^{-1}}$，这相当于已知

$$H_2(g)+\frac{1}{2}O_2(g) \xlongequal{\quad} H_2O(l) \qquad \Delta_r H_m^\ominus=-285.8\ \text{kJ·mol}^{-1}$$

$H_2(g)$在弹式热量计中燃烧反应是恒容反应，其热效应为 $\Delta_r U_m^\ominus$，由

$$\Delta_r H_m^\ominus=\Delta_r U_m^\ominus+\Delta\nu RT$$

得 $\Delta_r U_m^\ominus=\Delta_r H_m^\ominus-\Delta\nu RT$

$$=-285.8\times1\,000\ \text{J·mol}^{-1}-\left(-\frac{3}{2}\right)\times8.314\ \text{J·mol}^{-1}\text{·K}^{-1}\times298\ \text{K}$$

$$=-282.08\ \text{kJ·mol}^{-1}$$

由 0.30 mol $H_2(g)$完全燃烧，知反应进度 $\xi=0.30$ mol，则

$$\begin{aligned}\Delta_r U^\ominus&=\Delta_r U_m^\ominus\cdot\xi\\&=-282.08\ \text{kJ·mol}^{-1}\times0.30\ \text{mol}\\&=-84.624\ \text{kJ}\end{aligned}$$

即 84.624 kJ 热量使热量计的水温升高 5.212 K，由题设 2.345 g 正癸烷($C_{10}H_{22}$)燃烧使热量计的水温升高 6.862 K，可知其燃烧放热为

$$-84.624\ \text{kJ}\times\frac{6.862\ \text{K}}{5.212\ \text{K}}=-111.41\ \text{kJ}$$

即热反应式

$$C_{10}H_{22}(l)+\frac{31}{2}O_2(g) \xlongequal{\Delta V=0} 10\ CO_2(g)+11\ H_2O(l)$$

完全燃烧 2.345 g 正癸烷时，$\Delta_r U^\ominus=-111.41$ kJ。

正癸烷($C_{10}H_{22}$)的摩尔质量为 142 g·mol^{-1}，故

$$n=\frac{2.345\ \text{g}}{142\ \text{g·mol}^{-1}}=0.016\,51\ \text{mol}$$

即完全燃烧 2.345 g 正癸烷，$\xi=0.016\,51$ mol，则

$$\begin{aligned}\Delta_r U_m^\ominus&=\frac{\Delta_r U^\ominus}{\xi}\\&=\frac{-111.41\ \text{kJ}}{0.016\,51\ \text{mol}}\\&=-6\,748.03\ \text{kJ·mol}^{-1}\end{aligned}$$

燃烧热为恒压反应热效应，故

$\Delta_r H_m^\ominus=\Delta_r U_m^\ominus+\Delta\nu RT$

$$=-6\,748.03\times1\,000\ \text{J·mol}^{-1}+\left(-\frac{11}{2}\right)\times8.314\ \text{J·mol}^{-1}\text{·K}^{-1}\times298\ \text{K}$$

$$=-6\,761.7\ \text{kJ·mol}^{-1}$$

这就是正癸烷($C_{10}H_{22}$)的燃烧热。

例 3.6　1 g $C_2H_2(g)$在 298 K 的恒容条件下完全燃烧放出的热量为 50.1 kJ，求该温度下 C_2H_2 的标准摩尔燃烧热 $\Delta_c H_m^{\ominus}$。已知 $H_2(g)$和 C(石墨)的标准摩尔燃烧热分别为$-285.83\ kJ\cdot mol^{-1}$和$-393.51\ kJ\cdot mol^{-1}$。求 $C_2H_2(g)$的标准摩尔生成热。

解：由题设 1 g $C_2H_2(g)$恒容燃烧放热 50.1 kJ，而 $M(C_2H_2)=26\ g\cdot mol^{-1}$，故 1 mol $C_2H_2(g)$恒容燃烧时放热为

$$50.1\ kJ\times 26=1\,302.6\ kJ$$

即反应

$$C_2H_2(g)+\frac{5}{2}O_2(g)\xlongequal{\Delta V=0}2CO_2(g)+H_2O(l)$$

的恒容反应热　$\Delta_r U_m^{\ominus}=-1\,302.6\ kJ\cdot mol^{-1}$

而

$$C_2H_2(g)+\frac{5}{2}O_2(g)\xlongequal{\quad}2CO_2(g)+H_2O(l)$$

的恒压反应热 $\Delta_r H_m^{\ominus}$，才是 $C_2H_2(g)$的燃烧热 $\Delta_c H_m^{\ominus}(C_2H_2,g)$，即

$$\begin{aligned}&\Delta_c H_m^{\ominus}(C_2H_2,g)\\&=\Delta_r H_m^{\ominus}=\Delta_r U_m^{\ominus}+\Delta\nu RT\\&=-1\,302.6\times 1\,000\ J\cdot mol^{-1}+\left(-\frac{3}{2}\right)\times 8.314\ J\cdot mol^{-1}\cdot K^{-1}\times 298\ K\\&=-1\,306.3\ kJ\cdot mol^{-1}\end{aligned}$$

由题设知

$$\Delta_c H_m^{\ominus}(H_2,g)=-285.83\ kJ\cdot mol^{-1}$$

$$\Delta_c H_m^{\ominus}(C,石墨)=-393.5\ kJ\cdot mol^{-1}$$

$C_2H_2(g)$的生成反应为

$$2C(石墨)+H_2(g)\xlongequal{\quad}C_2H_2(g)$$

根据由燃烧热求反应热的公式得

$$\begin{aligned}\Delta_r H_m^{\ominus}&=\sum\nu_i\Delta_c H_m^{\ominus}(反应物)-\sum\nu_i\Delta_c H_m^{\ominus}(生成物)\\&=2\Delta_c H_m^{\ominus}(C,石墨)+\Delta_c H_m^{\ominus}(H_2,g)-\Delta_c H_m^{\ominus}(C_2H_2,g)\\&=[(-393.5)\times 2+(-285.83)\times 1-(-1\,306.3)\times 1]\ kJ\cdot mol^{-1}\\&=233.5\ kJ\cdot mol^{-1}\end{aligned}$$

例 3.7　产生水煤气的反应为 $C(s)+H_2O(g)\xlongequal{\quad}CO(g)+H_2(g)$，各气体分压均处在 1.013×10^5 Pa 下，体系达到平衡，求体系的温度。已知 $\Delta_f H_m^{\ominus}(H_2O,g)=-241.82\ kJ\cdot mol^{-1}$，$\Delta_f H_m^{\ominus}(CO,g)=-110.52\ kJ\cdot mol^{-1}$，$\Delta_f G_m^{\ominus}(H_2O,g)=-228.59\ kJ\cdot mol^{-1}$，$\Delta_f G_m^{\ominus}(CO,g)=-137.15\ kJ\cdot mol^{-1}$。

解：$\Delta_r H_m^{\ominus}=\sum_i\nu_i\Delta_f H_m^{\ominus}(生成物)-\sum_i\nu_i\Delta_f H_m^{\ominus}(反应物)$

$$=-110.52\ kJ\cdot mol^{-1}-(-241.82\ kJ\cdot mol^{-1})$$

$$=131.30\ \text{kJ·mol}^{-1}$$

同理，$\Delta_r G_m^\ominus = -137.15\ \text{kJ·mol}^{-1} - (-228.59\ \text{kJ·mol}^{-1}) = 91.44\ \text{kJ·mol}^{-1}$

由

$$\Delta_r G_m^\ominus = \Delta_r H_m^\ominus - T\Delta_r S_m^\ominus$$

$$\Delta_r S_m^\ominus = \frac{\Delta_r H_m^\ominus - \Delta_r G_m^\ominus}{T} = \frac{(131.30-91.44)\times 10^3\ \text{J·mol}^{-1}}{298\ \text{K}} = 133.76\ \text{J·mol}^{-1}\text{·K}^{-1}$$

$\Delta_r H$ 和 $\Delta_r S$ 随温度变化较小，可近似认为 $\Delta_r H$ 和 $\Delta_r S$ 不随温度变化而变化。反应达平衡时，$\Delta_r G_m^\ominus = 0 = \Delta_r H_m^\ominus - T\Delta_r S_m^\ominus$，故

$$T = \frac{\Delta_r H_m^\ominus}{\Delta_r S_m^\ominus} = \frac{131.30\ \text{kJ·mol}^{-1}}{133.76\times 10^{-3}\ \text{kJ·mol}^{-1}\text{·K}^{-1}} = 981.6\ \text{K}$$

例 3.8 已知 $\Delta_f H_m^\ominus(NH_3, g) = -46\ \text{kJ·mol}^{-1}$，$\Delta_f H_m^\ominus(H_2N—NH_2, g) = 95\ \text{kJ·mol}^{-1}$，$E(H—H) = 436\ \text{kJ·mol}^{-1}$，$E(N—H) = 391\ \text{kJ·mol}^{-1}$。求 $E(N—N)$。

解：由题设条件可知

(1) $\frac{1}{2}N_2(g) + \frac{3}{2}H_2(g) \xlongequal{} NH_3(g)$ $\qquad \Delta_r H_m^\ominus(1) = -46\ \text{kJ·mol}^{-1}$

(2) $N_2(g) + 2H_2(g) \xlongequal{} H_2N—NH_2(g)$ $\qquad \Delta_r H_m^\ominus(2) = 95\ \text{kJ·mol}^{-1}$

(1)×2−(2)×1 得

(3) $H_2(g) + H_2N—NH_2 \xlongequal{} 2NH_3(g)$

$$\begin{aligned}\Delta_r H_m^\ominus(3) &= \Delta_r H_m^\ominus(1)\times 2 - \Delta_r H_m^\ominus(2)\\ &= (-46\times 2 - 95)\ \text{kJ·mol}^{-1}\\ &= -187\ \text{kJ·mol}^{-1}\end{aligned}$$

根据键能与反应热的关系，有

$$\Delta_r H_m^\ominus(3) = E(H—H) + E(N—N) + 4E(N—H) - 6E(N—H)$$

所以

$$\begin{aligned}E(N—N) &= \Delta_r H_m^\ominus(3) - E(H—H) + 2E(N—H)\\ &= (-187 - 436 + 391\times 2)\ \text{kJ·mol}^{-1}\\ &= 159\ \text{kJ·mol}^{-1}\end{aligned}$$

例 3.9 利用下面热力学数据计算反应

$$CuS(s) + H_2(g) \xlongequal{} Cu(s) + H_2S(g)$$

可以发生的最低温度。

	$\Delta_f H_m^\ominus/(\text{kJ·mol}^{-1})$	$S_m^\ominus/(\text{J·mol}^{-1}\text{·K}^{-1})$
CuS(s)	−53.1	66.5
$H_2(g)$	0	130.57
$H_2S(g)$	−20.6	205.7
Cu(s)	0	33.15

解：反应的 $\Delta_r H_m^\ominus$ 和 $\Delta_r S_m^\ominus$ 可以由已知数据求出

$$\Delta_r H_m^\ominus = \Delta_f H_m^\ominus(H_2S,g) - \Delta_f H_m^\ominus(CuS,s)$$
$$= [-20.6-(-53.1)]\ kJ\cdot mol^{-1}$$
$$= 32.5\ kJ\cdot mol^{-1}$$

$$\Delta_r S_m^\ominus = S_m^\ominus(H_2S,g) + S_m^\ominus(Cu,s) - S_m^\ominus(CuS,s) - S_m^\ominus(H_2,g)$$
$$= (205.8+33.2-66.5-130.7)\ J\cdot mol^{-1}\cdot K^{-1}$$
$$= 41.8\ J\cdot mol^{-1}\cdot K^{-1}$$

$$\Delta_r G_m^\ominus = \Delta_r H_m^\ominus - T\Delta_r S_m^\ominus$$

当反应可以可逆进行时，$\Delta_r G_m^\ominus = 0$，即

$$\Delta_r H_m^\ominus = T\Delta_r S_m^\ominus$$

$$T = \frac{\Delta_r H_m^\ominus}{\Delta_r S_m^\ominus} = \frac{32.5\times 1\,000\ J\cdot mol^{-1}}{41.8\ J\cdot mol^{-1}\cdot K^{-1}} = 778\ K$$

当 $T>778$ K 时，反应即可发生。

例 3.10　用 CaO(s)吸收高炉废气中的 SO_3 气体，其反应方程式为

$$CaO(s) + SO_3(g) = CaSO_4(s)$$

根据下列数据计算该反应 373 K 时的 $\Delta_r G_m^\ominus$，说明反应进行的可能性；并计算反应逆转的温度，进一步说明应用此反应防止 SO_3 污染环境的合理性。

	$CaSO_4(s)$	$CaO(s)$	$SO_3(g)$
$\Delta_f H_m^\ominus/(kJ\cdot mol^{-1})$	$-1\,434.5$	-634.9	-395.7
$S_m^\ominus/(J\cdot mol^{-1}\cdot K^{-1})$	106.5	38.1	256.8

解：根据题设数据，可求出反应

$$CaO(s) + SO_3(g) = CaSO_4(s)$$

的 $\Delta_r H_m^\ominus$ 和 $\Delta_r S_m^\ominus$。

$$\Delta_r H_m^\ominus = \Delta_f H_m^\ominus(CaSO_4,s) - \Delta_f H_m^\ominus(CaO,s) - \Delta_f H_m^\ominus(SO_3,g)$$
$$= [-1\,434.5-(-634.9)-(-395.7)]\ kJ\cdot mol^{-1}$$
$$= -403.9\ kJ\cdot mol^{-1}$$

$$\Delta_r S_m^\ominus = S_m^\ominus(CaSO_4,s) - S_m^\ominus(CaO,s) - S_m^\ominus(SO_3,g)$$
$$= [106.5-38.1-256.8]\ J\cdot mol^{-1}\cdot K^{-1}$$
$$= -188.4\ J\cdot mol^{-1}\cdot K^{-1}$$

373 K 时

$$\Delta_r G_m^\ominus = \Delta_r H_m^\ominus - T\Delta_r S_m^\ominus$$
$$= -403.9\times 1\,000\ J\cdot mol^{-1} - 373\ K\times(-188.4\ J\cdot mol^{-1}\cdot K^{-1})$$
$$= -333.6\ kJ\cdot mol^{-1}$$

由于 $\Delta_r G_m^\ominus < 0$,故反应可以自发进行。

这是个放热反应,升高温度时有利于向 $CaSO_4$ 分解方向进行。当 $\Delta_r G_m^\ominus = 0$ 时,反应将以可逆方式进行,这时

$$\Delta_r H_m^\ominus = T\Delta_r S_m^\ominus$$

故

$$T = \frac{\Delta_r H_m^\ominus}{\Delta_r S_m^\ominus} = \frac{-403.9\times 1\,000\ \text{J}\cdot\text{mol}^{-1}}{-188.4\ \text{J}\cdot\text{mol}^{-1}\cdot\text{K}^{-1}} = 2\,144\ \text{K}$$

只有当温度高于 2 144 K 时,$CaSO_4$ 才能分解,而高炉废气的温度远小于反应

$$CaO(s) + SO_3(g) \xlongequal{} CaSO_4(s)$$

的逆转温度,所以用此反应吸收高炉废气中的 SO_3,以防止其污染环境是合理的。

例 3.11 通过查热力学数据表,估算常压下单质溴(Br_2,l)的沸点。

解: 单质 Br_2 的沸腾过程可表示为

$$Br_2(l) \xlongequal{} Br_2(g)$$

查热力学数据表得

	$\Delta_f H_m^\ominus/(\text{kJ}\cdot\text{mol}^{-1})$	$S_m^\ominus/(\text{J}\cdot\text{mol}^{-1}\cdot\text{K}^{-1})$
$Br_2(l)$	0	152.2
$Br_2(g)$	30.9	245.5

过程的焓变和熵变分别由下列计算求出

$$\begin{aligned}\Delta_r H_m^\ominus &= \Delta_f H_m^\ominus(Br_2,g) - \Delta_f H_m^\ominus(Br_2,l)\\ &= 30.9\ \text{kJ}\cdot\text{mol}^{-1} - 0\ \text{kJ}\cdot\text{mol}^{-1}\\ &= 30.9\ \text{kJ}\cdot\text{mol}^{-1}\end{aligned}$$

$$\begin{aligned}\Delta_r S_m^\ominus &= S_m^\ominus(Br_2,g) - S_m^\ominus(Br_2,l)\\ &= 245.5\ \text{J}\cdot\text{mol}^{-1}\cdot\text{K}^{-1} - 152.2\ \text{J}\cdot\text{mol}^{-1}\cdot\text{K}^{-1}\\ &= 93.3\ \text{J}\cdot\text{mol}^{-1}\cdot\text{K}^{-1}\end{aligned}$$

相变点下的相变可以认为是可逆过程,其 $\Delta_r G = 0$

根据公式 $\Delta_r G = \Delta_r H - T\Delta_r S$,当 $\Delta_r G = 0$ 时,有

$$T = \frac{\Delta_r H}{\Delta_r S}$$

将数据代入上式,得

$$T = \frac{30.9\ \text{kJ}\cdot\text{mol}^{-1}\times 1\,000\ \text{J}\cdot\text{kJ}^{-1}}{93.3\ \text{J}\cdot\text{mol}^{-1}\cdot\text{K}^{-1}}$$

$$=331.2\ \text{K}$$

例 3.12　已知　　$A(g)+B(s) = C(g)+D(s)$

$\Delta_r H=-52.99$ kJ，298 K，100 kPa 下发生反应，体系做了最大功并放热 1.49 kJ。求反应过程的 Q，W，$\Delta_r U$，$\Delta_r S$ 和 $\Delta_r G$。

解：由已知可直接得出 $Q=-1.49$ kJ。

根据题设可以看出，反应

$$A(g)+B(s) = C(g)+D(s)$$

体系做了最大功，所以其方式是可逆的，故热效应为 Q_r。于是

$$\Delta_r S=\frac{Q_r}{T}$$

$$=\frac{-1.49\times 1\,000\ \text{J}}{298\ \text{K}}$$

$$=-5.0\ \text{J}\cdot\text{K}^{-1}$$

$$\Delta_r H=\Delta_r U+\Delta(pV)$$

$$=\Delta_r U+p\Delta V$$

由反应式可以看出，反应前后无体积变化，故 $\Delta V=0$，所以

$$\Delta_r U=\Delta_r H$$

$$=-52.99\ \text{kJ}$$

由热力学第一定律

$$\Delta_r U=Q+W$$

所以

$$W=\Delta_r U-Q$$

$$=-52.99\ \text{kJ}-(-1.49\ \text{kJ})$$

$$=-51.5\ \text{kJ}$$

因为 $\Delta V=0$，无体积功，故过程只有非体积功。在可逆过程中，ΔG 与 $W_{非}$ 之间有如下关系

$$-\Delta_r G=-W_{非}$$

故

$$\Delta_r G=W_{非}=-51.5\ \text{kJ}$$

$\Delta_r G$ 也可以根据 $\Delta_r H$ 和 $T\Delta_r S$ 求出

$$\Delta_r G=\Delta_r H-T\Delta_r S$$

$$=-52.99\times 1\,000\ \text{J}-298\ \text{K}\times(-5.0\ \text{J}\cdot\text{K}^{-1})$$

$$=-51.5\ \text{kJ}$$

第二部分 习题

一、选择题

3.1 下列物质中，$\Delta_f H_m^\ominus$ 不等于零的是

(A) Fe(s)；　(B) C(石墨)；　(C) Ne(g)；　(D) Cl_2(l)。

3.2 已知 $\Delta_c H_m^\ominus$(C,石墨)＝－393.7 kJ·mol^{-1}，$\Delta_c H_m^\ominus$(C,金刚石)＝－395.6 kJ·mol^{-1}，则 $\Delta_f H_m^\ominus$(C,金刚石)为

(A) －789.5 kJ·mol^{-1}；　(B) 1.9 kJ·mol^{-1}；

(C) －1.9 kJ·mol^{-1}；　(D) 789.5 kJ·mol^{-1}。

3.3 已知在 298 K 时反应 $2N_2(g)+O_2(g) = 2N_2O(g)$ 的 $\Delta_r U_m^\ominus$ 为 166.5 kJ·mol^{-1}，则该反应的 $\Delta_r H_m^\ominus$ 为

(A) 164 kJ·mol^{-1}；　(B) 328 kJ·mol^{-1}；

(C) 146 kJ·mol^{-1}；　(D) 82 kJ·mol^{-1}。

3.4 已知键能数据

	C=C	C—C	C—H	H—H
E/(kJ·mol^{-1})	610	346	413	435

则反应 $C_2H_4(g)+H_2(g) = C_2H_6(g)$ 的 $\Delta_r H_m^\ominus$(kJ·mol^{-1})为

(A) 127；　(B) －127；　(C) 54；　(D) 172。

3.5 将固体 NH_4NO_3 溶于水中，溶液变冷，则该过程的 ΔG,ΔH,ΔS 的符号依次是

(A) ＋,－,－；　(B) ＋,＋,－；　(C) －,＋,－；　(D) －,＋,＋。

3.6 已知 $MnO_2(s) = MnO(s)+\frac{1}{2}O_2(g)$　$\Delta_r H_m^\ominus = 134.8$ kJ·mol^{-1}

$MnO_2(s)+Mn(s) = 2MnO(s)$　$\Delta_r H_m^\ominus = -250.1$ kJ·mol^{-1}

则 MnO_2 的标准摩尔生成热 $\Delta_f H_m^\ominus$ 为

(A) 519.7 kJ·mol^{-1}；　(B) －317.5 kJ·mol^{-1}；

(C) －519.7 kJ·mol^{-1}；　(D) 317.5 kJ·mol^{-1}。

3.7 冰的熔化热为 330.5 J·g^{-1}，0℃时将 1.0 g 水凝结为冰时的 ΔS 为

(A) －330.5 J·K^{-1}；(B) －1.21 J·K^{-1}；　(C) 0；　(D) 1.21 J·K^{-1}。

3.8 下列反应中，$\Delta_r H_m^\ominus$ 与产物的 $\Delta_f H_m^\ominus$ 相同的是

(A) $2H_2(g)+O_2(g) \longrightarrow 2H_2O(l)$；　(B) $NO(g)+\frac{1}{2}O_2(g) \longrightarrow NO_2(g)$；

(C) C(金刚石) ⟶ C(石墨)；　(D) $H_2(g)+\frac{1}{2}O_2(g) \longrightarrow H_2O(g)$。

3.9 下列物质中，标准摩尔熵最大的是

(A) MgF_2；　(B) MgO；　(C) $MgSO_4$；　(D) $MgCO_3$。

3.10 下列反应中，$\Delta_r S_m^\ominus$ 最大的是

(A) $C(s)+O_2(g) \longrightarrow CO_2(g)$；

(B) $2SO_2(g)+O_2(g) \longrightarrow 2SO_3(g)$；

(C) $3H_2(g)+N_2(g) \longrightarrow 2NH_3(g)$；

(D) $CuSO_4(s)+5H_2O(l) \longrightarrow CuSO_4\cdot 5H_2O(s)$。

3.11 下列反应在常温下均为非自发反应，在高温下仍为非自发的是

(A) $Ag_2O(s) \longrightarrow 2Ag(s)+\frac{1}{2}O_2(g)$；

(B) $Fe_2O_3(s)+\frac{3}{2}C(s) \longrightarrow 2Fe(s)+\frac{3}{2}CO_2(g)$；

(C) $N_2O_4(g) \longrightarrow 2NO_2(g)$；

(D) $6C(s)+6H_2O(g) \longrightarrow C_6H_{12}O_6(s)$。

3.12 液体沸腾过程中，下列几种物理量中数值增加的是

(A) 蒸气压； (B) 标准摩尔自由能； (C) 标准摩尔熵； (D) 液体质量。

3.13 下列过程中，$\Delta G=0$ 的是

(A) 氨在水中解离达平衡； (B) 理想气体向真空膨胀；

(C) 乙醇溶于水； (D) 炸药爆炸。

3.14 已知反应 $A_2(g)+2B_2(g) = 3C_2(g)$ 在恒压和温度 1 000 K 时的 $\Delta_r H_m$ 为 40 kJ·mol^{-1}，$\Delta_r S_m$ 为 40 J·mol^{-1}·K^{-1}，则下列关系中正确的是

(A) $\Delta_r U_m=\Delta_r H_m$； (B) $\Delta_r G_m=0$；

(C) $\Delta_r U_m=T\Delta_r S_m$； (D) 所有关系都正确。

二、填空题

3.15 2 mol Hg(l)在沸点温度(630 K)蒸发过程中所吸收的热量为 109.12 kJ。则汞的标准摩尔蒸发热 $\Delta_{vap}H_m^{\ominus}=$______；该过程对环境做功 $W=$______，$\Delta U=$______，$\Delta S=$______，$\Delta G=$______。

3.16 有 A,B,C,D 四个反应，在 298 K 时反应的热力学函数分别为

反 应	A	B	C	D
$\Delta_r H_m^{\ominus}/(kJ\cdot mol^{-1})$	10.5	1.80	−126	−11.7
$\Delta_r S_m^{\ominus}/(J\cdot mol^{-1}\cdot K^{-1})$	30.0	−113	84.0	−105

则在标准状态下，任何温度都能自发进行的反应是____，任何温度都不能自发进行的反应是____；另两个反应中，在温度高于____℃时可自发进行的反应是____，在温度低于__℃时可自发进行的反应是______。

3.17 1 mol 液态的苯完全燃烧生成 $CO_2(g)$ 和 $H_2O(l)$，则该反应的 Q_p 与 Q_V 的差值为__________kJ(温度 25 ℃)。

3.18 已知 25℃时，$\Delta_f H_m^{\ominus}(Br_2,g)=30.71$ kJ·mol^{-1}，$\Delta_f G_m^{\ominus}(Br_2,g)=3.14$ kJ·mol^{-1}，则 $Br_2(l)$ 的标准摩尔蒸发熵为________J·mol^{-1}·K^{-1}，正常沸点为______℃。

3.19 反应 $2HgO(s) = 2Hg(l)+O_2(g)$ $\Delta_r H_m^{\ominus}=181.4$ kJ·mol^{-1}，则 $\Delta_f H_m^{\ominus}(HgO,s)=$

________。已知 $A_r(Hg)=201$，生成 1 g Hg(l)的焓变是____________kJ。

3.20 已知反应 $CaCO_3(s) \longrightarrow CaO(s)+CO_2(g)$ 在 298 K 时 $\Delta_r G_m^\ominus=130\ kJ\cdot mol^{-1}$，1 200 K 时 $\Delta_r G_m^\ominus=-15.3\ kJ\cdot mol^{-1}$，则该反应的 $\Delta_r H_m^\ominus$ 为____________，$\Delta_r S_m^\ominus$ 为____________。

3.21 将下列物质按摩尔熵值由小到大排列，其顺序为____________________。
LiCl(s)， Li(s)， $Cl_2(g)$， $I_2(g)$， Ne(g)。

3.22 在25℃时，NaCl 在水中的溶解度为 6 $mol\cdot dm^{-3}$，在此温度下，若将 100 g NaCl 置于500 g 水中，则 NaCl 溶解过程的 $\Delta_r G$ ____ 0，$\Delta_r S$ ____ 0(填>或<号)。

3.23 若 3 mol 理想气体向真空膨胀，该过程的 $Q,W,\Delta U,\Delta H,\Delta S,\Delta G$ 中不为零的是______。

三、简答题和计算题

3.24 反应 $N_2(g)+3H_2(g) \longrightarrow 2NH_3(g)$ 在恒容热量器内进行，生成 2 mol NH_3 时放热 82.7 kJ，求反应的 $\Delta_r H_m^\ominus$。

3.25 制水煤气是将水蒸气从红热的煤中通过，有下列反应发生

$$C(s)+H_2O(g) \longrightarrow CO(g)+H_2(g)$$

$$CO(g)+H_2O(g) \longrightarrow CO_2(g)+H_2(g)$$

将此混合气体冷至室温即得水煤气，其中含有 CO，H_2 及少量 CO_2(水蒸气可忽略不计)。若 C 有 95%转化为 CO，5%转化为 CO_2，则 1 dm^3 此种水煤气燃烧产生的热量是多少(燃烧产物都是气体)？已知

	CO(g)	$CO_2(g)$	$H_2O(g)$
$\Delta_f H_m^\ominus/(kJ\cdot mol^{-1})$	−110.5	−393.5	−241.8

3.26 在一只弹式热量计中燃烧 0.20 mol $H_2(g)$ 生成 $H_2O(l)$，使热量计温度升高 0.88 K，当 0.010 mol 甲苯在此热量计中燃烧时，热量计温度升高 0.615 K，甲苯的燃烧反应为

$$C_7H_8(l)+9O_2(g) \longrightarrow 7CO_2(g)+4H_2O(l)$$

求该反应的 $\Delta_r H_m^\ominus$。已知 $\Delta_f H_m^\ominus(H_2O,l)=-285.8\ kJ\cdot mol^{-1}$。

3.27 已知丙烯 $C_3H_6(g)$ 的标准摩尔燃烧热 $\Delta_c H_m^\ominus=-2\,058.0\ kJ\cdot mol^{-1}$，求恒容反应

$$C_3H_6(g)+\frac{9}{2}O_2(g) \longrightarrow 3CO_2(g)+3H_2O(l)$$

的热效应。

3.28 阿波罗登月火箭用联氨(N_2H_4，l)作燃料，用 $N_2O_4(g)$ 作氧化剂，燃烧产物为 $N_2(g)$ 和 $H_2O(l)$。计算燃烧 1.0 kg 联氨所放出的热量，反应在 300 K，101.3 kPa 下进行，需要多少升 $N_2O_4(g)$？已知

	$N_2H_4(l)$	$N_2O_4(g)$	$H_2O(l)$
$\Delta_f H_m^\ominus/(kJ\cdot mol^{-1})$	50.6	9.16	−285.8

3.29 已知

$$2C(石墨)+O_2(g) \longrightarrow 2CO(g) \qquad \Delta_r H_m^\ominus(1)=-222\ kJ\cdot mol^{-1}$$

$$2H_2O(g) \longrightarrow O_2(g)+2H_2(g) \qquad \Delta_r H_m^\ominus(2)=484\ kJ\cdot mol^{-1}$$

$CO(g)+H_2O(g) \xlongequal{} CO_2(g)+H_2(g) \qquad \Delta_r H_m^{\ominus}(3)=-41\ kJ\cdot mol^{-1}$

求反应 $CO_2(g) \xlongequal{}$ C(石墨)$+O_2(g)$的 $\Delta_r H_m^{\ominus}$。

3.30 已知下列反应的热效应：

(1) $Fe_2O_3(s)+3CO(g) \longrightarrow 2Fe(s)+3CO_2(g) \qquad \Delta_r H_m^{\ominus}(1)=-27.61\ kJ\cdot mol^{-1}$

(2) $3Fe_2O_3(s)+CO(g) \longrightarrow 2Fe_3O_4(s)+CO_2(g) \qquad \Delta_r H_m^{\ominus}(2)=-58.58\ kJ\cdot mol^{-1}$

(3) $Fe_3O_4(s)+CO(g) \longrightarrow 3FeO(s)+CO_2(g) \qquad \Delta_r H_m^{\ominus}(3)=38.07\ kJ\cdot mol^{-1}$

求下面反应的反应热 $\Delta_r H_m^{\ominus}(4)$。

(4) $FeO(s)+CO(g) \longrightarrow Fe(s)+CO_2(g)$

3.31 试举例说明在什么情况下 $\Delta_r H_m^{\ominus}$，$\Delta_f H_m^{\ominus}$ 和 $\Delta_c H_m^{\ominus}$ 的数值相等。

3.32 已知 $CS_2(l)$在 101.3 kPa 和沸点温度(319.3 K)汽化时吸热 352 $J\cdot g^{-1}$，求 1 mol $CS_2(l)$ 在沸点温度汽化过程的 ΔH，ΔU 和 ΔS。

3.33 已知：液态甲醇氧化生成气态甲醛的反应焓变是 $-155.4\ kJ\cdot mol^{-1}$，气态甲醛恒容燃烧热为 $568.2\ kJ\cdot mol^{-1}$，$\Delta_f H_m^{\ominus}(CO_2,g)=-393.5\ kJ\cdot mol^{-1}$，$\Delta_f H_m^{\ominus}(H_2O,l)=-285.8\ kJ\cdot mol^{-1}$

试求：(1) 甲醇的燃烧热；

(2) 甲醇的生成热。

3.34 在 298 K 时，CS_2 的摩尔蒸发热 $\Delta_{vap} H_m^{\ominus}$ 为 $27.7\ kJ\cdot mol^{-1}$，$CS_2(l)$的标准熵 $S_m^{\ominus}$ 为 $151.3\ J\cdot mol^{-1}\cdot K^{-1}$，试求该温度条件下平衡时气态 CS_2 的标准熵 $S_m^{\ominus}(CS_2,g)$。

3.35 已知：$C_2H_4(g)$，C(s)，$H_2(g)$的燃烧热分别为 $-1\,411.2\ kJ\cdot mol^{-1}$，$-393.5\ kJ\cdot mol^{-1}$ 和 $-285.8\ kJ\cdot mol^{-1}$，试求

(1) $C_2H_4(g)$，$H_2(g)$，C(s)的燃烧反应的热化学反应方程式；

(2) $C_2H_4(g)$标准摩尔生成热。

3.36 已知下列数据：

$\Delta_f H_m^{\ominus}$(Sn,白)$=0$，　　$\Delta_f H_m^{\ominus}$(Sn,灰)$=-2.1\ kJ\cdot mol^{-1}$

$S_m^{\ominus}$(Sn,白)$=51.5\ J\cdot mol^{-1}\cdot K^{-1}$，$S_m^{\ominus}$(Sn,灰)$=44.3\ J\cdot mol^{-1}\cdot K^{-1}$

求 Sn(白) $\rightleftharpoons$ Sn(灰)的相变温度。

3.37 已知下列键能数据

键	N≡N	N—Cl	N—H	Cl—Cl	Cl—H	H—H
$E/(kJ\cdot mol^{-1})$	945	201	389	243	431	436

(1) 求反应 $2NH_3(g)+3Cl_2(g) \xlongequal{} N_2(g)+6HCl(g)$的 $\Delta_r H_m^{\ominus}$；

(2) 由标准生成热判断 $NCl_3(g)$和 $NH_3(g)$相对稳定性。

3.38 已知 $S_m^{\ominus}$(石墨)$=5.740\ J\cdot mol^{-1}\cdot K^{-1}$，$\Delta_f H_m^{\ominus}$(金刚石)$=1.897\ kJ\cdot mol^{-1}$，$\Delta_f G_m^{\ominus}$(金刚石)$=2.900\ kJ\cdot mol^{-1}$。根据计算结果说明石墨和金刚石的相对有序程度。

3.39 反应　　$2H_2(g)+O_2(g) \xlongequal{} 2H_2O(g)$

在氢能源的利用中具有重要的意义。根据下面的热力学数据计算 1 000 K，标准状态下，每克氢气最多可做多少非体积功？

	$H_2(g)$	$O_2(g)$	$H_2O(g)$
$\Delta_f H_m^{\ominus}/(kJ \cdot mol^{-1})$			-241.8
$S_m^{\ominus}/(J \cdot mol^{-1} \cdot K^{-1})$	130.7	205.2	188.8

第4章

化学反应速率

第一部分 例题

例 4.1 某温度下乙醛分解反应为

$$CH_3CHO(g) \longrightarrow CH_4(g) + CO(g)$$

根据下列实验数据：

t/s	42	105	242	384	665	1070
c(乙醛)/(10^{-3} mol·dm^{-3})	6.68	5.85	4.64	3.83	2.81	2.01

(1) 分别求算 42 s 到 242 s 和 242 s 到 665 s 时间间隔的平均反应速率，并说明两者大小不等的原因；

(2) 利用作图法求出 $t=100$ s 时的瞬时速率。

解：(1)

$$\bar{r}_1 = -\frac{\Delta_1 c}{\Delta_1 t} = -\frac{(4.64-6.68)\times10^{-3}\ \text{mol·dm}^{-3}}{(242-42)\ \text{s}} = 1.0\times10^{-5}\ \text{mol·dm}^{-3}\text{·s}^{-1}$$

$$\bar{r}_2 = -\frac{\Delta_2 c}{\Delta_2 t} = -\frac{(2.81-4.64)\times10^{-3}\ \text{mol·dm}^{-3}}{(665-242)\ \text{s}} = 4.3\times10^{-6}\ \text{mol·dm}^{-3}\text{·s}^{-1}$$

反应速率 $\bar{r}$ 正比于反应物浓度 c，在 242～665 s 时间间隔中反应物浓度远小于 42～242 s 的时间间隔中反应物的浓度，故平均反应速率 $\bar{r}_2<\bar{r}_1$。

(2) 根据题设中给出的数据，作 c-t 图，如图所示。

在曲线上 $t=100$ s 处作曲线的切线 l，利用直角三角形 ABC 求出 l 的斜率。

$$l\text{ 的斜率}=\frac{AC}{CB}$$

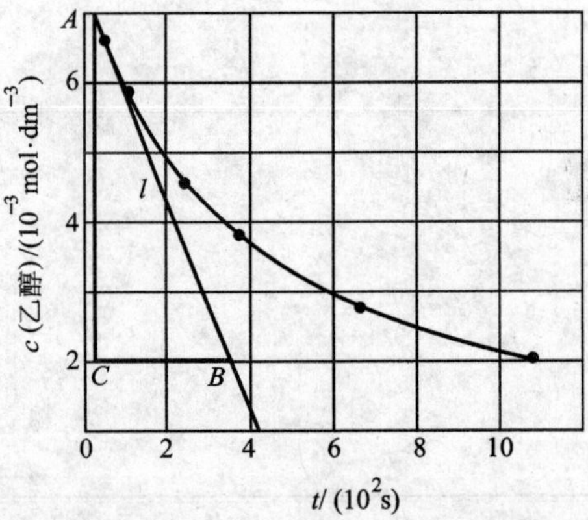

$$=\frac{(7-2)\times 10^{-3}\,\text{mol}\cdot\text{dm}^{-3}}{(3.5-0.2)\times 10^{2}\ \text{s}}$$

$$=1.5\times 10^{-5}\ \text{mol}\cdot\text{dm}^{-3}\cdot\text{s}^{-1}$$

即 $t=100$ s 时，反应速率为 1.5×10^{-5} mol·dm^{-3}·s^{-1}。

例 4.2 反应 $H_2(g)+I_2(g) \xlongequal{} 2HI(g)$可能有如下三个基元反应步骤：

① $I_2 \xlongequal{} I+I$

② $I+I \xlongequal{} I_2$

③ $H_2+2I \xlongequal{} 2HI$

试对每个基元反应步骤分别写出其速率方程，指出每个基元反应的反应级数和反应分子数并写出每个速率常数的单位。

解： ① $\bar{r}=k_1c(I_2)$，一级反应，单分子反应，k_1 的单位为 s^{-1}。

② $\bar{r}=k_2c(I)^2$，二级反应，双分子反应，k_2 的单位为 dm^3·mol^{-1}·s^{-1}。

③ $\bar{r}=k_3c(H_2)\cdot c(I)^2$，三级反应，三分子反应，$k_3$ 的单位为 dm^6·mol^{-2}·s^{-1}。

例 4.3 有人对反应 $C_2H_6+H_2 \longrightarrow 2CH_4$ 提出如下机理

① $C_2H_6 \rightleftharpoons 2CH_3$　　K

② $CH_3+H_2 \longrightarrow CH_4+H$　　k_2

③ $H+C_2H_6 \longrightarrow CH_4+CH_3$　　k_3

试用稳态近似法和平衡假设法推导生成 CH_4 的速率方程微分表达式，并用已知数据表示速率常数 k。

解： 反应②和反应③均生成 CH_4，故

$$\frac{d[CH_4]}{dt}=k_2[CH_3][H_2]+k_3[H][C_2H_6] \tag{1}$$

同时反应②为中间产物 H 的形成反应，而反应③为中间产物 H 的消耗反应，根据稳态近似法，反应②和反应③的速率相等，即

$$\frac{d[H]}{dt}=k_2[CH_3][H_2]$$

$$-\frac{d[H]}{dt}=k_3[H][C_2H_6]$$

$$k_2[CH_3][H_2]=k_3[H][C_2H_6]$$

式(1)变成

$$\frac{d[CH_4]}{dt}=2k_2[CH_3][H_2] \tag{2}$$

由题设的平衡条件,有

$$K=\frac{[CH_3]^2}{[C_2H_6]}$$

$$[CH_3]=K^{\frac{1}{2}}[C_2H_6]^{\frac{1}{2}}$$

将其代入式(2)

$$\frac{d[CH_4]}{dt}=2k_2K^{\frac{1}{2}}[H_2][C_2H_6]^{\frac{1}{2}}$$

令 $k=2k_2K^{\frac{1}{2}}$,则生成 CH_4 的速率方程为

$$\frac{d[CH_4]}{dt}=k[H_2][C_2H_6]^{\frac{1}{2}}$$

而其中速率常数 $k=2k_2K^{\frac{1}{2}}$。

例 4.4　说明可逆反应的速率常数 k_+,k_- 与其平衡常数 K 之间关系。若已知某温度下氢氟酸的解离反应

$$HF(aq) = H^+(aq)+F^-(aq)$$

的平衡常数为 $7.08\times10^{-4}\,mol\cdot dm^{-3}$。又已知基元反应

$$H^+(aq)+F^-(aq) = HF(aq)$$

的速率常数为 $1.00\times10^{11}\,dm^3\cdot mol^{-1}\cdot s^{-1}$,求氢氟酸解离反应的速率常数。

解: 对于可逆基元反应

$$aA \rightleftharpoons bB$$

$$r_+=k_+[A]^a$$

$$r_-=k_-[B]^b$$

当反应达到平衡时,$r_+=r_-$,故

$$k_+[A]^a_{平}=k_-[B]^b_{平}$$

所以

$$\frac{[B]^b_{平}}{[A]^a_{平}}=\frac{k_+}{k_-}$$

即

$$K=\frac{k_+}{k_-}$$

题中涉及的两个反应,根据微观可逆性原理,皆为基元反应。设反应

$$HF(aq) \xlongequal{\quad} H^+(aq) + F^-(aq)$$

为正反应，速率常数为 k_+，平衡常数为 K，则其逆反应

$$H^+(aq) + F^-(aq) \xlongequal{\quad} HF(aq)$$

的速率常数为 k_-。

由 $K=\dfrac{k_+}{k_-}$ 得

$$\begin{aligned} k_+ &= K \cdot k_- \\ &= 7.08\times10^{-4}\ \mathrm{mol \cdot dm^{-3}} \times 1.00\times10^{11}\ \mathrm{dm^3 \cdot mol^{-1} \cdot s^{-1}} \\ &= 7.08\times10^{7}\ \mathrm{s^{-1}} \end{aligned}$$

这就是氢氟酸解离反应的速率常数。

例 4.5 环丁烯异构化反应是一级反应：

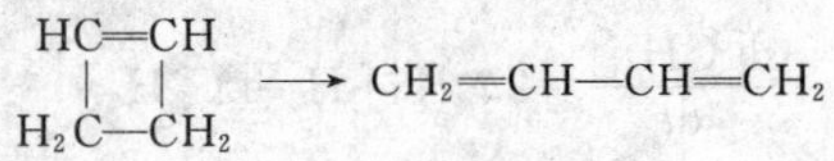

在150 ℃时 $k=2.0\times10^{-4}\ \mathrm{s^{-1}}$，气态环丁烯的初始浓度为 $1.89\times10^{-3}\ \mathrm{mol \cdot dm^{-3}}$。求：

(1) 20 min 时环丁烯的浓度；

(2) 环丁烯的浓度变成 $1.00\times10^{-3}\ \mathrm{mol \cdot dm^{-3}}$ 所需时间。

解：由题设知环丁烯异构化反应是一级反应。根据一级反应反应物的浓度与时间的关系式

$$\lg \frac{c}{c_0} = -\frac{k}{2.303} t$$

进行计算。

(1) 20 min 相当于 1 200 s。

$$\begin{aligned} \lg \frac{c}{c_0} &= -\frac{2.0\times10^{-4}\ \mathrm{s^{-1}}}{2.303} \times 1\,200\ \mathrm{s} \\ &= -0.104 \end{aligned}$$

$$\frac{c}{c_0} = 0.787$$

故 20 min 后环丁烯的浓度为

$$\begin{aligned} c &= 0.787\ c_0 \\ &= 0.787 \times 1.89\times10^{-3}\ \mathrm{mol \cdot dm^{-3}} \\ &= 1.49\times10^{-3}\ \mathrm{mol \cdot dm^{-3}} \end{aligned}$$

(2)
$$\begin{aligned} t &= -\frac{2.303 \lg \dfrac{c}{c_0}}{k} \\ &= -\frac{2.303 \lg \dfrac{1.00\times10^{-3}\ \mathrm{mol \cdot dm^{-3}}}{1.89\times10^{-3}\ \mathrm{mol \cdot dm^{-3}}}}{2.0\times10^{-4}\ \mathrm{s^{-1}}} \end{aligned}$$

$$=3.18\times10^{3}\ \text{s}$$

例 4.6　$SO_2Cl_2(g) \longrightarrow SO_2(g)+Cl_2(g)$ 为一级反应，某温度下速率常数 $k=3.8\times10^{-5}\ s^{-1}$，在该温度下反应 1.5 h 后，$SO_2Cl_2$ 的解离度是多少？

解： 1.5h 合 5 400 s。

依题意 $SO_2Cl_2(g) \longrightarrow SO_2(g)+Cl_2(g)$ 为一级反应，故其速率方程的积分表达式为

$$\lg c=\lg c_0-\frac{kt}{2.303}$$

即 $\lg\frac{c}{c_0}=-\frac{kt}{2.303}$，将题设条件代入其中，得

$$\lg\frac{c}{c_0}=-\frac{3.8\times10^{-5}\text{s}^{-1}\times5\,400\ \text{s}}{2.303}$$
$$=-0.089$$

所以

$$\frac{c}{c_0}=0.81$$

故

$$\frac{c_0-c}{c_0}=1-\frac{c}{c_0}=1-0.81=0.19$$

即 SO_2Cl_2 的解离度为 19%。

例 4.7　放射性同位素 ^{13}N 的放射强度经 18.6 min 后衰减为原来的 27.4%。求 ^{13}N 的半衰期。

解： 放射性同位素的衰变符合一级反应速率方程，且放射性强度与放射性同位素的原子个数成正比，或者说可以用其浓度 c 来体现。

由 $\lg c=\lg c_0-\frac{kt}{2.303}$ 得

$$k=-\frac{2.303}{t}\lg\frac{c}{c_0}$$

将题设条件代入其中，得

$$k=-\frac{2.303}{18.6\ \text{min}}\lg 0.274$$
$$=6.96\times10^{-2}\ \text{min}^{-1}$$

由一级反应的半衰期公式，得

$$t_{\frac{1}{2}}=\frac{0.693}{k}$$
$$=\frac{0.693}{6.96\times10^{-2}\ \text{min}^{-1}}$$
$$=9.96\ \text{min}$$

例 4.8　考古学者从古墓中取出的纺织品，经取样分析其 ^{14}C 含量为动植物活体的 85%。若放射性核衰变符合一级反应速率方程且已知 ^{14}C 的半衰期为 5 720 a，估算该纺织品年龄。

解： 由于放射性同位素 ^{14}C 的衰变相当于一级反应，根据一级反应的反应物浓度与时间的关

系进行计算。

$$t_{\frac{1}{2}}=\frac{0.693}{k}$$

所以
$$k=\frac{0.693}{t_{\frac{1}{2}}}=\frac{0.693}{5\,720\ \text{a}}=1.21\times10^{-4}\ \text{a}^{-1}$$

由
$$\lg\frac{c}{c_0}=-\frac{k}{2.303}t$$

得
$$t=-\frac{2.303\lg\frac{c}{c_0}}{k}=-\frac{2.303\lg\frac{85}{100}}{1.21\times10^{-4}\text{a}^{-1}}=1.3\times10^{3}\ \text{a}$$

例 4.9 在 19 世纪末，荷兰科学家 van't Hoff 根据大量实验指出，温度升高 10 K，反应速率扩大 2～4 倍。假定这些实验是在 27 ℃左右进行的，求所涉及的化学反应的活化能 E_a 的范围。

解： 反应活化能 E_a，反应温度 T 和速率常数 k 之间的关系符合公式：

$$\lg\frac{k_2}{k_1}=\frac{E_a}{2.303\,R}\left(\frac{1}{T_1}-\frac{1}{T_2}\right)$$

将 $\frac{k_2}{k_1}=2$，$T_1=(27+273)\ \text{K}=300\ \text{K}$，$T_2=310\ \text{K}$ 代入公式得

$$E_a=\frac{2.303\,R\lg\frac{k_2}{k_1}}{\frac{1}{T_1}-\frac{1}{T_2}}=\frac{2.303\times8.314\ \text{J}\cdot\text{mol}^{-1}\cdot\text{K}^{-1}\lg2}{\frac{1}{300\ \text{K}}-\frac{1}{310\ \text{K}}}=53.6\ \text{kJ}\cdot\text{mol}^{-1}$$

若将 $\frac{k_2}{k_1}=4$ 代入公式中，可得

$$E_a=107.2\ \text{kJ}\cdot\text{mol}^{-1}$$

故化学反应的活化能范围是 53.6 $\text{kJ}\cdot\text{mol}^{-1}$ 到 107.2 $\text{kJ}\cdot\text{mol}^{-1}$。

例 4.10 某一级反应 400 K 时的半衰期是 500 K 时的 100 倍，估算反应的活化能。

解： 由一级反应的半衰期公式

$$t_{\frac{1}{2}}=\frac{0.693}{k}$$

得

$$k=\frac{0.693}{t_{\frac{1}{2}}}$$

$$\frac{k_2}{k_1}=\frac{\dfrac{0.693}{t_{\frac{1}{2}}(2)}}{\dfrac{0.693}{t_{\frac{1}{2}}(1)}}=\frac{t_{\frac{1}{2}}(1)}{t_{\frac{1}{2}}(2)}$$

将其代入反应活化能 E_a，反应温度 T 和速率常数 k 的关系式

$$\lg\frac{k_2}{k_1}=\frac{E_a}{2.303\,R}\left(\frac{1}{T_1}-\frac{1}{T_2}\right)$$

可得

$$\lg\frac{t_{\frac{1}{2}}(1)}{t_{\frac{1}{2}}(2)}=\frac{E_a}{2.303\,R}\left(\frac{1}{T_1}-\frac{1}{T_2}\right)$$

将题设数据代入其中，得

$$E_a=\frac{2.303\,R\lg\dfrac{t_{\frac{1}{2}}(1)}{t_{\frac{1}{2}}(2)}}{\dfrac{1}{T_1}-\dfrac{1}{T_2}}$$

$$=\frac{2.303\times 8.314\ \text{J}\cdot\text{mol}^{-1}\cdot\text{K}^{-1}\ \lg 100}{\dfrac{1}{400\ \text{K}}-\dfrac{1}{500\ \text{K}}}$$

$$=76.6\ \text{kJ}\cdot\text{mol}^{-1}$$

例 4.11　蔗糖水解反应　$C_{12}H_{22}O_{11}+H_2O \longrightarrow 2C_6H_{12}O_6$

活化能 $E_a=110\ \text{kJ}\cdot\text{mol}^{-1}$；298 K 时其半衰期 $t_{\frac{1}{2}}=1.22\times10^4$ s，且 $t_{\frac{1}{2}}$ 与反应物浓度无关。

(1) 求此反应的反应级数；

(2) 写出其速率方程；

(3) 求 308 K 时的速率常数 k。

解：(1) 由题设知，反应的半衰期 $t_{\frac{1}{2}}$ 与反应物的浓度无关，故知该反应的反应级数为 1。

(2) 根据质量作用定律，其速率方程为

$$\bar{r}=k[C_{12}H_{22}O_{11}]$$

(3) 由公式 $t_{\frac{1}{2}}=\dfrac{0.693}{k}$，则 298 K 时的速率常数

$$k=\frac{0.693}{t_{\frac{1}{2}}}$$

$$=\frac{0.693}{1.22\times10^4\ \text{s}}$$

$$=5.68\times10^{-5}\ \text{s}^{-1}$$

反应的活化能 E_a，反应温度 T 和速率常数 k 之间的关系式为

$$\lg \frac{k_2}{k_1}=\frac{E_a}{2.303\ R}\left(\frac{1}{T_1}-\frac{1}{T_2}\right)$$

将 E_a，T_1 和 T_2 的数据代入其中，得

$$\lg \frac{k_2}{k_1}=\frac{110\times 1\,000\ \text{J}\cdot\text{mol}^{-1}}{2.303\times 8.314\ \text{J}\cdot\text{mol}^{-1}\cdot\text{K}^{-1}}\left(\frac{1}{298\ \text{K}}-\frac{1}{308\ \text{K}}\right)$$
$$=6.261\times 10^{-1}$$

所以

$$\frac{k_2}{k_1}=4.228$$

$$k_2=4.228\ k_1$$
$$=4.228\times 5.68\times 10^{-5}\ \text{s}^{-1}$$
$$=2.40\times 10^{-4}\ \text{s}^{-1}$$

例 4.12 合成氨反应一般在 773 K 下进行，没有催化剂时反应的活化能约为 326 kJ·mol^{-1}，使用还原铁粉作催化剂时，活化能降低至 175 kJ·mol^{-1}。计算加入催化剂后，反应速率扩大了多少倍？

解： 反应速率常数、温度和活化能的关系满足阿伦尼乌斯公式

$$\lg k=-\frac{E_a}{2.303\ RT}+\lg A$$

当温度一定、活化能 E_a 不同时，速率常数 k 不同，

于是

$$\lg k_1=-\frac{E_a(1)}{2.303\ RT}+\lg A \tag{1}$$

$$\lg k_2=-\frac{E_a(2)}{2.303\ RT}+\lg A \tag{2}$$

(2)－(1)得

$$\lg \frac{k_2}{k_1}=\frac{E_a(1)-E_a(2)}{2.303\ RT}$$

因为速率常数 k 与反应速率 r 成正比，故

$$\frac{k_2}{k_1}=\frac{r_2}{r_1}$$

公式变成 $\lg \frac{r_2}{r_1}=\frac{E_a(1)-E_a(2)}{2.303\ RT}$

$$=\frac{326\ \text{kJ}\cdot\text{mol}^{-1}-175\ \text{kJ}\cdot\text{mol}^{-1}}{(2.303\times 8.314\ \text{J}\cdot\text{mol}^{-1}\cdot\text{K}^{-1}\times 773\ \text{K})\times 1\,000\ \text{J}\cdot\text{kJ}^{-1}}$$

$$=10.2$$

故

$$\frac{r_2}{r_1}=1.6\times 10^{10}$$

即加入催化剂后，速率扩大了 1.6×10^{10} 倍。

第二部分　习题

一、选择题

4.1　当反应 $A_2+B_2 \longrightarrow 2AB$ 的速率方程为 $r=k[A_2][B_2]$ 时，则此反应

(A) 一定是基元反应；　(B) 一定是非基元反应；

(C) 不能肯定是否是基元反应；　(D) 反应为一级反应。

4.2　二级反应速率常数的量纲是

(A) s^{-1}；　(B) $mol\cdot dm^{-3}$；　(C) $mol\cdot dm^{-3}\cdot s^{-1}$；　(D) $mol^{-1}\cdot dm^{3}\cdot s^{-1}$。

4.3　反应 $2A+B \longrightarrow D$ 的有关实验数据在表中给出，此反应的速率常数 $k/(mol^{-2}\cdot dm^{6}\cdot min^{-1})$约为

初始浓度		最初速率
$[A]/(mol\cdot dm^{-3})$	$[B]/(mol\cdot dm^{-3})$	$r/(mol\cdot dm^{-3}\cdot min^{-1})$
0.05	0.05	4.2×10^{-2}
0.10	0.05	8.4×10^{-2}
0.10	0.10	3.4×10^{-1}

(A) 3.4×10^{2}；　(B) 6.7×10^{2}；　(C) 3.4×10^{3}；　(D) 6.7×10^{3}。

4.4　已知反应 $2O_3 = 3O_2$ 的反应机理为

$O_3 = O_2+O$　(慢)

$O_3+O = 2O_2$　(快)

当 O_2 的浓度增加时，其反应速率

(A) 加快；　(B) 减慢；　(C) 基本保持不变；　(D) 不能确定。

4.5　下列势能-反应历程图中，属放热反应的是

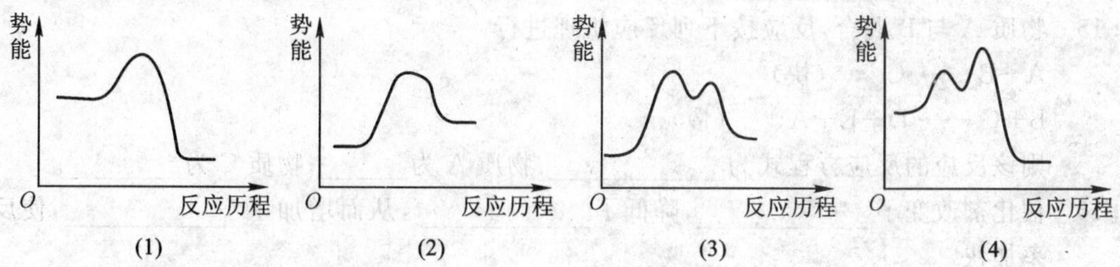

(A) (1)和(3)；　(B) (2)和(3)；　(C) (1)和(4)；　(D) (2)和(4)。

4.6　$A \rightleftharpoons B+C$ 是一放热的可逆基元反应，正反应的活化能为 E_a，逆反应的活化能为 E_a'，则下列活化能大小关系正确的是

(A) $E_a > E_a'$；　(B) $E_a < E_a'$；　(C) $E_a=\frac{1}{E_a'}$；　(D) 不能确定。

4.7　某化学反应进行 30 min 反应完成 50%，进行 60 min 反应完成 100%，则此反应是

(A) 三级反应；　(B) 二级反应；　(C) 一级反应；　(D) 零级反应。

4.8　已知反应 $2NO+O_2 \longrightarrow 2NO_2$ 为三级反应。下列操作会使反应速率常数改变的是

(A) 减小体系的压力；　(B) 在反应体系中加入大量的 NO；

(C) 降低反应温度；　(D) 在反应体系中加入 NO_2。

4.9　某一级反应的速率常数为 $9.5\times10^{-2}\ min^{-1}$。则此反应的半衰期为

(A) 3.65 min；　(B) 7.29 min；　(C) 0.27 min；　(D) 0.55 min。

4.10　下列陈述正确的是

(A) 对于一级反应，其半衰期与反应物的起始浓度有关；

(B) 对于二级反应，其半衰期与反应物的起始浓度有关；

(C) 半衰期 $t_{1/2}$ 是指完成该反应所需时间的 50%；

(D) 任何复杂反应都可以由速率方程式写出反应的级数。

4.11　放射性衰变过程是一级反应。某同位素的半衰期为 10^4 a，问此同位素试样由100 g 减少到1 g 约需

(A) 4×10^4 a；　(B) 5×10^4 a；　(C) 6×10^4 a；　(D) 7×10^4 a。

4.12　关于催化剂的说法，正确的是

(A) 不能改变反应的 $\Delta G, \Delta H, \Delta S, \Delta U$；

(B) 不能改变反应的 ΔG，但能改变 $\Delta H, \Delta S, \Delta U$；

(C) 不能改变反应的 $\Delta G, \Delta H$，但能改变 $\Delta S, \Delta U$；

(D) 不能改变反应的 $\Delta G, \Delta H, \Delta U$，但能改变 ΔS。

二、填空题

4.13　某温度下反应 $2NO(g)+O_2(g) \longrightarrow 2NO_2(g)$ 的速率常数 $k=8.8\times10^{-2}\ dm^6\cdot mol^{-2}\cdot s^{-1}$，已知反应对 O_2 来说是一级反应，则对 NO 为____级，速率方程为________________；当反应物浓度都是 $0.05\ mol\cdot dm^{-3}$时，反应的速率是________________。

4.14　反应 $A+B \longrightarrow C$ 的速率方程为 $r=k[A][B]^{1/2}$，其反应速率的单位是________，速率常数的单位是____________。(注：浓度用 $mol\cdot dm^{-3}$，时间用 s)

4.15　物质 A 与 B 混合，反应按下列反应机理进行

$A+B \longrightarrow C$　(快)

$B+C \longrightarrow D+E+A$　(慢)

则该反应的反应方程式为____________；物质 A 为______；物质 C 为________。

4.16　催化剂改变了____________，降低了____________，从而增加了____________，使反应速率加快。

4.17　若 $A \longrightarrow 2B$ 的活化能为 E_a，而 $2B \longrightarrow A$ 的活化能为 E'_a。加催化剂后 E_a 和 E'_a____________；加不同的催化剂则 E_a的数值变化____；提高反应温度，E_a 和 E'_a值__________；改变起始浓度后，E_a________。

4.18　由阿伦尼乌斯公式 $\ln k=-\dfrac{E_a}{RT}+\ln A$ 可以看出，升高温度，反应速率常数 k 将____；使用

催化剂时，反应速率常数 k 将____；而改变反应物或生成物浓度时，反应速率常数 k ____。

4.19 $CH_2(CH_2COOH)_2$ 在水溶液中分解成丙酮和二氧化碳。在 283 K 时分解反应速率常数为 $1.08\times10^{-4}\,mol\cdot dm^{-3}\cdot s^{-1}$，333 K 时为 $5.48\times10^{-2}\,mol\cdot dm^{-3}\cdot s^{-1}$。则该反应活化能________，303 K 时分解反应的速率常数为________。

4.20 某反应在温度由 20℃ 升至 30℃ 时，反应速率恰好增加 1 倍，则该反应的活化能为______ $kJ\cdot mol^{-1}$。

4.21 已知各基元反应的活化能如下表：

序　号	A	B	C	D	E
正反应的活化能/($kJ\cdot mol^{-1}$)	70	16	40	20	20
逆反应的活化能/($kJ\cdot mol^{-1}$)	20	35	45	80	30

在相同的温度时：

(1) 正反应是吸热反应的是______；

(2) 放热最多的反应是______；

(3) 正反应速率常数最大的反应是______；

(4) 反应可逆程度最大的反应是______；

(5) 正反应的速率常数 k 随温度变化最大的是______。

4.22 在常温常压下，HCl(g)的生成热为 $-92.3\ kJ\cdot mol^{-1}$，生成反应的活化能为 $113\ kJ\cdot mol^{-1}$，则其逆反应的活化能为________ $kJ\cdot mol^{-1}$。

三、简答题和计算题

4.23 反应 $2NO+2H_2 \longrightarrow N_2+2H_2O$ 的反应机理为

(1) $NO+NO \rightleftharpoons N_2O_2$ （快）

(2) $N_2O_2+H_2 \longrightarrow N_2O+H_2O$ （慢）

(3) $N_2O+H_2 \rightleftharpoons N_2+H_2O$ （快）

试确定总反应速率方程。

4.24 一氧化碳与氯气在高温下作用得到光气：$CO(g)+Cl_2(g) \xlongequal{} COCl_2(g)$，实验测得反应的速率方程为

$$d[COCl_2]/dt=k[CO][Cl_2]^{3/2}$$

有人提出其反应机理为

① $Cl_2 \underset{k_{-1}}{\overset{k_1}{\rightleftharpoons}} 2Cl\cdot$（快平衡）

② $Cl\cdot+CO \underset{k_{-2}}{\overset{k_2}{\rightleftharpoons}} COCl\cdot$（快平衡）

③ $COCl\cdot+Cl_2 \xrightarrow{k_3} COCl_2+Cl\cdot$（慢反应）

(1) 试说明这一机理与速率方程相符合；

(2) 指出反应速率方程中的 k 与反应机理中的速率常数(k_1,k_{-1},k_2,k_{-2})间的关系。

4.25 在 373 K 时，反应 $H_2PO_2^-+OH^- \longrightarrow HPO_3^{2-}+H_2$ 的实验数据如下：

初始浓度		$-\frac{d[H_2PO_2^-]}{dt}$/(mol·dm^{-3}·min^{-1})
$[H_2PO_2^-]$/(mol·dm^{-3})	$[OH^-]$/(mol·dm^{-3})	
0.10	1.0	3.2×10^{-5}
0.50	1.0	1.6×10^{-4}
0.50	4.0	2.56×10^{-3}

(1) 确定反应级数,写出速率方程;

(2) 计算此温度下的速率常数。

4.26 反应 $C_2H_6 \longrightarrow C_2H_4 + H_2$,开始阶段反应级数近似为 3/2 级,910 K 时速率常数为 1.13 dm$^{3/2}$·mol$^{-1/2}$·s^{-1}。试计算 C_2H_6(g)的压强为 1.33×10^4 Pa 时的起始分解速率 v_0。

4.27 在 28 ℃,鲜牛奶大约 4 h 变酸,但在 5 ℃的冰箱中可保持 48 h。假定反应速率与变酸时间成反比,求牛奶变酸反应的活化能。

4.28 已知反应 $CH_3CHO(g) \longrightarrow CH_4(g) + CO(g)$ 的活化能 $E_a = 188.3$ kJ·mol^{-1};如果以碘蒸气为催化剂,反应的活化能 $E'_a = 138.1$ kJ·mol^{-1}。计算温度为 800 K 时,加碘催化剂,反应速率增大为原来的多少倍。

4.29 若某化合物在 100 min 内被消耗掉 25%,若分别是零级、一级和二级反应,则 200 min 时,对于各级反应,该物质分别被消耗了多少?

4.30 某有机物的热分解是一级反应,活化能为 200 kJ·mol^{-1},600 K 时的半衰期为 360 min。问 700 K 时,多长时间可将该有机物分解 70%。

4.31 已知某气相反应的活化能 $E_a = 163$ kJ·mol^{-1},温度 390 K 时的速率常数 $k = 2.37\times10^{-2}$ dm^3·mol^{-1}·s^{-1}。求温度为 420 K 时的反应速率常数。

4.32 在某处高山上测得纯水 90 ℃沸腾。100 ℃下 3 min 可煮熟的鸡蛋,在这样的高山上需多少时间方可煮熟?假定鸡蛋被煮熟(即蛋白质变质)过程的活化能为 5.18×10^2 kJ·mol^{-1}。

4.33 在 600 K 时,某化合物分解反应的速率常数 $k = 3.3\times10^{-2}$ s^{-1},反应的活化能 $E_a = 18.88\times10^4$ J·mol^{-1},若控制反应在 10 min 内转化率达 90%,则反应的温度应控制为多少?

4.34 ^{203}Hg 可用于进行肾扫描。某医院购入 0.200 mg $^{203}Hg(NO_3)_2$ 试样,六个月(182 d)后,未发生衰变的试样还有多少?已知 ^{203}Hg 的半衰期为 46.1 d。

4.35 N_2O_5 分解为 NO_2 和 O_2 为一级反应,45 ℃时,其速率常数 $k = 4.8\times10^{-4}$ s^{-1}。

(1) 假设 N_2O_5 的起始浓度为 1.65×10^{-2} mol·dm^{-3},825 s 以后其浓度为多少?

(2) 多长时间后将由起始浓度减少到 1.00×10^{-2} mol·dm^{-3}?

第 5 章

化学平衡

第一部分　例题

例 5.1　27 ℃时，反应 $2NO_2(g) \rightleftharpoons N_2O_4(g)$实现平衡时，反应物和产物的分压分别为 p_1 和 p_2。写出 K_c，K_p 和 $K^\ominus$ 的表示式，并求出$\frac{K_c}{K^\ominus}$的值。（以 $p^\ominus = 100\ \text{kPa}$ 计算）

解：

$$2NO_2(g) \rightleftharpoons N_2O_4(g)$$

平衡分压　p_1　　p_2

故

$$K_p = \frac{p(N_2O_4, g)}{[p(NO_2, g)]^2} = \frac{p_2}{p_1^2}$$

$$K_c = K_p(RT)^{-\Delta\nu} = \frac{p_2}{p_1^2}RT$$

$$K^\ominus = \frac{\dfrac{p(N_2O_4, g)}{p^\ominus}}{\left[\dfrac{p(NO_2, g)}{p^\ominus}\right]^2} = \frac{\dfrac{p_2}{p^\ominus}}{\left(\dfrac{p_1}{p^\ominus}\right)^2} = \frac{p_2}{p_1^2}p^\ominus$$

$$\frac{K_c}{K^\ominus} = \frac{\dfrac{p_2}{p_1^2}RT}{\dfrac{p_2}{p_1^2}p^\ominus}$$

注意 K_c 的单位是$(\text{mol}\cdot\text{dm}^{-3})^{-1}$，而 $K^\ominus$ 是量纲一的量。所以

$$\frac{K_c}{K^\ominus} = \frac{\dfrac{p_2}{p_1^2} \times 8.314 \times 10^3\ \text{J}\cdot\text{mol}^{-1}\cdot\text{K}^{-1} \times (273+27)\ \text{K}}{\dfrac{p_2}{p_1^2} \times 100 \times 1\,000\ \text{J}\cdot\text{dm}^{-3}}$$

$$= 24.94\ \text{dm}^3\cdot\text{mol}^{-1}$$

例 5.2　某温度下，100 kPa 时反应 $2NO_2 \rightleftharpoons N_2O_4$ 的标准平衡常数 $K^\ominus = 3.06$，求 NO_2 的平衡转化率。

解： 设反应前 $n_{NO_2} = 1\ \text{mol}$，平衡时 $n_{平,NO_2} = x\ \text{mol}$，则有

$$\begin{array}{lccl} & 2NO_2 & \rightleftharpoons & N_2O_4 \\ t_0 & 1 & & 0 \\ t_{平} & x & & \frac{1}{2}(1-x) \quad 平衡\ n_{总}=\frac{1}{2}(1+x)\ \text{mol} \\ x_i & \dfrac{x}{\frac{1}{2}(1+x)} & & \dfrac{\frac{1}{2}(1-x)}{\frac{1}{2}(1+x)} \\ p_i & \dfrac{100\ \text{kPa}\ x}{\frac{1}{2}(1+x)} & & \dfrac{100\ \text{kPa}\ \frac{1}{2}(1-x)}{\frac{1}{2}(1+x)} \end{array}$$

$$K^\ominus=\frac{\dfrac{p(N_2O_4)}{p^\ominus}}{\left(\dfrac{p(NO_2)}{p^\ominus}\right)^2}$$

$$=\frac{\dfrac{\frac{1}{2}(1-x)}{\frac{1}{2}(1+x)}}{\left[\dfrac{x}{\frac{1}{2}(1+x)}\right]^2}=\frac{\frac{1}{4}(1-x)(1+x)}{x^2}$$

$$=3.06$$

解得 $x=0.275$

NO_2 的平衡转化率为

$$\frac{(1-0.275)\ \text{mol}}{1\ \text{mol}}\times 100\%=72.5\%$$

例 5.3 某温度下,反应 $H_2(g)+I_2(g) \rightleftharpoons 2HI(g)$的 $K_p=500$,求该温度时反应 $2HI(g) \rightleftharpoons H_2(g)+I_2(g)$的 K_p,并计算 HI 的解离度。

解: 互为逆反应的两个反应,其平衡常数互为倒数。故反应

$$2HI(g) \rightleftharpoons H_2(g) + I_2(g) \qquad K_p=\frac{1}{500}=2\times 10^{-3}$$

$$\begin{array}{llll} 起始分压/\text{kPa} & 100 & 0 & 0 \\ 平衡分压/\text{kPa} & 2x & \frac{1}{2}(100-2x) & \frac{1}{2}(100-2x) \end{array}$$

$$K_p=\frac{\dfrac{p(H_2,g)}{p^\ominus}\cdot\dfrac{p(I_2,g)}{p^\ominus}}{\left[\dfrac{p(HI,g)}{p^\ominus}\right]^2}$$

$$=\frac{\dfrac{\frac{1}{2}(100-2x)\ \text{kPa}}{p^\ominus}\times\dfrac{\frac{1}{2}(100-2x)\ \text{kPa}}{p^\ominus}}{\left(\dfrac{2x\ \text{kPa}}{p^\ominus}\right)^2}$$

故有
$$\left[\frac{\frac{1}{2}(100-2x)}{2x}\right]^2=2\times10^{-3}$$

解得
$$x=45.90$$

故 HI 的解离度为

$$\frac{(100-2x)\ \text{kPa}}{100\ \text{kPa}}\times100\%$$
$$=\frac{(100-45.90\times2)\ \text{kPa}}{100\ \text{kPa}}\times100\%$$
$$=8.20\%$$

例 5.4　某温度下，反应 $H_2(g)+Br_2(g) \rightleftharpoons 2HBr(g)$ 的 $K_c=8.10\times10^3$。求 $H_2(g)$ 和 $Br_2(g)$ 的起始浓度均为 1.00 $mol\cdot dm^{-3}$ 时，$H_2(g)$ 和 $Br_2(g)$ 的起始浓度分别为 10.00 $mol\cdot dm^{-3}$ 和 1.00 $mol\cdot dm^{-3}$ 时，Br_2 的转化率。

解：

	$H_2(g)$	$+Br_2(g) \rightleftharpoons$	$2HBr(g)$	$K_c=8.10\times10^3$
起始浓度/($mol\cdot dm^{-3}$)	1.00	1.00	0	
平衡浓度/($mol\cdot dm^{-3}$)	$1.00-x$	$1.00-x$	$2x$	

x 为平衡时已转化的 Br_2 的浓度，则

$$K_c=\frac{[HBr]^2}{[H_2][Br_2]}=\frac{(2x)^2}{(1.00-x)(1.00-x)}$$
$$=8.10\times10^3$$

故有
$$\frac{2x}{1.00-x}=90$$

解得
$$x=0.978$$

$$\text{转化率}=\frac{\text{已转化的 } Br_2 \text{ 的浓度}}{Br_2 \text{ 的起始浓度}}\times100\%$$
$$=\frac{0.978\ mol\cdot dm^{-3}}{1.00\ mol\cdot dm^{-3}}\times100\%$$
$$=97.8\%$$

	$H_2(g)$	$+Br_2(g) \rightleftharpoons$	$2HBr(g)$	$K_c=8.10\times10^3$
起始浓度/($mol\cdot dm^{-3}$)	10.00	1.00	0	
平衡浓度/($mol\cdot dm^{-3}$)	$10.00-y$	$1.00-y$	$2y$	

y 为平衡时已转化的 Br_2 的浓度，则

$$K_c=\frac{[HBr]^2}{[H_2][Br_2]}=\frac{(2y)^2}{(10.00-y)(1.00-y)}$$
$$=8.10\times10^3$$

解得
$$y=0.9999$$

$$\text{转化率}=\frac{\text{已转化的 } Br_2 \text{ 的浓度}}{Br_2 \text{ 的起始浓度}}\times100\%$$

$$=\frac{0.9999\ \text{mol}\cdot\text{dm}^{-3}}{1.00\ \text{mol}\cdot\text{dm}^{-3}}\times 100\%$$
$$=99.99\%$$

计算结果表明增大反应混合物中 H_2 的浓度,可以提高另一种反应物 Br_2 的利用率。

例 5.5 273 K 时,水的饱和蒸气压为 611 Pa,该温度下反应

$$SrCl_2\cdot 6H_2O(s) \rightleftharpoons SrCl_2\cdot 2H_2O(s)+4H_2O(g)$$

的 $K^{\ominus}=6.89\times10^{-12}$,利用计算结果说明实际发生的过程是 $SrCl_2\cdot 6H_2O(s)$ 失水风化,还是 $SrCl_2\cdot 2H_2O(s)$ 吸水潮解?

解: $$SrCl_2\cdot 6H_2O(s) \rightleftharpoons SrCl_2\cdot 2H_2O(s)+4H_2O(g)$$

$$K^{\ominus}=\left(\frac{p(H_2O)}{p^{\ominus}}\right)^4=6.89\times10^{-12}$$

所以 $$\frac{p(H_2O)}{p^{\ominus}}=1.62\times10^{-3}$$

故 $$p(H_2O)=p^{\ominus}\times1.62\times10^{-3}=100\ \text{kPa}\times1.62\times10^{-3}=162\ \text{Pa}$$

相对湿度为 $\frac{162\ \text{Pa}}{611\ \text{Pa}}=26.5\%$。

若相对湿度大于 26.5%,则 $SrCl_2\cdot 2H_2O$ 吸水潮解;若相对湿度小于 26.5%,则 $SrCl_2\cdot 6H_2O$ 失水风化。

例 5.6 根据下列热力学数据,计算 298 K 时 Hg 的饱和蒸气压和常压下 Hg 的沸点。

	Hg(l)	Hg(g)
$\Delta_f H_m^{\ominus}/(\text{kJ}\cdot\text{mol}^{-1})$	0	61.4
$S_m^{\ominus}/(\text{J}\cdot\text{mol}^{-1}\cdot\text{K}^{-1})$	75.9	175
$\Delta_f G_m^{\ominus}/(\text{kJ}\cdot\text{mol}^{-1})$	0	31.8

解: 汞的汽化过程可表示为

$$Hg(l) = Hg(g)$$

$$\Delta_r G_m^{\ominus}=\Delta_f G_m^{\ominus}(Hg,g)-\Delta_f G_m^{\ominus}(Hg,l)=31.8\ \text{kJ}\cdot\text{mol}^{-1}-0\ \text{kJ}\cdot\text{mol}^{-1}=31.8\ \text{kJ}\cdot\text{mol}^{-1}$$

由公式 $\Delta_r G_m^{\ominus}=-RT\ln K^{\ominus}$,得

$$\ln K^{\ominus}=-\frac{\Delta_r G_m^{\ominus}}{RT}=-\frac{31.8\ \text{kJ}\cdot\text{mol}^{-1}\times1000\ \text{J}\cdot\text{kJ}^{-1}}{8.314\ \text{J}\cdot\text{mol}^{-1}\cdot\text{K}^{-1}\times298\ \text{K}}=-12.8$$

故 $K^{\ominus}=2.76\times10^{-6}$

$$K^{\ominus}=\frac{p(\mathrm{Hg})}{p^{\ominus}}=2.76\times10^{-6}$$

所以

$$p(\mathrm{Hg})=p^{\ominus}\times2.76\times10^{-6}=100\ \mathrm{kPa}\times2.76\times10^{-6}=0.276\ \mathrm{Pa}$$

即 298 K 时 Hg 的饱和蒸气压为 0.276 Pa。

$$\begin{aligned}\Delta_r H_m^{\ominus}&=\Delta_f H_m^{\ominus}(\mathrm{Hg,g})-\Delta_f H_m^{\ominus}(\mathrm{Hg,l})\\&=61.4\ \mathrm{kJ\cdot mol^{-1}}-0\ \mathrm{kJ\cdot mol^{-1}}\\&=61.4\ \mathrm{kJ\cdot mol^{-1}}\end{aligned}$$

$$\begin{aligned}\Delta_r S_m^{\ominus}&=S_m^{\ominus}(\mathrm{Hg,g})-S_m^{\ominus}(\mathrm{Hg,l})\\&=175\ \mathrm{J\cdot mol^{-1}\cdot K^{-1}}-75.9\ \mathrm{J\cdot mol^{-1}\cdot K^{-1}}\\&=99.1\ \mathrm{J\cdot mol^{-1}\cdot K^{-1}}\end{aligned}$$

在正常沸点下的汽化过程可以认为是可逆的，过程的 $\Delta_r G_m^{\ominus}=0$，由公式

$$\Delta_r G_m^{\ominus}=\Delta_r H_m^{\ominus}-T\Delta_r S_m^{\ominus}$$

得

$$T\Delta_r S_m^{\ominus}=\Delta_r H_m^{\ominus}$$

$$\begin{aligned}T&=\frac{\Delta_r H_m^{\ominus}}{\Delta_r S_m^{\ominus}}\\&=\frac{61.4\ \mathrm{kJ\cdot mol^{-1}}\times1\,000\ \mathrm{J\cdot kJ^{-1}}}{99.1\ \mathrm{J\cdot mol^{-1}\cdot K^{-1}}}\\&=620\ \mathrm{K}\end{aligned}$$

相当于 347 ℃。

例 5.7　一定量的氯化铵受热分解 $NH_4Cl(s)\rightleftharpoons NH_3(g)+HCl(g)$。已知反应的 $\Delta_r H_m^{\ominus}=161\ \mathrm{kJ\cdot mol^{-1}}$，$\Delta_r S_m^{\ominus}=250\ \mathrm{J\cdot mol^{-1}\cdot K^{-1}}$，求在 700 K 达到平衡时体系的总压强。

解：

$$NH_4Cl(s)\rightleftharpoons NH_3(g)+HCl(g)$$

依题设条件

$$\begin{aligned}\Delta_r G_m^{\ominus}&=\Delta_r H_m^{\ominus}-T\Delta_r S_m^{\ominus}\\&=161\times1\,000\ \mathrm{J\cdot mol^{-1}}-700\ \mathrm{K}\times250\ \mathrm{J\cdot mol^{-1}\cdot K^{-1}}\\&=-14\,000\ \mathrm{J\cdot mol^{-1}}\end{aligned}$$

由于

$$\Delta_r G_m^{\ominus}=-RT\ln K^{\ominus}$$

所以

$$\begin{aligned}\ln K^{\ominus}&=-\frac{1}{RT}\Delta_r G_m^{\ominus}\\&=-\frac{1}{8.314\ \mathrm{J\cdot mol^{-1}\cdot K^{-1}}\times700\ \mathrm{K}}\times(-14\,000\ \mathrm{J\cdot mol^{-1}})\\&=2.41\end{aligned}$$

故

$$K^{\ominus}=11$$

$$K^{\ominus}=\frac{p(NH_3)}{p^{\ominus}}\cdot\frac{p(HCl)}{p^{\ominus}}$$

$$=11$$

因为
$$p(NH_3)=p(HCl)$$

故有
$$\left(\frac{p(NH_3)}{p^\ominus}\right)^2=11$$

所以
$$\frac{p(NH_3)}{p^\ominus}=3.3$$

$$p(NH_3)=3.3p^\ominus$$
$$=3.3\times10^2\ \text{kPa}$$

体系的总压为

$$p(NH_3)+p(HCl)=3.3\times10^2\ \text{kPa}+3.3\times10^2\ \text{kPa}$$
$$=6.6\times10^2\ \text{kPa}$$

例 5.8 某温度时将 2.00 mol PCl_5 与 1.00 mol PCl_3 相混合，发生反应

$$PCl_5(g) \rightleftharpoons PCl_3(g)+Cl_2(g)$$

平衡时总压强为 202 kPa，PCl_5(g)转化率为 91%。求该温度下反应的平衡常数 K_p 和 $K^\ominus$。

解：

	$PCl_5(g)$	$\rightleftharpoons$	$PCl_3(g)$	+	$Cl_2(g)$
起始时物质的量/mol	2.00		1.00		0
平衡时物质的量/mol	2.00(1−0.91) =0.18		1.00+2.00×0.91 =2.82		2.00×0.91 =1.82
x_i	$\frac{0.18}{4.82}$		$\frac{2.82}{4.82}$		$\frac{1.82}{4.82}$
p_i	$\frac{0.18}{4.82}\times202$ kPa		$\frac{2.82}{4.82}\times202$ kPa		$\frac{1.82}{4.82}\times202$ kPa
相对 p_i	$\frac{0.18\times202}{4.82\times100}$		$\frac{2.82\times202}{4.82\times100}$		$\frac{1.82\times202}{4.82\times100}$

$$K_p=\frac{\frac{1.82}{4.82}\times202\ \text{kPa}\times\frac{2.82}{4.82}\times202\ \text{kPa}}{\frac{0.18}{4.82}\times202\ \text{kPa}}$$

$$=1.20\times10^3\ \text{kPa}$$

$$K^\ominus=\frac{\frac{1.82\times202}{4.82\times100}\times\frac{2.82\times202}{4.82\times100}}{\frac{0.18\times202}{4.82\times100}}$$

$$=12$$

例 5.9 1.01325×10^5 Pa 时水的沸点为 373 K，若水的汽化热为44.0 kJ·mol^{-1}，试给出水的饱和蒸气压 p 与热力学温度 T 的函数关系式。

解： 由 $\Delta_r G_m^\ominus=\Delta_r H_m^\ominus-T\Delta_r S_m^\ominus$ 和 $\Delta_r G_m^\ominus=-RT\ln K^\ominus$ 得

$$\ln K^\ominus=-\frac{\Delta_r H_m^\ominus}{RT}+\frac{\Delta_r S_m^\ominus}{R}$$

即
$$\lg K^{\ominus}=-\frac{\Delta_r H_m^{\ominus}}{2.303RT}+\frac{\Delta_r S_m^{\ominus}}{2.303R}$$

对于反应
$$H_2O(l) \rightleftharpoons H_2O(g)$$

$K^{\ominus}=\frac{p(H_2O)}{p^{\ominus}}$，即 $K^{\ominus}$ 为以 10^5 Pa 为单位的 $p(H_2O)$ 的数值。所以其函数关系式为

$$\lg[p(H_2O)/10^5\ \text{Pa}]=-\frac{\Delta_r H_m^{\ominus}}{2.303RT}+\frac{\Delta_r S_m^{\ominus}}{2.303R} \tag{1}$$

将题设条件 373 K 时，$p(H_2O)$ 为 1.013×10^5 Pa 和 $\Delta_r H_m^{\ominus}=44.0\ \text{kJ·mol}^{-1}$ 代入式(1)中，求出

$$\Delta_r S_m^{\ominus}=118\ \text{J·mol}^{-1}\text{·K}^{-1}$$

所以式(1)又可表示为

$$\lg[p(H_2O)/10^5\ \text{Pa}]=-\frac{2\,298}{T/\text{K}}+6.16$$

式(1)说明，$\lg[p(H_2O)/10^5\ \text{Pa}]$ 对 $\frac{1}{T}$ 作图，可得一直线，其斜率为 $-\frac{\Delta_r H_m^{\ominus}}{2.303R}$，在纵轴上截距为 $\frac{\Delta_r S_m^{\ominus}}{2.303R}$。

由
$$\ln[p(H_2O)/10^5\ \text{Pa}]=-\frac{\Delta_r H_m^{\ominus}}{RT}+\frac{\Delta_r S_m^{\ominus}}{R}$$

得
$$p(H_2O)/10^5\ \text{Pa}=e^{\frac{\Delta_r S_m^{\ominus}}{R}}\cdot e^{-\frac{\Delta_r H_m^{\ominus}}{RT}} \tag{2}$$

将题设条件代入可得

$$p(H_2O)/10^5\ \text{Pa}=1.46\times10^6\ e^{-\frac{5\,292}{T/\text{K}}}$$

式(2)说明 $p(H_2O)/10^5$ Pa 对温度 T 作图得到的是指数函数。

例 5.10 反应 $2NaHCO_3(s) \rightleftharpoons Na_2CO_3(s)+CO_2(g)+H_2O(g)$ 的标准摩尔反应热为 $1.29\times10^2\ \text{kJ·mol}^{-1}$。若 303 K 时 $K^{\ominus}=1.66\times10^{-5}$，计算 393 K 的 $K^{\ominus}$。

解：
$$2NaHCO_3(s) \rightleftharpoons Na_2CO_3(s)+CO_2(g)+H_2O(g)$$

$$\lg K_1^{\ominus}=-\frac{\Delta_r H_m^{\ominus}}{2.303RT_1}+\frac{\Delta_r S_m^{\ominus}}{2.303R} \tag{1}$$

$$\lg K_2^{\ominus}=-\frac{\Delta_r H_m^{\ominus}}{2.303RT_2}+\frac{\Delta_r S_m^{\ominus}}{2.303R} \tag{2}$$

式(2)－式(1)得

$$\begin{aligned}\lg\frac{K_2^{\ominus}}{K_1^{\ominus}}&=\frac{\Delta_r H_m^{\ominus}}{2.303R}\left(\frac{1}{T_1}-\frac{1}{T_2}\right)\\&=\frac{129\,000\ \text{J·mol}^{-1}}{2.303\times8.314\ \text{J·mol}^{-1}\text{·K}^{-1}}\left(\frac{1}{303\ \text{K}}-\frac{1}{393\ \text{K}}\right)\\&=5.092\end{aligned}$$

$$\frac{K_2^{\ominus}}{K_1^{\ominus}}=1.236\times10^5$$

故 $K_2^\ominus = K_1^\ominus \times 1.236\times 10^5$

$= 1.66\times 10^{-5}\times 1.236\times 10^5$

$= 2.05$

所以 393 K 时，反应的平衡常数 $K^\ominus = 2.05$。

例 5.11 反应 $3H_2(g)+N_2(g) \rightleftharpoons 2NH_3(g)$ 200 ℃时的平衡常数 $K_1^\ominus = 0.64$，400 ℃时的平衡常数 $K_2^\ominus = 6.0\times 10^{-4}$，据此求该反应的标准摩尔反应热 $\Delta_r H_m^\ominus$ 和 $NH_3(g)$的标准摩尔生成热 $\Delta_f H_m^\ominus$。

解： $3H_2(g)+N_2(g) \rightleftharpoons 2NH_3(g)$

$$\lg K_1^\ominus = -\frac{\Delta_r H_m^\ominus}{2.303RT_1}+\frac{\Delta_r S_m^\ominus}{2.303R} \tag{1}$$

$$\lg K_2^\ominus = -\frac{\Delta_r H_m^\ominus}{2.303RT_2}+\frac{\Delta_r S_m^\ominus}{2.303R} \tag{2}$$

式(2)－式(1)得

$$\lg\frac{K_2^\ominus}{K_1^\ominus} = \frac{\Delta_r H_m^\ominus}{2.303R}\left(\frac{1}{T_1}-\frac{1}{T_2}\right)$$

所以反应的标准摩尔反应热

$$\Delta_r H_m^\ominus = \frac{2.303R\lg\dfrac{K_2^\ominus}{K_1^\ominus}}{\dfrac{1}{T_1}-\dfrac{1}{T_2}}$$

$$= \frac{2.303\times 8.314\ \mathrm{J\cdot mol^{-1}\cdot K^{-1}}\lg\dfrac{6.0\times 10^{-4}}{0.64}}{\dfrac{1}{(200+273)\mathrm{K}}-\dfrac{1}{(400+273)\mathrm{K}}}$$

$$= -92\ \mathrm{kJ\cdot mol^{-1}}$$

$NH_3(g)$的标准生成反应为

$$\frac{3}{2}H_2(g)+\frac{1}{2}N_2(g) = NH_3(g)$$

其化学计量数为题设的反应的一半，故其标准反应热为

$$-92\ \mathrm{kJ\cdot mol^{-1}}\times\frac{1}{2} = -46\ \mathrm{kJ\cdot mol^{-1}}$$

这就是 $NH_3(g)$的标准摩尔生成热 $\Delta_f H_m^\ominus$。

例 5.12 对于反应 $2C(s)+O_2(g) = 2CO(g)$ 反应的自由能变化($\Delta_r G_m^\ominus$)与温度(T)的关系为

$$\Delta_r G_m^\ominus = (-232\ 600-168T)\ \mathrm{J\cdot mol^{-1}}$$

由此可以说，随反应温度的升高，$\Delta_r G_m^\ominus$ 更负，反应会更彻底。这种说法是否正确？为什么？

解： 不正确。

由 $\Delta_r G_m^\ominus$ 的表达式可知，反应的焓变 $\Delta_r H_m^\ominus = -232\ 600\ J\cdot mol^{-1}$，反应的熵变 $\Delta_r S_m^\ominus = 168\ J\cdot mol^{-1}\cdot K^{-1}$。

按里·查德利原理，对于放热反应，升高温度时平衡向逆反应方向移动，也就是说，反应会更不彻底。

在温度条件发生变化时，一个反应是否比原温度条件下更彻底，应从其平衡常数变大还是变小来判断，由公式：

$$\lg\frac{K_2^\ominus}{K_1^\ominus}=\frac{\Delta_r H_m^\ominus}{R}\left(\frac{T_2-T_1}{T_1T_2}\right)$$

对于放热反应（$\Delta_r H_m^\ominus<0$），随反应温度升高，平衡常数变小（$K_2^\ominus<K_1^\ominus$），即升高温度时，反应更不彻底。

第二部分 习题

一、选择题

5.1 可逆反应达到平衡后，若反应速率常数 k 发生变化，则标准平衡常数

(A) 一定发生变化； (B) 一定不变； (C) 不一定变化； (D) 与 k 无关。

5.2 298K $H_2O(l) \rightleftharpoons H_2O(g)$ 达到平衡时，体系的水蒸气压为 3.13 kPa，则标准平衡常数 $K^\ominus$ 为

(A) 100； (B) 3.13×10^{-2}； (C) 3.13； (D) 1。

5.3 已知某温度条件下，反应 $A \rightleftharpoons D$ 的平衡常数为 $K_1^\ominus$，$D+B \rightleftharpoons C$ 的平衡常数为 $K_2^\ominus$。则反应 $A+B \rightleftharpoons C$ 的平衡常数 $K^\ominus$ 为

(A) $K_1^\ominus/K_2^\ominus$； (B) $K_1^\ominus\cdot K_2^\ominus$； (C) $K_1^\ominus+K_2^\ominus$； (D) $K_2^\ominus-K_1^\ominus$。

5.4 下列反应中，$K^\ominus$ 的值小于 K_p 值的是

(A) $H_2(g)+Cl_2(g) \rightleftharpoons 2HCl(g)$； (B) $H_2(g)+S(g) \rightleftharpoons H_2S(g)$；

(C) $CaCO_3(s) \rightleftharpoons CaO(s)+CO_2(g)$； (D) $C(s)+O_2(g) \rightleftharpoons CO_2(g)$。

5.5 某温度下，反应 $SO_2(g)+\frac{1}{2}O_2(g) \rightleftharpoons SO_3(g)$ 的平衡常数 $K^\ominus=50$；在同一温度下，反应 $2SO_3(g) \rightleftharpoons 2SO_2(g)+O_2(g)$ 的 $K^\ominus$ 值应为

(A) 2 500； (B) 100； (C) 4×10^{-4}； (D) 2×10^{-2}。

5.6 在容器中加入相同物质的量的 NO 和 Cl_2，在一定温度下发生反应 $NO(g)+\frac{1}{2}Cl_2(g) \rightleftharpoons NOCl(g)$ 达平衡，此时对有关各物质的分压判断正确的是

(A) $p(NO)=p(Cl_2)$； (B) $p(NO)=p(NOCl)$；

(C) $p(NO)<p(Cl_2)$； (D) $p(NO)>p(Cl_2)$。

5.7 在某温度下平衡 $A+B \rightleftharpoons G+F$ 的 $\Delta H<0$，升高温度平衡逆向移动的原因是

(A) $r_{正}$ 减小，$r_{逆}$ 增大； (B) $k_{正}$ 减小，$k_{逆}$ 增大；

(C) $r_{正}$ 和 $r_{逆}$ 都减小；　　(D) $r_{正}$ 增加的倍数小于 $r_{逆}$ 增加的倍数。

5.8　基元反应 $A+2B \rightleftharpoons 2C$,已知某温度下正反应速率常数 $k_{正}=1$,逆反应速率常数$k_{逆}=0.5$,则处于平衡状态的体系是

(A) $[A]=1\ mol\cdot dm^{-3}$, $[B]=[C]=2\ mol\cdot dm^{-3}$；

(B) $[A]=2\ mol\cdot dm^{-3}$, $[B]=[C]=1\ mol\cdot dm^{-3}$；

(C) $[A]=[C]=2\ mol\cdot dm^{-3}$, $[B]=1\ mol\cdot dm^{-3}$；

(D) $[A]=[C]=1\ mol\cdot dm^{-3}$, $[B]=2\ mol\cdot dm^{-3}$。

5.9　反应 $2SO_2(g)+O_2(g) \rightleftharpoons 2SO_3(g)$ 达平衡时,保持体积不变,加入惰性气体 He,使总压力增加一倍,则

(A) 平衡向右移动；　　(B) 平衡向左移动；

(C) 平衡不发生移动；　　(D) 无法判断。

5.10　对于反应 $2Cl_2(g)+2H_2O(g) = 4HCl(g)+O_2(g)$ 的 $\Delta_r H_m^{\ominus}<0$,将 $H_2O(g)$,$HCl(g)$,$Cl_2(g)$,$O_2(g)$混合并在反应达到平衡时,下列操作平衡不发生移动的是

(A) 增加容器体积；(B) 降低体系温度；　(C) 加入氧气；　(D) 加入催化剂。

5.11　反应 $NO_2(g)+NO(g) = N_2O_3(g)$ 的 $\Delta_r H_m^{\ominus}=-40.5\ kJ\cdot mol^{-1}$,反应达到平衡时,下列操作中能使平衡逆向移动的是

(A) 温度和体积不变,压入氖气；　　(B) 温度不变,减小体积；

(C) 体积和压力不变,降低温度；　　(D) 温度和压力不变,压入氦气。

5.12　在 298 K 反应 $BaCl_2\cdot H_2O(s) \rightleftharpoons BaCl_2(s)+H_2O(g)$ 达平衡时,$p(H_2O)=330$ Pa,则反应的 $\Delta_r G_m^{\ominus}$ 为

(A) $-14.2\ kJ\cdot mol^{-1}$；　　(B) $14.2\ kJ\cdot mol^{-1}$；

(C) $142\ kJ\cdot mol^{-1}$；　　(D) $-142\ kJ\cdot mol^{-1}$。

5.13　若反应商等于 1,下列关系正确的是

(A) $\Delta_r G_m^{\ominus}=0$；　(B) $\Delta_r G_m=0$；　(C) $\Delta_r G_m=\Delta_r G_m^{\ominus}$；　(D) $\Delta_r H_m^{\ominus}=T\Delta_r S_m^{\ominus}$。

5.14　某化合物 A 的水合晶体 $A\cdot 3H_2O$ 脱水反应过程：

$$A\cdot 3H_2O(s) = A\cdot 2H_2O(s)+H_2O(g) \qquad K_1^{\ominus}$$

$$A\cdot 2H_2O(s) = A\cdot H_2O(s)+H_2O(g) \qquad K_2^{\ominus}$$

$$A\cdot H_2O(s) = A(s)+H_2O(g) \qquad K_3^{\ominus}$$

为使 $A\cdot 2H_2O$ 晶体保持稳定(不发生潮解或风化),则容器中水蒸气压 $p(H_2O)$与平衡常数的关系应满足

(A) $K_2^{\ominus}>p(H_2O)/p^{\ominus}>K_3^{\ominus}$；　　(B) $p(H_2O)/p^{\ominus}>K_2^{\ominus}$；

(C) $p(H_2O)/p^{\ominus}>K_1^{\ominus}$；　　(D) $K_1^{\ominus}>p(H_2O)/p^{\ominus}>K_2^{\ominus}$。

5.15　反应 $I_2(s)+Cl_2(g) = 2ICl(g)$　$\Delta_r G_m^{\ominus}=-10.9\ kJ\cdot mol^{-1}$。25℃时,将分压为 $p_{Cl_2}=0.217$ kPa,$p_{ICl}=81.04$ kPa 的 Cl_2 和 ICl 与固体 I_2 放入一容器中,则混合时的反应的 $\Delta_r G_m$ 为

(A) $14.7\ kJ\cdot mol^{-1}$；　　(B) $1.18\ kJ\cdot mol^{-1}$；

(C) $3.25\ kJ\cdot mol^{-1}$；　　(D) $-4.7\ kJ\cdot mol^{-1}$。

二、填空题

5.16　在 25 ℃时，若两个反应的平衡常数之比为 10，则两个反应的 $\Delta_r G_m^\ominus$ 相差________ $kJ\cdot mol^{-1}$。

5.17　在 20 ℃时，甲醇的蒸气压为 11.83 kPa，则甲醇汽化过程的 $\Delta_r G_m^\ominus$ 为________ $kJ\cdot mol^{-1}$。甲醇在正常沸点时的 $\Delta_r G_m^\ominus$ 为________ $kJ\cdot mol^{-1}$。

5.18　在 100 ℃时，反应 $AB(g) \rightleftharpoons A(g)+B(g)$ 的平衡常数 $K_c=0.21\ mol\cdot dm^{-3}$，则标准平衡常数 $K^\ominus$ 的值为________。

5.19　已知环戊烷的汽化过程 $\Delta_r H_m^\ominus=28.7\ kJ\cdot mol^{-1}$，$\Delta_r S_m^\ominus=88\ J\cdot mol^{-1}\cdot K^{-1}$。环戊烷的正常沸点为____℃，在 25 ℃时的饱和蒸气压为________ kPa。

5.20　对于反应

$$SO_3(g) \longrightarrow SO_2(g)+\frac{1}{2}O_2(g) \qquad \Delta_r H_m^\ominus=98.7\ kJ\cdot mol^{-1}$$

将反应速率常数、反应速率、标准平衡常数 $K^\ominus$ 及平衡移动方向等随条件的变化填入下表。

	$k_{正}$	$k_{逆}$	$r_{正}$	$r_{逆}$	$K^\ominus$	平衡移动方向
增加总压						
升高温度						
加催化剂						

5.21　已知反应 $NiSO_4\cdot 6H_2O(s) \rightleftharpoons NiSO_4(s)+6H_2O(g)$ 的 $\Delta_r G_m^\ominus=77.7\ kJ\cdot mol^{-1}$，则平衡时 $NiSO_4\cdot 6H_2O$ 固体表面上水的蒸气压 $p(H_2O)$ 为________ Pa。

5.22　反应 $I_2(g) \rightleftharpoons 2I(g)$ 达平衡时：

(1) 升高温度，平衡常数________；原因是________________。

(2) 压缩气体时，$I_2(g)$的解离度________；原因是________________。

(3) 恒容时充入 N_2 气体，$I_2(g)$的解离度________；原因是________________。

(4) 恒压时充入 N_2 气体，$I_2(g)$的解离度________；原因是________________。

5.23　合成氨反应：$N_2(g)+3H_2(g) \longrightarrow 2NH_3(g)$，在 673 K 时，$K^\ominus=5.7\times10^{-4}$；在 473 K 时，$K^\ominus=0.61$。则 873 K 时，$K^\ominus=$________。

三、简答题和计算题

5.24　光气分解反应 $COCl_2(g) \longrightarrow CO(g)+Cl_2(g)$ 在 373 K 时，$K^\ominus=8.0\times10^{-9}$，$\Delta_r H_m^\ominus=104.6\ kJ\cdot mol^{-1}$，试求：

(1) 373 K 达平衡后总压为 200 kPa 时 $COCl_2$ 的解离度；

(2) 反应的 $\Delta_r S_m^\ominus$。

5.25　HI 分解反应为 $2HI(g) \rightleftharpoons H_2(g)+I_2(g)$，若开始时有 1 mol HI，平衡时有 24.4%的 HI 发生了分解。今欲将 HI 的分解分数降低到 10%，应往此平衡体系中加入多少摩尔 I_2？

5.26 在 308 K 和总压 100 kPa 时，N_2O_4 有 27.2%分解。

(1) 计算 $N_2O_4(g) \rightleftharpoons 2NO_2(g)$ 反应的 $K^{\ominus}$；

(2) 计算 308 K 时总压为 200 kPa 时，N_2O_4 的解离分数；

(3) 从计算结果说明压强对平衡移动的影响。

5.27 $PCl_5(g)$在 523 K 达分解平衡：

$$PCl_5(g) \rightleftharpoons PCl_3(g) + Cl_2(g)$$

平衡浓度：$[PCl_5]=1\ mol\cdot dm^{-3}$，$[PCl_3]=[Cl_2]=0.204\ mol\cdot dm^{-3}$。若温度不变而压强减小一半，在新的平衡体系中各物质的浓度为多少？

5.28 反应 $SO_2Cl_2(g) \rightleftharpoons SO_2(g)+Cl_2(g)$在 375 K 时平衡常数 $K^{\ominus}=2.4$。以 7.6 g SO_2Cl_2 和 100 kPa 的 Cl_2 作用于 1.0 dm^3 的烧瓶中。试计算平衡时 SO_2Cl_2，SO_2 和 Cl_2 的分压。

5.29 1 000 K 时，反应 $2SO_2(g)+O_2(g) \rightleftharpoons 2SO_3(g)$的 $K_p=3.4\times10^{-5}\ Pa^{-1}$。求反应$SO_2(g)+\frac{1}{2}O_2(g) \rightleftharpoons SO_3(g)$在该温度下的 K_p，K_c。

5.30 反应 $CaCO_3(s) = CaO(s)+CO_2(g)$ 在 1 037 K 时平衡常数 $K^{\ominus}=1.16$，若将 0.20 mol $CaCO_3$ 置于 10.0 dm^3 容器中并加热至 1 037 K。问达平衡时 $CaCO_3$ 的分解分数是多少？

5.31 反应 $PCl_5(g) = PCl_3(g)+Cl_2(g)$，在 523 K 时将 0.70 mol 的 PCl_5 注入 2.0 dm^3 密闭容器中，平衡时有 0.50 mol PCl_5 分解。试计算：

(1) 该温度下的平衡常数 K_c，$K^{\ominus}$ 及 PCl_5 分解分数；

(2) 若在上述平衡体系中再加入 0.10 mol Cl_2，计算 PCl_5 的分解分数，并与未加 Cl_2 时相比较；

(3) 若开始就注入 0.70 mol PCl_5 和 0.10 mol Cl_2，则平衡时 PCl_5 的分解分数是多少？与前面的结果比较，可以得出什么结论？

5.32 反应 $C_6H_5C_2H_5(g) = C_6H_5C_2H_3(g)+H_2(g)$ 在 873 K 和 100 kPa 压力下达到平衡。求下列两种情况下乙苯转化为苯乙烯的转化率。(873 K 时，平衡常数 $K^{\ominus}=8.9\times10^{-2}$)

(1) 以纯乙苯为原料；

(2) 原料气中加入不起反应的水蒸气，使物质的量之比 n(乙苯)∶n(水蒸气)=1∶10。

5.33 在 325 K，100 kPa 时 $N_2O_4(g)$的分解分数为 50.2%；该温度下，10×100 kPa 时，$N_2O_4(g)$的分解分数是多少？

5.34 在 250 ℃和 100 kPa，PCl_5 发生分解反应：

$$PCl_5(g) = PCl_3(g)+Cl_2(g)$$

达平衡时，测混合气体的密度为 2.695 $g\cdot dm^{-3}$。求反应的 $\Delta_r G_m^{\ominus}$ 和 $PCl_5(g)$的解离度。

5.35 在一定温度和压强下，某一定量的 PCl_5 气体的体积为 1 dm^3，此时 PCl_5 气体已有 50%解离为 PCl_3 和 Cl_2 气体。试判断在下列条件下，PCl_5 的解离度是增大还是减小。

(1) 减压使 PCl_5 的体积变为 2 dm^3；

(2) 保持压强不变，加入氮气使体积增至 2 dm^3；

(3) 保持体积不变，加入氮气使压强增加 1 倍；

(4) 保持压强不变，加入氯气体积变为 2 dm^3；

(5) 保持体积不变，加入氯气使压强增加1倍。

5.36 已知在427 ℃时各物质的热力学函数

	$N_2(g)$	$H_2(g)$	$NH_3(g)$
$\Delta_f H_m^\ominus/(kJ\cdot mol^{-1})$	0	0	−45.22
$S_m^\ominus/(J\cdot mol^{-1}\cdot K^{-1})$	217.0	155.9	243.5

在该温度下反应 $N_2(g)+3H_2(g) = 2NH_3(g)$ 达平衡时，$[N_2]=1.0\ mol\cdot dm^{-3}$，$[H_2]=3.0\ mol\cdot dm^{-3}$。求 NH_3 的浓度。

5.37 KOH 的溶解度很大，常温下约为 110 g/100 g H_2O，所以将几粒固体 KOH 放入 100 g 水中，可以溶解。上述过程明显放热。又有实验事实表明，KOH 的溶解度随温度升高而增大。从勒夏特列原理考虑，以上两种实验现象似乎矛盾。试给出合理解释。

第 6 章

原子结构与元素周期律

第一部分　例题

例 6.1　用量子数 n，l 和 m 对原子核外 $n=4$ 的所有可能的原子轨道分别进行描述。

解：$n=4$，则 $l=0,1,2,3$。

$$l=0 \quad m=0$$
$$l=1 \quad m=-1,0,+1$$
$$l=2 \quad m=-2,-1,0,+1,+2$$
$$l=3 \quad m=-3,-2,-1,0,+1,+2,+3$$

轨道数目：　　$1+3+5+7=16$

这 16 个原子轨道可以用量子数分别描述如下：

	n	l	m		n	l	m
1	4	0	0	9	4	2	2
2	4	1	−1	10	4	3	−3
3	4	1	0	11	4	3	−2
4	4	1	1	12	4	3	−1
5	4	2	−2	13	4	3	0
6	4	2	−1	14	4	3	1
7	4	2	0	15	4	3	2
8	4	2	1	16	4	3	3

例 6.2　用四个量子数 n，l，m 和 m_s 对原子核外 $n=3$ 的所有电子分别进行描述。

解：$n=3$，则 $l=0,1,2$。

$$l=0 \quad m=0$$
$$l=1 \quad m=-1,0,+1$$
$$l=2 \quad m=-2,-1,0,+1,+2$$

轨道数目：　　$1+3+5=9$

电子数：　　$2\times 9=18$

这 18 个电子的运动状态可以用量子数分别描述如下：

	n	l	m	m_s		n	l	m	m_s
1	3	0	0	$\frac{1}{2}$	10	3	2	-2	$-\frac{1}{2}$
2	3	0	0	$-\frac{1}{2}$	11	3	2	-1	$\frac{1}{2}$
3	3	1	-1	$\frac{1}{2}$	12	3	2	-1	$-\frac{1}{2}$
4	3	1	-1	$-\frac{1}{2}$	13	3	2	0	$\frac{1}{2}$
5	3	1	0	$\frac{1}{2}$	14	3	2	0	$-\frac{1}{2}$
6	3	1	0	$-\frac{1}{2}$	15	3	2	1	$\frac{1}{2}$
7	3	1	1	$\frac{1}{2}$	16	3	2	1	$-\frac{1}{2}$
8	3	1	1	$-\frac{1}{2}$	17	3	2	2	$\frac{1}{2}$
9	3	2	-2	$\frac{1}{2}$	18	3	2	2	$-\frac{1}{2}$

例 6.3　将氢原子核外电子从基态激发到 2s 或 2p 轨道，所需能量是否相同？为什么？若是 He 原子情况又怎样？若是 He^+ 或 Li^{2+} 情况又是怎样？

解：将氢原子核外电子从基态激发到 2s 或 2p 轨道，所需能量相同，原因是氢原子核外只有一个电子，这个电子仅受到原子核的作用，电子的能量只与主量子数有关，如下式所示

$$E=-13.6\times\frac{z^2}{n^2}\ \text{eV}$$

将 He^+ 或 Li^{2+} 核外电子从基态激发到 2s 或 2p 轨道，所需能量也相同，原因是这些类氢离子核外只有一个电子，这个电子也仅仅受到原子核的作用，电子的能量只与主量子数有关，不涉及内层电子屏蔽作用不同的问题。

若 He 原子核外电子从基态激发到 2s 或 2p 轨道，所需能量不同。原因是在多电子原子中，一个电子不仅受到原子核的引力，而且还要受到其他电子的斥力。He 第一层有 2 个电子，其中一个电子除了受原子核对它的引力之外，还受到另一个电子对它的排斥作用。这一电子的排斥作用可以考虑为它对核电荷的屏蔽效应，2s 和 2p 轨道受到的屏蔽不同，故两者的能量也不相同，所以电子从基态激发到 2s 和 2p 轨道，所需能量不同。

例 6.4　Cu 原子形成＋1 价离子时失去的是 4s 电子还是 3d 电子？用 Slater 规则的计算结果加以说明。

解：Cu 原子的电子结构式为

$$1s^2 2s^2 2p^6 3s^2 3p^6 3d^{10} 4s^1$$

4s 电子的 $\sigma_{4s}=(0.85\times18)+(1.00\times10)=25.3$

$$E_{4s}=-13.6\times\frac{(29-25.3)^2}{4^2}\ \text{eV}=-11.64\ \text{eV}$$

3d 电子的 $\sigma_{3d}=(0.35\times9)+(1.00\times18)=21.15$

$$E_{3d}=-13.6\times\frac{(29-21.15)^2}{3^2}\ \text{eV}=-93.12\ \text{eV}$$

计算结果是 $E_{4s}>E_{3d}$，说明 Cu 原子失去 4s 轨道中的电子。

例 6.5 分别写出原子序数为 24 和 41 的元素的名称、符号、电子结构式，并用四个量子数分别表示各价电子的运动状态。

解： 24 铬 Cr(chromium) [Ar]$3d^5 4s^1$

各价电子	n	l	m	m_s
$3d^5$	3	2	+2	$+\frac{1}{2}$
	3	2	+1	$+\frac{1}{2}$
	3	2	0	$+\frac{1}{2}$
	3	2	−1	$+\frac{1}{2}$
	3	2	−2	$+\frac{1}{2}$
$4s^1$	4	0	0	$+\frac{1}{2}$

41 铌 Nb(niobium) [Kr]$4d^4 5s^1$

各价电子	n	l	m	m_s
$4d^4$	4	2	+2	$+\frac{1}{2}$
	4	2	+1	$+\frac{1}{2}$
	4	2	0	$+\frac{1}{2}$
	4	2	−1	$+\frac{1}{2}$
$5s^1$	5	0	0	$+\frac{1}{2}$

例 6.6 已知离子 M^{2+} 3d 轨道中有 5 个电子，试推出

(1) M 原子的核外电子排布；

(2) M 元素的名称和元素符号；

(3) M 元素在周期表中的位置。

解： 先列出具有 $3d^{5\sim7}$ 的元素及其电子构型：

25 号 锰 Mn [Ar]$3d^5 4s^2$

26 号 铁 Fe [Ar]$3d^6 4s^2$

27 号 钴 Co [Ar]$3d^7 4s^2$

根据科顿原子轨道能级图，它们的 $E_{4s} > E_{3d}$，所以形成 M^{2+} 时，失去的是 2 个 4s 电子。由此可得出结论(1)M 原子的核外电子排布为[Ar]$3d^5 4s^2$；结论(2)M 元素是锰，其元素符号为 Mn。

[Ar]$3d^5 4s^2$ 中最高能级属于第 4 能级组，故 M 为第四周期元素。d 电子未充满，属于 d 区副族元素，其族数等于最高能级组中的电子总数，即(5+2)为 7。因此可推出结论(3)M 元素在周期表中位于 d 区，第四周期、ⅦB 族。

例 6.7　写出下列元素基态原子的电子结构式，并给出原子序数和元素名称：

(1) 第 4 个稀有气体；

(2) 第四周期的第 6 个过渡元素；

(3) 4p 轨道半充满的元素；

(4) 电负性最大的元素；

(5) 4f 轨道填充 4 个电子的元素；

(6) 第一个 4d 轨道全充满的元素。

解：电子排布式	原子序数	元素名称
(1) [Ar]$3d^{10}4s^2 4p^6$	36	氪 Kr
(2) [Ar]$3d^6 4s^2$	26	铁 Fe
(3) [Ar]$3d^{10}4s^2 4p^3$	33	砷 As
(4) [He]$2s^2 2p^5$	9	氟 F
(5) [Xe]$4f^4 6s^2$	60	钕 Nd
(6) [Kr]$4d^{10}$	46	钯 Pd

例 6.8　写出下列离子的电子结构式，并给出化学式：

(1) 与 Ar 电子构型相同的+2 价离子；

(2) 与 F^- 电子构型相同的+3 价离子；

(3) 核中质子个数最少的 3d 轨道全充满的+1 价离子；

(4) 与 Kr 电子构型相同的−1 价离子。

解：(1) $1s^2 2s^2 2p^6 3s^2 3p^6$　　Ca^{2+}

(2) $1s^2 2s^2 2p^6$　　Al^{3+}

(3) [Ar]$3d^{10}$　　Cu^+

(4) [Ar]$3d^{10}4s^2 4p^6$　　Br^-

例 6.9　某原子共有 6 个电子，其状态分别用四个量子数表示如下：

序号	n	l	m	m_s
①	3	2	−2	$\frac{1}{2}$
②	4	0	0	$-\frac{1}{2}$
③	2	0	0	$\frac{1}{2}$
④	4	0	0	$\frac{1}{2}$

续表

序号	n	l	m	m_s
⑤	2	1	0	$\frac{1}{2}$
⑥	3	1	-1	$\frac{1}{2}$

(1) 用主量子数与角量子数的光谱学符号相结合的方式(例如 2p,3s),表示每个电子所处的轨道;

(2) 将各个轨道按能量由高到低的次序排列起来。

解:(1) ① 3d　② 4s　③ 2s

④ 4s　⑤ 2p　⑥ 3p

(2) 该原子共有 6 个电子,这是激发态的碳原子,比照科顿原子轨道能级图各轨道按能量由高到低的次序排列如下:

4s,3d,3p,2p,2s

例 6.10　某元素在 Kr 之前,当它的原子失去 3 个电子后,其角量子数为 2 的轨道上的电子恰好是半充满。推断该元素的名称,并给出其基态原子的电子构型。

解:Kr 的电子结构式为[Ar]$3d^{10}4s^24p^6$。

角量子数为 2 的轨道是 d 轨道,d 轨道 5 重简并,半充满是指具有 d^5 结构。

在 Kr 之前,失去 3 个电子将涉及 3d 电子的原子中,肯定不含有 4p 电子。只有比[Ar]$3d^{10}4s^2$ 电子数少的原子,其 M^{3+} 离子才会改变其 3d 电子的结构。失去 2 个 4s 电子和 1 个 3d 电子后具有 $3d^5$ 构型的原子,其电子结构中应有 6 个 3d 电子。

因此该元素的原子的电子构型为[Ar]$3d^64s^2$,这是 26 号元素铁。

例 6.11　若四个量子数 n,l,m 和 m_s 的取值及相互关系重新规定如下:

n 为正整数。对于给定的 n 值,l 可以取下列 n 个值:

$$l=0,1,2,\cdots,(n-1)$$

对于给定的 l 值,m 可以取下列$(l+1)$个值:

$$m=0,+1,+2,\cdots,+l$$

$$m_s=\pm\frac{1}{2}$$

据此可以得到新的元素周期表。试根据新的周期表回答下列问题:

(1) 第二、第四周期各有多少种元素?

(2) p 区元素共有多少列?

(3) 位于第三周期、最右一列的元素的原子序数是多少?

(4) 原周期表中电负性最大的元素,在新的周期表中位于第几周期、第几列?

(5) 新的周期表中第一个具有 d 电子的元素,在原周期表中位于第几周期、第几列?

解:新规定的不同在于 m 的取值。

当 $l=0$ 时,m 只有 1 个取值 0;

$l=1$ 时，m 有 2 个取值 0，1；

$l=2$ 时，m 有 3 个取值 0，1，2。

这说明 $l=0$ 的 s 轨道只有 1 个取向，简并度为 1；

$l=1$ 的 p 轨道有 2 个不同的取向，简并度为 2；

$l=2$ 的 d 轨道有 3 个不同的取向，简并度为 3。

于是可得新周期表

H											He
Li	Be							B	C	N	O
F	Ne							Na	Mg	Al	Si
P	S	Cl	Ar	K	Ca	Sc	Ti	V	Cr	Mn	Fe
s 区元素		d 区元素						p 区元素			

根据新周期表回答问题如下：

(1) 第二周期有 6 种元素，第四周期有 12 种元素。

(2) p 区元素共有 4 列。

(3) 第三周期最右一列的元素为 Si，原子序数为 14。

(4) 原周期表中电负性最大的元素是 F，在新的周期表中位于第三周期、第 1 列。

(5) 新周期表中第一个具有 d 电子的元素是 Cl，它在原周期表中位于第三周期、第 17 列。

例 6.12　求算 Li 的第三电离能(用 $kJ\cdot mol^{-1}$ 表示)。

解： Li 的第三电离能是指 $Li^{2+} \longrightarrow Li^{3+} + e^-$ 过程所需能量。由于 Li^{2+} 为单电子离子，电子构型为 $1s^1$。

$$E_{1s}=-13.6\ \text{eV}\times\frac{z^2}{n^2}=-13.6\ \text{eV}\times\frac{3^2}{1^2}=-122.4\ \text{eV}$$

当 $n\to\infty$ 时，电子已失去，此时电子能量最高为 0，则 Li 的第三电离能为

$$\begin{aligned}I_3&=0-E_{1s}=122.4\ \text{eV}\\&=122.4\times1.602\times10^{-19}\times10^{-3}\ \text{kJ}\times6.02\times10^{23}\ \text{mol}^{-1}\\&=11\ 804\ \text{kJ}\cdot\text{mol}^{-1}\end{aligned}$$

第二部分　习题

一、选择题

6.1　原子轨道角度分布图中，从原点到曲面的距离表示

(A) ψ 值的大小；　(B) Y 值的大小；

(C) r 值的大小；　(D) $4\pi r^2 dr$ 值的大小。

6.2　下列轨道上的电子，在 xy 平面上的电子云密度为零的是

(A) 3s；　(B) $3p_x$；　(C) $3p_z$；　(D) $3d_{z^2}$。

6.3　第四周期元素原子中未成对电子数最多可达

(A) 4 个；　(B) 5 个；　(C) 6 个；　(D) 7 个。

6.4　基态原子的第五电子层只有 2 个电子，则该原子的第四电子层中的电子数肯定为

(A) 8 个；　(B) 18 个；　(C) 8～18 个；　(D) 8～32 个。

6.5　下列关于屏蔽效应的说法中，正确的是

(A) 4s 电子的屏蔽常数 σ_{4s} 反映了 4s 电子屏蔽原子核作用的大小；

(B) 当主量子数 n 和核电荷数 z 相同的两个电子，σ 值越大，电子的能量就越低；

(C) 主量子数 n 相同，角量子数 l 愈大，电子的屏蔽作用增大；

(D) 当屏蔽电子数目愈多或被屏蔽电子离核愈远时，σ 值也愈大。

6.6　下列元素中，原子半径最接近的一组是

(A) Ne, Ar, Kr, Xe；　(B) Mg, Ca, Sr, Ba；

(C) B, C, N, O；　(D) Cr, Mn, Fe, Co。

6.7　按原子半径由大到小排列，顺序正确的是

(A) Mg B Si；　(B) Si Mg B；　(C) Mg Si B；　(D) B Si Mg。

6.8　下列元素中，电子排布不正确的是

(A) Nb $4d^4 5s^1$；　(B) Nd $4f^4 5d^0 6s^2$；　(C) Ne $3s^2 3p^6$；　(D) Ni $3d^8 4s^2$。

6.9　下列基态原子的电子构型中，正确的是

(A) $3d^9 4s^2$；　(B) $3d^4 4s^2$；　(C) $4d^{10} 5s^0$；　(D) $4d^8 5s^2$。

6.10　元素周期表中，第一过渡系列与第二过渡系列元素性质的差异大于第二过渡系列与第三过渡系列元素性质的差异，主要原因是

(A) 惰性电子对效应；　(B) 价电子构型相似；

(C) 它们都是金属元素；　(D) 镧系收缩的影响。

6.11　镧系收缩使下列各对元素中性质相似的是

(A) Mn 和 Tc；　(B) Ru 和 Rh；　(C) Nd 和 Ta；　(D) Zr 和 Hf。

6.12　具有下列电子构型的元素中，第一电离能最小的是

(A) $ns^2 np^3$；　(B) $ns^2 np^4$；　(C) $ns^2 np^5$；　(D) $ns^2 np^6$。

6.13　Pb^{2+} 离子的价电子结构是

(A) $5s^2$；　(B) $6s^2 6p^2$；　(C) $5s^2 5p^2$；　(D) $5s^2 5p^6 5d^{10} 6s^2$。

6.14　下列各对元素中，第一电离能大小次序不正确的是

(A) Mg<Al；　(B) S<P；　(C) Cu<Zn；　(D) Cs<Au。

6.15　第二电离能最大的元素所具有的电子结构是

(A) $1s^2$；　(B) $1s^2 2s^1$；　(C) $1s^2 2s^2$；　(D) $1s^2 2s^2 2p^1$。

6.16　下列元素基态原子的第三电离能最大的是

(A) C；　(B) B；　(C) Be；　(D) Li。

6.17　某元素基态原子失去 3 个电子后，角量子数为 2 的轨道半充满，其原子序数为

(A) 24；　(B) 25；　(C) 26；　(D) 27。

6.18　下列元素中，属镧系元素的是

(A) Ta；　(B) Ti；　(C) Tl；　(D) Tm。

6.19　下列元素中，不是放射性元素的是

(A) Pa;　(B) Pd;　(C) Pm;　(D) Po。

6.20　下列元素中,属放射性元素的是

(A) Ta;　(B) Tb;　(C) Tc;　(D) Tm。

6.21　下列各组元素按电负性大小排列正确的是

(A) F>N>O;　(B) O>Cl>F;　(C) As>P>H;　(D) Cl>S>As。

6.22　如果氢原子的电离能是 13.6 eV,则 He^+ 的电离能为

(A) 122.4 eV;　(B) 54.4 eV;　(C) 27.2 eV;　(D) 13.6 eV。

6.23　下列各对元素中,第一电子亲和能大小排列正确的是

(A) O>S;　(B) F<C;　(C) Cl>Br;　(D) Si<P。

6.24　下列元素中第一电子亲和能最大的是

(A) O;　(B) F;　(C) S;　(D) Cl。

二、填空题

6.25　4p 亚层中轨道的主量子数为____,角量子数为____,该亚层的轨道最多可以有____种空间取向,最多可容纳____个电子。

6.26　第四周期元素中,4p 轨道半充满的是________,3d 轨道半充满的是________,4s 轨道半充满的是________,价层中 s 电子数与 d 电子数相同的是________。

6.27　周期表中最活泼的金属为________,最活泼的非金属为________;原子序数最小的放射性元素为第____周期元素,其元素符号为____。

6.28　给出下列元素的原子核外价电子排布式 W ________,Nb ________,Ru ________,Rh ______,Pd ________,Pt ________。

6.29　在各类原子轨道中,____轨道的钻穿能力最强,由此引起的后果是________________。

6.30　氢原子轨道的能量计算公式为____________;He^+ 基态电子的能量与 H 基态电子的能量之比为____。

6.31　镧系元素包括原子序数从____至____共____个元素;从 La 到 Lu 半径共减少____pm,这一事实称为________,其结果是____________________。

6.32　某元素在氪之前,该元素的原子失去 2 个电子后的离子在角量子数为 2 的轨道中有 1 个单电子,若只失去 1 个电子则离子的轨道中没有单电子。该元素的符号为____,其基态原子核外电子排布为__________,该元素在____区,第____族。

6.33　A 原子的 M 层比 B 原子的 M 层少 4 个电子,B 原子的 N 层比 A 原子的 N 层多 5 个电子。则 A 的元素符号为____,B 的元素符号为____,A 与 B 的单质在酸性溶液中反应得到的二种化合物为__________。

6.34　非放射性元素中,单电子数最多的元素单电子数为________个,它在周期表中位于第________周期,第________族。

三、简答题和计算题

6.35　指出下列用四个量子数表示的电子运动状态哪些是错误的,并说明出现错误的原因。

序号	n	l	m	m_s
①	3	2	−2	$\frac{1}{2}$
②	4	0	0	0
③	3	1	−1	$-\frac{1}{2}$
④	4	1	−2	$\frac{1}{2}$
⑤	2	−1	0	$-\frac{1}{2}$
⑥	−2	1	−1	$\frac{1}{2}$
⑦	3	3	1	$-\frac{1}{2}$

6.36　通过计算说明，原子序数为 25 的元素原子中，4s 和 3d 轨道哪个能量高？

6.37　由下列元素在周期表中的位置，给出元素名称、元素符号及其价层电子构型。

(1) 第四周期第ⅥB族；　(2) 第五周期第ⅠB族；

(3) 第五周期第ⅣA族；　(4) 第六周期第ⅡA族；

(5) 第四周期第ⅦA族。

6.38　有 A,B,C,D,E,F 元素，试按下列条件推断各元素在周期表中的位置、元素符号，给出各元素的价电子构型。

(1) A,B,C 为同一周期活泼金属元素，原子半径满足 A＞B＞C，已知 C 有 3 个电子层。

(2) D,E 为非金属元素，与氢结合生成 HD 和 HE。室温下 D 的单质为液体，E 的单质为固体。

(3) F 为金属元素，它有 4 个电子层并且有 6 个单电子。

6.39　A,B,C 三种元素的原子最后一个电子填充在相同的能级组轨道上，B 的核电荷比 A 大 9 个单位，C 的质子数比 B 多 7 个；1 mol 的 A 单质同酸反应置换出 1 g H_2，同时转化为具有氩原子的电子层结构的离子。判断 A,B,C 各为何元素，A,B 同 C 反应时生成的化合物的分子式。

6.40　A,B 两元素，A 原子的 M 层和 N 层的电子数分别比 B 原子的 M 层和 N 层的电子数少 7 个和 4 个。写出 A,B 的元素名称和电子排布式，给出推理过程。

6.41　如果发现 116 号元素，请给出

(1) 钠盐的化学式；　(2) 简单氢化物的化学式；

(3) 最高价态的氧化物的化学式；　(4) 该元素是金属还是非金属。

6.42　判断下列各对元素中哪一种元素的第一电离能大，并说明原因。

(1) S 与 P；　(2) Al 与 Mg；　(3) Sr 与 Rb；　(4) Cu 与 Zn；　(5) Cs 与 Au。

6.43　比较下列各对元素或离子的半径大小并说明原因。

(1) Sr 与 Ba；　(2) Ca 与 Sc；　(3) Ni 与 Cu；　(4) Zr 与 Hf；　(5) S^{2-} 与 S；　(6) Na^+ 与 Al^{3+}；　(7) Sn^{2+} 与 Pb^{2+}；　(8) Fe^{2+} 与 Fe^{3+}。

6.44　试根据原子结构理论预测：

(1) 第八周期将包括多少种元素？

(2) 核外出现第一个 5g 电子的元素其原子序数是多少？

(3) 第 114 号元素属于第几周期？第几族？

6.45 比较大小并简要说明原因。

(1) 第一电离能 O 与 N,Cd 与 In,Cr 与 W；

(2) 第一电子亲和能 C 与 N,S 与 P。

第 7 章

化学键理论概述

第一部分　例题

例 7.1　解释下列各组化合物熔点的高低关系。

(1) $NaCl>NaBr$；　(2) $CaO>KCl$；　(3) $MgO>Al_2O_3$。

解：三组化合物均为离子型化合物。离子晶体熔点主要由离子键的键能决定，键能越大，熔点越高。

键能和正、负离子电荷及半径有关。电荷高，离子键强。半径大，导致离子间距大，所以键能小；相反，半径小，则键能大。据此可以解释(1)和(2)。

(1) NaCl 和 NaBr 其正离子均为 Na^+，负离子电荷相同而半径为 $r(Cl^-)<r(Br^-)$，故键能 $E(NaCl)>E(NaBr)$，所以熔点 NaCl > NaBr。

(2) CaO 和 KCl，其键能的大小主要取决于离子电荷数。CaO 的正、负离子电荷数值均为 2，而 KCl 的均为 1，故 CaO 的键能比 KCl 的大，所以熔点 CaO > KCl 。

除正、负离子电荷和半径影响键能，从而影响化合物的熔点外，离子极化作用较强时，也可使离子化合物具有较多的共价成分，而使键能有所减小，熔点有所降低。

(3) MgO 与 Al_2O_3 相比，Al^{3+} 的电荷相当高，半径小，极化作用很强，因而使 Al_2O_3 具有较多的共价成分，离子键的键能有所减小，所以熔点 $MgO>Al_2O_3$。

例 7.2　已知 KF 晶体具有 NaCl 型结构，在 20℃时测出 KF 晶体密度为 2.481 $g\cdot cm^{-3}$，试计算 KF 晶胞的边长及在晶胞中相邻的 K^+ 和 F^- 离子间的距离。已知相对原子质量 $A_r(K)=39.10$，$A_r(F)=19.00$。

解：KF 晶体具有 NaCl 型结构，即 KF 晶体为立方面心晶格。一个 KF 晶胞中含有 4 个 K^+ 和 4 个 F^-。

KF 的晶胞体积为

$$V=\frac{4\times(39.10+19.00)\,g\cdot mol^{-1}}{2.481\,g\cdot cm^{-3}\times 6.023\times 10^{23}\ mol^{-1}}=1.555\times 10^{-22}\ cm^3$$

KF 的晶胞边长为

$$a=\sqrt[3]{V}=\sqrt[3]{1.555\times 10^{-22}\ cm^3}=5.38\times 10^{-8}\ cm=538\ pm$$

K^+ 与 F^- 间距离为

$$d=\frac{1}{2}a=269\ \text{pm}$$

例 7.3　根据下列已知数据，由玻恩－哈伯循环计算氯化钡的 $\Delta_f H_m^\ominus$。

氯分子的解离能	242.6 kJ·mol^{-1}
钡的原子化热	177.8 kJ·mol^{-1}
钡的第一电离能	520.9 kJ·mol^{-1}
钡的第二电离能	962.3 kJ·mol^{-1}
氯的电子亲和能	348.6 kJ·mol^{-1}
氯化钡的晶格能	2 026.7 kJ·mol^{-1}

解：玻恩－哈伯循环如图所示。

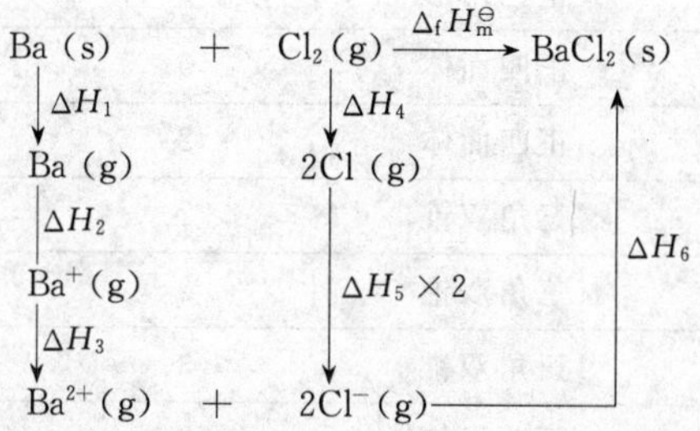

根据盖斯定律

$$\begin{aligned}\Delta_f H_m^\ominus(\text{BaCl}_2,\text{s}) &= \Delta H_1+\Delta H_2+\Delta H_3+\Delta H_4+\Delta H_5+\Delta H_6\\ &= 177.8\ \text{kJ·mol}^{-1}+520.9\ \text{kJ·mol}^{-1}+962.3\ \text{kJ·mol}^{-1}+\\ &\quad 242.6\ \text{kJ·mol}^{-1}-348.6\ \text{kJ·mol}^{-1}\times 2-\\ &\quad 2\,026.7\ \text{kJ·mol}^{-1}\\ &=-820.3\ \text{kJ·mol}^{-1}\end{aligned}$$

例 7.4　X 射线衍射法测得金属银的面心立方晶胞的边长为 408.6 pm，每立方厘米银的质量为 10.5 g，已知 Ag 的相对原子质量为 107.87。试据此计算阿伏伽德罗常数。

解：正立方体晶胞的边长为 408.6 pm，相当于 408.6×10^{-10} cm，故晶胞体积为

$$\begin{aligned}&(408.6\times10^{-10})^3\ \text{cm}^3\\ &=6.82\times10^{-23}\ \text{cm}^3\end{aligned}$$

依题意晶胞质量为

$$\begin{aligned}&10.5\ \text{g·cm}^{-3}\times6.82\times10^{-23}\ \text{cm}^3\\ &=7.16\times10^{-22}\ \text{g}\end{aligned}$$

立方面心晶胞中 Ag 原子的个数为

$$\frac{1}{8}\times8+\frac{1}{2}\times6=4$$

故每个 Ag 原子的质量为

$$7.16\times10^{-22}\ \text{g}\times\frac{1}{4}=1.79\times10^{-22}\ \text{g}$$

依题设，Ag 的摩尔质量为 107.87 g·mol^{-1}

故阿伏伽德罗常数 $N_A = \dfrac{107.87\ g \cdot mol^{-1}}{1.79 \times 10^{-22}\ g}$

$= 6.03 \times 10^{23}\ mol^{-1}$

例 7.5 用价层电子对互斥理论判断下列分子或离子的空间构型。

$BeCl_2$, BCl_3, NH_4^+, H_2O, ClF_3, PCl_5, I_3^-,

ICl_4^-, ClO_2^-, PO_4^{3-}, CO_2, SO_2, NOCl, $POCl_3$。

解：

分子或离子	价层电子对数	电子对构型	孤对电子对数	配体个数	分子或离子的几何构型
$BeCl_2$	2	直线形	0	2	直线形
BCl_3	3	正三角形	0	3	正三角形
NH_4^+	4	正四面体	0	4	正四面体
H_2O	4	正四面体	2	2	V 字形
ClF_3	5	三角双锥	2	3	T 字形
PCl_5	5	三角双锥	0	5	三角双锥
I_3^-	5	三角双锥	3	2	直线形
ICl_4^-	6	正八面体	2	4	正方形
ClO_2^-	4	正四面体	2	2	V 字形
PO_4^{3-}	4	正四面体	0	4	正四面体
CO_2	2	直线形	0	2	直线形
SO_2	3	正三角形	1	2	V 字形
NOCl	3	正三角形	1	2	V 字形
$POCl_3$	4	正四面体	0	4	四面体

例 7.6 用价层电子对互斥理论判断下列稀有气体化合物的空间构型，再用杂化轨道理论说明它们的成键情况。

XeF_2, XeF_4, XeO_3, XeO_4。

解：

化合物分子式	价层电子对数	配体个数	电子对构型	分子构型	杂化轨道类型	成键轨道	化学键类型
XeF_2	5	2	三角双锥	直线形	sp^3d 不等性杂化	sp^3d-2p	σ 键
XeF_4	6	4	正八面体	正方形	sp^3d^2 不等性杂化	sp^3d^2-2p	σ 键
XeO_3	4	3	正四面体	三角锥	sp^3 不等性杂化	sp^3-2p	σ 键
XeO_4	4	4	正四面体	正四面体	sp^3 等性杂化	sp^3-2p	σ 键

例 7.7　用杂化轨道理论解释为什么 BF_3 是平面三角形分子，而 NF_3 却是三角锥形分子。

解：BF_3 中心原子的价层电子结构为 $2s^2 2p^1$。

在 BF_3 分子中，中心原子 B 采取 sp^2 等性杂化，如图(a)所示，三条杂化轨道在空间呈正三角形分布，三个配体 F 与中心原子 B 成键。因此 BF_3 是平面三角形分子。

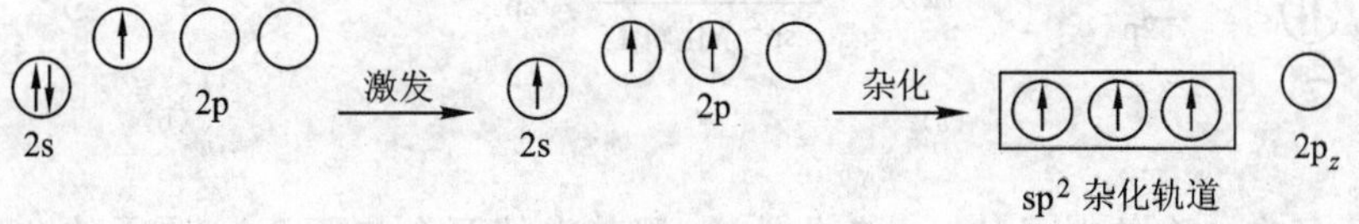

(a)

NF_3 中心原子 N 的价电子结构为 $2s^2 2p^3$，中心原子 N 采取 sp^3 不等性杂化，如图(b)所示，其中一个 sp^3 杂化轨道被孤对电子占据。四个杂化轨道在空间呈正四面体形状分布，三个配体 F 的单电子轨道与中心原子 N 的有单电子的 sp^3 杂化轨道成键。因此，NF_3 是三角锥形分子。

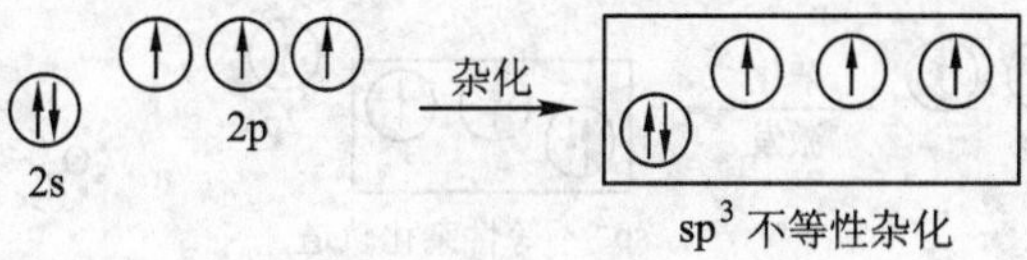

(b)

例 7.8　说明下列分子或离子的中心原子的杂化方式。

NCl_3，SF_4，$CHCl_3$，H_3O^+，NH_4^+，PCl_6^-，IF_3。

解：从价层电子对互斥理论出发计算出价层电子对对数，判断出电子对的几何构型，可以直接推出杂化轨道类型。若配体个数与价层电子对对数一致，则为等性杂化；若不一致则为不等性杂化。

分子或离子	价层电子对数	电子对构型	配体个数	杂化轨道类型
NCl_3	4	正四面体	3	sp^3 不等性杂化
SF_4	5	三角双锥	4	sp^3d 不等性杂化
$CHCl_3$	4	正四面体	4	sp^3 等性杂化
H_3O^+	4	正四面体	3	sp^3 不等性杂化
NH_4^+	4	正四面体	4	sp^3 等性杂化
PCl_6^-	6	正八面体	6	sp^3d^2 等性杂化
IF_3	5	三角双锥	3	sp^3d 不等性杂化

例 7.9　解释下列分子或离子中形成的共轭 π 键。

(1) NO_2，Π_3^3 或 Π_3^4；　　　(2) CO_3^{2-}，Π_4^6。

解：(1) N 原子电子构型为 $2s^2 2p^3$。一种看法是，N 原子 2s 轨道的 1 个电子激发到 2p 轨道，N 采取 sp^2 等性杂化。未参与杂化的 $2p_z$ 轨道，其中有一对电子。如图(a)所示。

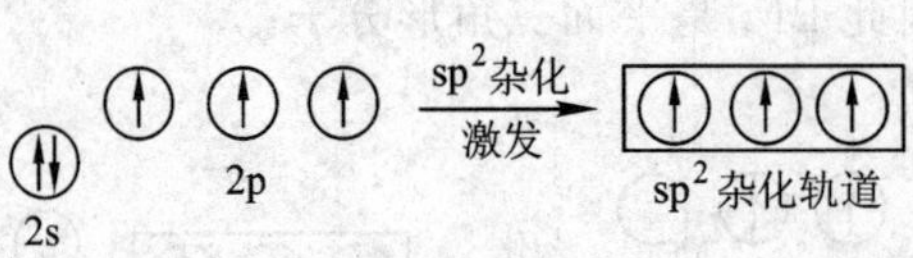

(a)

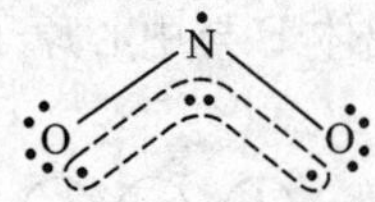

(b)

中心 N 原子有 3 个单电子的 sp^2 杂化轨道，用其中的两个与两个 O 原子的 $2p_x$ 轨道形成 2 个 σ 共价键，决定了 NO_2 分子的 V 字形结构，并确定了分子平面。N 原子未参与杂化的 $2p_z$ 轨道，其中有 2 个电子，两个 O 原子各有 1 个 $2p_z$ 轨道，其中各有 1 个单电子。这 3 个 $2p_z$ 轨道互相平行，且与分子平面垂直，互相重叠形成大 π 键 Π_3^4。如图(b)所示。

另一种看法是，N 原子采用 sp^2 不等性杂化。如图(c)所示，未参与杂化的 $2p_z$ 轨道，其中有 1 个电子。

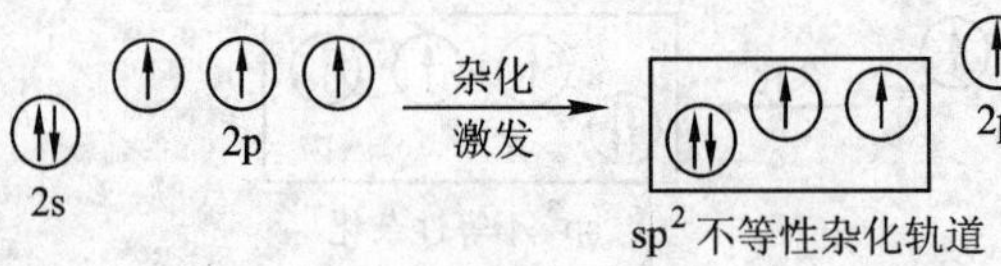

(c)

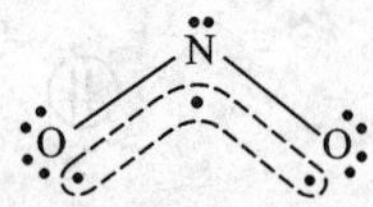

(d)

中心 N 原子的两个 sp^2 不等性杂化轨道中有单电子，与 O 原子的 $2p_x$ 轨道形成 σ 键，决定了 NO_2 分子的 V 字形结构，并确定了分子平面。N 原子中未参与杂化的 $2p_z$ 轨道，以及两个 O 原子的 $2p_z$ 轨道各有 1 个单电子。这 3 个 $2p_z$ 轨道形成大 π 键 Π_3^3。如图(d)所示。

(2) 在 CO_3^{2-} 离子中，中心碳原子采用 sp^2 等性杂化，如图(e)所示。中心碳原子用 3 个 sp^2 等性杂化轨道与 3 个氧原子的 $2p_x$ 轨道分别成 σ 键，确定了平面三角形离子，见图(f)。

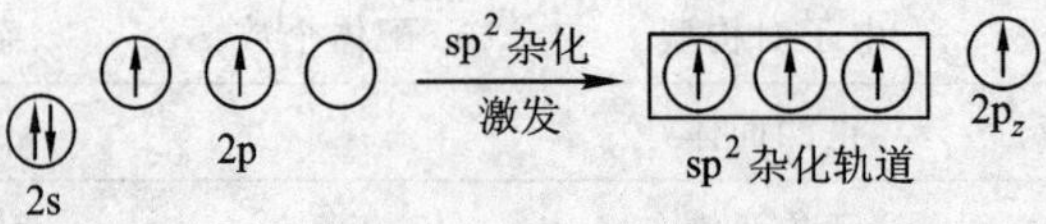

(e)

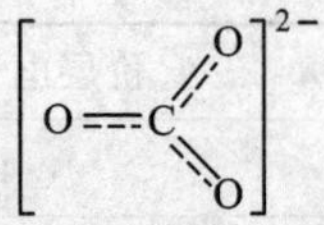

(f)

在垂直于离子所在平面的方向上，中心碳原子有未参加杂化的 $2p_z$ 轨道，其中有 1 个电子，3 个氧原子各有一个垂直于离子所在平面的 $2p_z$ 轨道，其中各有 1 个电子，另外 CO_3^{2-} 离子的 2 个电子也在这 4 个 $2p_z$ 轨道中运动。所以离子中有大 π 键 Π_4^6 存在。

例 7.10 写出 O_2^{2-}，O_2^-，O_2，O_2^+ 分子或离子的分子轨道式，指出它们的稳定性顺序。

解：分子轨道式：

O_2^{2-} $KK(\sigma_{2s})^2(\sigma_{2s}^*)^2(\sigma_{2p_x})^2(\pi_{2p_y})^2(\pi_{2p_z})^2(\pi_{2p_y}^*)^2(\pi_{2p_z}^*)^2$

O_2^-　$KK(\sigma_{2s})^2(\sigma_{2s}^*)^2(\sigma_{2p_x})^2(\pi_{2p_y})^2(\pi_{2p_z})^2(\pi_{2p_y}^*)^2(\pi_{2p_z}^*)^1$

O_2　$KK(\sigma_{2s})^2(\sigma_{2s}^*)^2(\sigma_{2p_x})^2(\pi_{2p_y})^2(\pi_{2p_z})^2(\pi_{2p_y}^*)^1(\pi_{2p_z}^*)^1$

O_2^+　$KK(\sigma_{2s})^2(\sigma_{2s}^*)^2(\sigma_{2p_x})^2(\pi_{2p_y})^2(\pi_{2p_z})^2(\pi_{2p_y}^*)^1$

氧分子和氧分子离子的键级及稳定性顺序

	O_2^{2-}	O_2^-	O_2	O_2^+
键级	1	1.5	2	2.5
稳定性	$O_2^{2-}<O_2^-<O_2<O_2^+$			

例 7.11　画出 NO 的分子轨道图，写出分子轨道式，指出它们的键级和磁性，并比较 NO^+，NO 和 NO^- 的稳定性。

解：NO 分子的分子轨道式为

$$KK(\sigma_{2s})^2(\sigma_{2s}^*)^2(\sigma_{2p_x})^2(\pi_{2p_y})^2(\pi_{2p_z})^2(\pi_{2p_y}^*)^1$$

NO 的分子轨道图如图所示。

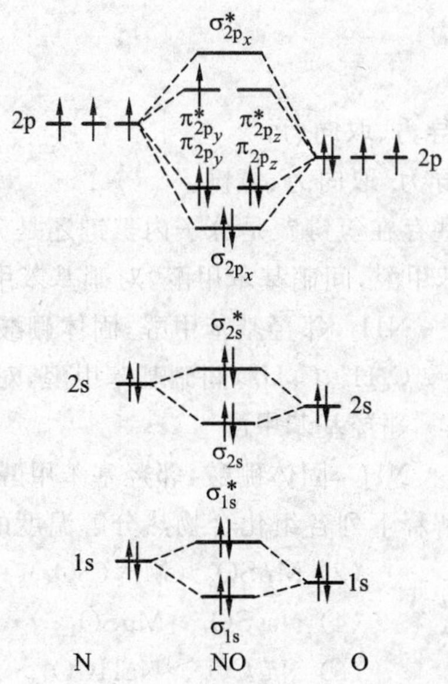

NO 分子的键级为 2.5，具有顺磁性。通过键级可以比较出 NO^+，NO 和 NO^- 的稳定性，见下表。

NO 分子和离子的键级及稳定性顺序

	NO^+	NO	NO^-
键级	3	2.5	2
稳定性	$NO^+>NO>NO^-$		

例 7.12 NF_3 的偶极矩远小于 NH_3 的偶极矩，但前者的电负性差远大于后者。如何解释这一矛盾现象？

解： NF_3 和 NH_3 分子都是三角锥构型。

分子的总偶极矩是分子内部各种因素所产生的分偶极矩的总矢量和。

NF_3 分子中成键电子对偏向电负性大的 F 原子，N 的孤电子对对偶极矩的贡献与键矩对偶极矩的贡献方向相反，即孤电子对的存在削弱了由键矩可能引起的分子偶极矩，故偶极矩较小，如图(a)所示；而 NH_3 分子中成键电子对偏向电负性大的 N 原子，即孤电子对对偶极矩的贡献与键矩对偶极矩的贡献方向相同，故 NH_3 分子有较大偶极矩，如图(b)所示。

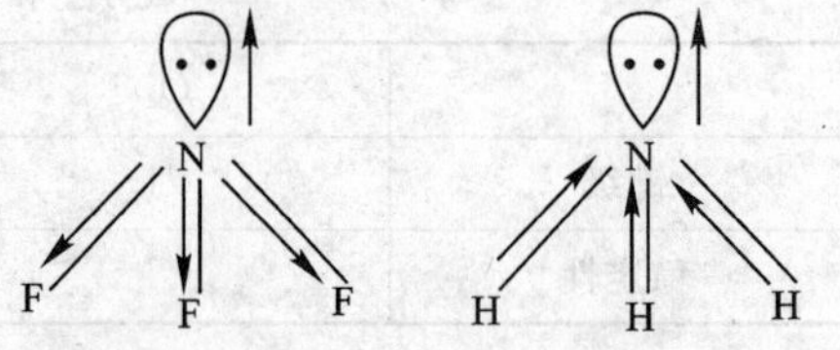

(a) (b)

例 7.13 判断下列各组分子之间存在什么形式的分子间作用力。

(1) 苯和 CCl_4； (2) 氦和水； (3) CO_2 气体；

(4) HBr 气体； (5) 甲醇和水。

解： (1) 苯和 CCl_4 色散力；

(2) 氦和水 色散力、诱导力；

(3) CO_2 气体 色散力；

(4) HBr 气体 色散力、诱导力、取向力；

(5) 甲醇和水 色散力、诱导力、取向力、氢键。

例 7.14 下列化合物中哪些存在氢键？是分子内氢键还是分子间氢键？

C_6H_6，NH_3，C_2H_6，邻羟基苯甲醛，间硝基苯甲醛，对硝基苯甲醛，固体硼酸。

解： 存在氢键的有 NH_3，邻羟基苯甲醛，固体硼酸

不存在氢键的有 C_6H_6，C_2H_6，间硝基苯甲醛，对硝基苯甲醛

存在分子内氢键的有 邻羟基苯甲醛

存在分子间氢键的有 NH_3，固体硼酸，邻羟基苯甲醛

例 7.15 用离子极化理论解释下列各组化合物热分解温度的高低关系。

(1) $CaSO_4 > CdSO_4$； (2) $MnSO_4 > Mn_2(SO_4)_3$；

(3) $SrSO_4 > MgSO_4$； (4) $Na_2SO_4 > MgSO_4$；

(5) $HNO_3 > HNO_2$ (6) $Na_2CO_3 > NaHCO_3$。

解： (1) 对于 $CaSO_4$ 和 $CdSO_4$，其正离子电荷相同而价电子构型不同，Ca^{2+} 是 8 电子构型，Cd^{2+} 是 18 电子构型，极化能力 $Cd^{2+} > Ca^{2+}$，所以稳定性 $CaSO_4 > CdSO_4$，分解温度 $CaSO_4 > CdSO_4$。

(2) 对于 $MnSO_4$ 和 $Mn_2(SO_4)_3$，其正离子是同种元素，离子电荷前者为+2，后者为+3，极化能力 $Mn^{2+} < Mn^{3+}$，所以热稳定性 $MnSO_4 > Mn_2(SO_4)_3$，分解温度 $MnSO_4 > Mn_2(SO_4)_3$。

(3) 对于 $SrSO_4$ 和 $MgSO_4$，其正离子是同一主族的+2 价离子，离子半径 $Sr^{2+} > Mg^{2+}$，极化能力 $Sr^{2+} < Mg^{2+}$，所以热稳定性 $SrSO_4 > MgSO_4$，分解温度 $SrSO_4 > MgSO_4$。

(4) 对于 Na_2SO_4 和 $MgSO_4$，其正离子的电荷数不同。Mg^{2+} 的电荷高，极化能力较强，所以

$MgSO_4$ 的热稳定性低于 Na_2SO_4，分解温度 Na_2SO_4＞$MgSO_4$。

(5) 对于 HNO_3 和 HNO_2，其正离子相同，对中心的反极化作用相同，但中心 N(Ⅴ)对 H^+ 的反极化作用的抵抗能力强于 N(Ⅲ)，故热稳定性 HNO_3＞HNO_2，分解温度 HNO_3＞HNO_2。

(6) 对于 Na_2CO_3 和 $NaHCO_3$，H^+ 的反极化能力极强，导致 $NaHCO_3$ 的热稳定性远小于 Na_2CO_3，故分解温度有 Na_2CO_3＞$NaHCO_3$。

第二部分　习题

一、选择题

7.1　下列化合物中含有极性共价键的是
(A) $KClO_3$；　(B) Na_2O_2；　(C) Na_2O；　(D) KI。

7.2　下列化合物中，键的极性最弱的是
(A) $FeCl_3$；　(B) $AlCl_3$；　(C) $SiCl_4$；　(D) PCl_5。

7.3　下列化合物中，含有非极性共价键的离子化合物是
(A) H_2O_2；　(B) Na_2CO_3；　(C) Na_2O_2；　(D) KO_3。

7.4　在 BrCH ═CHBr 分子中，C—Br 键采用的成键轨道是
(A) sp—p；　(B) sp^2—s；　(C) sp^2—p；　(D) sp^3—p。

7.5　中心原子采取 sp^2 杂化的分子是
(A) NH_3；　(B) BCl_3；　(C) PCl_3；　(D) H_2O。

7.6　下列分子或离子中，不含有孤对电子的是
(A) H_2O；　(B) H_3O^+；　(C) NH_3；　(D) NH_4^+。

7.7　下列分子中属于极性分子的是
(A) CCl_4；　(B) CH_3OCH_3；　(C) BCl_3；　(D) PCl_5。

7.8　下列分子中，中心原子采取等性杂化的是
(A) NCl_3；　(B) SF_4；　(C) CCl_4；　(D) H_2O。

7.9　下列离子中，中心原子采取不等性杂化的是
(A) H_3O^+；　(B) NH_4^+；　(C) PCl_6^-；　(D) BI_4^-。

7.10　下列分子中，属非极性分子的是
(A) SO_2；　(B) CO_2；　(C) NO_2；　(D) ClO_2。

7.11　下列分子或离子中，中心原子的杂化轨道与 NH_3 分子的中心原子杂化轨道最相似的是
(A) H_2O；　(B) H_3O^+；　(C) NH_4^+；　(D) BCl_3。

7.12　下列分子或离子中，构型不为直线形的是
(A) I_3^+；　(B) I_3^-；　(C) CS_2；　(D) $BeCl_2$。

7.13　下列分子或离子中键角∠ONO 最大的是
(A) NO_2^-；　(B) NO_2；　(C) NO_2^+；　(D) NO_3^-。

7.14　下列分子中含有不同长度共价键的是

(A) NH_3；　(B) SO_3；　(C) KI_3；　(D) SF_4。

7.15 按分子轨道理论，O_2 分子中最高能量的电子所处的分子轨道是

(A) π_{2p}；　(B) π_{2p}^*；　(C) σ_{2p}；　(D) σ_{2p}^*。

7.16 下列分子中属抗磁性的是

(A) O_2；　(B) CO；　(C) B_2；　(D) NO。

7.17 按分子轨道理论，最稳定的顺磁性粒子是

(A) O_2^+；　(B) O_2^{2+}；　(C) O_2；　(D) O_2^-。

7.18 熔融 SiO_2 晶体时，需要克服的作用力主要是

(A) 离子键；　(B) 氢键；　(C) 共价键；　(D) 范德华力。

7.19 下列化合物中，按沸点由高到低顺序排列正确的是

① 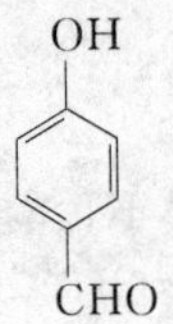　② 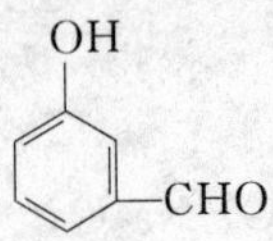　③ 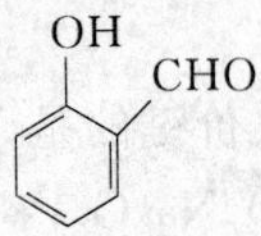

(A) ③②①；　(B) ②③①；　(C) ①②③；　(D) ③①②。

7.20 对化合物在水中的溶解度，下列判断中正确的是

(A) AgF>HF；　(B) CaF_2>$CaCl_2$；

(C) $HgCl_2$>HgI_2；　(D) LiF>NaCl。

7.21 下列离子中，变形性最大的是

(A) O^{2-}；　(B) S^{2-}；　(C) F^-；　(D) Cl^-。

7.22 下列化合物中，正、负离子间附加极化作用最强的是

(A) AgCl；　(B) HgS；　(C) ZnI_2；　(D) $PbCl_2$。

二、填空题

7.23 比较大小

(1) 晶格能　AlF_3 ________ $AlCl_3$，　NaCl ________ KCl；

(2) 溶解度　CuF_2 ________ $CuCl_2$，　$Ca(HCO_3)_2$ ________ $NaHCO_3$。

7.24 给出晶胞中离子总数：立方 ZnS ________；NaCl ________；CsCl ________。

7.25 已知 Cd^{2+} 半径为 97 pm，S^{2-} 半径为 184 pm，按正负离子半径比，CdS 应具有________型晶格，正、负离子的配位数之比应是________；但 CdS 却具有立方 ZnS 型晶格，正、负离子的配位数之比是________，这主要是由________________造成的。

7.26 比较各对化合物沸点高低（用>号和<号表示）

NaCl ______ $MgCl_2$，　AgCl ______ KCl，　NH_3 ______ PH_3，

CO_2 ______ SO_2，　O_3 ______ SO_2，　O_3 ______ O_2，

Ne ______ Ar，　HF ______ H_2O，　HF ______ NH_3，

H_2S ______ HCl，　HF ______ HI。

7.27 下列各物质中，是 CO 的等电子体的有________。

NO，　O_2，　N_2，　HF，　CN^-。

7.28 比较下列各对化合物中键的极性大小(用>号和<号表示)

PbO ____ PbS， $FeCl_3$ ____ $FeCl_2$， SnS ____ SnS_2，

AsH_3 ____ SeH_2， PH_3 ____ H_2S， HF ____ H_2O。

7.29 下列分子或离子中键角由大到小排列的顺序是________。

① BCl_3， ② NH_3， ③ H_2O， ④ PCl_4^+， ⑤ $HgCl_2$。

7.30 给出各分子或离子的几何构型和中心原子的杂化类型。

ICl_2^- ________，________；BrF_3 ________，________；

ICl_4^- ________，________；NO_2^+ ________，________。

7.31 下列分子或离子中，能形成分子内氢键的有______；不能形成分子间氢键的有______。

① NH_3，② H_2O，③ HNO_3，④ HF_2^-，⑤ NH_4^+，⑥ 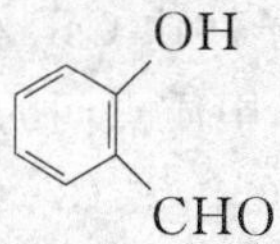 。

7.32 将 Na_2CO_3，$MgCO_3$，K_2CO_3，$MnCO_3$，$PbCO_3$ 按热稳定性由高到低排列，顺序为________________。

7.33 将 KCl，$CaCl_2$，$MnCl_2$，$ZnCl_2$ 按阳离子极化能力由强至弱排列，顺序为________________。

7.34 比较各对化合物的热稳定性(用>号和<号表示)。

HNO_3 ______ $NaNO_3$，Na_2SO_4 ______ Na_2SO_3，

Ag_2O ______ Cu_2O， $ZnCO_3$ ______ $HgCO_3$。

7.35 已知 P—P 键，C—C 键，OH…O 键的键能分别为 201 $kJ\cdot mol^{-1}$，345.6 $kJ\cdot mol^{-1}$，18.8 $kJ\cdot mol^{-1}$，试粗略估算：$P_4(g)$原子化热为______ $kJ\cdot mol^{-1}$，金刚石的原子化热为______ $kJ\cdot mol^{-1}$，冰的汽化热为______ $kJ\cdot mol^{-1}$。

7.36 在金属晶体中最常见的三种堆积方式有：(1)配位数为 8 的______堆积，(2) 配位数为____的立方面心堆积，(3) 配位数为____的______堆积。其中____和____空间利用率相等，____以 ABAB 方式堆积，____以 ABCABC 方式堆积，就金属原子的堆积层来看，二者的区别是在第____层。

7.37 金属 Cu 为面心立方密堆积结构，晶胞参数为 $a=361.4$ pm，金属原子配位数为____，晶胞中原子数为____，金属 Cu 原子半径为____pm，晶胞密度____ $g\cdot cm^{-3}$，Cu 的空间占有率是____。已知 $A_r(Cu)=63.54$。

7.38 金属钾晶体为体心立方结构，则在单位晶胞中钾原子的个数是______，已知金属钾的密度为 0.862 $g\cdot cm^{-3}$，则钾的半径为____pm。

7.39 给出金属晶体的空间占有率：面心立方密堆积______，体心立方密堆积______，六方密堆积______，金刚石型堆积______。

三、简答题和计算题

7.40 根据下列已知数据，由玻恩-哈伯循环计算 Al_2O_3 的晶格能。

$$\Delta_f H_m^\ominus(Al_2O_3,s) = -1\,676\ kJ\cdot mol^{-1}$$

$Al(s) \longrightarrow Al(g)$ $\Delta H = 326.4\ kJ \cdot mol^{-1}$

$Al(g) \longrightarrow Al^+(g) + e^-$ $I_1 = 578\ kJ \cdot mol^{-1}$

$Al^+(g) \longrightarrow Al^{2+}(g) + e^-$ $I_2 = 1\,817\ kJ \cdot mol^{-1}$

$Al^{2+}(g) \longrightarrow Al^{3+}(g) + e^-$ $I_3 = 2\,745\ kJ \cdot mol^{-1}$

$O_2(g) \longrightarrow 2O(g)$ $E = 498\ kJ \cdot mol^{-1}$

$O(g) + e^- \longrightarrow O^-(g)$ $E_1 = 141\ kJ \cdot mol^{-1}$

$O^-(g) + e^- \longrightarrow O^{2-}(g)$ $E_2 = -780\ kJ \cdot mol^{-1}$

7.41 已知NO(g)的生成热为90.25 $kJ \cdot mol^{-1}$，N_2 分子中三键的键能为941.69 $kJ \cdot mol^{-1}$，O_2 分子中双键的键能为493.59 $kJ \cdot mol^{-1}$，求NO(g)中N—O键的键能。

7.42 已知NaF中键的离子性比CsF小，但NaF的晶格能却比CsF的大。请解释原因。

7.43 指出下列物质在晶体中质点间的作用力、晶体类型、熔点高低。

(1) KCl，　(2) SiC，　(3) CH_3Cl，　(4) NH_3，　(5) Cu，　(6) Xe。

7.44 已知 CO_2，NO_2^-，BF_3 分别为直线形，V字形和平面三角形。试用等电子原理说明下列分子或离子的成键情况和几何构型。

O_3，NO_2^+，NO_3^-，N_3^-，CO_3^{2-}。

7.45 解释下列分子或离子中形成的共轭π键。

(1) NO_3^-，Π_4^6；　(2) O_3，Π_3^4。

7.46 计算金属面心立方最紧密堆积和体心立方紧密堆积的空间利用率。

7.47 在 BCl_3 和 NCl_3 分子中，中心原子的氧化数和配位数都相同，为什么二者的中心原子采取的杂化类型、分子构型却不同？

7.48 举例说明主族元素形成的 AB_3 型分子有几种几何构型？指出分子的中心原子A的轨道杂化类型、价层孤电子对数和分子是否有极性。

7.49 试用杂化轨道理论讨论下列分子的成键情况。

PCl_5，OF_2，ICl_3。

7.50 已知 NO_2，CO_2，SO_2 分子中键角分别为132°，180°，120°，判断它们的中心原子轨道的杂化类型，说明成键情况。

7.51 CO，N_2 和 CN^- 为等电子体。

(1) 用分子轨道理论说明CO，N_2 和 CN^- 的键能都很大的原因。

(2) 已知CO键能(1070 $kJ \cdot mol^{-1}$)比 N_2 键能(942 $kJ \cdot mol^{-1}$)大，为什么CO易被氧化而 N_2 却很稳定？

7.52 在下列各对化合物中，哪一种化合物的键角大？说明原因。

(a) CH_4 和 NH_3；　(b) OF_2 和 Cl_2O；　(c) NH_3 和 NF_3；　(d) PH_3 和 NH_3。

7.53 用价层电子对互斥理论推测下列分子或离子的空间结构。

$SnCl_2$，$SnCl_3^-$，$HgCl_2$，BrF_3，I_3^+，ICl_2^-，$IO_2F_2^-$，IF_5，SF_4，SO_2Cl_2，SO_3^{2-}，XeO_4。

7.54 HF分子间氢键比 H_2O 分子间氢键更强些，为什么HF的沸点及汽化热均比 H_2O 的低？

7.55 C和O的电负性差较大，CO分子极性却较弱，请说明原因。

7.56 为什么由不同种元素的原子生成的 PCl_5 分子为非极性分子，而由同种元素的原子形成的 O_3 分子却是极性分子？

7.57　请指出下列分子中哪些是极性分子，哪些是非极性分子？

NO_2，　$CHCl_3$，　NCl_3，　SO_3，　SCl_2，　$COCl_2$，　BCl_3。

7.58　判断下列化合物的分子间能否形成氢键，哪些分子能形成分子内氢键？

NH_3，H_2CO_3，HNO_3，CH_3COOH，$C_2H_5OC_2H_5$，HCl，

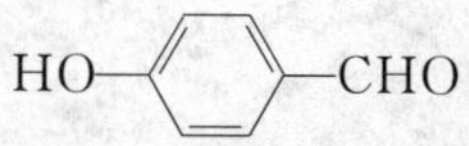，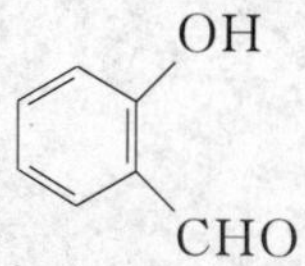，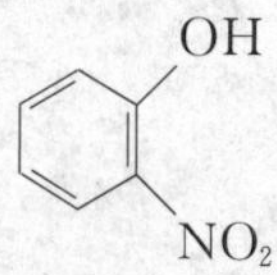。

7.59　判断下列各组分子之间存在何种形式的分子间作用力。

(1) CS_2 和 CCl_4；　(2) H_2O 与 H_2；　(3) CH_3Cl；　(4) H_2O 与 NH_3。

7.60　解释下列实验事实。

(1) 沸点 HF＞HI＞HCl，BiH_3＞NH_3＞PH_3；　(2) 熔点 BeO＞LiF；

(3) $SiCl_4$ 比 CCl_4 易水解；　(4) 金刚石比石墨硬度大。

7.61　C 和 Si 在同一族，为什么 CO_2 形成分子晶体而 SiO_2 却形成原子晶体？

7.62　元素 Si 和 Sn 的电负性相差不大，为什么常温下 SiF_4 为气态而 SnF_4 却为固态？

7.63　试比较如下两组化合物中正离子的极化能力大小：

(1) $ZnCl_2$，$FeCl_2$，$CaCl_2$，KCl；

(2) $SiCl_4$，$AlCl_3$，PCl_5，$MgCl_2$，NaCl。

7.64　试用离子极化理论排出下列各组化合物的熔点及溶解度由大到小的顺序

(1) $BeCl_2$，$CaCl_2$，$HgCl_2$；　(2) CaS，FeS，HgS；　(3) LiCl，KCl，CuCl。

7.65　判断下列化合物熔点高低顺序并说明理由。

MgO，BaO，BN，$CdCl_2$。

第 8 章 酸碱解离平衡

第一部分 例题

例 8.1 计算下列溶液的 pH。

(1) 0.01 $mol\cdot dm^{-3}$ HCN 溶液($K_a^\ominus=6.2\times10^{-10}$);

(2) 0.01 $mol\cdot dm^{-3}$ HNO_2 溶液($K_a^\ominus=5.1\times10^{-4}$);

(3) 0.01 $mol\cdot dm^{-3}$ H_2SO_4 溶液($K_{a_2}^\ominus=1.2\times10^{-2}$);

(4) 0.10 $mol\cdot dm^{-3}$ $NaHCO_3$ 溶液(H_2CO_3:$K_{a_1}^\ominus=4.2\times10^{-7}$,$K_{a_2}^\ominus=5.6\times10^{-11}$);

(5) 0.10 $mol\cdot dm^{-3}$ Na_2S 溶液(H_2S:$K_{a_1}^\ominus=1.1\times10^{-7}$,$K_{a_2}^\ominus=1.3\times10^{-13}$);

(6) 0.10 $mol\cdot dm^{-3}$ NH_4Cl 溶液($NH_3\cdot H_2O$ $K_b^\ominus=1.8\times10^{-5}$)。

解:(1) $c_0/K_a^\ominus=0.01/6.2\times10^{-10}=1.6\times10^7\gg400$ 可用最简式进行计算

$$[H^+]=\sqrt{K_a^\ominus\ c_0}\text{①}=\sqrt{6.2\times10^{-10}\times0.01}\ mol\cdot dm^{-3}=2.49\times10^{-6}mol\cdot dm^{-3}$$

$$pH=-\lg[H^+]=-\lg 2.49\times10^{-6}=5.60$$

(2) $c_0/K_a^\ominus=0.01/5.1\times10^{-4}=19.61<400$ 不能用最简式进行计算

$$HNO_2 \rightleftharpoons H^+ + NO_2^-$$

平衡浓度/($mol\cdot dm^{-3}$) $0.01-x$ x x

由 $K_a^\ominus=\dfrac{[H^+][NO_2^-]}{[HNO_2]}$ 得 $\dfrac{x^2}{0.01-x}=5.1\times10^{-4}$ $x=2.02\times10^{-3}$

$$[H^+]=2.02\times10^{-3}mol\cdot dm^{-3} \qquad pH=-\lg[H^+]=2.69$$

(3) H_2SO_4 第一步完全解离,则第一步解离后

$$[H^+]=[HSO_4^-]=0.01\ mol\cdot dm^{-3}$$

$$HSO_4^- \rightleftharpoons H^+ + SO_4^{2-}$$

平衡浓度/($mol\cdot dm^{-3}$) $0.01-x$ $0.01+x$ x

$$\frac{(0.01+x)x}{0.01-x}=1.2\times10^{-2}$$

① 依量纲推算,公式应为$[H^+]=c^\ominus\cdot\sqrt{K_a^\ominus c_0/c^\ominus}$,$c^\ominus=1\ mol\cdot dm^{-3}$。为简化起见,本书略去了 $c^\ominus$ 项。

解得　$x=4.52\times10^{-3}$

$[H^+]=0.01\ mol\cdot dm^{-3}+4.52\times10^{-3}\ mol\cdot dm^{-3}=1.45\times10^{-2}mol\cdot dm^{-3}$

$pH=-\lg[H^+]=1.84$

(4) HCO_3^- 为酸式盐，在水溶液中存在平衡

$$HCO_3^- \rightleftharpoons H^+ + CO_3^{2-}$$

$$HCO_3^- + H_2O \rightleftharpoons H_2CO_3 + OH^-$$

由 $K_{a_2}^\ominus\cdot c_0=5.6\times10^{-11}\times0.10=5.6\times10^{-12}>10^{-14}$，可采用最简式进行计算

$$[H^+]=\sqrt{K_{a_1}^\ominus K_{a_2}^\ominus}=\sqrt{4.2\times10^{-7}\times5.6\times10^{-11}}\ mol\cdot dm^{-3}=4.8\times10^{-9}\ mol\cdot dm^{-3}$$

$$pH=-\lg[H^+]=8.31$$

(5) S^{2-} 在水溶液中分两步水解，但 $K_{h_1}^\ominus \gg K_{h_2}^\ominus$，计算时只需考虑第一步水解

$$S^{2-} + H_2O \rightleftharpoons HS^- + OH^-$$

平衡浓度/$(mol\cdot dm^{-3})$　$0.1-x$　　x　　x

$$\frac{x^2}{0.1-x}=K_{h_1}^\ominus \qquad K_{h_1}^\ominus=\frac{K_w^\ominus}{K_{a_2}^\ominus}=\frac{1.0\times10^{-14}}{1.3\times10^{-13}}=7.7\times10^{-2}$$

解得　$x=0.057$　$[OH^-]=0.057\ mol\cdot dm^{-3}$

$$pH=-\lg[H^+]=-\lg\frac{K_w}{[OH^-]}=14-pOH=14-(-\lg[OH^-])$$

$$=12.76$$

(6) $NH_4^+ + H_2O \rightleftharpoons NH_3\cdot H_2O + H^+$

$$K_h^\ominus=\frac{K_w^\ominus}{K_b^\ominus}=\frac{1.0\times10^{-14}}{1.8\times10^{-5}}=5.56\times10^{-10}$$

$c_0/K_h^\ominus=0.10/5.6\times10^{-10}>400$ 可用最简式计算

$$[H^+]=\sqrt{K_h^\ominus c_0}=\sqrt{5.56\times10^{-10}\times0.10}\ mol\cdot dm^{-3}=7.46\times10^{-6}mol\cdot dm^{-3}$$

$pH=5.13$

例 8.2　通过计算说明：中和 50.0 cm^3，pH=3.80 的盐酸与中和 50.0 cm^3，pH=3.80 的醋酸溶液所需 NaOH 的物质的量是否相同？已知 $K_a^\ominus(HAc)=1.8\times10^{-5}$。

解：盐酸为强酸，在水中全部解离

$$[H^+]=[HCl]=10^{-3.8}\ mol\cdot dm^{-3}=1.6\times10^{-4}mol\cdot dm^{-3}$$

中和 50 cm^3 盐酸需 NaOH 的物质的量

$$50\times10^{-3}dm^3\times1.6\times10^{-4}mol\cdot dm^{-3}=8.0\times10^{-6}mol$$

醋酸为弱酸，在水中部分解离，则 pH=3.80 的醋酸溶液的浓度为

$$[HAc]=\frac{[H^+]^2}{K_a^\ominus}=\frac{(1.6\times10^{-4})^2}{1.8\times10^{-5}}\ mol\cdot dm^{-3}=1.4\times10^{-3}mol\cdot dm^{-3}$$

中和 50 cm^3 醋酸时需 NaOH 的物质的量为

$$50\times10^{-3}\,dm^3\times1.4\times10^{-3}\,mol\cdot dm^{-3}=7.0\times10^{-5}\,mol$$

计算结果表明，中和体积相同，pH 相同的盐酸和醋酸溶液时，由于[HAc]>[HCl]，所需 NaOH 的物质的量不同，中和弱酸所需的 NaOH 的物质的量要大于中和强酸时所需 NaOH 的物质的量。

例 8.3 298 K 时，测得 0.100 $mol\cdot dm^{-3}$ HF 溶液中$[H^+]$为 $7.63\times10^{-3}\,mol\cdot dm^{-3}$。求反应

$$HF(aq) \rightleftharpoons H^+(aq)+F^-(aq)$$

的 $\Delta_rG_m^\ominus$ 值。

解：

	$HF(aq)$	$\rightleftharpoons$	$H^+(aq)$	+	$F^-(aq)$
起始浓度/$(mol\cdot dm^{-3})$	0.100		0		0
平衡浓度/$(mol\cdot dm^{-3})$	$0.100-7.63\times10^{-3}$		7.63×10^{-3}		7.63×10^{-3}

$$K_a^\ominus=\frac{[H^+][F^-]}{[HF]}=\frac{(7.63\times10^{-3})^2}{0.100-7.63\times10^{-3}}=6.30\times10^{-4}$$

$$\Delta_rG_m^\ominus=-RT\ln K_a^\ominus=-8.314\,J\cdot mol^{-1}\cdot K^{-1}\times298\,K\times\ln6.30\times10^{-4}=18.3\,kJ\cdot mol^{-1}$$

例 8.4 已知氨水的 $K_b^\ominus=1.8\times10^{-5}$，现有 1.0 dm^3 0.10 $mol\cdot dm^{-3}$氨水，求

(1) 氨水的$[H^+]$；

(2) 加入 10.7 g NH_4Cl 后，溶液的$[H^+]$；(加入 NH_4Cl 后溶液体积的变化忽略不计)

(3) 加入 NH_4Cl 后，氨水解离度缩小的倍数。

解：(1)

	$NH_3\cdot H_2O$	$\rightleftharpoons$	NH_4^+	+	OH^-
起始浓度/$(mol\cdot dm^{-3})$	0.10		0		0
平衡浓度/$(mol\cdot dm^{-3})$	$0.10-x\approx0.10$		x		x

x 为解离完全的 $NH_3\cdot H_2O$ 的浓度。

$$K_b^\ominus=\frac{[NH_4^+][OH^-]}{[NH_3\cdot H_2O]}=\frac{x^2}{0.10}=1.8\times10^{-5}$$

解得 $x=1.34\times10^{-3}$

即 $[OH^-]=1.34\times10^{-3}\,mol\cdot dm^{-3}$

$$[H^+]=\frac{K_w^\ominus}{[OH^-]}$$

$$=\frac{1.0\times10^{-14}}{1.34\times10^{-3}}\ \text{mol·dm}^{-3}$$

$$=7.46\times10^{-12}\ \text{mol·dm}^{-3}$$

$$\text{解离度}\ \alpha_1=\frac{1.34\times10^{-3}}{0.10}\times100\%$$

$$=1.34\%$$

(2)
$$M(NH_4Cl)=53.5$$

$$n(NH_4Cl)=\frac{10.7}{53.5}\ \text{mol}=0.20\ \text{mol}$$

NH_4Cl 完全解离后，$[NH_4^+]=0.20\ \text{mol·dm}^{-3}$。

$$NH_3\cdot H_2O \rightleftharpoons NH_4^+ + OH^-$$

平衡浓度/(mol·dm^{-3})　　0.10　　0.20　　y

$$K_b^\ominus=\frac{[NH_4^+][OH^-]}{[NH_3\cdot H_2O]}$$

$$=\frac{0.20y}{0.10}$$

$$=1.8\times10^{-5}$$

解得
$$y=9.00\times10^{-6}$$

$$[OH^-]=9.00\times10^{-6}\ \text{mol·dm}^{-3}$$

$$[H^+]=1.11\times10^{-9}\ \text{mol·dm}^{-3}$$

$$\text{解离度}\ \alpha_2=\frac{9.00\times10^{-6}}{0.10}\times100\%$$

$$=(9.00\times10^{-3})\%$$

(3)
$$\frac{\alpha_1}{\alpha_2}=\frac{1.34\%}{(9.00\times10^{-3})\%}=149$$

例 8.5　计算 0.10 mol·dm^{-3} 的 Na_2CO_3 溶液中各离子的浓度。已知 H_2CO_3 的 $K_{a_1}^\ominus=4.5\times10^{-7}$，$K_{a_2}^\ominus=4.7\times10^{-11}$。

解：对于 CO_3^{2-} 的水解常数

$$K_{h_1}^\ominus=\frac{K_w^\ominus}{K_{a_2}^\ominus}=\frac{1.0\times10^{-14}}{4.7\times10^{-11}}=2.1\times10^{-4}$$

$$K_{h_2}^\ominus=\frac{K_w^\ominus}{K_{a_1}^\ominus}=\frac{1.0\times10^{-14}}{4.5\times10^{-7}}=2.2\times10^{-8}$$

$K_{h_1}^\ominus$ 比 $K_{h_2}^\ominus$ 大得多，CO_3^{2-} 二级水解很小，可由一级水解平衡求$[OH^-]$和$[HCO_3^-]$。

$$CO_3^{2-}+H_2O \rightleftharpoons HCO_3^- + OH^-$$

平衡浓度/(mol·dm^{-3})　　$0.1-x$　　x　　x

$$\frac{x^2}{0.1-x}=2.1\times10^{-4}$$

由最简式
$$x=\sqrt{K_{h_1}^\ominus c_0}=\sqrt{2.1\times10^{-4}\times0.10}=4.6\times10^{-3}$$

对于二级水解

$$HCO_3^- \quad + \quad H_2O \rightleftharpoons H_2CO_3 \quad + \quad OH^-$$

平衡浓度/($mol\cdot dm^{-3}$)　$4.6\times10^{-3}-y$　　y　　$4.6\times10^{-3}+y$

$$\frac{y(4.6\times10^{-3}+y)}{4.6\times10^{-3}-y}=2.2\times10^{-8}$$

$K_{h_2}^\ominus$ 很小，因而 y 很小

$$y\approx2.2\times10^{-8}$$

结果表明，[OH^-]和[HCO_3^-]几乎不受二级水解影响，溶液中各离子浓度归纳如下

$$[Na^+]=0.10\ mol\cdot dm^{-3}\times2=0.20\ mol\cdot dm^{-3}$$

$$[HCO_3^-]=[OH^-]=4.6\times10^{-3}\ mol\cdot dm^{-3}$$

$$[CO_3^{2-}]=0.10\ mol\cdot dm^{-3}-4.6\times10^{-3}\ mol\cdot dm^{-3}=9.5\times10^{-2}\ mol\cdot dm^{-3}$$

$$[H^+]=\frac{K_w^\ominus}{[OH^-]}=\frac{1.0\times10^{-14}}{4.6\times10^{-3}}\ mol\cdot dm^{-3}=2.2\times10^{-12}\ mol\cdot dm^{-3}$$

例 8.6 将 $0.10\ mol\cdot dm^{-3}$ HAc 和 $0.10\ mol\cdot dm^{-3}$ HCN 等体积混合，计算此溶液中[H^+]，[Ac^-]和[CN^-]。已知 $K_a^\ominus(HAc)=1.8\times10^{-5}$，$K_a^\ominus(HCN)=6.2\times10^{-10}$。

解：两种酸混合，其中 $K_a^\ominus(HAc)\gg K_a^\ominus(HCN)$，所以体系中[$H^+$]完全由 HAc 的解离来决定。等体积混合后，两种酸的浓度均为 $0.050\ mol\cdot dm^{-3}$。

$$HAc \rightleftharpoons H^+ + Ac^-$$

起始浓度/($mol\cdot dm^{-3}$)　0.050　0　0

平衡浓度/($mol\cdot dm^{-3}$)　$0.050-x$　x　x

x 为已解离的 HAc 的浓度。

$\frac{c_0}{K_a^\ominus}>400$，近似有 $0.050-x\approx0.050$，则

$$K_a^\ominus=\frac{[H^+][Ac^-]}{[HAc]}=\frac{x^2}{0.050}=1.8\times10^{-5}$$

解得　$x=9.5\times10^{-4}$

即溶液中　$[H^+]=9.5\times10^{-4}\ mol\cdot dm^{-3}$

$[Ac^-]=9.5\times10^{-4}\ mol\cdot dm^{-3}$

$$HCN \rightleftharpoons H^+ + CN^-$$

平衡时浓度/($mol\cdot dm^{-3}$)　0.050　9.5×10^{-4}　[CN^-]

$$K_a^\ominus(HCN)=\frac{[H^+][CN^-]}{[HCN]}$$

$$[CN^-]=\frac{K_a^\ominus(HCN)[HCN]}{[H^+]}$$

$$= \frac{6.2\times10^{-10}\times0.050}{9.5\times10^{-4}}\ \text{mol·dm}^{-3}$$

$$= 3.3\times10^{-8}\ \text{mol·dm}^{-3}$$

即溶液中$[CN^-]=3.3\times10^{-8}$ mol·dm^{-3}。

例 8.7　将 1.00 mol·dm^{-3} HAc 和 1.00 mol·dm^{-3} HF 等体积混合，若已知 HAc 的 $K_a^\ominus=1.8\times10^{-5}$，HF 的 $K_a^\ominus=6.3\times10^{-4}$。计算此溶液中的$[H^+]$，$[Ac^-]$和$[F^-]$。

解：

$$HAc \rightleftharpoons H^+ + Ac^-$$

$$HF \rightleftharpoons H^+ + F^-$$

两种酸等体积混合后，HAc 和 HF 的起始浓度均为 0.50 mol·dm^{-3}。

	HAc ＋	HF ⇌	2H$^+$ ＋	Ac$^-$ ＋	F$^-$
起始浓度/(mol·dm^{-3})	0.50	0.50	0	0	0
平衡浓度/(mol·dm^{-3})	$0.50-x$	$0.50-y$	$x+y$	x	y

x 为已解离的 HAc 的浓度，y 为已解离的 HF 的浓度，$(x+y)$为体系中 H$^+$ 浓度。采用近似计算，$0.50-x\approx0.50-y\approx0.50$。

$$K_a^\ominus(HAc)=\frac{[H^+][Ac^-]}{[HAc]}=\frac{(x+y)x}{0.50}=1.8\times10^{-5} \qquad (1)$$

$$K_a^\ominus(HF)=\frac{[H^+][F^-]}{[HF]}=\frac{(x+y)y}{0.50}=6.3\times10^{-4} \qquad (2)$$

式(1)/式(2)：　$$\frac{x}{y}=\frac{1.8\times10^{-5}}{6.3\times10^{-4}}=0.0286$$

所以

$$x=0.0286y$$

将其代入式(2)中，则

$$\frac{(0.0286y+y)y}{0.50}=6.3\times10^{-4}$$

解得

$$y=1.75\times10^{-2}$$

故

$$x=0.0286y=0.0286\times1.75\times10^{-2}=5.00\times10^{-4}$$

$$x+y=5.00\times10^{-4}+1.75\times10^{-2}=1.80\times10^{-2}$$

所以溶液中$[H^+]=1.80\times10^{-2}$ mol·dm^{-3}，$[Ac^-]=5.00\times10^{-4}$ mol·dm^{-3}，$[F^-]=1.75\times10^{-2}$ mol·dm^{-3}。

例 8.8　已知 H_2S 的 $K_1=1.1\times10^{-7}$，$K_2=1.3\times10^{-13}$，求 0.20 mol·dm^{-3} Na_2S 溶液中的$[Na^+]$，$[S^{2-}]$，$[HS^-]$，$[OH^-]$，$[H_2S]$和$[H^+]$。

解：

$$Na_2S = 2Na^+ + S^{2-}$$

0.20 mol·dm^{-3}的 Na_2S 完全解离，故溶液中的 Na^+ 浓度为 0.40 mol·dm^{-3}，而 S^{2-} 的起始浓度为 0.20 mol·dm^{-3}，则 S^{2-} 的水解分两步进行。

$$K_{h_1}^\ominus=\frac{K_w^\ominus}{K_{a_2}^\ominus}=\frac{1.0\times10^{-14}}{1.3\times10^{-13}}=7.7\times10^{-2}$$

$$K^{\ominus}_{h_2}=\frac{K^{\ominus}_{w}}{K^{\ominus}_{a_1}}=\frac{1.0\times10^{-14}}{1.1\times10^{-7}}=9.1\times10^{-8}$$

由于 $K^{\ominus}_{h_1}\gg K^{\ominus}_{h_2}$，故水解产生的[$OH^-$]由第一步水解决定。

$$S^{2-}+H_2O \rightleftharpoons HS^-+OH^-$$

起始浓度/($mol\cdot dm^{-3}$)　　0.20　　0　　0

平衡浓度/($mol\cdot dm^{-3}$)　　$0.20-x$　　x　　x

x 为已水解的 S^{2-} 的浓度。

$$K^{\ominus}_{h_1}=\frac{[HS^-][OH^-]}{[S^{2-}]}$$

$$=\frac{x^2}{0.20-x}=7.7\times10^{-2}$$

解得　$x=0.091$

即　$[OH^-]=0.091\ mol\cdot dm^{-3}$

$$[HS^-]=0.091\ mol\cdot dm^{-3}$$

$$[H^+]=\frac{K^{\ominus}_{w}}{[OH^-]}=\frac{1.0\times10^{-14}}{0.091}\ mol\cdot dm^{-3}=1.1\times10^{-13}\ mol\cdot dm^{-3}$$

$$[S^{2-}]=(0.20-x)\ mol\cdot dm^{-3}$$

$$=(0.20-0.091)\ mol\cdot dm^{-3}$$

$$=0.109\ mol\cdot dm^{-3}$$

$$HS^-+H_2O \rightleftharpoons H_2S+OH^-$$

平衡浓度/($mol\cdot dm^{-3}$)　　0.091　　y　　0.091

$$K^{\ominus}_{h_2}=\frac{[H_2S][OH^-]}{[HS^-]}=y$$

$$y=9.1\times10^{-8}$$

即[H_2S]$=9.1\times10^{-8}\ mol\cdot dm^{-3}$。

例 8.9　150 cm^3 0.10 $mol\cdot dm^{-3}$ HAc 溶液和 50 cm^3 0.10 $mol\cdot dm^{-3}$ NaOH 溶液混合，若已知 HAc 的 $pK^{\ominus}_{a}=4.74$，求混合溶液的[H^+]。

解：依题意 $V(HAc)=0.15\ dm^3$，$V(NaOH)=0.050\ dm^3$，则混合溶液

$$V=0.15\ dm^3+0.050\ dm^3=0.20\ dm^3$$

$$n(HAc)=0.10\ mol\cdot dm^{-3}\times0.15\ dm^3=0.015\ mol$$

$$n(NaOH)=0.10\ mol\cdot dm^{-3}\times0.050\ dm^3=0.0050\ mol$$

$$HAc+OH^- \rightleftharpoons Ac^-+H_2O$$

反应后剩余　$n(HAc)=0.015\ mol-0.0050\ mol=0.010\ mol$

生成　$n(Ac^-)=0.0050\ mol$

故在混合溶液中

$$c(HAc)=\frac{0.010\ mol}{0.20\ dm^3}=0.050\ mol\cdot dm^{-3}$$

$$c(\mathrm{Ac^-})=\frac{0.0050\ \mathrm{mol}}{0.20\ \mathrm{dm^3}}=0.025\ \mathrm{mol\cdot dm^{-3}}$$

因为　$$\mathrm{HAc} \rightleftharpoons \mathrm{H^+}+\mathrm{Ac^-} \qquad \mathrm{p}K_a^\ominus=4.74$$

$$K_a^\ominus=\frac{[\mathrm{H^+}][\mathrm{Ac^-}]}{[\mathrm{HAc}]}=1.8\times10^{-5}$$

所以　$$[\mathrm{H^+}]=K_a^\ominus\frac{[\mathrm{HAc}]}{[\mathrm{Ac^-}]}=1.8\times10^{-5}\times\frac{0.050}{0.025}\ \mathrm{mol\cdot dm^{-3}}=3.6\times10^{-5}\ \mathrm{mol\cdot dm^{-3}}$$

或用公式直接求出该缓冲溶液的 pH。

$$\mathrm{pH}=\mathrm{p}K_a^\ominus-\lg\frac{c_{酸}}{c_{盐}}=4.74-\lg\frac{0.050}{0.025}=4.44$$

故　$$[\mathrm{H^+}]=3.6\times10^{-5}\ \mathrm{mol\cdot dm^{-3}}$$

例 8.10　用强碱滴定某一元弱酸，在加入 3.50 $\mathrm{cm^3}$ 碱液时，体系的pH=4.15；在加入 5.70 $\mathrm{cm^3}$碱液时，体系的 pH=4.44。求该弱酸的解离平衡常数。

解：一元弱酸 HA 与强碱 $\mathrm{OH^-}$ 的反应为

$$\mathrm{HA}+\mathrm{OH^-} \rightleftharpoons \mathrm{A^-}+\mathrm{H_2O}$$

弱酸被强碱部分中和后得到弱酸盐与弱酸组成的缓冲溶液。其 pH 计算公式为

$$\mathrm{pH}=\mathrm{p}K_a^\ominus-\lg\frac{c_{酸}}{c_{盐}} \tag{1}$$

设酸的体积为 V_a，浓度为 c_a，加入的碱的体积为 V_b，浓度为 c_b，则反应后生成的盐的物质的量 $n_{盐}=V_bc_b$，浓度 $c_{盐}=\dfrac{V_bc_b}{V_a+V_b}$，剩余的酸的物质的量 $n_{酸}=V_ac_a-V_bc_b$，浓度 $c_{酸}=\dfrac{V_ac_a-V_bc_b}{V_a+V_b}$。

将 $c_{酸}$，$c_{盐}$ 代入式(1)得

$$\mathrm{pH}=\mathrm{p}K_a^\ominus-\lg\frac{\dfrac{V_ac_a-V_bc_b}{V_a+V_b}}{\dfrac{V_bc_b}{V_a+V_b}}$$

整理得　$$\mathrm{pH}=\mathrm{p}K_a^\ominus-\lg\left(\frac{\dfrac{V_ac_a}{c_b}}{V_b}-1\right)，令\frac{V_ac_a}{c_b}=A$$

则　$$\mathrm{pH}=\mathrm{p}K_a^\ominus-\lg\left(\frac{A}{V_b}-1\right)$$

依题意有　$$4.15=\mathrm{p}K_a^\ominus-\lg\left(\frac{A}{3.50\ \mathrm{cm^3}}-1\right) \tag{2}$$

$$4.44 = pK_a^\ominus - \lg\left(\frac{A}{5.70\ cm^3} - 1\right) \quad (3)$$

式(2)和式(3)联立，解得 $A = 16.8\ cm^3$，$pK_a^\ominus = 4.73$

故该弱酸的解离平衡常数 $K_a^\ominus = 1.86 \times 10^{-5}$。

例 8.11 80 cm^3 1.0 $mol \cdot dm^{-3}$ 的某一元弱酸与 50 cm^3 0.40 $mol \cdot dm^{-3}$ NaOH 溶液混合后，再稀释至 250 cm^3，测得溶液的 pH=2.72，求该弱酸的解离常数。

解：依题设条件，$V_{酸} = 0.080\ dm^3$，$V_{碱} = 0.050\ dm^3$

$$n_{酸} = c_{酸} V_{酸}$$
$$= 1.0\ mol \cdot dm^{-3} \times 0.080\ dm^3$$
$$= 0.080\ mol$$
$$n_{碱} = c_{碱} V_{碱}$$
$$= 0.40\ mol \cdot dm^{-3} \times 0.050\ dm^3$$
$$= 0.020\ mol$$

根据反应式
$$HA + NaOH \rightleftharpoons NaA + H_2O$$

中和反应后体系中有
$$n_{酸} = 0.060\ mol$$
$$n_{盐} = 0.020\ mol$$

稀释至 250 cm^3 即 0.250 dm^3 后，体系中

$$c_{酸} = \frac{n_{酸}}{V}$$
$$= \frac{0.060\ mol}{0.250\ dm^3}$$
$$= 0.240\ mol \cdot dm^{-3}$$
$$c_{盐} = \frac{n_{盐}}{V}$$
$$= \frac{0.020\ mol}{0.250\ dm^3}$$
$$= 0.080\ mol \cdot dm^{-3}$$

由弱酸和弱酸盐组成的缓冲体系的 pH 公式得

$$pH = pK_a^\ominus - \lg\frac{c_{酸}}{c_{盐}}$$

所以
$$pK_a^\ominus = pH + \lg\frac{c_{酸}}{c_{盐}}$$
$$= 2.72 + \lg\frac{0.240}{0.080}$$
$$= 2.72 + 0.4771$$
$$= 3.20$$

故 $K_a^\ominus = 6.3 \times 10^{-4}$。

例 8.12 甲溶液为一元弱酸，其$[H^+]=a\ mol\cdot dm^{-3}$，乙溶液为该一元弱酸的钠盐溶液，其$[H^+]=b\ mol\cdot dm^{-3}$，当上述甲溶液与乙溶液等体积混合后，测得其$[H^+]=c\ mol\cdot dm^{-3}$，求该一元弱酸的解离常数 $K_a^{\ominus}$。

解： 甲溶液中 $$HA \rightleftharpoons H^+ + A^-$$

解离度很小时，近似有$[HA]=c_0(HA)$，所以

$$[H^+]=\sqrt{K_a^{\ominus} c_0} =\sqrt{K_a^{\ominus}[HA]}=a$$

整理得
$$[HA]=\frac{a^2}{K_a^{\ominus}} \tag{1}$$

乙溶液中 $$A^- + H_2O \rightleftharpoons HA + OH^-$$

水解度很小时，近似有$[A^-]=c_0(A^-)$，所以

$$[OH^-]=\sqrt{\frac{K_w^{\ominus}}{K_a^{\ominus}}c_0}=\sqrt{\frac{K_w^{\ominus}}{K_a^{\ominus}}[A^-]}$$

$$[H^+]=\frac{K_w^{\ominus}}{[OH^-]}=\frac{K_w^{\ominus}}{\sqrt{\frac{K_w^{\ominus}}{K_a^{\ominus}}[A^-]}}=b$$

整理得

$$[A^-]=\frac{K_a^{\ominus}\cdot K_w^{\ominus}}{b^2} \tag{2}$$

甲溶液和乙溶液等体积混合后，形成弱酸-弱酸盐（HA-A⁻）缓冲体系，近似有$[HA]_{混}=\frac{1}{2}[HA]$和$[A^-]_{混}=\frac{1}{2}[A^-]$，即

$$K_a^{\ominus}=\frac{[H^+][A^-]_{混}}{[HA]_{混}} =\frac{c\times\frac{1}{2}[A^-]}{\frac{1}{2}[HA]}$$

将式(1)和式(2)代入其中，则

$$K_a^{\ominus}=\frac{c\times\frac{K_a^{\ominus}\cdot K_w^{\ominus}}{b^2}}{\frac{a^2}{K_a^{\ominus}}}$$

整理得

$$K_a^{\ominus}=\frac{a^2b^2}{cK_w^{\ominus}}$$

第二部分 习题

一、选择题

8.1 已知H_2CO_3 $K_{a_1}^{\ominus}=4.5\times10^{-7}$，$K_{a_2}^{\ominus}=4.7\times10^{-11}$

H_2S $K_{a_1}^{\ominus}=1.1\times10^{-7}$，$K_{a_2}^{\ominus}=1.3\times10^{-15}$

将相同浓度 H_2S 和 H_2CO_3 等体积混合后，下列对离子浓度相对大小表达正确的是

(A) $[CO_3^{2-}]<[S^{2-}]$； (B) $[CO_3^{2-}]>[S^{2-}]$；

(C) $[HCO_3^-]<[S^{2-}]$； (D) $[HS^-]<[CO_3^{2-}]$。

8.2 已知 H_3PO_4 的 $K_{a_1}^{\ominus}=6.9\times10^{-3}$，$K_{a_2}^{\ominus}=6.1\times10^{-8}$，$K_{a_3}^{\ominus}=4.8\times10^{-13}$，则在 0.1 $mol\cdot dm^{-3}$ NaH_2PO_4 溶液中离子浓度由大至小的顺序正确的是

(A) Na^+，$H_2PO_4^-$，HPO_4^{2-}，H_3PO_4，PO_4^{3-}；

(B) Na^+，$H_2PO_4^-$，HPO_4^{2-}，PO_4^{3-}，H_3PO_4；

(C) Na^+，HPO_4^{2-}，$H_2PO_4^-$，H_3PO_4，PO_4^{3-}；

(D) Na^+，HPO_4^{2-}，$H_2PO_4^-$，PO_4^{3-}，H_3PO_4。

8.3 将 0.1 $mol\cdot dm^{-3}$下列溶液加水稀释 1 倍后，pH 变化最小的是

(A) HCl； (B) H_2SO_4； (C) HNO_3； (D) HAc。

8.4 测得浓度 0.4 $mol\cdot dm^{-3}$一元弱酸 HA 溶液的 pH=4.0，该弱酸的解离常数为

(A) 2.5×10^{-8}； (B) 2.5×10^{-6}； (C) 1.0×10^{-4}； (D) 4.0×10^{-4}。

8.5 在下列溶液中 HCN 解离度最大的是

(A) 0.10 $mol\cdot dm^{-3}$ KCN；

(B) 0.20 $mol\cdot dm^{-3}$ NaCl；

(C) 0.10 $mol\cdot dm^{-3}$ KCN 和 0.10 $mol\cdot dm^{-3}$ KCl 混合溶液；

(D) 0.10 $mol\cdot dm^{-3}$ KCl 和 0.20 $mol\cdot dm^{-3}$ NaCl 混合溶液。

8.6 将 0.1 $mol\cdot dm^{-3}$ NaAc 溶液加水稀释时，下列各项数值中增大的是

(A) $[Ac^-]/[OH^-]$； (B) $[OH^-]/[Ac^-]$； (C) $[Ac^-]$； (D) $[OH^-]$。

8.7 在 0.10 $mol\cdot dm^{-3}$氨水中加入等体积的 0.10 $mol\cdot dm^{-3}$下列溶液后，使混合溶液的 pH 最大的是

(A) HCl； (B) H_2SO_4； (C) HNO_3； (D) HAc。

8.8 在 H_3PO_4 溶液中加入一定量 NaOH 后，溶液的 pH=10.00，在该溶液中下列物种中浓度最大的是

(A) H_3PO_4； (B) $H_2PO_4^-$； (C) HPO_4^{2-}； (D) PO_4^{3-}。

8.9 下列溶液中，具有明显缓冲作用的是

(A) Na_2CO_3； (B) $NaHCO_3$； (C) $NaHSO_4$； (D) Na_3PO_4。

8.10 配制 pH=7 的缓冲溶液时，选择最合适的缓冲对是〔$K_a^{\ominus}(HAc)=1.8\times10^{-5}$，$K_b^{\ominus}(NH_3)=$

1.8×10^{-5} H_2CO_3 $K^\ominus_{a_1}=4.5\times10^{-7}$，$K^\ominus_{a_2}=4.7\times10^{-11}$ H_3PO_4 $K^\ominus_{a_1}=6.9\times10^{-3}$，$K^\ominus_{a_2}=6.1\times10^{-8}$，$K^\ominus_{a_3}=4.8\times10^{-13}$]

(A) HAc－NaAc； (B) NH_3-NH_4Cl；

(C) $NaH_2PO_4-Na_2HPO_4$； (D) $NaHCO_3-Na_2CO_3$。

8.11 已知 H_2CO_3 的 $K^\ominus_{a_1}=4.5\times10^{-7}$，$K^\ominus_{a_2}=4.7\times10^{-11}$，则 0.10 mol·dm^{-3} $NaHCO_3$ 溶液的pH约为

(A) 5.6； (B) 7.0； (C) 8.3； (D) 13.0。

8.12 已知 H_3PO_4 的 $pK^\ominus_{a_1}=2.16$，$pK^\ominus_{a_2}=7.21$，$pK^\ominus_{a_3}=12.32$。0.10 mol·dm^{-3} Na_2HPO_4 溶液的 pH 约为

(A) 4.7； (B) 7.3； (C) 10.1； (D) 9.8。

8.13 不是共轭酸碱对的一组物质是

(A) NH_3，NH_2^-； (B) NaOH，Na^+；

(C) HS^-，S^{2-}； (D) H_2O，OH^-。

8.14 已知 $K^\ominus_b(NH_3)=1.8\times10^{-5}$，则其共轭酸的 $K^\ominus_a$ 为

(A) 1.8×10^{-9}； (B) 1.8×10^{-10}；

(C) 5.6×10^{-10}； (D) 5.6×10^{-5}。

二、填空题

8.15 已知0.10 mol·dm^{-3} HCN 溶液的解离度为0.0063%，则溶液的pH等于______，HCN的解离常数为______。

8.16 已知18 ℃时水的 $K^\ominus_w=6.4\times10^{-15}$，此时中性溶液中氢离子的浓度为______ mol·dm^{-3}，pH为______。

8.17 已知某二元弱酸 H_2A 的 $K^\ominus_{a_1}=1\times10^{-7}$，$K^\ominus_{a_2}=1\times10^{-14}$，则 0.10 mol·dm^{-3} H_2A 溶液中 $[A^{2-}]$为______ mol·dm^{-3}；在0.10 mol·dm^{-3} H_2A 和0.10 mol·dm^{-3}盐酸混合溶液中 $[A^{2-}]$为______ mol·dm^{-3}。

8.18 下列溶液中各物质的浓度均为 0.10 mol·dm^{-3}，则按 pH 由大到小排列的顺序为______。

(1) NH_4Cl 和 $NH_3\cdot H_2O$ 混合溶液； (2) NaAc 和 HAc 混合溶液；

(3) HAc； (4) $NH_3\cdot H_2O$；

(5) HCl； (6) NaOH。

8.19 在 0.10 mol·dm^{-3} HAc 溶液中加入少许 NaCl 晶体，溶液的 pH 将会______；若以 Na_2CO_3 代替 NaCl，则溶液的pH将会______。

8.20 实验室有 HCl，HAc($K^\ominus_a=1.8\times10^{-5}$)，NaOH，NaAc 四种浓度相同的溶液，现要配制 pH=4.44的缓冲溶液，共有三种配法，每种配法所用的两种溶液及其体积比分别为______；______；______。

8.21 在0.10 mol·dm^{-3} $NH_3\cdot H_2O$ 溶液中加入 NH_4Cl 固体，则 $NH_3\cdot H_2O$ 的浓度______，解离度______，pH将______，解离常数______。

8.22 2 mol·dm^{-3} $NH_3\cdot H_2O$ ($K^\ominus_b=1.8\times10^{-5}$)溶液的pH为______；将它与2 mol·dm^{-3}盐酸

等体积混合后,溶液的 pH 为______;若将氨水与 4 $mol\cdot dm^{-3}$ 盐酸等体积混合,则混合溶液的 pH 为______。

8.23 已知 H_3PO_4 的 $K_{a_1}^\ominus=6.9\times10^{-3}$,$K_{a_2}^\ominus=6.1\times10^{-8}$,$K_{a_3}^\ominus=4.8\times10^{-13}$。$H_3PO_4$ 的共轭碱为________,其 $K_b^\ominus$ 值为________。

8.24 在醋酸溶剂中,高氯酸的酸性比盐酸______,因为醋酸是______溶剂;在水中,高氯酸的酸性与盐酸的酸性______,这是因为水是______溶剂。

8.25 已知解离常数 HAc $K_a^\ominus=1.8\times10^{-5}$,HCN $K_a^\ominus=6.2\times10^{-10}$,HF $K_a^\ominus=6.3\times10^{-4}$,则相同浓度的稀溶液 NaAc,NaCN 和 NaF,水解度由大到小的顺序是__________。将 OH^-,Ac^-,CN^-,F^- 按碱性由强至弱顺序是________。

8.26 对于平衡反应 $HA+HE \rightleftharpoons A^-+H_2E^+$ $K^\ominus=1\times10^{-2}$,根据酸碱质子理论,反应式中的强酸为__________,强碱为__________。

8.27 根据酸碱质子理论,$[Fe(H_2O)_5(OH)]^{2+}$ 的共轭酸是______________,共轭碱是______________;HNO_3 的共轭酸是______________;NH_2^- 的共轭碱是______________。

三、简答题和计算题

8.28 三元酸 H_3AsO_4 的解离常数为 $K_1=5.5\times10^{-3}$,$K_2=1.7\times10^{-7}$,$K_3=5.1\times10^{-12}$。求多大起始浓度的 H_3AsO_4 可使溶液中$[AsO_4^{3-}]=4.0\times10^{-17}$ $mol\cdot dm^{-3}$?

8.29 向 0.10 $mol\cdot dm^{-3}$ 草酸($H_2C_2O_4$)溶液中滴加 NaOH 溶液至 pH=6.00,求溶液中 $H_2C_2O_4$,$HC_2O_4^-$ 和 $C_2O_4^{2-}$ 的浓度。已知 $H_2C_2O_4$ 的 $K_1=5.4\times10^{-2}$,$K_2=5.4\times10^{-5}$。

8.30 已知 HSO_4^- 的解离平衡常数为 1.0×10^{-2},求 0.010 $mol\cdot dm^{-3}$ H_2SO_4 溶液的$[H^+]$和 pH。

8.31 将 0.20 dm^3,0.40 $mol\cdot dm^{-3}$ HAc 和 0.60 dm^3,0.80 $mol\cdot dm^{-3}$ HCN 混合,求混合溶液中各离子的浓度。已知 $K_a^\ominus(HAc)=1.8\times10^{-5}$,$K_a^\ominus(HCN)=6.2\times10^{-10}$。

8.32 混合酸溶液中 HF 的浓度为 1.0 $mol\cdot dm^{-3}$,HAc 的浓度为 0.1 $mol\cdot dm^{-3}$。求溶液中 H^+,F^-,Ac^-,HF 和 HAc 的浓度。已知 $K_a^\ominus(HF)=6.6\times10^{-4}$,$K_a^\ominus(HAc)=1.8\times10^{-5}$。

8.33 将 0.20 $mol\cdot dm^{-3}$ 盐酸和 0.20 $mol\cdot dm^{-3}$ $H_2C_2O_4$ 溶液等体积混合后,求溶液中 $C_2O_4^{2-}$ 和 $HC_2O_4^-$ 的浓度。已知 $H_2C_2O_4$ 的 $K_{a_1}^\ominus=5.9\times10^{-2}$,$K_{a_2}^\ominus=6.4\times10^{-5}$。

8.34 欲配制 0.50 dm^3 pH=9,其中$[NH_4^+]=1.0$ $mol\cdot dm^{-3}$的缓冲溶液,求需密度为 0.904 $g\cdot cm^{-3}$,含氨质量分数为 26.0%的氨水的体积及所需固体氯化铵的质量。

8.35 在血液中 $H_2CO_3-NaHCO_3$ 缓冲对的作用之一是从细胞组织中迅速除去由运动产生的乳酸(简记为 HL)。

(1) 求 $HL+HCO_3^- \rightleftharpoons H_2CO_3+L^-$ 的平衡常数 $K^\ominus$;

(2) 若血液中$[H_2CO_3]=1.4\times10^{-3}$ $mol\cdot dm^{-3}$,$[HCO_3^-]=2.7\times10^{-2}$ $mol\cdot dm^{-3}$,求血液的 pH;

(3) 若向 1.0 dm^3 血液中加入 5.0×10^{-3}mol HL 后,pH 为多大?

8.36 在 20 cm^3 0.30 $mol\cdot dm^{-3}$ $NaHCO_3$ 溶液中加入 0.20 $mol\cdot dm^{-3}$ Na_2CO_3 溶液后,溶液的

pH=10.00。求加入 Na_2CO_3 的体积。已知 H_2CO_3 $K_{a_1}^{\ominus}=4.2\times10^{-7}$,$K_{a_2}^{\ominus}=5.6\times10^{-11}$。

8.37 通过计算判断在水溶液中,NH_3 与 HPO_4^{2-} 哪一个碱性较强?已知 $NH_3\cdot H_2O$ $K_b^{\ominus}=1.8\times10^{-5}$;$H_3PO_4$ $K_{a_1}^{\ominus}=6.9\times10^{-3}$,$K_{a_2}^{\ominus}=6.1\times10^{-8}$,$K_{a_3}^{\ominus}=4.8\times10^{-13}$。

8.38 根据酸碱质子理论,下列分子或离子中哪些是酸?哪些是碱?哪些既是酸又是碱?

HS^-,CO_3^{2-},$H_2PO_4^-$,NH_3,H_2S,HAc,OH^-,H_2O,NO_2^-。

8.39 根据酸碱质子理论,写出分子或离子的共轭酸(或碱)的化学式。

(1) SO_4^{2-};　(2) H_2SO_4;　(3) HSO_4^-;　(4) S^{2-};

(5) NH_3;　(6) H_2S;　(7) $H_2PO_4^-$。

第 9 章

沉淀溶解平衡

第一部分　例题

例 9.1　将 20 cm^3 0.01 $mol\cdot dm^{-3}$ $BaCl_2$ 和 20 cm^3 0.02 $mol\cdot dm^{-3}$ H_2SO_4 在强烈搅拌下与 960 cm^3 水相混合，利用计算结果判断是否有 $BaSO_4$ 沉淀生成。已知 $BaSO_4$ 的 $K_{sp}^{\ominus}=1.1\times10^{-10}$。

解：

$$V(Ba^{2+})=0.02\ dm^3$$

$$n(Ba^{2+})=0.01\ mol\cdot dm^{-3}\times0.02\ dm^3=2\times10^{-4}\ mol$$

$$V(SO_4^{2-})=0.02\ dm^3$$

$$n(SO_4^{2-})=0.02\ mol\cdot dm^{-3}\times0.02\ dm^3=4\times10^{-4}\ mol$$

混合后的总体积为

$$20\ cm^3+20\ cm^3+960\ cm^3=1\,000\ cm^3=1\ dm^3$$

所以混合溶液中

$$[Ba^{2+}]=\frac{2\times10^{-4}\ mol}{1\ dm^3}=2\times10^{-4}\ mol\cdot dm^{-3}$$

$$[SO_4^{2-}]=\frac{4\times10^{-4}\ mol}{1\ dm^3}=4\times10^{-4}\ mol\cdot dm^{-3}$$

$$\begin{aligned}Q_i&=[Ba^{2+}][SO_4^{2-}]\\&=2\times10^{-4}\times4\times10^{-4}\\&=8\times10^{-8}\end{aligned}$$

由于 $Q_i>K_{sp}^{\ominus}$，故有 $BaSO_4$ 沉淀生成。

例 9.2　某溶液中 Cr^{3+} 的浓度为 0.10 $mol\cdot dm^{-3}$，若已知 $Cr(OH)_3$ 的 $K_{sp}^{\ominus}=6.3\times10^{-31}$，求开始生成 $Cr(OH)_3$ 沉淀时的 pH。

解：

$$Cr(OH)_3 \rightleftharpoons Cr^{3+}+3OH^-$$

$$K_{sp}^{\ominus}=[Cr^{3+}][OH^-]^3$$

$$[OH^-]=\sqrt[3]{\frac{K_{sp}^{\ominus}}{[Cr^{3+}]}}$$

$$=\sqrt[3]{\frac{6.3\times10^{-31}}{0.10}}\ \text{mol·dm}^{-3}$$

$$=1.85\times10^{-10}\ \text{mol·dm}^{-3}$$

所以
$$\text{pOH}=9.7$$
故
$$\text{pH}=14-9.7=4.3$$

例 9.3 试比较 AgI 在纯水中和在 0.010 mol·dm^{-3} KI 溶液中的溶解度。已知 AgI 的 $K_{sp}^{\ominus}=8.5\times10^{-17}$。

解： AgI 在纯水中的溶解度

$$s_1=\sqrt{K_{sp}^{\ominus}}=\sqrt{8.5\times10^{-17}}\ \text{mol·dm}^{-3}=9.2\times10^{-9}\ \text{mol·dm}^{-3}$$

AgI 在 0.010 mol·dm^{-3} KI 溶液中溶解度为 s_2

$$\text{AgI} \rightleftharpoons \text{Ag}^+ + \text{I}^-$$

平衡浓度/(mol·dm^{-3})　　　s_2　　$0.010+s_2$

$$K_{sp}^{\ominus}=[\text{Ag}^+][\text{I}^-]=s_2(0.010+s_2)=9.3\times10^{-17}$$

因 s_2 很小，$0.010+s_2\approx0.010$ 代入上式得

$$s_2=\frac{8.5\times10^{-17}}{0.010}\ \text{mol·dm}^{-3}=8.5\times10^{-15}\ \text{mol·dm}^{-3}$$

$$\frac{s_1}{s_2}=\frac{9.2\times10^{-9}}{8.5\times10^{-15}}=1.1\times10^{6}$$

计算结果表明，同离子效应使 AgI 在 0.010 mol·dm^{-3} KI 溶液中的溶解度远小于其在纯水中的溶解度。

例 9.4 在下列溶液中不断通入 H_2S，计算溶液中最后残留的 Cu^{2+} 的浓度。

(1) 0.10 mol·dm^{-3} $CuSO_4$ 溶液；

(2) 0.10 mol·dm^{-3} $CuSO_4$ 与 1.0 mol·dm^{-3} HCl 的混合溶液。

解： (1) CuS 的 $K_{sp}^{\ominus}=6.3\times10^{-36}$，可见 0.10 mol·dm^{-3} Cu^{2+} 完全沉淀，生成 CuS 并产生 H^+，使 $[H^+]=0.20$ mol·dm^{-3}：

$$\text{Cu}^{2+}+\text{H}_2\text{S} = \text{CuS}+2\text{H}^+$$

同时，溶液中存在平衡

$$\text{H}^+ \quad + \quad \text{SO}_4^{2-} \quad = \quad \text{HSO}_4^-$$

$$0.20-x \quad\ 0.10-x \qquad\qquad x$$

$$\frac{x}{(0.20-x)(0.10-x)}=\frac{1}{K_{a_2}^{\ominus}}=\frac{1}{1.0\times10^{-2}}$$

解得 $x=0.09$

$$[\text{H}^+]=0.20\ \text{mol·dm}^{-3}-0.09\ \text{mol·dm}^{-3}=0.11\ \text{mol·dm}^{-3}$$

H_2S：$K_{a_1}^{\ominus}=1.1\times10^{-7}$，　$K_{a_2}^{\ominus}=1.3\times10^{-13}$

由　$H_2S \rightleftharpoons 2H^+ + S^{2-}$

$K_{a_1}^{\ominus} K_{a_2}^{\ominus}=\frac{[H^+]^2[S^{2-}]}{[H_2S]}$，饱和 H_2S 浓度为 0.10 $mol \cdot dm^{-3}$

得 $[S^{2-}]=\frac{K_{a_1}^{\ominus} K_{a_2}^{\ominus}[H_2S]}{[H^+]^2}=\frac{1.1\times10^{-7}\times1.3\times10^{-13}\times0.10}{(0.11)^2}\ mol \cdot dm^{-3}$

$=1.2\times10^{-19}\ mol \cdot dm^{-3}$

溶液中残留的 Cu^{2+} 浓度为

$$[Cu^{2+}]=\frac{K_{sp}^{\ominus}}{[S^{2-}]}=\frac{6.3\times10^{-36}}{1.2\times10^{-19}}=5.3\times10^{-17}\ mol \cdot dm^{-3}$$

(2) Cu^{2+} 完全沉淀产生 0.20 $mol \cdot dm^{-3}$ H^+ 则混合溶液中

$$[H^+]=1.0+0.20=1.20\ mol \cdot dm^{-3}$$

$$\begin{array}{ccccc} H^+ & + & SO_4^{2-} & \rightleftharpoons & HSO_4^- \\ 1.20-x & & 0.10-x & & x \end{array}$$

$$\frac{x}{(1.20-x)(0.10-x)}=\frac{1}{1.0\times10^{-2}}$$

解得 $x=0.10$

$$[H^+]=1.20-0.10=1.10\ mol \cdot dm^{-3}$$

$$[S^{2-}]=\frac{K_{a_1}^{\ominus} K_{a_2}^{\ominus}[H_2S]}{[H^+]^2}=\frac{1.1\times10^{-7}\times1.3\times10^{-13}\times0.10}{(1.10)^2}\ mol \cdot dm^{-3}$$

$$=1.2\times10^{-21}\ mol \cdot dm^{-3}$$

溶液中残留 Cu^{2+} 的浓度为

$$[Cu^{2+}]=\frac{K_{sp}^{\ominus}}{[S^{2-}]}=\frac{6.3\times10^{-36}}{1.2\times10^{-21}}\ mol \cdot dm^{-3}=5.3\times10^{-15}\ mol \cdot dm^{-3}$$

例 9.5 室温下测得 AgCl 饱和溶液中$[Ag^+]$和$[Cl^-]$的浓度均约为 $1.3\times10^{-5}\ mol \cdot dm^{-3}$。求反应

$$AgCl(s) \rightleftharpoons Ag^+(aq)+Cl^-(aq)$$

的 $\Delta_r G_m^{\ominus}$。

解：

$$AgCl(s) \rightleftharpoons Ag^+(aq)+Cl^-(aq)$$

$$K_{sp}^{\ominus}=[Ag^+][Cl^-]=1.3\times10^{-5}\times1.3\times10^{-5}=1.69\times10^{-10}$$

$$\Delta_r G_m^{\ominus}=-RT\ln K_{sp}^{\ominus}=-8.314\ J \cdot mol^{-1} \cdot K^{-1}\times298\ K\times\ln(1.69\times10^{-10})=55.7\ kJ \cdot mol^{-1}$$

例 9.6 Ba^{2+} 和 Sr^{2+} 的混合溶液中，二者的浓度均为 0.10 $mol \cdot dm^{-3}$，将极稀的 Na_2SO_4 溶液滴加到混合溶液中。已知 $BaSO_4$ 的 $K_{sp}^{\ominus}=1.1\times10^{-10}$，$SrSO_4$ 的 $K_{sp}^{\ominus}=3.4\times10^{-7}$。求

(1) 当 Ba^{2+} 已有 99%沉淀为 $BaSO_4$ 时的 $[Sr^{2+}]$；

(2) 当 Ba^{2+} 已有 99.99%沉淀为 $BaSO_4$ 时，Sr^{2+} 已经转化为 $SrSO_4$ 的百分数。

解：(1) 浓度为 0.10 $mol\cdot dm^{-3}$ 的 Ba^{2+}，已沉淀 99%，这时体系中

$$[Ba^{2+}]=0.10\ mol\cdot dm^{-3}\times(1-99\%)$$
$$=1.0\times10^{-3}\ mol\cdot dm^{-3}$$
$$BaSO_4 \rightleftharpoons Ba^{2+}+SO_4^{2-}$$
$$K_{sp}^{\ominus}=[Ba^{2+}][SO_4^{2-}]$$
$$[SO_4^{2-}]=\frac{K_{sp}^{\ominus}}{[Ba^{2+}]}$$
$$=\frac{1.1\times10^{-10}}{1.0\times10^{-3}}\ mol\cdot dm^{-3}$$
$$=1.1\times10^{-7}\ mol\cdot dm^{-3}$$
$$Q_i(SrSO_4)=[Sr^{2+}][SO_4^{2-}]$$
$$=0.10\times1.1\times10^{-7}$$
$$=1.1\times10^{-8}$$

由于 $Q_i(SrSO_4)<K_{sp}^{\ominus}(SrSO_4)$，故这时尚未生成 $SrSO_4$ 沉淀，因而 Sr^{2+} 的浓度仍为起始浓度 0.10 $mol\cdot dm^{-3}$。

(2) 浓度为 0.10 $mol\cdot dm^{-3}$ 的 Ba^{2+}，已沉淀 99.99%，这时体系中

$$[Ba^{2+}]=0.10\ mol\cdot dm^{-3}\times(1-99.99\%)$$
$$=1.0\times10^{-5}\ mol\cdot dm^{-3}$$
$$BaSO_4 \rightleftharpoons Ba^{2+}+SO_4^{2-}$$
$$K_{sp}^{\ominus}(BaSO_4)=[Ba^{2+}][SO_4^{2-}]$$
$$[SO_4^{2-}]=\frac{K_{sp}^{\ominus}(BaSO_4)}{[Ba^{2+}]}$$
$$=\frac{1.1\times10^{-10}}{1.0\times10^{-5}}\ mol\cdot dm^{-3}$$
$$=1.1\times10^{-5}\ mol\cdot dm^{-3}$$
$$K_{sp}^{\ominus}(SrSO_4)=[Sr^{2+}][SO_4^{2-}]$$
$$[Sr^{2+}]=\frac{K_{sp}^{\ominus}(SrSO_4)}{[SO_4^{2-}]}$$
$$=\frac{3.4\times10^{-7}}{1.1\times10^{-5}}\ mol\cdot dm^{-3}$$
$$=0.031\ mol\cdot dm^{-3}$$

则
$$\frac{0.10-0.031}{0.10}\times100\%=69\%$$

Sr^{2+} 已经转化成 $SrSO_4$ 的百分数为 69%。

例 9.7 已知 AgCl 的 $K_{sp}^{\ominus}=1.8\times10^{-10}$，求 AgCl 饱和溶液中 $[Ag^+]$；若加入盐酸，使溶液的 pH=3.0，再求溶液中 $[Ag^+]$。

解：

$$AgCl \rightleftharpoons Ag^+ + Cl^-$$
$$K_{sp}^{\ominus}=[Ag^+][Cl^-]$$
$$=1.8\times10^{-10}$$

在 AgCl 的饱和溶液中$[Ag^+]=[Cl^-]$，故

$$[Ag^+]=1.3\times10^{-5}\ mol\cdot dm^{-3}$$

体系 $pH=3.0$

则 $[HCl]=1.0\times10^{-3}\ mol\cdot dm^{-3}$

所以 $[Cl^-]=1.0\times10^{-3}\ mol\cdot dm^{-3}$

$$K_{sp}^{\ominus}=[Ag^+][Cl^-]$$
$$[Ag^+]=\frac{K_{sp}^{\ominus}}{[Cl^-]}$$
$$=\frac{1.8\times10^{-10}}{1.0\times10^{-3}}\ mol\cdot dm^{-3}$$
$$=1.8\times10^{-7}\ mol\cdot dm^{-3}$$

故在 $pH=3.0$ 的盐酸中$[Ag^+]=1.8\times10^{-7}\ mol\cdot dm^{-3}$。

例 9.8 向 $0.50\ mol\cdot dm^{-3}$的 $FeCl_2$ 溶液通 H_2S 气体至饱和，若控制不析出 FeS 沉淀，求溶液 pH 的范围。已知 FeS 的 $K_{sp}^{\ominus}=6.3\times10^{-18}$，$H_2S$ 的 $K_a^{\ominus}=1.3\times10^{-20}$。

解：

$$FeS \rightleftharpoons Fe^{2+}+S^{2-}$$
$$K_{sp}^{\ominus}=[Fe^{2+}][S^{2-}]$$

所以与 $0.50\ mol\cdot dm^{-3}$的 Fe^{2+}平衡的 S^{2-}，其浓度为

$$[S^{2-}]=\frac{K_{sp}^{\ominus}}{[Fe^{2+}]}$$
$$=\frac{6.3\times10^{-18}}{0.50}\ mol\cdot dm^{-3}$$
$$=1.26\times10^{-17}\ mol\cdot dm^{-3}$$

	$H_2S \rightleftharpoons$	$2H^+$	$+$	S^{2-}
平衡浓度/$(mol\cdot dm^{-3})$	0.10	$[H^+]$		1.26×10^{-17}

所以与饱和 $H_2S(0.10\ mol\cdot dm^{-3})$及 $1.26\times10^{-17}\ mol\cdot dm^{-3}$的 S^{2-}平衡的 H^+，其浓度可以由下面求出。因为

$$K_a^{\ominus}=\frac{[H^+]^2[S^{2-}]}{[H_2S]}$$

所以

$$[H^+]=\sqrt{\frac{K_a^{\ominus}[H_2S]}{[S^{2-}]}}$$
$$=\sqrt{\frac{1.3\times10^{-20}\times0.10}{1.26\times10^{-17}}}\ mol\cdot dm^{-3}$$
$$=0.0102\ mol\cdot dm^{-3}$$
$$pH=1.99$$

故 pH 应小于 1.99。

本题还可以采用如下方法进行计算。

$$Fe^{2+} + H_2S \rightleftharpoons FeS + 2H^+$$

平衡浓度/(mol·dm^{-3})　　0.50　0.10　　[H^+]

$$K^\ominus = \frac{[H^+]^2}{[Fe^{2+}][H_2S]}$$

$$= \frac{[H^+]^2}{[Fe^{2+}][H_2S]} \cdot \frac{[S^{2-}]}{[S^{2-}]} = \frac{\dfrac{[H^+]^2[S^{2-}]}{[H_2S]}}{[Fe^{2+}][S^{2-}]}$$

$$= \frac{K_a^\ominus}{K_{sp}^\ominus} = \frac{1.3\times10^{-20}}{6.3\times10^{-18}} = 2.1\times10^{-3}$$

$$K^\ominus = \frac{[H^+]^2}{[Fe^{2+}][H_2S]}$$

$$= \frac{[H^+]^2}{0.50\times0.10} = 2.1\times10^{-3}$$

所以

$$[H^+] = \sqrt{2.1\times10^{-3}\times0.50\times0.10}\ \text{mol·dm}^{-3}$$
$$= 0.0102\ \text{mol·dm}^{-3}$$
$$pH = 1.99$$

这种计算思路与题设的情景更相符合。

例 9.9　在 1.0 mol·dm^{-3} $CuCl_2$ 溶液中含有 10.0 mol·dm^{-3} HCl，通入 H_2S 至饱和。求达到平衡时，溶液中的[H^+]和[Cu^{2+}]。已知 CuS 的 $K_{sp}^\ominus = 6.3\times10^{-36}$，$H_2S$ 的 $K_a^\ominus = 1.3\times10^{-20}$。

解：反应过程中涉及两个平衡：

$$H_2S \rightleftharpoons 2H^+ + S^{2-} \qquad K_a^\ominus = 1.3\times10^{-20}$$
$$CuS \rightleftharpoons Cu^{2+} + S^{2-} \qquad K_{sp}^\ominus = 6.3\times10^{-36}$$

两式相减即得

$$Cu^{2+} + H_2S \rightleftharpoons CuS + 2H^+$$

$$K^\ominus = \frac{K_a^\ominus}{K_{sp}^\ominus}$$
$$= \frac{1.3\times10^{-20}}{6.3\times10^{-36}}$$
$$= 2.06\times10^{15}$$

1.0 mol·dm^{-3}的 Cu^{2+} 完全与 H_2S 反应，将生成 2 mol·dm^{-3} 的 H^+，故体系中[H^+]＝12 mol·dm^{-3}。

依题设 H_2S 饱和，故[H_2S]＝0.1 mol·dm^{-3}。

$$K^\ominus = \frac{[H^+]^2}{[Cu^{2+}][H_2S]}$$

$$[\mathrm{Cu}^{2+}]=\frac{[\mathrm{H}^+]^2}{K^\ominus[\mathrm{H_2S}]}$$
$$=\frac{12^2}{2.06\times10^{15}\times0.1}\ \mathrm{mol\cdot dm^{-3}}$$
$$=7.0\times10^{-13}\ \mathrm{mol\cdot dm^{-3}}$$

例 9.10 采用加入 KBr 溶液的方法，将 AgCl 沉淀转化为 AgBr。求 Br^- 的浓度必须保持大于 Cl^- 的浓度的多少倍？已知 AgCl 的 $K_{sp}^\ominus=1.8\times10^{-10}$，AgBr 的 $K_{sp}^\ominus=5.4\times10^{-13}$。

解： 转化过程涉及两个沉淀－溶解平衡：

$$\mathrm{AgCl} \rightleftharpoons \mathrm{Ag^+ + Cl^-} \qquad K_{sp}^\ominus(\mathrm{AgCl})=1.8\times10^{-10}$$
$$\mathrm{AgBr} \rightleftharpoons \mathrm{Ag^+ + Br^-} \qquad K_{sp}^\ominus(\mathrm{AgBr})=5.4\times10^{-13}$$

两式相减即得 AgCl 转化为 AgBr 的反应式：

$$\mathrm{AgCl+Br^-} \rightleftharpoons \mathrm{AgBr+Cl^-}$$
$$K^\ominus=\frac{K_{sp}^\ominus(\mathrm{AgCl})}{K_{sp}^\ominus(\mathrm{AgBr})}$$
$$=\frac{1.8\times10^{-10}}{5.4\times10^{-13}}$$
$$=3.3\times10^2$$
$$K^\ominus=\frac{[\mathrm{Cl^-}]}{[\mathrm{Br^-}]}$$
$$[\mathrm{Br^-}]=\frac{1}{K^\ominus}[\mathrm{Cl^-}]$$
$$=\frac{1}{3.3\times10^2}[\mathrm{Cl^-}]$$
$$[\mathrm{Br^-}]=3.0\times10^{-3}[\mathrm{Cl^-}]$$

故必须保持$[Br^-]>3.0\times10^{-3}[Cl^-]$，即$[Br^-]$大于$[Cl^-]$的 3.0×10^{-3} 倍。

例 9.11 将足量 ZnS 置于 1 dm^3 盐酸中，收集到 0.10 mol H_2S 气体。求溶液中$[H^+]$和$[Cl^-]$。已知 ZnS 的 $K_{sp}^\ominus=2.5\times10^{-22}$，$H_2S$ 的 $K_a^\ominus=1.3\times10^{-20}$。

解：
$$\mathrm{ZnS+2H^+} \rightleftharpoons \mathrm{Zn^{2+}+H_2S}$$

依题设收集到 0.10 mol H_2S 气体，这说明 4 个问题：

(1) 溶液已饱和，其中$[H_2S]=0.10\ mol\cdot dm^{-3}$；

(2) 逸出的和存在于饱和溶液中的 H_2S 共 0.20 mol；

(3) 生成 0.20 mol H_2S，同时 0.20 mol Zn^{2+} 存在于溶液中；

(4) 生成 0.20 mol H_2S，同时有 0.40 $mol\cdot dm^{-3}$ Cl^- 存在于溶液中。

$$K^\ominus=\frac{[\mathrm{Zn^{2+}}][\mathrm{H_2S}]}{[\mathrm{H^+}]^2}=\frac{[\mathrm{Zn^{2+}}][\mathrm{H_2S}]}{[\mathrm{H^+}]^2}\cdot\frac{[\mathrm{S^{2-}}]}{[\mathrm{S^{2-}}]}$$
$$=\frac{[\mathrm{Zn^{2+}}][\mathrm{S^{2-}}]}{\dfrac{[\mathrm{H^+}]^2[\mathrm{S^{2-}}]}{[\mathrm{H_2S}]}}=\frac{K_{sp}^\ominus(\mathrm{ZnS})}{K_a^\ominus}$$

$$=\frac{2.5\times10^{-22}}{1.3\times10^{-20}}$$

故 $$K^{\ominus}=1.92\times10^{-2}$$

$$[H^+]=\sqrt{\frac{[Zn^{2+}][H_2S]}{K^{\ominus}}}$$

$$=\sqrt{\frac{0.20\times0.10}{1.92\times10^{-2}}}\ mol\cdot dm^{-3}$$

$$=1.02\ mol\cdot dm^{-3}$$

这些 H^+ 存在于溶液中，同时也因此有 1.02 mol Cl^- 进入溶液中，故

$$[Cl^-]=1.02\ mol\cdot dm^{-3}+0.40\ mol\cdot dm^{-3}$$

$$=1.42\ mol\cdot dm^{-3}$$

例 9.12 某一元弱酸 HA 溶液的 $[H^+]=a\ mol\cdot dm^{-3}$，在此溶液中加入过量难溶盐 MA，实现沉淀溶解平衡时，溶液的 $[H^+]=b\ mol\cdot dm^{-3}$。设酸的浓度满足解离平衡的近似计算条件，求 MA 的溶度积常数 $K_{sp}^{\ominus}$。

解： 当体系中只有酸碱平衡时，即

$$HA \rightleftharpoons H^+ + A^- \tag{1}$$

$$K_a^{\ominus}=\frac{[H^+][A^-]}{[HA]}，其中[H^+]=[A^-]=a$$

由于符合近似计算条件，所以[HA]近似为起始浓度。

故 $$K_a^{\ominus}=\frac{a^2}{[HA]} \tag{2}$$

当沉淀溶解平衡实现后，即

$$MA \rightleftharpoons M^+ + A^- \tag{3}$$

溶液中 $[H^+]$ 依题意等于 b，显然这时的[HA]仍等于起始浓度，所以式(1)的平衡常数

$$K_a^{\ominus}=\frac{[H^+][A^-]}{[HA]}=\frac{b[A^-]}{[HA]} \tag{4}$$

结合式(2)，得

$$\frac{a^2}{[HA]}=\frac{b[A^-]}{[HA]}$$

所以有 $$[A^-]=\frac{a^2}{b} \tag{5}$$

从反应式(1)和(3)得出

$$[A^-]=[H^+]+[M^+]$$

即 $$[M^+]=[A^-]-[H^+]$$

所以两个平衡同时实现之时，有

$$[M^+]=\frac{a^2}{b}-b \tag{6}$$

对于沉淀溶解平衡式(3)，有

$$K_{sp}^{\ominus}=[M^+][A^-],$$

将式(5)和式(6)代入其中，得

$$K_{sp}^{\ominus}=\frac{a^2}{b}\left(\frac{a^2}{b}-b\right)$$

即
$$K_{sp}^{\ominus}=\frac{a^4-a^2b^2}{b^2}$$

第二部分 习题

一、选择题

9.1 已知 Ag_3PO_4 的 $K_{sp}^{\ominus}=8.9\times10^{-17}$，则 Ag_3PO_4 在 0.1 mol·dm^{-3} 的 Na_3PO_4 溶液中的溶解度为

(A) 7.6×10^{-5}；(B) 5.7×10^{-6}；(C) 3.2×10^{-6}；(D) 1.7×10^{-6}。

9.2 已知 $Sr_3(PO_4)_2$ 的溶解度为 1.0×10^{-6} mol·dm^{-3}，则该化合物的溶度积常数为

(A) 1.0×10^{-30}；(B) 1.1×10^{-28}；(C) 5.0×10^{-30}；(D) 1.0×10^{-12}。

9.3 已知 $Mg(OH)_2$ 的 $K_{sp}^{\ominus}=5.6\times10^{-12}$，则其饱和溶液的 pH 为

(A) 3.65；(B) 3.95；(C) 10.05；(D) 10.35。

9.4 $CaCO_3$ 在相同浓度的下列溶液中溶解度最大的是

(A) NH_4Ac；(B) $CaCl_2$；(C) NH_4Cl；(D) Na_2CO_3。

9.5 难溶盐 $Ca_3(PO_4)_2$ 在 a mol·dm^{-3} Na_3PO_4 溶液中的溶解度 s 与溶度积 $K_{sp}^{\ominus}$ 关系式中正确的是

(A) $K_{sp}^{\ominus}=108\ s^5$；(B) $K_{sp}^{\ominus}=(3s)^3\cdot(2s+a)^2$；

(C) $K_{sp}^{\ominus}=s^5$；(D) $K_{sp}^{\ominus}=s^3\cdot(s+a)^2$。

9.6 AgCl 和 Ag_2CrO_4 的溶度积分别为 1.8×10^{-10} 和 1.1×10^{-12}，则下面叙述中正确的是

(A) AgCl 与 Ag_2CrO_4 的溶解度相等；(B) AgCl 的溶解度大于 Ag_2CrO_4；

(C) AgCl 的溶解度小于 Ag_2CrO_4；(D) 都是难溶盐，溶解度无意义。

9.7 $BaSO_4$ 的相对分子质量为 233，$K_{sp}^{\ominus}=1.1\times10^{-10}$，把 1.0×10^{-3} mol 的 $BaSO_4$ 配成 10 dm^3 溶液，$BaSO_4$ 未溶解的质量是

(A) 0.0021 g；(B) 0.021 g；(C) 0.21 g；(D) 2.1 g。

9.8 已知 $Mg(OH)_2$ 的 $K_{sp}^{\ominus}=5.6\times10^{-12}$，则向 $Mg(OH)_2$ 饱和溶液中加 $MgCl_2$，使 Mg^{2+} 浓度为 0.010 mol·dm^{-3}，则该溶液的 pH 为

(A) 9.1； (B) 9.4； (C) 8.4； (D) 4.6。

9.9 已知 FeS 的 $K_{sp}^{\ominus}=6.3\times10^{-18}$；$H_2S$ 的 $K_{a_1}^{\ominus}\cdot K_{a_2}^{\ominus}=1.4\times10^{-20}$，在 0.10 mol·dm^{-3} Fe^{2+} 溶液中通入 H_2S 至饱和(0.10 mol·dm^{-3})，欲使 Fe^{2+} 不生成 FeS 沉淀，溶液的 pH 应是

(A) pH≥2.33； (B) pH≥3.53； (C) pH≤3.53； (D) pH≤2.33。

9.10 已知 $K_{sp}^{\ominus}$：AgCl 1.8×10^{-10}，AgBr 5.4×10^{-13}，AgSCN 1.0×10^{-12}，Ag_2CrO_4 1.1×10^{-12}，混合溶液中 KCl，KBr，KSCN 和 K_2CrO_4 浓度均为 0.010 mol·dm^{-3}，向溶液中滴加 0.010 mol·dm^{-3} $AgNO_3$ 溶液时，最先和最后沉淀的是

(A) Ag_2CrO_4，AgCl； (B) AgSCN，AgCl；

(C) AgBr，Ag_2CrO_4； (D) AgCl，Ag_2CrO_4。

9.11 已知 $K_{sp}^{\ominus}$：PbS 8.0×10^{-28}，Bi_2S_3 1.0×10^{-97}，CuS 8.0×10^{-36}，MnS 2.5×10^{-13}，CdS 8.0×10^{-27}，ZnS 2.5×10^{-22}，下列各对离子的混合溶液中均含有 0.30 mol·dm^{-3} HCl，不能用 H_2S 进行分离的是

(A) Cu^{2+}，Pb^{2+}； (B) Bi^{3+}，Cu^{2+}； (C) Mn^{2+}，Cd^{2+}； (D) Zn^{2+}，Pb^{2+}。

二、填空题

9.12 已知 $K_{sp}^{\ominus}(BaSO_4)=1.1\times10^{-10}$。若将 10 cm^3 0.2 mol·dm^{-3} $BaCl_2$ 与 30 cm^3 0.01 mol·dm^{-3} Na_2SO_4 混合，沉淀完全后溶液中$[Ba^{2+}][SO_4^{2-}]=$______________。

9.13 难溶电解质 $MgNH_4PO_4$ 和 $TiO(OH)_2$ 的溶度积表达式分别是______________，______________。

9.14 已知 PbF_2 的 $K_{sp}^{\ominus}=3.3\times10^{-8}$，则在 PbF_2 饱和溶液中，$[F^-]=$______mol·dm^{-3}，溶解度为______mol·dm^{-3}。

9.15 已知 $K_{sp}^{\ominus}$：FeS 6.3×10^{-18}，ZnS 2.5×10^{-22}，CdS 8.0×10^{-27}。在浓度相同的 Fe^{2+}，Zn^{2+} 和 Cd^{2+} 混合溶液中通入 H_2S 至饱和，最先生成沉淀的离子是________；最后生成沉淀的离子是______。

9.16 若 AgCl 在水中，0.010 mol·dm^{-3} $CaCl_2$ 中，0.010 mol·dm^{-3} NaCl 中及 0.050 mol·dm^{-3} $AgNO_3$中溶解度分别为 s_1，s_2，s_3 和 s_4，将这些溶解度按由大到小排列的顺序为________________。

9.17 已知 $Fe(OH)_3$ 的 $K_{sp}^{\ominus}=2.8\times10^{-39}$，欲使 0.10 mol $Fe(OH)_3$ 溶于 1 dm^3 溶液，则该溶液的最终 pH 应控制在__________。

9.18 同离子效应使难溶电解质的溶解度________，盐效应使难溶电解质的溶解度________；同离子效应较盐效应__________得多。

9.19 Ag_2CrO_4 固体加到 Na_2S 溶液中，大部分 Ag_2CrO_4 转化为 Ag_2S，这是由于________。

9.20 已知 $K_{sp}^{\ominus}$：$BaSO_4$ 1.1×10^{-10}，$BaCO_3$ 2.6×10^{-9}。溶液中 $BaSO_4$ 转化为 $BaCO_3$ 反应的标准平衡常数值为________。

9.21 向含有固体 AgI 的饱和溶液中：

(1) 加入固体 $AgNO_3$，则$[I^-]$变________；

(2) 若改加更多的 AgI，则$[Ag^+]$将________；

(3) 若改加 AgBr 固体，则$[I^-]$变________，而$[Ag^+]$________。

三、简答题和计算题

9.22 根据下列给定条件求溶度积常数。

(1) $FeC_2O_4 \cdot 2H_2O$ 在 1 dm^3 水中能溶解 0.10 g；

(2) $Ni(OH)_2$ 在 pH=9.00 的溶液中的溶解度为 1.6×10^{-6} $mol\cdot dm^{-3}$。

9.23 已知 Ag_2CO_3 的溶度积是 8.46×10^{-12}，若 Ag_2CO_3 在饱和溶液中完全解离，试计算

(1) Ag_2CO_3 饱和溶液中 Ag^+，CO_3^{2-} 的浓度(忽略 CO_3^{2-} 的水解)；

(2) Ag_2CO_3 在 0.01 $mol\cdot dm^{-3}$的 Na_2CO_3 溶液中的溶解度；

(3) Ag_2CO_3 在 0.01 $mol\cdot dm^{-3}$的 $AgNO_3$ 溶液中的溶解度。

9.24 1 g FeS 固体能否溶于 100 cm^3 1 $mol\cdot dm^{-3}$ 的盐酸溶液中？已知 FeS 的 $K_{sp}^{\ominus}=6.3\times10^{-18}$，$H_2S$ 的 $K_a^{\ominus}=K_{a_1}^{\ominus}\cdot K_{a_2}^{\ominus}=1.4\times10^{-20}$。

9.25 通过计算回答，0.010 mol 的 CuS 能否溶于 1.0 dm^3 盐酸中？

9.26 $Mg(OH)_2$ 在水中的溶解度为 1.12×10^{-4} $mol\cdot dm^{-3}$，求溶度积常数 $K_{sp}^{\ominus}$。如果在 0.10 dm^3 0.10 $mol\cdot dm^{-3}$ $MgCl_2$ 溶液中加入 0.10 dm^3 0.10 $mol\cdot dm^{-3}$ $NH_3\cdot H_2O$，求需加入多少克 NH_4Cl 固体才能够抑制 $Mg(OH)_2$ 沉淀的生成？已知 $NH_3\cdot H_2O$ 的 $K_b^{\ominus}=1.8\times10^{-5}$。

9.27 常温常压下，CO_2 在水中的溶解度为 0.033 $mol\cdot dm^{-3}$，求该条件下$CaCO_3$在饱和 CO_2 水溶液中的溶解度。已知 $CaCO_3$ 的 $K_{sp}^{\ominus}=2.8\times10^{-9}$，$H_2CO_3$ 的 $K_1=4.5\times10^{-7}$，$K_2=4.7\times10^{-11}$。

9.28 某溶液中含有 Fe^{2+} 和 Fe^{3+}，浓度均为 0.10 $mol\cdot dm^{-3}$，若要求沉淀完全 $Fe(OH)_3$ 而不产生 $Fe(OH)_2$ 沉淀，求溶液的 pH 应控制在什么范围？已知 $Fe(OH)_3$ 的 $K_{sp}^{\ominus}=2.8\times10^{-39}$，$Fe(OH)_2$ 的 $K_{sp}^{\ominus}=4.9\times10^{-17}$。

9.29 向浓度均为 0.025 $mol\cdot dm^{-3}$的 Pb^{2+} 和 Mn^{2+} 混合溶液中通入 H_2S 至饱和以分离 Pb^{2+} 和 Mn^{2+}，pH 应控制在什么范围？

9.30 将足量 FeS 置于 1 dm^3 盐酸溶液中，收集到 H_2S 气体在标准状态下为 2.24 dm^3。求盐酸溶液的浓度和 FeS 在该溶液中的溶解度。已知 $K_{sp}^{\ominus}(FeS)=6.3\times10^{-18}$，$K_a^{\ominus}(H_2S)=1.4\times10^{-20}$。

9.31 在 1 dm^3 0.20 $mol\cdot dm^{-3}$ $ZnSO_4$ 溶液中含有 Fe^{2+} 杂质为 0.056 g。加入氧化剂将 Fe^{2+} 氧化为 Fe^{3+} 后，调 pH 生成 $Fe(OH)_3$ 而除去杂质，问如何控制溶液的 pH？已知 $K_{sp}^{\ominus}[Zn(OH)_2]=3.0\times10^{-17}$，$K_{sp}^{\ominus}[Fe(OH)_3]=2.8\times10^{-39}$，$A_r(Fe)=56$。

9.32 如果 $BaCO_3$ 沉淀中尚有 0.010 mol $BaSO_4$，在 1.0 dm^3 此沉淀的饱和溶液中加入多少 mol Na_2CO_3 才能使 0.010 mol $BaSO_4$ 完全转化为 $BaCO_3$？

9.33 试通过计算说明，向含有 Ag_2CrO_4 固体的溶液中加入 KI 溶液有何现象产生？

已知 $K_{sp}^{\ominus}(Ag_2CrO_4)=1.1\times10^{-12}$，$K_{sp}^{\ominus}(AgI)=8.5\times10^{-17}$。

第 10 章

氧化还原反应

第一部分　例题

例 10.1　将下列氧化还原反应设计成两个半电池反应，并利用标准电极电势表的数据，求出 298 K 时反应的平衡常数 $K^\ominus$。

(1) $2Fe^{2+}+Cl_2 \longrightarrow 2Fe^{3+}+2Cl^-$

(2) $Zn+Hg_2Cl_2 \longrightarrow 2Hg+Zn^{2+}+2Cl^-$

(3) $Cl_2+H_2O \longrightarrow HClO+H^++Cl^-$

(4) $2H_2O \longrightarrow 2H_2+O_2$

解：(1) 正极　$\frac{1}{2}Cl_2+e^- \rightleftharpoons Cl^-$　　$E_+^\ominus=1.358\ V$

负极　$Fe^{3+}+e^- \rightleftharpoons Fe^{2+}$　　$E_-^\ominus=0.771\ V$

$$\begin{aligned}E^\ominus&=E_+^\ominus-E_-^\ominus\\&=1.358\ V-0.771\ V\\&=0.587\ V\end{aligned}$$

由
$$E^\ominus=\frac{0.059\ V}{z}\lg K^\ominus$$

得
$$\lg K^\ominus=\frac{zE^\ominus}{0.059\ V}=\frac{1\times0.587\ V}{0.059\ V}=9.949$$

故反应 $Fe^{2+}+\frac{1}{2}Cl_2 \longrightarrow Fe^{3+}+Cl^-$ 的 $K^\ominus=8.89\times10^9$，所以反应(1)的 $K^\ominus=(8.89\times10^9)^2=7.90\times10^{19}$。

(2) 正极　$Hg_2Cl_2+2e^- \rightleftharpoons 2Hg+2Cl^-$　　$E_+^\ominus=0.268\ V$

负极　$Zn^{2+}+2e^- \longrightarrow Zn$　　$E_-^\ominus=-0.7618\ V$

$$\begin{aligned}E^\ominus&=E_+^\ominus-E_-^\ominus\\&=0.268\ V-(-0.7618\ V)\\&=1.030\ V\end{aligned}$$

$$\lg K^\ominus=\frac{zE^\ominus}{0.059\ V}=\frac{2\times1.030\ V}{0.059\ V}=34.92$$

故反应 $Zn+Hg_2Cl_2 \longrightarrow 2Hg+Zn^{2+}+2Cl^-$ 的 $K^\ominus=8.32\times10^{34}$。

(3) 正极 $\frac{1}{2}Cl_2+e^- \rightleftharpoons Cl^-$ $E_+^\ominus=1.358\ V$

负极 $HClO+H^++e^- \rightleftharpoons \frac{1}{2}Cl_2+H_2O$ $E_-^\ominus=1.611\ V$

$$E^\ominus=E_+^\ominus-E_-^\ominus$$
$$=1.358\ V-1.611\ V=-0.253\ V$$

$$\lg K^\ominus=\frac{zE^\ominus}{0.059\ V}=\frac{-0.253\ V}{0.059\ V}=-4.288$$

故反应 $Cl_2+H_2O \longrightarrow HClO+H^++Cl^-$ 的 $K^\ominus=5.15\times10^{-5}$。

(4) 正极 $2H^++2e^- \rightleftharpoons H_2$ $E_+^\ominus=0\ V$

负极 $O_2+4H^++4e^- \longrightarrow 2H_2O$ $E_-^\ominus=1.229\ V$

$$E^\ominus=E_+^\ominus-E_-^\ominus$$
$$=0\ V-1.229\ V=-1.229\ V$$

$$\lg K^\ominus=\frac{zE^\ominus}{0.059\ V}$$
$$=\frac{4\times(-1.229\ V)}{0.059\ V}$$
$$=-83.32$$

故反应 $2H_2O \longrightarrow 2H_2+O_2$ 的 $K^\ominus=4.79\times10^{-84}$。

例 10.2 已知 $Mn+2H^+ \longrightarrow Mn^{2+}+H_2$ $\Delta_r G_m^\ominus=-228\ kJ\cdot mol^{-1}$

计算电对 Mn^{2+}/Mn 的 $E^\ominus$。

解: 将反应

$$Mn+2H^+ \longrightarrow Mn^{2+}+H_2$$

看成电池反应,并分解成两个电极反应

正极 $2H^++2e^- \rightleftharpoons H_2$ $E_+^\ominus=E^\ominus(H^+/H_2)=0\ V$

负极 $Mn^{2+}+2e^- \rightleftharpoons Mn$ $E_-^\ominus=E^\ominus(Mn^{2+}/Mn)$

由
$$\Delta_r G_m^\ominus=-zE^\ominus F$$

得
$$E^\ominus=-\frac{\Delta_r G_m^\ominus}{zF}$$
$$=-\frac{-228\,000}{2\times96\,500}\ V$$
$$=1.18\ V$$
$$E^\ominus=E_+^\ominus-E_-^\ominus$$

所以

$$E^\ominus(Mn^{2+}/Mn)=E_+^\ominus-E^\ominus$$
$$=0\ V-1.18\ V$$
$$=-1.18\ V$$

例 10.3 有如下两个电池

① $Fe|Fe^{3+}(c_2) \| Fe^{3+}(c_1)|Fe$

② $Pt|Fe^{3+}(c_2), Fe^{2+}(c_3) \| Fe^{2+}(c_3), Fe^{3+}(c_1)|Pt$

测得其电动势分别为 E_1 和 E_2。求 E_1 与 E_2 之比。

解: 电池① 正极反应 $Fe^{3+}(c_1)+3e^- \rightleftharpoons Fe$

$$E_+ = E^\ominus(Fe^{3+}/Fe) + \frac{0.059\ V}{3}\lg c_1$$

负极反应 $Fe^{3+}(c_2)+3e^- \rightleftharpoons Fe$

$$E_- = E^\ominus(Fe^{3+}/Fe) + \frac{0.059\ V}{3}\lg c_2$$

$$\begin{aligned} E_1 &= E_+ - E_- \\ &= E^\ominus(Fe^{3+}/Fe) + \frac{0.059\ V}{3}\lg c_1 - \left(E^\ominus(Fe^{3+}/Fe) + \frac{0.059\ V}{3}\lg c_2\right) \\ &= \frac{0.059\ V}{3}(\lg c_1 - \lg c_2) \\ &= \frac{0.059\ V}{3}\lg\frac{c_1}{c_2} \end{aligned}$$

电池② 正极反应 $Fe^{3+}(c_1)+e^- \rightleftharpoons Fe^{2+}(c_3)$

$$E_+ = E^\ominus(Fe^{3+}/Fe^{2+}) + 0.059\ V\lg\frac{c_1}{c_3}$$

负极反应 $Fe^{3+}(c_2)+e^- \rightleftharpoons Fe^{2+}(c_3)$

$$E_- = E^\ominus(Fe^{3+}/Fe^{2+}) + 0.059\ V\lg\frac{c_2}{c_3}$$

$$\begin{aligned} E_2 &= E_+ - E_- \\ &= E^\ominus(Fe^{3+}/Fe^{2+}) + 0.059\ V\lg\frac{c_1}{c_2} - \left(E^\ominus(Fe^{3+}/Fe^{2+}) + 0.059\ V\lg\frac{c_2}{c_3}\right) \\ &= 0.059\ V\left(\lg\frac{c_1}{c_3} - \lg\frac{c_2}{c_3}\right) \\ &= 0.059\ V\lg\frac{c_1}{c_2} \end{aligned}$$

$$\begin{aligned} \frac{E_1}{E_2} &= \frac{\frac{0.059\ V}{3}\lg\frac{c_1}{c_2}}{0.059\ V\lg\frac{c_1}{c_2}} \\ &= 1:3 \end{aligned}$$

例 10.4 已知:$Fe^{3+}+e^- \rightleftharpoons Fe^{2+}$ $E_A^\ominus = 0.77\ V$

$Fe(OH)_3$ 的 $K_{sp}^\ominus = 2.8\times10^{-39}$,$Fe(OH)_2$ 的 $K_{sp}^\ominus = 4.9\times10^{-17}$。求半反应 $Fe(OH)_3 + e^- \rightleftharpoons Fe(OH)_2 + OH^-$ 的 $E_B^\ominus$。

解: $Fe(OH)_3 + e^- \rightleftharpoons Fe(OH)_2 + OH^-$ 的 $E_B^\ominus$ 是[OH^-]=1.0 mol·dm^{-3}时的标准电极电势,通过 $K_{sp}^\ominus$ 可以求出这时的[Fe^{3+}]和[Fe^{2+}],结合 $Fe^{3+}+e^- \rightleftharpoons Fe^{2+}$ 的 $E_A^\ominus$,进而可以求出其非标

准态的 E_A，这个 E_A 值就是 $E_B^{\ominus}$。

由题设 $Fe(OH)_3 \rightleftharpoons Fe^{3+} + 3OH^-$ $K_{sp}^{\ominus} = 2.8 \times 10^{-39}$

$Fe(OH)_2 \rightleftharpoons Fe^{2+} + 2OH^-$ $K_{sp}^{\ominus} = 4.9 \times 10^{-17}$

当$[OH^-] = 1.0\ mol \cdot dm^{-3}$时，

$$[Fe^{3+}] = \frac{K_{sp}^{\ominus}}{[OH^-]^3} = \frac{2.8 \times 10^{-39}}{1.0^3} = 2.8 \times 10^{-39}$$

$$[Fe^{2+}] = \frac{K_{sp}^{\ominus}}{[OH^-]^2} = \frac{4.9 \times 10^{-17}}{1.0^2} = 4.9 \times 10^{-17}$$

将其代入 $Fe^{3+} + e^- \rightleftharpoons Fe^{2+}$ 电极反应式的 Nernst 方程式：

$$\begin{aligned} E &= E^{\ominus}(Fe^{3+}/Fe^{2+}) + 0.059\ V\ \lg \frac{[Fe^{3+}]}{[Fe^{2+}]} \\ &= 0.77\ V + 0.059\ V\ \lg \frac{2.8 \times 10^{-39}}{4.9 \times 10^{-17}} \\ &= -0.54\ V \end{aligned}$$

即 $E_B^{\ominus} = -0.54\ V$。

例 10.5 保持标准氢电极中 H_2 的压强不变，而将标准浓度的盐酸换成$0.10\ mol \cdot dm^{-3}$的醋酸。已知醋酸的 $K_a = 1.8 \times 10^{-5}$，求此时氢电极的电极电势。

解： 氢电极的电极反应为

$$2H^+ + 2e^- \rightleftharpoons H_2$$

其 Nernst 方程为

$$E = E^{\ominus}(H^+/H_2) + \frac{0.059\ V}{2} \lg \frac{\left(\frac{[H^+]}{c^{\ominus}}\right)^2}{\frac{p_{H_2}}{p^{\ominus}}}$$

$0.10\ mol \cdot dm^{-3}$ HAc 中，

$$\begin{aligned} [H^+] &= \sqrt{K_a^{\ominus} c_0} \\ &= \sqrt{1.8 \times 10^{-5} \times 0.10}\ mol \cdot dm^{-3} \\ &= \sqrt{1.8 \times 10^{-6}}\ mol \cdot dm^{-3} \end{aligned}$$

p_{H_2} 仍为标准状态。

所以上面的 Nernst 方程变成

$$\begin{aligned} E &= E^{\ominus}(H^+/H_2) + \frac{0.059\ V}{2} \lg \left(\frac{[H^+]}{c^{\ominus}}\right)^2 \\ &= 0\ V + \frac{0.059\ V}{2} \lg 1.8 \times 10^{-6} \\ &= -0.17\ V \end{aligned}$$

例 10.6　已知 $E^\ominus(Cu^{2+}/Cu^+)=+0.15\ V$，$E^\ominus(I_2/I^-)=+0.54\ V$，CuI 的 $K_{sp}^\ominus=1.3\times10^{-12}$。求：

(1) 氧化还原反应 $Cu^{2+}+2I^- \longrightarrow CuI+\frac{1}{2}I_2$ 298 K 时的平衡常数；

(2) 若溶液 Cu^{2+} 的起始浓度为 0.10 mol·dm^{-3}，I^- 的起始浓度为1.0 mol·dm^{-3}，计算达到平衡时留在溶液中的 Cu^{2+} 的浓度。

解：(1) 将氧化还原反应

$$Cu^{2+}+2I^- \longrightarrow CuI+\frac{1}{2}I_2$$

看成电池反应，其负极为 $\frac{1}{2}I_2+e^- \rightleftharpoons I^-$，$E_-^\ominus=0.54\ V$；其正极为 $Cu^{2+}+I^-+e^- \rightleftharpoons CuI$，$E_+^\ominus$。

将 $E_+^\ominus$ 看成 $Cu^{2+}+e^- \rightleftharpoons Cu^+$ 的非标准态 E，这个非标准态是由$[I^-]=1.0\ mol\cdot dm^{-3}$时的$[Cu^+]$决定的。

$$CuI \rightleftharpoons Cu^+ + I^- \qquad K_{sp}^\ominus=1.3\times10^{-12}$$

$$\begin{aligned}[Cu^+]&=\frac{K_{sp}^\ominus}{[I^-]}\\&=\frac{1.3\times10^{-12}}{1.0}\ mol\cdot dm^{-3}\\&=1.3\times10^{-12}\ mol\cdot dm^{-3}\end{aligned}$$

将其代入 Nernst 方程得

$$\begin{aligned}E_+&=E^\ominus+0.059\ V\ lg\frac{1}{[Cu^+]}\\&=0.15\ V+0.059\ V\ lg\frac{1}{1.3\times10^{-12}}\\&=0.85\ V\end{aligned}$$

电池的电动势

$$\begin{aligned}E^\ominus&=E_+^\ominus-E_-^\ominus\\&=0.85\ V-0.54\ V\\&=0.31\ V\end{aligned}$$

由

$$E^\ominus=\frac{0.059\ V}{z}\ lg\ K^\ominus$$

得

$$\begin{aligned}lgK^\ominus&=\frac{zE^\ominus}{0.059\ V}=\frac{0.31\ V}{0.059\ V}\\&=5.25\end{aligned}$$

所以

$$K^\ominus=1.8\times10^5$$

(2)	Cu^{2+}	+	$2I^-$	$\longrightarrow$ CuI	+	$\frac{1}{2}I_2$
起始浓度/(mol·dm^{-3})	0.10		1.0			
平衡浓度/(mol·dm^{-3})	x		1.0−0.10×2			

x 为平衡时溶液中的$[Cu^{2+}]$，由于 $K^{\ominus}$ 值大，反应彻底，可以认为0.10 mol·dm^{-3} 的 Cu^{2+} 几乎反应完全。故$[I^-]_平$ 为(1.0－0.10×2) mol·dm^{-3}。

$$K^{\ominus}=\frac{1}{[Cu^{2+}][I^-]^2}$$
$$=\frac{1}{x(1.0-0.10\times2)^2}$$
$$=1.8\times10^5$$
$$x=8.7\times10^{-6}$$

即溶液中 Cu^{2+} 的浓度为 8.7×10^{-6} mol·dm^{-3}。

例 10.7 298 K 时，测得如下原电池

$$(-)Cu|Cu^{2+}(1.0\times10^{-2}\,mol\cdot dm^{-3})\parallel Ag^+(c^{\ominus})|Ag(+)$$

的电动势 E＝0.52 V。

(1) 若已知 $E^{\ominus}(Ag^+/Ag)=0.80$ V，求 $E^{\ominus}(Cu^{2+}/Cu)$；

(2) 求该原电池的标准电动势 $E^{\ominus}_{池}$；

(3) 写出该原电池的电池反应，并计算其平衡常数 $K^{\ominus}$。

解：(1) 由公式 $E_{池}=E_+-E_-$ 得

$E_-=E_+-E_{池}$ 将题设条件代入其中，得

$$E_-=0.80\text{ V}-0.52\text{ V}$$
$$=0.28\text{ V}$$

负极的电极反应为 $$Cu^{2+}+2e^-=Cu$$

其 Nernst 方程为 $$E=E^{\ominus}+\frac{0.059\text{ V}}{z}\lg[Cu^{2+}]$$

所以 $$E^{\ominus}=E-\frac{0.059\text{ V}}{z}\lg[Cu^{2+}]$$
$$=0.28\text{ V}-\frac{0.059\text{ V}}{2}\lg(1.0\times10^{-2})$$
$$=0.34\text{ V}$$

(2) 题中的已知条件为 $E^{\ominus}_+=0.80$ V，(1)中已求出 $E^{\ominus}_-=0.34$ V，故

$$E^{\ominus}_{池}=E^{\ominus}_+-E^{\ominus}_-$$
$$=0.80\text{ V}-0.34\text{ V}$$
$$=0.46\text{ V}$$

(3) 电池反应为

$$2Ag^++Cu=2Ag+Cu^{2+}$$

由 $E^{\ominus}=\frac{0.059\text{ V}}{z}\lg K^{\ominus}$，得

$\lg K^{\ominus}=\dfrac{zE^{\ominus}}{0.059\ \text{V}}$，将(2)中求得的 $E^{\ominus}$ 值代入其中，得

$$\lg K^{\ominus}=\frac{2\times 0.46\ \text{V}}{0.059\ \text{V}}=15.6$$

故 $K^{\ominus}=4.0\times 10^{15}$。

例 10.8　将电对 IO_3^-/I_2 和电对 I_2/I^- 的电势－pH 图画在同一直角坐标系中。指出体系中涉及的歧化反应和逆歧化反应发生的具体 pH 范围。若在 298 K，pH＝11 时将所发生的反应以原电池方式完成，计算原电池的电动势 E 和电池反应的 $\Delta_r G_m$。

解：电对 IO_3^-/I_2 的电极反应式为

$$2IO_3^- + 12H^+ + 10e^- \rightleftharpoons I_2 + 6H_2O \qquad E^{\ominus}(1)=1.2\ \text{V}$$

$$E=E^{\ominus}(1)+\frac{0.059\ \text{V}}{10}\lg[H^+]^{12}$$

$$=1.2\ \text{V}+\frac{0.059\ \text{V}\times 12}{10}\lg[H^+]$$

故有
$$E=1.2\ \text{V}-0.07\ \text{V}\ \text{pH}$$

E 对 pH 作图为一直线，取两点（pH＝0，E＝1.2 V）和（pH＝14，E＝0.22 V），电势－pH 图见图中的 l_1 线。电对 I_2/I^- 的电极反应式为

$$I_2 + 2e^- \rightleftharpoons 2I^- \qquad E^{\ominus}(2)=0.54\ \text{V}$$

$E=E^{\ominus}$，E 与 pH 无关，为平行于横轴的直线，见图中的 l_2 线。

从图中看出，当 pH＜9.4 时 l_1 在 l_2 上方，即

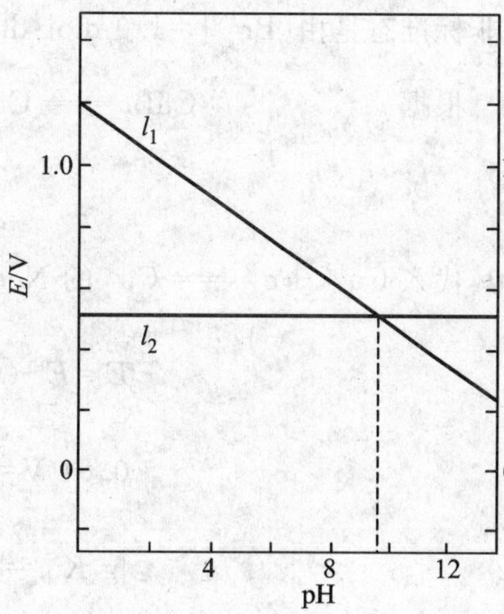

$$E(IO_3^-/I_2)>E(I_2/I^-)$$

IO_3^- 与 I^- 发生逆歧化反应，生成 I_2。

$$IO_3^- + 5I^- + 6H^+ = 3I_2 + 3H_2O$$

当 pH＞9.4 时 l_1 在 l_2 下方，即

$$E(IO_3^-/I_2)<E(I_2/I^-)$$

I_2 将发生歧化反应，生成 IO_3^- 和 I^-。

$$3I_2 + 3H_2O = IO_3^- + 5I^- + 6H^+$$

pH＝11 时发生歧化反应，这时

$$E_+=E(I_2/I^-)=0.54\ \text{V}$$

$$E_-=E(IO_3^-/I_2)=1.2\ \text{V}-0.07\ \text{V}\ \text{pH}=1.2\ \text{V}-0.07\ \text{V}\times 11=0.43\ \text{V}$$

故原电池的电动势 $E = E_{+} - E_{-}$

$= 0.54\ \text{V} - 0.43\ \text{V}$

$= 0.11\ \text{V}$

电池反应的 $\Delta_r G_m = -zEF$

$= (-5 \times 0.11 \times 96\ 500)\ \text{J} \cdot \text{mol}^{-1}$

$= -53\ \text{kJ} \cdot \text{mol}^{-1}$

例 10.9 已知 $Cu^{2+} + 2e^- \rightleftharpoons Cu$ $E^\ominus = 0.34\ \text{V}$

$Cu^{+} + e^- \rightleftharpoons Cu$ $E^\ominus = 0.52\ \text{V}$

$Cu^{2+} + Br^- + e^- \rightleftharpoons CuBr$ $E^\ominus = 0.64\ \text{V}$

求 CuBr 的 $K_{sp}^\ominus$。

解：将部分题设条件画在元素电势图上：

$$Cu^{2+} \text{———} Cu^{+} \xrightarrow{0.52\ \text{V}} Cu \quad (Cu^{2+} \to Cu:\ 0.34\ \text{V})$$

$$E^\ominus(Cu^{2+}/Cu) = \frac{E^\ominus(Cu^{2+}/Cu^{+}) \times 1 + E^\ominus(Cu^{+}/Cu) \times 1}{1+1}$$

所以 $E^\ominus(Cu^{2+}/Cu^{+}) = 2E^\ominus(Cu^{2+}/Cu) - E^\ominus(Cu^{+}/Cu)$

$= 0.34\ \text{V} \times 2 - 0.52\ \text{V}$

$= 0.16\ \text{V}$

即 $Cu^{2+} + e^- \rightleftharpoons Cu^{+}$ 的 $E^\ominus(Cu^{2+}/Cu^{+}) = 0.16\ \text{V}$。

将 $Cu^{2+} + Br^- + e^- \rightleftharpoons CuBr$ 的 $E^\ominus = 0.64\ \text{V}$ 看成是 $Cu^{2+} + e^- \rightleftharpoons Cu^{+}$ 的非标准态 E，这个非标准态是由$[Br^-] = 1.0\ \text{mol} \cdot \text{dm}^{-3}$时的$[Cu^{+}]$决定的。

根据 $CuBr \rightleftharpoons Cu^{+} + Br^-$ $K_{sp}^\ominus = [Cu^{+}][Br^-]$

得
$$[Cu^{+}] = \frac{K_{sp}^\ominus}{[Br^-]} = K_{sp}^\ominus$$

将其代入 $Cu^{2+} + e^- \rightleftharpoons Cu^{+}$ 的 Nernst 方程中，则

$$E = E^\ominus(Cu^{2+}/Cu^{+}) + 0.059\ \text{V}\ \lg \frac{1}{[Cu^{+}]}$$

$$0.64\ \text{V} = 0.16\ \text{V} + 0.059\ \text{V}\ \lg \frac{1}{K_{sp}^\ominus}$$

$$\lg K_{sp}^\ominus = \frac{0.16\ \text{V} - 0.64\ \text{V}}{0.059\ \text{V}} = -8.14$$

得 $K_{sp}^\ominus = 7.3 \times 10^{-9}$

例 10.10 下面是氧元素的电势图。根据此图回答下列问题：

$E_A^\ominus/\text{V}$

$$O_2 \xrightarrow{+0.695} H_2O_2 \text{———} H_2O \quad (O_2 \to H_2O:\ 1.23)$$

$E_B^\ominus/V$ $\quad O_2 \text{———} HO_2^- \overset{+0.88}{\text{———}} OH^-$（$O_2$ 至 OH^-：0.40）

(1) 计算后说明 H_2O_2 在酸性介质中的氧化性的强弱，在碱性介质中的还原性的强弱；

(2) 计算后说明 H_2O_2 在酸性介质中和碱性介质中的稳定性的强弱；

(3) 计算 H_2O 的离子积常数 K_w。

解：(1) 由酸性介质中的元素电势图得

$$E^\ominus(O_2/H_2O)=\frac{E^\ominus(O_2/H_2O_2)\times 1+E^\ominus(H_2O_2/H_2O)\times 1}{1+1}$$

所以
$$\begin{aligned}E^\ominus(H_2O_2/H_2O)&=2E^\ominus(O_2/H_2O)-E^\ominus(O_2/H_2O_2)\\&=1.23\ \text{V}\times 2-0.695\ \text{V}\\&=1.765\ \text{V}\end{aligned}$$

数据说明在酸性介质中 H_2O_2 是很强的氧化剂。

由碱性介质中的元素电势图得

$$E^\ominus(O_2/OH^-)=\frac{E^\ominus(O_2/HO_2^-)\times 1+E^\ominus(HO_2^-/OH^-)\times 1}{1+1}$$

所以
$$\begin{aligned}E^\ominus(O_2/HO_2^-)&=2E^\ominus(O_2/OH^-)-E^\ominus(HO_2^-/OH^-)\\&=0.40\ \text{V}\times 2-0.88\ \text{V}=-0.08\ \text{V}\end{aligned}$$

数据说明在碱性介质中 H_2O_2 是一种中等强度的还原剂。

(2) 将(1)中计算结果填入氧的元素电势图中

$E_A^\ominus/V$ $\quad O_2 \overset{0.695}{\text{———}} H_2O_2 \overset{1.765}{\text{———}} H_2O$（$O_2$ 至 H_2O：1.23）

$E_B^\ominus/V$ $\quad O_2 \overset{-0.08}{\text{———}} HO_2^- \overset{0.88}{\text{———}} OH^-$（$O_2$ 至 OH^-：0.40）

不论在酸性介质中，还是在碱性介质中，均有 $E_{右}^\ominus > E_{左}^\ominus$。这说明 H_2O_2 都是不稳定的，将会发生歧化反应。尽管从元素电势图上看，在热力学上 H_2O_2 在酸中歧化的可能性更大些，但实际上在碱中，由于动力学的原因，H_2O_2 分解的速率更快。

(3) 由元素电势图得

(a) $O_2+4H^++4e^- \rightleftharpoons 2H_2O$ $\qquad E^\ominus=1.23\ \text{V}$

(b) $O_2+2H_2O+4e^- \rightleftharpoons 4OH^-$ $\qquad E^\ominus=0.40\ \text{V}$

将(b)的 $E^\ominus$ 看成是(a)的非标准态 E，这个非标准态是由 $[OH^-]=1.0\ \text{mol}\cdot\text{dm}^{-3}$ 时的 $[H^+]$ 决定的。

$$[H^+]=\frac{K_w}{[OH^-]}=K_w$$

将其代入(a)的 Nernst 方程中

$$E=E^\ominus+\frac{0.059\ \text{V}}{4}\lg[H^+]^4$$

即 $$0.40\ \text{V}=1.23\ \text{V}+0.059\ \text{V}\lg K_w$$

$$\lg K_w=\frac{0.40\ \text{V}-1.23\ \text{V}}{0.059\ \text{V}}=-14.068,K_w=8.6\times10^{-15}$$

即水的离子积常数 $K_w=0.86\times10^{-14}$。

例 10.11 $E_A^\ominus/\text{V}$ $\quad Cr^{3+}\xrightarrow{-0.41}Cr^{2+}\xrightarrow{-0.91}Cr$

根据上面给出的部分 Cr 的元素电势图，计算下列各原电池的电动势 $E^\ominus$ 及其电池反应的 $\Delta_r G_m^\ominus$。

(1) $Cr|Cr^{2+}\parallel Cr^{3+},Cr^{2+}|Pt$

(2) $Cr|Cr^{3+}\parallel Cr^{3+},Cr^{2+}|Pt$

(3) $Cr|Cr^{2+}\parallel Cr^{3+}|Cr$

解：先求出 $E^\ominus(Cr^{3+}/Cr)$ 的数值，将元素电势图补充完整。

$$\begin{aligned}E^\ominus(Cr^{3+}/Cr)&=\frac{E^\ominus(Cr^{3+}/Cr^{2+})\times1+E^\ominus(Cr^{2+}/Cr)\times2}{1+2}\\&=\frac{(-0.41\ \text{V})\times1+(-0.91\ \text{V})\times2}{3}\\&=-0.74\ \text{V}\end{aligned}$$

(1)
$$\begin{aligned}E_{池}^\ominus&=E_+^\ominus-E_-^\ominus\\&=E^\ominus(Cr^{3+}/Cr^{2+})-E^\ominus(Cr^{2+}/Cr)\\&=(-0.41\ \text{V})-(-0.91\ \text{V})\\&=0.50\ \text{V}\end{aligned}$$

原电池的正极电极反应为 $\quad Cr^{3+}+e^-=\!=\!=Cr^{2+}$

原电池的负极电极反应为 $\quad Cr^{2+}+2e^-=\!=\!=Cr$

电池反应为 2 倍正极反应减去负极反应：$2Cr^{3+}+Cr=\!=\!=3Cr^{2+}$

故电子转移数 $z=2$。

$$\begin{aligned}\Delta_r G_m^\ominus&=-zE^\ominus F\\&=-2\times0.50\ \text{V}\times96\,500\ \text{C}\cdot\text{mol}^{-1}\\&=-96.5\ \text{kJ}\cdot\text{mol}^{-1}\end{aligned}$$

(2)
$$\begin{aligned}E_{池}^\ominus&=E_+^\ominus-E_-^\ominus\\&=E^\ominus(Cr^{3+}/Cr^{2+})-E^\ominus(Cr^{3+}/Cr)\\&=(-0.41\ \text{V})-(-0.74\ \text{V})\\&=0.33\ \text{V}\end{aligned}$$

原电池的正极反应为 $\quad Cr^{3+}+e^-=\!=\!=Cr^{2+}$

原电池的负极反应为 $\quad Cr^{3+}+3e^-=\!=\!=Cr$

电池反应为 3 倍正极反应减去负极反应：$2Cr^{3+}+Cr=\!=\!=3Cr^{2+}$

故电子转移数 $z=3$。

(3)
$$\begin{aligned}E_{池}^\ominus&=E_+^\ominus-E_-^\ominus\\&=E^\ominus(Cr^{3+}/Cr)-E^\ominus(Cr^{2+}/Cr)\end{aligned}$$

$$=(-0.74\ \text{V})-(-0.91\ \text{V})$$
$$=0.17\ \text{V}$$

原电池的正极电极反应为　　$Cr^{3+}+3e^- \longrightarrow Cr$

原电池的负极电极反应为　　$Cr^{2+}+2e^- \longrightarrow Cr$

电池反应为 2 倍正极反应减去 3 倍负极反应：$2Cr^{3+}+Cr \longrightarrow 3Cr^{2+}$

故电子转移数 $z=6$。

(2)、(3)中电池反应与(1)中相同，故电池反应的 $\Delta_r G_m^\ominus$ 与(1)中相同，均为 $-96.5\ \text{kJ}\cdot\text{mol}^{-1}$。三个原电池的电动势不同，但由于电子转移数不同，所以 $\Delta_r G_m^\ominus$ 仍保持一致。

例 10.12　试根据下面 pH=1 介质中 Bi 的元素电势图

$$Bi_2O_4 \xrightarrow{+1.59\ \text{V}} BiO^+ \xrightarrow{+0.32\ \text{V}} Bi \xrightarrow{-0.97\ \text{V}} BiH_3$$

(1) 求电对 Bi_2O_4/Bi，BiO^+/BiH_3，Bi_2O_4/BiH_3 的电极电势；

(2) 做出 Bi 元素的自由能-氧化数图。

解：(1)
$$E^\ominus(Bi_2O_4/Bi)=\frac{E^\ominus(Bi_2O_4/BiO^+)\times 1+E^\ominus(BiO^+/Bi)\times 3}{1+3}$$
$$=\frac{1.59\ \text{V}\times 1+0.32\ \text{V}\times 3}{4}$$
$$=0.64\ \text{V}$$

$$E^\ominus(BiO^+/BiH_3)=\frac{E^\ominus(BiO^+/Bi)\times 3+E^\ominus(Bi/BiH_3)\times 3}{3+3}$$
$$=\frac{0.32\ \text{V}\times 3+(-0.97\ \text{V})\times 3}{6}$$
$$=-0.32\ \text{V}$$

$$E^\ominus(Bi_2O_4/BiH_3)=\frac{E^\ominus(Bi_2O_4/BiO^+)\times 1+E^\ominus(BiO^+/Bi)\times 3+E^\ominus(Bi/BiH_3)\times 3}{1+3+3}$$
$$=\frac{1.59\ \text{V}\times 1+0.32\ \text{V}\times 3+(-0.97\ \text{V})\times 3}{7}$$
$$=-0.051\ \text{V}$$

(2) *A* 点　横坐标氧化数为 -3　BiH_3

$$Bi+3H^++3e^- \rightleftharpoons BiH_3 \qquad E^\ominus(A)=-0.97\ \text{V}$$
$$\Delta_r G_m^\ominus(A)=-zE^\ominus(A)F$$
$$=[-3\times(-0.97)\times 96\,500]\ \text{J}\cdot\text{mol}^{-1}$$
$$=281\ \text{kJ}\cdot\text{mol}^{-1}$$

A 点的纵坐标为 $281\ \text{kJ}\cdot\text{mol}^{-1}$。

B 点　横坐标氧化数为 $+3$　BiO^+

$$BiO^++2H^++3e^- \rightleftharpoons Bi+H_2O \qquad E^\ominus(B)=0.32\ \text{V}$$
$$\Delta_r G_m^\ominus(B)=-zE^\ominus(B)F$$
$$=(-3\times 0.32\times 96\,500)\ \text{J}\cdot\text{mol}^{-1}$$
$$=-93\ \text{kJ}\cdot\text{mol}^{-1}$$

按纵坐标的规定，B 点纵坐标为 93 $kJ\cdot mol^{-1}$。

C 点　横坐标氧化数为+4　Bi_2O_4

$$\frac{1}{2}Bi_2O_4+4H^++4e^- \rightleftharpoons Bi+2H_2O \qquad E^\ominus(C)=0.64\ V$$

$$\begin{aligned}\Delta_r G_m^\ominus(C)&=-zE^\ominus(C)F\\&=(-4\times 0.64\times 96\,500)\ J\cdot mol^{-1}\\&=-247\ kJ\cdot mol^{-1}\end{aligned}$$

按纵坐标的规定，C 点纵坐标为 247 $kJ\cdot mol^{-1}$。

A、B 和 C 三点，加上原点 $O(0,0)$，作 Bi 元素的自由能-氧化数图，如图所示。

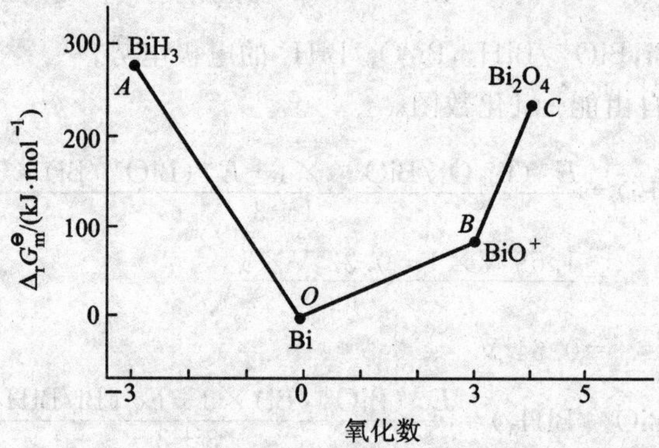

第二部分　习题

一、选择题

10.1　下列化合物中，氧呈现+2 价氧化态的是

(A) Cl_2O_5；　(B) BrO_2；　(C) $HClO_2$；　(D) F_2O。

10.2　某氧化剂 $YO(OH)_2^+$ 中元素 Y 的价态为+5，如果还原 7.16×10^{-4} mol $YO(OH)_2^+$ 溶液使 Y 至较低价态，则需用 0.066 $mol\cdot dm^{-3}$ 的 Na_2SO_3 溶液 26.98 mL。还原产物中 Y 元素的氧化态为

(A) −2；　(B) −1；　(C) 0；　(D) +1。

10.3　使下列电极反应中有关离子浓度减小一半，而 E 值增加的是

(A) $Cu^{2+}+2e^- = Cu$；　(B) $I_2+2e^- = 2I^-$；

(C) $2H^++2e^- = H_2$；　(D) $Fe^{3+}+e^- = Fe^{2+}$。

10.4　将下列反应设计成原电池时，不用惰性电极的是

(A) $H_2+Cl_2 = 2HCl$；　(B) $2Fe^{3+}+Cu = 2Fe^{2+}+Cu^{2+}$；

(C) $Ag^++Cl^- = AgCl$；　(D) $2Hg^{2+}+Sn^{2+} = Hg_2^{2+}+Sn^{4+}$。

10.5　下列氧化还原电对中，$E^\ominus$ 值最大的是

(A) Ag^+/Ag；　(B) $AgCl/Ag$；　(C) $AgBr/Ag$；　(D) AgI/Ag。

10.6　已知 $E^\ominus(Zn^{2+}/Zn)=-0.76\ V$，下列原电池反应的电动势为 0.46V，则氢电极溶液中的 pH 为

$$Zn+2H^+(a\ mol\cdot dm^{-3}) \longrightarrow Zn^{2+}(1\ mol\cdot dm^{-3})+H_2(1.013\times10^5\ Pa)$$

(A) 10.2；　(B) 2.5；　(C) 3.0；　(D) 5.1。

10.7　将标准氢电极与另一氢电极组成原电池，若使电池的电动势最大，另一氢电极所采用的酸性溶液应是

(A) $0.1\ mol\cdot dm^{-3}$ HCl；

(B) $0.1\ mol\cdot dm^{-3}$ HAc$+0.1\ mol\cdot dm^{-3}$ NaAc；

(C) $0.1\ mol\cdot dm^{-3}$ HAc；

(D) $0.1\ mol\cdot dm^{-3}$ H_2SO_4。

10.8　若要使电池$(-)Pt|H_2(p_1)|H^+(c_0)\parallel H^+(c_0)|H_2(p_2)|Pt(+)$的电动势 E 为正值，则 p_1 和 p_2 应满足的关系为

(A) $p_1=p_2$；　(B) $p_1<p_2$；

(C) $p_1>p_2$；　(D) p_1 和 p_2 可取任意值。

10.9　以惰性电极电解一段时间后，pH 增大的溶液是

(A) HCl；　(B) H_2SO_4；　(C) Na_2SO_4；　(D) $NaHSO_4$。

10.10　现有原电池$(-)Pt|Fe^{3+},Fe^{2+}\parallel Ce^{4+},Ce^{3+}|Pt(+)$，该原电池放电时所发生的反应是

(A) $Ce^{3+}+Fe^{3+} \longrightarrow Ce^{4+}+Fe^{2+}$；　(B) $3Ce^{4+}+Ce \longrightarrow 4Ce^{3+}$；

(C) $Ce^{4+}+Fe^{2+} \longrightarrow Ce^{3+}+Fe^{3+}$；　(D) $2Ce^{4+}+Fe \longrightarrow 2Ce^{3+}+Fe^{2+}$。

10.11　某氧化还原反应的标准摩尔吉布斯自由能变化为 $\Delta_rG_m^\ominus$，平衡常数为 $K^\ominus$，标准电动势为 $E^\ominus$，则下列对 $\Delta_rG_m^\ominus$，$K^\ominus$，$E^\ominus$ 的值判断合理的一组是

(A) $\Delta_rG_m^\ominus>0,E^\ominus<0,K^\ominus<1$；　(B) $\Delta_rG_m^\ominus>0,E^\ominus<0,K^\ominus>1$；

(C) $\Delta_rG_m^\ominus<0,E^\ominus<0,K^\ominus>1$；　(D) $\Delta_rG_m^\ominus<0,E^\ominus>0,K^\ominus<1$。

10.12　已知 $E^\ominus(M^{3+}/M^{2+})>E^\ominus[M(OH)_3/M(OH)_2]$，则溶度积 $K_{sp}^\ominus[M(OH)_3]$ 与 $K_{sp}^\ominus[M(OH)_2]$ 的关系应是

(A) $K_{sp}^\ominus[M(OH)_3]>K_{sp}^\ominus[M(OH)_2]$；　(B) $K_{sp}^\ominus[M(OH)_3]<K_{sp}^\ominus[M(OH)_2]$；

(C) $K_{sp}^\ominus[M(OH)_3]=K_{sp}^\ominus[M(OH)_2]$；　(D) 无法判断。

10.13　某电池$(-)A|A^{2+}(0.1\ mol\cdot dm^{-3})\parallel B^{2+}(1.0\times10^{-2}\ mol\cdot dm^{-3})|B(+)$的电动势 E 为 0.27V，则该电池的标准电动势 $E^\ominus$ 为

(A) 0.24V；　(B) 0.27 V；　(C) 0.30 V；　(D) 0.33V。

10.14　已知配合物的稳定常数 $K_{稳}^\ominus[Fe(CN)_6^{3-}]>K_{稳}^\ominus[Fe(CN)_6^{4-}]$，则下面对 $E^\ominus[Fe(CN)_6^{3-}/Fe(CN)_6^{4-}]$ 与 $E^\ominus(Fe^{3+}/Fe^{2+})$ 判断正确的是

(A) $E^\ominus[Fe(CN)_6^{3-}/Fe(CN)_6^{4-}]>E^\ominus(Fe^{3+}/Fe^{2+})$；

(B) $E^\ominus[Fe(CN)_6^{3-}/Fe(CN)_6^{4-}]<E^\ominus(Fe^{3+}/Fe^{2+})$；

(C) $E^\ominus[Fe(CN)_6^{3-}/Fe(CN)_6^{4-}]=E^\ominus(Fe^{3+}/Fe^{2+})$；

(D) 无法判断。

10.15　电极电势与 pH 无关的电对是

(A) H_2O_2/H_2O； (B) IO_3^-/I^-； (C) MnO_2/Mn^{2+}； (D) MnO_4^-/MnO_4^{2-}。

二、填空题

10.16 电池 (−)Pt|H_2(1.013×10^5 Pa)|H^+(1×10^{-3} mol·dm^{-3}) ‖ H^+(1 mol·dm^{-3})|H_2(1.013×10^5 Pa)|Pt(+)属于______电池，该电池的电动势为______V，电池反应为____________。

10.17 将 Ag−AgCl 电极[$E^\ominus$(AgCl/Ag)=0.224 V]与饱和甘汞电极[$E^\ominus$=0.242 V]组成原电池，该原电池的电池符号为____________；正极反应____________；负极反应____________；电池反应____________；电池反应的平衡常数为____________。

10.18 将 KI，$NH_3 \cdot H_2O$，$Na_2S_2O_3$ 和 Na_2S 溶液分别与 $AgNO_3$ 溶液混合(已知：$K_{sp}^\ominus$ AgI 8.5×10^{-17}，Ag_2S 6.3×10^{-50}；$K_{稳}^\ominus$：$[Ag(NH_3)_2]^+$ 1.1×10^7；$[Ag(S_2O_3)_2]^{3-}$ 2.9×10^{13})，则

(1) 当______存在时，Ag^+ 的氧化能力最强；

(2) 当______存在时，Ag 的还原能力最强。

10.19 标准状态下，下列反应均自发进行

$$2MnO_4^- + 5H_2O_2 + 6H^+ = 2Mn^{2+} + 5O_2 + 8H_2O$$

$$H_2O_2 + 2I^- + 2H^+ = 2H_2O + I_2$$

$$I_2 + 2S_2O_3^{2-} = 2I^- + S_4O_6^{2-}$$

由此判断反应所涉及的物质中还原性最强的是______，氧化性最强的是______。

10.20 电池 (−)Cu|Cu^+ ‖ Cu^+，Cu^{2+}|Pt(+)和(−)Cu|Cu^{2+} ‖ Cu^+，Cu^{2+}|Pt(+)的反应均可写成 $Cu + Cu^{2+} = 2Cu^+$，则此两电池的 $\Delta_r G_m^\ominus$______，$E^\ominus$______，$K^\ominus$______(填"相同"或"不同")。

10.21 已知 $E^\ominus(Cu^{2+}/Cu)$=0.342 V，$K_{sp}^\ominus[Cu(OH)_2]$=2.2×10^{-20}，则 $E^\ominus[Cu(OH)_2/Cu]$=______V。

10.22 在 $Fe^{3+} + e^- = Fe^{2+}$ 电极反应中，加入 Fe^{3+} 的配位剂 F^-，则使电极电势的数值______；在 $Cu^{2+} + e^- = Cu^+$ 电极反应中，加入 Cu^+ 的沉淀剂 I^- 可使其电极电势的数值______。

10.23 对某一自发的氧化还原反应，若将反应方程式中各物质的计量数扩大到原来的 2 倍，则此反应的$|\Delta_r G_m|$将______，电池电动势 E______。

10.24 已知 $MnO_4^- + 8H^+ + 5e^- = Mn^{2+} + 4H_2O$ $E^\ominus$=1.51 V，当 MnO_4^- 和 Mn^{2+} 处于标准状态时，电极电势与 pH 的关系是：E/V=______。

三、简答题和计算题

10.25 用离子电子法配平下列反应式(酸性介质)。

(1) $MnO_4^- + Cl^- \longrightarrow Mn^{2+} + Cl_2$；

(2) $Mn^{2+} + NaBiO_3 \longrightarrow MnO_4^- + Bi^{3+}$；

(3) $Cr^{3+} + PbO_2 \longrightarrow Cr_2O_7^{2-} + Pb^{2+}$；

(4) $C_3H_8O + MnO_4^- \longrightarrow C_3H_6O_2 + Mn^{2+}$；

(5) $HClO_3+P_4 \longrightarrow Cl^-+H_3PO_4$。

10.26 用离子电子法配平下列反应式(碱性介质)。

(1) $CrO_4^{2-}+HSnO_2^- \longrightarrow CrO_2^-+HSnO_3^-$;

(2) $H_2O_2+CrO_2^- \longrightarrow CrO_4^{2-}$;

(3) $CuS+CN^- \longrightarrow Cu(CN)_4^{3-}+S^{2-}+NCO^-$;

(4) $CN^-+O_2 \longrightarrow CO_3^{2-}+NH_3$;

(5) $Al+NO_2^- \longrightarrow Al(OH)_4^-+NH_3$。

10.27 已知 HCl 和 HI 溶液都是强酸,但 Ag 不能从 HCl 溶液置换出 H_2,却能从 HI 溶液中置换出 H_2。请通过计算加以解释。已知 $E^\ominus(Ag^+/Ag)=0.799$ V,AgCl 的 $K_{sp}^\ominus=1.8\times10^{-10}$,AgI 的 $K_{sp}^\ominus=8.5\times10^{-17}$。

10.28 某学生为测定 CuS 的溶度积常数,设计如下原电池:正极为铜片,在 0.1 mol·dm^{-3} Cu^{2+} 的溶液中,再通入 H_2S 气体使之达到饱和;负极为标准锌电极。测得电池电动势为 0.670 V。已知 $E^\ominus(Cu^{2+}/Cu)=0.342$ V,$E^\ominus(Zn^{2+}/Zn)=-0.763$ V,H_2S 的 $K_{a_1}^\ominus=1.1\times10^{-7}$,$K_{a_2}^\ominus=1.3\times10^{-13}$。试求 CuS 的溶度积常数。

10.29 已知 $H_3AsO_4+2H^++2e^- = H_3AsO_3+H_2O$ $E^\ominus=0.559$ V; $I_3^-+2e^- = 3I^-$ $E^\ominus=0.535$ V。求:

(1) 若溶液的 pH=7,反应向哪个方向自发进行?

(2) 溶液中$[H^+]=6$ mol·dm^{-3},反应向哪个方向自发进行?

10.30 求下列电池电动势和电池反应的标准平衡常数

(−)Cu|$[Cu(NH_3)_4]^{2+}$(0.10 mol·dm^{-3}),NH_3(1.0 mol·dm^{-3}) ‖ $AgNO_3$(0.010 mol·dm^{-3})|Ag(+)

已知 $E^\ominus(Ag^+/Ag)=0.80$ V,$E^\ominus(Cu^{2+}/Cu)=0.34$ V,$[Cu(NH_3)_4]^{2+}$ 的 $K_{稳}^\ominus=2.1\times10^{13}$。

10.31 已知 $E^\ominus(Cu^{2+}/Cu)=0.342$ V,$E^\ominus(Cu^{2+}/Cu^+)=0.153$ V,$K_{sp}^\ominus(CuCl)=1.72\times10^{-7}$。通过计算求反应 $Cu^{2+}+Cu+2Cl^- = 2CuCl$ 能否自发进行,并求反应的平衡常数 $K^\ominus$。

10.32 将下列非氧化还原反应设计成两个半电池反应,并利用标准电极电势表的数据,求出 298 K 时反应的平衡常数 $K^\ominus$。

(1) $H_2O = H^++OH^-$; (2) $Pt^{2+}+4Cl^- = PtCl_4$。

10.33 已知:$Cu^++e^- = Cu$ $E^\ominus=0.52$ V

CuCl 的 $K_{sp}^\ominus=1.7\times10^{-7}$,求电极反应 $CuCl+e^- = Cu+Cl^-$ 的 $E^\ominus$。

10.34 有一原电池(−)A|A^{2+} ‖ B^{2+}|B(+),当$[A^{2+}]=[B^{2+}]$时,电池的电动势为 0.78 V。现使该电池的电动势值减半,求此时的$[A^{2+}]/[B^{2+}]$。

10.35 已知 $E^\ominus(Tl^{3+}/Tl^+)=1.25$V,$E^\ominus(Tl^{3+}/Tl)=0.74$V,设计成下列三个标准电池:

(a) (−) Tl|Tl^+ ‖ Tl^{3+}|Tl(+)

(b) (−) Tl|Tl^+ ‖ Tl^{3+},Tl^+|Pt(+)

(c) (−) Tl|Tl^{3+} ‖ Tl^{3+},Tl^+|Pt(+)

(1) 请写出每一个电池的电池反应式; (2) 计算每一个电池的电动势和 $\Delta_r G_m^\ominus$。

10.36 在酸性条件下，将 $KMnO_4$ 滴加到过量 KI 溶液中，产物是什么？已知元素电势图如下

$E_A^\ominus/V$ $H_5IO_6 \xrightarrow{1.70} IO_3^- \xrightarrow{1.14} HOI \xrightarrow{1.45} I_3^- \xrightarrow{0.54} I^-$

$MnO_4^- \xrightarrow{0.56} MnO_4^{2-} \xrightarrow{2.26} MnO_2 \xrightarrow{0.95} Mn^{3+} \xrightarrow{1.51} Mn^{2+} \xrightarrow{-1.18} Mn$

10.37 向酸性的 1.0×10^{-3} $mol\cdot dm^{-3}$ Fe^{3+} 溶液中加入过量液态汞，发生反应为：$2Fe^{3+} + 2Hg = 2Fe^{2+} + Hg_2^{2+}$，达平衡时还有 4.6% Fe^{3+}。已知 $E^\ominus(Fe^{3+}/Fe^{2+})=0.77V$，求 $E^\ominus(Hg_2^{2+}/Hg)$。

10.38 已知 $E^\ominus(Ag^+/Ag)=0.80$ V，$E^\ominus(O_2/OH^-)=0.40$ V，$E^\ominus(H^+/H_2)=0$；$Ag(CN)_2^-$：$K^\ominus_{稳}=1\times10^{21}$。通过计算回答：

(1) 在碱性条件下通入空气时 Ag 能否溶于 KCN 溶液；

(2) Ag 能否从 KCN 溶液中置换出 H_2。

10.39 下图是铬体系的电势－pH 图。写出图中 DH，EF，FJ，IK，CF，DE，IJ 各线所表示的反应。

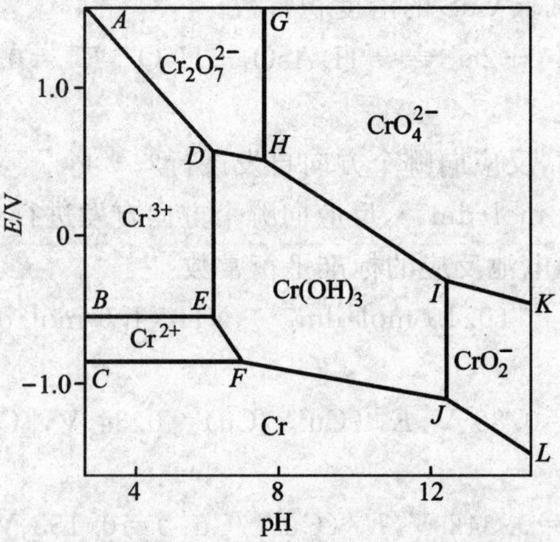

第 11 章

配位化学基础

第一部分　例题

例 11.1　指出下列配位化合物中配位单元的空间结构并画出可能存在的几何异构体。

(1) $[Cr(NH_3)_3(H_2O)_3]Cl_3$；　　(2) $[Co(NH_3)_2(en)_2]Cl_3$；

(3) $[Cr(H_2O)_4Cl_2]Cl\cdot 2H_2O$；　　(4) $[Pt(NH_3)_2(OH)_2Cl_2]$；

(5) $[Pt(NH_3)_2BrCl]$；　　(6) $[Co(NH_3)(en)Cl_3]$。

解：(1) 八面体，两个几何异构体，如图(a)所示。

(2) 八面体，两个几何异构体，如图(b)所示。

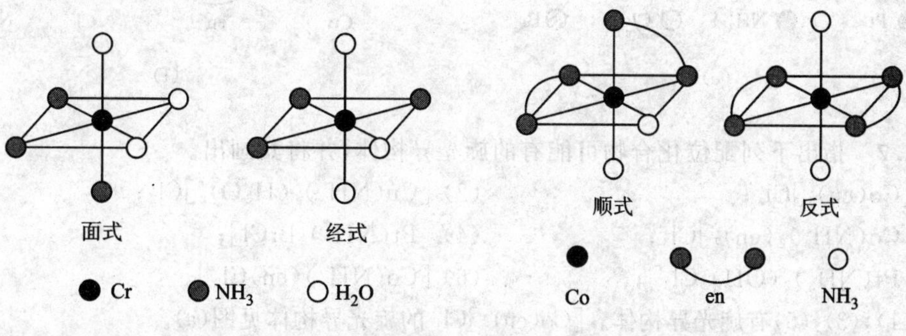

(a)　　(b)

(3) 八面体，两个几何异构体，如图(c)所示。

(4) 八面体，五个几何异构体，如图(d)所示。

(5) 平面四边形，两个几何异构体，如图(e)所示。

(6) 八面体，两个几何异构体，如图(f)所示。

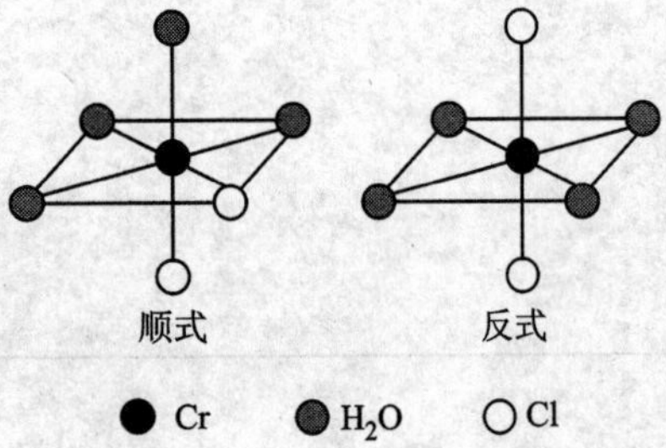

(c)

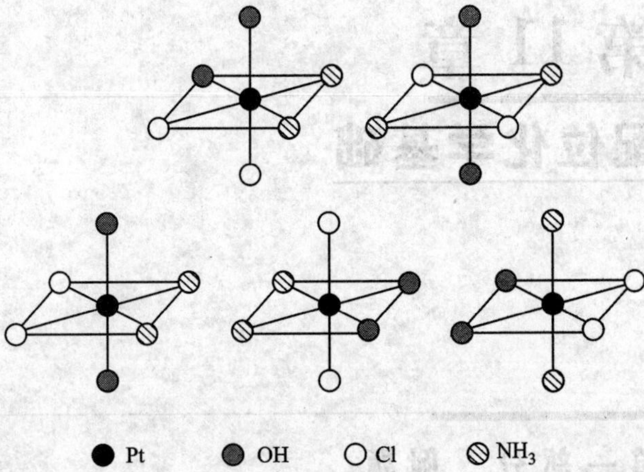

(d)

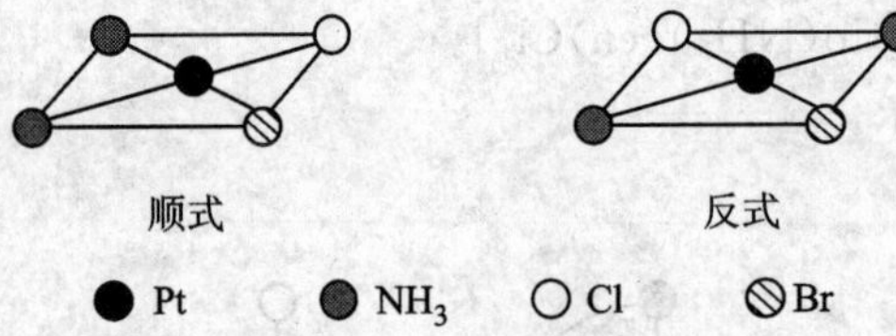

(e)

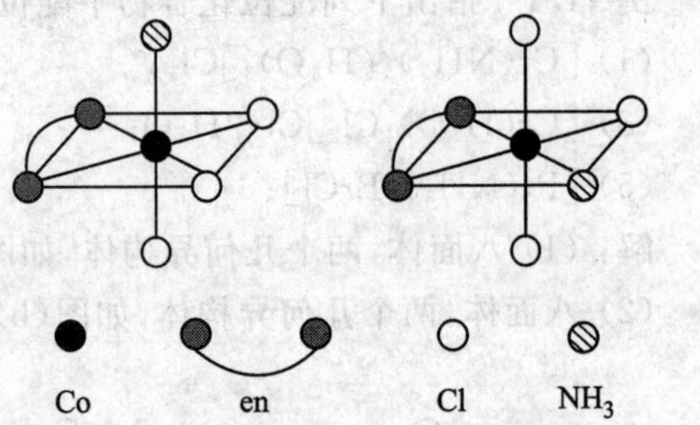

(f)

例 11.2 指出下列配位化合物可能有的旋光异构体,并将其画出。

(1) $[Co(en)_3]Cl_3$; (2) $[Cu(NH_3)_4(H_2O)_2]Cl_2$;

(3) $[Co(NH_3)_2(en)_2]Cl_3$; (4) $[Pt(NH_3)_2BrCl]$;

(5) $[Pt(NH_3)_2(OH)_2Cl_2]$; (6) $[Co(NH_3)(en)Cl_3]$。

解: (1),(3),(5)有旋光异构体。$[Co(en)_3]Cl_3$ 的旋光异构体见图(a)。

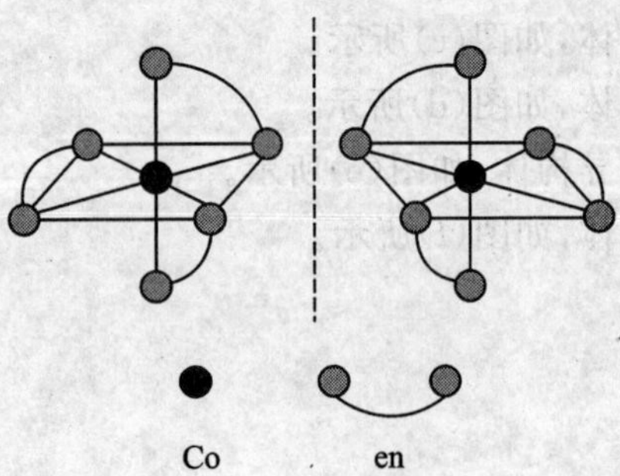

(a)

$[Co(NH_3)_2(en)_2]Cl_3$ 的旋光异构体见图(b)。

$[Pt(NH_3)_2(OH)_2Cl_2]$的旋光异构体见图(c)。

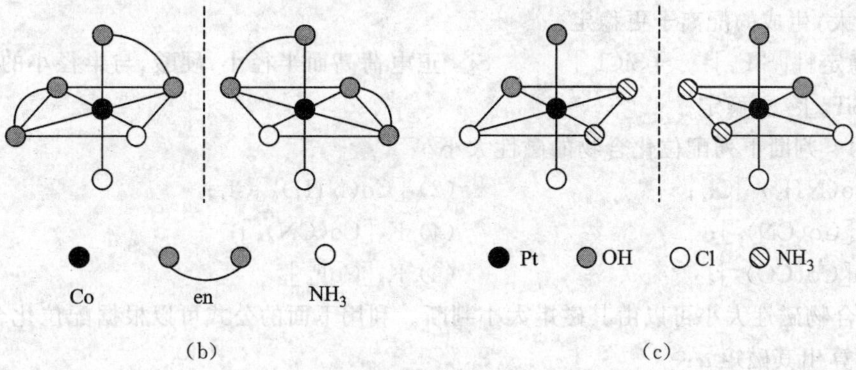

例 11.3　比较下列各对配位单元的相对稳定性并说明原因。

(1) $[Fe(SCN)_4]^-$,$[Co(SCN)_4]^{2-}$;

(2) $[Cu(NH_3)_4]^{2+}$,$[Zn(NH_3)_4]^{2+}$;

(3) $[Hg(CN)_4]^{2-}$,$[Zn(CN)_4]^{2-}$;

(4) $[Cu(en)_2]^{2+}$,$[Cu(H_2NCH_2CH_2COO)_2]$;

(5) $[Zn(CN)_4]^{2-}$,$[Ni(CN)_4]^{2-}$;

(6) $[Pt(NH_3)_4]^{2+}$,$[Cu(NH_3)_4]^{2+}$;

(7) $[Cu(CN)_2]^-$,$[Cu(NH_3)_2]^+$;

(8) $[Ni(NH_3)_6]^{2+}$,$[Ni(en)_3]^{2+}$;

(9) $[Cu(NH_3)_4]^{2+}$,$[Cu(NH_3)_4]^+$;

(10) $[SiF_6]^{2-}$,$[SiCl_6]^{2-}$。

解:(1) 稳定性$[Fe(SCN)_4]^- > [Co(SCN)_4]^{2-}$　　Fe^{3+} 正电荷比 Co^{2+} 高,Fe^{3+} 与阴离子配体 SCN^- 间静电引力大。

(2) 稳定性$[Cu(NH_3)_4]^{2+} > [Zn(NH_3)_4]^{2+}$　　$[Cu(NH_3)_4]^{2+}$ 为正方形结构,晶体场稳定化能大;$[Zn(NH_3)_4]^{2+}$ 为四面体结构,晶体场稳定化能小。

(3) 稳定性$[Hg(CN)_4]^{2-} > [Zn(CN)_4]^{2-}$　　CN^- 为软碱,与半径大的软酸 Hg^{2+} 结合生成的配离子稳定性高。

(4) 稳定性$[Cu(en)_2]^{2+} > [Cu(H_2NCH_2CH_2COO)_2]$　　乙二胺 en 以 2 个氮原子配位,$H_2NCH_2CH_2COO^-$ 以 1 个氮原子和 1 个氧原子配位,氮原子配位能力比氧原子配位能力强。

(5) 稳定性$[Zn(CN)_4]^{2-} < [Ni(CN)_4]^{2-}$　　Ni^{2+} 采取 dsp^2 杂化,$[Ni(CN)_4]^{2-}$ 为正方形结构,晶体场稳定化能大;Zn^{2+} 采取 sp^3 杂化,$[Zn(CN)_4]^{2-}$ 为四面体结构,晶体场稳定化能小。

(6) 稳定性$[Pt(NH_3)_4]^{2+} > [Cu(NH_3)_4]^{2+}$　　Pt 为高周期元素,d 轨道较为扩展,与配体的轨道重叠多,配位键强。

(7) 稳定性$[Cu(CN)_2]^- > [Cu(NH_3)_2]^+$　　对于 Cu^+,CN^- 是强配体,NH_3 是弱配体;Cu^+ 与 CN^- 间还有 d—pπ 配键,Cu^+ 与 NH_3 间只有 σ 配键。

(8) 稳定性$[Ni(NH_3)_6]^{2+}<[Ni(en)_3]^{2+}$　　$[Ni(en)_3]^{2+}$为螯合物，$[Ni(NH_3)_6]^{2+}$为简单配合物。

(9) 稳定性$[Cu(NH_3)_4]^{2+}>[Cu(NH_3)_4]^{+}$　　Cu^{2+}正电荷比Cu^{+}高，正电荷高的中心与配体的引力大，生成的配离子更稳定。

(10) 稳定性$[SiF_6]^{2-}>[SiCl_6]^{2-}$　　Si^{4+}正电荷高而半径小，硬酸，与半径小的硬碱F^-结合生成的$[SiF_6]^{2-}$更稳定。

例 11.4　判断下列配位化合物的磁性大小。

(1) $[Co(NH_3)_6]Cl_2$；　(2) $[Co(NH_3)_6]Cl_3$；

(3) $K_4[Co(CN)_6]$；　(4) $K_3[Co(CN)_6]$；

(5) $Na[Co(CO)_4]$；　(6) $K_3[CoF_6]$。

解：化合物磁性大小可以由其磁矩大小判断。利用下面的公式可以根据配位化合物中成单电子数 n 计算出其磁矩 μ：

$$\mu=\sqrt{n(n+2)}\mu_B$$

各化合物磁性大小计算结果如下：

题号	配位化合物	中心在球形场中的电子构型	配位化合物中心的电子轨道图	单电子数	理论磁矩 μ/μ_B
(1)	$[Co(NH_3)_6]Cl_2$	$3d^7 4s^0$	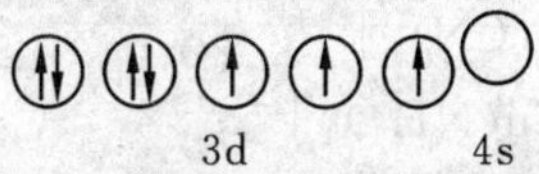	3	3.87
(2)	$[Co(NH_3)_6]Cl_3$	$3d^6 4s^0$	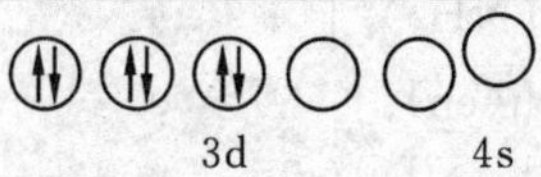	0	0
(3)	$K_4[Co(CN)_6]$	$3d^7 4s^0$	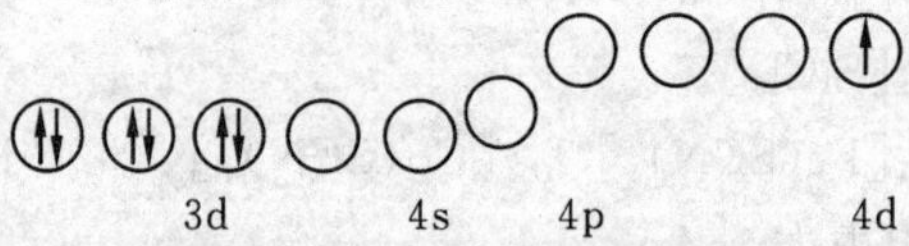	1	1.73
(4)	$K_3[Co(CN)_6]$	$3d^6 4s^0$	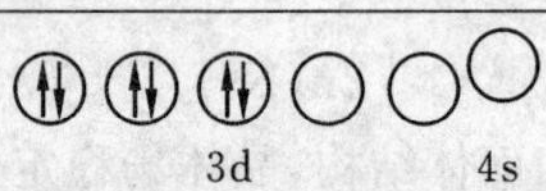	0	0
(5)	$Na[Co(CO)_4]$	$3d^8 4s^2$	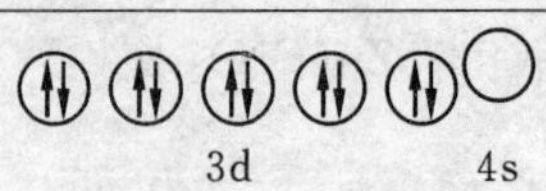	0	0
(6)	$K_3[CoF_6]$	$3d^6 4s^0$	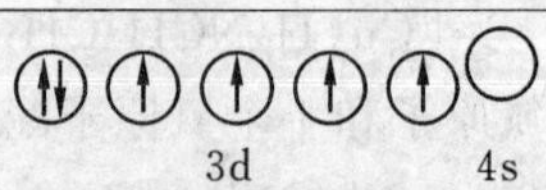	4	4.90

例 11.5　已知下列配位化合物的磁矩，根据配位化合物价键理论给出中心的轨道杂化方式、中心的价层电子排布、配位单元的几何构型。

(1) $[Co(NH_3)_6]^{2+}$　$\mu=3.9\ \mu_B$；　(2) $[Pt(CN)_4]^{2-}$　$\mu=0\ \mu_B$；

(3) $[Mn(SCN)_6]^{4-}$　$\mu=6.1\ \mu_B$；　(4) $[Co(NO_2)_6]^{4-}$　$\mu=1.8\ \mu_B$。

解：以$[Co(NO_2)_6]^{4-}$为例讨论问题。根据磁矩 μ 和单电子数 n 的关系式：

$$\mu=\sqrt{n(n+2)}\mu_B$$

由$[Co(NO_2)_6]^{4-}$的$\mu=1.8\mu_B$可以求得$n=1$。这说明强场NO_2^-使得Co^{2+}的3d轨道的7个电子发生了重排,3d轨道只排布3对电子,同时有1个3d轨道电子跃迁到4d轨道,如下图所示。中心采取d^2sp^3杂化,正八面体构型。

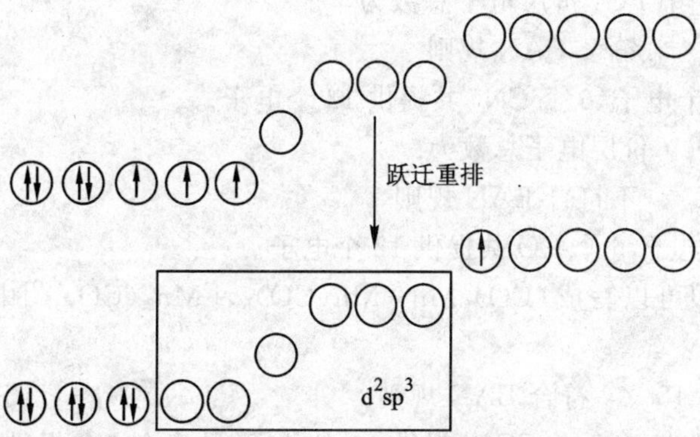

利用类似的方法对题设各配位化合物进行讨论,结果填入下表中。

配合单元中心杂化类型和几何构型

配位单元	磁矩/μ_B	单电子数	中心d轨道电子排布	中心杂化类型	几何构型
$[Co(NH_3)_6]^{2+}$	3.9	3	⇅ ⇅ ↑ ↑ ↑ 3d	sp^3d^2	八面体
$[Pt(CN)_4]^{2-}$	0	0	⇅ ⇅ ⇅ ⇅ ○ 5d	dsp^2	正方形
$[Mn(SCN)_6]^{4-}$	6.1	5	↑ ↑ ↑ ↑ ↑ 3d	sp^3d^2	八面体
$[Co(NO_2)_6]^{4-}$	1.8	1	⇅ ⇅ ⇅ ○ ○ 3d	d^2sp^3	八面体

例 11.6 通过计算判断下列配位化合物是否符合 EAN 规则。

(1) $K[Pt(C_2H_4)Cl_3]$; (2) $[Ru(C_5H_5)_2]$;

(3) $[Mo(CO)_6]$; (4) $K_4[Fe(CN)_6]$;

(5) $[V(CO)_6]$; (6) $[Mn_2(CO)_{10}]$。

解: EAN 规则就是 18 电子规则,即过渡金属在形成配位化合物时价层达到 18 个电子时配位化合物较稳定。

(1) $K[Pt(C_2H_4)Cl_3]$中Pt^{2+}价层电子总数为

$N=8+2+6=16$ 不符合 EAN 规则

其中Pt^{2+}提供 8 个电子,1 个C_2H_4提供 2 个电子,3 个Cl^-共提供 6 个电子。

(2) $[Ru(C_5H_5)_2]$中Ru^{2+}价层电子总数为

$N=6+2\times6=18$　　符合 EAN 规则

其中 Ru^{2+} 提供 6 个电子，2 个 $C_5H_5^-$ 共提供 12 个电子。

(3) $[Mo(CO)_6]$中 Mo 价层电子总数为

$N=6+2\times6=18$　　符合 EAN 规则

其中 Mo 提供 6 个电子，6 个 CO 共提供 12 个电子。

(4) $K_4[Fe(CN)_6]$中 Fe^{2+} 价层电子总数为

$N=6+2\times6=18$　　符合 EAN 规则

其中 Fe^{2+} 提供 6 个电子，6 个 CN^- 共提供 12 个电子。

(5) $[V(CO)_6]$中 V 价层电子总数为

$N=5+2\times6=17$　　不符合 EAN 规则

其中 V 提供 5 个电子，6 个 CO 共提供 12 个电子。

(6) $[Mn_2(CO)_{10}]$可以写成$(CO)_5Mn-Mn(CO)_5$，$[Mn_2(CO)_{10}]$中每个 Mn 价层电子总数为

$N=7+2\times5+1=18$　　符合 EAN 规则

其中 Mn 提供 7 个电子，5 个 CO 共提供 10 个电子，另一个 Mn 提供 1 个共用电子。

例 11.7 已知两个配离子的分裂能和成对能：

	$[Co(NH_3)_6]^{3+}$	$[Fe(H_2O)_6]^{2+}$
Δ/cm^{-1}	23 000	10 400
P/cm^{-1}	21 000	15 000

(1) 用价键理论及晶体场理论解释$[Fe(H_2O)_6]^{2+}$是高自旋的，$[Co(NH_3)_6]^{3+}$是低自旋的；

(2) 计算两种配离子的晶体场稳定化能。

解：(1) 由价键理论，H_2O 为弱配体，不能使 Fe^{2+} 的 d 轨道电子发生重排，因此$[Fe(H_2O)_6]^{2+}$是高自旋的；而 NH_3 对 Co^{3+} 强配体，能使 Co^{3+} 的 d 轨道电子发生重排，因此$[Co(NH_3)_6]^{3+}$是低自旋的。

由晶体场理论，$[Fe(H_2O)_6]^{2+}$的 $\Delta<P$，d 轨道电子采取高自旋排布；而$[Co(NH_3)_6]^{3+}$的 $\Delta>P$，d 轨道电子采取低自旋排布。

(2) $[Fe(H_2O)_6]^{2+}$的 d 轨道电子排布如图(a)所示：

$$\begin{aligned}\text{CFSE} &= 0-(-0.4\Delta\times4+0.6\Delta\times2)\\ &=0.4\Delta\\ &=10\,400\ \text{cm}^{-1}\times0.4\\ &=4\,160\ \text{cm}^{-1}\end{aligned}$$

$[Co(NH_3)_6]^{3+}$的 d 轨道电子排布如图(b)所示：

$$\begin{aligned}\text{CFSE} &= 0-(-0.4\Delta\times6+2P)\\ &=2.4\Delta-2P\\ &=2.4\times23\,000\ \text{cm}^{-1}-2\times21\,000\ \text{cm}^{-1}\\ &=13\,200\ \text{cm}^{-1}\end{aligned}$$

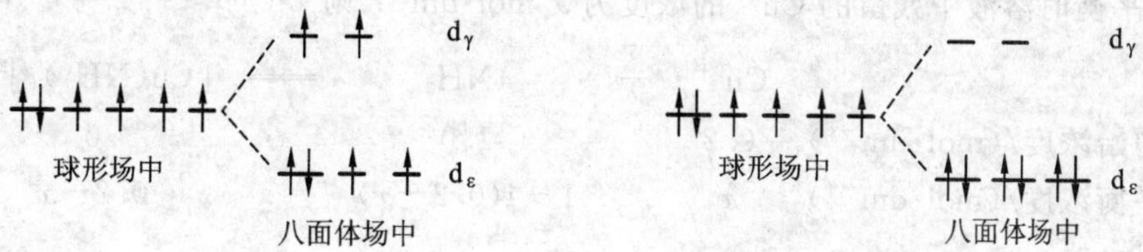

(a)　　　　(b)

例 11.8　请解释原因：

$[Fe(CN)_6]^{3-}$ 比 $[Fe(CN)_6]^{4-}$ 稳定，但与邻二氮菲（phen）生成的配位化合物却是 $[Fe(phen)_3]^{3+}$ 不如 $[Fe(phen)_3]^{2+}$ 稳定。

解：配离子 $[Fe(CN)_6]^{3-}$ 和 $[Fe(CN)_6]^{4-}$ 中心离子分别为 Fe^{3+} 和 Fe^{2+}，中心与配体 CN^- 间既有配体电子对向中心空的杂化轨道配位形成的 σ 配键，又有中心 d 轨道电子向配体 CN^- 的空 π^* 轨道配位形成 d－pπ 配键。带有正电荷的中心与带有负电荷的配体成键时以静电引力为主，d－pπ 配键对配离子稳定性影响较小。Fe^{3+} 与 CN^- 引力大于 Fe^{2+} 与 CN^- 引力，所以 $[Fe(CN)_6]^{3-}$ 比 $[Fe(CN)_6]^{4-}$ 稳定。

邻二氮菲的结构如图所示，分子中有离域大 π 键。

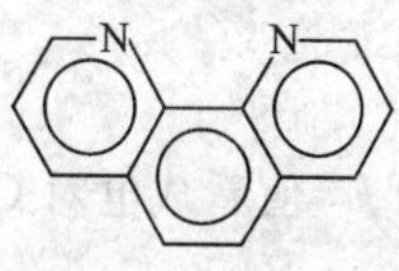

中性分子邻二氮菲与中心成键时，d－pπ 配键对配离子稳定性影响较大，中心与中性分子配体间静电引力对配离子稳定性影响较小。Fe^{2+} d 电子比 Fe^{3+} 多，向邻二氮菲的空 π^* 轨道反馈电子能力强，所以 $[Fe(phen)_3]^{2+}$ 比 $[Fe(phen)_3]^{3+}$ 稳定。

例 11.9　设计方案由 Pt 制备反式 $[Pt(NH_3)_2Cl_2]$，并用反应方程式表示之。

解：反位效应顺序：$NH_3 < Cl^-$，反式 $[Pt(NH_3)_2Cl_2]$ 可由 $[Pt(NH_3)_4]^{2+}$ 制备，制备路线如下：

$$Pt \longrightarrow [H_2PtCl_6] \longrightarrow [K_2PtCl_4] \longrightarrow [Pt(NH_3)_4]^{2+} \longrightarrow \text{反式}[Pt(NH_3)_2Cl_2]$$

Pt 溶于王水生成 $[H_2PtCl_6]$：

$$3Pt + 4HNO_3 + 18HCl = 3[H_2PtCl_6] + 4NO + 8H_2O$$

将 $[H_2PtCl_6]$ 与 KCl 作用生成溶解度较小的 $[K_2PtCl_6]$，加入还原剂得到 $[K_2PtCl_4]$：

$$[K_2PtCl_6] + K_2C_2O_4 = [K_2PtCl_4] + 2KCl + 2CO_2$$

将 $[K_2PtCl_4]$ 与浓氨水作用，得到 $[Pt(NH_3)_4]^{2+}$ 后，利用 Cl^- 比 NH_3 反位效应强的因素，将 $[Pt(NH_3)_4]^{2+}$ 转化为反式 $[Pt(NH_3)_2Cl_2]$。

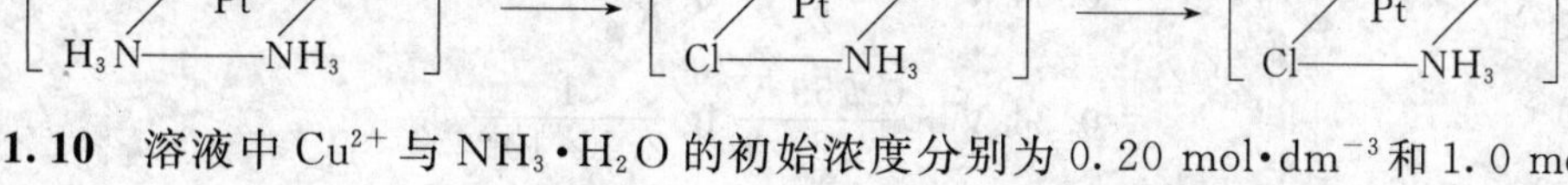

例 11.10　溶液中 Cu^{2+} 与 $NH_3 \cdot H_2O$ 的初始浓度分别为 0.20 $mol \cdot dm^{-3}$ 和 1.0 $mol \cdot dm^{-3}$，若反应生成的 $[Cu(NH_3)_4]^{2+}$ 的 $K^\ominus_{稳} = 2.1 \times 10^{13}$，计算平衡时溶液中残留的 Cu^{2+} 的浓度。

解：设平衡时溶液中残留的 Cu^{2+} 的浓度为 x mol·dm^{-3}，则

	Cu^{2+} +	$4NH_3$	$=\!=\!=$ $[Cu(NH_3)_4]^{2+}$
初始浓度/(mol·dm^{-3})	0.2	1.0	0
平衡浓度/(mol·dm^{-3})	x	$1-4(0.2-x)$	$0.2-x$

平衡常数表达式为

$$K_{稳}=\frac{[Cu(NH_3)_4^{2+}]}{[Cu^{2+}][NH_3]^4}$$

将平衡浓度代入该表达式，得

$$\frac{0.2-x}{x(0.2+4x)^4}=2.1\times10^{13}$$

由于 $[Cu(NH_3)_4]^{2+}$ 的 $K_{稳}$ 较大，则 x 值很小，$0.2-x\approx0.2$，$0.2+4x\approx0.2$，解得

$$x=6.0\times10^{-12}$$

即平衡时溶液中残留的 Cu^{2+} 的浓度为 6.0×10^{-12} mol·dm^{-3}。

例 11.11 已知 $Cu^{2+}+2e^- =\!=\!= Cu$ 的 $E^\ominus=0.34$ V，$[Cu(NH_3)_4]^{2+}$ 的 $K^\ominus_{稳}=2.1\times10^{13}$。求电对 $[Cu(NH_3)_4]^{2+}/Cu$ 的 $E^\ominus$。

解：电对 $[Cu(NH_3)_4]^{2+}/Cu$ 的电极反应式为

$$[Cu(NH_3)_4]^{2+}+2e^- =\!=\!= Cu+4NH_3$$

将它的 $E^\ominus$ 值看成电对 Cu^{2+}/Cu 的 E 值，即

$$[Cu(NH_3)_4^{2+}]=[NH_3]=1\ \text{mol·dm}^{-3}$$

时的 E 值。

由反应式 $$Cu^{2+}+4NH_3 =\!=\!= [Cu(NH_3)_4]^{2+}$$

得其平衡常数表达式为 $$K_{稳}=\frac{[Cu(NH_3)_4]^{2+}}{[Cu^{2+}][NH_3]^4}$$

所以有 $$[Cu^{2+}]=\frac{[Cu(NH_3)_4]^{2+}}{K_{稳}[NH_3]^4}=\frac{1}{K_{稳}}$$

根据 $Cu^{2+}+2e^- =\!=\!= Cu$ 的 Nernst 方程：

$$\begin{aligned}E&=E^\ominus(Cu^{2+}/Cu)+\frac{0.059\ \text{V}}{2}\lg[Cu^{2+}]\\&=0.34\ \text{V}+\frac{0.059\ \text{V}}{2}\lg\frac{1}{K_{稳}}\\&=0.34\ \text{V}+\frac{0.059\ \text{V}}{2}\lg\frac{1}{2.1\times10^{13}}\\&=-0.053\ \text{V}\end{aligned}$$

故电对$[Cu(NH_3)_4]^{2+}/Cu$ 的 $E^{\ominus}=-0.053\ V$。

例 11.12　已知

$$Fe^{3+}+e^{-} = Fe^{2+} \qquad E^{\ominus}=0.771\ V$$

$$[Fe(CN)_6]^{3-}+e^{-} = [Fe(CN)_6]^{4-} \qquad E^{\ominus}=0.358\ V$$

$$Fe^{3+}+6CN^{-} \rightleftharpoons [Fe(CN)_6]^{3-} \qquad K_{稳}=1.00\times10^{42}$$

求反应 $Fe^{2+}+6CN^{-} \rightleftharpoons [Fe(CN)_6]^{4-}$ 的 $K_{稳}^{\ominus}$。

解：将电极反应

$$[Fe(CN)_6]^{3-}+e^{-} = [Fe(CN)_6]^{4-}$$

的 $E^{\ominus}$ 值看成电极反应　　$Fe^{3+}+e^{-} = Fe^{2+}$

的 E 值，即

$$[Fe(CN)_6^{3-}]=[Fe(CN)_6^{4-}]=[CN^{-}]=1\ mol\cdot dm^{-3}$$

时 $Fe^{3+}+e^{-} = Fe^{2+}$ 的 E 值。

由反应式　　$Fe^{3+}+6CN^{-} = [Fe(CN)_6]^{3-}$

得其平衡常数表达式为　　$K_{稳}^{\ominus}(1)=\dfrac{[Fe(CN)_6^{3-}]}{[Fe^{3+}][CN^{-}]^6}$

所以有

$$[Fe^{3+}]=\frac{[Fe(CN)_6^{3-}]}{K_{稳}^{\ominus}(1)[CN^{-}]^6}=\frac{1}{K_{稳}^{\ominus}(1)}$$

同理有　　$[Fe^{2+}]=\dfrac{1}{K_{稳}^{\ominus}(2)}$

根据 $Fe^{3+}+e^{-} = Fe^{2+}$ 的 Nernst 方程：

$$E=E^{\ominus}(Fe^{3+}/Fe^{2+})+0.059\ V\lg\frac{[Fe^{3+}]}{[Fe^{2+}]}$$

$$=E^{\ominus}(Fe^{3+}/Fe^{2+})+0.059\ V\lg\frac{\dfrac{1}{K_{稳}^{\ominus}(1)}}{\dfrac{1}{K_{稳}^{\ominus}(2)}}$$

将数值代入上式，得

$$0.358\ V=0.771\ V+0.059\ V\lg\frac{K_{稳}^{\ominus}(2)}{1.00\times10^{42}}$$

解得　　$K_{稳}^{\ominus}(2)=1.00\times10^{35}$

即反应 $Fe^{2+}+6CN^{-} \rightleftharpoons [Fe(CN)_6]^{4-}$ 的 $K_{稳}^{\ominus}=1.00\times10^{35}$。

例 11.13　求在 100 cm^3 浓度为 10 $mol\cdot dm^{-3}$ 的氨水中能溶解多少克 AgCl 固体？已知 $[Ag(NH_3)_2]^{+}$ 的 $K_{稳}^{\ominus}=1.1\times10^{7}$，AgCl 的 $K_{sp}=1.8\times10^{-10}$。

解：$AgCl \rightleftharpoons Ag^+ + Cl^-$ $K_{sp}=1.8\times10^{-10}$

$Ag^+ + 2NH_3 \rightleftharpoons [Ag(NH_3)_2]^+$ $K^\ominus_{稳}=1.1\times10^7$

以上两式相加得

	$AgCl+2NH_3 \rightleftharpoons$	$[Ag(NH_3)_2]^+$	+	Cl^-
初始浓度/$(mol\cdot dm^{-3})$	10	0		0
平衡浓度/$(mol\cdot dm^{-3})$	$10-2x$	x		x

$$K=K_{sp}\cdot K^\ominus_{稳}=1.98\times10^{-3}$$

$$K=\frac{[Cl^-][Ag(NH_3)_2^+]}{[NH_3]^2}=\frac{x^2}{(10-2x)^2}=1.98\times10^{-3}$$

解得 $x=0.409$

即 1 dm^3 氨水中溶解 0.409 mol AgCl。

所以 100 cm^3 氨水中能溶解 AgCl 的质量为

$$m=143.5\ g\cdot mol^{-1}\times0.409\ mol\cdot dm^{-3}\times0.100\ dm^3$$
$$=5.9\ g$$

例 11.14 一原电池构成如下：

电极 A 铜片插入 2.0 $mol\cdot dm^{-3}$ $CuSO_4$ 和 10 $mol\cdot dm^{-3}$ 氨水的等体积混合溶液；

电极 B 铜片插入 1.0 $mol\cdot dm^{-3}$ $CuSO_4$ 溶液。

若该原电池的电动势 $E=0.39$ V，求 $[Cu(NH_3)_4]^{2+}$ 的稳定常数。

解：电极 B 是标准 Cu^{2+}/Cu 电极，其电极电势为 $E^\ominus(Cu^{2+}/Cu)$，电极 A 的电极反应是

$$[Cu(NH_3)_4]^{2+}+2e^- \rightleftharpoons Cu+4NH_3$$

可以将其 E 值看成是标准 Cu^{2+}/Cu 电极的非标准态，这个非标准态由 $[Cu(NH_3)_4]^{2+}$ 和 NH_3 的浓度来决定，所以有

$$E=E^\ominus(Cu^{2+}/Cu)+\frac{0.059\ V}{2}\lg[Cu^{2+}] \tag{1}$$

电极 A 中的 $CuSO_4$ 和氨水混合后浓度分别为 1.0 $mol\cdot dm^{-3}$ 和 5.0 $mol\cdot dm^{-3}$，且按下式反应

$$Cu^{2+}+4NH_3 \rightleftharpoons [Cu(NH_3)_4]^{2+} \tag{2}$$

充分反应后 Cu^{2+} 消耗殆尽，$[NH_3]=1.0\ mol\cdot dm^{-3}$

$[Cu(NH_3)_4]^{2+}=1.0\ mol\cdot dm^{-3}$，将其代入式(2)的平衡常数表达式中

$$K_{稳}=\frac{[Cu(NH_3)_4]^{2+}}{[Cu^{2+}][NH_3]^4}=\frac{1}{[Cu^{2+}]}$$

所以 $[Cu^{2+}]=\frac{1}{K_{稳}}$，将其代入式(1)中，得

$$E=E^\ominus(Cu^{2+}/Cu)+\frac{0.059\ V}{2}\lg\frac{1}{K_{稳}}$$

$$E_{池}=E_+-E_-$$

$$=E_A-E_B$$

$$=E^\ominus(Cu^{2+}/Cu)-\left[E^\ominus(Cu^{2+}/Cu)+\frac{0.059\ V}{2}\lg\frac{1}{K_{稳}}\right]$$

$$=-\frac{0.059\ V}{2}\lg\frac{1}{K_{稳}}$$

$$=\frac{0.059\ V}{2}\lg K_{稳}$$

依题意

$$E_{池}=0.39\ V$$

故

$$\lg K_{稳}=\frac{2E_{池}}{0.059\ V}=\frac{0.39V\times2}{0.059\ V}=13.2$$

所以 $K_{稳}=1.6\times10^{13}$。

第二部分　习题

一、选择题

11.1　已知 $E^\ominus(Hg^{2+}/Hg)=0.854$ V，$K^\ominus_{稳}(HgI_4^{2-})=6.8\times10^{29}$，则 $E^\ominus(HgI_4^{2-}/Hg)$值为

(A) -0.026 V；　(B) 0.026 V；　(C) -0.906 V；　(D) -0.052 V。

11.2　已知$[Ni(en)_3]^{2+}$的 $K^\ominus_{稳}=2.14\times10^{18}$，将 2.00 $mol\cdot dm^{-3}$ 的 en 溶液与 0.200 $mol\cdot dm^{-3}$ 的 $NiSO_4$ 溶液等体积混合，则平衡时$[Ni^{2+}]$)为

(A) 1.36×10^{-18} $mol\cdot dm^{-3}$；　(B) 2.91×10^{-18} $mol\cdot dm^{-3}$；

(C) 1.36×10^{-19} $mol\cdot dm^{-3}$；　(D) 4.36×10^{-20} $mol\cdot dm^{-3}$。

11.3　中心离子的 3d 电子排布为 $t_{2g}^3\ e_g^0$ 的八面体配合物是

(A) $[Mn(H_2O)_6]^{2+}$；　(B) $[FeF_6]^{3-}$；

(C) $[Co(CN)_6]^{3-}$；　(D) $[Cr(H_2O)_6]^{3+}$。

11.4　对下列各对配合物稳定性的判断，不正确的是

(A) $[Fe(CN)_6]^{3-}>[Fe(SCN)_6]^{3-}$；　(B) $[HgCl_4]^{2-}>[HgI_4]^{2-}$；

(C) $[AlF_6]^{3-}>[AlBr_6]^{3-}$；　(D) $[Cu(NH_3)_4]^{2+}>[Zn(NH_3)_4]^{2+}$。

11.5　下列配离子中，具有逆磁性的是

(A) $[Mn(CN)_6]^{4-}$；　(B) $[Cu(CN)_4]^{2-}$；

(C) $[Co(CN)_6]^{3-}$；　(D) $[Fe(CN)_6]^{3-}$。

11.6　下列配离子中，分裂能最大的是

(A) $[Ni(CN)_4]^{2-}$；　(B) $[Cu(NH_3)_4]^{2+}$；

(C) $[Fe(CN)_6]^{4-}$；　　(D) $[Zn(CN)_4]^{2-}$。

11.7 下列配合物中，除存在几何异构体外，还存在旋光异构体的是

(A) $[Pt(NH_3)_2Cl_2]$；　　(B) $[Co(NH_3)_4Cl_2]Cl$；

(C) $[Co(en)_2Cl_2]Cl$；　　(D) $[Pt(NH_3)ClBrPy]$。

11.8 下列配合物中，不存在旋光异构体的是

(A) $[PtCl_2(OH)_2(NH_3)_2]$；　　(B) $K_3[Cr(C_2O_4)_3]$；

(C) $[Co(en)_2Cl_2]Cl$；　　(D) $[Co(en)(NH_3)_4]Cl_3$。

11.9 下列配合物不具有平面四边形结构的

(A) $[Ni(CO)_4]$；　　(B) $[Cu(NH_3)_4]^{2+}$；

(C) $[AuCl_4]^-$；　　(D) $[PtCl_4]^{2-}$。

11.10 下列配合物中，不存在几何异构体的是

(A) $[CrCl_2(en)_2]Cl$；　　(B) $[Pt(en)Cl_4]$；

(C) $[Cu(NH_3)_4(H_2O)_2]SO_4$；　　(D) $[Ni(CO)_2(CN)_2]$。

11.11 在 $K[Co(C_2O_4)_2(en)]$ 中，中心离子的配位数为

(A) 3；　　(B) 4；　　(C) 5；　　(D) 6。

11.12 下列配离子具有正方形或八面体结构，其中 CO_3^{2-} 作螯合剂的是

(A) $[Co(NH_3)_5(CO_3)]^+$；　　(B) $K_2[Pt(en)(CO_3)_2]$；

(C) $[Pt(en)(NH_3)(CO_3)]$；　　(D) $[Co(NH_3)_4(CO_3)]$。

11.13 下列化合物中，肯定为无色的是

(A) ScF_3；　　(B) $TiCl_3$；　　(C) MnF_3；　　(D) CrF_3。

11.14 某金属离子生成的二种配合物的磁矩分别为 $\mu=4.90\ \mu_B$ 和 $\mu=0$，则该金属可能是

(A) Cr^{3+}；　　(B) Mn^{2+}；　　(C) Mn^{3+}；　　(D) Fe^{2+}。

11.15 下列配合物中，不能稳定存在的是

(A) $[Ni(NH_3)_6]^{2+}$；　　(B) $[Ni(H_2O)_6]^{2+}$；

(C) $[Ni(CN)_6]^{4-}$；　　(D) $[Ni(en)_3]^{2+}$。

二、填空题

11.16 命名下列配位化合物。

(1) $K_3[Co(NO_2)_6]$ ________；

(2) $[Pt(NH_3)_2(OH)_2Cl_2]$ ________；

(3) $[Cr(H_2O)_5Cl]Cl_2 \cdot H_2O$ ________；

(4) $[Ni(en)_3]Cl_2$ ________；

(5) $[Cu(NH_3)_4][PtCl_4]$ ________；

(6) $K_3[Fe(C_2O_4)_3] \cdot 3H_2O$ ________；

(7) $K_2[Cu(C_2O_4)_2]$ ________；

(8) $[Pt(py)_4][PtCl_4]$ ________；

(9) $[(CO)_3Co—(CO)_2—Co(CO)_3]$ ________。

11.17 根据下列配位化合物的名称写出其化学式。

(1) 氯化二异硫氰酸根·四氨合铬(Ⅲ)________________;
(2) 三氯·氨合铂(Ⅱ)酸钾________________;
(3) 氯·水·草酸根·乙二胺合铬(Ⅲ)________________;
(4) 四氯·二氨合铂(Ⅳ)________________。

11.18 配合物 $K_3[Fe(CN)_5(CO)]$ 中配离子的电荷数应为______,配离子的空间构型为______,配位原子为______,中心离子的配位数为______。d 电子在 t_{2g} 和 e_g 轨道上的排布方式为______,中心离子所采取的轨道杂化方式为______,该配合物属______磁性分子。

11.19 指出下列配合物或配离子存在的异构现象:
(1) $[CoBrCl(NH_3)_2(en)]^+$(顺式); (2) $[Co(NO_2)(NH_3)_5]^{2+}$;
(3) $[PtCl_2(NH_3)_2]$; (4) $[Cu(NH_3)_4][PtCl_4]$;
(5) $[PtCl(NH_3)_5]Br$。
几何异构____________,旋光异构______,解离异构______,键合______,配位异构______。

11.20 $[Ni(NH_3)_4]^{2+}$ 具有顺磁性,则它的几何构形为__________;$[Ni(CN)_4]^{2-}$ 几何构型为__________,具有______磁性。

11.21 已知$[PtCl_2(NH_3)_2]$有两种几何异构体,则中心离子所采取的杂化轨道应是______杂化;$[Zn(NH_3)_4]^{2+}$ 的中心离子所采取的杂化轨道应是______杂化。

11.22 指出下列配离子的中心离子中未成对电子数:
(1) $[CoCl_4]^{2-}$________; (2) $[MnF_6]^{4-}$________;
(3) $[Fe(H_2O)_6]^{2+}$________; (4) $[Ni(H_2O)_6]^{2+}$________;
(5) $[Mn(CN)_6]^{4-}$________; (6) $[Zn(CN)_4]^{2-}$________。

11.23 根据晶体场理论估计下列每一对配离子中,哪一个吸收光的波长较长?(用>号或<号表示)
(1) $[TiF_6]^{3-}$____$[Ti(CN)_6]^{3-}$; (2) $[CrCl_6]^{3-}$____$[Cr(NH_3)_6]^{3+}$;
(3) $[Ir(en)_3]^{3+}$____$[Co(en)_3]^{3+}$; (4) $[Fe(H_2O)_6]^{3+}$____$[Fe(H_2O)_6]^{2+}$。

11.24 按 EAN 规则(即 18 电子规则),化合物 $Mo(CO)_x(C_6H_6)$,$HCo(CO)_y$,$Mn_2(CO)_z$ 分子式中的 x,y,z 值分别为______,______和______。

11.25 已知:$[Co(NH_3)_6]^{3+}$ 的磁矩 $\mu=0\ \mu_B$,$[Co(NH_3)_6]^{2+}$ 的磁矩 $\mu=3.88\ \mu_B$,请指出:
(1) $[Co(NH_3)_6]^{2+}$ 配离子的成单电子数为________个;
(2) 按照价键理论,二个配离子中心的杂化轨道类型分别为________和________;形成的配合物分别属于________型和________型;
(3) 按照晶体场理论,两种配离子中 d 电子排布式分别为________和________;其 CFSE 分别为________和________;
(4) 分裂能(Δ)较大的是________配离子。

11.26 判断下列各对配合物的相对稳定性(用>号或<号表示)。
(1) $[Cd(CN)_4]^{2-}$____$[Cd(NH_3)_4]^{2+}$; (2) $[AgBr_2]^-$____$[AgI_2]^-$;
(3) $[Ag(S_2O_3)_2]^{3-}$____$[Ag(CN)_2]^-$; (4) $[FeF]^{2+}$____$[HgF]^+$;

三、简答题和计算题

11.27 指出下列配合物的空间构型并画出可能存在的几何异构体。

(1) $[Pt(NH_3)_2(NO_2)Cl]$； (2) $[Pt(Py)(NH_3)ClBr]$；

(3) $[Pt(NH_3)_2(OH)_2Cl_2]$； (4) $NH_4[Co(NH_3)_2(NO_2)_4]$；

(5) $[Co(NH_3)_3(OH)_3]$； (6) $[Cr(SCN)_2(en)_2]SCN$；

(7) $[Co(en)_3]Cl_3$； (8) $[Co(NH_3)(en)Cl_3]$。

11.28 画出下列配合物可能有的旋光异构体的结构。

(1) $[FeCl_2(C_2O_4)en]^-$； (2) $[Co(C_2O_4)_3]^{3-}$； (3) $[Co(en)_2Cl_2]^+$。

11.29 指出下列配位化合物哪些是内轨型配位化合物？哪些是外轨型配位化合物？

(1) $[Cr(H_2O)_6]Cl_3$； (2) $K_3[Cr(CN)_6]$；

(3) $K_2[PtCl_4]$； (4) $K_2[Ni(CN)_4]$；

(5) $K_4[Mn(CN)_6]$； (6) $K_3[Fe(C_2O_4)_3]$；

(7) $[Fe(CO)_5]$； (8) $K_3[Fe(CN)_6]$

11.30 计算下列配位化合物的磁矩和晶体场稳定化能。

(1) $[CoF_6]^{3-}$； (2) $[Fe(H_2O)_6]^{2+}$；

(3) $[Co(en)_3]^{2+}$； (4) $[Fe(SCN)_6]^{3-}$；

(5) $[Ni(CO)_4]$； (6) $[Mn(CN)_6]^{4-}$

11.31 有两种钴(Ⅲ)配合物组成均为 $Co(NH_3)_5Cl(SO_4)$，但分别只与 $AgNO_3$ 和 $BaCl_2$ 发生沉淀反应。写出两个配合物的化学结构式，并指出它们属于哪一类异构现象？

11.32 请解释原因：$[CoCl_4]^{2-}$ 和 $[NiCl_4]^{2-}$ 为四面体结构，而 $[CuCl_4]^{2-}$ 和 $[PtCl_4]^{2-}$ 却为正方形结构；

11.33 向 $Fe_2(SO_4)_3$ 溶液依次加入饱和 $(NH_4)_2C_2O_4$ 溶液、少量 KSCN 溶液、少量盐酸、过量 NH_4F 溶液，溶液的颜色如何变化？已知 $[Fe(C_2O_4)_3]^{3-}$ 为黄绿色，其 $K^{\ominus}_{稳}=1.6\times10^{20}$，$H_2C_2O_4$ 的 $K^{\ominus}_{a_1}=5.4\times10^{-2}$；$[Fe(SCN)_5]^{2-}$ 为红色，其 $K^{\ominus}_{稳}=2.5\times10^{6}$，HSCN 为强酸；$[FeF_5]^{2-}$ 为无色，其 $K^{\ominus}_{稳}=5.9\times10^{15}$。

11.34 二价铜的化合物中，$CuSO_4$ 为白色，而 $CuCl_2$ 为暗棕色，$CuSO_4\cdot5H_2O$ 为蓝色。请解释之。

11.35 向 Hg^{2+} 溶液中加入 KI 溶液时有红色 HgI_2 生成，继续加入过量的 KI 溶液时 HgI_2 溶解得无色的 HgI_4^{2-} 配离子。请说明 HgI_2 有颜色而 HgI_4^{2-} 无色的原因。

11.36 预测下列各对配离子稳定性相对高低，并简要说明原因。

(1) $[Co(NH_3)_6]^{3+}$ 与 $[Co(NH_3)_6]^{2+}$；

(2) $[Zn(EDTA)]^{2-}$ 与 $[Ca(EDTA)]^{2-}$；

(3) $[Cu(CN)_4]^{3-}$ 与 $[Zn(CN)_4]^{2-}$；

(4) $[AlF_6]^{3-}$ 与 $[AlCl_6]^{3-}$；

(5) $[Cu(NH_2CH_2COO)_2]$ 与 $[Cu(NH_2CH_2CH_2NH_2)_2]^{2+}$。

11.37 已知向 0.010 mol·dm^{-3} $ZnCl_2$ 溶液通 H_2S 至饱和，当溶液的 pH=1.0 时刚开始有 ZnS 沉淀产生。若在此浓度 $ZnCl_2$ 溶液中加入 1.0 mol·dm^{-3} KCN 后通入 H_2S 至饱和，求

在多大 pH 时会有 ZnS 沉淀产生？已知 $K^{\ominus}_{稳}[Zn(CN)_4^{2-}]=5.0\times10^{16}$。

11.38　已知 $E^{\ominus}(Au^+/Au)=1.69\ V$，$K^{\ominus}_{稳}[Au(CN)_2^-]=2\times10^{38}$，试求 $E^{\ominus}[Au(CN)_2^-/Au]$

11.39　已知 $E^{\ominus}(Fe^{3+}/Fe^{2+})=0.77\ V$，$E^{\ominus}(Sn^{4+}/Sn^{2+})=0.15\ V$，$K^{\ominus}_{稳}(FeF_6^{3-})=1.1\times10^{12}$。通过计算说明下列氧化还原反应能否发生，若能发生写出其化学反应式。（设有关物质的浓度为 $1.0\ mol\cdot dm^{-3}$）

(1) 向 $FeCl_3$ 溶液中加入 NaF，然后再加 $SnCl_2$。

(2) 向 $[Fe(SCN)_5]^{2-}$ 溶液中加入 $SnCl_2$。已知 $K^{\ominus}_{稳}[Fe(SCN)_5^{2-}]=2.6\times10^6$。

(3) 向 $[Fe(SCN)_5]^{2-}$ 溶液中加入 KI。已知 $E^{\ominus}(I_2/I^-)=0.54\ V$。

11.40　求在体积为 $1.5\ dm^3$ 的 $1.0\ mol\cdot dm^{-3}$ 的 NaS_2O_3 溶液中能溶解多少克 AgBr？已知 $M_r(AgBr)=188$，$K^{\ominus}_{稳}[Ag(S_2O_3)_2^{3-}]=2.8\times10^{13}$，$K^{\ominus}_{sp}(AgBr)=5.0\times10^{-13}$。

11.41　为什么在水溶液中，Co^{3+} 能氧化水，$[Co(NH_3)_6]^{3+}$ 却不能氧化水？已知 $K^{\ominus}_{稳}[Co(NH_3)_6^{3+}]=1.58\times10^{35}$，$K^{\ominus}_{稳}[Co(NH_3)_6^{2+}]=1.38\times10^5$，$K^{\ominus}_b(NH_3)=1.8\times10^{-5}$，$E^{\ominus}(Co^{3+}/Co^{2+})=1.81\ V$，$E^{\ominus}(O_2/OH^-)=0.40\ V$，$E^{\ominus}(O_2/H_2O)=1.23\ V$。

11.42　将 $50\ cm^3$ $0.20\ mol\cdot dm^{-3}$ $AgNO_3$ 溶液与 $50\ cm^3$ $0.40\ mol\cdot dm^{-3}$ KCN 溶液混合，加入 0.010 mol KCl 晶体，是否有 AgCl 沉淀生成？已知 $K^{\ominus}_{sp}(AgCl)=1.8\times10^{-10}$，$K^{\ominus}_{稳}[Ag(CN)_2^-]=1.25\times10^{21}$。

11.43　将铜电极浸在含有 $1.00\ mol\cdot dm^{-3}$ 氨和 $1.00\ mol\cdot dm^{-3}$ $[Cu(NH_3)_4]^{2+}$ 溶液里，以标准锌电极为负极，测得电池的电动势为 0.712 V。试计算 $[Cu(NH_3)_4]^{2+}$ 的稳定常数。已知 $E^{\ominus}(Cu^{2+}/Cu)=0.342\ V$，$E^{\ominus}(Zn^{2+}/Zn)=-0.763\ V$。

11.44　六配位单核配位化合物 $[MA_2(NO_2)_2]$ 的组成分析结果为：M：21.68%，N：31.04%，C：17.74%；未知配体 A 中不含氧；在配位化合物中已知的配体的氮氧键不等长。

(1) 通过计算推导出配位化合物的化学式，并命名之；

(2) 画出该配位化合物的结构及其几何异构体的结构。

11.45　某不活泼金属 M 在氯气中燃烧的产物溶于盐酸得黄色溶液，蒸发结晶，得到黄色晶体 Z，晶体中 M 的质量分数为0.4783。取 0.100 mol 晶体 Z 溶于水后投入铜片，反应完全后称得固体质量增加了为 10.17 g。求 Z 的化学式。

第 12 章

碱金属和碱土金属

第一部分 例题

例 12.1 完成并配平下列反应的化学方程式。

(1) $H_2 + Ca \xlongequal{500K}$　　(2) $Fe_2O_3 + Na_2O_2 \xlongequal{熔融}$

(3) $BaO_2 + H_2SO_4 \xlongequal{}$　　(4) $Li_2CO_3 \xlongequal{加热}$

(5) $Na_2O_2 + MnO_4^- + H^+ \xlongequal{}$　　(6) 过氧化钠与热水作用

(7) 二氧化碳与过氧化钠作用　　(8) 臭氧化钾溶于水

(9) 将氮化镁置于水中　　(10) 用钠还原四氯化钛

解: (1) $H_2 + Ca \xlongequal{500K} CaH_2$

(2) $Fe_2O_3 + 3Na_2O_2 \xlongequal{熔融} 2Na_2FeO_4 + Na_2O$

(3) $BaO_2 + H_2SO_4 \xlongequal{} BaSO_4 + H_2O_2$

(4) $Li_2CO_3 \xlongequal{加热} Li_2O + CO_2\uparrow$

(5) $5Na_2O_2 + 2MnO_4^- + 16H^+ \xlongequal{} 5O_2\uparrow + 2Mn^{2+} + 10Na^+ + 8H_2O$

(6) $2Na_2O_2 + 2H_2O \xlongequal{} 4NaOH + O_2$

(7) $2Na_2O_2 + 2CO_2 \xlongequal{} 2Na_2CO_3 + O_2$

(8) $4KO_3 + 2H_2O \xlongequal{} 4KOH + 5O_2$

(9) $Mg_3N_2 + 6H_2O \xlongequal{} 3Mg(OH)_2 + 2NH_3$

(10) $TiCl_4 + 4Na \xlongequal{} Ti + 4NaCl$

例 12.2 用反应方程式表示下列制备过程。

(1) 以重晶石为原料制备 $BaCl_2$,$BaCO_3$,BaO;

(2) 以食盐为原料制备过氧化钠;

(3) 以食盐、氨水和二氧化碳为原料制备纯碱。

解: (1) 工业上用炭在高温下还原重晶石粉,将其转化为可溶性的 BaS,由 BaS 进一步可制备其他钡的化合物:

$$BaSO_4 + 4C \xlongequal{高温} BaS + 4CO\uparrow$$

$$BaS + 2HCl(aq) = BaCl_2 + H_2S\uparrow$$
$$BaCl_2 + Na_2CO_3 = BaCO_3\downarrow + 2NaCl$$
$$BaCO_3 \xlongequal{高温} BaO + CO_2\uparrow$$

(2) 以 $CaCl_2$ 为助熔剂，电解 NaCl 制备金属钠。进一步可制备 Na_2O_2：

$$2NaCl(l) \xlongequal{高温} 2Na(l) + Cl_2(g)$$
$$4Na + O_2 \xlongequal{180\sim200\,℃} 2Na_2O$$
$$2Na_2O + O_2 \xlongequal{300\sim400\,℃} 2Na_2O_2$$

(3) 向吸足氨气的饱和食盐水中通入二氧化碳，析出溶解度小的 $NaHCO_3$，加热分解 $NaHCO_3$ 得到产品 Na_2CO_3，这种方法称为氨碱法：

$$NH_3 + CO_2 + H_2O = NH_4HCO_3$$
$$NH_4HCO_3 + NaCl = NaHCO_3 + NH_4Cl$$
$$2NaHCO_3 \xlongequal{\triangle} Na_2CO_3 + CO_2\uparrow + H_2O$$

例 12.3　鉴别下列各组物质。

(1) Na，K，Cs，Ba；　(2) $Be(OH)_2$，$Mg(OH)_2$；
(3) Na_2CO_3，$NaHCO_3$，NaOH；　(4) $BeCO_3$，$MgCO_3$；
(5) $Ca(OH)_2$，CaO，$CaSO_4$；　(6) Na_2CO_3，$MgCO_3$；
(7) Na_2CO_3，NaOH，Na_2O_2；　(8) $MgCO_3$，$PbCO_3$。

解：(1) 将极少量的四种金属单质放于高温火焰中，由其火焰的特征颜色可判断：

黄色——Na　紫色——K　蓝色——Cs　绿色——Ba

(2) 溶于过量 NaOH 溶液的是 $Be(OH)_2$，不溶于 NaOH 溶液的是 $Mg(OH)_2$：

$$Be(OH)_2 + 2NaOH = Na_2[Be(OH)_4]$$

(3) 与盐酸作用放出 CO_2 气体的是 Na_2CO_3 或 $NaHCO_3$，没有气体生成的是 NaOH。

将少量 Na_2CO_3 和 $NaHCO_3$ 分别溶于水，用 pH 试纸检验。溶液的 $pH>11$ 的是 Na_2CO_3，溶液的 $pH<9$ 的是 $NaHCO_3$。

(4) 将两种盐加热分解，分解物溶于过量 NaOH 溶液的是 $BeCO_3$，不溶于 NaOH 溶液的是 $MgCO_3$：

$$BeCO_3 = BeO + CO_2\uparrow$$
$$MgCO_3 = MgO + CO_2\uparrow$$
$$BeO + 2NaOH + H_2O = Na_2[Be(OH)_4]$$

(5) 将三种物质分别溶于水，溶液显强碱性的是 $Ca(OH)_2$ 或 CaO，溶液显中性的是 $CaSO_4$。溶于水放出大量热的是 CaO。

(6) 易溶于水的化合物是 Na_2CO_3，不易溶于水的化合物是 $MgCO_3$。

(7) 溶于热水有气体放出的是 Na_2O_2：

$$2Na_2O_2 + 2H_2O \xlongequal{} 4NaOH + O_2\uparrow$$

将另两种物质溶于稀酸，有 CO_2 气体放出的是 Na_2CO_3，没有气体生成的是 NaOH。

(8) 用煤气灯加热，产物为黄色的是 $PbCO_3$，不变色的是 $MgCO_3$：

$$PbCO_3 \xlongequal{} PbO(\text{黄色}) + CO_2\uparrow$$

例 12.4 为什么在配制黑火药时使用 KNO_3，而不用 $NaNO_3$？

解：Na^+ 半径比 K^+ 半径小，Na^+ 极化能力强，水合热大。因而 $NaNO_3$ 易吸水潮解，配制的黑火药不易长期保存，容易失效。而 KNO_3 不易潮解，配制的黑火药可长期保存，不容易失效。

例 12.5 钠和镁在空气中燃烧的主产物分别溶于水后，形成两种溶液。举例说明其性质的相同点和不同点。

解：Mg 在空气中燃烧主要生成普通氧化物 MgO；Na 在空气中燃烧主要生成过氧化物 Na_2O_2。

MgO 在水中溶解度较小，生成 $Mg(OH)_2$；Na_2O_2 在水中溶解度较大，生成 NaOH 和 H_2O_2。

钠和镁的燃烧产物分别溶于水都有氢氧化物生成，溶液都显碱性，这是两种溶液的相同点。

钠的燃烧产物溶于水有 H_2O_2 生成，溶液有氧化性和还原性；而镁的燃烧产物溶于水的溶液既无氧化性，也无还原性，这是两种溶液的不同点。

例 12.6 简要回答下列各题。

(1) LiF 溶解度比 AgF 小，LiI 溶解度却比 AgI 大；

(2) 在水中的溶解度 $LiClO_4 > NaClO_4 > KClO_4$；

(3) $Be(OH)_2$ 为两性物质而 $Mg(OH)_2$ 却显碱性；

(4) $BeCl_2$ 为共价化合物而 $MgCl_2$，$CaCl_2$ 等为离子化合物；

(5) $Mg(OH)_2$ 溶于 NH_4Cl 溶液而不溶于 NaOH 溶液；

(6) CsF 虽有最高的离子性，但 CsF 熔点却较低。

解：(1) LiF 和 AgF 都是离子型化合物，但 Li^+ 的半径(60 pm)却比 Ag^+ 的半径(126 pm)小得多，因而 LiF 的晶格能比 AgF 大。所以，LiF 在水中的溶解度比 AgF 的溶解度小。

LiI 与 AgI 相比，因 Ag^+ 有较大的变形性，Ag^+ 与 I^- 间的附加极化作用强，因而 AgI 分子的共价性比 LiI 强得多，使 AgI 溶解度远比 LiI 小。

(2) 阳离子半径 $Li^+ < Na^+ < K^+$；而复杂阴离子 ClO_4^- 的半径较大。一般来说，阴阳离子的半径若严重不匹配，则盐的稳定性较差，晶格能较小，盐的溶解度较大。因此，在水中的溶解度 $LiClO_4 > NaClO_4 > KClO_4$。

(3) 氢氧化物中 M—O—H 键在水中有两种解离方式：

$$M—O—H \longrightarrow MO^- + H^+ \quad \text{酸式解离}$$

$$M—O—H \longrightarrow M^+ + OH^- \quad \text{碱式解离}$$

采取哪种解离方式或以哪种解离方式为主，主要取决于金属阳离子的极化能力。

Mg^{2+} 半径较大，极化能力较弱，Mg—O 键比 O—H 键更易断开，$Mg(OH)_2$ 主要是碱式解离，所以 $Mg(OH)_2$ 显碱性。而 Be^{2+} 半径较小，极化能力较强，Be—O 键较强，使得 $Be(OH)_2$ 碱式解离与酸式解离相当，所以 $Be(OH)_2$ 为两性化合物。

(4) Be 的电负性较大(1.57)；Be^{2+} 的半径较小(约 31 pm)使其极化能力很强，所以 $BeCl_2$ 中

Be—Cl 键以共价性为主，$BeCl_2$ 为共价化合物。而其他碱土金属的电负性较小但离子半径却比 Be^{2+} 大得多（Mg^{2+} 为 65 pm，Ca^{2+} 为 95 pm），$MgCl_2$ 和 $CaCl_2$ 中的键以离子性为主，化合物为离子化合物。

(5) $Mg(OH)_2$ 为碱性氢氧化物，不溶于 NaOH 溶液和水。同时，$Mg(OH)_2$ 的 $K_{sp}^{\ominus}$ 不是很小，因而可溶于弱酸性的 NH_4Cl 溶液中。

$$Mg(OH)_2 + 2NH_4Cl = MgCl_2 + 2NH_3 + 2H_2O$$

(6) Cs^+ 半径较大（约 170 pm），Cs^+ 与 F^- 间的静电引力较小，使 CsF 晶格能较小。因此，虽然 Cs 与 F 的电负性差较大，CsF 有最高的离子性，但 CsF 的熔点却较低。

例 12.7　碱性土壤中含有 Na_2CO_3 和 K_2CO_3，试分析用 $CaSO_4$ 能否改良这种碱性土壤。

解：$CaCO_3$ 溶解度比 $CaSO_4$ 小，Na_2CO_3 和 K_2CO_3 与 $CaSO_4$ 缓慢反应：

$$Na_2CO_3 + CaSO_4 = CaCO_3 + Na_2SO_4$$

$$K_2CO_3 + CaSO_4 = CaCO_3 + K_2SO_4$$

强碱性 Na_2CO_3 和 K_2CO_3 转化为基本中性的 Na_2SO_4 和 K_2SO_4，降低了土壤的碱性，因此用 $CaSO_4$ 能改良含有 Na_2CO_3 和 K_2CO_3 的碱性土壤。但改良效果不是很好，因为 Na_2SO_4 和 K_2SO_4 使土壤板结，也影响植物体内外的渗透平衡，不利于植物生长。

例 12.8　在温度高于 1 020 K 条件下，$BeCl_2$ 气体以单分子形态存在，其中 Be 为 sp 杂化；当 $BeCl_2$ 气体温度低于该温度时，以二聚体形式存在，其中 Be 为 sp^2 杂化；无水固态 $BeCl_2$ 具有链状结构，其中 Be 为 sp^3 杂化。试分析上述各种 $BeCl_2$ 的成键形式与空间构型。

解：单分子中 Be 以 sp 方式杂化，形成两个有单电子的杂化轨道，在空间呈直线型分布。每个含有单电子的 sp 杂化轨道与 Cl 原子的单电子轨道重叠形成 σ 键，故 $BeCl_2$ 单分子呈直线型。

二聚体中，Be 以 sp^2 方式杂化，形成两个有单电子的杂化轨道和一个空的杂化轨道，杂化轨道为平面三角形。两个含有单电子的杂化轨道分别与两个 Cl 原子的单电子轨道形成 σ 键；其中一个 Cl 原子为端基 Cl，而另一个 Cl 原子除了以 σ 方式与 Be 生成共价键外，还提供孤对电子与另一个 Be 原子上的空 sp^2 杂化轨道形成配位键，因此分子中每个 Be 原子外均为平面三角形构型，如图(a)所示。

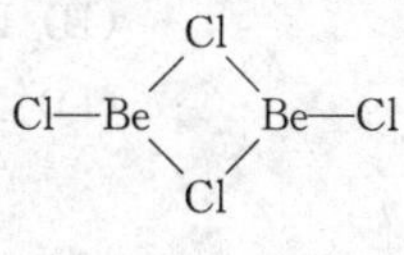

(a)

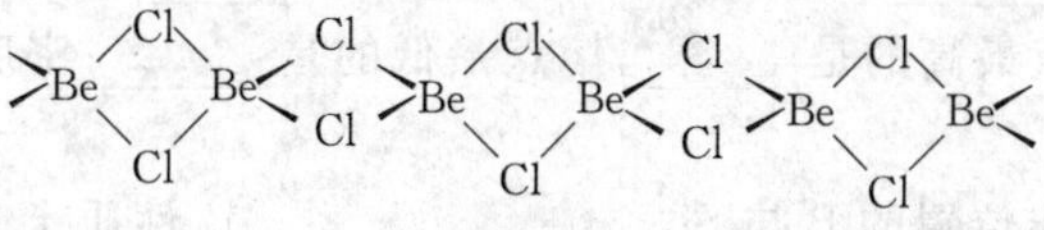

(b)

对于链状结构的 $BeCl_2$，Be 以 sp^3 方式杂化，形成两个有单电子的杂化轨道和两个空的杂化轨道，杂化轨道是呈正四面体分布。每个 Cl 原子除了以 σ 方式与 Be 生成共价键外，还提供孤对电子与 Be 上的空 sp^3 杂化轨道形成配位键，分子中每个 Be 原子均与 4 个 Cl 原子成键，且处于 4

个 Cl 原子构成的正四面体的中心。其结构如图(b)所示。

第二部分　习题

一、选择题

12.1　下列各对元素中,化学性质最相似的是

(A) Be 与 Mg;　(B) Mg 与 Al;　(C) Li 与 Be;　(D) Be 与 Al。

12.2　下列元素中,第一电离能最小的是

(A) Li;　(B) Be;　(C) Na;　(D) Mg。

12.3　下列氮化物中,最稳定的是

(A) Li_3N;　(B) Na_3N;　(C) K_3N;　(D) Ba_3N_2。

12.4　下列过氧化物中,最稳定的是

(A) Li_2O_2;　(B) Na_2O_2;　(C) K_2O_2;　(D) Rb_2O_2。

12.5　下列碳酸盐中,热稳定性最差的是

(A) $BaCO_3$;　(B) $CaCO_3$;　(C) K_2CO_3;　(D) Na_2CO_3。

12.6　下列化合物中,溶解度最小的是

(A) $NaHCO_3$;　(B) Na_2CO_3;　(C) $Ca(HCO_3)_2$;　(D) $CaCl_2$。

12.7　下列化合物中,溶解度最大的是

(A) LiF;　(B) $NaClO_4$;　(C) $KClO_4$;　(D) K_2PtCl_6。

12.8　下列钡盐中,在酸中溶解度最小的是

(A) $BaCO_3$;　(B) BaC_2O_4;　(C) $BaCrO_4$;　(D) $BaSO_4$。

12.9　下列化合物中,具有顺磁性的是

(A) Na_2O_2;　(B) SrO;　(C) KO_2;　(D) BaO_2。

12.10　下列各组化合物中,用煤气灯加热时分解产物类型不同的一组是

(A) $NaNO_3$,KNO_3;　(B) $LiNO_3$,$NaNO_3$;

(C) $LiNO_3$,$Mg(NO_3)_2$;　(D) $Mg(NO_3)_2$,$Cu(NO_3)_2$。

二、填空题

12.11　金属锂应保存在________中,金属钠和钾应保存在______中。

12.12　在 s 区金属中,熔点最高的是______,熔点最低的是______;密度最小的是________;硬度最小的是______。

12.13　周期表中,处于斜线位置的 B 与 Si,________,________性质十分相似,人们习惯上把这种现象称之为“斜线规则”或“对角线规则”。

12.14　给出下列物质的化学式。

(1) 萤石____________________;　(2) 岩盐____________________;

(3) 石膏____________________;　(4) 泻盐____________________;

(5) 芒硝________；　(6) 明矾________；
(7) 光卤石________；　(8) 重晶石________；
(9) 天青石________；　(10) 方解石________；
(11) 白云石________；　(12) 元明粉________。

12.15　$Be(OH)_2$ 与 $Mg(OH)_2$ 性质的最大差异是________________。

12.16　熔盐电解法制得的金属钠中一般含有少量的____，其原因是________。

12.17　电解熔盐 NaCl 制备金属钠时加入 $CaCl_2$ 的作用是________；电解熔盐 $BeCl_2$ 制备金属铍时加入 NaCl 的作用是________。

12.18　盛 $Ba(OH)_2$ 的试剂瓶在空气中放置一段时间后，瓶内壁出现一层白膜是____。

12.19　比较各对化合物溶解度大小：
(1) LiF ___ AgF；(2) LiI ___ AgI；(3) $NaClO_4$ ___ $KClO_4$；
(4) $CaCO_3$ ___ $Ca(HCO_3)_2$；(5) Li_2CO_3 ___ Na_2CO_3。

12.20　碱土金属的氧化物，从上至下晶格能依次___，硬度依次____，熔点依次____。

三、完成并配平下列反应方程式

12.21　在过氧化钠固体上滴加热水。

12.22　将二氧化碳通过过氧化钠。

12.23　将氮化镁投入水中。

12.24　向氯化锂溶液中滴加磷酸氢二钠溶液。

12.25　六水合氯化镁受热分解。

12.26　金属钠与氯化钾共热。

12.27　金属铍溶于氢氧化钠溶液。

12.28　用 NaH 还原四氯化钛。

12.29　将臭氧化钾投入水中。

四、简答题

12.30　金属钠是强还原剂，试写出它与下列物质反应的化学方程式。
(1) H_2O；(2) NH_3；(3) C_2H_5OH；(4) Na_2O_2；(5) MgO。

12.31　解释回答下列各题：
(1) 碱土金属比同周期的碱金属的熔点高、硬度大；
(2) 常用 Na_2O_2 来做制氧剂。

12.32　如何配制不含或含有极少碳酸钠的氢氧化钠溶液？

12.33　拟除掉 $BaCl_2$ 溶液中的少量 $FeCl_3$ 杂质，试分析加入 $Ba(OH)_2$ 和 $BaCO_3$ 哪种试剂更好。

12.34　碱金属中与水反应活泼性最低的是什么？这与用电极电势判断得出的结论是否一致？试给出适当的解释。

12.35 写出溶解度较小的碱金属盐类的化学式。

12.36 钾要比钠活泼，但可以通过下述反应制备金属钾，请解释原因并分析由此制备金属钾是否切实可行。

$$Na+KCl \xrightarrow{\text{高温熔融}} NaCl+K$$

12.37 举例说明锂与同族的钠、钾元素及化合物的不同点。

12.38 试举例说明锂与镁的相似性。

12.39 举例说明铍与铝的相似性。

12.40 一固体混合物可能含有 $MgCO_3$，Na_2SO_4，$Ba(NO_3)_2$，$AgNO_3$ 和 $CuSO_4$。混合物投入水中得到无色溶液和白色沉淀；将溶液进行焰色试验，火焰呈黄色；沉淀可溶于稀盐酸并放出气体。试判断哪些物质肯定存在，哪些物质可能存在，哪些物质肯定不存在，并分析原因。

12.41 在电炉法炼镁时，要用大量的冷氢气将炉口馏出的蒸气稀释、降温，以得到金属镁粉。请问能否用空气、氮气、二氧化碳代替氢气作冷却剂？为什么？

第 13 章

硼族元素

第一部分　例题

例 13.1　完成并配平下列反应方程式。

(1) $B+Cl_2 \xrightarrow{\text{高温}}$　　(2) $B+NaOH+NaNO_3 \xrightarrow{\text{熔融}}$

(3) $BCl_3+H_2 \xrightarrow{\text{无声放电}}$　　(4) $GaCl_3+NaOH =\!=\!=$

(5) $B_2H_6+Cl_2 =\!=\!=$　　(6) $BF_3+NH_3 =\!=\!=$

(7) $Al+Cr_2O_7^{2-}+H^+ =\!=\!=$　　(8) $LiAlH_4+BCl_3 \xrightarrow{\text{乙醚}}$

(9) $AlCl_3 \cdot 6H_2O \xrightarrow{\text{加热}}$　　(10) $Tl+HCl =\!=\!=$

解：(1) $2B+3Cl_2 \xrightarrow{\text{高温}} 2BCl_3$

(2) $2B+2NaOH+3NaNO_3 \xrightarrow{\text{熔融}} 2NaBO_2+3NaNO_2+H_2O$

(3) $2BCl_3+6H_2 \xrightarrow{\text{无声放电}} B_2H_6+6HCl$

(4) $GaCl_3+3NaOH =\!=\!= Ga(OH)_3\downarrow+3NaCl$

NaOH 过量时，

$Ga(OH)_3+3Na(OH) =\!=\!= Na_3GaO_3+3H_2O$

(5) $B_2H_6(g)+6Cl_2(g) =\!=\!= 2BCl_3(l)+6HCl(g)$

(6) $BF_3(g)+NH_3 =\!=\!= H_3NBF_3$

(7) $2Al+Cr_2O_7^{2-}+14H^+ =\!=\!= 2Al^{3+}+2Cr^{3+}+7H_2O$

(8) $3LiAlH_4+4BCl_3 \xrightarrow{\text{乙醚}} 2B_2H_6+3LiCl+3AlCl_3$

(9) $AlCl_3 \cdot 6H_2O \xrightarrow{\text{加热}} Al(OH)_2Cl+4H_2O+2HCl$

(10) $2Tl+2HCl =\!=\!= 2TlCl+H_2\uparrow$

例 13.2　判断下列反应过程能否实现，写出有关的反应方程式。

(1) 硼酸与氨水发生酸碱中和反应；

(2) 三氯化铊与硫化钠反应生成 Tl_2S_3；

(3) $Al(NO_3)_3$ 与 Na_2CO_3 作用生成 $Al_2(CO_3)_3$ 沉淀；

(4) 铝酸钠与 NH_4Cl 发生反应生成铝酸铵。

解: (1) 该反应能实现。其反应方程式为

$$H_3BO_3 + NH_3\cdot H_2O = NH_4[B(OH)_4]$$

该反应是弱酸和弱碱的中和反应。若参与反应的各种物质均处于标准状态,反应进行的方向应是盐的水解。

(2) 该反应不能实现。三氯化铊氧化性很强,硫化钠还原性很强,两者将发生氧化还原反应:

$$2TlCl_3 + 3Na_2S = Tl_2S\downarrow + 2S\downarrow + 6NaCl$$

(3) 该反应不能实现。$Al(OH)_3$ 的溶度积常数极小,因此 Al^{3+} 要与 Na_2CO_3 水解得到的 OH^- 反应,生成 $Al(OH)_3$:

$$2Al(NO_3)_3 + 3Na_2CO_3 + 3H_2O = 2Al(OH)_3\downarrow + 6NaNO_3 + 3CO_2\uparrow$$

(4) 该反应不能实现。铝酸钠是 Al(Ⅲ)在强碱性条件下的存在形式。在铝酸钠溶液中加入酸性的 NH_4Cl 时,体系失去强碱性,Al(Ⅲ)将 $Al(OH)_3$ 形式存在。实际将发生的过程是

$$NaAl(OH)_4 + NH_4Cl = Al(OH)_3\downarrow + NaCl + NH_3\uparrow + H_2O$$

例 13.3 试用化学反应方程式表示以硼砂为原料制备下列各化合物的过程

(1) H_3BO_3; (2) BF_3; (3) $NaBH_4$。

解: (1) $Na_2B_4O_7 + H_2SO_4 + 5H_2O = 4H_3BO_3 + Na_2SO_4$

(2) $2H_3BO_3 \xlongequal{\triangle} B_2O_3 + 3H_2O$

$B_2O_3 + 3CaF_2 + 3H_2SO_4 = 2BF_3\uparrow + 3CaSO_4 + 3H_2O$

(3) $2B_2O_3 + 4NaH = NaBH_4 + 3NaBO_2$

例 13.4 无水 $AlCl_3$ 如何制备?能否直接加热使 $AlCl_3\cdot 6H_2O$ 脱水制备无水 $AlCl_3$?

解: 无水三氯化铝可用干燥的氯气作氧化剂,在高温下氧化金属 Al 单质制备。化学反应方程式为

$$2Al + 3Cl_2(g) \xlongequal{\triangle} 2AlCl_3$$

$AlCl_3$ 遇水强烈水解,因此直接加热使 $AlCl_3\cdot 6H_2O$ 脱水制备无水 $AlCl_3$ 是不可能的。$AlCl_3\cdot 6H_2O$ 受热脱水时,发生的反应是

$$AlCl_3\cdot 6H_2O \xlongequal{\triangle} Al(OH)_2Cl + 4H_2O + 2HCl$$

最终产物是 Al_2O_3。

例 13.5 解释:

(1) 铝的抗腐蚀性能比铁强得多;

(2) 铝比铜活泼得多,但冷的浓 HNO_3 能溶解铜而不能溶解铝。

解: (1) Fe 在空气中被氧化,产物是一种疏松的含水氧化物。它与 Fe 的表面结合不紧密,

甚至于不断剥落，导致金属主体与空气接触进一步被氧化；Al 虽然比 Fe 活泼，但其在空气中被氧化的产物，是一种致密氧化物薄膜。它紧密地覆盖在 Al 的表面，使金属主体与空气隔绝，使氧化反应不能继续发生。所以铝的抗腐蚀性能比铁强得多。

(2) Al 虽然比 Cu 活泼，但其与冷的浓 HNO_3 反应，在 Al 的表面产生一种致密氧化物薄膜，发生钝化现象。而 Cu 与冷的浓 HNO_3 反应没有钝化现象发生，于是溶解于酸中。

例 13.6　根据铝在酸性介质和碱性介质中的标准电极电势说明：

(1) 铝在酸、碱、水中溶解的可能性，从而说明铝在这些溶液中和空气中的稳定性；

(2) 铝不溶于水，但能溶于 Na_2CO_3 溶液中。

解：$Al^{3+} + 3e^- \rightleftharpoons Al$　　$E^\ominus = -1.662V$

$Al(OH)_3 + 3e^- \rightleftharpoons Al + 3OH^-$　　$E^\ominus = -2.31V$

(1) 从铝在酸性介质和碱性介质中的标准电极电势看，铝在酸、碱、水中都是可溶的，而且在空气中可以被氧化成 Al_2O_3。正是由于 Al_2O_3 的生成，在金属铝表面形成致密的氧化膜，既阻碍了金属主体进一步被空气氧化，也隔绝了水与金属主体的接触，致使金属铝在水中不能真正溶解。

(2) 尽管金属铝在水中不能溶解，但 Na_2CO_3 溶液中水解生成的 OH^- 却可以将两性的 Al_2O_3 膜溶解掉，从而导致铝溶于 Na_2CO_3 溶液中。

例 13.7　举例说明 Tl(Ⅰ)与 Ag(Ⅰ)化合物性质的异同点。

解：Tl(Ⅰ)与 Ag(Ⅰ)的半径相近，电荷相同，极化能力相近，因而二者的化合物有相似之处：

(1) 化合物的难溶性。TlCl 和 AgCl 均为白色难溶化合物，Tl_2S 和 Ag_2S 均为难溶化合物。

(2) TlCl 和 AgCl 等卤化物见光均易分解。

Tl(Ⅰ)和 Ag(Ⅰ)的化合物有很多不同之处，现仅举几例加以说明：

(1) 氢氧化物稳定性不同。AgOH 室温下不稳定分解为 Ag_2O，而 TlOH 较稳定，TlOH 溶液为强碱，与 KOH 相似。

(2) Ag(Ⅰ)易生成稳定配合物，而 Tl(Ⅰ)则不易生成配合物。如 AgCl 易溶于氨水，生成 $[Ag(NH_3)_2]^+$，而 TlCl 则不溶。

(3) Ag(Ⅰ)有较强的氧化性，而 Tl(Ⅰ)有一定的还原性。

如
$$Ag^+ + Fe^{2+} = Ag + Fe^{3+}$$
$$TlCl + Cl_2 = TlCl_3$$

(4) Tl(Ⅰ)可以替代 K^+ 成矾，而 Ag(Ⅰ)则不能，如 $TlAl(SO_4)_2 \cdot 12H_2O$。

例 13.8　给出各方框中字母所代表的物质，并写出有关化学反应方程式。

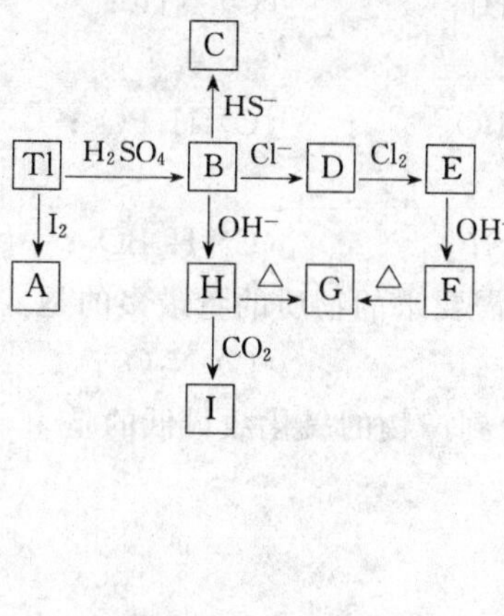

解：A—TlI；B—Tl_2SO_4；C—Tl_2S；D—TlCl；E—$TlCl_3$；F—Tl_2O_3；G—Tl_2O；H—TlOH；I—Tl_2CO_3。

金属 Tl ⟶ A　　$2Tl+I_2 = 2TlI$

金属 Tl ⟶ B　　$2Tl+H_2SO_4 = Tl_2SO_4+H_2\uparrow$

B ⟶ C　　$Tl_2SO_4+HS^- = Tl_2S\downarrow+HSO_4^-$

B ⟶ D　　$Tl_2SO_4+2Cl^- = 2TlCl\downarrow+SO_4^{2-}$

D ⟶ E　　$TlCl+Cl_2 = TlCl_3$

E ⟶ F　　$2TlCl_3+6OH^- = Tl_2O_3\downarrow+6Cl^-+3H_2O$

B ⟶ H　　$Tl_2SO_4+2OH^- = 2TlOH+SO_4^{2-}$

H ⟶ G　　$2TlOH \overset{\triangle}{=} Tl_2O+H_2O$

F ⟶ G　　$Tl_2O_3 \overset{\triangle}{=} Tl_2O+O_2\uparrow$

H ⟶ I　　$2TlOH+CO_2 = Tl_2CO_3\downarrow+H_2O$

第二部分　习题

一、选择题

13.1　在硼的化合物中，硼原子的最高配位数不超过 4，这是因为

(A) 硼原子半径小；　(B) 配位原子半径大；

(C) 硼与配位原子电负性差小；　(D) 硼原子无价层 d 轨道。

13.2　下列关于 BF_3 的叙述中，正确的是

(A) BF_3 易形成二聚体；　(B) BF_3 为离子化合物；

(C) BF_3 为路易斯酸；　(D) BF_3 常温下为液体。

13.3　下列金属单质中，熔点最低的是

(A) Cu；　(B) Zn；　(C) Na；　(D) Ga。

13.4　下列化合物中，熔点最低的是

(A) BCl_3；　(B) CCl_4；　(C) $SiCl_4$；　(D) $SnCl_4$。

13.5　下列物质中水解并能放出 H_2 的是

(A) B_2H_6；　(B) N_2H_4；　(C) NH_3；　(D) PH_3。

13.6　下列含氧酸中属于一元酸的是

(A) H_3AsO_3；　(B) H_3BO_3；　(C) H_3PO_3；　(D) H_2CO_3。

13.7　下列物质中，酸性最弱的是

(A) H_3PO_3；　(B) H_2S；　(C) H_3BO_3；　(D) H_5IO_6。

13.8　1 mol 下列物质生成正酸，需要水的物质的量最多的是

(A) I_2O_5；　(B) SO_2；　(C) N_2O_5；　(D) B_2O_3。

13.9　下列金属中，与硝酸反应得到产物的氧化数最低的是

(A) In；(B) Tl；(C) Fe；(D) Bi。

13.10 下列化合物中，氧化能力最强的是

(A) NO_2；(B) SO_3；(C) B_2O_3；(D) Tl_2O_3。

13.11 下列分子中，偶极矩最小的是

(A) B_2H_6；(B) SO_2；(C) NCl_3；(D) SF_4。

13.12 下列化合物中，氧化性与惰性电子对效应有关的是

(A) I_2O_5；(B) Tl_2O_3；(C) Mn_2O_7；(D) CrO_3。

二、填空题

13.13 硼的卤化物以 BX_3 单分子形式存在，其原因是分子内形成了____键。硼的卤化物的熔点由高到低的顺序排列为____________________。

13.14 无机苯的化学式为____，其结构为____，与____的结构相似。

13.15 硼酸为____状晶体，H_3BO_3 分子间以____键结合，层与层之间以____结合，故硼酸晶体具有____性，可作为____剂。

13.16 $GaCl_2$ 是____磁性物质，结构式应写成______。

13.17 硼砂的化学式为________，其为________元碱。

13.18 判断：(1) 化合物的热稳定性 $GaCl_3$ ____ $TlCl_3$；

(2) 酸性 $Al(OH)_3$ ____ $Ga(OH)_3$；

(3) 酸性溶液中，氧化性 Ga_2O_3 ____ Tl_2O_3；

13.19 TlCl 见光易分解，溶解度________，与一价阳离子的氯化物________相似；而 Tl^+ 的氢氧化物溶解度________，Tl^+ 易形成矾，与________的离子相似。

13.20 放在手中能够融化的金属有________，以液相存在的温度范围最大的金属是________。

13.21 硼酸与乙醇生成硼酸三乙酯的化学式为________，其火焰为________色，以此可以鉴定硼酸。

13.22 B_2O_3 与金属氧化物共熔生成的硼珠有特征的颜色，称为硼珠试验，如 CoO 的硼珠 $Co(BO_2)_2$ 为深蓝色，则 CuO 的硼珠为________色，MnO 的硼珠为________色，NiO 的硼珠为________色，Cr_2O_3 的硼珠为________色，Fe_2O_3 的硼珠为________色。

三、完成并配平下列反应方程式

13.23 硼砂溶液与稀硝酸混合。

13.24 将 Na_2CO_3 和 Al_2O_3 一起熔烧，然后将熔块打碎并投入水中。

13.25 铝溶于热 NaOH 溶液中。

13.26 向 $NaAlO_2$ 溶液中加 NH_4Cl。

13.27 向 TlOH 溶液中加 NaCl 溶液。

13.28 金属铊溶于稀硝酸。

13.29 向 KI 溶液中加入 $TlCl_3$。

四、简答题和计算题

13.30 简要解释下列各题：

(1) TlOH 易溶而 TlCl 难溶；

(2) BCl_3 的沸点比 $AlCl_3$ 低；

(3) $CuCl_2$ 为顺磁性而 $InCl_2$ 为逆磁性。

13.31 给出 BCl_3 和 BF_3 水解反应方程式，为什么二者水解产物不同？

13.32 试给出硼烷常见的五种键型。

13.33 根据标准摩尔生成吉布斯自由能的数值讨论，能否利用铝热法从 Fe_2O_3，Cr_2O_3，MnO_2，CaO 等氧化物中分别制取其金属单质。

13.34 由 BCl_3 制得的淡黄色固体 A，A 中含 B 23.4%，含 Cl 76.6%。取 0.0516 g A 在 69 ℃ 蒸发，在 2.96 kPa 时蒸气占有体积 0.268 dm^3。求 A 的化学式（已知 B 的相对原子质量为 10.81，Cl 的相对原子质量为 35.45）。

13.35 设计反应路线，从明矾制备氢氧化铝、硫酸钾和铝酸钾。

13.36 H_3BO_3 与 H_3PO_3 化学式相似，为什么 H_3BO_3 为一元酸，而 H_3PO_3 为二元酸？

13.37 二氯化镓（$GaCl_2$）为抗磁性化合物。已知 $GaCl_2$ 在溶液中解离成一种简单阳离子和一种四氯阴离子，试推测该化合物的可能结构。

第 14 章

碳族元素

第一部分 例题

例 14.1 完成并配平下列化学反应方程式。

(1) $CO+PdCl_2+H_2O =\!=\!=$

(2) $CaCO_3+CO_2+H_2O =\!=\!=$

(3) $MnCl_2(aq)+NaHCO_3(aq) =\!=\!=$

(4) $Si+NaOH =\!=\!=$

(5) $Si+HNO_3$(浓)$+HF =\!=\!=$

(6) $Na_2SiO_3+CO_2+H_2O =\!=\!=$

(7) $SiCl_4+H_2O =\!=\!=$

(8) $SiO_2+C \xlongequal{\triangle}$

(9) $SiCl_4+LiAlH_4 \xlongequal{\text{乙醚}}$

(10) $Ca_3(PO_4)_2+C+SiO_2 \xlongequal{\text{共热}}$

解: (1) $CO+PdCl_2+H_2O =\!=\!= CO_2+2HCl+Pd\downarrow$

(2) $CaCO_3+CO_2+H_2O =\!=\!= Ca(HCO_3)_2$

(3) $MnCl_2(aq)+NaHCO_3(aq) =\!=\!= MnCO_3\downarrow+NaCl(aq)+HCl(aq)$

(4) $Si+2NaOH+H_2O =\!=\!= Na_2SiO_3+2H_2\uparrow$

(5) $3Si+18HF+4HNO_3$(浓)$=\!=\!= 3H_2[SiF_6]+4NO\uparrow+8H_2O$

(6) $Na_2SiO_3+CO_2+H_2O =\!=\!= Na_2CO_3+H_2SiO_3\downarrow$

(7) $SiCl_4+4H_2O =\!=\!= H_4SiCl_4+4HCl$

(8) $SiO_2+C \xlongequal{\triangle} Si+2CO\uparrow$

(9) $SiCl_4+LiAlH_4 \xlongequal{\text{乙醚}} SiH_4+LiCl+AlCl_3$

(10) $2Ca_3(PO_4)_2+10C+6SiO_2 \xlongequal{\text{共热}} 6CaSiO_3+10CO\uparrow+P_4$

例 14.2 锗、锡、铅各单质分别与稀盐酸、稀硫酸、浓盐酸、浓硫酸作用,写出其化学反应方程式。

解: 锗的金属活性较弱,不能与盐酸、稀硫酸等非氧化性的酸作用。它能溶于热、浓硫酸中生成 Ge(Ⅳ)：

$$Ge + 4H_2SO_4 = Ge(SO_4)_2 + 2SO_2\uparrow + 4H_2O$$

锡的金属性比锗强些，可以与非氧化性的酸反应，生成 Sn(Ⅱ)，放出氢气。

在冷的稀盐酸中溶解缓慢，但能迅速溶于热浓盐酸中：

$$Sn + 2HCl = SnCl_2 + H_2\uparrow$$

在稀硫酸中反应也很缓慢：

$$Sn + H_2SO_4 = SnSO_4 + H_2\uparrow$$

锡与热、浓硫酸反应生成 Sn(Ⅳ)：

$$Sn + 4H_2SO_4 = Sn(SO_4)_2 + 2SO_2\uparrow + 4H_2O$$

铅与非氧化性的酸反应，产物为 Pb(Ⅱ)，如与稀盐酸、稀硫酸的反应：

$$Pb + 2HCl = PbCl_2 + H_2\uparrow$$
$$Pb + H_2SO_4 = PbSO_4 + H_2\uparrow$$

由于产物的溶解度小，覆盖于金属表面，使得反应速率很慢。但铅与浓盐酸反应，产物为 $PbCl_4^{2-}$，速率很快：

$$Pb + 4HCl = H_2PbCl_4 + H_2\uparrow$$

铅与热、浓硫酸反应生成 Pb(Ⅱ)：

$$Pb + 2H_2SO_4 = PbSO_4 + SO_2\uparrow + 2H_2O$$

例 14.3 Pb_3O_4 中 Pb 有两种不同的价态。试设计实验加以验证。

解：令 Pb_3O_4 与 HNO_3 反应，将产物中的棕黑色粉末滤出，令其在酸性介质中与 Mn^{2+} 反应：

$$5PbO_2 + 2Mn^{2+} + 4H^+ \xlongequal{Ag^+} 5Pb^{2+} + 2MnO_4^- + 2H_2O$$

有紫色 MnO_4^- 生成，说明 PbO_2 的存在。

滤液中加入 CrO_4^{2-}，则

$$Pb^{2+} + CrO_4^{2-} = PbCrO_4\downarrow$$

有黄色的 $PbCrO_4$ 沉淀生成，据此可以鉴定 Pb(Ⅱ)的存在。

例 14.4 设计实验以区别下列各对物质。

(1) Sb_2O_5 与 SnO；　(2) As_2S_3 与 SnS_2；

(3) $Pb(NO_3)_2$ 与 $Bi(NO_3)_3$；　(4) $Sn(OH)_2$ 与 $Pb(OH)_2$。

解：(1) 将 Sb_2O_5 和 SnO 分别溶于盐酸，滴加淀粉-碘化钾试液，有 I_2 生成使体系变蓝的是 Sb_2O_5。

(2) 将 As_2S_3 和 SnS_2 分别置于 6 $mol \cdot dm^{-3}$ 盐酸中，溶解的是 SnS_2，基本不溶解的是 As_2S_3。

(3) 溶于过量 NaOH 溶液的是 $Pb(NO_3)_2$，不溶于过量 NaOH 溶液的是 $Bi(NO_3)_3$。

(4) 溶于 NaOH 溶液后加入 H_2O_2 溶液,有棕黑色沉淀生成的是 $Pb(OH)_2$。

例 14.5 如何经过提纯除去气体中的少量杂质。

(1) 氢气中少量的一氧化碳;

(2) 一氧化碳中少量的二氧化碳。

解: (1) 将含有少量一氧化碳的氢气,通入 CuCl 的盐酸溶液。少量 CO 将被定量吸收:

$$CO + CuCl + 2H_2O \longrightarrow Cu(CO)Cl \cdot 2H_2O$$

则氢气被提纯。

(2) 将含有少量二氧化碳的一氧化碳,通入 $Ca(OH)_2$ 溶液。少量 CO_2 将被定量吸收:

$$CO_2 + Ca(OH)_2 \longrightarrow CaCO_3 \downarrow + H_2O$$

则一氧化碳被提纯。

例 14.6 碳和硅都是ⅣA 族元素,为什么由碳链构成的化合物有上千万种,而由硅链构成的化合物却仅有数种?为什么常温下 CO_2 是气体,而 SiO_2 却是固体?

解: 碳属于第二周期元素,原子半径很小,所以碳碳之间的 σ 键,其原子轨道的"头碰头"重叠程度很大,键很强。而且 π 键的轨道"肩并肩"重叠程度也很大。所以碳碳之间可以形成形形色色的链,以构成上千万种的有机化合物。

硅属于第三周期元素,原子半径比碳大,所以硅硅之间的 σ 键,其原子轨道的"头碰头"重叠程度远小于碳碳之间的 σ 键,键很弱。其 π 轨道"肩并肩"重叠的可能性十分小,以至于不能形成硅硅双键和三键。故硅链构成的化合物仅有数种。

CO_2 属于分子晶体,晶体中质点之间的结合力属于分子间力。这种力远小于离子键和共价键的结合作用,所以分子晶体一般来说熔点低,在室温下多以气体形式存在。

SiO_2 属于原子晶体,原子晶体中原子间都是以共价键相互连接的。由于共价键十分强,所以这类物质具有很高的熔点,在室温下多以固体形式存在。

总之,由于晶体类型的不同,所以常温下 CO_2 是气体,而 SiO_2 却是固体。

例 14.7 试说明为什么 Si 很难与酸作用,即使是与氧化性很强的酸也难作用,但却易于与碱发生反应。

解: 单质硅具有较强的非金属性,所以硅不易与酸反应。

氧化性的酸,例如 HNO_3,从电极电势看可以将 Si 氧化成 SiO_2,反应式为

$$3Si + 4HNO_3(\text{浓}) \longrightarrow 3SiO_2 + 4NO \uparrow + 2H_2O$$

但是生成物 SiO_2 不溶于水,附在反应物 Si 的表面,使反应不能进行下去。所以氧化性很强的酸也难与 Si 作用。

硅易与碱反应:

$$Si + 2NaOH + H_2O \longrightarrow Na_2SiO_3 + 2H_2$$

体现了硅的非金属性,且产物为可溶性 Na_2SiO_3,所以反应较为容易进行。

例 14.8 参照下面的 Ellingham 图,回答问题:

(1) 比较 CuO 和 Ag_2O 的热稳定性的高低;

(2) 给出用 C 还原 Al_2O_3，SiO_2 和 TiO_2 以制取相应单质的反应温度。

解：(1) 在图中所示的温度范围内，表示反应

$$4Ag+O_2 = 2Ag_2O$$

的吉布斯自由能 $\Delta_r G_m^\ominus$ 随温度 T 的变化的曲线，处于表示反应

$$2Cu_2O+O_2 = 4CuO$$

的曲线的上方。这说明 Ag_2O 的热稳定性低于 CuO。

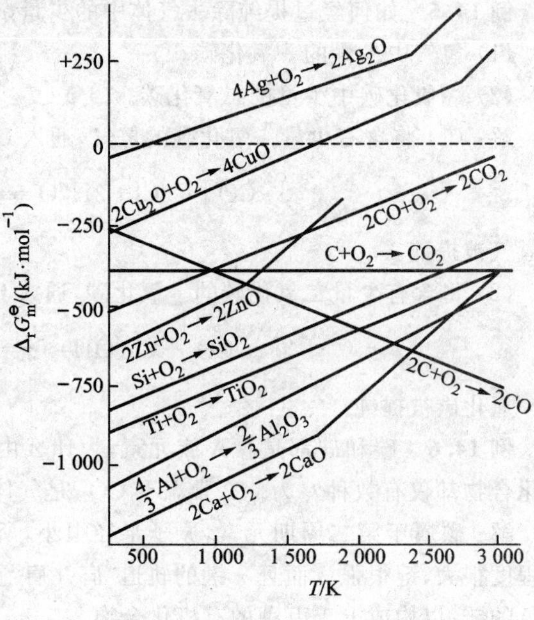

(2) 用 C 还原 Al_2O_3，SiO_2 和 TiO_2 以制取相应单质的反应及其温度如下：

$\frac{2}{3}Al_2O_3+2C = \frac{4}{3}Al+2CO$　2 300 K

$TiO_2+2C = Ti+2CO$　2 100 K

$SiO_2+2C = Si+2CO$　1 600 K

例 14.9 无色晶体 A 加热后有红棕色气体 B 生成。向 A 的水溶液中加入盐酸有白色沉淀 C 生成，盐酸过量时沉淀 C 溶解得到 D。若向 A 的水溶液中加入 KI 溶液，则有黄色沉淀 E 生成。向 A 的水溶液中滴加 NaOH 溶液有白色沉淀 F 生成，NaOH 过量则沉淀 F 溶解。将气体 B 通入水中生成 G，并放出无色气体 H。沉淀 F 溶于适量 G 中形成的溶液，结晶后可以得到 A。

试写出 A，B，C，D，E，F，G 和 H 所代表的物质的化学式，并用化学反应方程式表示各过程。

解：A—$Pb(NO_3)_2$；　B—NO_2；　C—$PbCl_2$；

D—$PbCl_4^{2-}$；　E—PbI_2；　F—$Pb(OH)_2$；

G—HNO_3；　H—NO。

各步反应方程式如下：

$$2Pb(NO_3)_2 = 2PbO+4NO_2\uparrow+O_2\uparrow$$
$$Pb^{2+}+2Cl^- = PbCl_2\downarrow$$
$$PbCl_2+2Cl^- = PbCl_4^{2-}$$
$$Pb^{2+}+2I^- = PbI_2\downarrow$$
$$Pb^{2+}+2OH^- = Pb(OH)_2\downarrow$$
$$3NO_2+H_2O = 2HNO_3+NO\uparrow$$
$$Pb(OH)_2+2HNO_3 = Pb(NO_3)_2+2H_2O$$

例 14.10 金属 A 在加热时与 Cl_2 反应生成无色液体化合物 B，B 经过量金属 A 处理转变为固体化合物 C。C 溶于盐酸形成无色透明溶液，用大量水稀释该溶液时产生白色沉淀 D。向 D 的盐酸溶液中通入 H_2S 气体生成褐色沉淀 E，沉淀 E 溶于过硫化钠溶液形成无色溶液 F。向 F 中加入稀盐酸生成黄色沉淀 G，并放出无色气体 H。

试写出 A,B,C,D,E,F,G 和 H 所代表的物质的化学式,并用化学反应方程式表示各过程。

解:A—Sn;　B—$SnCl_4$;　C—$SnCl_2$;　D—Sn(OH)Cl;

E—SnS;　F—Na_2SnS_3;　G—SnS_2;　H—H_2S。

各步反应方程式如下:

$$Sn+2Cl_2 \longrightarrow SnCl_4$$

$$Sn+SnCl_4 \longrightarrow 2SnCl_2$$

$$SnCl_2+H_2O \longrightarrow Sn(OH)Cl\downarrow +HCl$$

$$SnCl_2+H_2S \longrightarrow SnS\downarrow +2HCl$$

$$SnS+Na_2S_2 \longrightarrow SnS_2+Na_2S$$

$$SnS_2+Na_2S \longrightarrow Na_2SnS_3$$

$$Na_2SnS_3+2HCl \longrightarrow 2NaCl+SnS_2+H_2S\uparrow$$

第二部分　习题

一、选择题

14.1　下列各对物质中,中心原子的轨道杂化类型不同的是

(A) CH_4 与 SiH_4;　(B) H_3O^+ 与 NH_3;

(C) CH_4 与 NH_4^+;　(D) CF_4 与 SF_4。

14.2　下列物质在水中溶解度最小的是

(A) Na_2CO_3;　(B) $NaHCO_3$;

(C) $Ca(HCO_3)_2$;　(D) $KHCO_3$。

14.3　下列各组化合物中,对热稳定性判断正确的是

(A) $H_2CO_3>Ca(HCO_3)_2$;　(B) $Na_2CO_3>PbCO_3$;

(C) $(NH_4)_2CO_3>K_2CO_3$;　(D) $Na_2SO_3>Na_2SO_4$。

14.4　下列化合物中,不水解的是

(A) $SiCl_4$;　(B) CCl_4;　(C) BCl_3;　(D) PCl_5。

14.5　与 Na_2CO_3 溶液反应生成碱式盐沉淀的离子是

(A) Al^{3+};　(B) Ba^{2+};　(C) Cu^{2+};　(D) Hg^{2+}。

14.6　常温下不能稳定存在的是

(A) $GaCl_4^-$;　(B) $SnCl_4$;　(C) $PbCl_4$;　(D) $GeCl_4$。

14.7　下列氧化物中,氧化性最强的是

(A) SiO_2;　(B) GeO_2;　(C) SnO_2;　(D) Pb_2O_3。

14.8　下列化学式中代表金刚砂的是

(A) Al_2O_3;　(B) CaC_2;　(C) SiO_2;　(D) SiC。

14.9　下列物质中,酸性最强的是

(A) H_2SnO_3； (B) $Ge(OH)_4$； (C) $Sn(OH)_2$； (D) $Ge(OH)_2$。

14.10 下列物质中，酸性最弱的是

(A) H_2CO_3； (B) H_4SiO_4； (C) H_2SiF_6； (D) HBF_4。

14.11 下列物质中，与水作用放出氢气的是

(A) BCl_3； (B) NH_3； (C) F_2； (D) SiH_4。

14.12 下列单质中，与硝酸不反应的是

(A) Pb； (B) Sn； (C) Si； (D) C。

二、填空题

14.13 给出下列物质的化学式。

(1) 锗石矿_____； (2) 锡石矿_____； (3) 方铅矿_____； (4) 金刚石_____；
(5) 小苏打_____； (6) 石英_____； (7) 水玻璃_____； (8) 橄榄石_____；
(9) 钪硅石_____； (10) 密陀僧_____； (11) 铅黄_____； (12) 铅丹_____。

14.14 硅酸盐有一维链状、二维片状和三维网状结构，若不考虑边界，三种硅酸盐的酸根的结构通式依次为_____，_____，_____。

14.15 欲除去 CO 中有少量 CO_2，采取的方法是_____，欲除去 CO_2 中的少量 CO，采取的方法是_____。

14.16 溶解度：Na_2CO_3 ___ $NaHCO_3$，其原因是_____。

14.17 将各氧化物写成盐的形式为：三氧化二铅_____四氧化三铅_____，四氧化三铁_____。

14.18 $Pb(OH)_2$ 是___性氢氧化物，在过量的 NaOH 溶液中 Pb(Ⅱ)以_____形式存在，$Pb(OH)_2$溶于___酸或___酸得到无色清液。

14.19 Pb_3O_4 呈___色，俗称___，与 HNO_3 作用时，铅有___生成___，有___生成___。

14.20 将 $HClO_4$，H_2SiO_3，H_2SO_4，H_3PO_4 按酸性由高到低排列顺序为_____。

14.21 给出下列化合物的颜色：

$PbCl_2$ ___；PbI_2 ___；SnS ___；SnS_2 ___；
PbS ___；$PbSO_4$ ___；PbO ___；Pb_2O_3 ___。

三、完成并配平下列反应方程式

14.22 向浓氨水中通入过量 CO_2。

14.23 向 Na_2SiO_3 溶液中加入饱和 NH_4Cl 溶液。

14.24 向 $SnCl_2$ 溶液中加入过量 NaOH 溶液后滴加 $Bi(NO_3)_3$ 溶液。

14.25 将少量 $SnCl_2$ 溶液滴入 $HgCl_2$ 溶液中。

14.26 向 $Na_2[Sn(OH)_6]$溶液中通入 CO_2。

14.27 铅溶于热浓硝酸。

14.28 铅丹溶于过量 HI 溶液。

14.29 SnS 溶于$(NH_4)_2S_2$ 溶液。

14.30 将铅丹投入盐酸中。

14.31 用 $MnSO_4$ 和 H_2SO_4 混合溶液处理 PbO_2。

14.32　$PbCrO_4$ 溶于 NaOH 溶液。

14.33　用锌粉还原 $SiCl_4$。

14.34　炼铁中以石灰石除去矿石中的 SiO_2。

14.35　二氧化硅、炭粉与氯气共热。

14.36　石英与纯碱作用。

14.37　SnO_2 与 NaOH 共熔。

四、简答题和计算题

14.38　CS_2 和 CCl_4 都是非极性化合物，试比较二者的不同点。

14.39　下面图中(a)，(b)，(c)是碳或其氧化物与氧反应的自由能[$\Delta_r G_m^\ominus/(kJ\cdot mol^{-1})$]随温度变化的曲线，(d)是反应 $2\ Mn + O_2 \longrightarrow 2\ MnO$ 的自由能随温度变化的曲线。试回答：

(1) 给出(a)，(b)，(c)线表示的反应的方程式，并加以必要的说明。

(2) (d)线的拐点对应的温度是哪种物质的熔点？

(3) 给出温度在 $T_y \sim T_z$ 之间由 MnO 得到 Mn 的反应方程式。

(4) 给出温度在高于 T_z 后由 MnO 得到 Mn 的反应方程式。

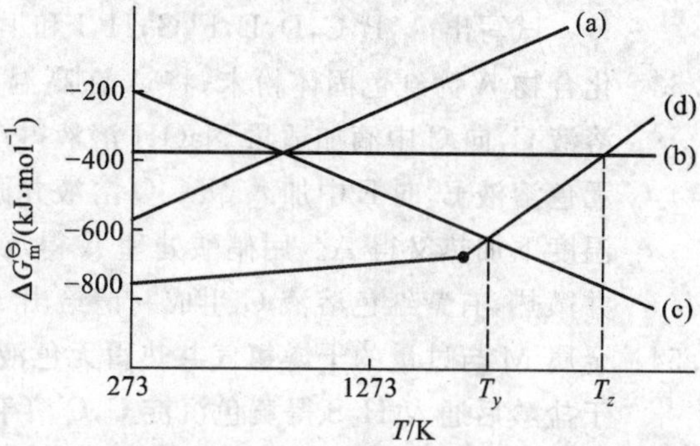

14.40　N_2 和 CO 具有相同的分子轨道和相似的分子结构，但 CO 与过渡金属形成配合物能力比 N_2 强得多，请解释原因。

14.41　简述 CO 和 CO_2 的实验室制法。

14.42　试用化学反应方程式表示下列制备过程。

(1) 以方铅矿(PbS)为原料，制取氧化铅、二氧化铅和铅单质；

(2) 以砂石中的 SiO_2 为原料，制取粗硅和高纯硅；

(3) 以偏硅酸钠(Na_2SiO_3)溶液为原料，制取变色硅胶。

14.43　如何用锡直接氯化的方法制取 $SnCl_4$？需要采取哪些防止产物水解的措施？

14.44　为什么 CCl_4 遇水不水解，而 $SiCl_4$，BCl_3，NCl_3 却易水解？

14.45　硅单质虽可有类似于金刚石结构，但其熔点、硬度却比金刚石差得多，请解释原因。

14.46　常温下 SiF_4 为气态，$SiCl_4$ 为液态；而 SnF_4 为固态，$SnCl_4$ 为液态，请解释原因。

14.47　如何配制 $SnCl_2$ 溶液？

14.48　用四种方法鉴别 $SnCl_4$ 和 $SnCl_2$ 溶液。

14.49　为什么铅易溶于浓盐酸和稀硝酸中，而难溶于稀盐酸和冷的浓硝酸？

14.50　试比较硅烷、硼烷和烷烃的热稳定性，并用化学反应方程式表示这些非金属氢化物的分解方式。

14.51　灰黑色固体单质 A，在常温下不与酸反应，与浓 NaOH 溶液作用时生成无色溶液 B 和气体 C。气体 C 在灼热的条件下可以将一黑色的氧化物还原成红色金属 D。A 在很高的温度下与氧气作用的产物为白色固体 E。E 与氢氟酸作用时能产生一无色气体 F。F 通入水中时生成白色沉淀 G 及溶液 H。G 用适量的 NaOH 溶液处理得溶液 B。

试写出 A,B,C,D,E,F,G,H 所代表的物质的化学式。

14.52 某白色固体 A,置于水中生成白色沉淀 B,加入浓盐酸 B 溶解。A 溶于稀 HNO_3 形成无色溶液 C。

将 $AgNO_3$ 溶液加入溶液 C,析出白色沉淀 D,D 溶于氨水得溶液 E。向 E 中加入 KI,生成浅黄色沉淀 F,再加入 NaCN 时沉淀 F 溶解。酸化溶液 E,又产生白色沉淀 D。

将 H_2S 通入溶液 C,产生褐色沉淀 G。G 溶于 Na_2S_2,形成溶液。酸化该溶液时得一黄色沉淀 H。

少量溶液 C 加入 $HgCl_2$ 溶液得白色沉淀 I,继续加入溶液 C,沉淀 I 逐渐变灰,最后变为黑色沉淀 J。

试写出 A,B,C,D,E,F,G,H,I 和 J 所代表的物质的化学式。

14.53 化合物 A 为红色固体粉末,将 A 在高温下加热最终得黄色固体 B。B 溶于硝酸得无色溶液 C,向 C 中滴加适量 NaOH 溶液得白色沉淀 D,加入过量 NaOH 溶液时,D 溶解得无色溶液 E,向 E 中加入 NaClO 溶液并微热,有棕黑色沉淀 F 生成。将 F 洗净后在一定温度下加热又得 A。用硝酸处理 A 得沉淀 F 和溶液 C。将 A 加入酸性 $MnSO_4$ 溶液中并微热,有紫红色溶液 G 生成。请给出 A,B,C,D,E,F,G 所代表的物质。

14.54 金属 M 与过量的干燥氯气共热得无色液体 A,A 与金属 M 作用转化为固体 B,将 A 溶于盐酸后通入 H_2S 得黄色沉淀 C,C 溶于 Na_2S 溶液得无色溶液 D。将 B 溶于稀盐酸后加入适量$HgCl_2$有白色沉淀 E 生成。向 B 的盐酸溶液中加入适量 NaOH 溶液有白色沉淀 F 生成。F 溶于过量 NaOH 溶液得无色溶液 G。向 G 中加入 $BiCl_3$ 溶液有黑色沉淀 H 生成。试给出 M,A,B,C,D,E,F,G,H 各为何物质。

14.55 无色晶体 A 易溶于水。将 A 在煤气灯上加热得到黄色固体 B 和棕色气体 C。B 溶于硝酸后又得 A 的水溶液。碱性条件下 A 与次氯酸钠溶液作用得黑色沉淀 D,D 不溶于硝酸。向 D 中加入盐酸有白色沉淀 E 和气体 F 生成,F 可使淀粉碘化钾试纸变色。将 E 和 KI 溶液共热,冷却后有黄色沉淀 G 生成,试确定 A,B,C,D,E,F,G 各为何物质。

14.56 将白色粉末 A 加热得黄色固体 B 和无色气体 C。B 溶于硝酸得无色溶液 D,向 D 中加入 K_2CrO_4 溶液得黄色沉淀 E。向 D 中加入 NaOH 溶液至碱性,有白色沉淀 F 生成,NaOH 过量时白色沉淀溶解得无色溶液。将气体 C 通入石灰水中产生白色沉淀 G,将 G 投入酸中,又有气体 C 放出。试给出 A,B,C,D,E,F,G 各代表何物质。

第 15 章

氮族元素

第一部分　例题

例 15.1　在稀硫酸介质中完成并配平下列反应的方程式。

(1) $I^- + NO_2^- ===$

(2) $NH_4^+ + NO_2^- \xlongequal{\triangle}$

(3) $MnO_4^- + NO_2^- ===$

(4) $MnO_4^- + As_2O_3 ===$

(5) $NaBiO_3 + Mn^{2+} ===$

(6) $H_3PO_3 + NO_2^- ===$

(7) $I^- + AsO_4^{3-} ===$

(8) $N_2H_4 + NO_2^- ===$

(9) $N_2H_4 + AgCl ===$

(10) $As_2O_3 + Zn ===$

解：(1) $2I^- + 2NO_2^- + 4H^+ === I_2 + 2NO\uparrow + 2H_2O$

(2) $NH_4^+ + NO_2^- \xlongequal{\triangle} N_2\uparrow + 2H_2O$

(3) $2MnO_4^- + 5NO_2^- + 6H^+ === 2Mn^{2+} + 5NO_3^- + 3H_2O$

(4) $4MnO_4^- + 5As_2O_3 + 9H_2O + 2H^+ === 4Mn^{2+} + 10H_2AsO_4^-$

(5) $5NaBiO_3 + 2Mn^{2+} + 14H^+ === 5Bi^{3+} + 2MnO_4^- + 5Na^+ + 7H_2O$

(6) $H_3PO_3 + 2NO_2^- + 2H^+ === H_3PO_4 + 2NO\uparrow + H_2O$

(7) $2I^- + AsO_4^{3-} + 2H^+ === I_2 + AsO_3^{3-} + H_2O$

(8) $N_2H_4 + NO_2^- + H^+ === HN_3 + 2H_2O$

(9) $N_2H_4 + 4AgCl === 4Ag + N_2\uparrow + 4HCl$

(10) $As_2O_3 + 6Zn + 12H^+ === 2AsH_3\uparrow + 6Zn^{2+} + 3H_2O$

例 15.2　完成并配平下列 NaOH 溶液参与的反应

(1) $NaOH + P_4 ===$

(2) NaOH(过量) $+ H_3PO_2 ===$

(3) $NaOH + As_2S_3 ===$

(4) $NaOH+Sb(OH)_3$ ══

(5) $NaOH+NCl_3$ ══

(6) $NaOH+NO_2$ ══

(7) NaOH(过量)$+As_2O_3$ ══

(8) NaOH(过量)$+H_3PO_3$ ══

解：(1) $3NaOH+P_4+3H_2O \xlongequal{} 3NaH_2PO_2+PH_3\uparrow$

(2) NaOH(过量)$+H_3PO_2 \xlongequal{} NaH_2PO_2+H_2O$

(3) $6NaOH+As_2S_3 \xlongequal{} Na_3AsO_3+Na_3AsS_3+3H_2O$

(4) $3NaOH+Sb(OH)_3 \xlongequal{} Na_3SbO_3+3H_2O$

(5) $3NaOH+NCl_3 \xlongequal{} NH_3+3NaClO$

(6) $2NaOH+2NO_2 \xlongequal{} NaNO_2+NaNO_3+H_2O$

(7) 6NaOH(过量)$+As_2O_3 \xlongequal{} 2Na_3AsO_3+3H_2O$

(8) 2NaOH(过量)$+H_3PO_3 \xlongequal{} Na_2HPO_3+2H_2O$

例 15.3 给出下列物质的水解反应方程式，并说明 NCl_3 水解产物与其他化合物的水解产物有何本质的区别？为什么？

(1) NCl_3；(2) PCl_3；(3) $AsCl_3$；(4) $SbCl_3$；(5) $BiCl_3$；(6) $POCl_3$。

解：(1) $NCl_3+3H_2O \xlongequal{} NH_3\uparrow+3HClO$

(2) $PCl_3+3H_2O \xlongequal{} H_3PO_3+3HCl$

(3) $AsCl_3+3H_2O \xlongequal{} H_3AsO_3+3HCl$

(4) $SbCl_3+H_2O \xlongequal{} SbOCl\downarrow+2HCl$

(5) $BiCl_3+H_2O \xlongequal{} BiOCl\downarrow+2HCl$

(6) $POCl_3+3H_2O \xlongequal{} H_3PO_4+3HCl$

NCl_3 水解产物既有酸 HClO，又有碱 NH_3，而同族 $AsCl_3$ 和 PCl_3 水解产物为两种酸。

P 和 As 的电负性都小于 Cl，$AsCl_3$ 和 PCl_3 水解时呈正电性的 P^{3+} 和 As^{3+} 与水解离出的 OH^- 结合，呈负电性的 Cl^- 与水解离出的 H^+ 结合，生成两种酸。

周期数较高的 Sb 和 Bi 金属性较强，Sb^{3+} 和 Bi^{3+} 与 OH^- 的结合较弱，故 $SbCl_3$ 和 $BiCl_3$ 水解不彻底，分别生成 SbOCl，BiOCl 沉淀和 HCl。

N 和 Cl 的电负性相近，NCl_3 中半径小的 N 的孤电子对向 H_2O 中的 H 配位，N 与 H 成键并脱去 Cl，最终生成 NH_3；NCl_3 中半径大的 Cl 和由 H_2O 释放出的 OH^- 结合，生成 HClO。

例 15.4 分别用三种方法鉴定下列各对物质。

(1) $NaNO_2$ 和 $NaNO_3$；(2) NH_4NO_3 和 NH_4Cl；(3) $SbCl_3$ 和 $BiCl_3$；

(4) $NaNO_3$ 和 $NaPO_3$；(5) Na_3PO_4 和 Na_2SO_4；(6) KNO_3 和 KIO_3。

解：(1) 向两种盐的溶液中分别加入酸性 $KMnO_4$ 溶液，能使 $KMnO_4$ 溶液褪色的是 $NaNO_2$，另一种盐是 $NaNO_3$：

$$2MnO_4^-+5NO_2^-+6H^+ \xlongequal{} 2Mn^{2+}+5NO_3^-+3H_2O$$

将两种盐的水溶液分别用 HAc 酸化，再加入 KI，颜色变黄、有 I_2 生成的是 $NaNO_2$，无明显变化的是 $NaNO_3$：

$$2HNO_2 + 2I^- + 2H^+ \longrightarrow I_2 + 2NO\uparrow + 2H_2O$$

向两种盐的溶液中加入 $AgNO_3$ 溶液，有黄色沉淀生成的是 $NaNO_2$，另一种盐是 $NaNO_3$：

$$Ag^+ + NO_2^- \longrightarrow AgNO_2\downarrow$$

(2) 向两种盐的溶液中加入 $AgNO_3$ 溶液，有白色沉淀生成的是 NH_4Cl，另一种盐是 NH_4NO_3：

$$Ag^+ + Cl^- \longrightarrow AgCl\downarrow$$

向两种盐的溶液中分别加入酸性 $KMnO_4$ 溶液，能使其褪色的是 NH_4Cl，另一种是 NH_4NO_3：

$$10Cl^- + 2MnO_4^- + 16H^+ \longrightarrow 2Mn^{2+} + 5Cl_2\uparrow + 8H_2O$$

取少量两种盐晶体分别装入两支试管中，加入 $FeSO_4$，加水溶解后沿着试管壁加浓硫酸，在浓硫酸与上层溶液的界面处有棕色环生成的是 NH_4NO_3，另一种盐是 NH_4Cl：

$$NO_3^- + 3Fe^{2+} + 4H^+ \longrightarrow NO + 3Fe^{3+} + 2H_2O$$
$$NO + Fe^{2+} \longrightarrow Fe(NO)^{2+}\text{（棕色）}$$

(3) 将两种盐溶于水，分别滴加 NaOH 溶液至过量，先有白色沉淀生成而后沉淀又溶解的是 $SbCl_3$，加 NaOH 溶液生成的白色沉淀不溶于过量 NaOH 溶液的是 $BiCl_3$：

$$Sb^{3+} + 3OH^- \longrightarrow Sb(OH)_3\downarrow$$
$$Sb(OH)_3 + 3OH^- \longrightarrow SbO_3^{3-} + 3H_2O$$
$$Bi^{3+} + 3OH^- \longrightarrow Bi(OH)_3\downarrow$$

将两种盐溶于稀盐酸，分别加入溴水，能使溴水褪色的是 $SbCl_3$，另一种盐是 $BiCl_3$：

$$Sb^{3+} + Br_2 \longrightarrow Sb^{5+} + 2Br^-$$

向两种盐溶液中加入 NaOH 和 NaClO 溶液，微热，有土黄色沉淀生成的是 $BiCl_3$，另一种盐是 $SbCl_3$：

$$Bi^{3+} + ClO^- + 4OH^- + Na^+ \longrightarrow NaBiO_3\downarrow + 2H_2O + Cl^-$$

(4) 向两种盐溶液中加入 $AgNO_3$ 溶液，有白色沉淀生成的是 $NaPO_3$，另一种盐是 $NaNO_3$：

$$Ag^+ + PO_3^- \longrightarrow AgPO_3\downarrow$$

分别将两种盐酸化后煮沸，这时偏磷酸盐 PO_3^- 将转化为正磷酸盐 PO_4^{3-}。再分别加入过量的 $(NH_4)_2MoO_4$，有特征的黄色沉淀磷钼酸铵生成的是偏磷酸钠，无此特征现象的是硝酸钠：

$$PO_4^{3-} + 12MoO_4^{2-} + 24H^+ + 3NH_4^+ \longrightarrow (NH_4)_3PMo_{12}O_{40}\cdot 6H_2O\downarrow + 6H_2O$$

分别将两种盐晶体加入 HNO_3 溶液，有棕色 NO_2 气体生成的是 $NaNO_2$，另一种盐是 $NaPO_3$：

$$NO_3^- + NO_2^- + 2H^+ \longrightarrow 2NO_2\uparrow + H_2O$$

(5) 向两种盐溶液中加入 $AgNO_3$ 溶液，有黄色沉淀生成的是 Na_3PO_4，有白色沉淀生成的是

Na_2SO_4：

$$3Ag^+ + PO_4^{3-} \longrightarrow Ag_3PO_4\downarrow \quad (黄色)$$
$$2Ag^+ + SO_4^{2-} \longrightarrow Ag_2SO_4\downarrow \quad (白色)$$

向两种盐溶液中加入 $BaCl_2$ 溶液后生成的白色沉淀不溶于硝酸的是 Na_2SO_4，生成的白色沉淀溶于硝酸的是 Na_3PO_4：

$$Ba^{2+} + SO_4^{2-} \longrightarrow BaSO_4\downarrow$$
$$3Ba^{2+} + 2PO_4^{3-} \longrightarrow Ba_3(PO_4)_2\downarrow$$
$$Ba_3(PO_4)_2 + 4H^+ \longrightarrow 3Ba^{2+} + 2H_2PO_4^-$$

向两种盐溶液中加入碘水溶液，能使碘水褪色的是 Na_3PO_4，不能使碘水褪色的是 Na_2SO_4。因为 Na_3PO_4 溶液碱性较强，碘水发生歧化反应：

$$3I_2 + 6PO_4^{3-} + 3H_2O \longrightarrow 5I^- + IO_3^- + 6HPO_4^{2-}$$

(6) 将两种盐溶液酸化后滴加 Na_2SO_3 溶液，颜色变黄、有 I_2 生成的是 KIO_3，另一种盐是 KNO_3：

$$2IO_3^- + 5SO_3^{2-} + 2H^+ \longrightarrow I_2 + 5SO_4^{2-} + H_2O$$

将两种盐分别与 $NaNO_2$ 晶体混合后滴加浓硫酸，有 NO_2 气态放出的是 KNO_3，另一种盐是 KIO_3：

$$NO_3^- + NO_2^- + 2H^+ \longrightarrow 2NO_2\uparrow + H_2O$$
$$2IO_3^- + 5NO_2^- + 2H^+ \longrightarrow I_2 + 5NO_3^- + H_2O$$

向两种盐溶液中分别加入 $BaCl_2$ 溶液，生成白色沉淀者为 KIO_3，另一种则为 KNO_3：

$$2KIO_3 + BaCl_2 \longrightarrow Ba(IO_3)_2\downarrow + 2KCl$$

例 15.5 提纯下列物质。

(1) 除去 N_2 气体中的少量 O_2 和 H_2O；

(2) 除去 NO 中的少量 NO_2；

(3) 除去 $NaNO_3$ 溶液中的少量 $NaNO_2$。

解：(1) 将 N_2 气通过赤热的铜粉，除去少量 O_2：

$$O_2 + 2Cu \longrightarrow 2CuO$$

再用 P_2O_5 干燥 N_2，除去少量 H_2O。

(2) 将气体通过水或 NaOH 溶液除去 NO_2，再用 P_2O_5 干燥：

$$3NO_2 + H_2O \longrightarrow 2HNO_3 + NO$$
$$2NO_2 + 2NaOH \longrightarrow NaNO_3 + NaNO_2 + H_2O$$

(3) 向溶液中加入少量 HNO_3 溶液后加热，可除去溶液中 NO_2^-：

$$2NO_2^- + 2H^+ \longrightarrow NO_2 + NO + H_2O$$

或向溶液中加入少量 NH_4NO_3 溶液后加热，可除去溶液中 NO_2^-：

$$NH_4^+ + NO_2^- \xlongequal{\quad} N_2 + 2H_2O$$

例 15.6 试分离下列各对离子。

(1) Sb^{3+} 和 Bi^{3+}；(2) PO_4^{3-} 和 NO_3^-；(3) PO_4^{3-} 和 SO_4^{2-}；(4) PO_4^{3-} 和 Cl^-。

解：(1) 向溶液中加入过量 NaOH 溶液，Sb^{3+} 生成可溶性的 SbO_3^{3-} 而 Bi^{3+} 生成 $Bi(OH)_3$ 沉淀：

$$Sb^{3+} + 6OH^- \xlongequal{\quad} SbO_3^{3-} + 3H_2O$$

$$Bi^{3+} + 3OH^- \xlongequal{\quad} Bi(OH)_3\downarrow$$

(2) 向溶液中加入 $AgNO_3$ 溶液，PO_4^{3-} 与 Ag^+ 生成 Ag_3PO_4 沉淀而 NO_3^- 留在溶液中。

(3) 将溶液用硝酸酸化后加入 $BaCl_2$ 溶液，SO_4^{2-} 转化为 $BaSO_4$ 沉淀而 PO_4^{3-} 转化为 $H_2PO_4^-$ 留在溶液中。

(4) 将溶液用硝酸酸化后加入 $AgNO_3$ 溶液，Cl^- 转化为 AgCl 沉淀而 PO_4^{3-} 转化为 $H_2PO_4^-$ 留在溶液中。

例 15.7 现有下列六种磷的含氧酸盐固体，试加以鉴定。

$Na_4P_2O_7$，$NaPO_3$，Na_2HPO_4，NaH_2PO_4，NaH_2PO_2，NaH_2PO_3。

解：向六种盐的水溶液中分别加入 $AgNO_3$ 溶液，生成白色沉淀的是 $Na_4P_2O_7$ 和 $NaPO_3$：

$$P_2O_7^{4-} + 4Ag^+ \xlongequal{\quad} Ag_4P_2O_7\downarrow(\text{白})$$

$$PO_3^- + Ag^+ \xlongequal{\quad} AgPO_3\downarrow(\text{白})$$

生成黄色沉淀的是 Na_2HPO_4 和 NaH_2PO_4：

$$HPO_4^{2-} + 3Ag^+ \xlongequal{\quad} Ag_3PO_4\downarrow(\text{黄}) + H^+$$

$$H_2PO_4^- + 3Ag^+ \xlongequal{\quad} Ag_3PO_4\downarrow(\text{黄}) + 2H^+$$

生成黑色沉淀的是 NaH_2PO_2 和 NaH_2PO_3：

$$H_2PO_2^- + 4Ag^+ + 2H_2O \xlongequal{\quad} 4Ag\downarrow(\text{黑}) + H_3PO_4 + 3H^+$$

$$H_2PO_3^- + 2Ag^+ + H_2O \xlongequal{\quad} 2Ag\downarrow(\text{黑}) + H_3PO_4 + H^+$$

$NaPO_3$ 能使蛋白液凝聚而 $Na_4P_2O_7$ 不能，可将 $NaPO_3$ 和 $Na_4P_2O_7$ 区分开。

Na_2HPO_4 溶液为弱碱性而 NaH_2PO_4 溶液为弱酸性，可将 Na_2HPO_4 和 NaH_2PO_4 区分开。

NaH_2PO_3 为酸式盐，其溶液有缓冲作用，加入少量强酸或强碱但溶液的 pH 基本不变；NaH_2PO_2 不是酸式盐，其溶液没有缓冲作用。由此可将 NaH_2PO_3 和 NaH_2PO_2 区分开。

例 15.8 解释下列实验现象。

(1) 向含有 Bi^{3+} 和 Sn^{2+} 的澄清溶液中加入 NaOH 溶液会有黑色沉淀生成。

(2) 向 Na_3PO_4 溶液中滴加 $AgNO_3$ 溶液时生成黄色沉淀，但向 $NaPO_3$ 溶液中滴加 $AgNO_3$ 溶液时却生成白色沉淀。

(3) 向 $AgNO_3$ 溶液中通入 NH_3 气体，先有棕褐色沉淀生成，而后沉淀溶解得到无色溶液；但向 $AgNO_3$ 溶液中通入 SbH_3 气体，生成的沉淀在 SbH_3 过量时也不溶解。

(4) 在煤气灯上加热 KNO_3 晶体时没有棕色气体生成，但 KNO_3 晶体混有 $CuSO_4$ 时有棕色气体生成。

(5) 分别向 NaH_2PO_4，Na_2HPO_4 和 Na_3PO_4 溶液中加入 $AgNO_3$ 溶液时，均得到黄色的 Ag_3PO_4 沉淀。

(6) 向 Na_2HPO_4 溶液中加入 $CaCl_2$ 溶液有白色沉淀生成，但向 NaH_2PO_4 溶液中加入 $CaCl_2$ 溶液没有沉淀生成。

解：(1) 在碱性条件下 Sn^{2+} 将 Bi^{3+} 还原为单质 Bi，生成的粉末产物为黑色：

$$3Sn^{2+} + 2Bi^{3+} + 18OH^- = 2Bi\downarrow + 3Sn(OH)_6^{2-}$$

(2) Na_3PO_4 溶液中滴加 $AgNO_3$ 溶液时生成黄色 Ag_3PO_4 沉淀，向 $NaPO_3$ 溶液中滴加 $AgNO_3$ 溶液时生成的是 $AgPO_3$ 沉淀，它显白色。

Ag^+ 离子的极化能力较强，其半径也较大，因而 Ag_3PO_4 中 Ag^+ 与负电荷多的 PO_4^{3-} 之间的附加极化作用较强，很容易发生电荷跃迁，吸收可见光显颜色。而 $AgPO_3$ 中 Ag^+ 与负电荷少的 PO_3^- 之间的附加极化作用较弱，很难发生电荷跃迁，即可见光照射后不发生电荷跃迁，因而为白色。

(3) 向 $AgNO_3$ 溶液中通入 NH_3 气体，先生成棕褐色 Ag_2O 沉淀，NH_3 过量则 Ag_2O 与 NH_3 生成配合物而溶解：

$$2Ag^+ + 2NH_3 + H_2O = Ag_2O\downarrow + 2NH_4^+$$
$$Ag_2O + 2NH_4^+ + 2NH_3 = 2Ag(NH_3)_2^+ + H_2O$$

向 $AgNO_3$ 溶液中通入 SbH_3 气体，发生氧化还原反应，生成的沉淀为单质 Ag 和 Sb_2O_3，过量 SbH_3 不能溶解 Ag 和 Sb_2O_3：

$$12Ag^+ + 2SbH_3 + 3H_2O = 12Ag\downarrow + Sb_2O_3\downarrow + 12H^+$$

(4) K^+ 极化能力弱，在煤气灯上加热 KNO_3 晶体时生成 KNO_2 和 O_2，不生成棕色 NO_2：

$$2KNO_3 = 2KNO_2 + O_2\uparrow$$

在 KNO_3 晶体中混有 $CuSO_4$，混合物受热时，NO_3^- 接触极化能力较强的 Cu^{2+} 使 NO_3^- 分解生成棕色 NO_2 气体：

$$4KNO_3 + 2CuSO_4 = 4NO_2\uparrow + O_2\uparrow + 2CuO + 2K_2SO_4$$

(5) AgH_2PO_4 和 Ag_2HPO_4 比 Ag_3PO_4 溶解度大得多，因此向 NaH_2PO_4，Na_2HPO_4 和 Na_3PO_4 溶液中加入 $AgNO_3$ 溶液时，都生成黄色的 Ag_3PO_4 沉淀。

(6) $CaHPO_4$ 不溶于水，$Ca(H_2PO_4)_2$ 溶于水。所以，向 Na_2HPO_4 溶液中加入 $CaCl_2$ 溶液有白色沉淀生成，向 NaH_2PO_4 溶液中加入 $CaCl_2$ 溶液没有沉淀生成。

例 15.9 完成下图所示物质转化的反应方程式并给出反应条件。

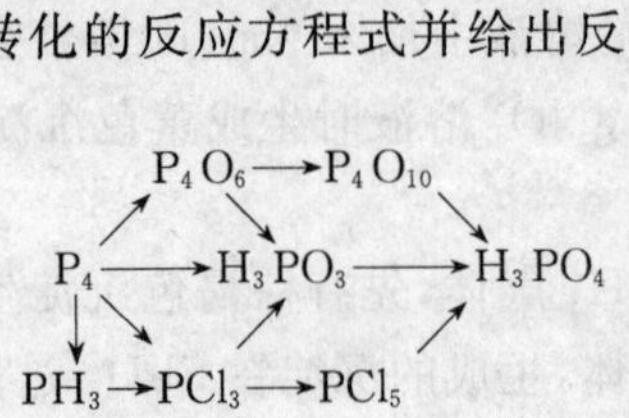

解：白磷在不充分的空气中燃烧，生成的氧化物为 P_4O_6：

$$P_4+3O_2 = P_4O_6$$

白磷缓慢与 H_2O_2 作用，产物中含有 H_3PO_3：

$$P_4+6H_2O_2 = 4H_3PO_3$$

白磷与不足量的干燥氯气反应，生成 PCl_3：

$$P_4+6Cl_2 = 4PCl_3$$

白磷在碱中歧化，生成 PH_3。加热有利于歧化反应进行（NaH_2PO_2 进一步歧化为 Na_3PO_4）：

$$P_4+3NaOH+3H_2O = PH_3\uparrow+3NaH_2PO_2$$

PH_3 与不足量的干燥氯气反应，生成 PCl_3：

$$2PH_3+3Cl_2 = 2PCl_3+6HCl$$

P_4O_6 与过量氧作用，生成 P_4O_{10}：

$$P_4O_6+2O_2 = P_4O_{10}$$

P_4O_6 缓慢溶于冷水，生成 H_3PO_3：

$$P_4O_6+6H_2O = 4H_3PO_3$$

PCl_3 水解生成 H_3PO_3：

$$PCl_3+3H_2O = H_3PO_3+3HCl$$

PCl_3 与过量干燥 Cl_2 作用，生成 PCl_5：

$$PCl_3+Cl_2 = PCl_5$$

P_4O_{10} 与过量水作用，最终生成 H_3PO_4：

$$P_4O_{10}+6H_2O = 4H_3PO_4$$

将 H_3PO_3 氧化，生成 H_3PO_4：

$$H_3PO_3+H_2O_2 = H_3PO_4+H_2O$$

PCl_5 彻底水解，生成 H_3PO_4：

$$PCl_5+4H_2O = H_3PO_4+5HCl$$

例 15.10　简要回答下列问题。

(1) 为什么 NH_3 溶液显碱性而 HN_3 溶液显酸性？

(2) 在 H_3PO_2，H_3PO_3 和 H_3PO_4 分子中都含有 3 个 H，为什么 H_3PO_2 为一元酸，H_3PO_3 为二元酸，而 H_3PO_4 为三元酸？

(3) 为什么与过渡金属的配位能力 $NH_3<PH_3$，$NF_3<PF_3$；而与 H^+ 的配位能力 $NH_3>PH_3$？

(4) 有人提出，可以由 NO_2 的磁性测定数据分析 NO_2 分子中的离域 π 键是 Π_3^3 还是 Π_3^4。你认为是否可行？为什么？

解：(1) 化合物在水溶液中的酸碱性，一般是由其在水中的解离情况决定的。

NH_3 是一种稳定的分子，在水中解离出 H^+ 的能力很弱。而 NH_3 中 N 的孤电子对有较强的配位能力，可以与 H_2O 解离出的 H^+ 结合，使体系中 OH^- 过剩，因此 NH_3 的水溶液显碱性：

$$NH_3 + H_2O = NH_3 \cdot H_2O \rightleftharpoons NH_4^+ + OH^- \qquad K_b^\ominus = 1.8 \times 10^{-5}$$

HN_3 的结构远不如 N_3^- 的结构稳定，故 HN_3 在水溶液中将解离出 H^+，生成稳定的 N_3^-。因此 HN_3 显酸性：

$$HN_3 \rightleftharpoons H^+ + N_3^- \qquad K_a^\ominus = 2.5 \times 10^{-5}$$

(2) 磷的含氧酸中，只有—OH 基团的 H 能解离出 H^+，而与 P 成键的 H 不能解离出 H^+。因此，磷的含氧酸是几元酸，是由分子中 H 形成几个—OH 基团决定的。

磷的含氧酸的结构如下图所示，(a) 表示的 H_3PO_2 分子中有 1 个—OH基团，为一元酸；(b) 表示的 H_3PO_3 分子中有 2 个—OH 基团，为二元酸；(c) 表示的 H_3PO_4 分子中有 3 个—OH 基团，为三元酸。

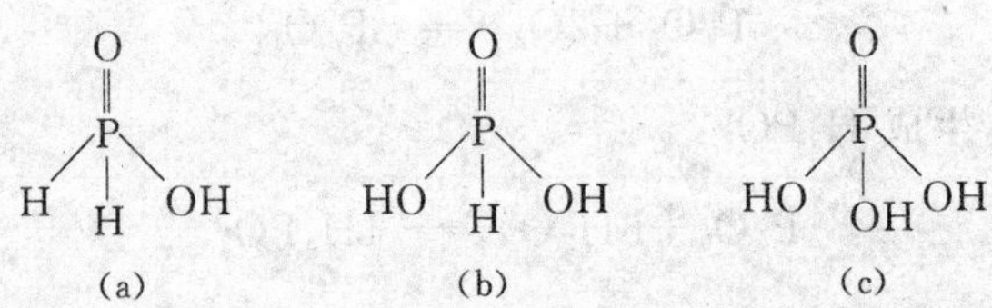

(3) NH_3 和 NF_3 利用 N 的孤电子对向过渡金属配位形成配位键；PH_3 和 PF_3 除利用 P 的孤电子对向过渡金属配位形成配位键外，而其中心原子 P 有空的 d 轨道，可以接受过渡金属 d 轨道电子的配位，形成 d—dπ 配键，使 PH_3 和 PF_3 与过渡金属生成的配合物更稳定。即与过渡金属的配位能力 $NH_3 < PH_3$，$NF_3 < PF_3$。

由于 H 不存在价层 d 轨道，在与 H^+ 配位时，NH_3 和 PH_3 只能以孤电子对向 H^+ 的 1s 空轨道配位。H^+ 的半径很小，与半径小的 N 形成的配位键较强，而与半径较大的 P 形成的配位键较弱。因此，与 H^+ 的配位能力 $NH_3 > PH_3$。

(4) 这种方法是不可行的。

测定 NO_2 的磁性应是 NO_2 处在液态或固态下，而随着温度的降低，NO_2 发生聚合反应：

$$2NO_2 \rightleftharpoons N_2O_4$$

实验结果表明，在 N_2O_4 沸点温度时，液体中含有 1% 的 NO_2，气体中含有 15.9% 的 NO_2；在 N_2O_4 熔点温度的液体中只含有 0.01% 的 NO_2，在低于 N_2O_4 的熔点温度时，固体中全部是 N_2O_4。

可见，液态或固态时 NO_2 几乎全部转化为 N_2O_4，无法测定液态或固态时 NO_2 的磁性。

例 15.11 无色晶体 A 受热得到无色气体 B，将 B 在更高的温度下加热后再恢复到原来的温度，发现气体体积增加了 50%。晶体 A 与等物质的量的 NaOH 固体共热得无色气体 C 和白色固体 D。将 C 通入 $AgNO_3$ 溶液先有棕黑色沉淀 E 生成，C 过量时则 E 消失得到无色溶液。

将 A 溶于浓盐酸后加入 KI 则溶液变黄。

试写出字母 A,B,C,D 和 E 所代表的物质的化学式,并用化学反应方程式表示各过程。

解: A—NH_4NO_3； B—N_2O； C—NH_3； D—$NaNO_3$； E—Ag_2O。

各步反应方程式如下：

$$NH_4NO_3 = N_2O\uparrow + 2H_2O$$
$$2N_2O = 2N_2 + O_2$$
$$NH_4NO_3 + NaOH = NH_3\uparrow + NaNO_3 + H_2O$$
$$2Ag^+ + 2NH_3 + H_2O = Ag_2O\downarrow + 2NH_4^+$$
$$Ag_2O + 4NH_3 + H_2O = 2Ag(NH_3)_2^+ + 2OH^-$$
$$2NO_3^- + 9I^- + 8H^+ = 2NO\uparrow + 3I_3^- + 4H_2O$$

例 15.12　无色晶体 A 溶于稀盐酸得无色溶液,再加入 NaOH 溶液得到白色沉淀 B。B 溶于过量 NaOH 溶液得到无色溶液 C。将 B 溶于盐酸后蒸发、浓缩后又析出 A。向 A 的稀盐酸溶液加入 H_2S 溶液生成橙色沉淀 D。D 与 Na_2S_2 可以发生氧化还原反应,反应产物之间作用得到无色溶液 E。将 A 置于水中生成白色沉淀 F。

试写出字母 A,B,C,D,E 和 F 所代表的物质的化学式,并用化学反应方程式表示各过程。

解: A—$SbCl_3$；　B—$Sb(OH)_3$；　C—Na_3SbO_3；
D—Sb_2S_3；　E—Na_3SbS_4；　F—SbOCl。

各步反应方程式如下：

$$SbCl_3 + 3NaOH = Sb(OH)_3\downarrow + 3NaCl$$
$$Sb(OH)_3 + 3NaOH = Na_3SbO_3 + 3H_2O$$
$$Sb(OH)_3 + 3HCl = SbCl_3 + 3H_2O$$
$$2SbCl_3 + 3H_2S = Sb_2S_3\downarrow + 6HCl$$
$$Sb_2S_3 + 2Na_2S_2 = Sb_2S_5 + 2Na_2S$$
$$Sb_2S_5 + 3Na_2S = 2Na_3SbS_4$$
$$SbCl_3 + H_2O = SbOCl\downarrow + 2HCl$$

第二部分　习题

一、选择题

15.1　干燥 NH_3 气可选择的干燥剂是

(A) 浓 H_2SO_4；　(B) $CaCl_2$；　(C) P_2O_5；　(D) CaO。

15.2　对下列化合物中的性质判断正确的是

(A) 碱性:$NH_3 > N_2H_4 > NH_2OH$；　(B) 熔点:$NH_3 > N_2H_4 > NH_2OH$；

(C) 还原性:$NH_3 > N_2H_4 > NH_2OH$；　(D) 热稳定性:$NH_2OH > N_2H_4 > NH_3$。

15.3 下列氢化物中，热稳定性最差的是

(A) NH_3； (B) PH_3； (C) AsH_3； (D) SbH_3。

15.4 分子中含 d—p 反馈 π 键的是

(A) HNO_3； (B) HNO_2； (C) H_3PO_2； (D) NH_3。

15.5 下列分子中，不存在 Π_3^4 离域键的是

(A) HNO_3； (B) HNO_2； (C) N_2O； (D) N_3^-。

15.6 下列物质中受热可得到 NO_2 的是

(A) $NaNO_3$； (B) $LiNO_3$； (C) KNO_3； (D) NH_4NO_3。

15.7 加热分解可以得到金属单质的是

(A) $Hg(NO_3)_2$； (B) $Cu(NO_3)_2$； (C) KNO_3； (D) $Mg(NO_3)_2$。

15.8 遇水后能放出气体并有沉淀生成的是

(A) $Bi(NO_3)_2$； (B) Mg_3N_2； (C) $(NH_4)_2SO_4$； (D) NCl_3。

15.9 与 $FeSO_4$ 和浓 H_2SO_4 发生棕色环反应的是

(A) $NaNH_2$； (B) $NaNO_2$； (C) $NaNO_3$； (D) NaN_3。

15.10 下列化合物中，最易发生爆炸反应的是

(A) $Pb(NO_3)_2$； (B) $Pb(N_3)_2$； (C) $PbCO_3$； (D) K_2CrO_4。

15.11 下列铵盐中，受热分解时有 NH_3 放出的是

(A) $(NH_4)_2SO_4$； (B) NH_4NO_3； (C) NH_4NO_2； (D) $(NH_4)_2Cr_2O_7$。

15.12 下列化合物中，不能将 I_2 还原的是

(A) H_3PO_3； (B) H_3PO_2； (C) HPO_3； (D) PH_3。

15.13 下列溶液中，与 $AgNO_3$ 溶液作用生成的沉淀颜色最深的是

(A) $NaPO_3$； (B) Na_2HPO_3； (C) Na_3PO_4； (D) $Na_4P_2O_7$。

15.14 下列酸中为一元酸的是

(A) $H_4P_2O_7$； (B) H_3PO_2； (C) H_3PO_3； (D) H_3PO_4。

15.15 下列物质的水解产物中既有酸又有碱的是

(A) NCl_3 (B) PCl_3 (C) $POCl_3$ (D) Mg_3N_2

15.16 下列物质中，不溶于氢氧化钠溶液的是

(A) $Sb(OH)_3$； (B) $Sb(OH)_5$； (C) H_3AsO_4； (D) $Bi(OH)_3$。

15.17 下列物质中与 HCl 反应能产生氯气的是

(A) H_3AsO_4； (B) H_3SbO_4； (C) Bi_2O_3； (D) $NaBiO_3$。

15.18 下列物质均有较强的氧化性，其中强氧化性与惰性电子对有关的是

(A) $K_2Cr_2O_7$； (B) $NaBiO_3$； (C) $(NH_4)_2S_2O_8$； (D) H_5IO_6。

15.19 下列化合物中，不能被 Br_2 氧化的是

(A) H_3PO_3； (B) H_3AsO_3； (C) $SbCl_3$； (D) $BiCl_3$。

二、填空题

15.20 给出下列物质的化学式。

(1) 雄黄______； (2) 雌黄______； (3) 辉锑矿______； (4) 锑硫镍矿______；

(5) 辉铋矿____；(6) 砷华____；(7) 锑华____；(8) 铋华____。

15.21 从 NH_3 的结构和 N 的价态考虑，应有____反应、____反应和____反应。

15.22 氮的氢化物中，碱性最强的是____，酸性最强的是____，配位能力最强的是____，最不稳定的是____，还原能力最差的是____，与 AgCl 反应有水生成的是____。

15.23 PH_3 的分子构型为____，其毒性比 NH_3 ____，溶解性比 NH_3 ____，碱性比 NH_3 ____，与过渡金属的配位能力比 NH_3 ____，热稳定性比 NH_3 ____。

15.24 稀酸的氧化性 HNO_3 ____ HNO_2；盐的热稳定性 $AgNO_3$ ____ $AgNO_2$；离子的配位能力 NO_3^- ____ NO_2^-。

15.25 依次给出次、亚、正、偏、焦磷酸的化学式。____，____，____，____，____。

15.26 H_3PO_3 为____元酸，H_3PO_4 为____元酸，而 $H_4P_2O_7$ 为____元酸。其酸性由强到弱依次为____。

15.27 $Ca(H_2PO_4)_2$，$CaHPO_4$，$Ca_3(PO_4)_2$ 在水中的溶解度大小次序为____。

15.28 $SbCl_3$ 的水解产物为____；$Cu(NO_3)_2 \cdot 2H_2O$ 在不太高温度时水解产物为____；温度较高时水解产物为____；$Mn(NO_3)_2$ 受热分解的产物为____。

15.29 在砷、锑、铋的硫化物中，能溶于 Na_2S 的是：____，____，____，____。

15.30 将 2 mol P_4O_{10} 转变为正磷酸，至少需要____ mol H_2O，NH_4NO_2 中 N 的平均氧化数为____。

15.31 在 NaH_2PO_4 溶液中加入 $AgNO_3$ 溶液时，生成的沉淀为____，沉淀为____色。

15.32 马氏试砷法中，把砷的化合物与锌和盐酸作用，产生分子式为____的气体，气体受热，在玻璃管中出现____。

15.33 As_2O_3 与 NaOH 溶液作用生成____，再加碘水生成____和____。

15.34 给出下列化合物或离子的颜色

As_2S_3 ____；As_2S_5 ____；Sb_2S_3 ____；Sb_2S_5 ____；$AgNO_2$ ____；

$K_3[Co(NO_2)_6]$ ____；$Fe(NO)^{2+}$ ____；NO_2 ____；N_2O_3 ____；N_2O_4 ____。

三、完成并配平下列反应方程式

15.35 将 NH_4Cl 和 $NaNO_2$ 溶液混合后加热。

15.36 氨气通过热的氧化铜。

15.37 用羟胺处理 AgBr。

15.38 将二氧化氮通入氢氧化钠溶液中。

15.39 向稀亚硝酸溶液滴入少量碘酸溶液。

15.40 叠氮酸铅受热分解。

15.41 向 $NaNO_2$ 溶液中加入浓硝酸。

15.42 金溶于王水。

15.43 铂溶于王水。

15.44 向红磷与水的混合物中滴加溴。

15.45 白磷溶于硝酸溶液中。

15.46 向次磷酸溶液中滴加硝酸银溶液。

15.47 向亚磷酸溶液中加入过量氢氧化钠溶液。

15.48 用稀盐酸处理 Zn_3P_2。

15.49 三硫化二砷溶于硫化钠。

15.50 向硫代砷酸钠溶液中加盐酸。

15.51 五硫化二锑溶于氢氧化钠溶液中。

15.52 将铋酸钠与少许酸化的硫酸锰溶液混合。

四、简答题

15.53 给出下列物质受热分解的反应方程式。

(1) $LiNO_3$； (2) KNO_3； (3) $AgNO_3$；

(4) $Bi(NO_3)_3$； (5) $Pb(NO_3)_2$； (6) $Fe(NO_3)_2$；

(7) NH_4NO_3； (8) $(NH_4)_2CO_3$； (9) $(NH_4)_2Cr_2O_7$；

(10) NH_4Cl； (11) $NaNH_2$； (12) $Pb(N_3)_2$；

(13) $NaNO_2$； (14) $AgNO_2$。

15.54 用反应方程式表示下列制备过程。

(1) 由 $NaNO_3$ 制备 HNO_2 溶液；

(2) 由 $BiCl_3$ 制备 $NaBiO_3$；

(3) 由 $SbCl_3$ 制备较纯净的 Sb_2S_5。

15.55 为什么氮族元素中 P,As,Sb 都可形成稳定的五氯化物,而 N 和 Bi 却不能形成五氯化物?

15.56 在与金属反应时,为什么浓 HNO_3 被还原的产物主要是 NO_2,而稀硝酸被还原的产物主要是 NO?

15.57 如何配制 $SbCl_3$ 和 $Bi(NO_3)_3$ 溶液?

15.58 在用铜与硝酸反应制备硝酸铜时,应选用稀硝酸还是浓硝酸?

15.59 用两种方法鉴定下列各对物质

(1) Na_3PO_3 和 Na_3PO_4； (2) NaH_2PO_4 和 Na_2HPO_4；

(3) KNO_3 和 $LiNO_3$； (4) $NaNO_3$ 和 NH_4NO_3。

15.60 实验室中 KNO_3 和 KNO_2 两种晶体试剂瓶的标签已脱落,实验室只有 KI,$FeSO_4$,$CoCl_2$,醋酸和浓硫酸,试设计四种方法加以鉴定。

15.61 除去下列物质中的杂质,给出相关的反应方程式。

(1) KNO_2 晶体中的少量 KNO_3 晶体；

(2) N_2O 气体中混有的少量 NO；

(3) Na_2SO_4 溶液中的少量$(NH_4)_2SO_4$。

15.62 H_3PO_2 和 H_3PO_3 各为几元酸？请说明原因。

15.63 $H_4P_2O_7$ 的解离常数 $K_1^\ominus=3.0\times10^{-2}$,$K_2^\ominus=4.4\times10^{-3}$,$K_3^\ominus=2.5\times10^{-7}$,$K_4^\ominus=5.6\times10^{-10}$,为什么 $K_1^\ominus$ 与 $K_2^\ominus$ 相近,$K_3^\ominus$ 与 $K_4^\ominus$ 相近,但 $K_2^\ominus$ 与 $K_3^\ominus$ 相差较大?

15.64 为什么向 $SbCl_5$ 溶液中通入 H_2S 得不到纯净的 Sb_2S_5？应如何制备 Sb_2S_5？

15.65 在酸性溶液中,按氧化能力由大到小排列下列离子,并简要说明之:NO_3^-,PO_4^{3-},AsO_4^{3-},SbO_4^{3-},BiO_3^-。

15.66　解释下列化合物熔点顺序

(1) $AsF_3 < AsCl_3 < AsBr_3 < AsI_3$；

(2) $SbF_3 > SbI_3 > SbBr_3 > SbCl_3$；

(3) $PCl_3 < PCl_5$，$SbF_3 > SbF_5$。

15.67　As_2O_3 在盐酸中的溶解度随酸的浓度增大而减小而后又增大，请解释原因。

15.68　钾盐 A 为白色粉末，A 溶于水后溶液显弱酸性。向 A 的水溶液中加入 $AgNO_3$ 溶液有黄色沉淀 B 生成。B 溶于硝酸得无色溶液 C。向 A 的水溶液中加入 $CaCl_2$ 无沉淀生成，再加入氨水则有白色沉淀 D 生成。试给出 A，B，C，D 所代表的物质。

15.69　化合物 A 为白色固体，A 在水中溶解度较小，但易溶于氢氧化钠溶液和浓盐酸。A 溶于浓盐酸得溶液 B，向 B 中通入 H_2S 得黄色沉淀 C，C 不溶于盐酸，易溶于氢氧化钠溶液。C 溶于硫化钠溶液得无色溶液 D，若将 C 溶于 Na_2S_2 溶液则得无色溶液 E。向 B 中滴加溴水，则溴被还原，而 B 转为无色溶液 F，向所得 F 的酸性溶液中加入淀粉碘化钾溶液，则溶液变蓝，给出 A，B，C，D，E，F 所代表的物质。

15.70　无色钠盐晶体 A 溶于水后加入 $AgNO_3$ 有浅黄色沉淀 B 生成。用 NaOH 溶液处理 B，得到棕黑色沉淀 C。B 溶于硝酸并放出棕色气体 D。D 通入 NaOH 溶液后经蒸发、浓缩析出晶体 E。E 受热分解得无色气体 F 和 A 的粉末。

试写出字母 A，B，C，D，E 和 F 所代表的物质的化学式。

15.71　化合物 A 是一种易溶于水的无色液体。当 A 的水溶液与 HNO_3 共热并加入 $AgNO_3$ 时，形成白色沉淀 B，B 溶于氨水形成溶液 C，加入 HNO_3 时重新得到沉淀 B。如果 A 的水溶液通 H_2S 至饱和，生成黄色沉淀 D，D 不溶于稀 HNO_3，但溶于 KOH 和 KHS 的混合溶液并得到溶液 E。酸化 E 时又得沉淀 D。D 又能溶于 KOH 和 H_2O_2 的混合溶液，生成溶液 F。F 用 $Mg(NO_3)_2$ 和 NH_4NO_3 的混合物处理，形成白色沉淀 G。G 溶于 HAc 后用 $AgNO_3$ 处理，得到红棕色沉淀 H。试确定各字母所代表的物质。

15.72　化合物 A 为白色固体，不溶于水。A 受热剧烈分解，生成固体 B 和气体 C。固体 B 不溶于水或盐酸，但溶于热的稀硝酸得无色溶液 D 和无色气体 E。E 在空气中变棕色。向溶液 D 中加入盐酸时得白色沉淀 F。气体 C 与普通试剂不起反应，但与热的金属镁作用生成白色固体 G。G 与水作用得白色沉淀 H 及气体 I。I 能使湿润的红色石蕊试纸变蓝。H 可溶于稀硫酸得溶液 J。化合物 A 以 H_2S 溶液处理时得黑色沉淀 K，无色溶液 L 和气体 C。过滤后，固体 K 溶于浓硝酸得气体 E，黄色沉淀 M 和溶液 D。用 NaOH 溶液处理滤液 L 又得气体 I。请指出 A，B，C，D，E，F，G，H，I，J，K，L，M 所代表的物质的化学式。

15.73　化合物 A 加入水中得白色沉淀 B 和无色溶液 C。取溶液 C 与饱和 H_2S 溶液作用生成棕黑色沉淀 D，D 不溶于 NaOH 溶液，能溶于盐酸。向溶液 C 中加入 NaOH 溶液有白色沉淀 E 生成，E 不溶于 NaOH 溶液。向 $SnCl_2$ 溶液中加入过量 NaOH 溶液后滴加溶液 C，有黑色沉淀 F 生成。向溶液 C 中加入 $AgNO_3$ 溶液有白色沉淀 G 生成，G 不溶于硝酸易溶于氨水，试给出 A，B，C，D，E，F 和 G 的化学式。

第 16 章

氧族元素

第一部分　例题

例 16.1　完成并配平下列反应方程式。

(1) $H_2S + ClO_3^- + H^+$ ══

(2) $Na_2S_2O_4 + O_2 + NaOH$ ══

(3) $PbO_2 + H_2O_2$ ══

(4) $PbS + H_2O_2$ ══

(5) $S + NaOH$(浓) ══

(6) $Cu + H_2SO_4$(浓) ══

(7) $S + H_2SO_4$(浓) ══

(8) $H_2S + H_2SO_4$(浓) ══

(9) $SO_2Cl_2 + H_2O$ ══

(10) $HSO_3Cl + H_2O$ ══

解：(1) $5H_2S + 8ClO_3^-$ ══ $5SO_4^{2-} + 2H^+ + 4Cl_2 + 4H_2O$

(2) $Na_2S_2O_4 + O_2 + 2NaOH$ ══ $Na_2SO_3 + Na_2SO_4 + H_2O$

(3) $PbO_2 + H_2O_2$ ══ $PbO + H_2O + O_2\uparrow$

(4) $PbS + 4H_2O_2$ ══ $PbSO_4 + 4H_2O$

(5) $3S + 6NaOH$(浓碱) ══ $2Na_2S + Na_2SO_3 + 3H_2O$

(6) $Cu + 2H_2SO_4$(浓) ══ $CuSO_4 + SO_2\uparrow + 2H_2O$

(7) $S + 2H_2SO_4$(浓) ══ $3SO_2\uparrow + 2H_2O$

(8) $H_2S + H_2SO_4$(浓) ══ $S\downarrow + SO_2 + 2H_2O$

(9) $SO_2Cl_2 + 2H_2O$ ══ $H_2SO_4 + 2HCl$

(10) $HSO_3Cl + H_2O$ ══ $H_2SO_4 + HCl$

例 16.2　完成下列各反应的化学方程式。

(1) Na_2O_2 与过量冷水作用；

(2) 几滴热水滴在 Na_2O_2 固体上；

(3) 电解硫酸和硫酸铵的混合溶液；

(4) 将难溶于水和酸的 Al_2O_3 变成可溶于水的硫酸盐；

(5) 无氧条件下 Zn 粉还原酸式亚硫酸钠溶液；
(6) 将 SeO_2 溶于水，然后通 SO_2 气体；
(7) 用盐酸酸化多硫化铵溶液；
(8) 向硫代硫酸钠溶液中滴加少量硝酸银溶液；
(9) 向硝酸银溶液中滴加少量硫代硫酸钠溶液；
(10) 在中等酸度的钛(Ⅳ)盐溶液中加入 H_2O_2。

解：(1) $Na_2O_2+2H_2O \xlongequal{\quad} 2NaOH+H_2O_2$

(2) $2Na_2O_2+2H_2O \xlongequal{\quad} 4NaOH+O_2\uparrow$

(3) $2HSO_4^- \xlongequal{电解} S_2O_8^{2-}+H_2$

(4) $Al_2O_3+3K_2S_2O_7 \xlongequal{共熔} Al_2(SO_4)_3+3K_2SO_4$

(5) $2NaHSO_3+Zn \xlongequal{\quad} Na_2S_2O_4+Zn(OH)_2$

(6) $2SO_2+H_2SeO_3+H_2O \xlongequal{\quad} 2H_2SO_4+Se\downarrow$

(7) $2HCl+(NH_4)_2S_x \xlongequal{\quad} H_2S\uparrow+(x-1)S\downarrow+2NH_4Cl$

(8) $Ag^++2S_2O_3^{2-} \xlongequal{\quad} Ag(S_2O_3)_2^{3-}$

(9) $2Ag^++S_2O_3^{2-} \xlongequal{\quad} Ag_2S_2O_3\downarrow$(白)

$Ag_2S_2O_3+H_2O \xlongequal{\quad} Ag_2S\downarrow$(黑)$+2H^++SO_4^{2-}$

(10) $TiO^{2+}+H_2O_2 \xlongequal{\quad} Ti(O_2)^{2+}+H_2O$

例 16.3　用化学反应方程式表示物质的转化：

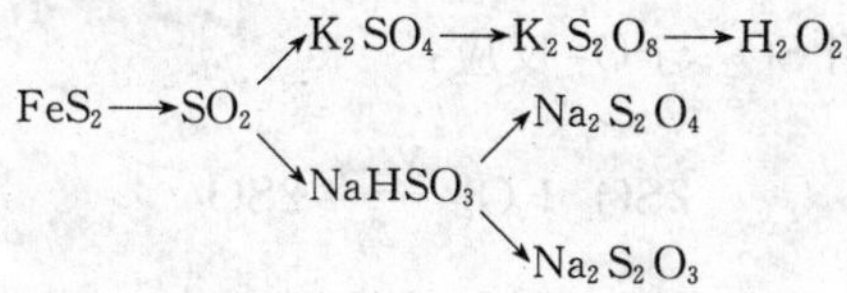

解：$4FeS_2+11O_2 \xlongequal{\triangle} 2Fe_2O_3+8SO_2$

$2SO_2(g)+O_2(g) \xlongequal[723\ K]{V_2O_5} 2SO_3$

$2KOH+SO_3 \xlongequal{\quad} K_2SO_4+H_2O$

$K_2SO_4+H_2SO_4 \xlongequal{\quad} 2KHSO_4$

$2KHSO_4 \xlongequal{电解} K_2S_2O_8+H_2\uparrow$

$K_2S_2O_8+2H_2O \xlongequal{H_2SO_4} 2KHSO_4+H_2O_2$

$2SO_2$(过量)$+Na_2CO_3+H_2O \xlongequal{\quad} 2NaHSO_3+CO_2\uparrow$

$2NaHSO_3+Zn \xlongequal{\quad} Na_2S_2O_4+Zn(OH)_2$

$NaHSO_3+NaOH \xlongequal{\quad} Na_2SO_3+H_2O$

$Na_2SO_3+S \xlongequal{\quad} Na_2S_2O_3$

例 16.4　按如下要求，制备 H_2S，SO_2 和 SO_3，写出相关化学反应方程式。
(1) 化合物中 S 的氧化数不变的反应；
(2) 化合物中 S 的氧化数变化的反应。

解:(1) S 氧化数不变的反应:

H_2S 用金属硫化物与非氧化性的稀酸反应,例如

$$FeS + 2HCl(稀) \xlongequal{} FeCl_2 + H_2S\uparrow$$

SO_2 用 Na_2SO_3 与稀盐酸反应:

$$Na_2SO_3 + 2HCl \xlongequal{} 2NaCl + SO_2\uparrow + H_2O$$

SO_3 用加热分解硫酸盐的方法:

$$CaSO_4 \xlongequal{\triangle} CaO + SO_3\uparrow$$

(2) S 氧化数变化的反应:

H_2S 用 NaI 与浓 H_2SO_4 反应:

$$8NaI + 9H_2SO_4(浓) \xlongequal{} 4I_2 + 8NaHSO_4 + H_2S + 4H_2O$$

SO_2 ① 金属单质与浓硫酸反应:

$$Zn + 2H_2SO_4(浓) \xlongequal{} ZnSO_4 + SO_2\uparrow + 2H_2O$$

② 单质 S 或硫化物矿在空气中燃烧:

$$S + O_2 \xlongequal{} SO_2$$

$$4FeS_2 + 11O_2 \xlongequal{} 2Fe_2O_3 + 8SO_2$$

SO_3 以 V_2O_5 为催化剂用 SO_2 与 O_2 反应:

$$2SO_2 + O_2 \xlongequal[\triangle]{V_2O_5} 2SO_3$$

例 16.5 用化学反应方程式表示下列制备过程。

(1) 以碳酸钠和硫黄为原料制备硫代硫酸钠;

(2) 工业上以硫化钠、碳酸钠和二氧化硫为原料制备硫代硫酸钠;

(3) 工业上以硫酸和硫酸铵为原料制备过二硫酸铵。

解:(1) 将部分硫黄在空气中燃烧制备 SO_2:

$$S + O_2 \xlongequal{} SO_2$$

将 SO_2 通入 Na_2CO_3 溶液中,发生反应:

$$SO_2 + Na_2CO_3 \xlongequal{} Na_2SO_3 + CO_2$$

使硫黄粉与沸腾的 Na_2SO_3 溶液反应,制备 $Na_2S_2O_3$:

$$S + Na_2SO_3 \xlongequal{} Na_2S_2O_3$$

(2) 将 Na_2S 和 Na_2CO_3 按摩尔比 2:1 配成溶液,然后向其中通入 SO_2 制备 $Na_2S_2O_3$,发生如下反应:

$$2Na_2S + Na_2CO_3 + 4SO_2 \xlongequal{} 3Na_2S_2O_3 + CO_2$$

(3) 将硫酸和硫酸铵溶液混合,制备硫酸氢铵:

$$H_2SO_4 + (NH_4)_2SO_4 \longrightarrow 2NH_4HSO_4$$

以 Pt 为电极，电解 NH_4HSO_4 的饱和溶液，制备过二硫酸铵：

$$2NH_4HSO_4 \longrightarrow (NH_4)_2S_2O_8 + H_2\uparrow$$

例 16.6 试解释由同种元素原子构成的 O_3 分子为什么具有极性？

解： 分子的极性可以由分子的偶极矩来衡量。分子的偶极矩等于分子内各种因素所产生的分偶极矩的矢量和。

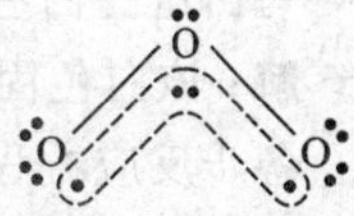

O_3 分子的结构：中心氧原子用 sp^2 杂化轨道与配位氧键连，整个分子还有一个大 π 键(Π_3^4)，故 O_3 分子呈 V 形，如图所示。

由此可见，虽然 O_3 分子中成键原子之间的元素电负性差为零，但中心原子有一孤电子对，而配位氧各有两对孤电子对，这些孤电子对产生偶极不能完全抵消。此外，O_3 的大 π 键对分子极性也有贡献。所以 O_3 分子具有极性，其偶极矩 μ 为 1.93×10^{-30} C·m。

例 16.7 由硫酸盐构成的矾通常有两种形式，试给出通式并各举一例。

解： 一类的组成符合通式：$M_2^ISO_4\cdot M^{II}SO_4\cdot 6H_2O$。式中 M^I 为 NH_4^+，Na^+，K^+，Rb^+，Cs^+；M^{II} 为 Fe^{2+}，Co^{2+}，Ni^{2+}，Zn^{2+}，Cu^{2+}，Hg^{2+}。如著名的莫尔盐 $(NH_4)_2SO_4\cdot FeSO_4\cdot 6H_2O$，镁钾矾 $K_2SO_4\cdot MgSO_4\cdot 6H_2O$。

另一类的组成符合通式：$M_2^ISO_4\cdot M_2^{III}(SO_4)_3\cdot 24H_2O$。式中 M^{III} 为 V^{3+}，Cr^{3+}，Fe^{3+}，Co^{3+}，Al^{3+}，Ga^{3+} 等。如明矾 $K_2SO_4\cdot Al_2(SO_4)_3\cdot 24H_2O$，铬矾 $K_2SO_4\cdot Cr_2(SO_4)_3\cdot 24H_2O$。

例 16.8 为什么硫酸盐的热稳定性比碳酸盐高，而硅酸盐的热稳定性更高。

解： 对于相同金属离子的硫酸盐和碳酸盐来说，金属离子的极化能力相同，含氧酸根(SO_4^{2-}，CO_3^{2-})电荷相同，且半径都较大。因此，两者热稳定性差异主要是含氧酸根的中心原子氧化数的不同。一般情况，中心原子氧化数越大，抵抗金属离子的极化能力越强，含氧酸盐越稳定。因此中心原子氧化数为+6 的硫酸盐的稳定性比中心原子氧化数+4 的碳酸盐高。

硅酸盐热稳定性更高的原因与前两种盐不同，前两种盐分解均产生气体如 SO_2，CO_2，是熵驱动反应。而硅酸盐分解反应无气体产生，除金属氧化物外，就是 SiO_2，反应的熵增很少。这就是硅酸盐热稳定性高的原因。

例 16.9 某溶液中可能含 Cl^-，S^{2-}，SO_3^{2-}，$S_2O_3^{2-}$，SO_4^{2-} 离子，进行下列实验并产生如下的实验现象：

(1) 向一份未知液中加过量 $AgNO_3$ 溶液产生白色沉淀；

(2) 向另一份未知液中加入 $BaCl_2$ 溶液也产生白色沉淀；

(3) 取第三份未知液，用 H_2SO_4 酸化后加入溴水，溴水不褪色。

试判断哪几种离子存在？哪几种离子不存在？哪几种离子可能存在？

解： 由实验(1) 可知：溶液中不含 S^{2-}，$S_2O_3^{2-}$，因为：Ag_2S 为黑色沉淀，$Ag_2S_2O_3$ 虽为白色沉淀，但其不稳定会分解，由白色转变为黑色的 Ag_2S。

由实验(2) 可知：溶液中应含有 SO_4^{2-}。

由实验(3) 酸化的溴水不褪色，说明溶液中不含 S^{2-}，$S_2O_3^{2-}$ 及 SO_3^{2-} 具有还原性的离子。

由此可得出结论：SO_4^{2-} 肯定存在，S^{2-}，$S_2O_3^{2-}$，SO_3^{2-} 肯定不存在，Cl^-可能存在。

例 16.10 有一种能溶于水的白色固体，其水溶液进行下列实验而产生如下的实验现象：

(1) 用铂丝沾少量液体在火焰上灼烧，产生黄色火焰；

(2) 它使酸化的 $KMnO_4$ 溶液褪色而产生无色溶液，该溶液与 $BaCl_2$ 溶液作用生成不溶于稀 HNO_3 的白色沉淀；

(3) 加入硫粉，并加热，硫溶解生成无色溶液，此溶液酸化时产生乳白色或浅黄色沉淀；此溶液也能使 KI_3 溶液褪色，也能溶解 AgCl 或 AgBr 沉淀。

写出这一白色固体的分子式，并完成各步反应方程式。

解： 该白色固体的化学式为 Na_2SO_3。

各步反应方程式如下：

$$5SO_3^{2-}+2MnO_4^-+6H^+ = 5SO_4^{2-}+2Mn^{2+}+3H_2O$$

$$SO_4^{2-}+Ba^{2+} = BaSO_4$$

$$Na_2SO_3+S = Na_2S_2O_3$$

$$Na_2S_2O_3+2HCl = 2NaCl+S\downarrow+SO_2\uparrow+H_2O$$

$$2Na_2SO_3+I_2 = Na_2S_2O_4+2NaI$$

$$AgBr+2Na_2S_2O_3 = Na_3[Ag(S_2O_3)_2]+NaBr$$

例 16.11 一种盐 A 溶于水后，加入稀 HCl，有刺激性气体 B 产生，同时有黄色沉淀 C 析出，气体 B 能使 $KMnO_4$ 溶液褪色；若通 Cl_2 于 A 溶液，Cl_2 即消失并得到溶液 D，D 与钡盐作用，即产生白色沉淀 E。

试写出字母 A，B，C，D 和 E 所代表的物质的化学式，并用化学反应方程式表示各过程。

解： A—$Na_2S_2O_3$； B—SO_2； C—S； D—Na_2SO_4，H_2SO_4； E—$BaSO_4$。

各步反应方程式如下：

$$Na_2S_2O_3+2HCl = 2NaCl+S\downarrow+SO_2\uparrow+H_2O$$

$$5SO_2+2MnO_4^-+2H_2O = 5SO_4^{2-}+2Mn^{2+}+4H^+$$

$$Na_2S_2O_3+4Cl_2+5H_2O = Na_2SO_4+H_2SO_4+8HCl$$

$$SO_4^{2-}+Ba^{2+} = BaSO_4\downarrow$$

例 16.12 将无色钠盐溶于水得无色溶液 A，用 pH 试纸检验知 A 显酸性。向 A 中滴加 $KMnO_4$ 溶液，则紫红色褪去，说明 A 被氧化为 B，向 B 中加入 $BaCl_2$ 溶液得不溶于强酸的白色沉淀 C。向 A 中加入稀盐酸有无色气体 D 放出，将 D 通入 $KMnO_4$ 溶液则又得到无色的 B。向含有淀粉的 KIO_3 溶液中滴加少许 A 则溶液立即变蓝，说明有 E 生成，A 过量时蓝色消失得无色溶液。

试写出字母 A，B，C，D 和 E 所代表的物质的化学式，并用化学反应方程式表示各过程。

解： A—$NaHSO_3$； B—SO_4^{2-}； C—$BaSO_4$； D—SO_2； E—I_2。

各步反应方程式如下：

$$HSO_3^- = H^+ + SO_3^{2-}$$

$$5HSO_3^-+2MnO_4^-+H^+ = 5SO_4^{2-}+2Mn^{2+}+3H_2O$$

$$SO_4^{2-}+Ba^{2+} = BaSO_4\downarrow$$

$$HSO_3^-+H^+ = SO_2\uparrow+H_2O$$

$$5SO_2+4MnO_4^-+4H_2O = 5SO_4^{2-}+2Mn^{2+}+4H^+$$

$$2IO_3^-+5HSO_3^- = I_2+5SO_4^{2-}+H_2O+3H^+$$

第二部分 习题

一、选择题

16.1 常温下最稳定的晶体硫的分子式为

(A) S_2； (B) S_4； (C) S_6； (D) S_8。

16.2 下列物质中酸性最强的是

(A) H_2S； (B) H_2SO_3； (C) H_2SO_4； (D) $H_2S_2O_7$。

16.3 干燥 H_2S 气体，可选用的干燥剂是

(A) 浓 H_2SO_4； (B) KOH； (C) P_2O_5； (D) $CuSO_4$。

16.4 少量 H_2O_2 与 H_2S 反应的主要产物是

(A) H_2SO_4； (B) H_2SO_3； (C) $H_2S_2O_3$； (D) S。

16.5 下列物质中，只有还原性的是

(A) $Na_2S_2O_3$； (B) Na_2S； (C) Na_2SO_3； (D) Na_2S_2。

16.6 下列四个电极反应中，$E^\ominus$ 值最大的是

(A) $H_2O_2+2H^++2e^- \Longrightarrow 2H_2O$； (B) $HO_2^-+H_2O+2e^- \Longrightarrow 3OH^-$；

(C) $O_2+2H^++2e^- \Longrightarrow H_2O_2$； (D) $O_2+H_2O+2e^- \Longrightarrow HO_2^-+OH^-$。

16.7 为使已变暗的古油画恢复原来的白色，使用的方法为

(A) 用 SO_2 气体漂白； (B) 用稀 H_2O_2 溶液擦洗；

(C) 用氯水擦洗； (D) 用 O_3 漂白。

16.8 关于 O_3 的下列叙述中正确的是

(A) O_3 比 O_2 稳定； (B) O_3 是非极性分子；

(C) O_3 是顺磁性物质； (D) O_3 比 O_2 的氧化性强。

16.9 下列叙述中不正确的是

(A) H_2O_2 分子构型为直线形； (B) H_2O_2 是弱酸；

(C) H_2O_2 既有氧化性又有还原性；

(D) H_2O_2 和 $K_2Cr_2O_7$ 的酸性溶液反应生成 CrO_5。

16.10 下列分子或离子中，属于平面三角形构型的是

(A) SO_3； (B) O_3； (C) ICl_3； (D) H_3O^+。

16.11 下列分子中，结构和中心原子杂化类型都与 O_3 相同的是

(A) SO_3； (B) SO_2； (C) CO_2； (D) Cl_2O。

16.12 下列化合物中，在标准状态下氧化能力最弱的是

(A) H_2SO_3； (B) H_2SO_4； (C) $H_2S_2O_8$； (D) H_2O_2。

16.13 下列各对物质中，能发生反应的是

(A) CuS 和 HCl； (B) Ag 和 HCl； (C) $AlCl_3$ 和 H_2S； (D) Na_2SO_3 和 I_2。

16.14 下列化合物中，与 H_2S 和 HNO_3 都能发生氧化还原反应的是

(A) $FeCl_3$； (B) SO_2； (C) KI； (D) SO_3。

16.15 下列离子的溶液与 Na_2S 溶液反应，生成黄色沉淀的一组是

(A) Fe^{3+}，Bi^{3+}； (B) Cd^{2+}，Fe^{3+}； (C) Pb^{2+}，As^{3+}； (D) Sn^{4+}，Cd^{2+}。

16.16 下列各组硫化物中，难溶于稀盐酸，但能溶于浓盐酸的是

(A) Bi_2S_3 和 ZnS； (B) CuS 和 Sb_2S_3；

(C) CdS 和 SnS； (D) As_2S_3 和 HgS。

16.17 下列硫化物中，既能溶于 Na_2S 溶液又能溶于 Na_2S_2 溶液的是

(A) ZnS； (B) SnS； (C) Sb_2S_3； (D) HgS。

16.18 下列硫化物中，不溶于 Na_2S_2 溶液的是

(A) SnS； (B) As_2S_3； (C) Sb_2S_3； (D) ZnS。

16.19 按酸性由强至弱排列，顺序正确的是

(A) H_2Te，H_2S，H_2Se； (B) H_2Se，H_2Te，H_2S；

(C) H_2Te，H_2Se，H_2S； (D) H_2S，H_2Se，H_2Te。

16.20 用于制备 $K_2S_2O_8$ 的方法是

(A) 酸性条件下以 $KMnO_4$ 氧化 K_2SO_4； (B) 用 Cl_2 氧化 K_2SO_4；

(C) 用 H_2O_2 氧化 $K_2S_2O_3$； (D) 电解 $KHSO_4$ 溶液。

二、填空题

16.21 比较大小：

(1) 氧化性 O_3 ____ O_2，O_3 ____ H_2O_2，SO_2 ____ SO_3，O_2 ____ SO_3。

(2) 稳定性 O_3 ____ O_2，SO_2 ____ SO_3，Na_2SO_3 ____ Na_2SO_4。

16.22 H_2O_2 分子中 O—O 键级为______，O_2 分子中 O—O 键级为______，O_3 分子中 O—O 键级为______。

16.23 在 SO_3 中，S 采取的杂化方式为______，而在 $(SO_3)_3$ 中，S 采取的杂化方式为______。

16.24 用<或>填空：

(1) 氧化性 H_2SO_3 ______ I_2； (2) 还原性 H_2SO_3 ______ I_2；

(3) 稳定性 $K_2S_2O_8$ ______ K_2SO_4； (4) 酸性 H_5IO_6 ______ H_6TeO_6；

(5) 熔点 K_2SO_4 ______ K_2S。

16.25 给出下列离子的结构式。

硫代硫酸根 ________；过二硫酸根________；

连二亚硫酸根________；连四硫酸根________。

16.26 向各离子浓度均为 0.1 mol·dm^{-3} 的 Mn^{2+}，Zn^{2+}，Cu^{2+}，Ag^+，Hg^{2+}，Pb^{2+} 混合溶液中通入 H_2S，可被沉淀的离子有________。

16.27 若除去氢气中少量的 SO_2，H_2S 和水蒸气，应将氢气先通过______溶液，再通过______。

16.28 硫化物 ZnS，CuS，MnS，SnS，HgS 中，易溶于稀盐酸的是______；不溶于稀盐酸，但溶于浓盐酸的是______；不溶于浓盐酸，但可溶于硝酸的是______；只溶于王水的是______。

16.29 $AgNO_3$ 溶液与过量的 $Na_2S_2O_3$ 溶液反应生成______色的______。过量的 $AgNO_3$ 溶液

与 $Na_2S_2O_3$ 溶液反应生成______色的______，后变为______色的______。

16.30　$NaHSO_3$ 受热分解产物为______；$Na_2S_2O_8$ 受热分解产物为________；Na_2SO_3 受热分解产物为______。

16.31　H_2S 水溶液长期放置后变混浊，原因是________。

16.32　酸化某溶液析出 S 并放出 SO_2，则原溶液中的含硫化合物可能为______，______，______或______。

16.33　写出下列物质的化学式。

(1) 方铅矿______；(2) 朱砂______；(3) 闪锌矿______；(4) 黄铜矿______；

(5) 黄铁矿______；(6) 芒硝______；(7) 海波______；(8) 保险粉______。

16.34　比较组成为 $M_2S_2O_x$ 的三种盐，它们各自符合下面所述的某些性质：

(1) 阴离子以 —O—O— 键为特征；

(2) 阴离子以 S—S 键为特征；

(3) 阴离子以 S—O—S 键为特征；

(4) 它是由酸式硫酸盐缩合而成；

(5) 它是由酸式硫酸盐阳极氧化形成；

(6) 它是由亚硫酸盐水溶液与硫反应形成；

(7) 它的水溶液使溴化银溶解；

(8) 它的水溶液与氢氧化物(MOH)反应生成硫酸盐；

(9) 在水溶液中能把 Mn^{2+} 氧化成 MnO_4^-。

试将 x 的正确数值填入下表中角标括号内，并将上述各性质以序号填入相应盐的横栏内：

$M_2S_2O_{(\ )}$			
$M_2S_2O_{(\ )}$			
$M_2S_2O_{(\ )}$			

16.35　给出下列化合物的颜色：

ZnS ______；MnS ______；CdS ______；SnS ______；As_2S_3 ______；

As_2S_5 ______；Sb_2S_3 ______；Sb_2S_5 ______；$Ag_2S_2O_3$ ______；PbS_2O_3 ______。

三、完成并配平下列反应方程式

16.36　H_2S 通入 H_2O_2 溶液中。

16.37　H_2S 通入酸性 $KClO_3$ 溶液中。

16.38　向 Na_2S 和 Na_2SO_3 混合溶液中加入稀酸。

16.39　向 $Na_2S_2O_3$ 溶液中加入碘水。

16.40　将 SO_2 通入氯水中。

16.41　向 H_2O_2 溶液中加入酸性 $KMnO_4$ 溶液。

16.42　用 O_3 处理 PbS。

16.43　硫代硫酸钠溶液加入氯水中。

16.44 向溴水中通入少量 H_2S。

16.45 向 Na_2S_2 溶液中滴加盐酸。

16.46 将 Cr_2S_3 投入水中。

16.47 过氧化钠分别与冷水、热水作用。

16.48 向 HI 溶液中通入 O_3。

16.49 向 $Ag(S_2O_3)_2^{3-}$ 的弱酸性溶液中通入 H_2S。

四、简答题

16.50 回答下列问题。

(1) 为什么 O_2 具有顺磁性,而 O_3 具有反磁性?

(2) SO_2Cl_2 易水解,SF_6 不水解;

(3) 从分子结构角度解释为什么 O_3 比 O_2 的氧化能力强?

16.51 已知 O_2F_2 结构与 H_2O_2 相似,但 O_2F_2 中 O—O 键长 121 pm,H_2O_2 中 O—O 键长 148 pm,请给出 O_2F_2 的结构,并解释两个化合物中 O—O 键长不同的原因。

16.52 回答下列问题。

(1) 给出 SO_2,SO_3,O_3 分子中离域大 π 键类型;

(2) 叙述 SO_3,H_2SO_4 和发烟硫酸的相互关系;

(3) 为什么 $SOCl_2$ 既可做 lewis 酸又可做 Lewis 碱?

(4) 给出 SOF_2,$SOCl_2$,$SOBr_2$ 分子中 S—O 键强度的变化规律,并解释原因。

16.53 由 H_2S 的制备过程来分析 H_2S 的性质。

16.54 有四种试剂:Na_2SO_4,Na_2SO_3,$Na_2S_2O_3$,$Na_2S_2O_6$,其标签已脱落,设计一简便方法鉴别它们。

16.55 现有五瓶无色溶液分别是 Na_2S,Na_2SO_3,$Na_2S_2O_3$,Na_2SO_4,$Na_2S_2O_8$,试加以确认,并写出有关的反应方程式。

16.56 将硫黄粉、石灰与水混合,经煮沸、摇匀制得石硫合剂。试解释石硫合剂呈橙色至樱桃红色的原因,并写出相应的反应方程式。

16.57 试设计方案分离下列各组离子。

(1) Ag^+,Pb^{2+},Fe^{2+};　　(2) Al^{3+},Zn^{2+},Fe^{3+},Cu^{2+}。

16.58 为什么不宜采用高温浓缩的办法获得 $NaHSO_3$ 晶体?

16.59 试用价层电子对互斥理论判断 SOF_2 和 $SOCl_2$ 的空间构型。说明在 O 原子和 S 原子之间的 d—pπ 配键是怎么形成的。试比较两者的 d—pπ 配键的强弱。

16.60 将 0.108 g 白色固体 A 置于干燥箱中于 105 ℃干燥一段时间后,得到 0.72 g 黄色固体 B。将 B 在 400 ℃加热,失重 0.16 g,得到白色固体 C。将 A 与 KI 晶体混合后熔于稀盐酸得到黄色溶液 D。向溶液 D 中加入过量固体 C,则溶液变成无色溶液 E 和白色沉淀 F。少量 C 溶于水后加入 Na_2CO_3 溶液有白色沉淀 G 生成。试确定 A,B,C,D,E,F 各为何物质?

16.61 无色晶体 A 溶于 NaOH 溶液后加热有无色气体 B 放出。将 B 通入 $AgNO_3$ 溶液先有棕黑色沉淀析出,过量后黑色沉淀溶解得无色溶液 C。向 C 中加入盐酸有白色沉淀 D 生成。向 A 的水溶液中加入 KI 溶液则溶液变黄，再加入 $BaCl_2$ 溶液则有不溶于酸的白色沉淀 E 生成。试确定 A，B，C，D，E 各为何物质？

16.62　向白色固体钾盐 A 中加入酸 B 有紫黑色固体 C 和无色气体 D 生成，C 微溶于水，但易溶于 A 的溶液中得棕黄色溶液 E，向 E 中加入 NaOH 溶液得无色溶液 F。将气体 D 通入 $Pb(NO_3)_2$ 溶液得黑色沉淀 G。若将 D 通入 $NaHSO_3$ 溶液则有乳白色沉淀 H 析出。回答 A，B，C，D，E，F，G，H 各为何物质。

16.63　向无色溶液 A 中加入 HI 溶液有无色气体 B 和黄色沉淀 C 生成，C 在 KCN 溶液中部分溶解得无色溶液 D，向 D 中通入 H_2S 时析出黑色沉淀 E，E 不溶于浓盐酸。若向 A 中加入 KI 溶液有黄色沉淀 F 生成，将 F 投入 KCN 溶液则 F 全部溶解。请给出 A，B，C，D，E，F 所代表的物质。

16.64　将无水钠盐固体 A 溶于水，滴加稀硫酸有无色气体 B 生成，B 通入碘水溶液，则碘水褪色，说明 B 转化为 C。晶体 A 在 600 ℃以上加热至恒重后生成混合物 D。用 pH 试纸检验发现 D 的水溶液的碱性大大高于 A 的水溶液。向 D 的水溶液中加 $CuCl_2$ 溶液，有不溶于盐酸的黑色沉淀 E 生成。若用 $BaCl_2$ 溶液代替 $CuCl_2$ 进行实验，则有白色沉淀 F 生成，F 不溶于硝酸、氢氧化钠溶液及氨水。试写出字母 A，B，C，D，E 和 F 所代表的物质的化学式。

第 17 章

卤素

第一部分 例题

例 17.1 完成并配平下列反应方程式。

(1) $Cl_2 + HgO + H_2O =\!=\!=$

(2) $Br_2 + Na_2CO_3 =\!=\!=$

(3) $KBrO_3 + KBr + H_2SO_4 =\!=\!=$

(4) $CaSiO_3 + HF =\!=\!=$

(5) $KClO_3(s) \xlongequal{\triangle}$

(6) $NaCl(s) + NaHSO_4(s) \xlongequal{\triangle}$

(7) $NaBr + H_2SO_4$(浓) $=\!=\!=$

(8) $NaI + H_2SO_4$(浓) $=\!=\!=$

(9) $MnO_4^- + Cl^- + H^+ =\!=\!=$

(10) $FeBr_2 + Cl_2$(过量) $=\!=\!=$

解：(1) $2Cl_2 + 2HgO + H_2O =\!=\!= HgO\cdot HgCl_2 + 2HClO$

(2) $3Br_2 + 3Na_2CO_3 =\!=\!= NaBrO_3 + 5NaBr + 3CO_2\uparrow$

(3) $KBrO_3 + 5KBr + 3H_2SO_4 =\!=\!= 3Br_2 + 3K_2SO_4 + 3H_2O$

(4) $CaSiO_3 + 6HF =\!=\!= CaF_2 + SiF_4\uparrow + 3H_2O$

(5) $4KClO_3(s) \xlongequal{\triangle} 3KClO_4 + KCl$

(6) $NaCl(s) + NaHSO_4(s) \xlongequal{\triangle} Na_2SO_4(s) + HCl(g)$

(7) $2NaBr + 3H_2SO_4$(浓) $=\!=\!= Br_2 + 2NaHSO_4 + SO_2\uparrow + 2H_2O$

(8) $8NaI + 9H_2SO_4$(浓) $=\!=\!= 4I_2 + 8NaHSO_4 + H_2S\uparrow + 4H_2O$

(9) $2MnO_4^- + 10Cl^- + 16H^+ =\!=\!= 2Mn^{2+} + 5Cl_2\uparrow + 8H_2O$

(10) $2FeBr_2 + 3Cl_2$(过量) $=\!=\!= 2FeCl_3 + 2Br_2$

例 17.2 以反应方程式表示下列反应过程，并给出实验现象。

(1) 用过量 $HClO_3$ 处理 I_2；

(2) 氯水滴入 KBr 和 KI 混合溶液中；

(3) 向 KI 溶液中滴加 H_2O_2；

(4) 向酸性的 KIO_3 和淀粉混合溶液中滴加 Na_2SO_3 溶液；

(5) 将次氯酸钠溶液滴入硝酸铅溶液。

解：(1) $2HClO_3 + I_2 = 2HIO_3 + Cl_2\uparrow$

紫黑色的碘消失，并有气体放出。

(2) $Cl_2 + 2I^- = I_2 + 2Cl^-$

溶液先变成黄色或橙色。

$5Cl_2 + I_2 + 6H_2O = 10Cl^- + 2IO_3^- + 12H^+$

然后变成无色。

$Cl_2 + 2Br^- = 2Cl^- + Br_2$

最后溶液又变成黄色或橙色。

(3) $H_2O_2 + 2I^- + 2H^+ = I_2 + 2H_2O$

先观察到溶液由无色变成黄色。

$5H_2O_2 + I_2 = 2HIO_3 + 4H_2O$

$2HIO_3 + 5H_2O_2 = 6H_2O + I_2 + 5O_2\uparrow$

溶液由黄色变成无色，同时有气体生成。

(4) $2IO_3^- + 5SO_3^{2-} + 2H^+ = I_2 + 5SO_4^{2-} + H_2O$

溶液变蓝。

(5) $Pb^{2+} + ClO^- + 2OH^- = PbO_2\downarrow + Cl^- + H_2O$

有黑色沉淀析出。

例 17.3 以 NaCl 为基本原料制备下列化合物，写出各主要步骤的反应方程式。

(1) NaClO；　　(2) $KClO_3$；

(3) $HClO_4$；　　(4) $Ca(ClO)_2$。

解：(1) $2NaCl + 2H_2O \xlongequal{电解} 2NaOH + Cl_2\uparrow + H_2\uparrow$

$Cl_2 + 2NaOH = NaCl + NaClO + H_2O$

(2) $2NaCl + 2H_2O \xlongequal{电解} 2NaOH + Cl_2\uparrow + H_2\uparrow$

$3Cl_2 + 6KOH \xlongequal{\triangle} 5KCl + KClO_3 + 3H_2O$

将溶液冷却，$KClO_3$ 即沉淀析出。

(3) $2NaCl+2H_2O \xlongequal{电解} 2NaOH+Cl_2\uparrow+H_2\uparrow$

$3Cl_2+6KOH \xlongequal{\triangle} 5KCl+KClO_3+3H_2O$

$4KClO_3 \xlongequal{\triangle} 3KClO_4+KCl$

$KClO_4$ 溶解度比 KCl 小，可分离。

$$KClO_4+H_2SO_4 \xlongequal{} KHSO_4+HClO_4$$

减压蒸馏出 $HClO_4$。

(4) $2NaCl+2H_2O \xlongequal{电解} 2NaOH+Cl_2\uparrow+H_2\uparrow$

$2Cl_2+2Ca(OH)_2 \xlongequal{} Ca(ClO)_2+CaCl_2+2H_2O$

例 17.4 用反应方程式表示下列制备过程，并注明反应条件。

(1) 以萤石(CaF_2)为原料制取单质氟； (2) 从盐酸制备氯气；

(3) 从氯酸钾制备高氯酸； (4) 以盐酸为原料制备次氯酸；

(5) 由海水制备溴； (6) 从液溴制备溴酸钾水溶液。

解：(1) $CaF_2+H_2SO_4(浓) \xlongequal{\triangle} CaSO_4+2HF\uparrow$

向液态 HF 中加入强电解质 KF，形成导电性强且熔点较低的混合物。

电解 KHF_2 制单质 F_2。

阳极反应为

$$2F^- \xlongequal{} F_2+2e^-$$

得到的 F_2 压入镍制的特种钢瓶内储存。

(2) 使 MnO_2 与浓盐酸在加热的条件下反应：

$$MnO_2+HCl(浓) \xlongequal{\triangle} MnCl_2+Cl_2\uparrow+H_2O$$

(3) $4KClO_3 \xlongequal{\triangle} 3KClO_4+KCl$

$KClO_4$ 溶解度比 KCl 小，可分离。

$$KClO_4+H_2SO_4 \xlongequal{} KHSO_4+HClO_4$$

减压蒸馏出 $HClO_4$。

(4) 先加热浓 HCl 与 MnO_2 的混合物制备 Cl_2：

$$MnO_2+4HCl(浓) \xlongequal{\triangle} MnCl_2+Cl_2\uparrow+2H_2O$$

然后，Cl_2 歧化生成 HClO 和 HCl，向体系中加入 HgO 或 Ag_2O 以除去 H^+，使歧化反应能够进行：

$$2HgO+2Cl_2+H_2O \xlongequal{} HgO\cdot HgCl_2+2HClO$$

$$Ag_2O+2Cl_2+H_2O \xlongequal{} 2AgCl+2HClO$$

也可在 $CaCO_3$ 悬浮液中通入 Cl_2，利用 CO_3^{2-} 与形成的 H^+ 结合成 CO_2 使歧化反应能够进行，形成较高浓度的 HClO：

$$CaCO_3+2Cl_2+H_2O \xlongequal{} Ca^{2+}+2Cl^-+CO_2+2HClO$$

（5）先将海水日照浓缩，调成酸性，通入 Cl_2，将 Br^- 氧化成 Br_2：

$$2Br^-+Cl_2 \xlongequal{} 2Cl^-+Br_2$$

然后鼓入空气将 Br_2 吹出，用 Na_2CO_3 溶液吸收：

$$3Br_2+3Na_2CO_3 \xlongequal{} 5NaBr+NaBrO_3+3CO_2\uparrow$$

最后加酸制得 Br_2：

$$5HBr+HBrO_3 \xlongequal{} 3Br_2+3H_2O$$

（6）使液态的 Br_2 在 KOH 溶液中发生歧化反应：

$$3Br_2+6KOH \xlongequal{} 5KBr+KBrO_3+H_2O$$

反应温度应在 50～80 ℃之间。

例 17.5 试解释下列现象。

（1）I_2 溶解在 CCl_4 中得到紫色溶液，而 I_2 溶解在乙醚中却是红棕色溶液；

（2）I_2 难溶于水，却易溶于 KI 溶液；

（3）溴能从含有碘离子的溶液中取代出碘，碘又能从溴酸钾溶液中取代出溴；

（4）AlF_3 熔点高达 1 563 K，而 $AlCl_3$ 的熔点却只有 463 K；

（5）分别向 $FeCl_2$ 和 $NaHCO_3$ 溶液中加入碘水，碘水都不褪色。向二者的混合溶液中加入碘水，则褪色。

解：（1）一般认为溶液呈紫色表明溶解了的“碘分子”并未和溶剂分子发生较强的结合。CCl_4 为非极性溶剂，碘溶于 CCl_4 溶液后仍为分子状态，显示出碘单质在蒸气时的紫色。乙醚为极性溶剂，碘溶于乙醚时与溶剂间有溶剂合作用，形成的溶剂合物不再是其单质蒸气时的紫色，而是红棕色。

（2）I_2 的特征之一是能形成多碘化物 KI_3，所以可较好地溶解在 KI 水溶液中，其中 I_3^- 是直线形离子，在溶液中呈现黄色，并且在溶液中，I_2 或多碘化物的浓度越大，溶液的颜色越深。

（3）溴可从 KI 溶液中置换 I_2。

查表得 $E^\ominus(Br_2/Br^-)=1.07$ V，$E^\ominus(I_2/I^-)=0.54$ V。因为 $E^\ominus(Br_2/Br^-)>E^\ominus(I_2/I^-)$；$Br_2$ 有氧化性，I^- 有还原性，故

$$Br_2+2KI \xlongequal{} 2KBr+I_2$$

碘又能够从 $KBrO_3$ 溶液中置换出单质 Br_2。

查表得 $E^\ominus(BrO_3^-/Br_2)=1.48$ V，$E^\ominus(IO_3^-/I_2)=1.20$ V。因为 $E^\ominus(BrO_3^-/Br_2)>E^\ominus(IO_3^-/I_2)$，$BrO_3^-$ 作氧化剂，氧化单质 I_2：

$$I_2 + 2KBrO_3 = 2KIO_3 + Br_2$$

(4) 一般把元素电负性差值大于 1.7 的化合物看做是离子型化合物。若两种元素电负性的差值小于 1.7,可以判断它们之间主要形成共价键。

查得 Al,F,Cl 的电负性分别为 1.61,3.98 和 3.16。

可见,AlF_3 $\Delta\chi$ 大于 1.7 为典型的离子型化合物,其熔点很高;而 $AlCl_3$ $\Delta\chi$ 小于 1.7 为共价化合物,其熔点较低。

(5) 因为 $E^{\ominus}(Fe^{3+}/Fe^{2+}) > E^{\ominus}(I_2/I^-)$,所以 I_2 不能将 Fe^{2+} 氧化而褪色。

因为 $NaHCO_3$ 溶液的碱性较弱,所以碘在 $NaHCO_3$ 溶液中不发生歧化反应,故碘水也不褪色。

当向 $FeCl_2$ 和 $NaHCO_3$ 的混合溶液中加入碘水时,由于 Fe^{2+} 离子生成氢氧化物沉淀,将导致铁电对的电极电势数值发生改变:

$$Fe^{2+} + 2HCO_3^- = Fe(OH)_2\downarrow + 2CO_2$$

使 $E^{\ominus}[Fe(OH)_3/Fe(OH)_2] < E^{\ominus}(I_2/I^-)$,$Fe(OH)_2$ 能将 I_2 还原而褪色:

$$2Fe(OH)_2 + I_2 + 2HCO_3^- = 2Fe(OH)_3 + 2CO_2 + 2I^-$$

例 17.6 简要回答下列各题。

(1) 为什么单质氟不能用电解相应的氟化物水溶液来制备?

(2) F_2 的化学性质极为活泼,为什么电解 KHF_2 时可用 Cu,Ni 及其合金作电解槽?

(3) 向溴水中通入氯气,能否有 $HBrO_3$ 生成? 为什么?

(4) 为什么从氟到氯活泼性的变化有一个突变?

(5) 为什么不能用玻璃容器盛 NH_4F 溶液?

(6) 为什么很浓($5\sim15\ mol\cdot dm^{-3}$)的 HF 水溶液是强酸?

(7) 在卤化物中,为什么各种元素最高氧化态都是以氟化物存在,而不是以碘化物存在?

解: (1) 由于 OH^- 或 H_2O 比 F^- 更容易给出电子而被氧化,因此电解应在无水条件下进行。

(2) 因为在 Cu,Ni 及其合金的电解槽表面可形成致密的,且难溶的氟化物保护膜,阻止 F_2 与 Cu,Ni 进一步反应,故可以用铜、镍等作电解槽。

(3) 查得 $E^{\ominus}(BrO_3^-/Br_2) = 1.48\ V$, $E^{\ominus}(Cl_2/Cl^-) = 1.36\ V$。因为 $E^{\ominus}(Cl_2/Cl^-) < E^{\ominus}(BrO_3^-/Br_2)$,所以向溴水中通入氯气,不能生成 $HBrO_3$。

(4) 由于 F 的半径特别小,F_2 分子中孤电子对之间有较大的排斥作用,使得 F_2 分子的解离能远小于 Cl_2;由于 F 的半径特别小,形成的离子键非常强,远强于 Cl 形成的同类离子键;由于 F 的半径特别小,氟离子的水合时放出的热量远多于氯离子的水合时放出的热量。所以从氟到氯活泼性有一个突变。

(5) NH_4F 水解生成 NH_3 和 HF:

$$NH_4F + H_2O = NH_3\cdot H_2O + HF$$

HF 和 SiO_2 反应,使玻璃容器被腐蚀:

$$SiO_2 + 4HF = SiF_4\uparrow + 2H_2O$$

因而 NH_4F 只能储存在塑料瓶中。

(6) HF 是弱酸，在水溶液中的解离为

$$HF(aq) \rightleftharpoons H^+(aq) + F^-(aq) \quad (a) \quad K_a^\ominus = 6.3\times10^{-4}$$

当 HF 浓度增大时，其酸性增强，因为存在下列反应：

$$HF(aq) + F^-(aq) \rightleftharpoons HF_2^-(aq) \quad (b) \quad K^\ominus = 5.2$$

反应(b)$K^\ominus$ 值大，表明 HF_2^- 浓度较大，由于 F^- 的消耗，使反应(a)右移，所以氢离子浓度增大。

(7) 由于 F_2 的氧化能力最强，可以将其他元素氧化成最高价，所以元素形成氟化物往往表现最高价。如 SiF_4，SF_6，IF_7，OsF_8。而 I_2 与 F_2 相比氧化能力小得多，所以元素在形成碘化物时，往往表现较低的氧化态。如 CuI，Hg_2I_2。

同时 F 的原子半径很小，在形成高价氟化物时，排列在中心原子周围的空间效应有利；而原子半径较大的 I 在中心原子周围排列时空间效应不利。

例 17.7　将下列各组物质的有关性质按由大到小排序，并简要说明理由。

(1) 键解离能 Cl_2，Br_2，I_2；　　(2) 酸强度 HF，HCl，HBr，HI；

(3) 氧化性 HClO，$HClO_3$，$HClO_4$；　(4) 稳定性 ClO_2，I_2O_5。

解：(1) 从 Cl_2 到 Br_2 到 I_2 键的解离能逐渐下降。这与卤素原子的半径大小密切相关。从 Cl_2 到 Br_2 到 I_2，因为原子半径增大，在卤素双原子分子中，核对成键电子对的引力随原子半径增大而减小，所以导致解离能呈现逐渐下降的趋势。

(2) 氢卤酸的酸性由大到小排序为 HI，HBr，HCl，HF。除 HF 是弱酸外，其余均为强酸。

X^- 对 H^+ 的吸引能力弱，则解离度大，溶液的酸性强；反之，X^- 对 H^+ 的吸引能力强，则解离度小，溶液的酸性弱。这种吸引能力取决于 X^- 离子本身所带电荷和离子半径，即 X^- 离子本身的电子密度。按 I^-—Br^-—Cl^-—F^- 顺序，尽管离子所带电荷相同，而离子的半径逐渐减小，则电荷密度逐渐升高，于是 X^- 对 H^+ 的吸引能力逐渐增大。结果导致 HI，HBr，HCl，HF 在水溶液中的解离度依次减小，酸性逐渐减弱。

(3) 氯的含氧酸氧化性由大到小排序为 HClO，$HClO_3$，$HClO_4$。因为高价态含氧酸的中心原子抵抗 H^+ 的极化作用的能力较强，而且酸根的对称性高，其稳定性好。所以酸中的氧不易与中心脱离，酸不易被还原。

(4) I_2O_5 的稳定性远大于 ClO_2。I_2O_5 是碘酸的酸酐，I(Ⅴ)是常见的稳定价态，而 ClO_2 分子中 Cl(Ⅳ)是不稳定价态。因此常温常压下 I_2O_5 是较稳定的固体，ClO_2 是不稳定的气体。

例 17.8　某一试液能使 $KMnO_4$ 的酸性溶液褪色，但不能使碘-淀粉溶液褪色。试指出下列阴离子哪些可能存在于试液中。

(1) $S_2O_3^{2-}$；　(2) S^{2-}；　(3) Br^-；　(4) I^-；　(5) NO_2^-；　(6) SO_3^{2-}。

已知：$E^\ominus(MnO_4^-/Mn^{2+}) = 1.51$ V，$E^\ominus(I_2/I^-) = 0.535$ V。

解：查电极电势表得 $E^\ominus(S_4O_6^{2-}/S_2O_3^{2-}) = 0.08$ V，$E^\ominus(S/H_2S) = 0.142$ V，$E^\ominus(Br_2/Br^-) = 1.07$ V，$E^\ominus(NO_3^-/HNO_2) = 0.934$ V，$E^\ominus(SO_4^{2-}/H_2SO_3) = 0.172$ V。

因为 $E^\ominus(MnO_4^-/Mn^{2+})$ 大于 $E^\ominus(S_4O_6^{2-}/S_2O_3^{2-})$，$E^\ominus(S/H_2S)$，$E^\ominus(Br_2/Br^-)$，$E^\ominus(I_2/I^-)$，

$E^{\ominus}(NO_3^-/HNO_2)$和$E^{\ominus}(SO_4^{2-}/H_2SO_3)$。

所以，在酸性溶液中$S_2O_3^{2-}$，S^{2-}，Br^-，I^-，NO_2^-，SO_3^{2-}均能使$KMnO_4$褪色；而$E^{\ominus}(I_2/I^-)$只比$E^{\ominus}(S_4O_6^{2-}/S_2O_3^{2-})$，$E^{\ominus}(S/H_2S)$和$E^{\ominus}(SO_4^{2-}/H_2SO_3)$大，故$S_2O_3^{2-}$，$S^{2-}$，$SO_3^{2-}$能使碘-淀粉溶液褪色，而$Br^-$，$I^-$，$NO_2^-$则不能。

因此，Br^-，I^-，NO_2^-离子可能存在。

例 17.9 在淀粉碘化钾溶液中加入少量NaClO时，得到蓝色溶液，说明有A生成；加入过量NaClO时，蓝色褪去溶液变为无色，说明有B生成；然后酸化之并加入少量固体Na_2SO_3，则溶液的蓝色复原；当Na_2SO_3过量时蓝色又褪去成为无色溶液，说明有C生成；再加入$NaIO_3$溶液，溶液的蓝色又出现。试判断A，B和C各为何种物质，并写出各步反应的方程式。

解： A—I_2； B—KIO_3； C—KI。

各步反应方程式如下：

$$2I^- + ClO^- + H_2O \xlongequal{} I_2 + Cl^- + 2OH^-$$

$$I_2 + 5ClO^- + 2OH^- \xlongequal{} 2IO_3^- + 5Cl^- + H_2O$$

$$2IO_3^- + 5SO_3^{2-} + 2H^+ \xlongequal{} I_2 + 5SO_4^{2-} + H_2O$$

$$I_2 + SO_3^{2-} + H_2O \xlongequal{} 2I^- + SO_4^{2-} + 2H^+$$

$$5I^- + IO_3^- + 6H^+ \xlongequal{} 3I_2 + 3H_2O$$

例 17.10 白色固体A与油状无色液体B反应生成C。纯净的C为紫黑色固体，微溶于水，易溶于A的溶液中，得到红棕色溶液D。将D分成两份，一份中加入无色溶液E，另一份中通入黄绿色气体单质F，两份均褪色成无色透明溶液。无色溶液E遇酸生成淡黄色沉淀G，同时放出无色气体H。将气体F通入溶液E，在所得溶液中加入$BaCl_2$，有白色沉淀I生成，I不溶于HNO_3。

试写出字母A，B，C，D，E，F，G，H和I所代表的物质的化学式，并用化学反应方程式表示各过程。

解： A—KI； B—浓H_2SO_4； C—I_2； D—KI_3+I_2；

E—$Na_2S_2O_3$； F—Cl_2； G—S； H—SO_2； I—$BaSO_4$。

各步反应方程式如下：

$$8KI + 9H_2SO_4(浓) \xlongequal{} 4I_2 + H_2S\uparrow + 8KHSO_4 + 4H_2O$$

$$I_2 + KI \xlongequal{} KI_3$$

$$2Na_2S_2O_3 + I_2 \xlongequal{} Na_2S_4O_6 + 2NaI$$

$$I_2 + 5Cl_2 + 6H_2O \xlongequal{} 2IO_3^- + 10Cl^- + 12H^+$$

$$Na_2S_2O_3 + 2H^+ \xlongequal{} 2Na^+ + S\downarrow + SO_2\uparrow + H_2O$$

$$Na_2S_2O_3 + 4Cl_2 + 5H_2O \xlongequal{} Na_2SO_4 + H_2SO_4 + 8HCl$$

$$Ba^{2+} + SO_4^{2-} \xlongequal{} BaSO_4\downarrow$$

由于A中和E中的阳离子未加限定，故Na^+，K^+等均可考虑。

第二部分 习题

一、选择题

17.1 制备 F_2 实际所采用的方法是
(A) 电解 HF； (B) 电解 CaF_2； (C) 电解 KHF_2； (D) 电解 NH_4F。

17.2 下列各对试剂混合后能产生氯气的是
(A) NaCl 与浓 H_2SO_4； (B) NaCl 与 MnO_2；
(C) NaCl 与浓 HNO_3； (D) $KMnO_4$ 与浓 HCl。

17.3 欲由 KBr 固体制备 HBr 气体，应选择的酸是
(A) H_2SO_4； (B) HAc； (C) HNO_3； (D) H_3PO_4。

17.4 在热碱溶液中，Cl_2 的歧化产物为
(A) Cl^- 和 ClO^-； (B) Cl^- 和 ClO_2^-； (C) Cl^- 和 ClO_3^-； (D) Cl^- 和 ClO_4^-。

17.5 下列含氧酸中酸性最弱的是
(A) HClO； (B) HIO； (C) HIO_3； (D) HBrO。

17.6 下列含氧酸中，酸性最强的是
(A) $HClO_3$； (B) HClO； (C) HIO_3； (D) HIO。

17.7 下列酸中，酸性由强至弱排列顺序正确的是
(A) HF＞HCl＞HBr＞HI； (B) HI＞HBr＞HCl＞HF；
(C) $HClO＞HClO_2＞HClO_3＞HClO_4$； (D) $HIO_4＞HClO_4＞HBrO_4$。

17.8 下列有关卤素的论述不正确的是
(A) 溴可由氯作氧化剂制得； (B) 卤素单质都可由电解熔融卤化物得到；
(C) I_2 是最强的还原剂； (D) F_2 是最强的氧化剂。

17.9 下列含氧酸的氧化性递变不正确的是
(A) $HClO_4＞H_2SO_4＞H_3PO_4$； (B) $HBrO_4＞HClO_4＞H_5IO_6$；
(C) $HClO＞HClO_3＞HClO_4$； (D) $HBrO_3＞HClO_3＞HIO_3$。

17.10 下列物质中，关于热稳定性判断正确的是
(A) HF＜HCl＜HBr＜HI； (B) HF＞HCl＞HBr＞HI；
(C) $HClO＞HClO_2＞HClO_3＞HClO_4$； (D) $HCl＞HClO_4＞HBrO_4＞HIO_4$。

17.11 卤素的氧化物中，热稳定性最高的是
(A) ClO_2； (B) OF_2； (C) I_2O_5； (D) I_2O_7。

17.12 下列物质在酸性溶液中，能将 Mn^{2+} 氧化为 MnO_4^- 的是
(A) Cl_2； (B) $HClO_3$； (C) H_5IO_6； (D) H_2O_2。

二、填空题

17.13 F，Cl，Br 三元素中电子亲和能最大的是______，单质的解离能最小的是______。

17.14 给出下列物质的化学式。

(1) 萤石________； (2) 冰晶石________； (3) 氟磷灰石________；

(4) 光卤石________； (5) 光气________。

17.15 下列物质的颜色为：I_2________，I_2 溶于 CCl_4 中________，I_2 溶于乙醇中________，少量 I_2 溶于 KI 溶液中________。

A. 紫色； B. 紫黑色； C. 红棕色； D. 黄色。

17.16 将 $Cl_2(g)$ 通入热的 $Ca(OH)_2$ 溶液中，反应产物是________，低温下 Br_2 与 Na_2CO_3 溶液反应的产物是________，常温下 I_2 与 NaOH 溶液反应的产物是________。

17.17 反应 $KX(s)+H_2SO_4(浓) = KHSO_4+HX$，卤化物 KX 是指________和________。

17.18 导致氢氟酸的酸性与其他氢卤酸明显不同的因素主要是________小，而________特别大。

17.19 比较下列各对物质的热稳定性

(1) ClO_2 ______ I_2O_5； (2) $HClO_2$ ______ $HClO_4$；

(3) IF_7 ______ BrF_7； (4) $NaICl_4$ ______ $CsICl_4$。

17.20 含氧酸的酸性常随非羟基氧(或酰氧)原子数的增多而______。

17.21 氧化性 $HClO_3$ ________ HClO，酸性 $HClO_3$ ________ HClO。

17.22 Cl_2O 是______的酸酐，I_2O_5 是______的酸酐。

17.23 $HClO_4$ 的酸酐是______，它具有强________性，受热容易发生______。

17.24 高碘酸是________元________酸，其酸根离子的空间构型为______，其中碘原子的杂化方式为______，高碘酸具有强________性。

17.25 Cl_2O 和 ClO_2 分子结构均为______；但 ClO_2 分子中的 Cl—O 键长比 Cl_2O 分子中的 Cl—O 键长______；原因是______。

三、完成并配平反应方程式

17.26 将氟通入溴酸钠碱性溶液中。

17.27 次氯酸钠溶液与硫酸锰反应。

17.28 氯气通入碳酸钠热溶液中。

17.29 将 I_2O_5 和 KI 混合后加入稀硫酸。

17.30 向碘化亚铁溶液中滴加过量氯水。

17.31 向碘化铬溶液中加入次氯酸钠溶液。

17.32 用氢碘酸溶液处理氧化铜。

17.33 将氯气通入碘酸钾的碱性溶液中。

17.34 向 KI 溶液中滴加 KClO 溶液。

17.35 将 KClO 溶液与浓盐酸混合。

17.36 向 KClO 溶液中加入 $Pb(NO_3)_2$ 溶液。

四、简答题

17.37 氟的电子亲和能比氯小，但 F_2 却比 Cl_2 活泼，请解释原因。

17.38 以反应方程式表示反应过程,并给出实验现象:氯气长时间通入 KI 溶液中。

17.39 写出下列物质受热脱水的反应方程式。

(1) $BeCl_2 \cdot 4H_2O$; (2) $MgCl_2 \cdot 6H_2O$;

(3) $CaCl_2 \cdot 6H_2O$; (4) $FeCl_3 \cdot 6H_2O$。

17.40 实验室常用浓盐酸与 MnO_2 或 $KMnO_4$ 反应制备 Cl_2,试分析两种方法的优缺点。

17.41 用反应方程式表示下列制备过程并注明反应条件。

(1) 从盐酸制次氯酸; (2) 由氯化钾制备氧气。

17.42 实验室中制取少量 HBr 所采用的方法是将红磷与 H_2O 混合后滴加 Br_2。为什么不能将红磷与 Br_2 混合后滴加 H_2O 制备 HBr?

17.43 为什么 I_2 溶于 KI 溶液后可能呈现不同颜色?

17.44 给出实验现象和反应方程式,并加以说明

(1) 向 KI 溶液中滴加 H_2O_2 溶液;

(2) 向 HIO_3 溶液中滴加 Na_2SO_3 淀粉溶液;

(3) 向 Na_2SO_3 淀粉溶液中滴加 HIO_3 溶液。

17.45 用化学反应方程式表示下列提纯和鉴别过程。

(1) 工业碘中常常含有 ICl 或 IBr 杂质,试设计方案提纯碘,并说明方案的理论根据;

(2) 某 NaCl 样品中混有少量 NaBr,试设法提纯该样品;

(3) 一白色粉末,可能是 KCl,KBr 或 KI,试设计方案加以鉴别;

(4) 一固体样品,可能是 $KClO_4$ 或 K_5IO_6,试设计方案加以鉴别。

17.46 四支试管分别盛有 HCl,HBr,HI,H_2SO_4 溶液。如何鉴别?

17.47 漂白粉长期暴露于空气中为什么会失效?

17.48 有三瓶白色固体失去标签,它们分别是 KClO,$KClO_3$ 和 $KClO_4$,用什么方法加以鉴别?

17.49 比较 KI_3,$KIBr_2$ 和 KI_2Br 的稳定性并说明原因。

17.50 解释实验现象:

(1) 向 KI 溶液中滴加少量 KClO,溶液变黄。但向 KClO 溶液中滴加入少量 KI,溶液不变黄。

(2) 向 $KClO_3$ 溶液中加入少量浓盐酸,溶液不变黄;向浓盐酸中加入 $KClO_3$ 晶体,则溶液变黄。

(3) 向 $FeSO_4$ 溶液中加入碘水,碘水不褪色;再加入 NH_4F 溶液,则碘水褪色。

17.51 用价层电子对互斥理论,判断下列分子或离子的空间结构,并写出中心原子的杂化轨道类型。

(1) ClF_3; (2) BrF_5; (3) IBr; (4) IF_7; (5) ICl_4^-。

17.52 将易溶于水的钠盐 A 与浓硫酸混合后微热得无色气体 B。将 B 通入酸性高锰酸钾溶液后有气体 C 生成。将 C 通入另一钠盐 D 的水溶液中则溶液变黄、变橙,最后变为棕色,说明有 E 生成,向 E 中加入氢氧化钠溶液得无色溶液 F,当酸化该溶液时又有 E 出现。请给出 A,B,C,D,E,F 的化学式。

17.53 今有白色的钠盐晶体 A 和 B。A 和 B 都溶于水,A 的水溶液呈中性,B 的水溶液呈碱性。

A 溶液与 $FeCl_3$ 溶液作用，溶液呈棕色。A 溶液与 $AgNO_3$ 溶液作用，有黄色沉淀析出。晶体 B 与浓盐酸反应，有黄绿色气体产生，此气体同冷 NaOH 溶液作用，可得到含 B 的溶液。向 A 溶液中开始滴加 B 溶液时，溶液呈红棕色；若继续滴加过量的 B 溶液，则溶液的红棕色消失。试判断白色晶体 A 和 B 各为何物？

17.54 少量白色粉末 A 溶于水，溶液显酸性；向该溶液中加入少量淀粉溶液后滴加 Na_2SO_3 溶液，则溶液变蓝；Na_2SO_3 溶液过量溶液变无色。一定量的 A 在干燥的氮气流中于 200 ℃ 加热一段时间后，失重约 5%，冷却得到白色粉末 B。B 溶于水后蒸发、浓缩又析出 A。请给出相关反应方程式及 A 和 B 的化学式。

17.55 无色钾盐晶体 A 易溶于水。向盛 A 的水溶液试管中加入少量 CCl_4 和氯水，充分反应并摇动试管，试管下部变黄；然后加入少量 $FeSO_4$ 溶液，试管下部变无色；若再加入少量 KI 溶液并摇动试管，则管下部变红。向 A 的水溶液中加入 $AgNO_3$，有淡黄色沉淀生成，该沉淀易溶于 $Na_3S_2O_3$ 溶液。试给出 A 的化学式。

第 18 章

氢和稀有气体

第一部分　例题

例 18.1　完成并配平下列反应方程式。

(1) $H_2 + Na \xlongequal{高温}$

(2) $WO_3 + H_2 \xlongequal{高温}$

(3) $TiCl_4 + H_2 \xlongequal{高温}$

(4) $LiH + B_2H_6 \xlongequal{乙醚}$

(5) $LiH + AlCl_3 \xlongequal{高温}$

解：(1) $H_2 + 2Na \xlongequal{高温} 2NaH$

(2) $WO_3 + 3H_2 \xlongequal{高温} W + 3H_2O$

(3) $TiCl_4 + 2H_2 \xlongequal{高温} Ti + 4HCl$

(4) $2LiH + B_2H_6 \xlongequal{乙醚} 2LiBH_4$

(5) $4LiH + AlCl_3 \xlongequal{高温} LiAlH_4 + 3LiCl$

例 18.2　完成并配平下列反应方程式。

(1) $XeF_4 + Xe =\!=\!=$

(2) $XeF_2 + H_2 =\!=\!=$

(3) $XeF_4 + Hg =\!=\!=$

(4) $XeF_4(s) + Pt(s) =\!=\!=$

(5) $XeF_2 + I^- =\!=\!=$

解：(1) $XeF_4 + Xe =\!=\!= 2XeF_6$

(2) $XeF_2 + H_2 =\!=\!= Xe + 2HF$

(3) $XeF_4 + 4Hg =\!=\!= Xe\uparrow + 2Hg_2F_2$

(4) $XeF_4(s) + Pt(s) =\!=\!= Xe\uparrow + PtF_4$

(5) $XeF_2 + 2I^- =\!=\!= Xe\uparrow + I_2 + 2F^-$

例 18.3 根据价层电子对互斥理论，讨论下列分子的几何形状，并根据杂化轨道理论，讨论其中 Xe 的轨道杂化方式。

(1) XeF_6； (2) $XeOF_4$。

解：(1) XeF_6 中心 Xe 的周围共有 8＋1×6＝14 个电子，价层电子对数为 7，6 个配体，1 个孤电子对。可以认为 7 对电子呈五角双锥分布，其中 6 对成键电对呈变形八面体分布。孤电子对指向八面体一棱的中点或指向一面的中心。如图(a)所示。

Xe 的电子构型为 $5s^2 5p^6$，电子轨道图为

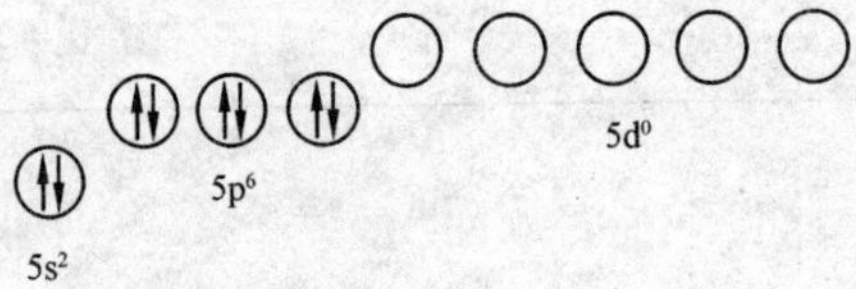

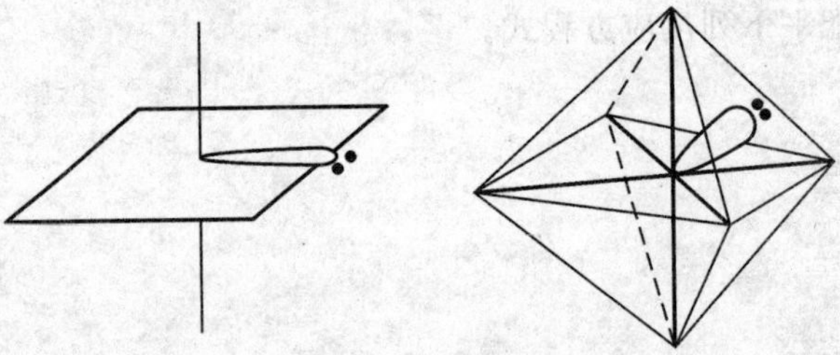

(a)

激发杂化后重排成

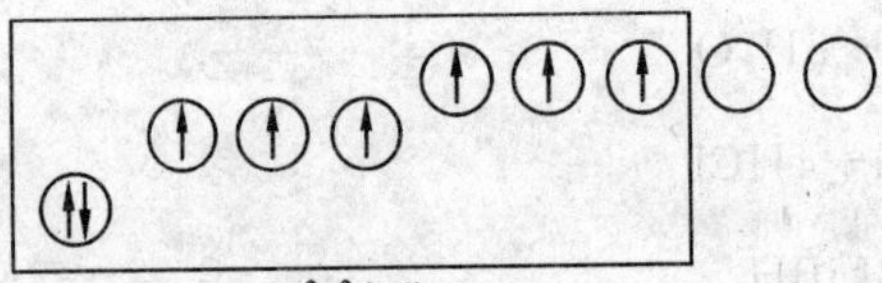

sp^3d^3杂化

形成 sp^3d^3 杂化轨道，其中 6 条单电子轨道呈八面体分布，与 6 个 F 的 2p 轨道成 σ 键。故 XeF_6 分子呈八面体构型。但由于孤电子对的存在，对于各 F 的斥力，使得八面体构型有些扭曲和改变。

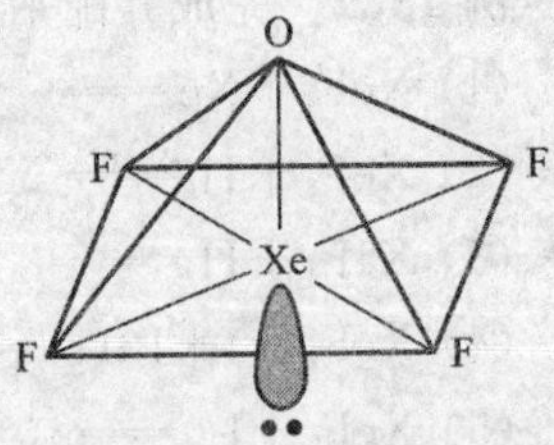

(b)

(2) $XeOF_4$ 中心 Xe 的周围共有 8＋0＋1×4＝12 个电子，价层电子对数为 6，5 个配体，1 个孤电子对。价层电子对构型为八面体，分子构型为四角锥形。如图(b)所示。

基态 Xe 的电子经激发重排形成 sp^3d^2 杂化

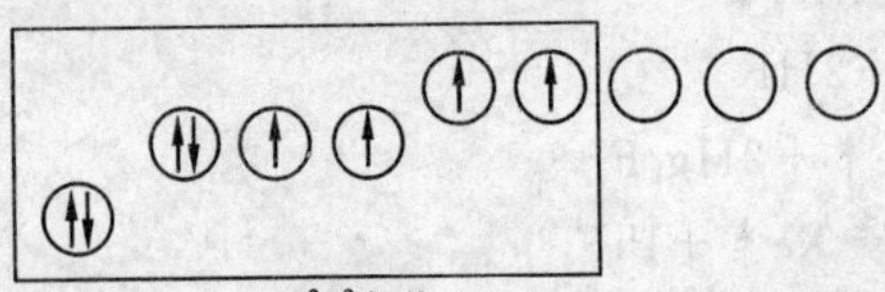

sp^3d^2杂化

6 条杂化轨道在空间呈八面体分布，其中 4 条有单电子的杂化轨道和 1 条有对电子的杂化轨道分别与 4 个 F 和 1 个 O 成键，而余下一条轨道中有孤对电子。

所以 $XeOF_4$ 的分子构型为四角锥形。

例 18.4　从分子轨道理论出发讨论下列分子和离子存在的可能性。

(1) HeH；(2) HeH^+；(3) He_2^+；(4) He_2。

解： HeH，HeH^+，He_2^+ 和 He_2 的分子轨道能级图见下图，它们存在的可能性可以由它们键级的大小决定，现分别讨论如下。

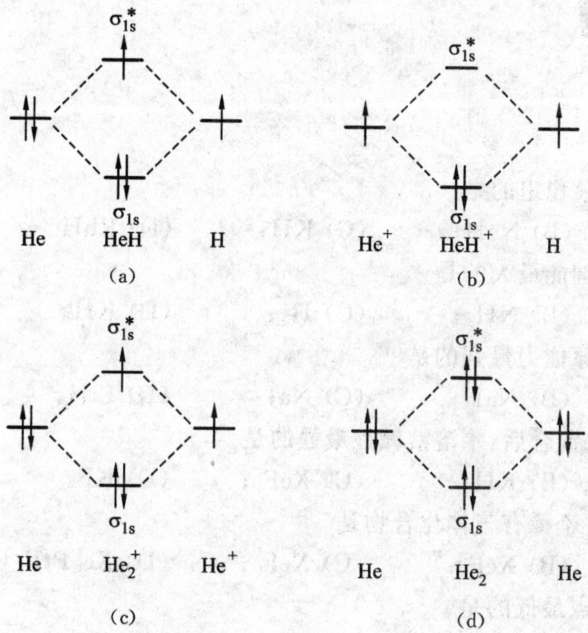

(1) HeH　由图(a)，HeH 的键级为$\frac{1}{2}$，He 与 H 之间键较弱，但键级不为 0，因此，HeH 有存在的可能性。

(2) HeH^+　由图(b)，HeH^+ 的键级为 1，He 与 H 之间形成共价单键，因此，HeH^+ 有存在的可能性。

(3) He_2^+　由图(c)，He_2^+ 的键级为$\frac{1}{2}$，共价键较弱，但键级不为 0，因此，He_2^+ 有存在的可能性。

(4) He_2　由图(d)，He_2 的键级为 0，He 与 He 之间不存在共价键，因此，He_2 没有存在的可能性。

例 18.5　根据 VSEPR 预言 $XeOF_2$，XeO_2F_2 和 XeO_3F_2 的结构。

解： 根据 VSEPR(价层电子对互斥理论)，Xe 有 8 个价电子，与 O 和 F 形成的几个化合物的结构见下表。

分子式	$XeOF_2$	XeO_2F_2	XeO_3F_2
Xe 价层电子对数	5	5	5
Xe 价层电子对构型	三角双锥	三角双锥	三角双锥
孤电子对数	2	1	0
分子结构	T 字形	变形四面体	三角双锥

第二部分 习题

一、选择题

18.1 下列氢化物中，最稳定的是

(A) LiH；(B) NaH；(C) KH；(D) RbH。

18.2 下列化合物中，键能最大的是

(A) HBr；(B) NH_3；(C) H_2；(D) KH。

18.3 下列物质中，还原能力最强的是

(A) HI；(B) NaH；(C) Na；(D) LiH。

18.4 下列化合物与水混合后，水溶液碱性最强的是

(A) HCl；(B) KH；(C) XeF_4；(D) KF。

18.5 合成出来的第一个稀有气体化合物是

(A) XeF_2；(B) XeF_4；(C) XeF_6；(D) $Xe[PtF_6]$。

18.6 下列气体中，沸点最低的是

(A) 氢；(B) 氦；(C) 氮；(D) 氧。

18.7 下列分子或离子中，中心原子的杂化类型相同的是

(A) XeO_3 和 $XeOF_4$；(B) XeF_2 和 XeF_4；

(C) $XeOF_4$ 和 XeO_6^{4-}；(D) XeF_4 和 XeO_4。

18.8 下列氢化物中，与水不发生氧化还原反应的是

(A) B_2H_6；(B) SiH_4；(C) PH_3；(D) KH。

18.9 下列制备方法中，能够得到比较纯净 H_2 的是

(A) 稀盐酸与锌金属作用；(B) 电解 25%的 NaOH 溶液；

(C) 催化裂解天然气；(D) 水蒸气通过红热的炭层。

二、填空题

18.10 水溶液中没有独立存在的 H^+，H^+ 的存在形式为________。

18.11 氢的同位素有 3 种，其名称分别是________、________、________，符号分别为________、________、________。

18.12 工业上用________通过红热的________来获得 H_2，分离产物中 H_2 的方法是将________

连同________一起通过红热的________，然后将混合物在 2×10^6 Pa 下用________洗涤，吸收掉________后得到 H_2。

18.13　稀有气体中，不能在常压下固化的是________，可用来制霓虹灯的是________，产生的白光特别明亮而用来舞台照明的灯填充了________气体。

18.14　XeF_6 不完全水解产物是________，完全水解产物是________。

18.15　按原子计，在海洋中丰度最高的元素是________。

三、完成并配平下列反应方程式。

18.16　$KH + H_2O =\!=\!=$

18.17　$TiCl_4 + NaH \xlongequal{高温}$

18.18　$UO_2 + CaH_2 \xlongequal{高温}$

18.19　$CO_2 + BaH_2 \xlongequal{高温}$

18.20　$LiAlH_4 + H_2O =\!=\!=$

18.21　$Na_4XeO_6 + MnSO_4 + H_2SO_4 =\!=\!=$

18.22　$XeF_4 + ClO_3^- =\!=\!=$

18.23　$XeF_2 + IF_5 =\!=\!=$

18.24　$XeF_4 + CF_3CF{=}CF_2 =\!=\!=$

18.25　$XeF_4 + SF_4 =\!=\!=$

18.26　$XeF_6 + SiO_2 =\!=\!=$

四、简答题

18.27　对于稀有气体化合物的研究，为什么多集中于元素氙？

18.28　合成 XeF_2，XeF_4 和 XeF_6 要采取哪些措施以保证目标产物较纯净？采取这些措施的理论依据是什么？

18.29　用价层电子对互斥理论讨论下列分子和离子的几何形状。

(1) XeF_2；　(2) XeF_4；　(3) XeF_6；　(4) XeO_3；　(5) $XeOF_4$。

第 19 章

铜副族元素和锌副族元素

第一部分　例题

例 19.1　完成并配平下列反应方程式。

(1) 金属铜在有空气存在的条件下与稀硫酸作用；

(2) 金属铜溶于氰化钠的水溶液；

(3) 在有铵离子存在的条件下，氢氧化铜溶于氨水；

(4) 向$[Ag(S_2O_3)_2]^{3-}$溶液中通入硫化氢气体；

(5) 溴化银在光的作用下分解；

(6) 金溶于王水。

解：(1) $2Cu+O_2+H_2SO_4(稀) = Cu(OH)_2 \cdot CuSO_4$

(2) $Cu+4CN^-+H_2O = [Cu(CN)_4]^{3-}+OH^-+\frac{1}{2}H_2\uparrow$

(3) $Cu(OH)_2+4NH_3 \cdot H_2O = [Cu(NH_3)_4]^{2+}+2OH^-+4H_2O$

(4) $2[Ag(S_2O_3)_2]^{3-}+H_2S+6H^+ = Ag_2S\downarrow+4S\downarrow+4SO_2+4H_2O$

(5) $2AgBr \xlongequal{h\nu} 2Ag+Br_2$

(6) $Au+4HCl+HNO_3 = HAuCl_4+NO\uparrow+2H_2O$

例 19.2　完成并配平下列反应的化学方程式。

(1) 向 $ZnCl_2$ 的稀溶液中不断滴加氢氧化钠溶液；

(2) 向 $CdCl_2$ 的稀溶液中不断滴加氢氧化钠溶液；

(3) 向 $ZnCl_2$ 的稀溶液中不断滴加氨水；

(4) 向 $Hg(NO_3)_2$ 溶液滴加氢氧化钠溶液；

(5) 向 $HgCl_2$ 中滴加氨水；

(6) 向 $Hg(NO_3)_2$ 溶液中不断滴加碘化钾溶液；

(7) 奈斯勒试剂与 NH_4^+ 作用；

(8) 氯化汞与亚锡离子反应。

解：(1) $ZnCl_2+2NaOH = Zn(OH)_2\downarrow+2NaCl$

$Zn(OH)_2+2NaOH = Na_2[Zn(OH)_4]$

(2) $CdCl_2+2NaOH = Cd(OH)_2\downarrow+2NaCl$

(3) $ZnCl_2 + 2NH_3 \cdot H_2O \xlongequal{} Zn(OH)_2 \downarrow + 2NH_4Cl$

$Zn(OH)_2 + 4NH_3 \cdot H_2O \xlongequal{} [Zn(NH_3)_4]^{2+} + 2OH^- + 4H_2O$

(4) $Hg(NO_3)_2 + 2NaOH \xlongequal{} HgO \downarrow + 2NaNO_3 + H_2O$

(5) $HgCl_2 + 2NH_3 \xlongequal{} Hg(NH_2)Cl \downarrow + NH_4Cl$

(6) $Hg^{2+} + 2I^- \xlongequal{} HgI_2 \downarrow$

$HgI_2 + 2I^- \xlongequal{} [HgI_4]^{2-}$

(7) $2[HgI_4]^{2-} + NH_4^+ + 4OH^- \xlongequal{}$ 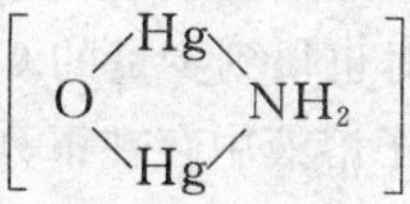 $I \downarrow + 7I^- + 3H_2O$

(8) $2HgCl_2 + Sn^{2+} \xlongequal{} Hg_2Cl_2 \downarrow + Sn^{4+} + 2Cl^-$

$Hg_2Cl_2 + Sn^{2+} \xlongequal{} 2Hg + Sn^{4+} + 2Cl^-$

例 19.3　$CuCl$,$AgCl$,Hg_2Cl_2 都是难溶于水的白色粉末,试区别这三种物质。

解:将不溶于水的 $CuCl$,$AgCl$ 和 Hg_2Cl_2 分别用氨水处理。

有灰黑色沉淀的是 Hg_2Cl_2:

$$Hg_2Cl_2 + 2NH_3 \xlongequal{} Hg(NH_2)Cl \downarrow (\text{白色}) + Hg \downarrow (\text{黑色}) + NH_4Cl$$

先变成无色溶液,后又变成蓝色的是 $CuCl$:

$$CuCl + 2NH_3 \xlongequal{} [Cu(NH_3)_2]^+ + Cl^-$$

无色的$[Cu(NH_3)_2]^+$不稳定,遇到空气则变成深蓝色的$[Cu(NH_3)_4]^{2+}$:

$$4[Cu(NH_3)_2]^+ + O_2 + 8NH_3 + 2H_2O \xlongequal{} 4[Cu(NH_3)_4]^{2+} + 4OH^-$$

溶解得到无色溶液的是 $AgCl$:

$$AgCl + 2NH_3 \xlongequal{} [Ag(NH_3)_2]^+ + Cl^-$$

例 19.4　如何用化学方法除去金属银中少量的金属铜杂质。

解:方法一　将银溶于硝酸,蒸发,浓缩,冷却得到 $AgNO_3$ 和 $Cu(NO_3)_2$ 混合物,控制加热温度在 200～400 ℃,$Cu(NO_3)_2$ 分解为 CuO,而 $AgNO_3$ 不分解。将 CuO 和 $AgNO_3$ 混合物溶于水,过滤除去不溶的 CuO,滤液经蒸发,浓缩,冷却得到 $AgNO_3$ 晶体,将 $AgNO_3$ 在较高温度下加热,分解产物为金属银。

方法二　将得到的 $AgNO_3$ 和 $Cu(NO_3)_2$ 混合物在较高温度下加热,$AgNO_3$ 分解产物为金属银,$Cu(NO_3)_2$ 分解为 CuO;用稀硫酸处理 Ag 和 CuO 混合物,CuO 溶解而除去。

例 19.5　试设计方案,分离下列各离子:

Cu^{2+},Ag^+,Zn^{2+},Hg_2^{2+}。

解:离子分离方案见下图。

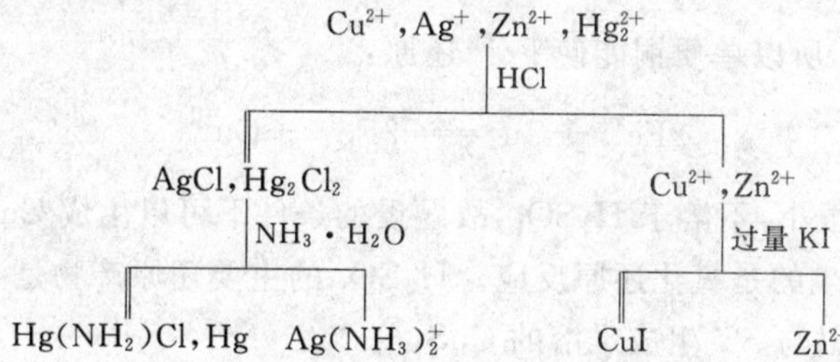

例 19.6 解释下列实验现象。

(1) $[Ag(NH_3)_2]Cl$ 遇到硝酸时，析出沉淀。

(2) 稀释 $CuCl_2$ 的浓溶液时，体系的颜色由黄色经绿色变为蓝色。

(3) 将 SO_2 通入 $CuSO_4$ 和 NaCl 的浓的混合溶液，有白色沉淀生成。

(4) 单质铁能使 Cu^{2+} 还原，单质铜却能使 Fe^{3+} 还原。

(5) 在用 H_2SO_4 酸化的 $CuSO_4$ 溶液中通入 H_2S，可以得到黑色的 CuS 沉淀。当 Cu 与浓硫酸共热，主要的含硫产物为 SO_2，同时也得到少量的 CuS 沉淀。

解： (1) 在 $[Ag(NH_3)_2]^+$ 配离子溶液中存在下列配合-解离平衡：

$$[Ag(NH_3)_2]^+ \rightleftharpoons Ag^+ + 2NH_3$$

当向该体系中加入硝酸时，有下列相互作用：

$$NH_3 + H^+ = NH_4^+$$

由于生成 NH_4^+，使配离子 $[Ag(NH_3)_2]^+$ 的解离得到加强。当 Ag^+ 离子浓度增加到足以形成 AgCl 沉淀时，则发生下式的反应：

$$[Ag(NH_3)_2]Cl + HNO_3 = AgCl\downarrow + NH_4NO_3$$

(2) 在很浓的 $CuCl_2$ 水溶液中，可形成黄色的 $[CuCl_4]^{2-}$，而 $CuCl_2$ 的稀溶液为浅蓝色，这是因为溶液中存在 $[Cu(H_2O)_4]^{2+}$ 的缘故：

$$\underset{(黄)}{[CuCl_4]^{2-}} + 4H_2O \rightleftharpoons \underset{(浅蓝)}{[Cu(H_2O)_4]^{2+}} + 4Cl^-$$

稀释 $CuCl_2$ 的浓溶液时，依次观察到黄色、黄绿色、绿色、蓝绿色和蓝色。颜色变化的原因是溶液中黄色的 $[CuCl_4]^{2-}$ 配离子和浅蓝色 $[Cu(H_2O)_4]^{2+}$ 配离子的相对量不同所致。

(3) 白色沉淀为氯化亚铜，为使 Cu^{2+} 转变为 Cu(Ⅰ)，在有还原剂 SO_2 存在的同时，还必须有 Cu(Ⅰ)的沉淀剂或络合剂 Cl^- 存在，以降低溶液中 Cu^+ 的浓度，使之成为难溶物或难解离的化合物：

$$2Cu^{2+} + SO_2 + 2Cl^- + 2H_2O = 2CuCl\downarrow + SO_4^{2-} + 4H^+$$

(4) 查得 Fe^{2+}/Fe 的 $E^\ominus(1) = -0.447$ V，Fe^{3+}/Fe^{2+} 的 $E^\ominus(2) = 0.771$ V，Cu^{2+}/Cu 的 $E^\ominus(3) = 0.34$ V。

因为 $E^\ominus(1) < E^\ominus(3)$，所以单质铁能使 Cu^{2+} 还原：

$$Fe + Cu^{2+} = Fe^{2+} + Cu$$

而 $E^\ominus(3) < E^\ominus(2)$，所以单质铜能使 Fe^{3+} 还原：

$$2Fe^{3+} + Cu = 2Fe^{2+} + Cu^{2+}$$

(5) CuS 的溶解度很小，不溶于 H_2SO_4，故题设的条件下可以生成 CuS 沉淀。

铜与浓硫酸之间发生的是氧化还原反应。H_2SO_4 的主要还原产物是 SO_2，但也有少量 S^{2-}。Cu 的氧化产物 Cu^{2+} 可以与 S^{2-} 生成难溶的 CuS。

例 19.7 化合物 A 是一种红色固体，它不溶于水，与稀硫酸反应生成蓝色的溶液 B 和暗红色沉淀 C。往 B 中加入氨水，生成 D 的深蓝色溶液，再加入适量 KCN，得无色溶液，说明有 E 生成。C 与浓硫酸反应生成 B，同时放出有刺激性气味的气体 F。

试写出字母 A，B，C，D，E 和 F 所代表的物质的化学式，并用化学反应方程式表示各过程。

解：A—Cu_2O； B—$CuSO_4$； C—Cu； D—$[Cu(NH_3)_4]SO_4$；

E—$[Cu(CN)_x]^{1-x}$（$x=2\sim4$）； F—SO_2。

各步反应方程式如下：

$$Cu_2O + H_2SO_4(稀) = Cu + CuSO_4 + H_2O$$

$$CuSO_4 + 4NH_3 \cdot H_2O = [Cu(NH_3)_4]SO_4 + 4H_2O$$

$$Cu(NH_3)_4^{2+} + (x+2)CN^- + 4H_2O = [Cu(CN)_x]^{1-x} + (CN)_2\uparrow + 4NH_3 \cdot H_2O\ (x=2\sim4)$$

$$Cu + 2H_2SO_4(浓) = CuSO_4 + SO_2\uparrow + 2H_2O$$

例 19.8 白色固体 A 不溶于水和氢氧化钠溶液，溶于盐酸形成无色溶液 B 和气体 C。向溶液 B 中滴加氨水先有白色沉淀 D 生成，而后 D 又溶于过量氨水中形成无色溶液 E；将气体 C 通入 $CdSO_4$ 溶液中得黄色沉淀，若将 C 通入溶液 E 中则析出固体 A。

试写出字母 A，B，C，D 和 E 所代表的物质的化学式，并用化学反应方程式表示各过程。

解：A—ZnS； B—$ZnCl_2$； C—H_2S；

D—$Zn(OH)_2$； E—$[Zn(NH_3)_4]^{2+}$。

各步反应方程式如下：

$$ZnS + 2HCl = ZnCl_2 + H_2S\uparrow$$

$$ZnCl_2 + 2NH_3 \cdot H_2O = Zn(OH)_2\downarrow + 2NH_4Cl$$

$$Zn(OH)_2 + 4NH_3 \cdot H_2O = [Zn(NH_3)_4](OH)_2 + 4H_2O$$

$$CdSO_4 + H_2S = CdS\downarrow + H_2SO_4$$

$$H_2S + [Zn(NH_3)_4](OH)_2 = ZnS\downarrow + 4NH_3 + 2H_2O$$

第二部分 习题

一、选择题

19.1 既易溶于稀氢氧化钠又易溶于氨水的是

(A) $Cu(OH)_2$； (B) Ag_2O； (C) $Zn(OH)_2$； (D) $Cd(OH)_2$。

19.2 下列化合物中，在 NaOH 溶液中溶解度最小的是

(A) $Sn(OH)_2$； (B) $Pb(OH)_2$； (C) $Cu(OH)_2$； (D) $Zn(OH)_2$。

19.3 和稀硫酸作用有金属单质生成的是

(A) Ag_2O； (B) Cu_2O； (C) ZnO； (D) HgO。

19.4 为除去铜粉中少量氧化铜，应采取的操作是

(A) 浓盐酸洗； (B) KCN 溶液洗； (C) 稀硝酸洗； (D) 稀硫酸洗。

19.5 欲除去 $Cu(NO_3)_2$ 溶液中的少量 $AgNO_3$，最好加入：

(A) 铜粉；(B) NaOH；(C) Na_2S；(D) $NaHCO_3$。

19.6 下列分子中，具有顺磁性的是

(A) CuCl；(B) $CuCl_2$；(C) Hg_2Cl_2；(D) $HgCl_2$。

19.7 向 $Hg_2(NO_3)_2$ 溶液中加入 NaOH 溶液，生成的沉淀是

(A) Hg_2O；(B) HgOH；(C) HgO+Hg；(D) $Hg(OH)_2$+Hg。

19.8 下列化合物中，在硝酸和氨水中都能溶解的是

(A) AgCl；(B) Ag_2CrO_4；(C) $HgCl_2$；(D) CuS。

19.9 在分析气体时可用于吸收 CO 的试剂为

(A) $PdCl_2$；(B) CuCl；(C) AgCl；(D) Hg_2Cl_2。

19.10 下列化合物中，颜色最深的是

(A) CuO；(B) ZnO；(C) HgO；(D) PbO。

19.11 下列化合物中，在氨水、盐酸、氢氧化钠溶液中均不溶解的是

(A) $ZnCl_2$；(B) $CuCl_2$；(C) Hg_2Cl_2；(D) AgCl。

19.12 下列试剂中可将 Hg_2Cl_2，CuCl，AgCl 鉴别开的是

(A) Na_2S；(B) $NH_3\cdot H_2O$；(C) Na_2SO_4；(D) KNO_3。

二、填空题

19.13 给出下列物质的化学式。

(1) 黄铜矿______；(2) 辉铜矿______；(3) 赤铜矿______；(4) 黑铜矿______；

(5) 孔雀石______；(6) 胆矾______；(7) 闪锌矿______；(8) 菱锌矿______；

(9) 朱砂______；(10) 锌白______；(11) 立德粉______；(12) 镉黄______；

(13) 甘汞______；(14) 升汞______。

19.14 给出组成合金的金属：黄铜________，青铜________，康铜________。

19.15 向 $AgNO_3$ 溶液中滴加 NaH_2PO_4 溶液生成的沉淀的化学式为________。

19.16 Hg_2Cl_2 分子构型为________，中心原子采取的杂化类型为________。用氨水处理 Hg_2Cl_2 得到的沉淀是________。

19.17 黄色 HgO 在一定温度下加热一段时间转化为红色的 HgO，这是因为____________；ZnO 长时间加热后将由白色变成黄色，这是由于在加热过程中____________。

19.18 欲将 Ag^+ 从 Pb^{2+}，Sn^{4+}，Al^{3+}，Hg^{2+} 混合溶液中分离出来，可加入的试剂为________。

19.19 Cu(Ⅰ)在水溶液中不稳定，容易发生________反应，该反应的离子方程式为________。因此，Cu(Ⅰ)在水溶液中只能以________和________形式存在，如____________和____________。

19.20 由汞的元素电势图 $Hg^{2+}\xrightarrow{0.92\ V}Hg_2^{2+}\xrightarrow{0.79\ V}Hg$ 可知，Hg_2^{2+} 在酸性条件下不发生________反应，若使该反应发生则需加入________或________。向 $Hg(NO_3)_2$ 中加入单质汞后得到的产物是__________。

19.21 Hg_2Cl_2 是利尿剂。有时服用含有 Hg_2Cl_2 的药剂会引起中毒，其原因是____________。

19.22 五支试管分别盛有以下五种试液，请用一种试剂把它们区别开，并给出产物和现象。

产物与现象 \ 试液 / 试剂	NaCl	Na_2S	$K_2Cr_2O_7$	$Na_2S_2O_3$	K_2HPO_4

19.23 给出下列离子的颜色。
$[Cu(H_2O)_4]^{2+}$ ________；$[CuCl_4]^{2-}$ ________；$[Cu(CN)_4]^{3-}$ ________；$[CuCl_2]^-$ ________；
$[Cu(NH_3)_4]^{2+}$ ________；$[Cu(OH)_4]^{2-}$ ________；$[Cu(NH_3)_2]^+$ ________；
$[Cu(CN)_4]^{2-}$ ________；$[HgI_4]^{2-}$ ________；$[Hg(SCN)_4]^{2-}$ ________。

19.24 给出下列化合物的颜色。
$CuSO_4$ ________；$CuCl_2$ ________；$CuCl_2 \cdot 2H_2O$ ________；$K_2[Cu(C_2O_4)_2] \cdot 2H_2O$ ________；$Cu(OH)_2$ ________；$Cu(OH)_2 \cdot CuCO_3$ ________；CuBr ________；CuI ________；
CuCN ________；CuO ________；Cu_2O ________；Ag_2O ________；$AgPO_3$ ________；
Ag_3PO_4 ________；$Ag_4P_2O_7$ ________；AgCl ________；AgBr ________；AgI ________；
$Ag_2S_2O_3$ ________；$Zn[Hg(SCN)_4]$ ________；ZnO ________；ZnS ________；CdO ________；HgO ________；Hg_2Cl_2 ________；Hg_2I_2 ________；HgI_2 ________。

19.25 比较大小。
(1) 在水中溶解度 CuCl ____ AgCl，$AgClO_4$ ____ $KClO_4$；
(2) 在氨水中溶解度 $Cr(OH)_3$ ____ $Zn(OH)_2$，$ZnCl_2$ ____ ZnO；
(3) 在 KI 溶液中的溶解度 HgI_2 ____ PbI_2，PbI_2 ____ AgI。

三、完成并配平下列反应方程式

19.26 氯化铜溶液与亚硫酸氢钠溶液混合后微热。
19.27 向 $CuSO_4$ 溶液中滴加 NaCN 溶液。
19.28 铜在潮湿的空气中被缓慢氧化。
19.29 氯化亚铜暴露于空气中。
19.30 向 $Na_2Sn(OH)_4$ 溶液中滴加硝酸银溶液。
19.31 硝酸银与亚磷酸反应。
19.32 向 $Ag(S_2O_3)_2^{3-}$ 溶液中通入氯气。
19.33 氯化锌用作焊药溶解 FeO。
19.34 锌溶于氢氧化钠溶液。
19.35 硝酸汞溶液与单质汞作用后，再加入盐酸。
19.36 用氨水处理甘汞。
19.37 氧化汞溶于氢碘酸。
19.38 用盐酸处理 Ag_2O。
19.39 在碱性介质中用 Al 还原 HgS。

19.40 向 $Hg_2(NO_3)_2$ 溶液中加入 NaOH 溶液。

四、简答题和计算题

19.41 解释下列实验事实。

(1) 加热 $CuCl_2 \cdot 2H_2O$ 得不到无水 $CuCl_2$；

(2) HgC_2O_4 难溶于水，但可溶于盐酸；

(3) $Hg(NO_3)_2$ 溶液中有 NH_4NO_3 存在时，加入氨水得不到 $HgNH_2NO_3$ 沉淀。

19.42 选择合适的配合剂，分别将下列各种微溶盐溶解。

(1) CuCl；(2) AgBr；(3) CuS；(4) HgI_2；(5) CuI；(6) $HgNH_2Cl$。

19.43 解释下列实验现象。

(1) 向盛 $CuSO_4$ 溶液试管中加入 NaOH 溶液析出浅蓝色沉淀，然后将试管水浴加热则沉淀变黑；

(2) 向 $HgCl_2$ 溶液中加入 NaOH 溶液析出黄色沉淀，而向 $HgCl_2$ 溶液中加入氨水析出白色沉淀；

(3) $Hg(NO_3)_2$ 溶于水时析出黄色沉淀，而 $HgCl_2$ 溶于水时没有明显的沉淀析出；

(4) 向 $Hg_2(NO_3)_2$ 溶液中滴加 KI 溶液，先有黄色沉淀析出，KI 溶液过量，则沉淀最后变成黑色。

19.44 用简单方法将下列各组混合物分离。

(1) Hg_2Cl_2 与 $HgCl_2$；(2) $CuSO_4$ 与 $CdSO_4$；(3) $Hg(NO_3)_2$ 与 $Pb(NO_3)_2$；(4) $Cu(NO_3)_2$ 与 $AgNO_3$；(5) $ZnCl_2$ 与 $SnCl_2$。

19.45 请将下列合成用反应式表示出来。

(1) 由 $CuSO_4$ 合成 CuBr；(2) 由 ZnS 合成无水 $ZnCl_2$；

(3) 由 Hg 制备 $K_2[HgI_4]$；(4) 由 $ZnCO_3$ 提取 Zn。

19.46 定影过程是用 $Na_2S_2O_3$ 溶解胶片上未曝光的 AgBr，但将胶片在用久了的定影液中定影，胶片会"发花"，为什么？

19.47 给出下列过程的实验现象和相关的反应式。

(1) 向 $Cu(NH_3)_4^{2+}$ 溶液中滴加盐酸；

(2) 将 $[Cu(NH_3)_4]SO_4$ 溶液加热；

(3) 向 $CuCl_4^{2-}$ 溶液中滴加 KI 溶液，再加入适量的 Na_2SO_3 溶液。

19.48 设计方案将下列离子分离并复原：

Al^{3+}，Cr^{3+}，Ag^+，Zn^{2+}，Hg^{2+}。

19.49 试设计一个不用生成硫化物而能将下列离子分离的方案。

Ag^+，Hg_2^{2+}，Cu^{2+}，Zn^{2+}，Cd^{2+}，Hg^{2+}，Al^{3+}。

19.50 通过计算说明，为什么铜能溶于氰化钾溶液并置换出氢气，而银在通入空气时才能溶于氰化钾溶液。已知 $E^\ominus(Ag^+/Ag) = 0.799\ V$，$E^\ominus(Cu^+/Cu) = 0.52\ V$，$K^\ominus_{稳}[Cu(CN)_2^-] = 1.0\times10^{24}$，$K^\ominus_{稳}[Ag(CN)_2^-] = 1.0\times10^{21}$。

19.51 黑色化合物 A 不溶于水，溶于浓盐酸后得黄色溶液 B。用水稀释 B 则转化为蓝色溶液 C。向 C 中加入碘化钾溶液则有黄色沉淀 D 生成，再加入适量 $Na_2S_2O_3$ 溶液后沉淀转为白色，说明有 E 存在。E 溶于过量 $Na_2S_2O_3$ 溶液得无色溶液 F。若向 B 中通入二氧化硫后加水稀释则有白色沉淀 G 生成。G 溶于氨水后很快转为蓝色溶液，说明有 H 生成。请给出 A,B,C,D,E,F,G,H 所代表的化合物或离子。

19.52　无色晶体 A 溶于水后加入盐酸得白色沉淀 B。分离后将 B 溶于 $Na_2S_2O_3$ 溶液得无色溶液 C。向 C 中加入盐酸得白色沉淀混合物 D 和无色气体 E。E 与碘水作用后转化为无色溶液 F。向 A 的水溶液中滴加少量 $Na_2S_2O_3$ 溶液立即生成白色沉淀 G，该沉淀由白变黄、变橙、变棕最后转化为黑色，说明有 H 生成。请给出 A,B,C,D,E,F,G,H 所代表的化合物或离子。

19.53　白色固体溶于水后得无色溶液 A。向 A 中加入氢氧化钠溶液得黄色沉淀 B，B 不溶于过量的氢氧化钠溶液。B 溶于盐酸又得到 A。向 A 中滴加少量氯化亚锡溶液有白色沉淀 C 生成。用过量碘化钾溶液处理 C 得黑色沉淀 D 和无色溶液 E。向无色溶液 E 中通入硫化氢气体得黑色沉淀 F，F 不溶于硝酸。将 F 溶于王水后得黄色沉淀 G、无色溶液 H 和气体 I，I 可使酸性高锰酸钾溶液褪色。请给出 A,B,C,D,E,F,G,H,I 所代表的化合物或离子。

19.54　固体混合物中可能含有 $CuSO_4$，$ZnSO_4$，$AgNO_3$，$HgCl_2$，$SnCl_2$，NaCl。通过下列实验，判断哪些物质肯定存在，哪些物质肯定不存在。并分析原因。

(1) 取少量混合物投入水中并微热。有白色沉淀生成，溶液最后为无色。

(2) 将沉淀分离后与氨水作用，沉淀全部消失，溶液变为蓝色。向蓝色溶液中加过量盐酸，无沉淀生成。

(3) 取(1)的溶液加适量氢氧化钠溶液，有白色沉淀生成。该白色沉淀溶于过量的氢氧化钠，但在氨水中只有部分溶解。

19.55　向无色溶液 A 中加入过量硝酸时有白色沉淀 B 和无色溶液 C 生成。向 C 中加入过量铜粉得蓝色溶液 D 并放出红棕色气体 E。浓缩溶液 D，颜色逐渐变黄，最后析出浅棕色晶体；晶体与稀硫酸反应得蓝色溶液并有白色沉淀 F 析出。

(1) 给出 B,E,F 各代表何种物质？

(2) 浓缩 D 时，溶液为什么变黄？

(3) 溶液 C 中除 H^+ 外，还有哪两种阳离子？

19.56　白色固体 A 为三种硝酸盐的混合物，进行如下实验：

(1) 取少量固体 A 溶于水后，加 NaCl 溶液，有白色沉淀生成。

(2) 将(1)的沉淀离心分离，离心液分成三份：一份加入少量 Na_2SO_4，有白色沉淀生成；第二份加入 K_2CrO_4 溶液，有黄色沉淀生成；第三份加入 NaClO 有棕黑色沉淀生成。

(3) 在(1)所得沉淀中加入过量氨水，白色沉淀部分溶解，部分转化为灰白色沉淀。

(4) 在(3)所得离心液中加入过量硝酸，又有白色沉淀产生。

试确定 A 中含哪三种硝酸盐。

19.57　化合物 A 的溶液为绿色，将铜丝与其共煮渐渐生成土黄色溶液 B。用大量的水稀释 B 得到白色沉淀 C。C 溶于稀硫酸得到蓝色溶液 D 和红色单质 E。向蓝色溶液 D 中不断滴入氨水，先有蓝色沉淀 F 生成，最后得到深蓝色溶液 G；红色单质 E 不溶于稀硫酸和稀氢氧化钠溶液，但可溶于浓硫酸生成蓝色溶液 D 和无色气体 H。

试写出字母 A,B,C,D,E,F,G 和 H 所代表的物质的化学式。

19.58 某络酸的钠盐 A 与稀盐酸作用,有刺激性气体 B 和黑色沉淀 C 生成,同时溶液中出现极浅的黄色浑浊,说明有 D 产生。气体 B 能使 $KMnO_4$ 溶液褪色。若通氯气于 A 的溶液中,得到白色沉淀 E 和化合物 F 的溶液。F 与 $BaCl_2$ 作用,有不溶于酸的白色沉淀 G 产生。若在 A 的溶液中加入 KI,则生成黄色沉淀 H,再加入 NaCN 溶液,H 溶解,形成 I 的无色溶液,再向其中通入 H_2S 气体,又得到 C。

试写出字母 A,B,C,D,E,F,G,H 和 I 所代表的物质的化学式。

19.59 将无水硫酸铜溶于水得到溶液 A。用过量的浓盐酸处理 A 得到溶液 B。将 SO_2 通入 B 后用水稀释有沉淀 C 生成。将沉淀滤出并用蒸馏水洗净后溶于氨水得无色溶液 D,D 迅速转化为溶液 E。如向溶液 E 中加入过量铜屑,则又生成 D。

(1) 给出 A,B,C,D,E 的颜色及含铜组分化学式或配离子;

(2) 给出由 D 生成 E 的反应式。

第 20 章

钛副族元素和钒副族元素

第一部分　例题

例 20.1　完成并配平下列反应方程式。

(1) $TiO_2 + 6HF(aq) =\!=\!=$

(2) $TiO_2 + H_2SO_4$(浓) $\xlongequal{\triangle}$

(3) $TiO_2 + KOH \xlongequal{熔融}$

(4) $Ti^{3+} + CuCl_2 + H_2O =\!=\!=$

(5) $TiCl_4(g) + H_2 =\!=\!=$

(6) $TiCl_4 + HCl$(浓)$+ NH_4Cl =\!=\!=$

(7) $TiO_2 + BaCO_3 \xlongequal{熔融}$

(8) $TiO_2 + CCl_4 \xlongequal{高温}$

解：(1) $TiO_2 + 6HF =\!=\!= H_2TiF_6 + 2H_2O$

(2) $TiO_2 + 2H_2SO_4$(浓) $\xlongequal{\triangle} Ti(SO_4)_2 + 2H_2O$

(3) $TiO_2 + 2KOH \xlongequal{熔融} K_2TiO_3 + H_2O$

(4) $Ti^{3+} + CuCl_2 + H_2O =\!=\!= TiO^{2+} + CuCl\downarrow + 2H^+ + Cl^-$

(5) $2TiCl_4(g) + H_2 =\!=\!= 2TiCl_3 + 2HCl$

(6) $TiCl_4 + 2HCl$(浓)$+ NH_4Cl =\!=\!= (NH_4)_2[TiCl_6] + 2HCl$

(7) $TiO_2 + BaCO_3 \xlongequal{熔融} BaTiO_3 + CO_2\uparrow$

(8) $TiO_2 + CCl_4 \xlongequal{高温} TiCl_4 + CO_2\uparrow$

例 20.2　完成并配平下列反应方程式。

(1) 金属钒与氢氟酸作用；

(2) 高温下金属钒与氧气反应；

(3) 高温下金属钒与氯气反应；

(4) 真空条件下，碳与三氧化二钒共热；

(5) 五氧化二钒溶于冷浓氢氧化钠溶液；

(6) 五氧化二钒溶于硫酸；

(7) 五氧化二铌与氢氟酸反应；

(8) 五氧化二钽在熔融条件下与氢氧化钠反应。

解：(1) $2V + 12HF \xlongequal{\quad} 2H_3VF_6 + 3H_2 \uparrow$

(2) $4V + 5O_2 \xlongequal{高温} 2V_2O_5$

(3) $V + 2Cl_2 \xlongequal{高温} VCl_4$

(4) $V_2O_3 + 3C \xlongequal[\triangle]{真空} 2V + 3CO \uparrow$

(5) $V_2O_5 + 6NaOH \xlongequal{\quad} 2Na_3VO_4 + 3H_2O$

(6) $V_2O_5 + H_2SO_4 \xlongequal{\quad} (VO_2)_2SO_4 + H_2O$

(7) $Nb_2O_5 + 12HF \xlongequal{\quad} 2HNbF_6 + 5H_2O$

(8) $Ta_2O_5 + 10NaOH \xlongequal{熔融} 2Na_5TaO_5 + 5H_2O$

例 20.3 打开盛装 $TiCl_4$ 试剂的玻璃瓶时会冒白烟，试写出相关反应的方程式。如果水量充分，反应产物将有什么不同？

解：$TiCl_4$ 遇潮湿的空气发生部分水解，生成钛酰氯：

$$TiCl_4 + H_2O \xlongequal{\quad} TiOCl_2 + 2HCl$$

生成的 HCl 遇水蒸气凝结成小颗粒，呈雾状，即所谓的“白烟”。

如果水量充分，$TiCl_4$ 将完全水解生成水合二氧化钛($TiO_2 \cdot nH_2O$)：

$$TiCl_4 + (n+2)H_2O \xlongequal{\quad} TiO_2 \cdot nH_2O + 4HCl$$

例 20.4 试指出下列离子中，哪些在水溶液中不能存在，并说明理由。

(1) $[Ti(H_2O)_6]^{2+}$；　　(2) $[Ti(H_2O)_6]^{3+}$；

(3) $[Ti(H_2O)_6]^{4+}$；　　(4) $[Zr(H_2O)_6]^{2+}$。

解：$[Ti(H_2O)_6]^{2+}$ 不能存在。见下面的元素电势图

$$TiO^{2+} \xrightarrow{0.1\ V} Ti^{3+} \xrightarrow{-0.37\ V} Ti^{2+} \xrightarrow{-1.63\ V} Ti$$

由于 Ti^{2+} 的还原性极强，在水中将被氧化成 Ti^{3+}。

$[Ti(H_2O)_6]^{4+}$ 不能存在。因为 Ti^{4+} 的电荷过高，且半径很小，约为 61 pm，在水中将发生水解，变成 TiO^{2+} 形式。

$[Zr(H_2O)_6]^{2+}$ 不能存在。Zr 的低氧化态不稳定，基本上以 Zr(Ⅳ)形式存在。

只有$[Ti(H_2O)_6]^{3+}$ 可以在水中存在。但是由于其还原性较强，可以被空气中的 O_2 氧化，所以也要注意保护。

例 20.5 试解释现象。

(1) 向 V^{3+} 的绿色溶液中，滴加酸性 $KMnO_4$ 溶液，在反应的一定阶段可以得到绿色溶液。

(2) 存在 VF_5，不存在 VCl_5；但是对于 Nb 和 Ta，既存在 MF_5 又存在 MCl_5。

解：(1) 酸性条件下，向 V^{3+} 溶液中滴加 $KMnO_4$ 溶液，先后发生如下反应：

$$5V^{3+} + MnO_4^- + H_2O = 5VO^{2+} + Mn^{2+} + 2H^+$$

产物 VO^{2+} 为蓝色。

继续滴加 $KMnO_4$，VO^{2+} 被氧化为黄色的 VO_2^+：

$$5VO^{2+} + MnO_4^- + H_2O = 5VO_2^+ + Mn^{2+} + 2H^+$$

当蓝色的 VO^{2+} 和黄色的 VO_2^+ 浓度相当时，溶液显绿色。

(2) V(Ⅴ)有较强的氧化性，遇到 Cl^- 时，可将其氧化生成 Cl_2：

$$V_2O_5 + 6HCl = 2VOCl_2 + Cl_2\uparrow + 3H_2O$$

故 VCl_5 不存在。而 F^- 不能被 V(Ⅴ)氧化，故存在 VF_5。

对于 Nb(Ⅴ)，Ta(Ⅴ)，高氧化态稳定，即氧化能力较差，不能氧化 Cl^-，所以 $NbCl_5$，$TaCl_5$ 能稳定存在。

例 20.6　浅黄色晶体 A 受热分解生成棕黄色粉末 B 和无色气体 C。B 不溶于水，与浓盐酸作用放出强刺激性气体 D。将气体 C 通入 $CuSO_4$ 溶液有淡蓝色沉淀 E 生成，C 过量则沉淀溶解得到深蓝色溶液 F。B 溶于稀硫酸后，加入适量草酸，经充分反应得到蓝色溶液 G。向溶液 G 中放入足量金属 Zn，最终生成紫色溶液 H。

试写出 A，B，C，D，E，F，G 和 H 所代表的物质的化学式，并用化学反应方程式表示各过程。

解：A—NH_4VO_3；　B—V_2O_5；　C—NH_3；
D—Cl_2；　E—$Cu(OH)_2$；　F—$[Cu(NH_3)_4]^{2+}$；
G—VO^{2+}；　H—V^{2+}。

各步反应方程式如下：

$$2NH_4VO_3 = V_2O_5 + 2NH_3\uparrow + H_2O$$
$$V_2O_5 + 6HCl(浓) = 2VOCl_2 + Cl_2\uparrow + 3H_2O$$
$$2NH_3 + CuSO_4 + 2H_2O = Cu(OH)_2\downarrow + (NH_4)_2SO_4$$
$$Cu(OH)_2 + 4NH_3 = [Cu(NH_3)_4]^{2+} + 2OH^-$$
$$V_2O_5 + H_2SO_4 = (VO_2)_2SO_4 + H_2O$$
$$2VO_2^+ + H_2C_2O_4 + 2H^+ = 2VO^{2+}(蓝) + 2CO_2\uparrow + 2H_2O$$
$$VO^{2+} + Zn + 2H^+ = V^{2+}(紫) + Zn^{2+} + H_2O$$

第二部分　习题

一、选择题

20.1　下列金属中，在地壳中丰度最高的是
(A) Cu；　(B) Zn；　(C) Ti；　(D) V。

20.2　下列各对元素的性质最相似的是
(A) Cr 和 Mn；　(B) Cu 和 Zn；　(C) Ti 和 V；　(D) Nd 和 Ta。

20.3 下列各对元素的性质差异最大的是

(A) Ti 和 V； (B) Mo 和 W； (C) Nb 和 Ta； (D) Zr 和 Hf。

20.4 下列金属中，易溶于 HF 溶液的是

(A) Ti； (B) Cu； (C) Ni； (D) Si。

20.5 下列金属中，与硝酸作用的产物氧化数最低的是

(A) Sb； (B) V； (C) Mo； (D) W。

20.6 与其他溶液颜色明显不同的是

(A) $TiCl_3$； (B) $V(H_2O)_6^{2+}$； (C) $V(H_2O)_6^{3+}$； (D) $KMnO_4$。

20.7 下列化合物中，在酸性介质中氧化性最强的是

(A) TiO_2； (B) V_2O_5； (C) MoO_3； (D) Sb_2O_5。

20.8 下列物质中，具有金属光泽的是

(A) TiO_2； (B) $TiCl_4$； (C) TiC； (D) $TiO(NO_3)_2$。

20.9 常温下以液态形式存在的是

(A) $TiOSO_4$； (B) $BaTiO_3$； (C) TiO_2； (D) $TiCl_4$。

20.10 下列无机材料中，具有压电效应的是

(A) $BaCO_3$； (B) $BaSO_4$； (C) $BaTiO_3$； (D) $BaCrO_4$。

20.11 下列试剂中，能将 TiO^{2+} 还原为 Ti^{3+} 的是

(A) H_2S； (B) SO_2； (C) KI； (D) Al。

20.12 在强酸介质中，五价钒的主要存在形式为

(A) V^{5+}； (B) VO^{3+}； (C) VO_2^+； (D) V_2O_5。

二、填空题

20.13 钛溶于热的浓盐酸的氧化产物是________，钛与干燥的氯在高温下的反应产物是________；钒与稀硝酸反应的氧化产物是________。

20.14 给出下列物质的化学式。

(1) 金红石______； (2) 钛铁矿______； (3) 钙钛矿______； (4) 榍石______；
(5) 锆英石______； (6) 斜锆石______； (7) 绿硫钒石______； (8) 钒铅矿______。

20.15 Ti(Ⅳ)在酸性溶液中的存在形式为________，V(Ⅳ)在酸性溶液中的存在形式为________。

20.16 用 $Ti(CO_3)_4$，TiI_4，$Ti(NO_3)_4$，$Ti(OH)_4$ 表示的化合物中，其中________可以从溶液中析出，实际上不可能存在的是________。

20.17 用过量 Zn 还原 VO^{2+} 溶液，最终的还原产物为________；用 Fe^{3+} 溶液氧化 V^{3+}，最终的氧化产物为________。

20.18 五价钒的溶液与 H_2O_2 发生________反应，在酸性条件下反应产物为________，在碱性条件下反应产物为________。

20.19 给出下列离子在溶液中的颜色。

Ti^{3+}________，V^{2+}________，V^{3+}________，VO^{2+}________，VO_2^+________，
VO_4^{3-}________，$V_{10}O_{28}^{6-}$________，$[TiO(H_2O_2)_2]^{2+}$________，$[V(O_2)]^{3+}$________，

$[VO_2(O_2)_2]^{3-}$ ________。

三、完成并配平下列反应方程式

20.20 钛溶于氢氟酸。

20.21 向三氯化钛溶液中加入稀硝酸。

20.22 由 TiO_2 制备 $TiCl_4$。

20.23 向硫酸氧钛溶液中加入过氧化氢。

20.24 用 NaH 还原四氯化钛。

20.25 五氧化二钒溶于稀硫酸。

20.26 向 VO_2^+ 溶液中加入硫酸亚铁。

20.27 酸性条件下用 $KMnO_4$ 滴定四价钒。

四、简答题和计算题

20.28 解释下列实验现象。

(1) 冷却浓的 $TiCl_3$ 溶液析出的 $TiCl_3 \cdot 6H_2O$ 晶体为紫色，用乙醚萃取 $TiCl_3$ 溶液在一定条件下析出的 $TiCl_3 \cdot 6H_2O$ 晶体为绿色。

(2) $TiCl_3$ 溶液与 $CuCl_2$ 溶液反应后加水稀释有白色沉淀析出。

(3) 向酸性的 $VOSO_4$ 溶液中滴加 $KMnO_4$ 溶液，溶液由蓝色变黄。

20.29 给出实验现象和反应方程式。

(1) 向 $TiCl_4$ 溶液中加入浓盐酸和金属锌后充分反应。

(2) 向前面反应后的溶液中缓慢加入 NaOH 溶液至溶液呈碱性。

(3) 将(2)的沉淀过滤出来，用硝酸将其溶解后再加入稀碱。

20.30 用反应方程式表示由钛铁矿制备无水 $TiCl_3$。

20.31 钛缓慢溶于盐酸，生成钛(Ⅲ)离子的紫色溶液；该溶液在室温下迅速使酸化的高锰酸钾水溶液脱色。写出相关的离子反应方程式。

20.32 试写出钛白、锌白、铅白的化学组成，并指出钛白作为染料的优点。

20.33 已知 V^{3+} 为绿色。在酸性的 V^{3+} 溶液中滴加适量 $KMnO_4$ 溶液时，也得到绿色溶液。请释解原因。

20.34 向酸性的 V^{2+} 溶液中滴加 $KMnO_4$ 溶液，溶液的颜色如何变化？指出各颜色所对应的钒的存在形式。

20.35 解释下列化合物的熔点和颜色变化。

化合物	TiF_4	$TiCl_4$	$TiBr_4$	TiI_4
熔点/K	557	249	311	428
颜　色	白色	无色	橙色	深棕色

20.36 将 N_2O_5 与 $TiCl_4$ 作用可制备无水 $Ti(NO_3)_4$。已知 $Ti(NO_3)_4$ 熔点为 58 ℃，试分析它比一般的硝酸盐熔点低的原因。

20.37 化合物 A 为无色液体。A 在潮湿的空气中冒白烟。取 A 的水溶液加入 $AgNO_3$ 溶液则有不溶于硝酸的白色沉淀 B 生成，B 易溶于氨水。取锌粒投入 A 的盐酸溶液中，最终得到紫色溶液 C。向 C 中加入 NaOH 溶液至碱性则有紫色沉淀 D 生成。将 D 洗净后置于稀硝酸中得无色溶液 E。将溶液 E 加热得白色沉淀 F。请给出各字母所代表的物质。

20.38 白色化合物 A 在煤气灯上加热转为橙色固体 B 并有无色气体 C 生成。B 溶于硫酸得黄色溶液 D。向 D 中滴加适量 NaOH 溶液又析出橙黄色固体 B，NaOH 过量时 B 溶解得无色溶液 E。向 D 中通入 SO_2 得蓝色溶液 F，F 可使酸性高锰酸钾溶液褪色。将少量 C 通入 $AgNO_3$ 溶液有棕褐色沉淀 G 生成，通入过量的 C 后沉淀 G 溶解得无色溶液 H。请给出各字母所代表的物质。

20.39 无色液体 A 与干燥氧气在高温下反应，生成不溶于水的白色粉末 B，B 和锌粉混合后与盐酸缓慢作用，最后得到紫红色溶液，说明有化合物 C 生成。向 C 的溶液中加入 $CuCl_2$ 溶液得白色沉淀 D。紫色化合物 C 溶于过量硝酸得无色溶液 E。将溶液 E 蒸干后，在较高温度下加热又得到 B。A 与铝粉混合，在高温下反应有化合物 C 生成。试写出 A，B，C，D 和 E 所代表的物质的化学式。

第 21 章

铬副族元素和锰副族元素

第一部分　例题

例 21.1　完成并配平下列在酸性溶液中反应的方程式。

(1) $Cr_2O_7^{2-} + H_2S =\!=\!=$

(2) $Cr_2O_7^{2-} + Fe^{2+} =\!=\!=$

(3) $Cr_2O_7^{2-} + Br^- =\!=\!=$

(4) $Cr^{3+} + NaBiO_3 =\!=\!=$

(5) $Mn^{2+} + PbO_2 =\!=\!=$

(6) $MnO_4^- + H_2O_2 =\!=\!=$

(7) $MnO_4^- + Cr^{3+} =\!=\!=$

(8) $MnO_2 + Fe^{2+} =\!=\!=$

解：(1) $Cr_2O_7^{2-} + 3H_2S + 8H^+ =\!=\!= 2Cr^{3+} + 3S\downarrow + 7H_2O$

$Cr_2O_7^{2-} + S + 8H^+ =\!=\!= 2Cr^{3+} + H_2SO_4 + 3H_2O$

(2) $Cr_2O_7^{2-} + 6Fe^{2+} + 14H^+ =\!=\!= 2Cr^{3+} + 6Fe^{3+} + 7H_2O$

(3) $Cr_2O_7^{2-} + 6Br^- + 14H^+ =\!=\!= 2Cr^{3+} + 3Br_2 + 7H_2O$

(4) $2Cr^{3+} + 3NaBiO_3 + 4H^+ =\!=\!= Cr_2O_7^{2-} + 3Bi^{3+} + 2H_2O + 3Na^+$

(5) $2Mn^{2+} + 5PbO_2 + 4H^+ =\!=\!= 2MnO_4^- + 5Pb^{2+} + 2H_2O$

(6) $2MnO_4^- + 5H_2O_2 + 6H^+ =\!=\!= 2Mn^{2+} + 5O_2\uparrow + 8H_2O$

(7) $6MnO_4^- + 10Cr^{3+} + 11H_2O =\!=\!= 6Mn^{2+} + 5Cr_2O_7^{2-} + 22H^+$

(8) $MnO_2 + 2Fe^{2+} + 4H^+ =\!=\!= Mn^{2+} + 2Fe^{3+} + 2H_2O$

例 21.2　完成并配平下列在碱性介质中反应的方程式。

(1) $Cr(OH)_4^- + H_2O_2 =\!=\!=$

(2) $Cr(OH)_3 + I_2 =\!=\!=$

(3) $Mn(OH)_2 + H_2O_2 =\!=\!=$

(4) $MnO_4^{2-} + Cl_2 =\!=\!=$

(5) $MnO_4^- + NO_2^- =\!=\!=$

解：(1) $2Cr(OH)_4^- + 3H_2O_2 + 2OH^- =\!=\!= 2CrO_4^{2-} + 8H_2O$

(2) $2Cr(OH)_3+3I_2+10OH^- \longrightarrow 2CrO_4^{2-}+6I^-+8H_2O$

(3) $Mn(OH)_2+H_2O_2 \longrightarrow MnO(OH)_2+H_2O$

或 $Mn(OH)_2+H_2O_2 \longrightarrow MnO_2+2H_2O$

(4) $2MnO_4^{2-}+Cl_2 \longrightarrow 2MnO_4^-+2Cl^-$

(5) $2MnO_4^-+NO_2^-+2OH^- \longrightarrow 2MnO_4^{2-}+NO_3^-+H_2O$

例 21.3 实验室经常用$(NH_4)_2S_2O_8$，PbO_2，$NaBiO_3$为氧化剂鉴定Mn^{2+}，试给出鉴定反应的方程式和反应条件。

解： 反应须在酸性条件下进行，但酸化时不能用还原性酸，如 HCl 等。

$(NH_4)_2S_2O_8$氧化能力虽强，但与Mn^{2+}反应速率小，需要加入Ag^+催化而且加热条件下反应：

$$2Mn^{2+}+5S_2O_8^{2-}+8H_2O \xrightarrow[\triangle]{Ag^+} 2MnO_4^-+10SO_4^{2-}+16H^+$$

由标准电极电势$E^\ominus(PbO_2/Pb^{2+})=1.46V$可知，在标准状态下$PbO_2$氧化能力不如$MnO_4^-$。为提高氧化能力，在$PbO_2$与$Mn^{2+}$反应时，用$H_2SO_4$酸化，$Pb^{2+}$生成溶解度小的$PbSO_4$使$E(PbO_2/Pb^{2+})$增大，为加快反应需要加热：

$$2Mn^{2+}+5PbO_2+4H^++5SO_4^{2-} \xrightarrow{\triangle} 2MnO_4^-+5PbSO_4+2H_2O$$

$NaBiO_3$氧化能力强，与Mn^{2+}反应速率较快，反应时用硫酸和硝酸酸化均可，也无需加热：

$$2Mn^{2+}+5NaBiO_3+14H^+ \longrightarrow 2MnO_4^-+5Bi^{3+}+5Na^++7H_2O$$

例 21.4 $K_2Cr_2O_7$溶液分别与$BaCl_2$，KOH，热的浓 HCl，酸性H_2O_2作用，将分别转变为何产物？

解： $K_2Cr_2O_7$溶液与$BaCl_2$作用，生成黄色的$BaCrO_4$沉淀：

$$K_2Cr_2O_7+2BaCl_2+H_2O \longrightarrow 2BaCrO_4\downarrow+2KCl+2HCl$$

$K_2Cr_2O_7$溶液与 KOH 作用，生成黄色的K_2CrO_4溶液：

$$K_2Cr_2O_7+2KOH \longrightarrow 2K_2CrO_4+H_2O$$

$K_2Cr_2O_7$溶液与热的浓 HCl 作用，生成氯气：

$$K_2Cr_2O_7+14HCl \xrightarrow{\triangle} 2KCl+2CrCl_3+3Cl_2\uparrow+7H_2O$$

$K_2Cr_2O_7$溶液与酸性H_2O_2作用，生成蓝色的CrO_5：

$$K_2Cr_2O_7+4H_2O_2+H_2SO_4 \longrightarrow 2CrO_5+5H_2O+K_2SO_4$$

CrO_5在酸性溶液中不稳定（萃取进入乙醚或戊醇中较稳定），很快分解：

$$4CrO_5+12H^+ \longrightarrow 4Cr^{3+}+7O_2\uparrow+6H_2O$$

例 21.5　试描述以软锰矿为原料制备高锰酸钾的实验步骤，并写出各步反应的方程式。

解：软锰矿即二氧化锰。

将氧化剂 $KClO_3$ 或 KNO_3（也可以用空气中的 O_2 做氧化剂）和 MnO_2，KOH（或 K_2CO_3）按一定比例混合，用固相熔融法制备 K_2MnO_4：

$$3MnO_2+KClO_3+6KOH \xlongequal{熔融} 3K_2MnO_4+KCl+3H_2O$$

电解 K_2MnO_4 溶液得到 $KMnO_4$：

$$2K_2MnO_4+2H_2O \xlongequal{电解} 2KMnO_4+2KOH+H_2\uparrow$$

产物中的 KOH 可以循环使用于制取 K_2MnO_4 的步骤。

例 21.6　论证下列各组离子能否大量共存，写出有关化学反应的方程式。

(1) 溶液中含有 Na^+，K^+，$Al(OH)_4^-$，NO_3^-，$Cr_2O_7^{2-}$，NO_2^-；

(2) 溶液中含有 K^+，MnO_4^-，SO_4^{2-}，Mn^{2+}，I^-。

解：判断溶液中离子能否共存，应从两个方面加以考虑：一是离子之间是否发生化学反应，能发生反应的离子不能共存；二是酸碱等介质条件能否保证所有离子的形态都稳定存在。

(1) 不能大量共存。

$Cr_2O_7^{2-}$ 只能存在于酸性介质中，而$[Al(OH)_4]^-$，NO_2^- 只能存在于碱性介质中。

且 $Cr_2O_7^{2}$ 与 NO_2^- 之间可发生氧化还原反应：

$$Cr_2O_7^{2-}+3NO_2^-+8H^+ = 2Cr^{3+}+3NO_3^-+4H_2O$$

(2) 不能大量共存。

MnO_4^- 可以将 Mn^{2+}，I^- 氧化，反应为：

$$2MnO_4^-+3Mn^{2+}+2H_2O = 5MnO_2\downarrow+4H^+$$

$$2MnO_4^-+10I^-+16H^+ = 2Mn^{2+}+5I_2+8H_2O$$

例 21.7　解释下列实验现象。

(1) $CrCl_3\cdot 6H_2O$ 溶于水的溶液为绿色，将溶液煮沸一段时间后冷至室温，溶液变为蓝紫色。

(2) 向 $MnSO_4$ 溶液中加入 NaOH 溶液，生成白色沉淀；该白色沉淀暴露在空气中则逐渐变成棕黑色；加入稀硫酸沉淀不溶解，再加入双氧水沉淀消失。

(3) 将 MnO_2，$KClO_3$，KOH 固体混合后用煤气灯加热，得绿色固体；用大量水处理绿色固体得到紫色溶液和棕黑色沉淀，再通入过量 NO_2 则溶液颜色和沉淀消失得到无色溶液。

(4) $[Cr(H_2O)_6]^{3+}$ 内界中的配位 H_2O 逐步被 NH_3 取代后，溶液的颜色发生一系列变化，从紫色→浅红→橙红→橙黄→黄色。

解：(1) $CrCl_3\cdot 6H_2O$ 溶于水主要以$[Cr(H_2O)_4Cl_2]^+$形式存在，溶液为绿色；将溶液煮沸一段时间后冷至室温，溶液中有紫色的$[Cr(H_2O)_6]^{3+}$及其水解产物$[Cr(OH)(H_2O)_5]^{2+}$等，溶液为蓝紫色：

$$[Cr(H_2O)_6]^{3+} \rightleftharpoons [Cr(OH)(H_2O)_5]^{2+}+H^+$$

(2) 向 $MnSO_4$ 溶液中加入 NaOH 溶液，生成白色的 $Mn(OH)_2$ 沉淀：

$$MnSO_4 + 2NaOH = Mn(OH)_2 \downarrow + Na_2SO_4$$

$Mn(OH)_2$ 还原能力强，在空气中被氧化为棕黑色的 MnO_2：

$$2Mn(OH)_2 + O_2 = 2MnO_2 + 2H_2O$$

MnO_2 不溶于稀硫酸，但在酸性条件下与双氧水反应生成 Mn^{2+}，沉淀消失：

$$MnO_2 + H_2O_2 + 2H^+ = Mn^{2+} + O_2 \uparrow + 2H_2O$$

(3) 将 MnO_2，$KClO_3$，KOH 固体混合后用煤气灯加热，得绿色 K_2MnO_4：

$$3MnO_2 + KClO_3 + 6KOH = 3K_2MnO_4 + KCl + 3H_2O$$

加入大量水时，溶液中碱的浓度降低，K_2MnO_4 歧化得到紫色 $KMnO_4$ 溶液和棕黑色 MnO_2 沉淀：

$$3K_2MnO_4 + 2H_2O = 2KMnO_4 + MnO_2 \downarrow + 4KOH$$

NO_2 为酸性氧化物，有还原性，过量的 NO_2 能将 $KMnO_4$ 和 MnO_2 还原为近无色的 Mn^{2+}：

$$MnO_4^- + 5NO_2 + H_2O = Mn^{2+} + 5NO_3^- + 2H^+$$

$$MnO_2 + 2NO_2 = Mn^{2+} + 2NO_3^-$$

所以，溶液的紫色和沉淀都消失，得到无色溶液。

(4) $[Cr(H_2O)_6]^{3+}$ 内界中的 H_2O 逐步被 NH_3 取代后，随着配离子内界配体的变化则颜色发生如下变化：

$$\underset{\text{紫色}}{[Cr(H_2O)_6]^{3+}} \longrightarrow \underset{\text{紫红}}{[Cr(NH_3)_2(H_2O)_4]^{3+}} \longrightarrow \underset{\text{浅红}}{[Cr(NH_3)_3(H_2O)_3]^{3+}}$$

$$\longrightarrow \underset{\text{橙红}}{[Cr(NH_3)_4(H_2O)_2]^{3+}} \longrightarrow \underset{\text{橙黄}}{[Cr(NH_3)_5(H_2O)]^{3+}} \longrightarrow \underset{\text{黄色}}{[Cr(NH_3)_6]^{3+}}$$

由于 NH_3 是比 H_2O 更强的配体，分裂能大。当 NH_3 逐级取代 H_2O 后，Δ_o 逐渐增大，d-d 跃迁所需能量相应增大，吸收可见光的波长逐渐变短，从黄绿光→蓝绿光→蓝光，透射和反射出的光波长逐渐变长，于是看到的颜色从紫色至黄色。

例 21.8 橙红色固体 A 受热后生成深绿色的固体 B 和无色的气体 C，加热时 C 能与镁反应生成黄色的固体 D。未经过高温灼烧的固体物质 B 与 NaOH 共熔后溶于水生成绿色的溶液 E，在 E 中加适量 H_2O_2 则生成黄色溶液 F。将 F 酸化变为橙色的溶液 G，在 G 中加 $BaCl_2$ 溶液，得黄色沉淀 H。在 G 的浓溶液中加 KCl 固体，反应完全后蒸发、浓缩，然后冷却有橙红色晶体 I 析出。I 受强热得到的固体产物中有 B，同时得到能支持燃烧的气体 J。

试写出字母 A，B，C，D，E，F，G，H，I 和 J 所代表的物质的化学式，并用化学反应方程式表示各过程。

解： A—$(NH_4)_2Cr_2O_7$； B—Cr_2O_3； C—N_2； D—Mg_3N_2；
E—CrO_2^-； F—CrO_4^{2-}； G—$Cr_2O_7^{2-}$； H—$BaCrO_4$；

I—$K_2Cr_2O_7$；　　　　J—O_2。

各步反应方程式如下：

$$(NH_4)_2Cr_2O_7 \xlongequal{\triangle} N_2 + Cr_2O_3 + 4H_2O$$

$$3Mg + N_2 \xlongequal{\triangle} Mg_3N_2$$

$$Cr_2O_3 + 2NaOH = 2NaCrO_2 + H_2O$$

$$2CrO_2^- + 3H_2O_2 + 2OH^- = 2CrO_4^{2-} + 4H_2O$$

$$2CrO_4^{2-} + 2H^+ = Cr_2O_7^{2-} + H_2O$$

$$Cr_2O_7^{2-} + 2Ba^{2+} + H_2O = 2BaCrO_4\downarrow + 2H^+$$

$$Na_2Cr_2O_7 + KCl = K_2Cr_2O_7 + NaCl$$

$$2K_2Cr_2O_7 \xlongequal{\triangle} 2K_2O + 2Cr_2O_3 + 3O_2\uparrow$$

例 21.9　绿色固体 A 易溶于水，其水溶液中通入 CO_2 即得棕黑色固体 B 和紫红色溶液 C。B 与浓 HCl 溶液共热时得黄绿色气体 D 和近乎无色溶液 E。将此溶液和溶液 C 混合能生成沉淀 B。将气体 D 通入 A 的溶液，可得 C。

试写出字母 A,B,C,D 和 E 所代表的物质的化学式，并用化学反应方程式表示各过程。

解：A—K_2MnO_4；　　　　B—MnO_2；　　　C—MnO_4^-；

D—Cl_2；　　　　E—Mn^{2+}。

各步反应方程式如下：

$$3K_2MnO_4 + CO_2 + 2H^+ = 2KMnO_4 + MnO_2\downarrow + K_2CO_3 + H_2O$$

$$MnO_2 + 4HCl(浓) \xlongequal{\triangle} MnCl_2 + 2H_2O + Cl_2\uparrow$$

$$3Mn^{2+} + 2MnO_4^- + 2H_2O = 5MnO_2\downarrow + 4H^+$$

$$2MnO_4^- + Cl_2 = 2MnO_4^- + 2Cl^-$$

例 21.10　一种固体混合物可能含有 $AgNO_3$,CuS,$AlCl_3$,$KMnO_4$,K_2SO_4 和 $ZnCl_2$ 中的一种或几种。将此混合物置于水中，并用少量盐酸酸化，得白色沉淀物 A 和无色溶液 B。白色沉淀 A 可溶于氨水中。将滤液 B 分成两份，一份中加入少量氢氧化钠溶液，有白色沉淀产生，再加入过量氢氧化钠溶液则白色沉淀溶解。另一份中加入少量氨水，也产生白色沉淀，当加入过量氨水时，白色沉淀溶解。

试根据上述现象，判断在混合物中，哪些物质肯定存在，哪些肯定不存在，哪些可能存在。说明理由，并用方程式表示。

解：肯定存在的有：$AgNO_3$,$ZnCl_2$

肯定不存在的有：CuS,$AlCl_3$,$KMnO_4$

可能存在的有：K_2SO_4

混合物加水，酸化，过滤后得到白色沉淀和无色溶液，证明混合物中没有 CuS,$KMnO_4$。

白色沉淀 A 溶于氨水，为 AgCl，肯定有 $AgNO_3$ 存在。

滤液 B 加 NaOH 生成白色沉淀，加过量 NaOH 沉淀又溶解，说明溶液中有两性离子(Zn^{2+}，

Al^{3+})。滤液 B 加 $NH_3 \cdot H_2O$ 生成白色沉淀，加过量 $NH_3 \cdot H_2O$ 沉淀消失，证明有 $ZnCl_2$ 没有 $AlCl_3$。

无法确证 K_2SO_4 存在与否，只能说可能存在。

相关反应方程式如下：

$$Ag^+ + Cl^- \longrightarrow AgCl\downarrow$$
$$AgCl + 2NH_3 \cdot H_2O \longrightarrow [Ag(NH_3)_2]Cl + 2H_2O$$
$$ZnCl_2 + 2NH_3 \cdot H_2O \longrightarrow Zn(OH)_2\downarrow + 2NH_4Cl$$
$$Zn(OH)_2 + 4NH_3 \cdot H_2O \longrightarrow [Zn(NH_3)_4](OH)_2 + 4H_2O$$
$$Zn^{2+} + 2OH^- \longrightarrow Zn(OH)_2\downarrow$$
$$Zn(OH)_2 + 2OH^- \longrightarrow [Zn(OH)_4]^{2-}$$

第二部分 习题

一、选择题

21.1 下列金属中，硬度最高的是

(A) Cr； (B) Mo； (C) W； (D) Mn。

21.2 下列金属中，熔点最高的是

(A) Cr； (B) Mo； (C) W； (D) Mn。

21.3 下列各对元素的性质最相似的是

(A) Cr 和 Mo； (B) Mo 和 W； (C) Mn 和 Re； (D) Cr 和 Mn。

21.4 与其他化合物颜色明显不同的是

(A) $Cu(OH)_2 \cdot CuCO_3$； (B) $NaCrO_2$； (C) K_2MnO_4； (D) K_2CrO_4。

21.5 下列硝酸盐中，受热分解时金属的氧化数升高的是

(A) $Pb(NO_3)_2$； (B) $Mn(NO_3)_2$； (C) $Al(NO_3)_3$； (D) $Cu(NO_3)_2$。

21.6 下列化合物中，还原性最强的是

(A) $Mg(OH)_2$； (B) $Al(NO_3)_3$； (C) $Cu(NO_3)_2$； (D) $Mn(OH)_2$。

21.7 某金属离子在八面体强场中的磁矩与在八面体弱场中的磁矩几乎相等，则该离子可能是

(A) Mn^{2+}； (B) Cr^{3+}； (C) Mn^{3+}； (D) Fe^{3+}。

21.8 由 Cr_2O_3 制备 K_2CrO_4，应选择的试剂是

(A) 王水； (B) $H_2O_2 + H_2SO_4$；

(C) Cl_2； (D) $KOH(s) + KClO_3(s)$。

21.9 下列物质中，强氧化性与惰性电子对效应无关的是

(A) PbO_2； (B) $NaBiO_3$； (C) $K_2Cr_2O_7$； (D) $TlCl_3$。

21.10 下列化合物中，不为黄颜色的是

(A) $BaCrO_4$； (B) Ag_2CrO_4； (C) $PbCrO_4$； (D) PbI_2。

21.11 欲分离溶液中 Cr^{3+} 和 Zn^{2+}，应加入的试剂为

(A) NaOH； (B) $NH_3 \cdot H_2O$； (C) H_2S； (D) Na_2CO_3。

21.12 酸性介质中，不能将 Mn^{2+} 氧化为 MnO_4^- 的是

(A) $(NH_4)_2S_2O_8$； (B) $NaBiO_3$； (C) $K_2Cr_2O_7$； (D) PbO_2。

21.13 下列金属氧化物中，熔点最低的是

(A) Na_2O； (B) HgO； (C) V_2O_5； (D) Mn_2O_7。

21.14 在酸性介质中可使 Cr^{3+} 转化为 $Cr_2O_7^{2-}$ 的试剂是

(A) H_2O_2； (B) MnO_2； (C) $KMnO_4$； (D) HNO_3。

21.15 酸性介质中发生歧化反应的离子是

(A) Mn^{2+}； (B) Mn^{3+}； (C) Cr^{3+}； (D) Ti^{3+}。

二、填空题

21.16 铬缓慢溶于盐酸生成的蓝色产物是______；该产物不稳定，很容易被氧化为绿色的______。

21.17 $KMnO_4$ 溶液被 Na_2SO_3 还原的产物与溶液的酸碱性有关，在酸性溶液中的还原产物为______；在碱性溶液中的还原产物为______；在中性溶液中的还原产物为______。

21.18 给出下列物质的化学式。

(1) 铬铁矿______；(2) 铬铅矿______；(3) 铬赭石矿______；(4) 辉钼矿______；

(5) 钼铅矿______；(6) 白钨矿______；(7) 软锰矿______；(8) 黑锰矿______；

(9) 方锰矿______；(10) 菱锰矿______。

21.19 给出下列离子的颜色。

$Cr(H_2O)_6^{3+}$______，$[Cr(H_2O)_5Cl]^{2+}$______，$[Cr(NH_3)_6]^{3+}$______，

$Cr(OH)_4^-$______，$[Cr(NH_3)_3(H_2O)_3]^{3+}$______，$CrO_4^{2-}$______，

$Cr_2O_7^{2-}$______，$Mn(H_2O)_6^{2+}$______，MnO_4^{2-}______，MnO_4^-______。

21.20 给出下列化合物的颜色。

$Cr_2(SO_4)_3 \cdot 18H_2O$______，$Cr_2(SO_4)_3$______，

$CrCl_3 \cdot 6H_2O$______，Cr_2O_3______，CrO_3______，CrO_5______，

$Cr(OH)_3$______，CrO_2Cl_2______，$BaCrO_4$______，$PbCrO_4$______，

Ag_2CrO_4______，$MnSO_4 \cdot 7H_2O$______，K_2MnO_4______，$KMnO_4$______，

$Mn(OH)_2$______，MnO_2______。

21.21 Mn^{2+} 在酸性条件下还原能力差，需强氧化剂才能将其氧化为 MnO_4^-。实验室常用于在酸性条件下将 Mn^{2+} 氧化为 MnO_4^- 的试剂有______，______和______，若用______做氧化剂时须加入______催化剂。

21.22 向 $CrCl_3$ 溶液中滴加 Na_2CO_3 溶液，产生的沉淀组成为______，沉淀的颜色为______。

21.23 为检验 Cr(Ⅵ)，可向酸性溶液中加入______和______，生成______色的______，该物质的结构式为______，其中 Cr 的价态为______。

21.24 向 K_2MnO_4 溶液中滴加稀硫酸时，发生______反应，产物为______。

21.25 锰的常见氧化物有 MnO，Mn_2O_3，MnO_2，Mn_2O_7，其中碱性最强的是______，酸性最强的

是______。

21.26 十二钨磷杂多酸的化学式为______________。

三、完成并配平下列反应方程式

21.27 在酸性介质中用 $KMnO_4$ 氧化 $Cr_2(SO_4)_3$。

21.28 将 Cr_2O_3 与 Al 粉混合后加热。

21.29 $MnCO_3$ 受热分解。

21.30 将 MnO_2 与浓硫酸混合后水浴加热。

21.31 酸性介质中用 $NaBiO_3$ 氧化 Mn^{2+}。

21.32 向 Na_2SO_3 溶液中滴加 $KMnO_4$ 溶液。

21.33 向 Na_2SO_3 和 NaOH 混合溶液中滴加 $KMnO_4$ 溶液。

21.34 向酸性 $K_2Cr_2O_7$ 溶液中加入 H_2O_2 生成绿色溶液。

21.35 三氧化二铬与焦硫酸钾共熔。

21.36 在碱性介质中氯与三碘化铬作用。

21.37 高锰酸钾晶体与浓硫酸作用。

21.38 室温下用浓盐酸处理二氧化锰。

21.39 在稀硫酸溶液中二氧化锰与过氧化氢作用。

21.40 $K_2Cr_2O_7$ 与 KCl 和浓硫酸混合后加热。

21.41 Cr_2O_3 与 NaOH 和 $NaNO_3$ 混合后加热熔融。

21.42 $(NH_4)_2Cr_2O_7$ 受热分解。

21.43 在 200 ℃温度下加热 $KMnO_4$ 晶体。

21.44 $MnSO_4$ 晶体受热分解。

四、简答题和计算题

21.45 根据下列实验现象，给出反应方程式。

(1) 向 $Cr_2(SO_4)_3$ 溶液中滴加 NaOH 溶液，先有灰蓝色沉淀生成，后沉淀溶解得绿色溶液。再加入 H_2O_2，溶液由绿色变为黄色。

(2) 在酸性介质中，用 Zn 还原 $Cr_2O_7^{2-}$ 时，溶液由橙色经绿色最后变为蓝色，放置一段时间后又变为绿色。

(3) 向酸性 $K_2Cr_2O_7$ 溶液中通入 SO_2 时，溶液由橙色变为绿色。

(4) 向 $MnSO_4$ 溶液中滴加 NaOH 溶液有白色沉淀生成，在空气中放置沉淀逐渐变为棕褐色。

(5) 向酸性 $KMnO_4$ 溶液中通入 H_2S，溶液由紫色变成近无色，并有乳白色沉淀析出。

21.46 解释下列实验现象。

(1) 向 $K_2Cr_2O_7$ 与 H_2SO_4 溶液中加入 H_2O_2，再加入乙醚并摇动，乙醚层为蓝色。水层逐渐变绿。

(2) 向 $BaCrO_4$ 固体加浓盐酸时无明显变化，经加热后溶液变绿。

(3) 向 $K_2Cr_2O_7$ 溶液中滴加 $AgNO_3$ 溶液，有砖红色沉淀析出，再加入 NaCl 溶液并煮沸，沉淀变为白色。

21.47　完成下列物质相互转化的反应方程式。

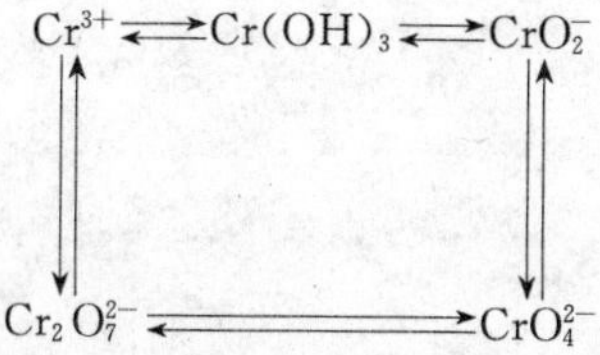

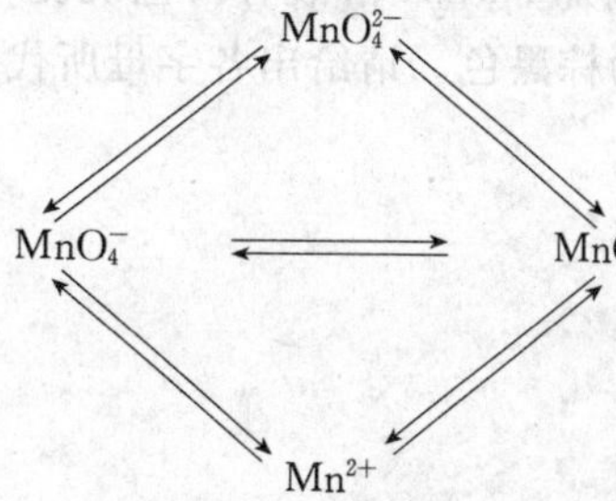

21.48　试描述以铬铁矿为原料制备重铬酸钾的实验步骤，并写出各步反应的方程式。

21.49　设计方案分离溶液中共存的离子：Mn^{2+}，Zn^{2+}，Cr^{3+}，Al^{3+}。

21.50　测定水中溶解氧量的方法是，在隔绝空气的条件下向一定量的水样中加入适量的 $MnCl_2$ 及过量的 NaOH 溶液。然后以过量的 H_2SO_4 酸化该溶液，再加入过量的 KI 溶液。充分反应后用已知浓度的标准 $Na_2S_2O_3$ 溶液滴定生成的 I_2。

试写出有关的反应式，并给出 O_2 和消耗 $Na_2S_2O_3$ 的物质的量之比。

21.51　$BaCrO_4$ 与 $BaSO_4$ 的溶度积常数相近$[K_{sp}^{\ominus}(BaCrO_4)=1.2\times10^{-10}, K_{sp}^{\ominus}(BaSO_4)=1.1\times10^{-10}]$，但 $BaCrO_4$ 可溶于硝酸而 $BaSO_4$ 却不溶于硝酸。为什么？

21.52　在酸性溶液中，MnO_4^- 与 Mn^{2+} 反应生成 MnO_2 沉淀，在分析 Fe^{2+} 含量时却可由 MnO_4^- 与 Fe^{2+} 在酸性条件下定量反应。二者是否矛盾？

21.53　A 的水合物为紫色晶体。向 A 的水溶液中加入 Na_2CO_3 溶液有灰蓝色沉淀 B 生成。B 溶于过量 NaOH 溶液得到绿色溶液 C。向 C 中滴加 H_2O_2 得黄色溶液 D。取少量 D 经醋酸酸化后加入 $BaCl_2$ 溶液则析出黄色沉淀 E。将 D 用硫酸酸化后通入 SO_2 得到绿色溶液 F。将 A 溶于浓盐酸后加入 KI 溶液经鉴定有 I_2 生成，同时放出无色气体 G。G 在空气中逐渐变为棕色。请给出各字母所代表的物质。

21.54　将黄色晶体 A 溶于水后通入 SO_2 得绿色溶液 B。向 B 中加入过量的 NaOH 溶液得绿色溶液 C。向 C 中滴加 H_2O_2 得黄色溶液 D。将 D 酸化至弱酸性后加入 $Pb(NO_3)_2$ 有黄色沉淀 E 生成。向 B 中加入氨水至过量有沉淀 F 生成。过滤后将 F 与 $KClO_3$ 和 KOH 共熔又得到 A。请给出各字母所代表的物质。

21.55　混合溶液中含有三种阴离子。向该溶液中加入 $AgNO_3$ 至不再有沉淀生成并稍过量后得红色沉淀 A 和紫色溶液 B。用硝酸处理沉淀 A 时沉淀部分溶解余下的沉淀变为白色，溶液为橙色。向溶液 B 中通入 SO_2 则紫色消失并有白色沉淀生成。请根据以上实验现象判断混合溶液中有哪三种阴离子并给出沉淀 A 的化学式。

21.56　将绿色固体 A 溶于水后通入过量 SO_2 得溶液 B。向 B 中加入 NaOH 溶液得白色沉淀 C，C 不溶于过量的 NaOH 溶液，再加入 H_2O_2 后沉淀变为暗棕色，说明有 D 生成。将 D 过滤后与 $KClO_3$ 和 KOH 共熔又得 A。请给出 A，B，C，D 的化学式。

21.57　棕黑色粉末 A 不溶于水。将 A 与稀硫酸混合后加入 H_2O_2 并微热得无色溶液 B。向酸性的 B 中加入些 $NaBiO_3$ 粉末后得紫红色溶液 C。向 C 中加入 NaOH 溶液至碱性后滴

加 Na_2SO_3 溶液有绿色溶液 D 生成。向 D 中滴加稀硫酸又生成 A 和 C。少量 A 与浓盐酸作用在室温下生成暗黄色溶液 E,加热 E 后有黄绿色气体 F 和近无色的溶液 G 生成。向 B 中滴加 NaOH 溶液有白色沉淀 H 生成,H 不溶于过量的 NaOH。但在空气中 H 逐渐变为棕黑色。请给出各字母所代表的物质。

第 22 章

铁系元素和铂系元素

第一部分　例题

例 22.1　完成并配平下列化学反应方程式。

(1) $FeCl_3 + Fe =\!=\!=$

(2) $FeCl_3 + SnCl_2 =\!=\!=$

(3) $FeCl_3 + H_2S =\!=\!=$

(4) $FeCl_3 + KI =\!=\!=$

(5) $Ni^{2+} + Br_2 + OH^- =\!=\!=$

(6) $NiO(OH) + HCl =\!=\!=$

(7) $Ni(OH)_2 + Br_2 =\!=\!=$

(8) $Co_3O_4 + HCl =\!=\!=$

(9) $Co(OH)_3 + HCl =\!=\!=$

(10) $Co^{3+} + Mn^{2+} =\!=\!=$

解：(1) $2FeCl_3 + Fe =\!=\!= 3FeCl_2$

(2) $2FeCl_3 + SnCl_2 =\!=\!= 2FeCl_2 + SnCl_4$

(3) $2FeCl_3 + H_2S =\!=\!= 2FeCl_2 + S + 2HCl$

(4) $2FeCl_3 + 2KI =\!=\!= 2FeCl_2 + I_2 + 2KCl$

(5) $2Ni^{2+} + Br_2 + 6OH^- =\!=\!= 2NiO(OH)\downarrow + 2Br^- + 2H_2O$

(6) $2NiO(OH) + 6HCl =\!=\!= 2NiCl_2 + Cl_2\uparrow + 4H_2O$

(7) $2Ni(OH)_2 + Br_2 + 2OH^- =\!=\!= 2Ni(OH)_3 + 2Br^-$

(8) $Co_3O_4 + 8HCl =\!=\!= 3CoCl_2 + Cl_2\uparrow + 4H_2O$

(9) $2Co(OH)_3 + 6HCl =\!=\!= 2CoCl_2 + Cl_2\uparrow + 6H_2O$

(10) $5Co^{3+} + Mn^{2+} + 4H_2O =\!=\!= 5Co^{2+} + MnO_4^- + 8H^+$

例 22.2　完成下列物质的转化，并给出相关的反应方程式。

(1) $Fe \rightarrow FeSO_4\cdot 7H_2O \rightarrow FeCl_3\cdot 6H_2O \rightarrow K_3[Fe(C_2O_4)_3]\cdot 3H_2O$

(2) $Co \rightarrow CoSO_4\cdot 7H_2O \rightarrow CoCl_2\cdot 6H_2O \rightarrow [Co(NH_3)_6]Cl_3$

(3) $Ru \rightarrow Na_2RuO_4 \rightarrow RuO_4$

解：(1) 将铁屑溶于稀硫酸，过滤除去杂质，滤液经水浴蒸发浓缩后，冷却结晶，得到绿色的

$FeSO_4\cdot 7H_2O$ 晶体：

$$Fe+H_2SO_4+7H_2O \longrightarrow FeSO_4\cdot 7H_2O+H_2\uparrow$$

向热的 $FeSO_4$ 溶液中加入 NaOH 和 H_2O_2，生成 $Fe(OH)_3$ 沉淀：

$$2FeSO_4+H_2O_2+4NaOH \longrightarrow 2Fe(OH)_3\downarrow+2Na_2SO_4$$

将 $Fe(OH)_3$ 沉淀过滤、洗涤后溶于盐酸，蒸发浓缩后冷却结晶，析出 $FeCl_3\cdot 6H_2O$ 晶体：

$$Fe(OH)_3+3HCl+3H_2O \longrightarrow FeCl_3\cdot 6H_2O$$

将饱和 $K_2C_2O_4$ 溶液与 $FeCl_3$ 溶液按物质的量的比为 3.5 : 1 混合，蒸发浓缩，冷却则析出绿色 $K_3[Fe(C_2O_4)_3]\cdot 3H_2O$ 晶体：

$$3K_2C_2O_4+FeCl_3+3H_2O \longrightarrow K_3[Fe(C_2O_4)_3]\cdot 3H_2O+3KCl$$

(2) 将金属钴溶于稀硫酸，过滤除去杂质，滤液经水浴蒸发浓缩后，冷却结晶，得到粉红色的 $FeSO_4\cdot 7H_2O$ 晶体：

$$Co+H_2SO_4+7H_2O \longrightarrow CoSO_4\cdot 7H_2O+H_2\uparrow$$

向 $CoSO_4$ 溶液中加入 NaOH 溶液，生成粉红色 $Co(OH)_2$ 沉淀：

$$CoSO_4+2NaOH \longrightarrow 2Co(OH)_2\downarrow+Na_2SO_4$$

过滤，洗涤沉淀。将 $Co(OH)_2$ 溶于盐酸后，蒸发、浓缩，冷却后析出 $CoCl_2\cdot 6H_2O$ 粉红色晶体：

$$Co(OH)_2+2HCl+4H_2O \longrightarrow CoCl_2\cdot 6H_2O$$

向 $CoCl_2$ 溶液中加入少量 NH_4Cl 和过量氨水，加入活性炭作催化剂，H_2O_2 为氧化剂，水浴加热，生成的 $[Co(NH_3)_6]Cl_3$ 吸附在活性炭上：

$$2CoCl_2+H_2O_2+10NH_3+2NH_4Cl \longrightarrow 2[Co(NH_3)_6]Cl_3+2H_2O$$

过滤，用稀盐酸将吸附在活性炭上的 $[Co(NH_3)_6]Cl_3$ 溶解，除去活性炭，加入少量浓盐酸，冷却，析出橙黄色 $[Co(NH_3)_6]Cl_3$。

(3) 单质 Ru 与 Na_2O_2 共熔融，可制得钌酸钠：

$$Ru+3Na_2O_2 \longrightarrow Na_2RuO_4+2Na_2O$$

使钌酸钠与 $NaClO_3$ 及 H_2SO_4 共热，可制得四氧化钌：

$$3Na_2RuO_4+NaClO_3+3H_2SO_4 \longrightarrow 3RuO_4+NaCl+3Na_2SO_4+3H_2O$$

例 22.3 设计方案分离共存于溶液中的下列离子：

$$Al^{3+}, Cr^{3+}, Fe^{3+}, Co^{2+}, Ni^{2+}。$$

解： 分离方案如图所示。

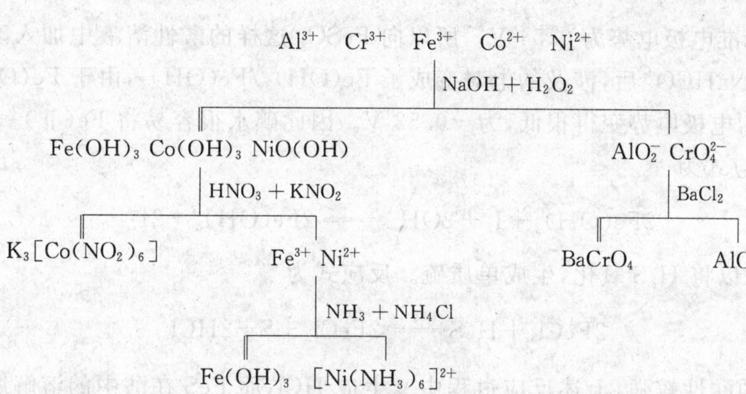

例 22.4　现有三瓶黑色固体试剂，分别为二氧化锰、二氧化铅和四氧化三铁。试设计方案将其一一鉴别出来，并写出相关化学反应方程式。

解：(1) 取少许固体试剂，加入 $MnSO_4$ 溶液和 H_2SO_4。微热，若溶液变红（有 MnO_4^- 生成），则该固体为 PbO_2：

$$5PbO_2 + 2Mn^{2+} + 5SO_4^{2-} + 4H^+ = 2MnO_4^- + 5PbSO_4 + 2H_2O$$

(2) 剩余二种固体试剂，分别加入浓 HCl。加热后放出 Cl_2 气体的为 MnO_2 试剂：

$$MnO_2 + 4HCl \xrightarrow{\triangle} MnCl_2 + Cl_2\uparrow + 2H_2O$$

(3) 余下的一种则为 Fe_3O_4。

例 22.5　选择适当方法实现下列转化而不引入杂质离子：

(1) 将 $FeCl_3$ 溶液转变为 $FeCl_2$ 溶液；

(2) 将 $FeCl_2$ 溶液转变为 $FeCl_3$ 溶液。

解：(1) 向 $FeCl_3$ 溶液中加入纯净的铁粉，充分反应后过滤：

$$2FeCl_3 + Fe = 3FeCl_2$$

(2) 向 $FeCl_2$ 溶液中加入 H_2O_2 和盐酸，充分反应后加热除去过量的 H_2O_2 即可：

$$2FeCl_2 + H_2O_2 + 2HCl = 2FeCl_3 + 2H_2O$$

例 22.6　请解释下列问题：

(1) 向 $FeCl_3$ 溶液加入 KSCN 溶液，溶液立即变红，加入适量 $SnCl_2$ 后溶液变成无色；

(2) 向 $FeSO_4$ 溶液加入碘水，碘水不褪色，再加入 $NaHCO_3$ 后，碘水褪色；

(3) 向 $FeCl_3$ 溶液中通入 H_2S，并没有硫化物沉淀生成。

解：(1) 向 $FeCl_3$ 溶液加入 KSCN 溶液，生成红色的 $[Fe(SCN)_n]^{3-n}$：

$$Fe^{3+} + nSCN^- = [Fe(SCN)_n]^{3-n} \quad (n=1\sim6)$$

加入 $SnCl_2$ 使 $[Fe(SCN)_n]^{3-n}$ 中 Fe^{3+} 还原为 Fe^{2+}，故红色消失，因为较稀的 Fe^{2+} 溶液近于无色：

$$2[Fe(SCN)_n]^{3-n} + Sn^{2+} = 2Fe^{2+} + Sn^{4+} + 2nSCN^-$$

(2) 酸性条件下，电对 Fe^{3+}/Fe^{2+} 的标准电极电势为 0.77 V，用碘水不能将 Fe(Ⅱ)氧化，因

为电对 I_2/I^- 的标准电极电势为 0.54 V。所以向 $FeSO_4$ 这样的酸性溶液中加入碘水，碘水不褪色。体系中加入 $NaHCO_3$ 后，涉及的电对变成了 $Fe(OH)_3/Fe(OH)_2$，由于 $Fe(OH)_3$ 的溶度积远小于 $Fe(OH)_2$，电极电势变得很低，为 −0.52 V。因此碘水很容易将 Fe(Ⅱ)氧化为 Fe(Ⅲ)，故碘水褪色。反应式为

$$2Fe(OH)_2 + I_2 + 2OH^- \longrightarrow 2Fe(OH)_3 + 2I^-$$

(3) $FeCl_3$ 可以将 H_2S 氧化，生成单质硫。反应式为

$$2FeCl_3 + H_2S \longrightarrow 2FeCl_2 + S + 2HCl$$

$FeCl_3$ 溶液的酸性较强，上述反应过程中又生成 HCl，而 FeS 在酸中的溶解度较大，不能沉淀。所以向 $FeCl_3$ 溶液中通入 H_2S，不会有硫化物沉淀生成。

例 22.7 试比较配位化合物$[NiCl_4]^{2-}$与$[PtCl_4]^{2-}$的稳定性并说明原因。

解：稳定性$[NiCl_4]^{2-} < [PtCl_4]^{2-}$。

Ni^{2+} 和 Pt^{2+} 电子构型均为 d^8。

按配位化合物价键理论，对于 Ni^{2+} 而言，Cl^- 为弱配体，不能使 Ni^{2+} 的 d 轨道电子重排，Ni^{2+} 只能采取 sp^3 杂化，与 Cl^- 形成外轨型配位化合物，稳定性较差，如图(a)所示。而 Pt 为高周期元素，d 轨道伸展较远，与配体 Cl^- 形成较强的配位键；结果 Cl^- 可以起到强配体的作用，使 Pt^{2+} 的 d 轨道电子重排，Pt^{2+} 采取 dsp^2 杂化，与 Cl^- 形成内轨型配合物，稳定性较高，如图(b)所示。

按晶体场理论，Ni^{2+} 在 Cl^- 的四面体场中分裂能小，晶体场稳定化能较小，如图(a)所示，故$[NiCl_4]^{2-}$ 稳定性较差；而 Pt^{2+} 在 Cl^- 的正方形场中分裂能大，在高能量 $d_{x^2-y^2}$ 轨道未填充电子，晶体场稳定化能大，如图(b)所示，故$[PtCl_4]^{2-}$ 稳定性较高。

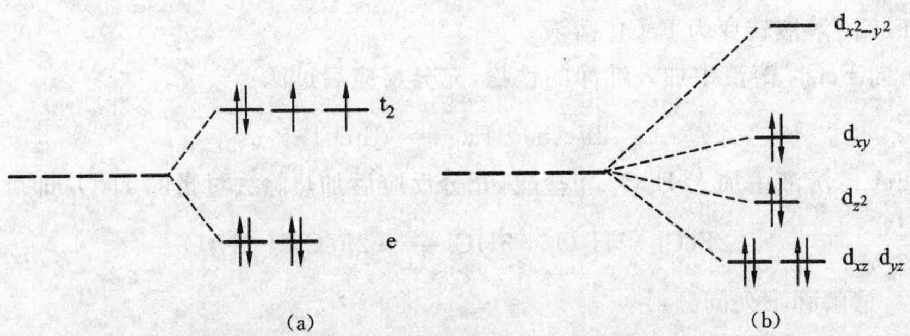

例 22.8 给出下列过程的实验现象及反应方程式：

(1) 向 $NiSO_4$ 溶液中缓慢滴加稀氨水；

(2) 向$[Co(NH_3)_6]^{2+}$溶液中缓慢滴加稀盐酸。

解：(1) 向 $NiSO_4$ 溶液中缓慢滴加稀氨水，先有绿色沉淀生成：

$$NiSO_4 + 2NH_3 + 2H_2O \longrightarrow Ni(OH)_2\downarrow + (NH_4)_2SO_4$$

氨水过量则绿色沉淀溶解，生成蓝色$[Ni(NH_3)_6]^{2+}$溶液：

$$Ni(OH)_2 + 6NH_3 \longrightarrow [Ni(NH_3)_6]^{2+} + 2OH^-$$

(2) 向$[Co(NH_3)_6]^{2+}$溶液中缓慢滴加稀盐酸，先有蓝绿色沉淀生成：

$$[Co(NH_3)_6]^{2+} + HCl + H_2O \longrightarrow Co(OH)Cl \downarrow + 4NH_3 + 2NH_4^+$$

盐酸过量则蓝绿色沉淀溶解，生成粉红色$[Co(H_2O)_6]^{2+}$溶液：

$$Co(OH)Cl + HCl + 5H_2O \longrightarrow [Co(H_2O)_6]^{2+} + 2Cl^-$$

例 22.9 向绿色水合晶体 A 的溶液中加入碱和过氧化氢，有沉淀 B 生成。B 溶于草酸氢钾溶液得到黄绿色溶液 C，将 C 蒸发浓缩后缓慢冷却，析出绿色晶体 D。光照 D 分解为黄色固体 E。E 受热分解最后得到黑色的粉末 F。

试写出 A，B，C，D，E 和 F 所代表的物质的化学式，并用化学反应方程式表示各过程。

解：A—$FeSO_4 \cdot 7H_2O$；　B—$Fe(OH)_3$；　C—$[Fe(C_2O_4)_3]^{3-}$；
D—$K_3[Fe(C_2O_4)_3] \cdot 3H_2O$；　E—$FeC_2O_4$；　F—FeO。

$$2FeSO_4 + 4NaOH + H_2O_2 \longrightarrow 2Fe(OH)_3 \downarrow + 2Na_2SO_4$$

$$Fe(OH)_3 + 3KHC_2O_4 \longrightarrow K_3[Fe(C_2O_4)_3] + 3H_2O$$

$$2K_3[Fe(C_2O_4)_3] \cdot 3H_2O \xlongequal{光} 2FeC_2O_4 + 3K_2C_2O_4 + 2CO_2 \uparrow + 3H_2O$$

$$FeC_2O_4 \xlongequal{\triangle} FeO + CO_2 \uparrow + CO \uparrow$$

例 22.10 向粉红色溶液 A 中加入过量 NaOH 溶液有粉红色沉淀 B 生成，随后加入氯水，沉淀变为棕褐色沉淀 C，将 C 分离出后溶于浓盐酸得蓝色溶液 D 和气体 E。若将 B 溶于浓盐酸也得溶液 D。

试写出 A，B，C，D 和 E 所代表的物质的化学式，并用化学反应方程式表示各过程。

解：A—$Co(H_2O)_6Cl_2$；　B—$Co(OH)_2$；　C—$Co(OH)_3$；
D—$[CoCl_4]^{2-}$；　E—Cl_2。

各步反应方程式如下：

$$Co(H_2O)_6^{2+} + 2OH^- \longrightarrow Co(OH)_2 \downarrow + 6H_2O$$

$$2Co(OH)_2 + Cl_2 + 2OH^- \longrightarrow 2Co(OH)_3 + 2Cl^-$$

$$2Co(OH)_3 + 10HCl \longrightarrow 2CoCl_4^{2-} + Cl_2 \uparrow + 6H_2O + 4H^+$$

$$Co(OH)_2 + 4HCl \longrightarrow CoCl_4^{2-} + 2H_2O + 2H^+$$

第二部分 习题

一、选择题

22.1 下列过渡金属中，密度最大的是

(A) W；　(B) Os；　(C) Ir；　(D) Au。

22.2 下列金属中，最活泼的是

(A) Fe；　(B) Co；　(C) Ni；　(D) Pd。

22.3 $FeCl_3$ 溶液遇 KSCN 溶液变红，欲使红色褪去，可加入试剂

① Fe 粉 ② $SnCl_2$ ③ $CoCl_2$ ④ NH_4F

(A) ①②③; (B) ①②④; (C) ②③④; (D) ①③④。

22.4 下列物质不能在溶液中大量共存的是

(A) $[Fe(CN)_6]^{3-}$ 和 OH^-; (B) $[Fe(CN)_6]^{3-}$ 和 I^-;

(C) $[Fe(CN)_6]^{4-}$ 和 I_2; (D) Fe^{3+} 和 Br^-。

22.5 能用 NaOH 溶液分离的离子对是

(A) Cr^{3+} 和 Al^{3+}; (B) Cu^{2+} 和 Zn^{2+};

(C) Cr^{3+} 和 Fe^{3+}; (D) Cu^{2+} 和 Fe^{3+}。

22.6 下列化合物中,与浓盐酸作用没有氯气放出的是

(A) Pb_2O_3; (B) Fe_2O_3; (C) Co_2O_3; (D) Ni_2O_3。

22.7 某金属离子在八面体弱场中磁矩为 5.9 μ_B,在八面体强场中的磁矩不为零,则该离子可能是

(A) Fe^{2+}; (B) Fe^{3+}; (C) Co^{2+}; (D) Co^{3+}。

22.8 下列配离子中,按还原性由强至弱排列,顺序正确的是

① $[Co(H_2O)_6]^{2+}$ ② $[Co(NH_3)_6]^{2+}$ ③ $[Co(CN)_6]^{4-}$ ④ $[Fe(CN)_6]^{4-}$

(A) ①②③④; (B) ④③②①; (C) ③④②①; (D) ③②④①。

22.9 下列水合晶体中,加热脱水时不生成碱式盐的是

(A) $MgCl_2 \cdot 6H_2O$; (B) $NiCl_2 \cdot 6H_2O$; (C) $CoCl_2 \cdot 6H_2O$; (D) $CuCl_2 \cdot 2H_2O$。

22.10 下列新制出的沉淀在空气中放置,颜色不发生变化的是

(A) $Mn(OH)_2$; (B) $Fe(OH)_2$; (C) $Co(OH)_2$; (D) $Ni(OH)_2$。

22.11 与 Na_2S 溶液作用均生成黑色沉淀的一对离子是

(A) Fe^{2+},Co^{2+}; (B) Fe^{2+},Mn^{2+}; (C) Ni^{2+},Zn^{2+}; (D) Cu^{2+},Zn^{2+}。

22.12 可以形成记忆合金的一对金属单质是

(A) Ni 与 Fe; (B) Ni 与 Ti; (C) Cu 与 Ni; (D) Ti 与 Co。

22.13 下列金属单质中,耐碱能力最强的是

(A) Cu; (B) Cr; (C) Ni; (D) Pt。

22.14 下列气体中可由 $PdCl_2$ 溶液检出的是

(A) CO_2; (B) CO; (C) O_3; (D) NO_2。

22.15 下列金属单质中,能与王水反应的是

(A) Ta; (B) Os; (C) Ir; (D) Pt。

22.16 过渡金属 M 与有机磷形成的配合物可能形成 π 键,这种 π 键属于

(A) $M(d\pi) \longrightarrow L(p\pi)$; (B) $M(d\pi) \longrightarrow L(d\pi)$;

(C) $L(p\pi) \longrightarrow M(d\pi)$; (D) $L(p\pi) \longrightarrow M(p\pi)$。

二、填空题

22.17 向 $FeCl_3$ 溶液中加入 KSCN 溶液后,溶液变为________色,再加入过量 NH_4F 溶液后,溶液又变为________色。最后滴加 NaOH 溶液时,又有____________生成。

22.18 离子 V^{3+},Cr^{3+},Mn^{2+},Fe^{2+} 与弱场配体生成配合物,按顺磁性由大到小排这些金属离

子，其顺序是________。

22.19　向热的氢氧化铁浓碱性悬浮液中通入氯气，溶液变为______色；再加入 $BaCl_2$ 溶液，则有______色的______生成。

22.20　给出下列物质的化学式。

(1) 赤铁矿______；(2) 磁铁矿______；(3) 褐铁矿______；
(4) 菱铁矿______；(5) 砷钴矿______；(6) 辉钴矿______；
(7) 硫钴矿______；(8) 赤血盐______；(9) 黄血盐______；
(10) 绿矾______；(11) 莫尔盐______；(12) 铁铵矾______；
(13) 二茂铁______；(14) 蔡斯盐______；(15) 顺铂______。

22.21　在配制 $FeSO_4$ 溶液时，常向溶液中加入一些______和______，其目的是________________。

22.22　$FeCl_3$ 的蒸气中含有________分子，其结构类似于______蒸气；其中 Fe^{3+} 的杂化方式为______。$FeCl_3$ 易溶于有机溶剂，原因是____________。

22.23　现有四瓶绿色溶液，分别含有 Ni(Ⅱ)，Cu(Ⅱ)，Cr(Ⅲ)，MnO_4^{2-}。

(1) 加水稀释后，溶液变蓝的是______；
(2) 加入过量酸性 Na_2SO_3 溶液后，变为无色的是____；
(3) 加入适量 NaOH 溶液有沉淀生成，NaOH 过量时沉淀溶解，又得到绿色溶液的是______；
(4) 加入适量氨水有绿色沉淀生成，氨水过量时得到蓝色溶液的是______。

22.24　在 Cr^{3+}，Mn^{2+}，Fe^{2+}，Fe^{3+}，Co^{2+}，Ni^{2+} 中，易溶于过量氨水的是______。

22.25　向 $CoSO_4$ 溶液中加入过量 KCN 溶液，则有______生成，放置后逐渐转化为______。

22.26　给出下列离子的颜色。

$Fe(H_2O)_6^{2+}$ ______，$Co(H_2O)_6^{2+}$ ______，$Ni(H_2O)_6^{2+}$ ______，
$Fe(H_2O)_6^{3+}$ ______，$FeCl_4^-$ ______，$Fe(SCN)_6^{3-}$ ______，
FeF_5^{2-} ______，$Fe(C_2O_4)_3^{3-}$ ______，$[Fe(H_2O)_5OH]^{2+}$ ______，
$Co(NH_3)_6^{2+}$ ______，$CoCl_4^{2-}$ ______，$Co(SCN)_4^{2-}$ ______，
$Ni(NH_3)_6^{3+}$ ______，$Ni(CN)_4^{2-}$ ______，$PtCl_4^{2-}$ ______。

22.27　给出下列化合物的颜色

$FeSO_4\cdot 7H_2O$ ______，$FeSO_4$ ______，$FeSO_4\cdot(NH_4)_2SO_4\cdot 6H_2O$ ______，
$Fe(OH)_2$ ______，$K_4[Fe(CN)_6]\cdot 3H_2O$ ______，$Fe(C_5H_5)_2$ ______，
$FeCl_3$ ______，$FeCl_3\cdot 6H_2O$ ______，$K_3[Fe(CN)_6]$ ______，
$K_3[Fe(C_2O_4)_3]\cdot 3H_2O$ ______，Fe_2O_3 ______，$Fe(OH)_3$ ______，
$CoSO_4\cdot 7H_2O$ ______，$CoCl_2\cdot 6H_2O$，______ $CoCl_2$ ______，
$Co(OH)_2$ ______，$K_3[Co(NO_2)_6]$ ______，$Co[Hg(SCN)_4]$ ______，
$NiSO_4\cdot 7H_2O$ ______，$NiCl_2\cdot 6H_2O$ ______ $Ni(OH)_2$ ______，
$Pt(NH_3)_2Cl_2$ ______，$K[Pt(C_2H_4)Cl_3]\cdot H_2O$ ______。

三、完成并配平下列反应方程式

22.28　将 SO_2 通入 $FeCl_3$ 溶液中。

22.29 稀硫酸溶液中五氧化二钒与硫酸亚铁作用。

22.30 硫酸亚铁溶液与赤血盐混合。

22.31 强碱性条件下向 $Fe(OH)_3$ 加过量次氯酸钠。

22.32 过量氯水滴入 FeI_2 溶液中。

22.33 硫酸亚铁受热分解。

22.34 用浓盐酸处理三氧化二钴。

22.35 用浓硫酸处理 $Co(OH)_3$。

22.36 向 $CoCl_2$ 和溴水的混合溶液中滴加 NaOH 溶液。

22.37 弱酸性条件下向 $CoSO_4$ 溶液中滴加饱和 KNO_2 溶液。

22.38 碱性条件下向 $NiSO_4$ 溶液中加入 NaClO 溶液。

22.39 铂溶于王水。

22.40 将一氧化碳通入 $PdCl_2$ 溶液。

四、简答题和计算题

22.41 写出与下述实验现象有关的反应方程式。

向含有 Fe^{2+} 的溶液中加入 NaOH 溶液后生成蓝绿色沉淀，空气中放置沉淀逐渐变棕色。过滤后，用盐酸溶解棕色沉淀得黄色溶液。向黄色溶液中加入几滴 KSCN 溶液则溶液立即变红，再通入 SO_2 则红色消失。向溶液中再滴入 $KMnO_4$ 溶液，则 $KMnO_4$ 紫色褪去。最后加入黄血盐溶液时，生成蓝色沉淀。

22.42 解释下列问题。

(1) 在 $FeCl_3$ 溶液中加入 KSCN 溶液时出现血红色，再加入少许铁粉后血红色逐渐消失。

(2) 向少量 $FeCl_3$ 溶液中加入过量饱和$(NH_4)_2C_2O_4$ 溶液后，滴加少量 KSCN 溶液并不出现红色，但再滴加盐酸则溶液立即变红。请解释原因。

(3) I_2 不能氧化 Fe^{2+}，但在 KCN 存在下，I_2 可以氧化 Fe^{2+}。

(4) 蓝色的变色硅胶吸水后变成粉红色。

22.43 给出鉴别 Fe^{3+}，Fe^{2+}，Co^{2+}，Ni^{2+} 的常用方法。

22.44 根据铂的化学性质，指出在铂制容器中能否进行下述各试剂参与的化学反应。

(1) HF；(2) 王水；(3) H_2O_2+HCl；(4) Na_2O_2+NaOH；(5) Na_2CO_3；(6) $NaHSO_4$；(7) Na_2CO_3+S。

22.45 $K_4[Fe(CN)_6]$可由 $FeSO_4$ 与 KCN 直接在溶液中制备，但 $K_3[Fe(CN)_6]$却不能由 $Fe_2(SO_4)_3$和 KCN 直接在水溶液中制备，为什么？应如何制备 $K_3[Fe(CN)_6]$？

22.46 给出下列实验的现象和反应方程式。

(1) 向黄血盐溶液中滴加碘水；

(2) 将 $3\ mol\cdot dm^{-3}$ $CoCl_2$ 溶液加热，再滴加 $AgNO_3$ 溶液；

(3) 将$[Ni(NH_3)_6]SO_4$ 溶液水浴加热一段时间再加氨水；

(4) 用浓盐酸处理 $Fe(OH)_3$，$Co(OH)_3$，$Ni(OH)_3$。

22.47 当氯化钴溶于水时，生成粉红色溶液 A。向 A 中加浓盐酸得到蓝色的溶液 B。如果溶液 A 用浓氨水处理，则生成蓝绿色沉淀，当进一步加入浓氨水后，将空气通入该混合物，产生棕黄色的溶液 C。

(1) 写出在 A,B 和 C 中存在的各种含钴物质的化学式；

(2) 指出在 A 和 B 中，配离子的几何构型。

22.48　现有三个标签脱落的试剂瓶，分别盛有 MnO_2，PbO_2，Fe_3O_4 棕黑色粉末。请加以鉴别并写出反应式。

22.49　不用硫化氢和硫化物，设计方案分离含有 Ba^{2+}，Al^{3+}，Cr^{3+}，Fe^{3+}，Co^{2+}，Ni^{2+} 的混合溶液。

22.50　将浅蓝绿色晶体 A 溶于水后加入氢氧化钠溶液和 H_2O_2 并微热，得到棕色沉淀 B 和溶液 C。B 和 C 分离后将溶液 C 加热有碱性气体 D 放出。B 溶于盐酸得黄色溶液 E。向 E 中加 KSCN 溶液有红色的 F 生成。向 F 中滴加 $SnCl_2$ 溶液则红色褪去，F 转化为 G。向 G 中滴加赤血盐溶液有蓝色沉淀 H 生成。向 A 的水溶液中滴加 $BaCl_2$ 溶液有不溶于硝酸的白色沉淀生成。给出 A～H 所代表的主要化合物或离子。

22.51　金属 M 溶于稀盐酸时生成 MCl_2，其磁矩为 5.0B. M.。在无氧操作条件下，MCl_2 溶液遇 NaOH 溶液生成白色沉淀 A。A 接触空气逐渐变绿或蓝绿，最后变成棕色沉淀 B。灼烧时，B 转化为棕红色粉末 C。B 不溶于 NaOH 溶液，B 与草酸氢钾溶液在加热条件下得黄色溶液，蒸发、浓缩后有绿色晶体 D 析出。

B 溶于盐酸生成黄色溶液 E。E 与 KI 溶液作用有 I_2 生成，再加过量的 NaF，I_2 又消失。若向 B 的浓 NaOH 悬浮液中通入 Cl_2 气时可得到紫红色溶液 F。向 F 中加入 $BaCl_2$ 时有红棕色沉淀 G 生成。G 为强氧化剂。请给出 A,B,C,D,E,F,G 所代表的化合物。

22.52　蓝色化合物 A 溶于水得粉红色溶液 B。向 B 中加入过量氢氧化钠溶液得粉红色沉淀 C。用次氯酸钠溶液处理 C 则转化为黑色沉淀 D。洗涤、过滤后将 D 与浓盐酸作用得蓝色溶液 E。将 E 用水稀释后又得粉红色溶液 B。请给出 A,B,C,D,E 所代表的物质。

22.53　混合溶液 A 为紫红色。向 A 中加入浓盐酸并微热得蓝色溶液 B 和气体 C。A 中加入 NaOH 溶液则得棕黑色沉淀 D 和绿色溶液 E。向 A 中通入过量 SO_2 则溶液最后变为粉红色溶液 F。向 F 中加入过量氨水得白色沉淀 G 和棕黄色溶液 H。G 在空气中缓慢转变为棕黑色沉淀。将 D 与 G 混合后加入硫酸又得溶液 A。请给出 A,B,C,D,E,F,G,H 所代表的主要化合物或离子。

22.54　某固体混合物中可能含有 KI，$SnCl_2$，$CuSO_4$，$ZnSO_4$，$FeCl_3$，$CoCl_2$ 和 $NiSO_4$。通过下列实验判断哪些物质肯定存在，哪些物质肯定不存在，并分析原因。

(1) 取少许固体溶入稀硫酸中，没有沉淀生成。

(2) 将盐的水溶液与过量氨水作用，有灰绿色沉淀生成，溶液为蓝色。

(3) 将盐的水溶液与 KSCN 作用，无明显变化。再加入戊醇，也无明显变化。

(4) 向盐的水溶液中加入过量 NaOH 溶液有沉淀生成，溶液无明显颜色。过滤后，向溶液缓慢滴加盐酸时，有白色沉淀生成。

(5) 向盐的溶液中滴加 $AgNO_3$ 溶液时，得到不溶于硝酸的白色沉淀。沉淀溶于氨水。

22.55　某同学在确定所合成的 $K_3[Fe(C_2O_4)_3]\cdot 3H_2O$ 晶体中 FeC_2O_4 杂质的含量时，进行了以下实验：将一定量样品加入稀硫酸中，微热溶解后用 0.0500 $mol\cdot dm^{-3}$ 的高锰酸钾溶液滴定，用去 108.00 cm^3；再加入适量还原剂将三价铁还原为二价铁后，用 $KMnO_4$ 溶液滴定，恰好用去 20.00 cm^3。

(1) 给出滴定反应的离子反应式；

(2) 计算所合成产品的组成(不考虑结晶水)。

22.56 金属 A 溶于稀盐酸，生成化合物 B 的溶液。在无氧操作条件下，将 NaOH 加到 B 溶液中，生成淡绿色沉淀 C。C 接触空气颜色逐渐变深，最后成为棕红色沉淀 D。灼烧 D 可生成棕红色粉末 E，E 经不彻底还原而生成铁磁性黑色物质 F。D 溶于稀盐酸生成 G 的溶液，该溶液能将 KI 氧化成 I_2，但在加入 KI 之前，先加入 NaF，则不能氧化 KI。若向 D 的浓 NaOH 悬浮液中通入氯气，可得到 H 的紫红色溶液，向该溶液中加入 $BaCl_2$ 后就会有红棕色固体 I 析出，I 是一种强氧化剂。试写出 A，B，C，D，E，F，G，H 和 I 所代表的物质的化学式。

22.57 A 为黑色粉末，B 为白色粉末，向 A 和 B 的混合物中加稀盐酸，先得蓝色溶液，逐渐变为淡绿色，同时析出紫红色沉淀 C，过滤后，得滤液 D。沉淀 C 溶于热浓硫酸，得溶液 E 并放出气体 F。将 E 蒸干、灼烧又得到白色粉末 B。向滤液 D 中加入 NaOH 溶液并鼓入空气，生成棕红色沉淀 G；把 G 灼烧后，得红色粉末 H；H 与铝粉混合燃烧得到黑色物质 A。试写出 A，B，C，D，E，F，G 和 H 所代表的物质的化学式。

22.58 有一固体混合物可能含有 $FeCl_3$，$NaNO_2$，$Ca(OH)_2$，$AgNO_3$，$CuCl_2$，NaF，NH_4Cl 七种物质中的若干种。若将此混合物加水后，可得白色沉淀和无色溶液，在此无色溶液中加入 KSCN 没有变化；无色溶液可使酸化后 $KMnO_4$ 溶液紫色褪去；将无色溶液加热有气体放出。另外，白色沉淀可溶于 $NH_3 \cdot H_2O$ 中。

试根据上述现象，判断在混合物中，哪些物质肯定存在，哪些肯定不存在，哪些可能存在，说明理由，并用化学反应方程式表示。

习题参考答案

第 2 章

一、选择题

2.1 A　2.2 C　2.3 D　2.4 B　2.5 C　2.6 D　2.7 A　2.8 B　2.9 A　2.10 C
2.11 D　2.12 B　2.13 C　2.14 C　2.15 A　2.16 D

二、填空题

2.17　$\left(p+\frac{a}{V^2}\right)(V-b)=RT$。

2.18　大，小。

2.19　17 $g\cdot mol^{-1}$，NH_3。

2.20　0.350。

2.21　2.026×10^4，1.013×10^5，8.104×10^4。

2.22　0.48。

2.23　6.08×10^4 Pa。

2.24　9.69。

2.25　35.93 g/100 g (H_2O)；26.44%，5.42 $mol\cdot dm^{-3}$；6.14 $mol\cdot kg^{-1}$；0.10；0.90。

2.26　3.86 $K\cdot kg\cdot mol^{-1}$。

2.27　④ ② ① ③。

2.28　低，$\Delta T_f=K_f\cdot m$。

三、简答题和计算题

2.29　反应前气体的物质的量为

$$n_1=\frac{p_1V}{RT}=\frac{1.23\times10^5\ \mathrm{Pa}\times0.5\times10^{-3}\ \mathrm{m^3}}{8.314\ \mathrm{Pa\cdot m^3\cdot mol^{-1}\cdot K^{-1}}\times298\ \mathrm{K}}=0.024\ 8\ \mathrm{mol}$$

反应后气体的物质的量为

$$n_2=\frac{p_2V}{RT}=\frac{8.3\times10^4\ \mathrm{Pa}\times0.5\times10^{-3}\ \mathrm{m^3}}{8.314\ \mathrm{Pa\cdot m^3\cdot mol^{-1}\cdot K^{-1}}\times298\ \mathrm{K}}=0.016\ 8\ \mathrm{mol}$$

设反应后生成 x mol NO_2 气体，由

$$2NO+O_2=\!=\!=2NO_2$$

$$\left(0.0248-\frac{3}{2}x\right)\text{mol} \quad x\ \text{mol}$$

$$n_2=(0.0248\ \text{mol}-\frac{3}{2}x\text{mol})+x\text{mol}$$

$$=0.0168\ \text{mol}$$

得 $x=0.016$

生成 NO_2 的质量为 $0.016\ \text{mol}\times 46\ \text{g}\cdot\text{mol}^{-1}=0.74\ \text{g}$

2.30 (1) 混合气体中的水蒸气最后全部被干燥剂吸收，则混合气体中氮气的分压为

$$p(N_2)=99.3\ \text{kPa}$$

混合气体中水蒸气的分压为

$$p(H_2O)=101.3\ \text{kPa}-99.3\ \text{kPa}=2.0\ \text{kPa}$$

由公式 $p_i=x_i\,p(\text{总})$，则有

混合气体中氮气的摩尔分数为

$$x(N_2)=\frac{p(N_2)}{p(\text{总})}=\frac{99.3\ \text{kPa}}{101.3\ \text{kPa}}=0.98$$

混合气体中水蒸气的摩尔分数为

$$x(H_2O)=\frac{p(H_2O)}{p(\text{总})}=\frac{2.0\ \text{kPa}}{101.3\ \text{kPa}}=0.02$$

(2) 根据题意，混合气体中水蒸气的质量等于干燥剂增加的质量，则水蒸气中水的物质的量为

$$\frac{0.150\times 10^{-3}\times 10^{3}\ \text{g}}{18\ \text{g}\cdot\text{mol}^{-1}}=8.33\times 10^{-3}\ \text{mol}$$

由理想气体状态方程 $pV=nRT$，得到瓶的体积为

$$V(\text{瓶})=V(H_2O)=\frac{n(H_2O)RT}{p(H_2O)}=\frac{8.33\times 10^{-3}\ \text{mol}\times 8.314\ \text{Pa}\cdot\text{m}^3\cdot\text{mol}^{-1}\cdot\text{K}^{-1}\times 293\ \text{K}}{2.0\times 10^3\ \text{Pa}}$$

$$=10.15\times 10^{-3}\ \text{m}^3=10.15\ \text{dm}^3$$

2.31 电解反应为 $H_2O = H_2+\frac{1}{2}O_2$，则 1 mol H_2O 可生成 1.5 mol 气体。氧气和氢气的分压之和为

$$p(H_2)+p(O_2)=p(\text{总})-p(N_2)=1.88\times 10^5\ \text{Pa}-(1.01\times 10^5\ \text{Pa}-4.04\times 10^3\ \text{Pa})$$

$$=9.104\times 10^4\ \text{Pa}$$

氧气和氢气的物质的量为

$$n(H_2)+n(O_2)=\frac{[p(H_2)+p(O_2)]V}{RT}$$

$$=\frac{9.104\times 10^4\ \text{Pa}\times 3\times 10^{-3}\ \text{m}^3}{8.314\ \text{Pa}\cdot\text{m}^3\cdot\text{mol}^{-1}\cdot\text{K}^{-1}\times 302\ \text{K}}$$

$$=0.1088\ \text{mol}$$

容器中水的质量为

$$0.1088\ \text{mol}\times\frac{2}{3}\times 18\ \text{g}\cdot\text{mol}^{-1}=1.306\ \text{g}$$

2.32 氧气的分压为

$$p(O_2)=7.97\times10^4\ \text{Pa}-4.23\times10^3\ \text{Pa}=7.547\times10^4\ \text{Pa}$$

由理想气体状态方程 $pV=nRT$ 得氧气的物质的量

$$n(O_2)=\frac{p(O_2)\cdot V}{RT}$$

$$=\frac{7.547\times10^4\ \text{Pa}\times1.5\times10^{-3}\ \text{m}^3}{8.314\ \text{Pa}\cdot\text{m}^3\cdot\text{mol}^{-1}\cdot\text{K}^{-1}\times303\ \text{K}}$$

$$=4.49\times10^{-2}\ \text{mol}$$

由反应式 $2KClO_3 \xlongequal{} 2KCl+3O_2$

分解的 $KClO_3$ 的质量为

$$4.49\times10^{-2}\ \text{mol}\times\frac{2}{3}\times122.6\ \text{g}\cdot\text{mol}^{-1}=3.67\ \text{g}$$

2.33 设原混合气体中 C_2H_4 的物质的量为 n_1，H_2 的物质的量为 n_2

反应	C_2H_4+	H_2	$\xlongequal{}$ C_2H_6	
反应前	n_1	n_2	0	$n(总)=n_1+n_2$
反应后	0	n_2-n_1	n_1	$n(总)=(n_2-n_1)+n_1=n_2$

原混合气体中 C_2H_4 的摩尔分数为

$$x(C_2H_4)=\frac{n_1}{n_1+n_2}$$

$$=1-\frac{n_2}{n_1+n_2}=1-\frac{p(终)}{p(始)}$$

$$=1-\frac{4\,530\ \text{Pa}}{6\,930\ \text{Pa}}=0.346$$

2.34 根据理想气体状态方程 $pV=nRT$，2.3 g 乙醇气体所占的体积为

$$V=\frac{nRT}{p}$$

$$=\frac{2.3\ \text{g}/46\ \text{g}\cdot\text{mol}^{-1}\times8.314\ \text{Pa}\cdot\text{m}^3\cdot\text{mol}^{-1}\cdot\text{K}^{-1}\times293\ \text{K}}{5\,866.2\ \text{Pa}}$$

$$=2.076\times10^{-2}\text{m}^3=20.76\ \text{dm}^3$$

在 20.76 dm^3 气体中，空气的分压为

$$p(空)=1.013\times10^5\ \text{Pa}-5\,866\ \text{Pa}=9.54\times10^4\ \text{Pa}$$

通入 1.013×10^5Pa 的空气的体积为

$$V(空)=\frac{9.54\times10^4\text{Pa}\times20.76\ \text{dm}^3}{1.013\times10^5\text{Pa}}=19.55\ \text{dm}^3$$

或 $V(空)=20.76\ \text{dm}^3\left(1-\frac{5\,866\ \text{Pa}}{1.013\times10^5\ \text{Pa}}\right)$

$=19.56\ \text{dm}^3$

2.35 通入空气的物质的量为

$$n(空)=\frac{pV}{RT}=\frac{1.013\times10^5\ \text{Pa}\times1.0\times10^{-3}\text{m}^3}{8.314\ \text{Pa}\cdot\text{m}^3\cdot\text{mol}^{-1}\cdot\text{K}^{-1}\times273\ \text{K}}=0.044\,6\ \text{mol}$$

被空气带走的二甲醚蒸气的物质的量为

$$n(\text{甲})=\frac{0.0335\ \text{g}}{46\ \text{g}\cdot\text{mol}^{-1}}=7.28\times10^{-4}\ \text{mol}$$

依题意，混合气体的总压等于外压(1.013×10^5 Pa)，二甲醚蒸气的分压为

$$\begin{aligned}p(\text{甲})&=\frac{n(\text{甲})}{n(\text{甲})+n(\text{空})}\cdot p(\text{总})\\&=\frac{7.28\times10^{-4}}{7.28\times10^{-4}+4.46\times10^{-2}}\times1.013\times10^5\ \text{Pa}\\&=1.63\times10^3\ \text{Pa}\end{aligned}$$

2.36 反应式 $2H_2(g)+O_2(g) = 2H_2O(l)$

		$2H_2(g)$	$O_2(g)$	$2H_2O(l)$
反应前	n_0/mol	$2a$	$2a$	0
反应后	n_t/mol	0	a	$2a$

反应后的体积是 a mol O_2 和饱和水蒸气形成的混合气体。其中水蒸气的分压为 $p(H_2O)$，由题设可知 $p(H_2O)=3.17$ kPa。

下面求取氧气的分压 $p(O_2)$，根据分压的定义，当 a mol 氧气单独占有容器总体积 V 时，其压强即为 $p(O_2)$。

由 $pV=nRT$，得出当 V、R、T 不变时有 $p\propto n$，即压强与物质的量成正比。根据题设 $4a$ mol 气体形成的压强为 100 kPa，可知 a mol 氧气形成的 $p(O_2)$为

$$\frac{100\ \text{kPa}}{4}=25\ \text{kPa}$$

由分压定律 $p_{\text{总}}=\sum_i p_i$，故

$$p_{\text{总}}=p(O_2)+p(H_2O)$$

即 $$p_{\text{总}}=25\ \text{kPa}+3.17\ \text{kPa}=28.17\ \text{kPa}$$

2.37 剩余的 H_2SO_4 与 NaOH 发生反应

$$H_2SO_4+2NaOH = Na_2SO_4+2H_2O$$

与 NH_3 反应所消耗 H_2SO_4 的物质的量为

$$50\times10^{-3}\text{dm}^3\times0.50\ \text{mol}\cdot\text{dm}^{-3}-\frac{1}{2}\times10.4\times10^{-3}\text{dm}^3\times1.0\ \text{mol}\cdot\text{dm}^{-3}=0.0198\ \text{mol}$$

NH_3 与 H_2SO_4 的反应为

$$2NH_3+H_2SO_4 = (NH_4)_2SO_4$$

饱和溶液中 NH_3 的物质的量为

$$0.0198\ \text{mol}\times2=0.0396\ \text{mol}$$

溶液中 NH_3 的质量为

$$0.0396\ \text{mol}\times17.0\ \text{g}\cdot\text{mol}^{-1}=0.6732\ \text{g}$$

饱和溶液中水的质量为

$$3.018\ \text{g}-0.6732\ \text{g}=2.3448\ \text{g}$$

NH_3 在水中的溶解度为

$$\frac{0.6732\ \text{g}}{2.3448\ \text{g}}\times100\ \text{g}/100\ \text{g}(H_2O)=28.71\ \text{g}/100\ \text{g}(H_2O)$$

2.38 由 $p=p_A^* x_A$ 得丙酮的摩尔分数为

$$x(丙酮)=\frac{p}{p^*(丙酮)}=\frac{35\ 570\ \mathrm{Pa}}{37\ 330\ \mathrm{Pa}}=0.952\,9$$

设非挥发性有机物的摩尔质量为 M,由

$$x(丙酮)=\frac{\dfrac{120\ \mathrm{g}}{58\ \mathrm{g\cdot mol^{-1}}}}{\dfrac{120\ \mathrm{g}}{58\ \mathrm{g\cdot mol^{-1}}}+\dfrac{6\ \mathrm{g}}{M}}=0.952\,9$$

得 $M=58.2\ \mathrm{g\cdot mol^{-1}}$

2.39 根据题意,$\Delta T_b=K_b\cdot b=K_b\cdot\dfrac{\dfrac{W_B}{M_B}}{W_A}$

$$\begin{aligned}M_B&=\frac{K_bW_B}{W_A\Delta T_b}\\&=\frac{2.53\ \mathrm{K\cdot kg\cdot mol^{-1}}\times3.24\ \mathrm{g}}{40\ \mathrm{g}\times0.81\ \mathrm{K}}\\&=253\ \mathrm{g\cdot mol^{-1}}\end{aligned}$$

设此硫分子的分子式为 S_n,则 $32n=253$,$n=8$。

因此,此溶液中的硫分子是由 8 个硫原子组成的。

2.40 以葡萄糖水溶液为例进行计算。

先求出葡萄糖水溶液的质量摩尔浓度,依题意,100 g H_2O 中溶解 10 g 葡萄糖,按此比例 1 000 g H_2O 中有 100 g 葡萄糖。设溶液的质量摩尔浓度为b,则

$$\begin{aligned}b&=\frac{100\ \mathrm{g\cdot kg^{-1}}}{180\ \mathrm{g\cdot mol^{-1}}}\\&=0.556\ \mathrm{mol\cdot kg^{-1}}\end{aligned}$$

$$\Delta T_f=k_fb$$

已知 H_2O 溶液的 $k_f=1.86\ \mathrm{K\cdot kg\cdot mol^{-1}}$,将其与 b 值代入公式中

$$\begin{aligned}\Delta T_f&=1.86\ \mathrm{K\cdot kg\cdot mol^{-1}}\times0.556\ \mathrm{mol\cdot kg^{-1}}\\&=1.034\ \mathrm{K}\end{aligned}$$

由 ΔT_f(凝固点降低值)的定义式

$$\Delta T_f=T_f^0-T_f$$

故

$$\begin{aligned}T_f&=T_f^0-\Delta T_f\\&=273\ \mathrm{K}-1.034\ \mathrm{K}\\&=271.97\ \mathrm{K}\end{aligned}$$

同理对甘油有 $b=1.087\ \mathrm{mol\cdot kg^{-1}}$,$\Delta T_f=2.022\ \mathrm{K}$,$T_f=270.98\ \mathrm{K}$。

2.41 对于 $Pb(NO_3)_2$:

其质量摩尔浓度 $b_1=\dfrac{\dfrac{0.570\ \mathrm{g}}{331.2\ \mathrm{g\cdot mol^{-1}}}}{120\times10^{-3}\ \mathrm{kg}}=0.014\,3\ \mathrm{mol\cdot kg^{-1}}$

通过测定凝固点降低值，溶液的质量摩尔浓度

$$b_2=\frac{0.08\ \text{K}}{1.86\ \text{K}\cdot\text{kg}\cdot\text{mol}^{-1}}=0.0430\ \text{mol}\cdot\text{kg}^{-1}$$

溶液中的粒子数目 $\frac{0.0430\ \text{mol}}{0.0143\ \text{mol}}=3$

可见 $Pb(NO_3)_2$ 在水中是完全解离的。

对于 $PbCl_2$：

其质量摩尔浓度 $b_2=\frac{\frac{0.570\ \text{g}}{278.2\ \text{g}\cdot\text{mol}^{-1}}}{100\times10^{-3}\text{kg}}=0.0205\ \text{mol}\cdot\text{kg}^{-1}$

通过测定凝固点降低值，溶液的质量摩尔浓度

$$b_2=\frac{0.0381\ \text{K}}{1.86\ \text{K}\cdot\text{kg}\cdot\text{mol}^{-1}}=0.0205\ \text{mol}\cdot\text{kg}^{-1}$$

溶液中的粒子数目 $\frac{0.0205\ \text{mol}}{0.0205\ \text{mol}}=1$

可见 $PbCl_2$ 在水中溶解度很小，几乎不解离，以分子形式存在。

2.42 $\Delta T_f=K_f\cdot m$

$$=1.86\ \text{K}\cdot\text{kg}\cdot\text{mol}^{-1}\times\frac{2\ \text{g}}{60\ \text{g}\cdot\text{mol}^{-1}}\div(75\times10^{-3}\text{kg})$$

$$=0.83\ \text{K}$$

纯水的凝固点 273 K，则所配溶液的凝固点为

$$T=273\ \text{K}-0.83\ \text{K}=272.17\ \text{K}$$

2.43 (1) 通入空气的物质的量为

$$n(\text{空})=\frac{pV}{RT}=\frac{1.013\times10^5\ \text{Pa}\times4.0\times10^{-3}\text{m}^3}{8.314\ \text{Pa}\cdot\text{m}^3\cdot\text{mol}^{-1}\cdot\text{K}^{-1}\times293\ \text{K}}=0.1663\ \text{mol}$$

被空气带走的苯蒸气物质的量为

$$n(\text{苯})=\frac{1.185\ \text{g}}{78.0\ \text{g}\cdot\text{mol}^{-1}}=0.0152\ \text{mol}$$

混合气体的总压为 1.013×10^5 Pa，则苯蒸气分压为

$$p(\text{苯})=\frac{n(\text{苯})}{n(\text{空})+n(\text{苯})}\times p(\text{总})$$

$$=\frac{0.0152}{0.1663+0.0152}\times1.013\times10^5\ \text{Pa}$$

$$=8.48\times10^3\ \text{Pa}$$

混合气体中苯的蒸气压就是苯溶液的蒸气压。由拉乌尔定律，$p=p_A^{\ominus}\cdot x_A$ 得苯的摩尔分数为

$$x(\text{苯})=\frac{p(\text{苯})}{p^{\ominus}(\text{苯})}=\frac{8.48\times10^3\ \text{Pa}}{1\times10^4\ \text{Pa}}=0.848$$

设溶质的摩尔质量为 M，由摩尔分数定义得

$$x(\text{苯})=\frac{\frac{100\ \text{g}}{78\ \text{g}\cdot\text{mol}^{-1}}}{\frac{100\ \text{g}}{78\ \text{g}\cdot\text{mol}^{-1}}+\frac{15\ \text{g}}{M}}=0.848$$

解得 $M=65.3\ g\cdot mol^{-1}$

(2) 苯溶液的质量摩尔浓度为

$$b=\frac{\dfrac{15\ g}{65.3\ g\cdot mol^{-1}}}{100\times10^{-3}\ kg}=2.297\ mol\cdot kg^{-1}$$

由 $\Delta T_f=K_f\cdot b=5.1\ K\cdot mol^{-1}\cdot kg\times2.297\ mol\cdot kg^{-1}=11.7\ K$

苯溶液凝固点为

$$T=T_f-\Delta T_f=278.4\ K-11.7\ K=266.7\ K$$

由 $\Delta T_b=K_b\cdot b=2.53\ K\cdot mol^{-1}\cdot kg\times2.297\ mol\cdot kg^{-1}=5.8\ K$

该苯溶液的沸点为

$$T=T_b+\Delta T_b=353.1\ K+5.8\ K=358.9\ K$$

2.44 由 $\Delta T_f=K_f\cdot b$ 得溶液的质量摩尔浓度

$$b=\frac{\Delta T_f}{K_f}=\frac{0.543\ K}{1.86\ K\cdot mol^{-1}\cdot kg}=0.292\ mol\cdot kg^{-1}$$

该葡萄糖溶液的质量分数为

$$w=\frac{0.292\ mol\times180\ g\cdot mol^{-1}}{0.292\ mol\times180\ g\cdot mol^{-1}+1\,000\ g}\times100\%=5.0\%$$

根据 $\Pi=cRT$，且稀溶液中 $c\approx b$

血液的温度约为 37℃，即 $T=310\ K$。则血液的渗透压为

$$\Pi=cRT\approx0.292\ mol\cdot dm^{-3}\times8.314\times10^{3}\ Pa\cdot dm^{3}\cdot mol^{-1}\cdot K^{-1}\times310\ K$$
$$=752.6\times10^{3}\ Pa=752.6\ kPa$$

第 3 章

一、选择题

3.1 D　3.2 B　3.3 A　3.4 B　3.5 D　3.6 C　3.7 B　3.8 D　3.9 C　3.10 A
3.11 D　3.12 C　3.13 A　3.14 D

二、填空题

3.15 54.56 kJ，10.48 kJ，98.64 kJ，173.2 $J\cdot K^{-1}$，0。

3.16 C，B，77，A，−161.6，D。

3.17 −3.72。

3.18 92.52，58.93。

3.19 $-90.7\ kJ\cdot mol^{-1}$，0.451。

3.20 $178\ kJ\cdot mol^{-1}$，$161\ J\cdot mol^{-1}\cdot K^{-1}$。

3.21 Li(s)，LiCl(s)，Ne(g)，$Cl_2(g)$，$I_2(g)$。

3.22 <，>。

3.23 ΔS，ΔG。

三、简答题和计算题

3.24 反应在恒容条件下进行，则有

$$\Delta_r U_m^\ominus = \Delta_r U/\xi = Q_V/\xi$$

反应进度 $\xi = \dfrac{\Delta n(NH_3)}{\nu(NH_3)} = \dfrac{2\ mol - 0}{2} = 1\ mol$

$$Q_V = -82.7\ kJ$$

则 $\Delta_r U_m^\ominus = Q_V/\xi = \dfrac{-82.7\ kJ}{1\ mol} = -82.7\ kJ\cdot mol^{-1}$

$\Delta_r H_m^\ominus = \Delta_r U_m^\ominus + \Delta\nu RT$

$= -82.7\ kJ\cdot mol^{-1} + (-2)\times 8.314\times 10^{-3}\ kJ\cdot mol^{-1}\cdot K^{-1}\times 298\ K$

$= -87.66\ kJ\cdot mol^{-1}$

3.25 设产生 1 dm^3 水煤气时消耗的碳为 $n(C)$。

根据题意，CO 和 CO_2 总量为 $n(C)$，其中 CO 为 0.95 $n(C)$，CO_2 为 0.05 $n(C)$，而 H_2 为 1.05 $n(C)$

由 $pV=nRT$ 得

$$n(总) = \frac{pV}{RT}$$

$$= \frac{1.0\times 10^5\ Pa\times 1\ dm^3}{8.314\times 10^3\ Pa\cdot dm^3\cdot mol^{-1}\cdot K^{-1}\times 298\ K}$$

$$= 0.040\ mol$$

$$n(总) = n(CO) + n(CO_2) + n(H_2)$$

$$= 0.95\ n(C) + 0.05 n(C) + 1.05 n(C)$$

得 $n(C) = 0.019\,5\ mol$

其中CO 为 $0.019\,5\ mol\times 0.95 = 0.019\ mol$

H_2 为 $0.019\,5\ mol\times 1.05 = 0.020\ mol$

水煤气的燃烧反应

$$CO(g) + \frac{1}{2}O_2(g) = CO_2(g) \qquad (1)$$

$$H_2(g) + \frac{1}{2}O_2(g) = H_2O(g) \qquad (2)$$

$\Delta_r H_m^\ominus(1) = -393.5\ kJ\cdot mol^{-1} - (-110.5\ kJ\cdot mol^{-1}) = -283.0\ kJ\cdot mol^{-1}$

$\Delta_r H_m^\ominus(2) = -241.8\ kJ\cdot mol^{-1}$

1 dm^3 水煤气燃烧产生的热量为

$\Delta_r H = n(CO)\cdot\Delta_r H_m^\ominus(1) + n(H_2)\cdot\Delta_r H_m^\ominus(2)$

$= 0.019\ mol\times(-283.0\ kJ\cdot mol^{-1}) + 0.020\ mol\times(-241.8\ kJ\cdot mol^{-1})$

$= -10.21\ kJ$

3.26 由 $\Delta_f H_m^\ominus(H_2O,l) = -285.8\ kJ\cdot mol^{-1}$ 得

$$H_2(g) + \frac{1}{2}O_2(g) \xlongequal{\quad} H_2O(l) \qquad \Delta_r H_m^\ominus = -285.8\ kJ\cdot mol^{-1}$$

即 $$\begin{aligned}\Delta_r U_m^\ominus &= \Delta_r H_m^\ominus - \Delta\nu RT \\ &= -285.8\ \text{kJ·mol}^{-1} - (-1.5)\times 8.314\times 10^{-3}\ \text{kJ·mol}^{-1}\text{·K}^{-1}\times 298\ \text{K} \\ &= -282.1\ \text{kJ·mol}^{-1}\end{aligned}$$

生成水的恒容反应热为

$$Q_V = n\Delta_r U_m^\ominus = 0.2\ \text{mol}\times(-282.1\ \text{kJ·mol}^{-1}) = -56.42\ \text{kJ}$$

由题意，0.2 mol $H_2(g)$燃烧生成 $H_2O(l)$时所放出的热量等于热量计所吸收的热量，则热量计的热容为

$$C = \frac{-Q_V}{T} = \frac{56.42\ \text{kJ}}{0.88\ \text{K}} = 64.11\ \text{kJ·K}^{-1}$$

同理，0.01 mol 甲苯燃烧放出的热量等于热量计吸收的热量：

$$\begin{aligned}Q_V &= -64.11\ \text{kJ·K}^{-1}\times 0.615\ \text{K} \\ &= -39.43\ \text{kJ}\end{aligned}$$

甲苯燃烧反应的 $\Delta_r U_m^\ominus$ 为

$$\Delta_r U_m^\ominus = \frac{Q_V}{\xi} = \frac{-39.43\ \text{kJ}}{0.01\ \text{mol}} = -3\,943\ \text{kJ·mol}^{-1}$$

甲苯燃烧反应的 $\Delta_r H_m^\ominus$ 为

$$\begin{aligned}\Delta_r H_m^\ominus &= \Delta_r U_m^\ominus + \Delta\nu RT \\ &= -3\,943\ \text{kJ·mol}^{-1} + (-2)\times 8.314\times 10^{-3}\ \text{kJ·mol}^{-1}\text{·K}^{-1}\times 298\ \text{K} \\ &= -3\,948\ \text{kJ·mol}^{-1}\end{aligned}$$

3.27 $C_3H_6(g)$的标准摩尔燃烧热 $\Delta_c H_m^\ominus$ 即为反应

$$C_3H_6(g) + \frac{9}{2}O_2(g) = 3CO_2(g) + 3H_2O(l)$$

的恒压反应热 $\Delta_r H_m^\ominus$。其恒容反应热用 $\Delta_r U_m^\ominus$ 表示。

该反应气相物质的化学计量数改变量为 $\Delta\nu$

$$\Delta\nu = 3 - \left(1 + \frac{9}{2}\right) = -\frac{5}{2}$$

由公式 $\Delta_r H_m^\ominus = \Delta_r U_m^\ominus + \Delta\nu RT$，得

$$\Delta_r U_m^\ominus = \Delta_r H_m^\ominus - \Delta\nu RT$$

将 $\Delta\nu$ 值代入，得

$$\begin{aligned}\Delta_r U_m^\ominus &= -2\,058.0\ \text{kJ·mol}^{-1} - \left(-\frac{5}{2}\right)\times 8.314\ \text{J·mol}^{-1}\text{·K}^{-1}\times 298\ \text{K}\times 10^{-3}\ \text{kJ·J}^{-1} \\ &= -2\,051.8\ \text{kJ·mol}^{-1}\end{aligned}$$

3.28 反应 $2N_2H_4(l) + N_2O_4(g) = 3N_2(g) + 4H_2O(l)$

$$\begin{aligned}\Delta_r H_m^\ominus &= 4\times(-285.8\ \text{kJ·mol}^{-1}) - 2\times 50.6\ \text{kJ·mol}^{-1} - 9.16\ \text{kJ·mol}^{-1} \\ &= -1\,253.56\ \text{kJ·mol}^{-1}\end{aligned}$$

燃烧 1 kg $N_2H_4(l)$所放出的热量为

$$Q=\frac{1\,000\ \text{g}}{32\ \text{g}\cdot\text{mol}^{-1}}\times\frac{-1\,253.56\ \text{kJ}\cdot\text{mol}^{-1}}{2}$$
$$=-19\,587\ \text{kJ}$$
$$\approx-1.96\times10^{4}\ \text{kJ}$$

燃烧 1 kg N_2H_4 需 $N_2O_4(g)$的体积为

$$V=\frac{nRT}{p}$$
$$=\frac{\frac{1\,000\ \text{g}}{32\ \text{g}\cdot\text{mol}^{-1}}\times\frac{1}{2}\times8.314\times10^{3}\ \text{Pa}\cdot\text{dm}^{3}\cdot\text{mol}^{-1}\cdot\text{K}^{-1}\times300\ \text{K}}{1.013\times10^{5}\ \text{Pa}}$$
$$=384.7\ \text{dm}^{3}$$

3.29 根据题设，可得

$$2\text{C(石墨)}+\text{O}_2(\text{g})=\!=\!=2\text{CO(g)}\qquad\times\left(-\frac{1}{2}\right)$$
$$2\text{H}_2\text{O(g)}=\!=\!=\text{O}_2(\text{g})+2\text{H}_2(\text{g})\qquad\times\left(+\frac{1}{2}\right)$$
$$+)\ \text{CO(g)}+\text{H}_2\text{O(g)}=\!=\!=\text{CO}_2(\text{g})+\text{H}_2(\text{g})\qquad\times(-1)$$
$$\text{CO}_2(\text{g})=\!=\!=\text{C(石墨)}+\text{O}_2(\text{g})$$

所以根据盖斯定律，所得的化学反应的摩尔反应热为

$$\Delta_r H_m^\ominus=\Delta_r H_m^\ominus(1)\times\left(-\frac{1}{2}\right)+\Delta_r H_m^\ominus(2)\times\left(+\frac{1}{2}\right)+\Delta_r H_m^\ominus(3)\times(-1)$$
$$=\left[(-222)\times\left(-\frac{1}{2}\right)+484\times\left(+\frac{1}{2}\right)+(-41)\times(-1)\right]\ \text{kJ}\cdot\text{mol}^{-1}$$
$$=394\ \text{kJ}\cdot\text{mol}^{-1}$$

3.30 由盖斯定律得$(4)=\frac{1}{6}[(1)\times3-(2)-(3)\times2]$

$$\Delta_r H_m^\ominus(4)=\frac{1}{6}[\Delta_r H_m^\ominus(1)\times3-\Delta_r H_m^\ominus(2)-\Delta_r H_m^\ominus(3)\times2]$$
$$=\frac{1}{6}[(-27.61\ \text{kJ}\cdot\text{mol}^{-1})\times3-(-58.58\ \text{kJ}\cdot\text{mol}^{-1})-38.07\ \text{kJ}\cdot\text{mol}^{-1}\times2]$$
$$=-16.73\ \text{kJ}\cdot\text{mol}^{-1}$$

3.31 $\Delta_r H_m^\ominus$ 表示的是处于标准状态的反应物生成标准状态的产物的焓变，即反应热。

$\Delta_f H_m^\ominus$ 表示的是由处于标准状态的各种元素的指定单质生成标准状态的 1 mol 某纯物质时的热效应。

$\Delta_c H_m^\ominus$ 表示的是在标准大气压下 1 mol 物质完全燃烧时的热效应。完全燃烧在热力学上有严格的规定：碳、氮、硫燃烧产物分别为气体 CO_2，N_2，SO_2，氢、氯的燃烧产物分别液态 H_2O 和 HCl 水溶液。

一个反应同时满足以上三个热力学函数的条件时，则 $\Delta_r H_m^\ominus=\Delta_f H_m^\ominus=\Delta_c H_m^\ominus$，如 1 mol H_2 完全燃烧反应：

$$H_2(g)+1/2O_2(g) \longrightarrow H_2O(l)$$

该反应的反应热等于 $H_2(g)$的标准摩尔燃烧热，也等于 $H_2O(l)$的标准摩尔生成热，即

$$\Delta_c H_m^\ominus(H_2,g)=\Delta_f H_m^\ominus(H_2O,l)=\Delta_r H_m^\ominus$$

注意：如果上述反应的产物是 $H_2O(g)$，则 $\Delta_c H_m^\ominus(H_2,g)\neq\Delta_f H_m^\ominus(H_2O,g)$，因为 $H_2(g)$完全燃烧的产物应是液态 H_2O，而不是气态 H_2O。

再如，1 mol 石墨完全燃烧反应的 $\Delta_r H_m^\ominus$、$\Delta_f H_m^\ominus$ 和 $\Delta_c H_m^\ominus$ 在数值上相等：

$$C(石墨)+O_2(g) \longrightarrow CO_2(g)$$

即该反应的反应热 $\Delta_r H_m^\ominus$ 值等于C(石墨)的标准摩尔燃烧热 $\Delta_c H_m^\ominus$ 值，也等于气态 CO_2 的标准摩尔生成热值，所以有：

$$\Delta_c H_m^\ominus(石墨)=\Delta_f H_m^\ominus(CO_2,g)=\Delta_r H_m^\ominus$$

3.32 $\Delta H=352\ \text{J}\cdot\text{g}^{-1}\times 76.15\ \text{g}\cdot\text{mol}^{-1}\times 1\ \text{mol}$

$=26\ 805\ \text{J}$

$\approx 26.8\ \text{kJ}$

$\Delta U=\Delta H-\Delta nRT$

$=26.8\ \text{kJ}-1\ \text{mol}\times 8.314\times10^{-3}\text{kJ}\cdot\text{mol}^{-1}\cdot\text{K}^{-1}\times 319.3\ \text{K}$

$=24.1\ \text{kJ}$

$\Delta S=\dfrac{\Delta H}{T}=\dfrac{26\ 805\ \text{J}}{319.3\ \text{K}}=83.95\ \text{J}\cdot\text{K}^{-1}$

3.33 (1) $HCHO(g)+O_2(g) \longrightarrow CO_2(g)+H_2O(l)$

$$\begin{aligned}\Delta_c H_m^\ominus(CH_2O,g)&=\Delta_r U_m^\ominus+\Delta\nu RT\\&=-568.2\ \text{kJ}\cdot\text{mol}^{-1}+(1-2)\times 8.314\times10^{-3}\text{kJ}\cdot\text{mol}^{-1}\cdot\text{K}^{-1}\times 298\ \text{K}\\&=-570.7\ \text{kJ}\cdot\text{mol}^{-1}\end{aligned}$$

$$CH_3OH(l)+\frac{1}{2}O_2(g) \longrightarrow HCHO(g)+H_2O(l)$$

$$\Delta_r H_m^\ominus=\sum_i \nu_i\Delta_c H_m^\ominus(反应物)-\sum_i \nu_i\Delta_c H_m^\ominus(生成物)$$

$$\Delta_r H_m^\ominus=\Delta_c H_m^\ominus(CH_3OH,l)-\Delta_c H_m^\ominus(CH_2O,g)$$

$$-155.4\ \text{kJ}\cdot\text{mol}^{-1}=\Delta_c H_m^\ominus(CH_3OH,l)-(-570.7\ \text{kJ}\cdot\text{mol}^{-1})$$

$$\Delta_c H_m^\ominus(CH_3OH,l)=-726.1\ \text{kJ}\cdot\text{mol}^{-1}$$

(2) $CH_3OH(l)+\frac{3}{2}O_2(g) \longrightarrow CO_2(g)+2H_2O(l)$

$$\Delta_r H_m^\ominus=\sum_i \nu_i\Delta_f H_m^\ominus(生成物)-\sum_i \nu_i\Delta_f H_m^\ominus(反应物)$$

$$\begin{aligned}\Delta_r H_m^\ominus=\Delta_c H_m^\ominus(CH_3OH,l)&=(-393.5\ \text{kJ}\cdot\text{mol}^{-1})+2\times(-285.8\ \text{kJ}\cdot\text{mol}^{-1})-\Delta_f H_m^\ominus(CH_3OH,l)\\&=-726.1\ \text{kJ}\cdot\text{mol}^{-1}\end{aligned}$$

$$\Delta_f H_m^\ominus(CH_3OH,l)=-239.0\ \text{kJ}\cdot\text{mol}^{-1}$$

3.34 $CS_2(l) \xlongequal{} CS_2(g)$

在298 K达平衡时，液态的CS_2与气态的CS_2的相变可以视为可逆过程。恒温可逆过程中的熵变为

$$\Delta S=\frac{Q_r}{T}$$

故$CS_2(l)$变为$CS_2(g)$的熵变为

$$\Delta S=\frac{Q_r}{T}=\frac{\Delta_v H_m^\ominus}{T}=\frac{27.7\times10^3\ J\cdot mol^{-1}}{298\ K}=92.95\ J\cdot mol^{-1}\cdot K^{-1}$$

由 $\Delta S^\ominus=S_m^\ominus(CS_2,g)-S_m^\ominus(CS_2,l)$

得 $S_m^\ominus(CS_2,g)=S_m^\ominus(CS_2,l)+\Delta S_m^\ominus$

$$=151.3\ J\cdot mol^{-1}\cdot K^{-1}+92.95\ J\cdot mol^{-1}\cdot K^{-1}$$
$$=244.25\ J\cdot mol^{-1}\cdot K^{-1}$$

3.35 (1) $C_2H_4(g)$，$H_2(g)$，$C(s)$的燃烧反应的热化学反应方程式

$C_2H_4(g)+3O_2(g) \xlongequal{} 2CO_2(g)+2H_2O(l)$ $\quad \Delta_c H_m^\ominus(1)=-1\,411.2\ kJ\cdot mol^{-1}$

$C(s)+O_2(g) \xlongequal{} CO_2(g)$ $\quad \Delta_c H_m^\ominus(2)=-393.5\ kJ\cdot mol^{-1}$

$H_2(g)+\frac{1}{2}O_2(g) \xlongequal{} H_2O(l)$ $\quad \Delta_c H_m^\ominus(3)=-285.8\ kJ\cdot mol^{-1}$

(2) 解法一：由燃烧热求化学反应的反应热。

$C_2H_4(g)$生成反应方程式

$$2C(s)+2H_2(g) \xlongequal{} C_2H_4(g)$$

由关系式 $\Delta_r H_m^\ominus=\sum_i \nu_i \Delta_c H_m^\ominus(\text{反应物})-\sum_i \nu_i \Delta_c H_m^\ominus(\text{生成物})$

$C_2H_4(g)$标准摩尔生成热

$$\Delta_f H_m^\ominus=\Delta_r H_m^\ominus=[2\times\Delta_c H_m^\ominus(2)+2\times\Delta_c H_m^\ominus(3)]-\Delta_c H_m^\ominus(1)$$
$$=[2\times(-393.5\ kJ\cdot mol^{-1})+2\times(-285.8\ kJ\cdot mol^{-1})]-(-1\,411.2\ kJ\cdot mol^{-1})$$
$$=52.6\ kJ\cdot mol^{-1}$$

解法二：由生成热求化学反应的反应热。

由反应式可知，$\Delta_c H_m^\ominus(2)=\Delta_f H_m^\ominus(CO_2,g)$， $\quad \Delta_c H_m^\ominus(3)=\Delta_f H_m^\ominus(H_2O,l)$

$C_2H_4(g)$标准摩尔生成热可通过反应

$$C_2H_4(g)+3O_2(g) \xlongequal{} 2\ CO_2(g)+2H_2O(l)$$

的反应热（燃烧热）求得。

$$\Delta_r H_m^\ominus=\sum_i \nu_i \Delta_f H_m^\ominus-\sum_i \nu_i \Delta_f H_m^\ominus$$

$$\Delta_c H_m^\ominus(C_2H_4,g)=[2\times\Delta_f H_m^\ominus(CO_2,g)+2\times\Delta_f H_m^\ominus(H_2O,l)]-\Delta_f H_m^\ominus(C_2H_4,g)$$

$$\Delta_f H_m^\ominus(C_2H_4,g)=[2\times\Delta_f H_m^\ominus(CO_2,g)+2\times\Delta_f H_m^\ominus(H_2O,l)]-\Delta_c H_m^\ominus(C_2H_4,g)$$
$$=[2\times(-393.5\ kJ\cdot mol^{-1})+2\times(-285.8\ kJ\cdot mol^{-1})]-$$
$$(-1\,411.2\ kJ\cdot mol^{-1})$$

$=52.6\ kJ\cdot mol^{-1}$

3.36 $$\Delta_r H_m^\ominus=\Delta_f H_m^\ominus(Sn,灰)-\Delta_f H_m^\ominus(Sn,白)=-2.1\ kJ\cdot mol^{-1}$$

$$\Delta_r S_m^\ominus=S_m^\ominus(Sn,灰)-S_m^\ominus(Sn,白)=44.3\ J\cdot mol\cdot K^{-1}-51.5\ J\cdot mol^{-1}\cdot K^{-1}$$

$$=-7.2\ J\cdot mol^{-1}\cdot K^{-1}$$

相变过程 $\Delta_r G_m^\ominus=0$，即 $\Delta_r H_m^\ominus-T\Delta_r S_m^\ominus=0$

得相变温度为

$$T=\frac{\Delta_r H_m^\ominus}{\Delta_r S_m^\ominus}=\frac{-2.1\ kJ\cdot mol^{-1}}{-7.2\times10^{-3}\ kJ\cdot mol^{-1}\cdot K^{-1}}=291.7\ K$$

3.37 (1) $2NH_3(g)+3Cl_2(g)=\!=\!=N_2(g)+6HCl(g)$

$\Delta_r H_m^\ominus=2\times3E(N-H)+3E(Cl-Cl)-E(N\equiv N)-6E(Cl-H)$

$=6\times389\ kJ\cdot mol^{-1}+3\times243\ kJ\cdot mol^{-1}-945\ kJ\cdot mol^{-1}-6\times431\ kJ\cdot mol^{-1}$

$=-468\ kJ\cdot mol^{-1}$

(2) $\frac{1}{2}N_2(g)+\frac{3}{2}Cl_2(g)=\!=\!=NCl_3(g)$,

$\frac{1}{2}N_2(g)+\frac{3}{2}H_2(g)=\!=\!=NH_3(g)$

$\Delta_f H_m^\ominus(NCl_3,g)$

$=\frac{1}{2}E(N\equiv N)+\frac{3}{2}E(Cl-Cl)-3E(N-Cl)$

$=\frac{1}{2}\times945\ kJ\cdot mol^{-1}+\frac{3}{2}\times243\ kJ\cdot mol^{-1}-3\times201\ kJ\cdot mol^{-1}$

$=234\ kJ\cdot mol^{-1}$

$\Delta_f H_m^\ominus(NH_3,g)$

$=\frac{1}{2}E(N\equiv N)+\frac{3}{2}E(H-H)-3E(N-H)$

$=\frac{1}{2}\times945\ kJ\cdot mol^{-1}+\frac{3}{2}\times436\ kJ\cdot mol^{-1}-3\times389\ kJ\cdot mol^{-1}$

$=-40.5\ kJ\cdot mol^{-1}$

计算结果表明，NH_3 稳定而 NCl_3 不稳定。

3.38 对于反应 C(石墨)⟶C(金刚石)

$\Delta_r H_m^\ominus=\Delta_f H_m^\ominus$(金刚石)，$\Delta_r G_m^\ominus=\Delta_f G_m^\ominus$(金刚石)

由 $\Delta_r G_m^\ominus=\Delta_r H_m^\ominus-T\Delta_r S_m^\ominus$

$$\Delta_r S_m^\ominus=\frac{\Delta_r H_m^\ominus-\Delta_r G_m^\ominus}{T}$$

$$=\frac{(1.897-2.900)\times10^3\ J\cdot mol^{-1}}{298\ K}$$

$$=-3.366\ J\cdot mol^{-1}\cdot K^{-1}$$

$\Delta_r S_m^\ominus=S_m^\ominus$(金刚石)$-S_m^\ominus$(石墨)

$S_m^\ominus$(金刚石)$=\Delta_r S_m^\ominus+S_m^\ominus$(石墨)

$=-3.366\ J\cdot mol^{-1}\cdot K^{-1}+5.740\ J\cdot mol^{-1}\cdot K^{-1}$

$=2.374\ J\cdot mol^{-1}\cdot K^{-1}$

由于 $S_m^\ominus$(石墨)$>S_m^\ominus$(金刚石),说明金刚石中碳原子排列更有序。

3.39 在恒温恒压条件下,体系可做非体积功的最大值是反应的 $\Delta_r G$ 的相反数。

根据题设的数据,可以求得反应

$$2H_2(g)+O_2(g) = 2H_2O(g)$$

的 $\Delta_r G_m^\ominus$ 值。

$$\begin{aligned}\Delta_r H_m^\ominus &= 2\Delta_f H_m^\ominus(H_2O,g)-2\Delta_f H_m^\ominus(H_2,g)-\Delta_f H_m^\ominus(O_2,g)\\ &=(-241.8\times 2)\ kJ\cdot mol^{-1}\\ &=-483.6\ kJ\cdot mol^{-1}\end{aligned}$$

$$\begin{aligned}\Delta_r S_m^\ominus &= 2S_m^\ominus(H_2O,g)-2S_m^\ominus(H_2,g)-S_m^\ominus(O_2,g)\\ &=(188.8\times 2-130.7\times 2-205.2)\ J\cdot mol^{-1}\cdot K^{-1}\\ &=-89\ J\cdot mol^{-1}\cdot K^{-1}\end{aligned}$$

故

$$\begin{aligned}\Delta_r G_m^\ominus &= \Delta_r H_m^\ominus - T\Delta_r S_m^\ominus\\ &=[-483.6\times 1\,000-1\,000\times(-89)]\ J\cdot mol^{-1}\\ &=-394.6\ kJ\cdot mol^{-1}\end{aligned}$$

即 2 mol 氢气可做非体积功 394.6 kJ。

氢气的摩尔质量为 $M=2\ g\cdot mol^{-1}$,故 2 mol 氢气的质量 $m=M\cdot n=2\ g\cdot mol^{-1}\times 2\ mol=4\ g$

所以每克氢气可做的非体积功为

$$394.6\ kJ\times\frac{1}{4}=98.7\ kJ$$

第 4 章

一、选择题

4.1 C 4.2 D 4.3 A 4.4 C 4.5 C 4.6 B 4.7 D 4.8 C 4.9 B 4.10 B
4.11 D 4.12 A

二、填空题

4.13 二、$r=k[NO]^2[O_2]$,$1.1\times 10^{-5}\ mol\cdot dm^{-3}\cdot s^{-1}$。

4.14 $mol\cdot dm^{-3}\cdot s^{-1}$,$mol^{-1/2}\cdot dm^{3/2}\cdot s^{-1}$。

4.15 $2B = D+E$;催化剂;中间产物。

4.16 反应历程,反应所需的活化能,活化分子百分数。

4.17 同等程度降低,不同,基本不变,不变。

4.18 增大,增大,不变。

4.19 $97.63\ kJ\cdot mol^{-1}$,$1.67\times 10^{-3}\ mol\cdot dm^{-3}\cdot s^{-1}$

4.20 51。

4.21 (1) A,(2) D,(3) B,(4) C,(5) A

4.22 205.3。

三、简答题和计算题

4.23 反应机理中各步反应都是基元反应,总反应的速率由速率最慢的那一步基元反应决定。所以总反应的速率方程应为

$$r=k_2[N_2O_2][H_2] \quad ①$$

N_2O_2 是反应(1)的产物,该步反应为快反应,立即达平衡,则

$$K_1=\frac{[N_2O_2]}{[NO]^2}$$

即
$$[N_2O_2]=K_1[NO]^2$$

代入①得 $r=k_2K_1[NO]^2[H_2]=k[NO]^2[H_2]$

4.24 (1) 机理中③为慢反应,因此整个反应的速率取决于反应③,故有

$$\frac{d[COCl_2]}{dt}=k_3[COCl\cdot][Cl_2] \quad (a)$$

速率方程中出现活性很大的自由基 COCl·的浓度,我们必须设法在速率方程中消去它,使速率方程中只包含反应物的浓度。为此我们需找到自由基的浓度和反应物浓度的关系。因反应①②速率很快,几乎一直处于平衡态,因此,由①,②得

$$r_+=r_-$$

即 $k_1[Cl_2]=k_{-1}[Cl\cdot]^2$

得
$$[Cl\cdot]=\frac{k_1^{1/2}}{k_{-1}^{1/2}}[Cl_2]^{1/2} \quad (b)$$

$$k_2[CO][Cl\cdot]=k_{-2}[COCl\cdot]$$

得
$$[COCl\cdot]=\frac{k_2}{k_{-2}}[CO][Cl\cdot] \quad (c)$$

将(b),(c)代入(a)得

$$\frac{d[COCl_2]}{dt}=k_3\frac{k_2k_1^{1/2}}{k_{-2}k_{-1}^{1/2}}[CO][Cl_2]^{3/2}$$

令
$$k=\frac{k_1^{1/2}k_2k_3}{k_{-1}^{1/2}k_{-2}}$$

$$\frac{d[COCl_2]}{dt}=k[CO][Cl_2]^{3/2}$$

可见建议的机理与速率方程相符合

(2) $k=\frac{k_1^{1/2}k_2\ k_3}{k_{-1}^{1/2}k_{-2}}$

4.25 (1) 设反应的速率方程为 $r=k[H_2PO_2^-]^m[OH^-]^n$

当$[OH^-]$不变时,有

$$\frac{3.2\times10^{-5}}{1.6\times10^{-4}}=\frac{k(0.10)^m(1.0)^n}{k(0.50)^m(1.0)^n}$$

即得 $m=1$

当$[H_2PO_2^-]$不变时，有

$$\frac{1.6\times10^{-4}}{2.56\times10^{-3}}=\frac{k(0.50)^m(1.0)^n}{k(0.50)^m(4.0)^n}$$

得 $n=2$

反应级数为 $n+m=3$

反应速率方程为 $r=k[H_2PO_2^-][OH^-]^2$

(2) 将任一组数据代入速率方程得

$$k=\frac{r}{[H_2PO_2^-][OH^-]^2}$$
$$=\frac{3.2\times10^{-5}\,mol\cdot dm^{-3}\cdot min^{-1}}{0.1\ mol\cdot dm^{-3}\times(1.0\ mol\cdot dm^{-3})^2}$$
$$=3.2\times10^{-4}\,mol^{-2}\cdot dm^{6}\cdot min^{-1}$$

4.26　以$[C_2H_6]$的变化表示起始分解速率

$$r_0=-\frac{d[C_2H_6]}{dt}=k[C_2H_6]^{3/2}$$

由理想气体状态方程 $pV=nRT$

$$[C_2H_6]=\frac{n}{V}=\frac{p}{RT}$$

$$r_0=k\left(\frac{p}{RT}\right)^{3/2}=1.13\ dm^{3/2}\cdot mol^{-1/2}\cdot s^{-1}\times\left(\frac{1.33\times10^4\ Pa}{8.314\times10^3\ Pa\cdot dm^3\cdot mol^{-1}\cdot K^{-1}\times910\ K}\right)^{3/2}$$
$$=8.3\times10^{-5}\ mol\cdot dm^{-3}\cdot s^{-1}$$

注意：$R=8.314\ J\cdot mol^{-1}\cdot K^{-1}=8.314\ Pa\cdot m^3\cdot mol^{-1}\cdot K^{-1}$
$=8.314\times10^3\ Pa\cdot dm^3\cdot mol^{-1}\cdot K^{-1}$

4.27　反应速率与变酸时间成反比　$\frac{k_2}{k_1}=\frac{t_1}{t_2}=\frac{48}{4}$

$$\lg\frac{k_2}{k_1}=\frac{E_a}{2.303\,R}\left(\frac{T_2-T_1}{T_1T_2}\right)$$

$$\lg\frac{48}{4}=\frac{E_a}{2.303\times8.314\times10^{-3}\ kJ\cdot mol^{-1}\cdot K^{-1}}\left(\frac{301\ K-278\ K}{301\ K\times278\ K}\right)$$

解得活化能为　$E_a=75\ kJ\cdot mol^{-1}$

4.28　反应速率之比等于反应速率常数之比。

加催化剂前 $\lg k=-\frac{E_a}{2.303RT}+\lg A$　(1)

加催化剂后 $\lg k'=-\frac{E'_a}{2.303\,RT}+\lg A'$　(2)

对于同一反应，$A=A'$。(2)式－(1)式得

$$\lg\frac{k'}{k}=-\frac{E'_a-E_a}{2.303\,RT}$$
$$=\frac{-(138.1-188.3)\times10^3\,J\cdot mol^{-1}}{2.303\times8.314\ J\cdot mol^{-1}\cdot K^{-1}\times800\ K}$$
$$=3.277$$

所以$\frac{k'}{k}=1.89\times10^3$

4.29 零级反应

$$c=c_0-kt$$

即

$$c_0-c=kt$$

$$\frac{(c_0-c)_{100\text{ min}}}{(c_0-c)_{200\text{ min}}}=\frac{t_{100\text{ min}}}{t_{200\text{ min}}}$$

$$\frac{0.25}{(c_0-c)_{200\text{ min}}}=\frac{100\text{ min}}{200\text{ min}}$$

解得

$$c_0-c=0.5=50\%$$

一级反应

$$\lg c=\lg c_0-\frac{k}{2.303}t$$

$$\lg\frac{c_0}{c}=\frac{k}{2.303}t$$

$$\frac{\lg\left(\frac{c_0}{c}\right)_{100\text{ min}}}{\lg\left(\frac{c_0}{c}\right)_{200\text{ min}}}=\frac{t_{100\text{ min}}}{t_{200\text{ min}}}$$

$$\frac{\lg\left(\frac{1}{0.75}\right)_{100\text{ min}}}{\lg\left(\frac{1}{c}\right)_{200\text{ min}}}=\frac{100\text{ min}}{200\text{ min}}$$

$$c=0.56\text{，即消耗掉 }44\%$$

二级反应

$$\frac{1}{c}-\frac{1}{c_0}=kt$$

$$\frac{\left(\frac{1}{c}-\frac{1}{c_0}\right)_{100\text{ min}}}{\left(\frac{1}{c}-\frac{1}{c_0}\right)_{200\text{ min}}}=\frac{t_{100\text{ min}}}{t_{200\text{ min}}}$$

$$\frac{\left(\frac{1}{0.75}-1\right)_{100\text{ min}}}{\left(\frac{1}{c}-1\right)_{200\text{ min}}}=\frac{100\text{ min}}{200\text{ min}}$$

解得

$$c=0.60\text{，即消耗掉 }40\%$$

4.30 一级反应的半衰期

$$t_{1/2}=\frac{0.693}{k}$$

则速率常数为

$$k=\frac{0.693}{360\text{ min}}=1.93\times10^{-3}\text{ min}^{-1}$$

由阿伦尼乌斯公式得

$$\lg\frac{k_{700\text{ K}}}{k_{600\text{ K}}}=\frac{E_a}{2.303R}\left(\frac{1}{T_{600\text{ K}}}-\frac{1}{T_{700\text{ K}}}\right)$$

$$\lg\frac{k_{700\text{ K}}}{1.93\times10^{-3}\text{ min}^{-1}}=\frac{200\text{ kJ}\cdot\text{mol}^{-1}}{2.303\times8.314\times10^{-3}\text{ kJ}\cdot\text{mol}^{-1}\cdot\text{K}^{-1}}\left(\frac{1}{600\text{ K}}-\frac{1}{700\text{ K}}\right)$$

解得，700 K 时速率常数为 $k_{700\ \mathrm{K}}=0.59\ \mathrm{min}^{-1}$

由 $$\lg c=\lg c_0-\frac{k}{2.303}t$$

得 $$\lg\frac{c_0}{c}=\frac{k}{2.303}t$$

$$\lg\frac{1}{0.3}=\frac{0.59\ \mathrm{min}^{-1}}{2.303}t$$

解得 $$t=2.04\ \mathrm{min}$$

4.31 反应活化能 E_a，反应温度 T 和速率常数 k 之间的关系符合公式：

$$\lg\frac{k_2}{k_1}=\frac{E_a}{2.303\ R}\left(\frac{1}{T_1}-\frac{1}{T_2}\right)$$

将题设条件 $E_a=163\ \mathrm{kJ\cdot mol^{-1}}$，$T_1=390\ \mathrm{K}$，$T_2=420\ \mathrm{K}$ 和 $R=8.314\ \mathrm{J\cdot mol^{-1}\cdot K^{-1}}$ 代入公式得

$$\lg\frac{k_2}{k_1}=\frac{163\times1\,000\ \mathrm{J\cdot mol^{-1}}}{2.303\times8.314\ \mathrm{J\cdot mol^{-1}\cdot K^{-1}}}\left(\frac{1}{390\ \mathrm{K}}-\frac{1}{420\ \mathrm{K}}\right)$$
$$=1.559$$

所以 $$\frac{k_2}{k_1}=36.22$$

故 $$k_2=36.22\ k_1$$
$$=36.22\times2.37\times10^{-2}\ \mathrm{dm^3\cdot mol^{-1}\cdot s^{-1}}$$
$$=8.58\times10^{-1}\ \mathrm{dm^3\cdot mol^{-1}\cdot s^{-1}}$$

4.32 速率常数 k 与反应速率 r 成正比，反应速率 r 与完成反应所需时间 t 成反比，故有 k 与 t 成反比，即

$$\frac{k_2}{k_1}=\frac{t_1}{t_2}$$

将鸡蛋煮熟即蛋白质变质的过程看成一个复杂的化学反应。其速率常数、反应温度和活化能之间满足阿伦尼乌斯公式。经变换得

$$\lg\frac{k_2}{k_1}=\frac{E_a}{2.303\ R}\left(\frac{T_2-T_1}{T_2T_1}\right)$$

即 $$\lg\frac{t_1}{t_2}=\frac{E_a}{2.303\ R}\left(\frac{T_2-T_1}{T_2T_1}\right)$$

$$=\frac{(373\ \mathrm{K}-363\ \mathrm{K})\times5.18\times10^2\ \mathrm{kJ\cdot mol^{-1}}\times1\,000\ \mathrm{J\cdot kJ^{-1}}}{2.303\times8.314\ \mathrm{J\cdot mol^{-1}\cdot K^{-1}}\times373\ \mathrm{K}\times363\ \mathrm{K}}$$

$$=2.00$$

故 $$\frac{t_1}{t_2}=1.00\times10^2$$

$$t_1 = 1.00\times10^2\ t_2 = 1.00\times10^2\times3\ \text{min} = 3.00\times10^2\ \text{min}$$

4.33 根据速率常数单位知该反应为一级反应

$$\lg c = \lg c_0 - \frac{k}{2.303}t$$

即
$$\lg\frac{c_0}{c} = \frac{k}{2.303}t$$

$$\lg\frac{1}{0.1} = \frac{k}{2.303}\times600\ \text{s}$$

解得
$$k = 3.8\times10^{-3}\ \text{s}^{-1}$$

由阿伦尼乌斯公式
$$\lg\frac{k_2}{k_1} = \frac{E_a}{2.303R}\left(\frac{1}{T_1}-\frac{1}{T_2}\right)$$

$$\lg\frac{3.8\times10^{-3}\ \text{s}^{-1}}{3.3\times10^{-2}\ \text{s}^{-1}} = \frac{18.88\times10^4\ \text{J}\cdot\text{mol}^{-1}}{2.303\times8.314\ \text{J}\cdot\text{mol}^{-1}\cdot\text{K}^{-1}}\left(\frac{1}{600\ \text{K}}-\frac{1}{T_2}\right)$$

解得
$$T_2 = 567.8\ \text{K}$$

4.34 由题意 $T_{1/2}=46.1$ d，反应为一级，$m_0=0.200$ mg

由 $T_{1/2}=\frac{0.693}{k}$ 得 $k=\frac{0.693}{T_{1/2}}$

$$\lg\frac{m}{m_0} = -\frac{kt}{2.303} = -\frac{0.693t}{2.303T_{1/2}} = -\frac{0.693\times182}{2.303\times46.1} = -1.19$$

剩余试样质量 $m=0.0129$ mg

4.35 (1) 对于一级反应 $\lg\frac{c}{c_0} = -\frac{k}{2.303}t$

因此 $\lg\frac{[N_2O_5]}{1.65\times10^{-2}\ \text{mol}\cdot\text{dm}^{-3}} = -\frac{4.80\times10^{-4}\ \text{s}^{-1}\times825\ \text{s}}{2.303} = -0.172$

解得 $[N_2O_5] = 0.011\ \text{mol}\cdot\text{dm}^{-3}$

(2) 由
$$\lg\frac{c}{c_0} = -\frac{k}{2.303}t$$

$$\lg\frac{1.00\times10^{-2}\ \text{mol}\cdot\text{dm}^{-3}}{1.65\times10^{-2}\ \text{mol}\cdot\text{dm}^{-3}} = -\frac{4.80\times10^{-4}\ \text{s}^{-1}\cdot t}{2.303} = -0.217$$

解得 $t = 1\,041$ s

第 5 章

一、选择题

5.1 C　5.2 B　5.3 B　5.4 C　5.5 C　5.6 C　5.7 D　5.8 C　5.9 C　5.10 D
5.11 D　5.12 B　5.13 C　5.14 D　5.15 C

二、填空题

5.16 5.7。

5.17 5.23，0。

5.18 6.43。

5.19 53.1， 37.3。

5.20 不变，不变，增大，增大，不变，逆向移动；
增大，增大，增大，增大，增大，正向移动；
增大，增大，增大，增大，不变，不移动。

5.21 537。

5.22 (1) 增大，I_2 解离是吸热反应（$\Delta_r H_m^\ominus > 0$）；
(2) 减少，总体积减小，压强增大，平衡向气体粒子数减少的方向移动；
(3) 不变，$I_2(g)$ 和 $I(g)$ 的分压都不变；
(4) 增大，体积变大时则 $I_2(g)$ 和 $I(g)$ 的分压同时减小，平衡向粒子数多的方向移动。

5.23 1.3×10^{-5}。

三、简答题和计算题

5.24 (1) 设 $COCl_2$ 起始浓度为 $1\ mol\cdot dm^{-3}$，解离度为 α。

$$COCl_2(g) \rightleftharpoons CO(g) + Cl_2(g)$$

平衡时 $(1-\alpha)mol \qquad \alpha mol \qquad \alpha mol$

$$n(总) = (1-\alpha) + \alpha + \alpha = (1+\alpha)(mol)$$

$$p(COCl_2) = \frac{1-\alpha}{1+\alpha}p = \frac{1-\alpha}{1+\alpha}\times 2.0\times10^5\ Pa$$

$$p(CO) = p(Cl_2) = \frac{\alpha}{1+\alpha}p$$

$$= \frac{\alpha}{1+\alpha}\times 2.0\times10^5\ Pa$$

$$K^\ominus = \frac{[p(CO)/p^\ominus][p(Cl_2)/p^\ominus]}{p(COCl_2)/p^\ominus}$$

$$= \frac{\left(\frac{\alpha}{1+\alpha}\times\frac{2.0\times10^5}{1.0\times10^5}\right)^2}{\frac{1-\alpha}{1+\alpha}\times\frac{2.0\times10^5}{1.0\times10^5}}$$

$$= 8.0\times10^{-9}$$

解得 $\alpha = 6.32\times10^{-5} = 6.32\times10^{-3}\%$

(2) $\Delta_r G_m^\ominus = -2.303RT\lg K^\ominus$

$= -2.303\times 8.314\ J\cdot mol^{-1}\cdot K^{-1}\times 373\ K\times \lg 8.0\times10^{-9}$

$= 57.8\times10^3\ J\cdot mol^{-1}$

$$\Delta_r S_m^\ominus = \frac{\Delta_r H_m^\ominus - \Delta_r G_m^\ominus}{T}$$

$$=\frac{(104.6\times10^3-57.8\times10^3)\ \mathrm{J\cdot mol^{-1}}}{373\ \mathrm{K}}$$

$$=125.5\ \mathrm{J\cdot mol^{-1}K^{-1}}$$

5.25 设容器的体积为 V，应向平衡体系中加入 x mol I_2，

	$2HI \rightleftharpoons$	H_2 +	I_2
起始浓度/($mol\cdot dm^{-3}$)	$\frac{1}{V}$	0	0
平衡浓度/($mol\cdot dm^{-3}$)	$\frac{1-0.244}{V}$	$\frac{0.122}{V}$	$\frac{0.122}{V}$
新平衡浓度/($mol\cdot dm^{-3}$)	$\frac{1-0.10}{V}$	$\frac{0.05}{V}$	$\frac{0.05+x}{V}$

根据题意，温度不变则平衡常数不变：

$$\frac{\left(\frac{0.122}{V}\right)\left(\frac{0.122}{V}\right)}{\left(\frac{1-0.244}{V}\right)^2}=\frac{\left(\frac{0.05}{V}\right)\left(\frac{0.05+x}{V}\right)}{\left(\frac{1-0.10}{V}\right)^2}$$

解得 $x=0.372$

5.26 (1) 设起始态 N_2O_4 为 1 mol。N_2O_4 解离度为 $\alpha=0.272$

$$N_2O_4(g) \rightleftharpoons 2NO_2(g)$$

平衡时 $(1-\alpha)$mol　　2αmol

$$n(\text{总})=(1-\alpha)+2\alpha=1+\alpha=1.272\ (\mathrm{mol})$$

$$p(NO_2)=\frac{2\alpha}{1.272}\times p(\text{总})=\frac{0.544}{1.272}p^\ominus,\ p(N_2O_4)=\frac{(1-\alpha)}{1.272}p(\text{总})=\frac{0.728}{1.272}p^\ominus$$

$$K^\ominus=\frac{[p(NO_2)/p^\ominus]^2}{p(N_2O_4)/p^\ominus}=\frac{(0.544/1.272)^2}{0.728/1.272}=0.32$$

(2)
$$N_2O_4(g) \rightleftharpoons 2NO_2$$

平衡时 $(1-\alpha)$mol　　2αmol

$$n(\text{总})=(1+\alpha)\mathrm{mol}$$

$$p(NO_2)=\frac{2\alpha}{1+\alpha}p(\text{总})=\frac{2\alpha}{1+\alpha}\times2.0\times10^5\ \mathrm{Pa}$$

$$p(N_2O_4)=\frac{1-\alpha}{1+\alpha}p(\text{总})=\frac{1-\alpha}{1+\alpha}\times2.0\times10^5\ \mathrm{Pa}$$

$$K^\ominus=\frac{[p(NO_2)/p^\ominus]^2}{p(N_2O_4)/p^\ominus}=\frac{\left(\frac{2\alpha}{1+\alpha}\times2.0\times10^5\ \mathrm{Pa}/1.0\times10^5\ \mathrm{Pa}\right)^2}{\frac{1-\alpha}{1+\alpha}\times2.0\times10^5\ \mathrm{Pa}/1.0\times10^5\ \mathrm{Pa}}=0.32$$

解得 $\alpha=0.196=19.6\%$

(3) 计算结果表明，增大体系的压强，平衡向气体分子数目减少的方向移动。

5.27 若压强减小一半，则新的平衡体系中各物质的起始浓度为原来的 $\frac{1}{2}$：

	$PCl_5(g) \rightleftharpoons$	$PCl_3(g)$ +	$Cl_2(g)$
平衡浓度/($mol\cdot dm^{-3}$)	1	0.204	0.204

新平衡浓度/$(mol\cdot dm^{-3})$ $0.5-x$ $\quad$ $0.102+x$ $\quad$ $0.102+x$

若温度不变,则平衡常数不变

$$\frac{(0.102+x)^2}{0.5-x}=\frac{(0.204)^2}{1.0}$$

解得 $x=0.0368$

在新的平衡体系中,各物质的浓度为

$$[PCl_5]=0.5\ mol\cdot dm^{-3}-0.0368\ mol\cdot dm^{-3}\approx 0.463\ mol\cdot dm^{-3}$$

$$[PCl_3]=[Cl_2]=0.102\ mol\cdot dm^{-3}+0.0368\ mol\cdot dm^{-3}\approx 0.139\ mol\cdot dm^{-3}$$

5.28 设平衡时 SO_2 的分压为 xPa。

$$\text{始态时 } p(SO_2Cl_2)=\frac{\dfrac{7.6\ g}{135\ g\cdot mol^{-1}}\times 8.314\times 10^3\ Pa\cdot dm^3\cdot mol^{-1}\cdot K^{-1}\times 375\ K}{1.0\ dm^3}=1.755\times 10^5\ Pa$$

$$SO_2Cl_2 \rightleftharpoons SO_2 + Cl_2$$

平衡分压/Pa $\quad$ $1.755\times 10^5-x$ $\quad$ x $\quad$ $1.0\times 10^5+x$

$$K^{\ominus}=\frac{(x/p^{\ominus})[(1.0\times 10^5+x)/p^{\ominus}]}{(1.755\times 10^5-x)/p^{\ominus}}=2.4$$

解得 $\quad x=0.97\times 10^5$

所以 $\quad p(SO_2Cl_2)=1.755\times 10^5\ Pa-0.97\times 10^5\ Pa=0.79\times 10^5\ Pa=7.9\times 10^4\ Pa$

$$p(SO_2)=0.97\times 10^5\ Pa=9.7\times 10^4\ Pa$$

$$p(Cl_2)=1.0\times 10^5\ Pa+0.97\times 10^5\ Pa=1.97\times 10^5\ Pa$$

5.29 当化学反应方程式中计量数扩大 n 倍时,反应的平衡常数 K 将变成 K^n。故反应

$$SO_2(g)+\frac{1}{2}O_2(g) \rightleftharpoons SO_3(g)$$

$$K_p=(3.40\times 10^{-5}\ Pa^{-1})^{0.5}$$
$$=5.83\times 10^{-3}\ Pa^{-0.5}$$

联系 K_p 和 K_c 的关系式是理想气体的状态方程式 $pV=nRT$,$p=\frac{n}{V}RT$ 和 $p=cRT$ 等。

必须注意的是 K_p 表示式中的 p,其单位是 Pa,而 K_c 表示式中的 c 的单位经常是 $mol\cdot dm^{-3}$,体积不是 m^3,而是 dm^3。于是 c 的数值比以 $mol\cdot dm^{-3}$ 为单位时扩大了 10^3 倍。为了保证公式 $p=cRT$ 两边数值相等,应有

$$R=8.314\times 10^3\ Pa\cdot dm^3\cdot mol^{-1}\cdot K^{-1}$$

由 p 和 c 的关系式得到 K_p 和 K_c 的关系式

$$K_p=K_c(RT)^{\Delta\nu}$$

$\Delta\nu$ 为气体分子计量数的改变量。故

$$K_c=K_p(RT)^{-\Delta\nu}$$
$$=5.83\times 10^{-3}\ Pa^{-0.5}\times(8.314\times 10^3\ Pa\cdot dm^3\cdot mol^{-1}\cdot K^{-1}\times 1000\ K)^{0.5}$$

$=16.8\ \text{mol}^{-0.5}\cdot\text{dm}^{1.5}$

5.30 $K^{\ominus}=p(CO_2)/p^{\ominus}$

$p(CO_2)=1.16\times1.0\times10^5=1.16\times10^5\ \text{Pa}$

在 1 037 K 达平衡时，CO_2 的物质的量为

$$n=\frac{pV}{RT}$$

$$=\frac{1.16\times10^5\ \text{Pa}\times10\ \text{dm}^3}{8.314\times10^3\ \text{Pa}\cdot\text{dm}^3\cdot\text{mol}^{-1}\cdot\text{K}^{-1}\times1\,037\ \text{K}}$$

$$=0.135\ \text{mol}$$

$CaCO_3$ 分解分数为 $\dfrac{0.135}{0.20}\times100\%=68\%$

5.31 (1)

$$PCl_5(g) \rightleftharpoons PCl_3(g)+Cl_2(g)$$

平衡浓度/$(\text{mol}\cdot\text{dm}^{-3})$ $\quad \dfrac{0.70-0.50}{2} \quad \dfrac{0.50}{2} \quad \dfrac{0.50}{2}$

$$K_c=\frac{[PCl_3][Cl_2]}{[PCl_5]}=\frac{(0.25\ \text{mol}\cdot\text{dm}^{-3})^2}{0.10\ \text{mol}\cdot\text{dm}^{-3}}$$

$$=0.625\ \text{mol}\cdot\text{dm}^{-3}$$

$$K^{\ominus}=K_p\left(\frac{1}{p^{\ominus}}\right)^{\Delta\nu}=K_c(RT)^{\Delta\nu}\left(\frac{1}{p^{\ominus}}\right)^{\Delta\nu}$$

$$=0.625\ \text{mol}\cdot\text{dm}^{-3}\times8.314\times10^3\ \text{Pa}\cdot\text{dm}^3\cdot\text{mol}^{-1}\cdot\text{K}^{-1}\times523\ \text{K}\times\frac{1}{1.0\times10^5\ \text{Pa}}$$

$$=27.18$$

PCl_5 的分解分数$\dfrac{0.25}{0.35}=71.43\%$

(2) 再注入 0.10 mol Cl_2 后平衡向生成 PCl_5 方向移动，设 PCl_5 浓度又增加 $x\ \text{mol}\cdot\text{dm}^{-3}$。

$$PCl_5(g) \rightleftharpoons PCl_3(g) + Cl_2(g)$$

新平衡 $\quad 0.10+x \quad 0.25-x \quad 0.25+0.05-x$

$$K_c=\frac{(0.25-x)(0.30-x)}{0.1+x}=0.625$$

解得 $x=0.011$

PCl_5 分解分数为$\dfrac{0.25-0.011}{0.35}=68.29\%$

比较(1)，(2)的计算结果表明，增加生成物浓度，平衡向增大反应物浓度的方向移动，反应物的分解分数降低。

(3) 设平衡时 PCl_3 的浓度为 $x\ \text{mol}\cdot\text{dm}^{-3}$，则

$$PCl_5(g) \rightleftharpoons PCl_3(g)+Cl_2(g)$$

平衡时 $\quad 0.35-x \quad x \quad 0.05+x$

$$K_c=\frac{x(0.05+x)}{0.35-x}=0.625$$

解得 $x=0.239$

PCl_5 分解分数为$\frac{0.239}{0.35}=68.29\%$

PCl_5 分解百分数与(2)的结果相同，说明在相同条件下，体系平衡状态的组成与达到平衡的途径无关。

5.32 (1) 设起始态有1.0 mol 乙苯气体，达平衡时乙苯的转化率为x，则达平衡时各物质的物质的量(mol)为

$$C_6H_5C_2H_5(g) \rightleftharpoons C_6H_5C_2H_3(g)+H_2(g)$$
$$1.0-x \qquad x \qquad x$$

达平衡时总的物质的量为

$$n=1-x+x+x=1+x(\text{mol})$$

平衡时各物质的分压为

$$p(C_6H_5C_2H_5)=\frac{1.0-x}{1.0+x}p,$$

$$p(C_6H_5C_2H_3)=p(H_2)=\frac{x}{1+x}p$$

$$p=p^\ominus=1.0\times10^5\ \text{Pa}$$

$$K^\ominus=\frac{[p(C_6H_5C_2H_3)/p^\ominus][p(H_2)/p^\ominus]}{p(C_6H_5C_2H_5)/p^\ominus}$$

$$=\frac{\left(\frac{x}{1.0+x}\right)^2}{\left(\frac{1.0-x}{1.0+x}\right)}=8.9\times10^{-2}$$

解得 $x=0.286$

乙苯转化率为 $0.286\times100\%=28.6\%$

(2) 设起始态有1.0 mol 乙苯，则水蒸气为10 mol，乙苯的转化率为x，则

$$C_6H_5C_2H_5(g)=C_6H_5C_2H_3(g)+H_2(g)$$

平衡时物质的量/mol $\quad 1.0-x \qquad x \qquad x$

平衡时总的物质的量

$$n=1-x+x+x+10=11+x(\text{mol})$$

平衡时各物质的分压为

$$p(C_6H_5C_2H_5)=\frac{1-x}{11+x}p$$

$$p(C_6H_5C_2H_3)=p(H_2)=\frac{x}{11+x}p$$

$$K^\ominus=\frac{\left(\frac{x}{11+x}\right)^2}{\left(\frac{1-x}{11+x}\right)}=8.9\times10^{-2}$$

解得 $x=0.624$

乙苯的转化率为 $0.624\times100\%=62.4\%$

5.33 设起始态有1 mol N_2O_4，平衡时解离度α

$$N_2O_4(g) \rightleftharpoons 2NO_2(g)$$

平衡时物质的量/mol　　$1-\alpha$　　2α

$$n(\text{总})=(1-\alpha)+2\alpha=1+\alpha$$

$$p(N_2O_4)=p\cdot\frac{1-\alpha}{1+\alpha}\quad p(NO_2)=p\cdot\frac{2\alpha}{1+\alpha}$$

$$K^{\ominus}=\frac{[p(NO_2)/p^{\ominus}]^2}{p(N_2O_4)/p^{\ominus}}=\frac{p}{p^{\ominus}}\cdot\frac{4\alpha^2}{1-\alpha^2}$$

$p=1.0\times10^5$ Pa 时，$\alpha=50.2\%=0.502$，

$$p^{\ominus}=1.0\times10^5\ \text{Pa}$$

$$K^{\ominus}=1\times\frac{4\times0.502^2}{1-0.502^2}=1.35$$

温度相同，$K^{\ominus}$ 不变。若 $p=10\times1.0\times10^5$ Pa

$K^{\ominus}=10\times\frac{4\alpha^2}{1-\alpha^2}=1.35$　得 $\alpha=0.181=18.1\%$

5.34　设平衡时体积为 1 dm^3，因分解前后质量不变，因此分解前 $PCl_5(g)$ 的物质的量为 $\frac{2.695}{208.5}$ mol。

若 $PCl_5(g)$ 的解离度为 α，则有

$$PCl_5(g) \ = \ PCl_3(g) + Cl_2(g)$$

平衡时物质的量/mol　　$0.012\,93(1-\alpha)$　　$0.012\,93\alpha$　　$0.012\,93\alpha$

每升中气体的物质的量为

$$n=\frac{pV}{RT}=\frac{1.0\times10^5\ \text{Pa}\times1\ \text{dm}^3}{8.314\times10^3\ \text{Pa}\cdot\text{dm}^3\cdot\text{mol}^{-1}\cdot\text{K}^{-1}\times(250+273)\text{K}}=0.023\ \text{mol}$$

$0.023=0.012\,93(1-\alpha)+0.012\,93\times2\alpha$

得 $\alpha=0.779$

$$p(PCl_5)=\frac{0.012\,93(1-0.779)}{0.023}\times1.0\times10^5\ \text{Pa}$$

$$=0.124\times10^5\ \text{Pa}$$

$$p(PCl_3)=p(Cl_2)=\frac{0.012\,93\times0.779}{0.023}\times1.0\times10^5\ \text{Pa}=0.438\times10^5\ \text{Pa}$$

$$K^{\ominus}=\frac{[p(Cl_2)/p^{\ominus}][p(PCl_3)/p^{\ominus}]}{p(PCl_5)/p^{\ominus}}$$

$$=\frac{(0.438\times10^5/1.0\times10^5)^2}{0.124\times10^5/1.0\times10^5}=1.55$$

$$\Delta_r G_m^{\ominus}=-RT\ln K^{\ominus}$$

$$=-8.314\ \text{J}\cdot\text{mol}^{-1}\cdot\text{K}^{-1}\times523\ \text{K}\times2.303\times\lg1.55$$

$$=1\,906\ \text{J}\cdot\text{mol}^{-1}$$

$$=1.91\ \text{kJ}\cdot\text{mol}^{-1}$$

5.35　PCl_5 的分解反应为

$$PCl_5(g) \rightleftharpoons PCl_3(g)+Cl_2(g)$$

当 PCl_5 已有 50%分解时，PCl_5，PCl_3，Cl_2 的平衡分压相等，设 $p=p(PCl_5)=p(PCl_3)=$

$p(Cl_2)$，则平衡常数 $K_p=p$。

(1) 体积增大1倍，则压力减小1倍，各物质的分压亦都减小1倍。则

$$\frac{p(PCl_3)p(Cl_2)}{p(PCl_5)}=\frac{\left(\frac{1}{2}p\right)^2}{\frac{1}{2}p}=\frac{1}{2}p=\frac{1}{2}K_p$$

即 $\frac{p(PCl_3)p(Cl_2)}{p(PCl_5)}<K_p$，平衡向正反应方向移动，故解离度必然增加。

(2) 加入的氮气不参与化学反应，但体积增大1倍，使 PCl_5，PCl_3 和 Cl_2 的分压都减小1倍，使平衡向正反应方向移动，PCl_5 的解离度增加。

(3) 加入氮气不参与化学反应，但使压力增大1倍而体积不变，因此 PCl_5，PCl_3 和 Cl_2 气体的分压不变，不影响化学平衡。故 PCl_5 的解离度不变。

(4) 加入氯气使体积增加至 2 dm^3 而总压不变，则 PCl_5 和 PCl_3 分压减小而 Cl_2 分压增大

$$p(PCl_5)=p(PCl_3)=\frac{1}{2}p \qquad p(Cl_2)=3p-\frac{1}{2}p\times 2=2p$$

$$\frac{p(PCl_3)p(Cl_2)}{p(PCl_5)}=\frac{\frac{1}{2}p\times 2p}{\frac{1}{2}p}=2p=2K_p>K_p$$

则加入氯气后平衡向反应物方向移动，PCl_5 解离度减小。

(5) 加 Cl_2 体积不变，$p(PCl_5)=p(PCl_3)=p$，$p(Cl_2)=6p-2p=4p$

$\frac{p(PCl_3)p(Cl_2)}{p(PCl_5)}=4p=4K_p>K_p$，$PCl_5$ 解离度减小。

5.36 对于反应 $N_2(g)+3H_2(g) \longrightarrow 2NH_3(g)$

有 $$\Delta_r H_m^\ominus=2\Delta_f H_m^\ominus(NH_3)=2\times(-45.22\ kJ\cdot mol^{-1})=-90.4\ kJ\cdot mol^{-1}$$

$$\Delta_r S_m^\ominus=2S_m^\ominus(NH_3)-[S_m^\ominus(N_2)+3S_m^\ominus(H_2)]$$
$$=2\times 243.5\ J\cdot mol^{-1}\cdot K^{-1}-(217.0\ J\cdot mol^{-1}\cdot K^{-1}+3\times 155.9\ J\cdot mol^{-1}\cdot K^{-1})$$
$$=-197.7\ J\cdot mol^{-1}\cdot K^{-1}$$

由吉布斯公式，则

$$\Delta_r G_m^\ominus=\Delta_r H_m^\ominus-T\Delta_r S_m^\ominus$$
$$=-90.4\ kJ\cdot mol^{-1}-700\ K\times(-197.7\times 10^{-3}\ kJ\cdot mol^{-1}\cdot K^{-1})$$
$$=48\ kJ\cdot mol^{-1}$$

因为 $$\Delta_r G_m^\ominus=-RT\ln K^\ominus$$

所以 $$\ln K^\ominus=-\frac{\Delta_r G_m^\ominus}{RT}=\frac{48\ kJ\cdot mol^{-1}}{8.314\times 10^{-3}\ kJ\cdot mol^{-1}\cdot K^{-1}\times 700\ K}$$
$$=-8.25$$

得 $$K^\ominus=2.6\times 10^{-4}$$

由 $$K^\ominus=K_c\left(\frac{RT}{p^\ominus}\right)^{\Delta\nu}$$

$$K_c = K^\ominus \left(\frac{RT}{p^\ominus}\right)^{-\Delta\nu}$$

$$= 2.6 \times 10^{-4} \times \left(\frac{8.314 \times 10^3 \text{ Pa·dm}^3\text{·mol}^{-1}\text{·K}^{-1} \times 700 \text{ K}}{1.0 \times 10^5 \text{ Pa}}\right)^2$$

$$= 0.88 \text{ mol}^{-2}\text{·dm}^6$$

平衡时　　　　$[N_2] = 1.0\ \text{mol·dm}^{-3}$　　$[H_2] = 3.0\ \text{mol·dm}^{-3}$

根据平衡关系式：

$$\frac{[NH_3]^2}{[N_2][H_2]^3} = \frac{[NH_3]^2}{1.0\ \text{mol·dm}^{-3} \times (3.0\ \text{mol·dm}^{-3})^3} = 0.88\ \text{mol}^{-2}\text{·dm}^6$$

$$[NH_3] = \sqrt{0.88\ \text{mol}^{-2}\text{·dm}^6 \times 1.0\ \text{mol·dm}^{-3} \times (3.0\ \text{mol·dm}^{-3})^3}$$

$$= 4.87\ \text{mol·dm}^{-3}$$

5.37　勒夏特列原理的表述是，如果对平衡体系施加外部影响，平衡将向着减小该影响的方向移动，就是说原理适用的是平衡体系(至少是接近平衡的体系)。

在 KOH 饱和溶液中加入少许固体 KOH，加热时这些 KOH 溶解，说明溶解度随温度的升高而增大。由此可以判断 KOH 溶解是吸热反应。

KOH 溶解度很大，将几粒固体 KOH 放入 100 g 水中，这个溶解过程远远偏离平衡状态，可以放热，但不说明在接近平衡状态时整个溶解过程是放热的。

第 6 章

一、选择题

6.1 B　6.2 C　6.3 C　6.4 C　6.5 D　6.6 D　6.7 C　6.8 C　6.9 C　6.10 D

6.11 D　6.12 B　6.13 D　6.14 A　6.15 B　6.16 C　6.17 C　6.18 D　6.19 B　6.20 C

6.21 D　6.22 B　6.23 C　6.24 D

二、填空题

6.25　4，1，3，6。

6.26　As，Cr 和 Mn，K，Cr 和 Cu，Ti。

6.27　Fr，F，五，Tc。

6.28　$5d^4 6s^2$，$4d^4 5s^1$，$4d^7 5s^1$，$4d^8 5s^1$，$4d^{10} 5s^0$，$5d^9 6s^1$。

6.29　s，s 轨道能量降低，造成能级交错。

6.30　$E = -13.6 \dfrac{1^2}{n^2}(\text{eV})$；4∶1。

6.31　57，71，15；11，镧系收缩，使第二过渡元素和第三过渡元素原子半径相近。

6.32　Cu，$[Ar]3d^{10}4s^1$，ds，IB。

6.33　Fe，Br，$FeBr_2$ 和 $FeBr_3$。

6.34　8，六，ⅢB

三、简答题和计算题

6.35 错误的有②④⑤⑥⑦。

② 错在自旋量子数 m_s 的取值没有 0 这个值。

④ 错在角量子数 $l=1$ 时，磁量子数 m 不能取 -2 这个值。

⑤ 错在角量子数不能为 -1。

⑥ 错在主量子数不能为 -2。

⑦ 错在主量子数 $n=3$ 时，角量子数不能取 3 这个值。

6.36 25 号元素的基态原子电子排布式为 $1s^2 2s^2 2p^6 3s^2 3p^6 3d^5 4s^2$

$$\sigma_{4s}=1\times0.35+13\times0.85+10\times1.0=21.40$$

$$E_{4s}=-13.6\ \text{eV}\ \frac{(25-21.40)^2}{4^2}=-11.02\ \text{eV}$$

$$\sigma_{3d}=4\times0.35+18\times1.0=19.40$$

$$E_{3d}=-13.6\ \text{eV}\times\frac{(25-19.40)^2}{3^2}=-47.39\ \text{eV}$$

可见对 25 号元素 $E_{4s}>E_{3d}$。

6.37 (1) 铬 Cr $3d^5 4s^1$；(2) 银 Ag $4d^{10} 5s^1$；

(3) 锡 Sn $5s^2 5p^2$；(4) 钡 Ba $6s^2$；

(5) 溴 Br $4s^2 4p^5$。

6.38 见下表

	周期	族	元素符号	价层电子构型
A	三	ⅠA	Na	$3s^1$
B	三	ⅡA	Mg	$3s^2$
C	三	ⅢA	Al	$3s^2 3p^1$
D	四	ⅦA	Br	$4s^2 4p^5$
E	五	ⅦA	I	$5s^2 5p^5$
F	四	ⅥB	Cr	$3d^5 4s^1$

6.39 A:K,B:Ni,C:Br,KBr,$NiBr_2$。

6.40 A 为钒(V)　$1s^2 2s^2 2p^6 3s^2 3p^6 3d^3 4s^2$

B 为硒(Se)　$1s^2 2s^2 2p^6 3s^2 3p^6 3d^{10} 4s^2 4p^4$

推理过程：

(1) 元素 B 的 N 层比 A 的 N 层多 4 个电子，这 4 个电子一定要填入 4p 轨道，于是 3d 轨道必定全填满(即 $3d^{10}$)。由此可知 B 的 K,L,M 层均填满电子。

(2) A 原子的 M 层比 B 原子的 M 层少 7 个电子，所以 A 的 M 层电子排布为 $3s^2 3p^6 3d^3$，这样 A 的 K,L 层全填满电子，4s 轨道也填满电子($E_{4s}<E_{3d}$)。于是 A 原子的电子排布为：$1s^2 2s^2 2p^6 3s^2 3p^6 3d^3 4s^2$。

(3) 元素B的N层比元素A的N层多4个电子，A的N层已有$4s^2$，所以元素B的N层必为$4s^24p^4$，即B原子的电子排布为：$1s^22s^22p^63s^23p^63d^{10}4s^24p^4$。

6.41 若以A代表116号元素，则有

(1) Na盐的化学式Na_2A；(2) 氢化物H_2A；

(3) 最高价态氧化物AO_3；(4) 该元素为金属。

6.42 题中各对元素均为同周期元素。一般来说，在同一周期中，从左至右随有效核电荷的增加，半径减小，第一电离能总的趋势是增大。但由于电子构型对电离能影响较大，可能会造成某些反常现象。

(1) P>S 因p电子构型为$3s^23p^3$，3p轨道半充满；而S的电子构型为$3s^23p^4$，失去一个电子后3p半充满。

(2) Mg>Al Mg失去的是3s电子，而Al失去的是3p电子；$E_{3s}<E_{3p}$，3p电子能量高而更易失去。同时，Mg电子构型为$3s^2$，3s轨道全充满；Al的电子构型为$3s^23p^1$，失去一个电子后变为$3s^23p^0$稳定结构。

(3) Sr>Rb Sr的核电荷比Rb多，半径也比Rb小。其次Sr的$5s^2$较稳定。

(4) Zn>Cu Zn的核电荷比Cu多。同时Zn的3d轨道全充满，4s轨道也全充满；Cu的4s轨道半充满，失一个电子后为$3d^{10}4s^0$稳定结构。

(5) Au>Cs Au为IB族元素，电子构型为$5d^{10}6s^1$，由于5d电子对6s电子的屏蔽作用较小，有效核电荷大，半径小；Cs为IA族元素，电子构型为$(5s^25p^6)6s^1$，失去一个电子后变为$5s^25p^6$稳定结构。

6.43 (1) Ba>Sr 同族元素，Ba比Sr多一电子层；

(2) Ca>Sc 同周期元素，Sc核电荷多；

(3) Cu>Ni 同周期元素，Cu次外层为18电子，屏蔽作用大，有效核电荷小，外层电子受引力小；

(4) Zr≈Hf 镧系收缩的结果；

(5) $S^{2-}>S$ 同一元素，电子数越多，半径越大；

(6) $Na^+>Al^{3+}$ 同一周期元素，Al^{3+}正电荷高；

(7) $Pb^{2+}>Sn^{2+}$ 同一族元素的离子，正电荷数相同，但Pb^{2+}比Sn^{2+}多一电子层；

(8) $Fe^{2+}>Fe^{3+}$ 同一元素离子，电子越少，正电荷越高则半径越小。

6.44 (1) 第八周期包括第八能级组，最多可容纳50个电子($8s^25g^{18}6f^{14}7d^{10}8p^6$)，即共有50种元素。

(2) 该元素原子价层电子结构为$8s^25g^1$。该元素原子序数为121。

(3) 第114号元素原子电子排布为[Rn]$7s^25f^{14}6d^{10}7p^2$。该元素属于第七周期，第ⅣA族。

6.45 (1) 第一电离能N>O，N的电子构型$1s^22s^22p^3$，其2p轨道为半充满，比较稳定；而O的电子构型为：$1s^22s^22p^4$，其2p轨道失去一个电子后为半充满。

Cd>In Cd价电子构型：$4d^{10}5s^2$，5s轨道全充满较稳定；而In的价电子构型：$4d^{10}5s^25p^1$，失去5p电子后为稳定结构。

W>Cr Cr与W同族，W比Cr的核电荷增加很多，但W半径比Cr增大不多，核对外层引力W>Cr

(2) 第一电子亲和能

C>N，因 N 的 2p 轨道半充满，为较稳定状态，若再结合一个电子，要克服较多的成对能，体系能量升高，第一电子亲和能较小；而 C 的 2p 轨道未达半充满，再结合一个电子才达到半充满稳定结构，因而第一电子亲和能较大。

S>P，P 与 N 同族，3p 轨道已达半充满，再结合电子时要克服较大的电子成对能；而 S 原子 3p 轨道有 4 个电子，超过半充满，此外，S 的有效核电荷比 P 大，半径 S 比 P 小，因而 S 容易得电子，电子亲和能比P大。

第7章

一、选择题

7.1 A　7.2 D　7.3 C　7.4 C　7.5 B　7.6 D　7.7 B　7.8 C　7.9 A
7.10 B　7.11 B　7.12 A　7.13 C　7.14 D　7.15 B　7.16 B　7.17 A　7.18 C
7.19 C　7.20 C　7.21 B　7.22 B

二、填空题

7.23　(1) >，>；　(2) <，<。

7.24　8，8，2。

7.25　NaCl，6∶6，4∶4，正负离子之间相互极化作用。

7.26　NaCl<$MgCl_2$　$MgCl_2$ 的离子键强于 NaCl。

AgCl<KCl　Ag^+ 极化能力强使 AgCl 百分数降低；

NH_3>PH_3　NH_3 分子间形成氢键。

CO_2<SO_2　CO_2 为非极性分子，SO_2 为极性分子；CO_2 半径小于 SO_2，色散力 CO_2<SO_2。

O_3<SO_2　O_3 分子极性小于 SO_2；色散力 O_3<SO_2。

O_3>O_2　O_3 为极性分子而 O_2 为非极性分子；O_3 半径大于 O_2 的半径，O_3 色散力比 O_2 分子大。

Ne<Ar　半径 Ar>Ne，色散力 Ne<Ar。

HF<H_2O　H_2O 分子间形成的氢键多；HF 气化时只断开部分氢键。

HF>NH_3　HF 分子间氢键比 NH_3 分子间氢键强。

H_2S>HCl　半径 H_2S>HCl，色散力 H_2S>HCl。

HF>HI　HF 分子间氢键很强，HI 分子间不能形成氢键。

7.27　N_2，CN^-。

7.28　PbO>PbS，$FeCl_3$<$FeCl_2$，SnS>SnS_2，

AsH_3<SeH_2，PH_3<H_2S，HF>H_2O。

7.29　⑤①④②③。

7.30　ICl_2^-　直线形，sp^3d；BrF_3　T 字形，sp^3d；

ICl_4^-　正方形，sp^3d^2；NO_2^+　直线形，sp。

7.31　③④⑥,④⑤。

HF_2^- 结构为 F—H---F,没有可形成分子间氢键的 H 原子。

NH_4^+:N 上无孤对电子,不能形成分子间氢键。

7.32　K_2CO_3,Na_2CO_3,$MgCO_3$,$MnCO_3$,$PbCO_3$。

7.33　$ZnCl_2$,$MnCl_2$,$CaCl_2$,KCl。

7.34　$HNO_3 < NaNO_3$,$Na_2SO_4 > Na_2SO_3$,$Ag_2O < Cu_2O$,$ZnCO_3 > HgCO_3$。

7.35　1 206, 691.2, 37.6。

7.36　(1) 体心立方,(2) 12,(3) 12,六方紧密,(2),(3),(3),(2),三。

7.37　12, 4, 127.8, 8.94, 74.05%。

7.38　2, 230。

说明:由密度 $d=\frac{m}{V}$,得晶胞体积为

$$V=\frac{m}{d}=\frac{2\times 39.10\ \text{g}\cdot\text{mol}^{-1}}{0.862\ \text{g}\cdot\text{cm}^{-3}\times 6.023\times 10^{23}\ \text{mol}^{-1}}$$
$$=1.506\times 10^{-22}\ \text{cm}^3$$

晶胞边长 $a=\sqrt[3]{V}=5.32\times 10^{-8}$ cm

立方体对角线长为$\sqrt{3}a$

则 K 的半径为

$$r=\frac{\sqrt{3}a}{4}=\frac{\sqrt{3}\times 5.32\times 10^{-8}\ \text{cm}}{4}$$
$$=2.30\times 10^{-8}\ \text{cm}$$
$$=230\ \text{pm}$$

7.39　74.05%, 68.02%, 74.05%, 34.01%。

三、简答题和计算题

7.40　玻恩-哈伯循环设计如下

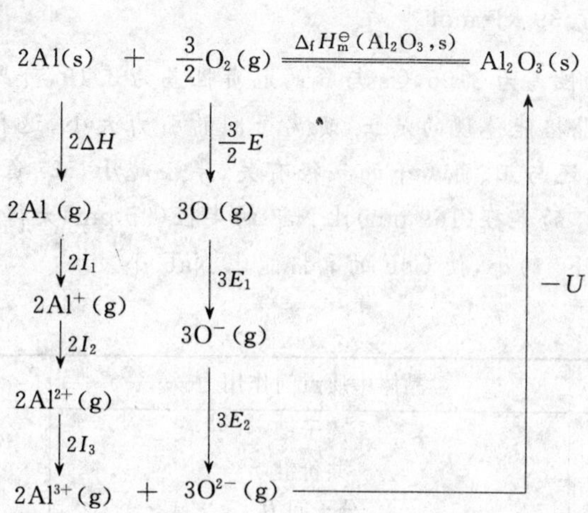

根据盖斯定律

$$\Delta_f H_m^{\ominus}(Al_2O_3, s) = 2\Delta H + 2I_1 + 2I_2 + 2I_3 + \frac{3}{2}E - 3E_1 - 3E_2 - U$$

所以 $U = 2\Delta H + 2(I_1 + I_2 + I_3) + \frac{3}{2}E - 3(E_1 + E_2) - \Delta_f H_m^{\ominus}(Al_2O_3, s)$

$= 326.4\ \text{kJ·mol}^{-1} \times 2 + (578\ \text{kJ·mol}^{-1} + 1\,817\ \text{kJ·mol}^{-1} + 2\,745\ \text{kJ·mol}^{-1})$

$\times 2 + 498\ \text{kJ·mol}^{-1} \times \frac{3}{2} - (141\ \text{kJ·mol}^{-1} - 780\ \text{kJ·mol}^{-1}) \times 3$

$+ 1\,676\ \text{kJ·mol}^{-1}$

$= 1.53 \times 10^4\ \text{kJ·mol}^{-1}$

7.41　根据题中给出的热力学数据，设计热力学循环：

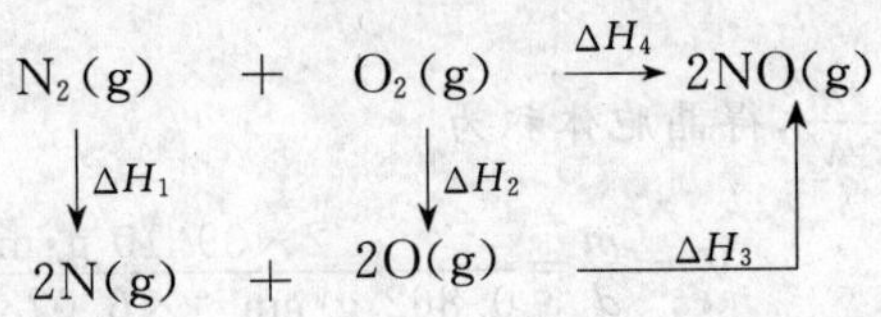

$\Delta H_1 = D(N{\equiv}N) = 941.69\ \text{kJ·mol}^{-1}$

$\Delta H_2 = D(O{=}O) = 493.59\ \text{kJ·mol}^{-1}$

$\Delta H_4 = 2\Delta_f H_m^{\ominus}(NO, g) = 2 \times 90.25\ \text{kJ·mol}^{-1}$

$= 180.50\ \text{kJ·mol}^{-1}$

$\Delta H_3 = -2E(N{-}O)$

由盖斯定律：

$$\Delta H_4 = \Delta H_1 + \Delta H_2 + \Delta H_3$$

则 $\Delta H_3 = \Delta H_4 - \Delta H_1 - \Delta H_2$

$= 180.50\ \text{kJ·mol}^{-1} - 941.69\ \text{kJ·mol}^{-1} - 493.59\ \text{kJ·mol}^{-1}$

$= -1\,254.78\ \text{kJ·mol}^{-1}$

$E(N{-}O) = -\frac{1}{2}\Delta H_3$

$= 627.39\ \text{kJ·mol}^{-1}$

7.42　Na 与 F 的电负性差为 3.05，Cs 与 F 的电负性差为 3.19，可见 NaF 中键的极性比 CsF 中键的极性小。晶格能体现的是正、负离子间的引力大小，这种静电引力不仅和离子键的极性大小有关，还与正、负离子的半径有关，半径越小，正、负离子间的引力越大，晶格能越大。由于 Cs^+ 的半径(169 pm)比 Na^+ 的半径(95 pm)大得多，因而 Cs^+ 与 F^- 间的静电引力比 Na^+ 与 F^- 的小，使 CsF 的晶格能比 NaF 小。

7.43　结果见下表：

化合物	晶体中质点间作用力	晶体类型	熔点
KCl	离子键	离子晶体	较高
SiC	共价键	原子晶体	很高
CH_3Cl	分子间力	分子晶体	较低
NH_3	氢键，分子间力	分子晶体	较低

续表

化合物	晶体中质点间作用力	晶体类型	熔点
Cu	金属键	金属晶体	较高
Xe	色散力	分子晶体	很低

7.44 根据等电子原理,原子数相同的分子或离子中,若电子数也相同,则这些分子或离子具有相似的电子结构和相似的几何构型。将各分子或离子的电子总数算出来,分别与 CO_2, NO_2^-, BF_3 对照,即可得出其电子结构和几何构型:

电子总数	分子或离子	σ键类型	π键类型	电子结构	几何构型
	CO_2	sp—p	2个 Π_3^4	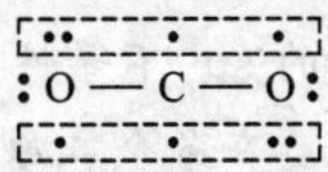	直线形
16	NO_2^+	sp—p	2个 Π_3^4	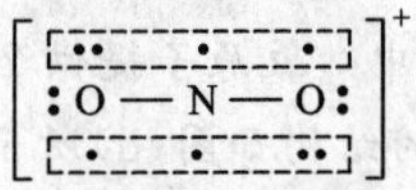	直线形
	N_3^-	sp—p	2个 Π_3^4	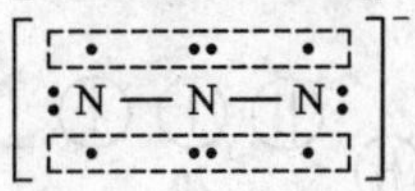	直线形
18	NO_2^-	sp^2—p	Π_3^4	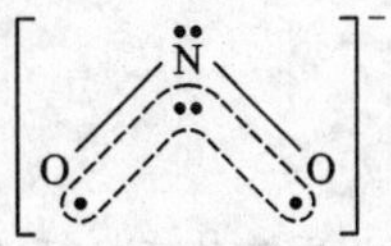	V字形
	O_3	sp^2—p	Π_3^4	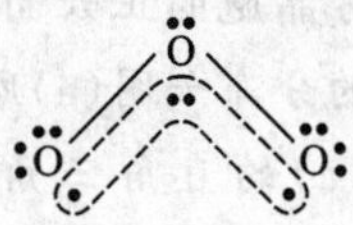	V字形
	BF_3	sp^2—p	Π_4^6	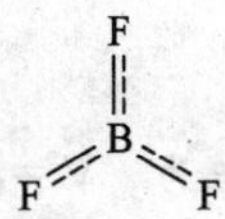	平面三角形
24	NO_3^-	sp^2—p	Π_4^6	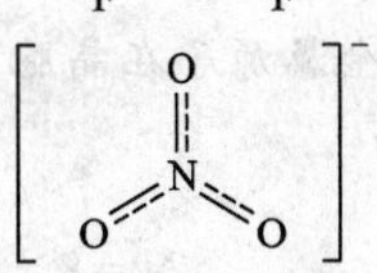	平面三角形
	CO_3^{2-}	sp^2—p	Π_4^6	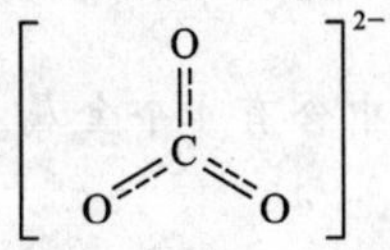	平面三角形

7.45 (1) 在 NO_3^- 离子中,中心氮原子采用 sp^2 等性杂化,如图(a)所示。中心氮原子用 3 个 sp^2 等性杂化轨道与 3 个氧原子的 $2p_x$ 轨道分别成 σ 键,确定了平面三角形离子。在垂直

于离子所在平面的方向上，中心氮原子有未参加杂化的 $2p_z$ 轨道，其中有 2 个电子；3 个氧原子各有一个垂直于离子所在平面的 $2p_z$ 轨道，其中各有 1 个电子。另外 NO_3^- 离子的 1 个电子也在这 4 个 $2p_z$ 轨道中运动。所以离子中有大 π 键 Π_4^6 存在，如图(b)所示。

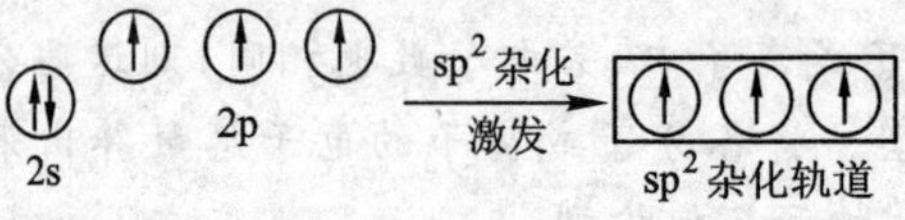

(a)

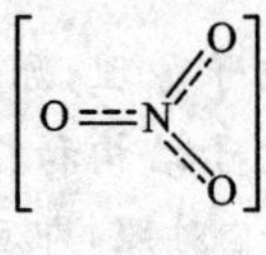

(b)

(2) 在臭氧 O_3 分子中，中心氧原子采用 sp^2 不等性杂化，如图(c)所示。中心氧原子用 2 个有单电子的 sp^2 不等性杂化轨道与 2 个配体氧原子的 $2p_x$ 轨道分别成 σ 键，确定了平面三角形分子。在 3 个氧原子之间还存在着一个垂直于分子平面的大 π 键 Π_3^4，这个离域的 π 键是由中心氧原子提供 2 个 p 电子、另外 2 个配位氧原子各提供 1 个 p 电子形成的。O_3 分子的结构如图(d)所示。

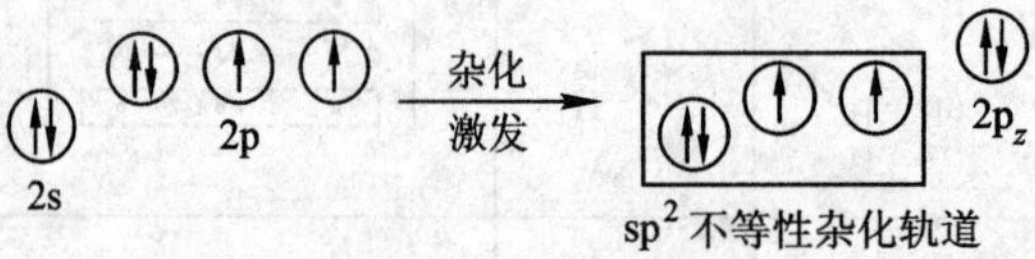

(c)

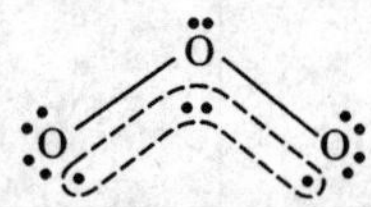

(d)

7.46 在面心立方晶胞的正六面体中，设边长为 a，金属原子的半径为 r，立方体六个面中每一面金属原子的分布如图(a)所示。

由图(a)的直角三角形△ABC 知，$(AC)^2+(BC)^2=(AB)^2$。

因为 $AC=BC=a$，$AB=4r$，所以 $2a^2=(4r)^2$，故 $a=2\sqrt{2}r$。

晶胞体积为 $V=a^3=(2\sqrt{2}r)^3=16\sqrt{2}r^3$。

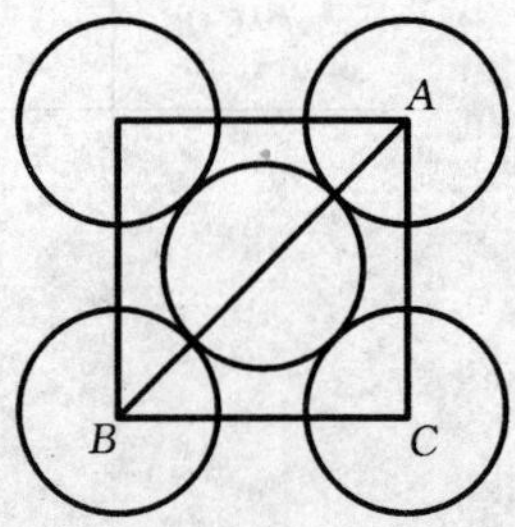

(a)

根据金属原子在晶胞中不同位置，晶胞中金属原子的数目 N 为

$$N=8\times\frac{1}{8}+6\times\frac{1}{2}=4$$

每个晶胞中含有 4 个金属原子，故金属的总体积为

$$V_{金属}=4\times\frac{4}{3}\pi r^3=\frac{16}{3}\pi r^3$$

所以，金属面心立方最紧密堆积的空间利用率为

$$\frac{V_{金属}}{V}\times100\%=\frac{\frac{16}{3}\pi r^3}{16\sqrt{2}r^3}\times100\%=\frac{\pi}{3\sqrt{2}}\times100\%=74.05\%$$

在体心立方晶胞的正六面体中，设边长为 a，金属原子的半径为 r，如图(b)所示。正六面体中有直角三角形$\triangle ABC$，如图(c)所示。

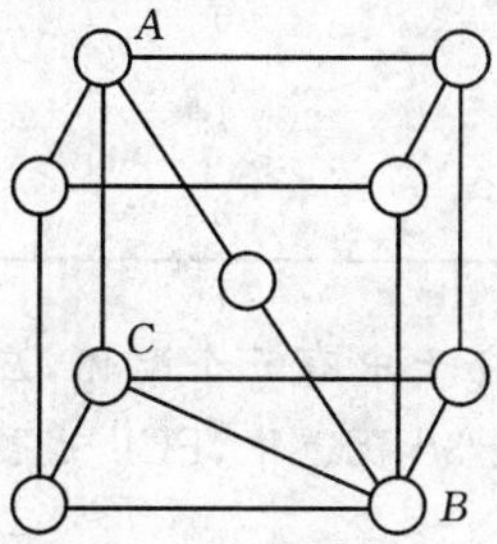

(b)

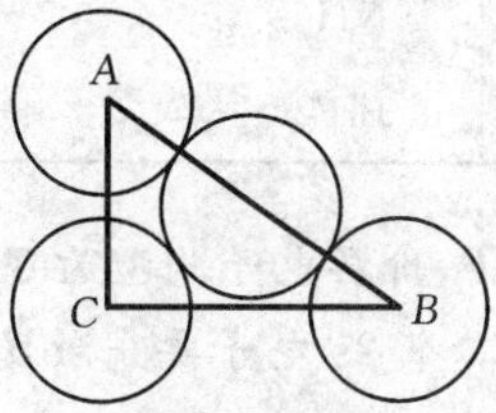

(c)

因为 $AB=\sqrt{3}AC$，且 $AB=4r$，$AC=a$，所以有 $4r=\sqrt{3}a$，即 $a=\frac{4\sqrt{3}}{3}r$。

晶胞体积为
$$V=a^3=\left(\frac{4\sqrt{3}}{3}r\right)^3=\frac{64\sqrt{3}}{9}r^3$$

晶胞内金属原子的数目 N 为

$$N=8\times\frac{1}{8}+1=2$$

每个晶胞中含有 2 个金属原子，故金属的总体积为

$$V_{金属}=2\times\frac{4}{3}\pi r^3=\frac{8}{3}\pi r^3$$

所以，金属体心立方紧密堆积的空间利用率为

$$\frac{V_{金属}}{V}\times100\%=\frac{\frac{8}{3}\pi r^3}{\frac{64\sqrt{3}}{9}r^3}\times100\%=\frac{\sqrt{3}}{8}\pi\times100\%=68.02\%$$

7.47　中心原子的杂化类型、分子的几何构型是由分子中的中心原子价层电子数、价层轨道数和配位数共同决定的。只从中心原子的化合价和配位数不能决定中心原子采取的杂化类型和分子的几何构型。

在 NCl_3 分子中，N 原子电子构型 $2s^22p^3$，4 个轨道有 5 个电子，因孤对电子占有杂化轨道，每个 N—Cl 键占一个杂化轨道，N 只能采取 sp^3 杂化方式。因有一对孤对电子，分子构型为三角锥形。

在 BCl_3 分子中，B 原子电子构型为 $2s^22p^1$，3 个价电子占有 4 个价轨道中的二个。因配位数为 3，应形成 3 个 σ 键，用去 3 个杂化轨道。为保证 3 个杂化轨道中都有一个可供配对的电子，2s 轨道的 2 个电子先激发一个到 p 轨道中。价电子数和配位数(成键轨道数)决定了 B 原子只能采取 sp^2 杂化方式。

7.48　AB_3 型分子共有三种几何构型，有关结果见下表：

几何构型	实例	A 的杂化轨道类型	价层孤电子对数	是否有极性
平面三角形	BCl_3	sp^2	0	无极性
三角锥形	NH_3	sp^3	1	有极性
T 字形	BrF_3	sp^3d	2	有极性

7.49 PCl_5：中心原子 P，价层电子构型为 $3s^23p^3$，分子中有五个配体，应形成五个 σ 键，需五个单电子，杂化前二个 2s 电子要先激发一个到 3d 轨道中，PCl_5 成键过程：

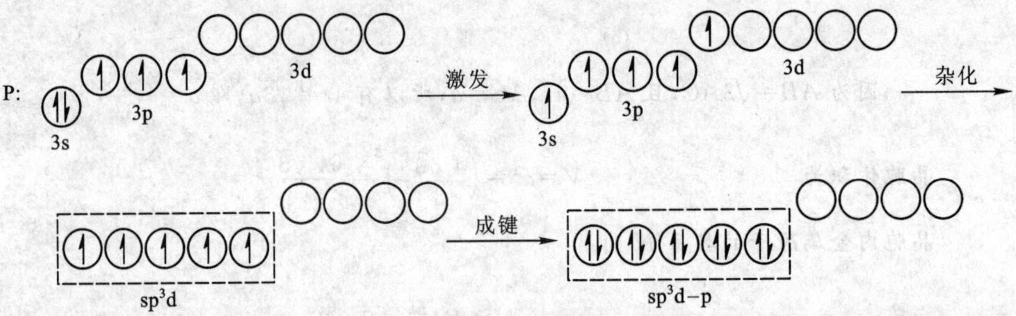

OF_2：中心原子 O，价层电子构型为 $2s^22p^4$，有二个单电子，OF_2 中有二个配体，中心原子采取 sp^3 杂化，其中二个杂化轨道被二对孤对电子占用。OF_2 成键过程：

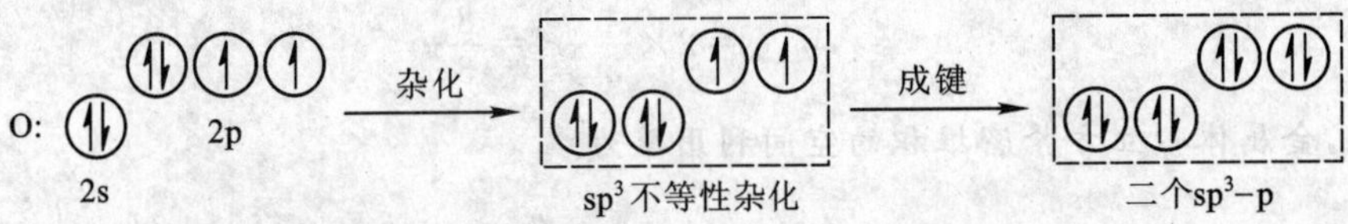

由于中心原子 O 上有二对孤对电子，OF_2 分子呈 V 字形。

ICl_3：中心原子 I，价层电子构型为 $5s^25p^5$，价层只有一个单电子，而 ICl_3 有三个配体，中心原子在杂化前必激发一个电子。中心原子还有二对孤对电子占有杂化轨道，因而中心原子 I 采取 sp^3d 杂化方式，ICl_3 成键过程：

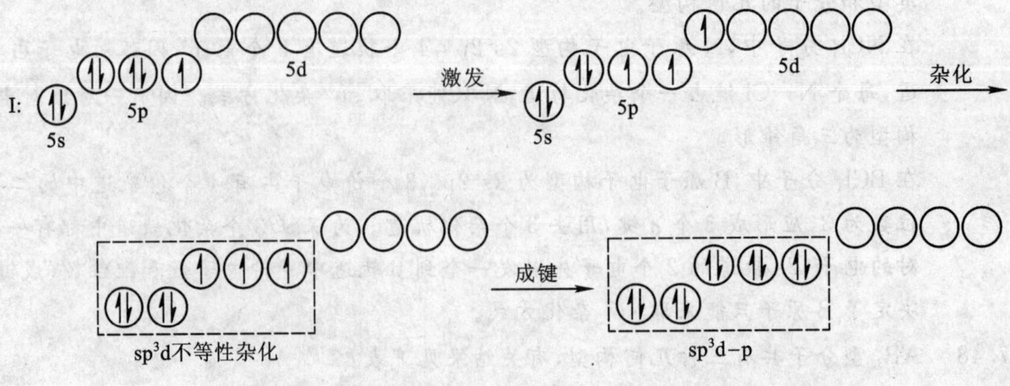

有二对孤对电子占有杂化轨道，分子为 T 字形：

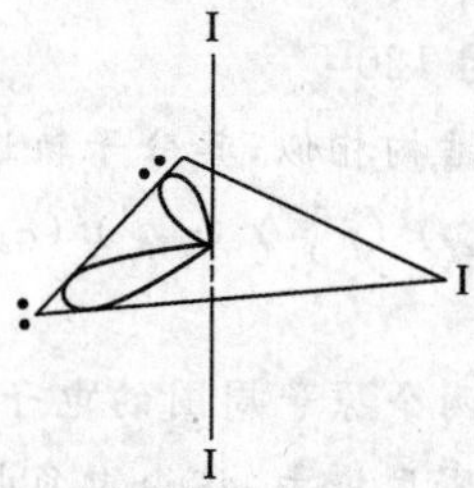

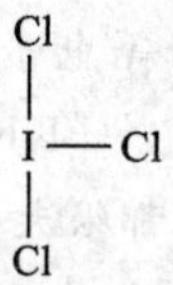

7.50 NO_2 中心原子 N 外层电子构型为 $2s^2 2p^3$，与 O 成键时，N 采取 sp^2 杂化，孤对电子不占有杂化轨道，而是激发后留下一对电子占有 p 轨道，不参与杂化而形成大 π 键：

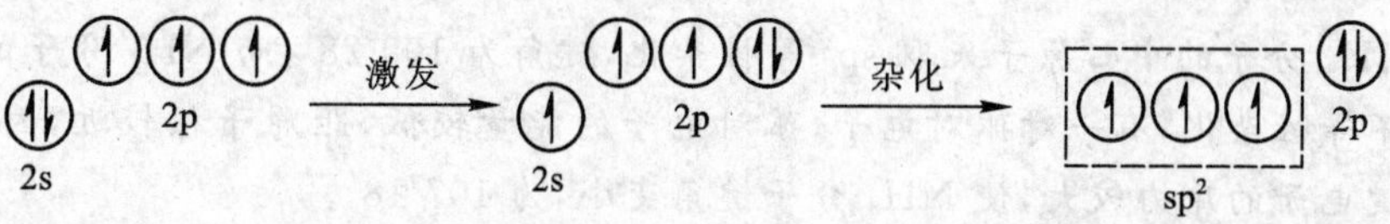

杂化后的三个单电子有两个与 O 成两个 σ 键，另一个为不成键的单电子。不成键的单电子与成键电子间的斥力较小，因而键角远大于 120°（即 132°）。

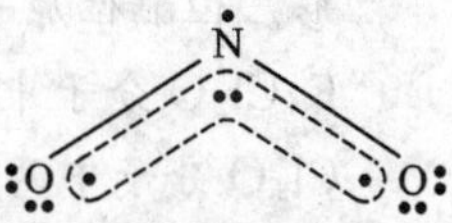

另外，分子中还有一个 Π_3^4 键。但也有不同的观点，认为分子中有单电子是不稳定的，NO_2 分子中 N 上不成键的应是孤对电子，除 N 与 O 间的两个 σ 键外，分子中还有一个离域的 Π_3^3 键。在解释键角大于 120°时，可以从另一个角度来解释：由于氮和氧的电负性较大且半径较小，N—O 间距离较小，因而两个氧原子间有较大斥力（氧上还有二对孤对电子），因此造成键角远大于 120°。但这不是 N 上的不成键电子决定的。

NO_2 分子中究竟含有 Π_3^3 还是 Π_3^4 键，还有待进一步研究。

CO_2 中心原子 C 外层电子构型为 $2s^2 2p^2$，在与 O 成键时，C 原子 2s 两个电子激发后，采取 sp 杂化。两个 sp 杂化轨道上的单电子与两个 O 原子形成二个 σ 键。按价键理论，C 原子上两个未参与杂化的 2p 电子，与两个氧原子形成二个 π 键。而按分子轨道理论，C 上的二个未杂化的 2p 单电子与二个 O 原子形成二个 Π_3^4 键：

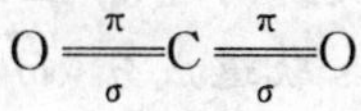

价键理论结果

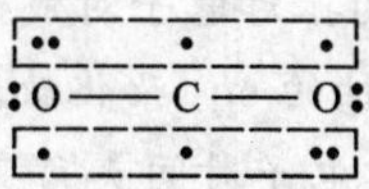

分子轨道理论结果

由于 C 采取 sp 杂化，因此，CO_2 分子为直线形。

SO_2 分子中 S 原子的外层电子构型为 $3s^2 3p^4$，与 O 成键时 S 采取 sp^2 杂化，余下的一对 3p 电子与两个 O 原子形成 Π_3^4 键：

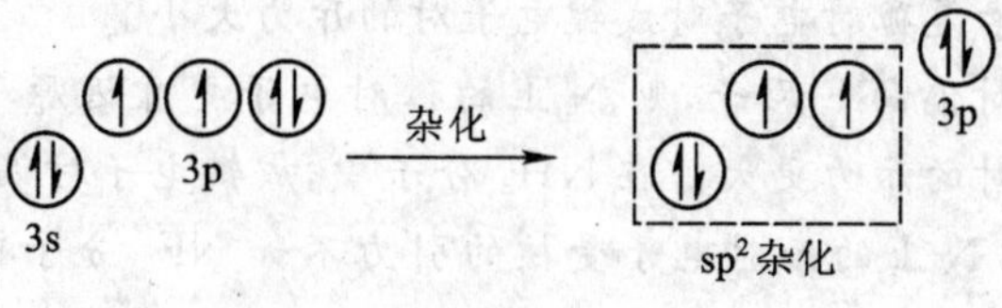

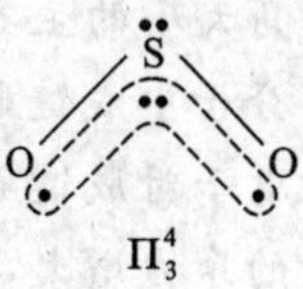

Π_3^4

由于S上的孤对电子中有一对占有杂化轨道，因而SO_2分子为V字形。由于S原子半径较大，两个氧原子间斥力不大，两个氧原子间的斥力与S上的孤对电子对成键电子的斥力相当，因而SO_2分子中键角恰好为120°。

7.51 (1) CO，N_2和CN^-为等电子体，分子结构相似，其分子轨道式为

$$[KK(\sigma_{2s})^2(\sigma_{2s}^*)^2(\pi_{2p_y})^2(\pi_{2p_z})^2(\sigma_{2p_x})^2]$$

键级均为3，所以键能都很大。

(2) CO分子由两种元素的原子形成，两个原子周围的电子密度不同，对称性低；同时，由于有O向C的配键，使C周围的电子密度增大，这个电负性小而电子密度大的C易失去电子而被氧化。N_2键能虽然比CO小，但分子的对称性高，加之N的电负性大使其束缚电子能力强，不易失去电子。

7.52 (a) 键角$CH_4 > NH_3$

CH_4分子的中心原子采取sp^3等性杂化，键角为109°28′，而NH_3分子的中心原子为sp^3不等性杂化，有一对孤对电子，孤对电子的能量较低，距原子核较近，因而孤对电子对成键电子的斥力较大，使NH_3分子键角变小，为107°18′。

(b) 键角$Cl_2O > OF_2$

OF_2和Cl_2O分子的中心原子氧均为sp^3不等性杂化，有二对孤对电子，分子构型为V字形。但配位原子F的电负性远大于Cl的电负性，OF_2分子中成键电子对偏向配位原子F，Cl_2O分子中成键电子对偏向中心原子O，在OF_2分子中两成键电子对间的斥力小而Cl_2O分子中两成键电子对斥力大，因而Cl_2O分子的键角大于OF_2分子的键角。一般都用配位原子与中心原子电负性来解释键角大小。

仅从成键电子对间的斥力来解释分子键角的大小不尽合理。在分子中，孤对电子的能量要比成键电子对能量低，孤对电子距中心原子的核更近，因而孤对电子与成键电子对间的斥力要大于成键电子对与成键电子对间的斥力。显然这与OF_2分子的键角小于Cl_2O分子的键角相矛盾。实际上，Cl_2O分子的键角为111°，比sp^3等性杂化轨道间的键角还要大。那么，怎样解释OF_2键角小于Cl_2O键角更合理呢？

在OF_2和Cl_2O分子中，中心原子O的半径较小且电负性较大。在OF_2分子中，成键电子对偏向F原子，结果使O原子上的孤对电子更靠近O原子，孤对电子的能量进一步降低，则使O的孤对电子对成键电子对斥力增大。同时，O上孤对电子的能量降低，则孤对电子在不等性的sp^3杂化轨道中占有更多的s轨道成分，而成键电子中有较多的p轨道成分，使成键电子对间夹角变小。另外，OF_2分子中两个F原子半径较小，两个F原子间的斥力可忽略；但在Cl_2O分子中，两个Cl原子间的斥力则较大，因Cl原子的半径远大于F原子的半径。

(c) 键角$NH_3 > NF_3$

NH_3和NF_3分子中，H和F的半径都较小，分子中H与H及F与F间斥力可忽略。决定键角大小的主要因素是孤对电子对成键电子对的斥力大小。

NF_3分子中成键电子对偏向F原子，则N上的孤对电子更靠近原子核，能量更低，因此孤对电子对成键电子对的斥力更大。在NH_3分子中，成键电子对偏向N原子，成键电子对间的斥力增大，同时N上的孤对电子受核的引力不如NF_3分子中大。孤对电子的能

量与成键电子对能量相差不大。造成孤对电子与成键电子对的压力与成键电子对和成键电子对的斥力相差不大。所以,NH_3 分子中键角与 109°28′相差不大(107°18′)。

(d) 键角 $NH_3 > PH_3$

NH_3分子和 PH_3 分子的构型均为三角锥形。配体相同,但中心原子不同。N 的电负性大而半径小,P 的电负性小而半径大。半径小电负性大的 N 原子周围的孤对电子和成键电子对间尽量保持最大角度才能保持斥力均衡,因而 NH_3 分子中的键角接近 109°28′。此外,PH_3 键角接近 90°(实际为 93°18′)也可能与 P 有与 sp^3 轨道能量相近的 3d 轨道有关,如 AsH_3,PH_3,PF_3 及 H_2S 等键角都接近 90°。

7.53 结果见下表:

分子或离子	价层电子对数	电子对几何构型	孤对电子数	分子或离子结构
$SnCl_2$	3	三角形	1	V 字形
$SnCl_3^-$	4	四面体	1	三角锥形
$HgCl_2$	2	直线形	0	直线形
BrF_3	5	三角双锥	2	T 字形
I_3^+	4	四面体	2	V 字形
ICl_2^-	5	三角双锥	3	直线形
$IO_2F_2^-$	5	三角双锥	1	变形四面体
IF_5	6	八面体	1	四角锥形
SF_4	5	三角双锥	1	变形四面体
SO_2Cl_2	4	四面体	0	四面体
SO_3^{2-}	4	四面体	1	三角锥形
XeO_4	4	四面体	0	四面体

7.54 F—H---F 氢键的键能为 28.0 $kJ \cdot mol^{-1}$,而 O—H---O 氢键的键能为 18.8 $kJ \cdot mol^{-1}$。可见 HF 分子间的氢键比 H_2O 分子间氢键强。

H_2O 分子有二对孤对电子,二个 H 原子,因此,水分子最多可与周围分子形成 4 个氢键;而 HF 分子中只有一个 H 原子,最多可与周围 HF 分子形成二个氢键,即 H_2O 分子间氢键比 HF 分子间氢键多。另外,H_2O 汽化时,气态的 H_2O 均为单分子而没有二聚、三聚分子,说明水汽化时要断开全部氢键;而 HF 汽化时,气相中仍有二聚体$(HF)_2$,即 HF 汽化时不必断开全部的氢键。综上所述,由于 H_2O 分子间氢键多而汽化时需断开全部氢键,HF 分子间氢键数较 H_2O 少且汽化时 HF 不必断开全部氢键,结果是 H_2O 汽化热要比 HF 汽化热大,H_2O 沸点比 HF 沸点高。

7.55 CO 分子的偶极矩为 0.12 D,偶极矩比较小。而 C 与 O 的电负性差为 0.89,显然,偶极矩大小与电负性差不符。

按分子轨道理论,CO 分子中 C 与 O 间为三重键:一个 σ 键,二个 π 键。二个 π 键中有一

个为氧原子提供电子对形成的 π 配键。CO 分子结构可表示为

$$:C \overset{\leftarrow}{\equiv} O:$$

CO 分子的三重键中，两个共价键的电子对偏向 O 原子产生的偶极矩方向指向 O 原子；另一个由 O 原子提供电子对的配键产生的偶极方向指向 C 原子。由于共价键产生的偶极方向与配键产生的偶极方向相反，互相抵消大部分，因而 CO 分子的偶极矩很小。

7.56 在 PCl_5 分子中，虽然 P—Cl 为极性键，但由于 PCl_5 分子为三角双锥构型，键的偶极矩互相抵消，使分子的正电荷中心和负电荷中心重合，分子的偶极矩为零。因此，PCl_5 为非极性分子。在 O_3 分子中，虽然分子中的原子为同种元素原子，由于 O_3 分子为 V 字形构型，分子中有 Π_3^4 离域键，使中心氧原子与端氧原子的孤电子对数不同、电子密度不同，使 O—O 键有极性，从而 O_3 分子的偶极矩不为零，分子有微弱的极性。

7.57 极性分子有 NO_2，$CHCl_3$，NCl_3，SCl_2，$COCl_2$。

非极性分子有 SO_3，BCl_3。

7.58 不能形成分子间氢键的分子有 $C_2H_5OC_2H_5$，HCl 能形成分子内氢键的有 HNO_3，

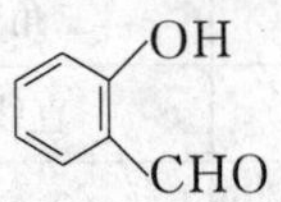，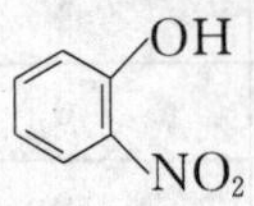

7.59 (1) CS_2 和 CCl_4 色散力。

(2) H_2O 与 N_2 诱导力，色散力。

(3) CH_3Cl 取向力，诱导力，色散力。

(4) H_2O 与 NH_3 取向力，诱导力，色散力，氢键。

7.60 (1) 分子半径 HI＞HCl＞HF，色散力 HI＞HCl＞HF，但 HF 分子间形成最强的氢键，结果使 HF 沸点高于 HI。

但在氮族元素的氢化物中，NH_3 分子间氢键较弱，沸点顺序不是 $NH_3>BiH_3>PH_3$，而是 $BiH_3>NH_3>PH_3$。

(2) BeO 和 LiF 都是离子型晶体，Be^{2+} 电荷比 Li^+ 高但半径却较小，+2 价的 Be^{2+} 与 −2 价的 O^{2-} 之间的静电引力要比 +1 价的 Li^+ 与 −1 价的 F^- 的静电引力大得多，BeO 晶格能比 LiF 晶格能大。所以 BeO 熔点比 LiF 高。

(3) 在 $SiCl_4$ 分子中，中心原子 Si 有和 3s，3p 轨道能量相近的 3d 空轨道，该 3d 空轨道可接受水分子中 O 所提供的电子对，因而 $SiCl_4$ 易水解。在 CCl_4 分子中，中心原子 C 的价层无空的轨道，2s 和 2p 轨道都已用来成键，不能接受水分子中 O 原子提供的电子对，因此，CCl_4 不易水解。

(4) 金刚石是典型的原子晶体，每个碳原子都以 sp^3 杂化轨道与四个碳原子形成共价单键，四面体分布的碳原子的杂化轨道通过共顶点连接方式形成三维空间骨架，因此，金刚石硬度大。石墨属层状晶体，晶体中的碳原子以 sp^2 杂化轨道与相邻的三个碳原子形成共价单键，每个碳原子还有一个与 sp^2 杂化轨道平面相垂直的 2p 轨道，形成离域大 π 键。因此，石墨中的碳原子按层状排列，层与层之间以分子间力相结合，距离较大，所以层与层之间容易发生滑动，造成石墨晶体较软。

7.61 CO_2 为分子晶体而 SiO_2 为原子晶体，无论从宏观上还是从微观上来讨论，结果都是一样

的。从宏观上看，C 与 O 形成双键的键能（798.9 kJ·mol^{-1}）比形成单键的键能（357.7 kJ·mol^{-1}）的二倍要大，因而 C 与 O 形成双键时，以 CO_2 形式存在更稳定；而 Si 与 O 形成双键的键能要比形成单键的键能的二倍要小，因而 Si 与 O 以单键相结合形成巨型的原子晶体而不是 O＝Si＝O 分子晶体。从微观角度看，C 的半径小，C 与 O 的 p 轨道以肩并肩形式重叠能形成较强的 π 键，因而 CO_2 分子中 C 与 O 之间以双键相结合，CO_2 为分子晶体；而 Si 的半径较大，Si 与 O 的 p 轨道以肩并肩形式重叠较少则不能形成稳定的 π 键，Si 与 O 间只能形成稳定的 σ 单键，每个 Si 采取 sp^3 杂化并与 4 个 O 形成 SiO_4 四面体，SiO_4 四面体共顶点氧形成骨架结构，—Si—O—Si—O 无限连接而构成原子晶体。

7.62 Si 的电负性为 1.90，Sn 的电负性为 1.96，二者的电负性相差很小。但 SiF_4 为气态，SnF_4 为固态。其主要原因是 Si^{4+} 的半径（41 pm）比 Sn^{4+} 的半径（71 pm）小得多，Si^{4+} 有强的极化能力，SiF_4 为共价化合物而 SnF_4 为离子化合物。所以 SiF_4 的熔、沸点很低，常温时为气态，而 SnF_4 熔、沸点较高，常温下为固态。

7.63 (1) 极化能力 $Zn^{2+}>Fe^{2+}>Ca^{2+}>K^+$

K，Ca，Fe，Zn 四个元素在同一周期，K^+ 只有一个正电荷，极化能力最弱。Ca^{2+}，Fe^{2+}，Zn^{2+} 带正电荷数相同，离子半径 $Ca^{2+}>Fe^{2+}\approx Zn^{2+}$；$Ca^{2+}$ 为 8 电子构型，Fe^{2+} 为 9～17 电子构型，Zn^{2+} 为 18 电子构型，阳离子的有效核电荷数 $Zn^{2+}>Fe^{2+}>Ca^{2+}$。所以极化能力 $Zn^{2+}>Fe^{2+}>Ca^{2+}$。

(2) 极化能力 $P^{5+}>Si^{4+}>Al^{3+}>Mg^{2+}>Na^+$

离子半径 $P^{5+}<Si^{4+}<Al^{3+}<Mg^{2+}<Na^+$

离子电荷 $P^{5+}>Si^{4+}>Al^{3+}>Mg^{2+}>Na^+$

电荷数越高，半径越小，离子的极化能力越强。实际上由于高电荷的强极化能力及其元素的电负性较大，PCl_5 和 $SiCl_4$ 为共价型化合物，$AlCl_3$ 以共价键为主的化合物，只有 $MgCl_2$ 和 NaCl 为离子型化合物。

7.64 化合物的熔点高低与溶解度大小基本是一致的：

(1) $CaCl_2>BeCl_2>HgCl_2$

离子极化能力 $Ca^{2+}<Be^{2+}<Hg^{2+}$

化合物的共价性 $CaCl_2<BeCl_2<HgCl_2$

(2) CaS>FeS>HgS

原因同(1)

(3) KCl>LiCl>CuCl

阳离子半径	K^+	Li^+	Cu^+
	133 pm	70 pm	96 pm

因 Cu^+ 为 d^{10} 结构，有效核电荷数大且有一定的变形性，因而极化能力按 $K^+<Li^+<Cu^+$，化合物的离子性按 KCl>LiCl>CuCl 顺序变化。

7.65 熔点：BN > MgO> BaO > $CdCl_2$。

BN 为原子晶体，键能大，熔点高；MgO 和 BaO 为离子晶体。离子半径 $Mg^{2+}<Ba^{2+}$，离

子键强度 MgO > BaO；$CdCl_2$ 过渡型晶体，熔点较低。同时，MgO 和 BaO 与 $CdCl_2$ 相比，−2 价阴离子与阳离子的引力大于−1 价阴离子与阳离子的引力，结果是 $CdCl_2$ 晶体离子键强度低，熔点低。

第 8 章

一、选择题

8.1 B　8.2 A　8.3 D　8.4 A　8.5 D　8.6 B　8.7 D　8.8 C　8.9 B
8.10 C　8.11 C　8.12 D　8.13 B　8.14 C

二、填空题

8.15　5.20，4.0×10^{-10}。

8.16　8×10^{-8}，7.10。

8.17　1×10^{-14}，1×10^{-20}。

8.18　(6)，(4)，(1)，(2)，(3)，(5)。

8.19　减小，增大。

8.20　HAc−NaAc，2:1；HCl−NaAc，2:3；HAc−NaOH，3:1。

8.21　增大，变小，变小，不变。

8.22　11.78，4.63，0.00。

8.23　$H_2PO_4^-$，1.3×10^{-12}。

8.24　强，示差；相近，拉平。

8.25　NaCN，NaAc，NaF；$OH^- > CN^- > Ac^- > F^-$。

8.26　H_2E^+，A^-。

8.27　$[Fe(H_2O)_6]^{3+}$，$[Fe(H_2O)_4(OH)_2]^+$；$H_2NO_3^+$；NH^{2-}。

三、简答题和计算题

8.28　由 $H_3AsO_4 \rightleftharpoons 3H^+ + AsO_4^{3-}$ 得

$$K_1K_2K_3 = \frac{[H^+]^3[AsO_4^{3-}]}{[H_3AsO_4]} \tag{1}$$

因为 $K_2 \ll K_1$，故体系的$[H^+]$由第一步解离决定

$$H_3AsO_4 \rightleftharpoons H^+ + H_2AsO_4^-$$

$$K_1 = \frac{[H^+][H_2AsO_4^-]}{[H_3AsO_4]} \text{ 即}$$

$$K_1 = \frac{[H^+]^2}{[H_3AsO_4]} \tag{2}$$

将其代入式(1)中，得

$$K_2K_3=[H^+][AsO_4^{3-}]$$

故 $$[H^+]=\frac{K_2K_3}{[AsO_4^{3-}]}$$

$$=\frac{1.7\times10^{-7}\times5.1\times10^{-12}}{4.0\times10^{-17}}\ mol\cdot dm^{-3}$$

$$=2.17\times10^{-2}\ mol\cdot dm^{-3}$$

将其代入式(2)中，得

$$K_1=\frac{(2.17\times10^{-2})^2}{[H_3AsO_4]}$$

所以 $$[H_3AsO_4]=\frac{(2.17\times10^{-2})^2}{K_1}\ mol\cdot dm^{-3}$$

$$=\frac{(2.17\times10^{-2})^2}{5.5\times10^{-3}}\ mol\cdot dm^{-3}$$

$$=0.086\ mol\cdot dm^{-3}$$

H_3AsO_4 的起始浓度为平衡浓度$[H_3AsO_4]$与$[H^+]$之和

$$0.086\ mol\cdot dm^{-3}+2.17\times10^{-2}\ mol\cdot dm^{-3}=0.11\ mol\cdot dm^{-3}$$

8.29 第一步解离 $$H_2C_2O_4 \rightleftharpoons HC_2O_4^- + H^+$$

$$K_1=\frac{[HC_2O_4^-][H^+]}{[H_2C_2O_4]}$$

得 $$\frac{[HC_2O_4^-]}{[H_2C_2O_4]}=\frac{K_1}{[H^+]}=\frac{5.4\times10^{-2}}{1.0\times10^{-6}}=5.4\times10^4$$

第二步解离 $$HC_2O_4^- \rightleftharpoons H^+ + C_2O_4^{2-}$$

$$K_2=\frac{[C_2O_4^{2-}][H^+]}{[HC_2O_4^-]}$$

得 $$\frac{[C_2O_4^{2-}]}{[HC_2O_4^-]}=\frac{K_2}{[H^+]}=\frac{5.4\times10^{-5}}{1.0\times10^{-6}}=54$$

所以 $$[C_2O_4^{2-}]=54[HC_2O_4^-] \tag{1}$$

$$[HC_2O_4^-]=5.4\times10^4[H_2C_2O_4] \tag{2}$$

由式(1)和式(2)得

$$[C_2O_4^{2-}]=2.9\times10^6[H_2C_2O_4] \tag{3}$$

体系中草酸的起始总浓度为 $0.10\ mol\cdot dm^{-3}$，以三种形式分配在平衡体系中，故

$$[H_2C_2O_4]+[HC_2O_4^-]+[C_2O_4^{2-}]=0.10\ mol\cdot dm^{-3}$$

即 $$[H_2C_2O_4]+5.4\times10^4[H_2C_2O_4]+2.9\times10^6[H_2C_2O_4]=0.10\ mol\cdot dm^{-3}$$

解得 $$[H_2C_2O_4]=3.4\times10^{-8}\ mol\cdot dm^{-3}$$

$$[HC_2O_4^-]=3.4\times10^{-8}\ mol\cdot dm^{-3}\times5.4\times10^4=1.8\times10^{-3}\ mol\cdot dm^{-3}$$

$$[C_2O_4^{2-}]=3.4\times10^{-8}\ mol\cdot dm^{-3}\times2.9\times10^6=0.099\ mol\cdot dm^{-3}$$

8.30 $0.010\ mol\cdot dm^{-3}$的 H_2SO_4 第一步完全解离，故有 $0.010\ mol\cdot dm^{-3}$ 的 H^+ 和 HSO_4^- 存在

于第二步解离之中。

$$HSO_4^- \rightleftharpoons H^+ + SO_4^{2-}$$

起始浓度/($mol\cdot dm^{-3}$)　　0.010　　0.010　　0

平衡浓度/($mol\cdot dm^{-3}$)　　$0.010-x$　　$0.010+x$　　x

x 为第二步解离出的$[H^+]$。

$$K^\ominus=\frac{[H^+][SO_4^{2-}]}{[HSO_4^-]}=\frac{x(0.010+x)}{0.010-x}=1.0\times10^{-2}$$

解得　$x=4.14\times10^{-3}$

故平衡时

$$[H^+]=(0.010+x)\ mol\cdot dm^{-3}=(0.010+4.14\times10^{-3})\ mol\cdot dm^{-3}=0.014\ mol\cdot dm^{-3}$$

即　$pH=1.85$

8.31 由于 HAc 的解离常数比 HCN 大 10^5 倍，HAc 在溶液中的解离占主导地位，求溶液中$[H^+]$时可以忽略 HCN 解离所提供的 H^+。混合溶液中两种酸的浓度：

$$[HAc]=0.40\ mol\cdot dm^{-3}\times\frac{0.20\ dm^3}{0.20\ dm^3+0.60\ dm^3}=0.10\ mol\cdot dm^{-3}$$

$$[HCN]=0.80\ mol\cdot dm^{-3}\times\frac{0.60\ dm^3}{0.20\ dm^3+0.60\ dm^3}=0.60\ mol\cdot dm^{-3}$$

溶液中$[H^+]$与$[Ac^-]$相同：

$$[Ac^-]=[H^+]=\sqrt{K_a^\ominus(HAc)[HAc]}=\sqrt{1.8\times10^{-5}\times0.10}=1.3\times10^{-3}\ mol\cdot dm^{-3}$$

求 CN^- 浓度时，应考虑 HAc 解离出 H^+ 的同离子效应：

$$HCN \rightleftharpoons H^+ + CN^-$$

平衡浓度/($mol\cdot dm^{-3}$)　$0.60-y$　　$1.3\times10^{-3}+y$　　y

$$\frac{(1.3\times10^{-3}+y)y}{0.60-y}=6.2\times10^{-10}$$

解得　$y=2.9\times10^{-7}$，$[CN^-]=2.9\times10^{-7}\ mol\cdot dm^{-3}$

溶液中$[OH^-]$为

$$[OH^-]=\frac{K_w}{[H^+]}=\frac{1.0\times10^{-14}}{1.3\times10^{-3}}\ mol\cdot dm^{-3}=7.7\times10^{-12}\ mol\cdot dm^{-3}$$

8.32 HF 和 HAc 的解离常数相差不大，应同时考虑 HF 和 HAc 的解离。设平衡时$[F^-]$为 $x\ mol\cdot dm^{-3}$，$[Ac^-]$为 $y\ mol\cdot dm^{-3}$

$$HF \rightleftharpoons H^+ + F^- \qquad HAc \rightleftharpoons H^+ + Ac^-$$

平衡浓度/($mol\cdot dm^{-3}$)　$1.0-x$　$x+y$　x　　$0.1-y$　$x+y$　y

则有 $\dfrac{(x+y)x}{1.0-x}=6.6\times10^{-4}$ $\dfrac{(x+y)y}{0.1-y}=1.8\times10^{-5}$

两种酸的浓度较大，平衡常数很小，可以进行近似处理：

$$1.0-x\approx1.0 \qquad 0.1-y\approx0.1$$

得 $$(x+y)x=6.6\times10^{-4} \tag{1}$$

$$(x+y)y=1.8\times10^{-6} \tag{2}$$

将(1)式除以(2)式得 $\dfrac{x}{y}=366.67$

即 $x=366.67\,y$

代入(2)式得 $y=7.0\times10^{-5}$

则 $x=366.67\quad y=2.6\times10^{-2}$

$[H^+]=(x+y)mol\cdot dm^{-3}=2.6\times10^{-2}mol\cdot dm^{-3}$

$[F^-]=x\ mol\cdot dm^{-3}=2.6\times10^{-2}\ mol\cdot dm^{-3}$

$[Ac^-]=y\ mol\cdot dm^{-3}=7.0\times10^{-5}\ mol\cdot dm^{-3}$

$[HF]=(1.0-x)\ mol\cdot dm^{-3}=0.97\ mol\cdot dm^{-3}$

$[HAc]=(0.1-y)\ mol\cdot dm^{-3}=0.1\ mol\cdot dm^{-3}$

8.33 由于 $K_{a_2}^{\ominus}(H_2C_2O_4)$ 较小，加之HCl中 H^+ 的同离子效应，在求溶液中 $HC_2O_4^-$ 浓度时，只考虑第一步解离即可：

$$H_2C_2O_4 \rightleftharpoons H^+ + HC_2O_4^-$$

平衡浓度/($mol\cdot dm^{-3}$) $0.1-x$ $\quad 0.1+x$ $\quad x$

$$\frac{(0.1+x)x}{0.1-x}=K_{a_1}^{\ominus}=5.9\times10^{-2}$$

解得 $x=3.1\times10^{-2}$

$C_2O_4^{2-}$ 由 $H_2C_2O_4$ 的第二步解离求得

$$HC_2O_4^- \rightleftharpoons H^+ + C_2O_4^{2-}$$

平衡浓度/($mol\cdot dm^{-3}$) $0.031-y$ $\quad 0.131+y$ $\quad y$

$$\frac{(0.131+y)y}{0.031-y}=K_{a_2}^{\ominus}=6.4\times10^{-5}$$

解得 $y=1.5\times10^{-5}$

则混合溶液中 $[C_2O_4^{2-}]=1.5\times10^{-5}\ mol\cdot dm^{-3}$

$[HC_2O_4^-]=3.1\times10^{-2}\ mol\cdot dm^{-3}$

8.34 $K_b^{\ominus}(NH_3\cdot H_2O)=1.8\times10^{-5}$

$$pH=14-pK_b^{\ominus}+\lg\frac{[NH_3]}{[NH_4^+]}$$

$$\lg\frac{[NH_3]}{[NH_4^+]}=pH+pK_b^{\ominus}-14=9+4.74-14=-0.26$$

$$\frac{[NH_3]}{[NH_4^+]}=0.55$$

$$[NH_3]=0.55\times[NH_4^+]=0.55\ mol\cdot dm^{-3}$$

浓氨水的浓度为

$$\frac{0.904\times10^{3}\ \text{g}\cdot\text{dm}^{-3}\times26.0\%}{17\ \text{g}\cdot\text{mol}^{-1}}=13.83\ \text{mol}\cdot\text{dm}^{-3}$$

需浓氨水的体积为

$$\frac{0.50\ \text{dm}^{3}\times0.55\ \text{mol}\cdot\text{dm}^{-3}}{13.83\ \text{mol}\cdot\text{dm}^{-3}}=1.99\times10^{-2}\ \text{dm}^{3}$$

需 NH_4Cl 的质量

$$1.0\ \text{mol}\cdot\text{dm}^{-3}\times0.50\ \text{dm}^{3}\times53.5\ \text{g}\cdot\text{mol}^{-1}=26.75\ \text{g}$$

8.35 (1) $HL+HCO_3^- \rightleftharpoons H_2CO_3+L^-$

$$K^{\ominus}=\frac{[H_2CO_3][L^-]}{[HL][HCO_3^-]}\cdot\frac{[H^+]}{[H^+]}$$

$$=\frac{K_a^{\ominus}(HL)}{K_{a_1}^{\ominus}(H_2CO_3)}=3.3\times10^{2}$$

(2) $$\text{pH}=\text{p}K_{a_1}^{\ominus}-\lg\frac{[H_2CO_3]}{[HCO_3^-]}$$

$$=6.38-\lg\frac{1.4\times10^{-3}}{2.7\times10^{-2}}=7.66$$

(3) 由于HL酸性比 H_2CO_3 强得多,可近似处理成 HL 与 HCO_3^- 全部反应生成 H_2CO_3。则

$$[H_2CO_3]=1.4\times10^{-3}\ \text{mol}\cdot\text{dm}^{-3}+5.0\times10^{-3}\ \text{mol}\cdot\text{dm}^{-3}$$

$$=6.4\times10^{-3}\ \text{mol}\cdot\text{dm}^{-3}$$

$$[HCO_3^-]=2.7\times10^{-2}\ \text{mol}\cdot\text{dm}^{-3}-5.0\times10^{-3}\ \text{mol}\cdot\text{dm}^{-3}$$

$$=2.2\times10^{-2}\ \text{mol}\cdot\text{dm}^{-3}$$

$$\text{pH}=\text{p}K_{a_1}^{\ominus}-\lg\frac{[H_2CO_3]}{[HCO_3^-]}$$

$$=6.38-\lg\frac{6.4\times10^{-3}}{2.2\times10^{-2}}=6.92$$

8.36 pH 恰好在 $\text{p}K_{a_2}^{\ominus}$ 与 $\text{p}K_{a_1}^{\ominus}$ 之间且接近 $\text{p}K_{a_2}^{\ominus}$,说明溶液为 $HCO_3^--CO_3^{2-}$ 缓冲溶液。

设加入 Na_2CO_3 的体积为 V,则有

$$[HCO_3^-]=\frac{0.30\times20}{20+V}=\frac{6}{20+V}\ \text{mol}\cdot\text{dm}^{-3}$$

$$[CO_3^{2-}]=\frac{0.20\,V}{20+V}\ \text{mol}\cdot\text{dm}^{-3}$$

$$\frac{[HCO_3^-]}{[CO_3^{2-}]}=\frac{6.0}{0.20V}$$

由 $\text{pH}=\text{p}K_{a_2}^{\ominus}-\lg\dfrac{[HCO_3^-]}{[CO_3^{2-}]}$

$$10=-\lg5.6\times10^{-11}-\lg\frac{6.0}{0.20\,V}$$

$$\frac{6.0}{0.20V}=1.78,V=16.85\ \text{cm}^{3}$$

加入 Na_2CO_3 16.85 cm^3。

8.37 根据酸碱质子理论：

$$H_2PO_4^- \rightleftharpoons H^+ HPO_4^{2-}$$

$H_2PO_4^-$ 与 HPO_4^{2-} 是共轭酸碱对。

$$HPO_4^{2-} + H_2O \rightleftharpoons H_2PO_4^- + OH^-$$

$$K_b^\ominus(HPO_4^{2-}) = \frac{[H_2PO_4^-][OH^-]}{[HPO_4^{2-}]} = \frac{[H_2PO_4^-][OH^-][H^+]}{[HPO_4^{2-}][H^+]} = \frac{K_w^\ominus}{K_{a_2}^\ominus}$$

$$= \frac{1.0\times10^{-14}}{6.1\times10^{-8}} = 1.6\times10^{-7}$$

$K_b^\ominus(HPO_4^{2-}) < K_b^\ominus(NH_3 \cdot H_2O)$

所以 NH_3 的碱性比 HPO_4^{2-} 强。

8.38 酸：H_2S，HAc；

碱：CO_3^{2-}，OH^-，NO_2^-；

既是酸又是碱：HS^-，$H_2PO_4^-$，H_2O，NH_3。

8.39 (1) SO_4^{2-} 共轭酸为 HSO_4^-；

(2) H_2SO_4 共轭碱为 HSO_4^-；

(3) HSO_4^- 共轭酸为 H_2SO_4；共轭碱为 SO_4^{2-}；

(4) S^{2-} 共轭酸为 HS^-；

(5) NH_3 共轭酸为 NH_4^+；

(6) H_2S 共轭碱为 HS^-；

(7) $H_2PO_4^-$ 共轭酸为 H_3PO_4，共轭碱为 HPO_4^{2-}。

第9章

一、选择题

9.1 C　9.2 B　9.3 C　9.4 C　9.5 B　9.6 C　9.7 C　9.8 B　9.9 D
9.10 C　9.11 B

二、填空题

9.12 1.1×10^{-10}。

9.13 $K_{sp}^\ominus(MgNH_4PO_4) = [Mg^{2+}][NH_4^+][PO_4^{3-}]$，

$K_{sp}^\ominus[TiO(OH)_2] = [TiO^{2+}][OH^-]^2$。

9.14 4.0×10^{-3}，2.0×10^{-3}。

9.15 Cd^{2+}，Fe^{2+}。

9.16 $s_1 > s_3 > s_2 > s_4$。

9.17 $\leqslant 1.48$。

9.18 减小，增大，大。

9.19 Ag_2CrO_4 的溶解度比 Ag_2S 的大。

9.20 4.0×10^{-2}。

9.21　(1) 小;(2) 不变;(3) 小,增大。

三、简答题和计算题

9.22　(1) $FeC_2O_4 \cdot 2H_2O$ 在水中的溶解度为

$$\frac{0.10}{180}=5.6\times10^{-4}\ mol\cdot dm^{-3}$$

$$FeC_2O_4 \rightleftharpoons Fe^{2+}+C_2O_4^{2-}$$

$$K_{sp}^{\ominus}=[Fe^{2+}][C_2O_4^{2-}]=(5.6\times10^{-4})^2$$
$$=3.1\times10^{-7}$$

(2) pH=9　$[OH^-]=1\times10^{-5}\ mol\cdot dm^{-3}$

$$Ni(OH)_2 \rightleftharpoons Ni^{2+} + 2OH^-$$
$$s \qquad 1\times10^{-5}+2s$$

$$s=1.6\times10^{-6}\ mol\cdot dm^{-3}$$

$$K_{sp}^{\ominus}=s(1\times10^{-5}+2s)^2=1.6\times10^{-6}\times(1\times10^{-5}+2\times1.6\times10^{-6})^2$$
$$=2.7\times10^{-16}$$

9.23　(1) 设 Ag_2CO_3 在水中的溶解度为 s

$$Ag_2CO_3 \rightleftharpoons 2Ag^+ + CO_3^{2-}$$

平衡时相对浓度　　$2s$　　s

$$K_{sp}^{\ominus}=[Ag^+]^2[CO_3^{2-}]$$
$$=(2s)^2s$$
$$=4s^3$$

所以

$$s=\sqrt[3]{\frac{K_{sp}^{\ominus}}{4}}=\sqrt[3]{\frac{8.46\times10^{-12}}{4}}\ mol\cdot dm^{-3}$$
$$=1.28\ mol\cdot dm^{-3}$$

$$[Ag^+]=2s=2.56\times10^{-4}\ mol\cdot dm^{-3}$$
$$[CO_3^{2-}]=s=1.28\times10^{-4}\ mol\cdot dm^{-3}$$

(2) Ag_2CO_3 在 0.01 $mol\cdot dm^{-3}$ Na_2CO_3 溶液中溶解度为 s

$$[CO_3^{2-}]\approx0.01\ mol\cdot dm^{-3}$$

$$Ag_2CO_3 \rightleftharpoons 2Ag^+ + CO_3^{2-}$$

平衡时相对浓度　　$2s$　　$0.01+s\approx0.01$

$$K_{sp}^{\ominus}=[Ag^+]^2[CO_3^{2-}]$$
$$=(2s)^2\times0.01$$
$$=0.04s^2$$

所以

$$s=\sqrt{\frac{K_{sp}^{\ominus}}{0.04}}=\sqrt{\frac{8.46\times10^{-12}}{0.04}}\ mol\cdot dm^{-3}$$
$$=1.45\times10^{-5}\ mol\cdot dm^{-3}$$

(3) Ag_2CO_3 在 0.01 $mol\cdot dm^{-3}$ 的 $AgNO_3$ 溶液中溶解度为 s

$$[Ag^+]=0.01\ mol\cdot dm^{-3}$$

$$Ag_2CO_3 \rightleftharpoons 2Ag^+ + CO_3^{2-}$$

平衡时相对浓度 $\qquad 0.01+s\approx 0.01 \qquad s$

$$K_{sp}^{\ominus}=[Ag^+]^2[CO_3^{2-}]$$
$$=0.01^2\times s$$

所以
$$s=\frac{K_{sp}^{\ominus}}{0.01^2}=\frac{8.46\times10^{-12}}{0.01^2}\ mol\cdot dm^{-3}$$
$$=8.46\times10^{-8}\ mol\cdot dm^{-3}$$

9.24 1g FeS 为 0.0114 mol，若溶于 100 cm^3 1 $mol\cdot dm^{-3}$ 盐酸

$$FeS + 2H^+ \rightleftharpoons Fe^{2+} + H_2S$$

平衡浓度/$(mol\cdot dm^{-3})$ $\qquad 1-2\times0.114 \qquad 0.114 \qquad 0.114$

但 H_2S 饱和浓度为 0.1 $mol\cdot dm^{-3}$，即$[H_2S]=0.1\ mol\cdot dm^{-3}$，过多的 H_2S 以气体形式释放出来。

由 $K_{sp}^{\ominus}=[Fe^{2+}][S^{2-}]$，FeS 全溶解时 S^{2-} 浓度为

$$[S^{2-}]\leqslant\frac{K_{sp}^{\ominus}}{[Fe^{2+}]}=\frac{6.3\times10^{-18}}{0.114}\ mol\cdot dm^{-3}$$
$$=5.5\times10^{-17}\ mol\cdot dm^{-3}$$

由 $K_a^{\ominus}(H_2S)=\frac{[H^+]^2[S^{2-}]}{[H_2S]}$，FeS 全溶解时 H^+ 浓度

$$[H^+]\geqslant\sqrt{\frac{K_a^{\ominus}(H_2S)\cdot[H_2S]}{[S^{2-}]}}$$
$$=\sqrt{\frac{1.4\times10^{-20}\times0.10}{5.5\times10^{-17}}}\ mol\cdot dm^{-3}$$
$$=5.0\times10^{-3}\ mol\cdot dm^{-3}$$

按 FeS 全溶解，溶液中剩余$[H^+]$为

$$[H^+]=(1-2\times0.114)\ mol\cdot dm^{-3}=0.772\ mol\cdot dm^{-3}$$

计算结果表明 FeS 能完全溶解。

9.25
$$CuS + 2H^+ \rightleftharpoons Cu^{2+} + H_2S$$
$$x-2\times0.010 \qquad 0.010 \qquad 0.010$$

$$K^{\ominus}=\frac{[Cu^{2+}][H_2S]}{[H^+]^2}=\frac{[Cu^{2+}][H_2S][S^{2-}]}{[H^+]^2[S^{2-}]}=\frac{K_{sp}^{\ominus}}{K_{a_1}^{\ominus}K_{a_2}^{\ominus}}$$

已知 CuS $K_{sp}^{\ominus}=6.3\times10^{-36}$，$H_2S$ 的 $K_{a_1}^{\ominus}\cdot K_{a_2}^{\ominus}=1.4\times10^{-20}$

所以
$$K^{\ominus}=\frac{6.3\times10^{-36}}{1.4\times10^{-20}}=4.5\times10^{-16}$$

$$\frac{(0.010)^2}{(x-2\times0.010)^2}=4.5\times10^{-16}$$

因 $K^{\ominus}$ 很小，即$(x-2\times0.010)$很大，$x-2\times0.010\approx x$

解得 $\quad x=2.1\times10^6$，即$[HCl]=2.1\times10^6\ mol\cdot dm^{-3}$

可见，在 1 dm^3 盐酸溶液中溶解 0.010 mol 的 CuS 需盐酸浓度在 $2.1\times10^6\ mol\cdot dm^{-3}$。实

际上盐酸最大浓度约为 12 $mol \cdot dm^{-3}$，说明 CuS 不能溶于盐酸中。

9.26
$$Mg(OH)_2 \rightleftharpoons Mg^{2+} + 2OH^-$$
$$K_{sp}^{\ominus} = [Mg^{2+}][OH^-]^2 \quad (1)$$

其中$[Mg^{2+}]$与溶解度 s 相等，而$[OH^-]=2s$

故有
$$K_{sp}^{\ominus} = s \times (2s)^2 = 4s^3$$

将题设条件代入其中，得
$$K_{sp}^{\ominus} = 4 \times (1.12 \times 10^{-4})^3 = 5.62 \times 10^{-12}$$

依题意 0.10 $mol \cdot dm^{-3}$ 的 $MgCl_2$ 溶液和 0.10 $mol \cdot dm^{-3}$ 的 $NH_3 \cdot H_2O$ 等体积混合后，
$$[Mg^{2+}] = [NH_3 \cdot H_2O] = 0.050\ mol \cdot dm^{-3}$$

由式(1)得，使 0.050 $mol \cdot dm^{-3}$ 的 Mg^{2+} 沉淀，需要的
$$[OH^-] = \sqrt{\frac{K_{sp}^{\ominus}}{[Mg^{2+}]}}$$

将求得的 $K_{sp}^{\ominus}$ 值代入其中，得
$$[OH^-] = \sqrt{\frac{5.62 \times 10^{-12}}{0.050}}\ mol \cdot dm^{-3} = 1.06 \times 10^{-5}\ mol \cdot dm^{-3}$$

这个$[OH^-]$由 $NH_3 \cdot H_2O$ 和加入的$[NH_4^+]$共同维持，由缓冲体系的 pH 公式
$$pOH = pK_b^{\ominus} - \lg \frac{c_{碱}}{c_{盐}}$$

得
$$c_{盐} = \frac{K_b^{\ominus} c_{碱}}{[OH^-]}$$

式中
$$c_{碱} = [NH_3 \cdot H_2O] = 0.050\ mol \cdot dm^{-3}$$
$$c_{盐} = [NH_4^+]$$

故
$$[NH_4^+] = \frac{1.8 \times 10^{-5} \times 0.050}{1.06 \times 10^{-5}}\ mol \cdot dm^{-3} = 8.49 \times 10^{-2}\ mol \cdot dm^{-3}$$

不考虑加入 NH_4Cl 后体积的变化，则溶液的体积
$$V = 0.10\ dm^3 + 0.10\ dm^3 = 0.20\ dm^3$$

加入的 NH_4Cl 的
$$n = cV = 8.49 \times 10^{-2}\ mol \cdot dm^{-3} \times 0.20\ dm^3 = 0.0170\ mol$$

NH_4Cl 的质量
$$m = nM = 0.0170\ mol \times 53.5\ g \cdot mol^{-1} = 0.910\ g$$

即加入 0.910 g 以上 NH_4Cl 可以抑制 $Mg(OH)_2$ 的生成。

9.27 该溶解过程用化学反应方程式表示为

$$CaCO_3 + H_2CO_3 \longrightarrow Ca^{2+} + 2HCO_3^-$$

其平征常数

$$K^\ominus = \frac{[Ca^{2+}][HCO_3^-]^2}{[H_2CO_3]}$$

在平衡常数表示式的分子和分母中同时乘以$[CO_3^{2-}][H^+]$

得

$$K^\ominus = \frac{[Ca^{2+}][CO_3^{2-}]\cdot\dfrac{[H^+][HCO_3^-]}{[H_2CO_3]}}{\dfrac{[H^+][CO_3^{2-}]}{[HCO_3^-]}} = \frac{K_{sp}^\ominus \cdot K_1}{K_2}$$

所以

$$K^\ominus = \frac{2.8\times10^{-9}\times4.5\times10^{-7}}{4.7\times10^{-11}} = 2.68\times10^{-5}$$

反应过程中 1 mol $CaCO_3$ 溶解，则得到 1 mol Ca^{2+} 和 2 mol HCO_3^-，故平衡时$[Ca^{2+}]$等于 $CaCO_3$ 的溶解度 s，$[HCO_3^-]=2s$。

所以上式可以表示为

$$K^\ominus = \frac{s\times(2s)^2}{0.033} = 2.68\times10^{-5}$$

解得 $s=6.0\times10^{-3}$，故 $CaCO_3$ 在该条件下的溶解度为 6.0×10^{-3} $mol\cdot dm^{-3}$。

9.28 由 $Fe(OH)_3 \rightleftharpoons Fe^{3+} + 3OH^-$ 得

$$K_{sp}^\ominus = [Fe^{3+}][OH^-]^3$$

$$[OH^-] = \sqrt[3]{\frac{K_{sp}^\ominus}{[Fe^{3+}]}}$$

Fe^{3+} 沉淀完全，即$[Fe^{3+}]=1.0\times10^{-5}$ $mol\cdot dm^{-3}$时，有

$$[OH^-] = \sqrt[3]{\frac{2.8\times10^{-39}}{1.0\times10^{-5}}}\ mol\cdot dm^{-3} = 6.54\times10^{-12}\ mol\cdot dm^{-3}$$

这时体系的 pOH=11.2，pH=2.8

由 $Fe(OH)_2 \rightleftharpoons Fe^{2+} + 2OH^-$ 得

$$K_{sp}^\ominus = [Fe^{2+}][OH^-]^2$$

$$[OH^-] = \sqrt{\frac{K_{sp}^\ominus}{[Fe^{2+}]}} = \sqrt{\frac{4.9\times10^{-17}}{0.10}}\ mol\cdot dm^{-3} = 2.21\times10^{-8}\ mol\cdot dm^{-3}$$

这时体系的 pOH=7.7，pH=6.3

因此分离 Fe^{3+} 和 Fe^{2+}，pH 应控制在 2.8～6.3 之间。

9.29 $K_{sp}^\ominus(PbS)=8.0\times10^{-28}$，$K_{sp}^\ominus(MnS)=2.5\times10^{-13}$

Pb^{2+} 和 Mn^{2+} 浓度相同，生成沉淀的类型相同，因而 $K_{sp}^\ominus$ 小的 PbS 先生成沉淀。

Pb^{2+}沉淀完全时，溶液中S^{2-}浓度为

$$[S^{2-}]=\frac{K_{sp}^{\ominus}(PbS)}{[Pb^{2+}]}=\frac{8.0\times10^{-28}}{1.0\times10^{-5}}\ mol\cdot dm^{-3}=8.0\times10^{-23}\ mol\cdot dm^{-3}$$

此时溶液中H^+浓度应为

$$[H^+]=\sqrt{\frac{K_{a_1}^{\ominus}K_{a_2}^{\ominus}[H_2S]}{[S^{2-}]}}=\sqrt{\frac{1.1\times10^{-7}\times1.3\times10^{-13}\times0.10}{1.0\times10^{-23}}}\ mol\cdot dm^{-3}$$

$$=4.23\ mol\cdot dm^{-3}$$

$$pH=-0.63$$

Mn^{2+}开始沉淀时，溶液中S^{2-}浓度为

$$[S^{2-}]=\frac{K_{sp}^{\ominus}(MnS)}{[Mn^{2+}]}=\frac{2.5\times10^{-13}}{0.025}\ mol\cdot dm^{-3}=1.0\times10^{-11}\ mol\cdot dm^{-3}$$

此时溶液中H^+浓度为

$$[H^+]=\sqrt{\frac{1.1\times10^{-7}\times1.3\times10^{-13}\times0.10}{1.0\times10^{-11}}}\ mol\cdot dm^{-3}=1.2\times10^{-5}\ mol\cdot dm^{-3}$$

$$pH=4.92$$

控制pH范围为$-0.63\sim4.92$。

9.30 产生的气体物质的量为0.10 mol，饱和溶液中H_2S浓度为0.10 $mol\cdot dm^{-3}$。则FeS与HCl反应共生成0.20 mol H_2S。

$$\begin{array}{ccccc} FeS & + & 2H^+ & = & Fe^{2+} & + & H_2S \\ & & x-2\times0.20 & & 0.10\times2 & & 0.10 \end{array}$$

$$K^{\ominus}=\frac{[Fe^{2+}][H_2S]}{[H^+]^2}=\frac{[Fe^{2+}][H_2S]}{[H^+]^2}\cdot\frac{[S^{2-}]}{[S^{2-}]}$$

$$=\frac{K_{sp}^{\ominus}(FeS)}{K_a^{\ominus}(H_2S)}=\frac{6.3\times10^{-18}}{1.4\times10^{-20}}=4.5\times10^2$$

即 $\frac{0.20\times0.10}{(x-0.40)^2}=4.5\times10^2$

解得 $x=0.40$，$[HCl]=0.40\ mol\cdot dm^{-3}$

则盐酸溶液初始浓度为0.40 $mol\cdot dm^{-3}$，FeS在该盐酸溶液中的溶解度为0.20 $mol\cdot dm^{-3}$。

9.31 溶液中Fe^{3+}浓度为

$$[Fe^{3+}]=\frac{0.056}{56}\ mol\cdot dm^{-3}=1.0\times10^{-3}\ mol\cdot dm^{-3}$$

欲使Fe^{3+}沉淀完全(浓度低于$1.0\times10^{-5}\ mol\cdot dm^{-3}$)，溶液中$OH^-$浓度至少为

$$[OH^-]=\sqrt[3]{\frac{2.8\times10^{-39}}{1.0\times10^{-5}}}\ mol\cdot dm^{-3}=6.5\times10^{-12}\ mol\cdot dm^{-3}$$

$$pH=14-pOH=2.8$$

欲使Zn^{2+}不沉淀，OH^-浓度应低于

$$[OH^-]=\sqrt{\frac{3.0\times10^{-17}}{0.20}}\ mol\cdot dm^{-3}=1.2\times10^{-8}\ mol\cdot dm^{-3}$$

$$pH = 14 - pOH = 6.1$$

故应控制溶液 pH 在 2.8～6.1 之间。

9.32 $K_{sp}^{\ominus}(BaCO_3) = 2.6\times10^{-9}$，$K_{sp}^{\ominus}(BaSO_4) = 1.1\times10^{-10}$

$$BaSO_4 + CO_3^{2-} = BaCO_3 + SO_4^{2-}$$

平衡浓度/$(mol\cdot dm^{-3})$　　$x - 0.010$　　　0.010

$$K^{\ominus} = \frac{[SO_4^{2-}]}{[CO_3^{2-}]} = \frac{[SO_4^{2-}]}{[CO_3^{2-}]}\cdot\frac{[Ba^{2+}]}{[Ba^{2+}]} = \frac{K_{sp}^{\ominus}(BaSO_4)}{K_{sp}^{\ominus}(BaCO_3)} = \frac{1.1\times10^{-10}}{2.6\times10^{-9}}$$

$$= 4.2\times10^{-2}$$

$$\frac{0.010}{x-0.010} = 4.2\times10^{-2} \qquad 得\ x = 0.25$$

所以，加入 0.25 mol Na_2CO_3 于 1.0 dm^3 饱和溶液中便能实现沉淀的转化。

9.33 若 Ag_2CrO_4 饱和溶液中加入 KI 溶液，存在下列平衡：

$$Ag_2CrO_4 + 2I^- \rightleftharpoons 2AgI + CrO_4^{2}$$

$$K^{\ominus} = \frac{[CrO_4^{2-}]}{[I^-]^2} = \frac{[CrO_4^{2-}]}{[I^-]^2}\cdot\frac{[Ag^+]^2}{[Ag^+]^2} = \frac{1.1\times10^{-12}}{(8.5\times10^{-17})^2}$$

$$= 1.5\times10^{20}$$

平衡常数很大，所以在含有 Ag_2CrO_4 沉淀的溶液中滴加 KI 溶液，Ag_2CrO_4 溶解，将会产生 AgI 沉淀，如果加入足量的 KI，即可使砖红色的 Ag_2CrO_4 固体完全转变为黄色的 AgI 沉淀。

第 10 章

一、选择题

10.1 D　10.2 C　10.3 B　10.4 C　10.5 A　10.6 D　10.7 B　10.8 C　10.9 A
10.10 C　10.11 A　10.12 B　10.13 C　10.14 B　10.15 D

二、填空题

10.16 浓差；0.177；$H^+(1\ mol\cdot dm^{-3}) \longrightarrow H^+(1\times10^{-3}\ mol\cdot dm^{-3})$。

10.17 (－) Ag|AgCl|$Cl^-(1\ mol\cdot dm^{-3})$ ¦¦ KCl(饱和)|Hg_2Cl_2|Hg(＋)

$Hg_2Cl_2 + 2e^- = 2Hg + 2Cl^-$

$Ag + Cl^- = AgCl + e^-$

$Hg_2Cl_2 + 2Ag = 2Hg + 2AgCl$

$K^{\ominus} = 4.1$。

10.18 (1) $NH_3\cdot H_2O$；(2) Na_2S。

10.19 $S_2O_3^{2-}$；MnO_4^-。

10.20 相同；不同；相同。

10.21 －0.24 V。

10.22 减小，增大。

10.23 变大；不变。

10.24 1.51—0.094 pH。

三、简答题和计算题

10.25 (1) $2MnO_4^- + 10Cl^- + 16H^+ \xlongequal{} 2Mn^{2+} + 5Cl_2 + 8H_2O$

(2) $2Mn^{2+} + 5NaBiO_3 + 14H^+ \xlongequal{} 2MnO_4^- + 5Bi^{3+} + 5Na^+ + 7H_2O$

(3) $2Cr^{3+} + 3PbO_2 + H_2O \xlongequal{} Cr_2O_7^{2-} + 3Pb^{2+} + 2H^+$

(4) $5C_3H_8O + 4MnO_4^- + 12H^+ \xlongequal{} 5C_3H_6O_2 + 4Mn^{2+} + 11H_2O$

(5) $10HClO_3 + 3P_4 + 18H_2O \xlongequal{} 10Cl^- + 12H_3PO_4 + 10H^+$

10.26 (1) $2CrO_4^{2-} + 3HSnO_2^- + H_2O \xlongequal{} 2CrO_2^- + 3HSnO_3^- + 2OH^-$

(2) $3H_2O_2 + 2CrO_2^- + 2OH^- \xlongequal{} 2CrO_4^{2-} + 4H_2O$

(3) $2CuS + 9CN^- + 2OH^- \xlongequal{} 2[Cu(CN)_4]^{3-} + 2S^{2-} + NCO^- + H_2O$

(4) $2CN^- + O_2 + 2OH^- + 2H_2O \xlongequal{} 2CO_3^{2-} + 2NH_3$

(5) $2Al + NO_2^- + OH^- + 5H_2O \xlongequal{} 2[Al(OH)_4]^- + NH_3$

10.27 假设各物质均处于标准状态

$$\begin{aligned} E^\ominus(AgCl/Ag) &= E^\ominus(Ag^+/Ag) + 0.059\ \lg[Ag^+] \\ &= E^\ominus(Ag^+/Ag) + 0.059\ \lg K_{sp}^\ominus \\ &= 0.799\ V + 0.059\ V\ \lg 1.8\times10^{-10} \\ &= 0.224\ V \end{aligned}$$

因 $E^\ominus(H^+/H_2)=0$，而 $E^\ominus(AgCl/Ag) > E^\ominus(H^+/H_2)$，因而 Ag 不能与 H^+ 反应生成 AgCl，故不能置换出 H_2。

$$\begin{aligned} E^\ominus(AgI/Ag) &= E^\ominus(Ag^+/Ag) + 0.059\ \lg[Ag^+] \\ &= E^\ominus(Ag^+/Ag) + 0.059\ \lg K_{sp}^\ominus(AgI) \\ &= 0.799\ V + 0.059\ V\ \lg 8.5\times10^{-17} \\ &= -0.149\ V \end{aligned}$$

由于 $E^\ominus(AgI/Ag) < E^\ominus(H^+/H_2)$，则 Ag 能与 H^+ 反应生成 AgI，故能从 HI 溶液中置换出 H_2。

10.28 设生成 CuS 沉淀后，正极溶液中 Cu^{2+} 的浓度为 $x\ mol\cdot dm^{-3}$。

所组成电池为：$(-)Zn|Zn^{2+}(1\ mol\cdot dm^{-3}) \parallel Cu^{2+}(x\ mol\cdot dm^{-3})|Cu(+)$

电池反应为：
$$Cu^{2+} + Zn \xlongequal{} Cu + Zn^{2+}$$

由
$$E = E^\ominus - \frac{0.059\ V}{2}\lg\frac{[Zn^{2+}]}{[Cu^{2+}]}$$

$$0.670\ V = [0.342\ V - (-0.763\ V)] - \frac{0.059\ V}{2}\lg\frac{1}{x}$$

得　$x = 1.80\times10^{-15}$，$[Cu^{2+}] = 1.80\times10^{-15}\ mol\cdot dm^{-3}$

平衡时，Cu^{2+} 浓度很小，$0.1\ mol\cdot dm^{-3}$ 的 Cu^{2+} 几乎全部转化为 CuS：

$$Cu^{2+} + H_2S \xlongequal{} CuS\downarrow + 2H^+$$

则溶液中 $[H^+] = 2\times0.1\ mol\cdot dm^{-3} = 0.2\ mol\cdot dm^{-3}$

由 $H_2S \rightleftharpoons 2H^+ + S^{2-}$ $K_{a_1}^\ominus \cdot K_{a_2}^\ominus = \dfrac{[H^+]^2[S^{2-}]}{[H_2S]}$

得 $[S^{2-}] = \dfrac{K_{a_1}^\ominus \cdot K_{a_2}^\ominus \cdot [H_2S]}{[H^+]^2}$

饱和溶液时$[H_2S] = 0.1\ mol \cdot dm^{-3}$

$$[S^{2-}] = \frac{1.1\times10^{-7}\times1.3\times10^{-13}\times0.1\ mol\cdot dm^{-3}}{(0.2\ mol\cdot dm^{-3})^2}$$

$$= 3.58\times10^{-20}\ mol\cdot dm^{-3}$$

$$K_{sp}^\ominus(CuS) = [Cu^{2+}][S^{2-}]$$

$$= 1.80\times10^{-15}\times3.58\times10^{-20}$$

$$= 6.44\times10^{-35}$$

10.29 $H_3AsO_3 + I_3^- + H_2O \rightleftharpoons H_3AsO_4 + 3I^- + 2H^+$

(1) pH=7 时，$[H^+] = 1\times10^{-7}\ mol\cdot dm^{-3}$

$$E(H_3AsO_4/H_3AsO_3) = E^\ominus + \frac{0.059\ V}{2}\lg\frac{[H_3AsO_4][H^+]^2}{[H_3AsO_3]}$$

$$= 0.559\ V + \frac{0.059\ V}{2}\lg(1\times10^{-7})^2$$

$$= 0.146\ V$$

由于$E^\ominus(I_2/I^-)$不随$[H^+]$变化而改变，即$E^\ominus(I_2/I^-)$大于$E(H_3AsO_4/H_3AsO_3)$反应朝正反应方向进行。

(2) 当$[H^+] = 6\ mol\cdot dm^{-3}$时

$$E(H_3AsO_4/H_3AsO_3) = E^\ominus + \frac{0.059\ V}{2}\lg\frac{[H_3AsO_4][H^+]^2}{[H_3AsO_3]}$$

$$= 0.559\ V + \frac{0.059\ V}{2}\lg 6^2 = 0.60\ V$$

由于$E^\ominus(I_2/I^-) < E(H_3AsO_4/H_3AsO_3)$，所以反应逆向自发进行。

10.30 $E_+ = E^\ominus + 0.059\ V\lg[Ag^+]$

$$= 0.80\ V + 0.059\ V\lg 0.010$$

$$= 0.68\ V$$

由

$$K_稳^\ominus = \frac{[Cu(NH_3)_4^{2+}]}{[Cu^{2+}][NH_3]^4}$$

$$[Cu^{2+}] = \frac{[Cu(NH_3)_4^{2+}]}{K_稳^\ominus[NH_3]^4} = \frac{0.10}{2.1\times10^{13}\times1.0^4}\ mol\cdot dm^{-3}$$

$$= 4.8\times10^{-15}\ mol\cdot dm^{-3}$$

$$E_- = 0.34\ V + \frac{0.059\ V}{2}\lg(4.8\times10^{-15})$$

$$= -0.082\ V$$

电池电动势 $E = 0.68\ V - (-0.082\ V) = 0.76\ V$

电池标准电极电势：

$$E_+^\ominus = E^\ominus(Ag^+/Ag) = 0.80\ V$$

$$E_-^{\ominus}=E^{\ominus}[Cu(NH_3)_4^{2+}/Cu]=0.34\ V+\frac{0.059\ V}{2}\lg\left(\frac{1}{2.1\times10^{13}}\right)$$

$$=-0.053\ V$$

电池的电动势 $E^{\ominus}=E_+^{\ominus}-E_-^{\ominus}=0.80\ V-(-0.053\ V)$

$$=0.85\ V$$

$$\lg K^{\ominus}=\frac{zE^{\ominus}}{0.059\ V}=\frac{2\times0.85}{0.059}$$

$$=28.81$$

电池反应的标准平衡常数 $K^{\ominus}=6.46\times10^{28}$

10.31 由元素电势图

$$E^{\ominus}/V\quad Cu^{2+}\ \xrightarrow{0.153}\ Cu^{+}\ \text{——}\ Cu\qquad (Cu^{2+}\text{——}Cu:\ 0.342)$$

得 $E^{\ominus}(Cu^+/Cu)=2\times0.342\ V-0.153\ V=0.531\ V$

解法一：对于反应 $Cu^{2+}+Cu+2\ Cl^-=2\ CuCl$

正极反应 $Cu^{2+}+Cl^-+e^-=CuCl$

负极反应 $Cu+Cl^-=CuCl+e^-$

$$E^{\ominus}(Cu^{2+}/CuCl)=E^{\ominus}(Cu^{2+}/Cu)+0.059\ V\lg\frac{[Cu^{2+}]}{[Cu^+]}$$

$$=E^{\ominus}(Cu^{2+}/Cu)+0.059\ V\lg\frac{1}{K_{sp}^{\ominus}(CuCl)}$$

$$=0.153\ V+0.059\ V\lg\frac{1}{1.72\times10^{-7}}$$

$$=0.552\ V$$

$$E^{\ominus}(CuCl/Cu)=E^{\ominus}(Cu^+/Cu)+0.059\ V\lg[Cu^+]$$

$$=E^{\ominus}(Cu^+/Cu)+0.059\ V\lg K_{sp}^{\ominus}(CuCl)$$

$$=0.531\ V+0.059\lg(1.72\times10^{-7})$$

$$=0.132\ V$$

$$E^{\ominus}=E_+^{\ominus}-E_-^{\ominus}=E^{\ominus}(Cu^{2+}/CuCl)-E^{\ominus}(CuCl/Cu)$$

$$=0.552\ V-0.132\ V$$

$$=0.42\ V$$

$E^{\ominus}>0$，反应向正反应方向进行。

由 $$\lg K^{\ominus}=\frac{zE^{\ominus}}{0.059\ V}=\frac{1\times0.42\ V}{0.059\ V}=7.12$$

得 $$K^{\ominus}=1.3\times10^7$$

解法二： $Cu^{2+}+Cu=2\ Cu^+$ (1)

$$\lg K_1^{\ominus}=\frac{1\times[E^{\ominus}(Cu^{2+}/Cu)-E^{\ominus}(Cu^+/Cu)]}{0.059\ V}$$

$$=\frac{1\times(0.153\ V-0.531\ V)}{0.059\ V}=-0.64$$

$K_1^\ominus = 3.98\times10^{-7}$

$$2\,Cu^+ + 2Cl^- \longrightarrow 2CuCl \qquad (2)$$

$$K_2^\ominus = \frac{1}{[K_{sp}^\ominus(CuCl)]} = \frac{1}{(1.72\times10^{-7})^2} = 3.38\times10^{13}$$

上两式(1)+(2)得 $Cu^{2+} + Cu + 2Cl^- \longrightarrow 2CuCl$

即 $K^\ominus = K_1^\ominus \cdot K_2^\ominus = 3.98\times10^{-7}\times3.38\times10^{13} = 1.3\times10^7$

由于 $K^\ominus > 1$，故反应正向进行。

10.32 (1) 正极 $\frac{1}{4}O_2 + \frac{1}{2}H_2O + e^- \rightleftharpoons OH^-$ $E_+^\ominus = 0.401\ V$

负极 $\frac{1}{4}O_2 + H^+ + e^- \rightleftharpoons \frac{1}{2}H_2O$ $E_-^\ominus = 1.229\ V$

$$\begin{aligned} E^\ominus &= E_+^\ominus - E_-^\ominus \\ &= 0.401\ V - 1.229\ V \\ &= -0.828\ V \end{aligned}$$

$$\begin{aligned} \lg K^\ominus &= \frac{zE^\ominus}{0.059\ V} \\ &= \frac{1\times(-0.828\ V)}{0.059\ V} \\ &= -14.0 \end{aligned}$$

故反应 $H_2O \longrightarrow H^+ + OH^-$ 的 $K^\ominus = 1.0\times10^{-14}$。

(2) 正极 $Pt^{2+} + 2e^- \rightleftharpoons Pt$ $E_+^\ominus = 1.18\ V$

负极 $PtCl_4^{2-} + 2e^- \rightleftharpoons Pt + 4Cl^-$ $E_-^\ominus = 0.755\ V$

$$\begin{aligned} E^\ominus &= E_+^\ominus - E_-^\ominus \\ &= 1.18\ V - 0.755\ V \\ &= 0.425\ V \end{aligned}$$

$$\begin{aligned} \lg K^\ominus &= \frac{zE^\ominus}{0.059\ V} \\ &= \frac{2\times0.425\ V}{0.059\ V} \\ &= 14.41 \end{aligned}$$

故反应 $Pt^{2+} + 4Cl^- \longrightarrow PtCl_4^{2-}$ 的 $K^\ominus = 2.57\times10^{14}$。

10.33 将 $CuCl + e^- \rightleftharpoons Cu + Cl^-$ 的标准电极电势 $E^\ominus$ 看成为 $Cu^+ + e^- \rightleftharpoons Cu$ 的非标准态电极电势 E，而这个非标准态是由 $[Cl^-] = 1.0\ mol\cdot dm^{-3}$ 时的 $[Cu^+]$ 决定的。

$$CuCl \rightleftharpoons Cu^+ + Cl^-$$

$$\begin{aligned} [Cu^+] &= \frac{K_{sp}^\ominus}{[Cl^-]} \\ &= \frac{1.7\times10^{-7}}{1.0}\ mol\cdot dm^{-3} \\ &= 1.7\times10^{-7}\ mol\cdot dm^{-3} \end{aligned}$$

将其代入 $Cu^+ + e^- \rightleftharpoons Cu$ 的 Nernst 方程式，则

$$E = E^\ominus + 0.059\ \text{V} \lg[Cu^+]$$
$$= 0.52\ \text{V} + 0.059\ \text{V} \lg(1.7\times10^{-7})$$
$$= 0.12\ \text{V}$$

即 $E^\ominus(CuCl/Cu) = 0.12\ \text{V}$。

10.34 题设中电池符号所表示的电池，其反应为 $B^{2+} + A \rightleftharpoons A^{2+} + B$，电子转移数 $z=2$，其电动势的 Nernst 方程为

$$E = E^\ominus - \frac{0.059\ \text{V}}{z}\lg\frac{[A^{2+}]}{[B^{2+}]}$$

依题设当 $[A^{2+}]=[B^{2+}]$ 时，$E=0.78$ V，故

$$E = E^\ominus - \frac{0.059\ \text{V}}{2}\lg 1$$

所以 $$E^\ominus = E = 0.78\ \text{V}$$

电动势减半，即 $E=\frac{1}{2}\times0.78\ \text{V}=0.39\ \text{V}$，代入 Nernst 方程得

$$\lg\frac{[A^{2+}]}{[B^{2+}]} = \frac{E^\ominus - E}{\frac{0.059\ \text{V}}{2}}$$
$$= \frac{0.78\ \text{V} - 0.39\ \text{V}}{\frac{0.059\ \text{V}}{2}}$$
$$= 13.22$$

所以 $[A^{2+}]/[B^{2+}] = 1.7\times10^{13}$。

10.35 (1) 三个电池的电池反应式完全相同：

$Tl^{3+} + 2Tl = 3Tl^+$

(2) 三个电池的电极反应式不同，则电池的电动势 $E^\ominus$ 不同。

$$E^\ominus(Tl^+/Tl) = 3\times E^\ominus(Tl^{3+}/Tl) - 2\times E^\ominus(Tl^{3+}/Tl^+)$$
$$= 3\times0.741\ \text{V} - 2\times1.25\ \text{V}$$
$$= -0.28\ \text{V}$$

(a) 电池，电子转移数为 3

正极反应 $Tl^{3+} + 3e = Tl$

负极反应 $Tl = Tl^+ + e^-$

$$E^\ominus(a) = E^\ominus(Tl^{3+}/Tl) - E^\ominus(Tl^+/Tl)$$
$$= 0.74\ \text{V} - (-0.28\ \text{V})$$
$$= 1.02\ \text{V}$$

$\Delta_r G_m^\ominus = -zE^\ominus F = -3\times1.02\times96.5\ \text{kJ·mol}^{-1} = -295.3\ \text{kJ·mol}^{-1}$

(b) 电池，电子转移数为 2

正极反应： $Tl^{3+} + 2e = Tl^+$

负极反应： $Tl = Tl^+ + e^-$

$E^\ominus(b)=E^\ominus(Tl^{3+}/Tl^+)-E^\ominus(Tl^+/Tl)$

$=1.25\ V-(-0.28\ V)=1.53\ V$

$\Delta_r G_m^\ominus=-zE^\ominus F=-2\times1.53\times96.5\ kJ\cdot mol^{-1}=-295.3\ kJ\cdot mol^{-1}$

(c) 电池，电子转移数为 6

正极反应： $Tl^{3+}+2e^- \Longrightarrow Tl^+$

负极反应： $Tl \Longrightarrow Tl^{3+}+3e^-$

$E^\ominus(c)=E^\ominus(Tl^{3+}/Tl^+)-E^\ominus(Tl^{3+}/Tl)$

$=1.25V-0.74V$

$=0.51V$

$\Delta_r G_m^\ominus=-zE^\ominus F=-6\times0.51\times96\,500\ kJ\cdot mol^{-1}=-295.29\ kJ\cdot mol^{-1}$

计算结果表明，三个电池反应的 $\Delta_r G_m^\ominus$ 相同。因为三个电池反应均相同

$$Tl^{3+}+2Tl \Longrightarrow 3Tl^+$$

所以 $\Delta_r G_m^\ominus$ 相同。G 是状态函数。

10.36 从元素电势图可知，HIO，MnO_4^{2-}，Mn^{3+} 能发生歧化反应，在酸性介质中不能稳定存在，这些物质不可能是反应产物。

在酸性介质中，单质 Mn 能与 H^+ 反应，因而 Mn 不是反应产物：

$Mn+2H^+ \Longrightarrow Mn^{2+}+H_2$

题中给出 KI 溶液过量，因此，凡能与 I^- 发生反应的物质也不能是反应产物，应予以排除。则反应产物不能是 IO_3^-，H_5IO_6 和 MnO_2：

$$IO_3^-+5I^-+6H^+ \Longrightarrow 3I_2+3H_2O,$$

$$3H_5IO_6+I^- \Longrightarrow 4IO_3^-+3H^++6H_2O$$

$$3MnO_2+I^-+6H^+ \Longrightarrow IO_3^-+3Mn^{2+}+3H_2O$$

从以上分析结果，反应产物只能是 I_3^-，Mn^{2+}：

$$2MnO_4^-+15I^-+16H^+ \Longrightarrow 5I_3^-+2Mn^{2+}+8H_2O$$

10.37 达平衡时，各离子的浓度为

$[Fe^{3+}]=1.0\times10^{-3}\ mol\cdot dm^{-3}\times4.6\%=4.60\times10^{-5}\ mol\cdot dm^{-3}$

$[Fe^{2+}]=1.0\times10^{-3}\ mol\cdot dm^{-3}-4.6\times10^{-5}\ mol\cdot dm^{-3}=9.54\times10^{-4}\ mol\cdot dm^{-3}$

$[Hg_2^{2+}]=\frac{1}{2}[Fe^{2+}]=4.77\times10^{-4}\ mol\cdot dm^{-3}$

平衡常数为

$$K^\ominus=\frac{[Hg_2^{2+}][Fe^{2+}]^2}{[Fe^{3+}]^2}=\frac{(4.77\times10^{-4})(9.54\times10^{-4})^2}{(4.6\times10^{-5})^2}=0.205$$

电池的电动势为

$$E^\ominus=\frac{0.059\ V}{2}\lg K^\ominus=\frac{0.059\ V}{2}\lg 0.205=-0.020\ V$$

由 $E^\ominus=E^\ominus(Fe^{3+}/Fe^{2+})-E^\ominus(Hg_2^{2+}/Hg)$

得 $E^\ominus(Hg_2^{2+}/Hg)=E^\ominus(Fe^{3+}/Fe^{2+})-E^\ominus=0.77\ V-(-0.02\ V)$

$=0.79\ V$

10.38 (1) $E^\ominus[Ag(CN)_2^-/Ag]=E^\ominus(Ag^+/Ag)+0.059\ \lg[Ag^+]$

由 $Ag^+ + 2CN^- \longrightarrow Ag(CN)_2^-$

当 $[CN^-]=[Ag(CN)_2^-]=1\ mol\cdot dm^{-3}$

$$K^\ominus_{稳}=\frac{[Ag(CN)_2^-]}{[Ag^+][CN^-]^2}=\frac{1}{[Ag^+]}$$

则 $[Ag^+]=\frac{1}{K^\ominus_{稳}}$

$$E^\ominus[Ag(CN)_2^-/Ag]=0.80\ V+0.059\ V\ \lg\frac{1}{1\times10^{21}}$$

$$=-0.44\ V$$

对反应 $4Ag+O_2+8KCN+2H_2O \longrightarrow 4K[Ag(CN)_2]+4KOH$

$E^\ominus=E^\ominus(O_2/OH^-)-E^\ominus[Ag(CN)_2^-/Ag]$

$=0.40\ V-(-0.44\ V)$

$=0.84\ V$

说明在碱性条件下通入空气时 Ag 能溶于 KCN 溶液。

(2) 在 KCN 溶液中，由于 CN^- 的水解，溶液呈弱碱性

$$[H^+]\approx10^{-10}(mol\cdot dm^{-3})$$

对反应 $2H_2O+2e^- \longrightarrow H_2+2OH^-$

$$E(H_2O/H_2)=E^\ominus(H^+/H_2)+\frac{0.059\ V}{2}\lg[H^+]^2$$

$=0\ V+0.059\ V\ \lg10^{-10}$

$=-0.59\ V$

反应 $2Ag+2H_2O+4CN^- \longrightarrow 2Ag(CN)_2^- + H_2 + 2OH^-$

$$E=E(H_2O/H_2)-E^\ominus[Ag(CN)_2^-/Ag]$$

$=-0.59\ V-(-0.44\ V)$

$=-0.15\ V$

由于 $E<0$，Ag 不能从 KCN 溶液中置换出 H_2。

10.39

DH	$Cr_2O_7^{2-}+8H^++6e^- \rightleftharpoons 2Cr(OH)_3+H_2O$
EF	$Cr(OH)_3+e^- \rightleftharpoons Cr^{2+}+3OH^-$
FJ	$Cr(OH)_3+3e^- \rightleftharpoons Cr+3OH^-$
IK	$CrO_4^{2-}+2H_2O+3e^- \rightleftharpoons CrO_2^-+4OH^-$
CF	$Cr^{2+}+2e^- \rightleftharpoons Cr$
DE	$Cr^{3+}+3OH^- \rightleftharpoons Cr(OH)_3$
IJ	$Cr(OH)_3+OH^- \rightleftharpoons CrO_2^-+2H_2O$

第 11 章

一、选择题

11.1 A　11.2 C　11.3 D　11.4 B　11.5 C　11.6 A　11.7 C　11.8 D　11.9 A

11.10 B　11.11 D　11.12 D　11.13 A　11.14 D　11.15 C

二、填空题

11.16 (1) 六硝基合钴(Ⅲ)酸钾;

(2) 二氯·二羟·二氨合铂(Ⅳ);

(3) 一水合二氯化氯·五水合铬(Ⅲ);

(4) 二氯化三(乙二胺)合镍(Ⅱ);

(5) 四氯合铂(Ⅱ)酸四氨酮(Ⅱ);

(6) 三水合三草酸根合铁(Ⅲ)酸钾;

(7) 二草酸根合铜(Ⅱ)酸钾;

(8) 四氯合铂(Ⅱ)酸四吡啶合铂(Ⅱ);

(9) 二(μ-羰基)·二(三羰基合钴)。

11.17 (1) $[Cr(NCS)_2(NH_3)_4]Cl$;

(2) $K[PtCl_3(NH_3)]$;

(3) $[CrCl(C_2O_4)(H_2O)en]$;

(4) $[PtCl_4(NH_3)_2]$。

11.18 −3,八面体,C(或碳),6,$t_{2g}^6e_g^0$,d^2sp^3,反

11.19 几何异构(3),旋光异构(1),解离异构(5),键合异构(2),配位异构(4)。

11.20 四面体;正方形,反。

11.21 dsp^2,sp^3。

11.22 (1) 3 个;(2) 5 个;(3) 4 个;(4) 2 个;(5) 1 个;(6) 0。

11.23 (1) >; (2) >; (3) <; (4) <。

11.24 3,4,10。

11.25 (1) 3;

(2) sp^3d^2,d^2sp^3;内轨,外轨;

(3) $d_\varepsilon^6d_\gamma^0$(或 $t_{2g}^6e_g^0$),$d_\varepsilon^5d_\gamma^2$(或 $t_{2g}^5e_g^2$);$24D_q-2P$,$8D_q$;

(4) $[Co(NH_3)_6]^{3+}$。

11.26 (1) >;(2) <;(3) <;(4) >。

三、简答题和计算题

11.27 (1) $[Pt(NH_3)_2(NO_2)Cl]$　平面正方形,2 种异构体

(2) $[Pt(Py)(NH_3)ClBr]$　平面正方形,有 3 种异构体

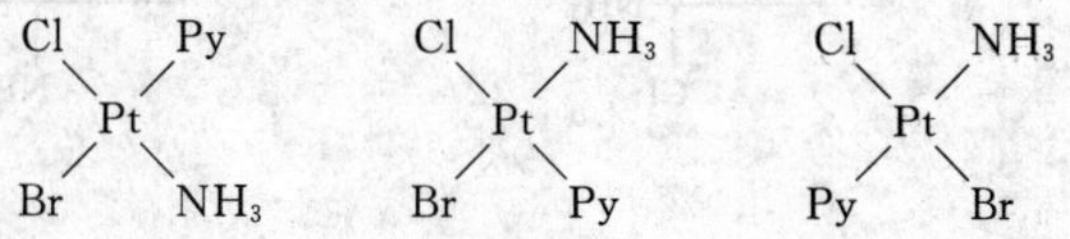

(3) $[Pt(NH_3)_2(OH)_2Cl_2]$ 八面体,5 种异构体(中心原子未画出)

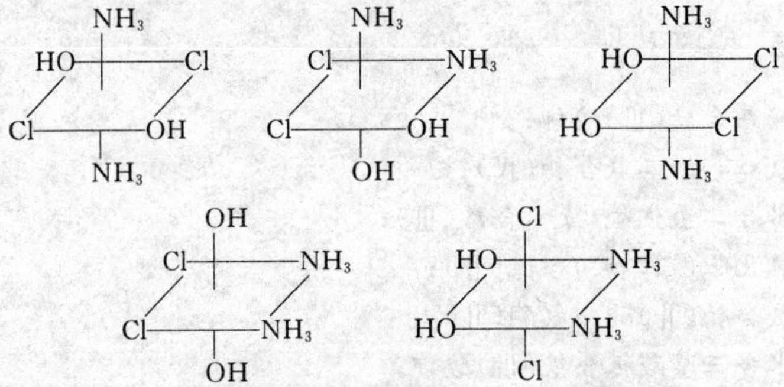

(4) $[Co(NH_3)_2(NO_2)_4]$ 八面体,2 种异构体

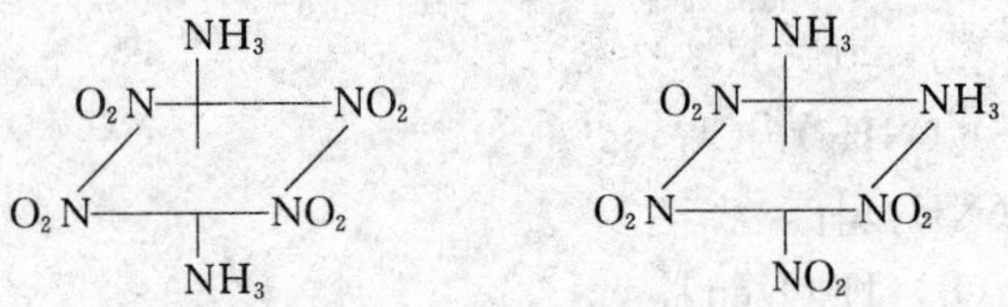

(5) $[Co(NH_3)_3(OH)_3]$ 八面体,2 种异构体

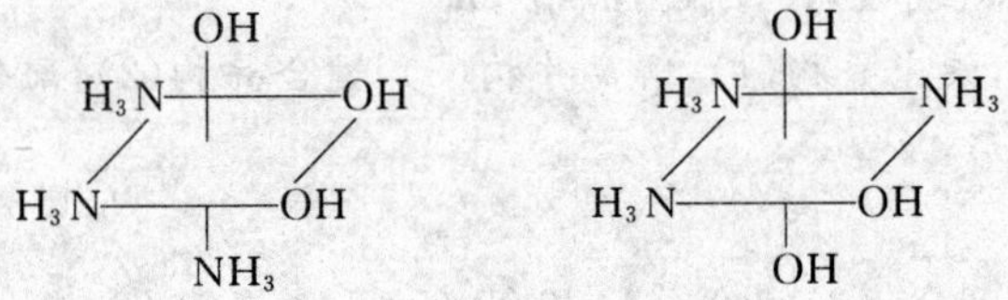

(6) $[Cr(SCN)_2(en)_2]^-$ 八面体,2 种异构体

(7) $[Co(en)_3]^{3+}$ 八面体,1 种异构体

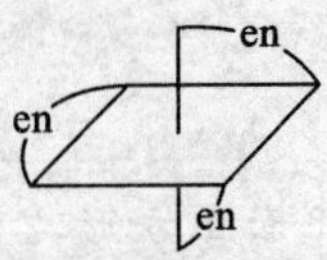

(8) $[Co(NH_3)(en)Cl_3]$ 八面体,2 种异构体

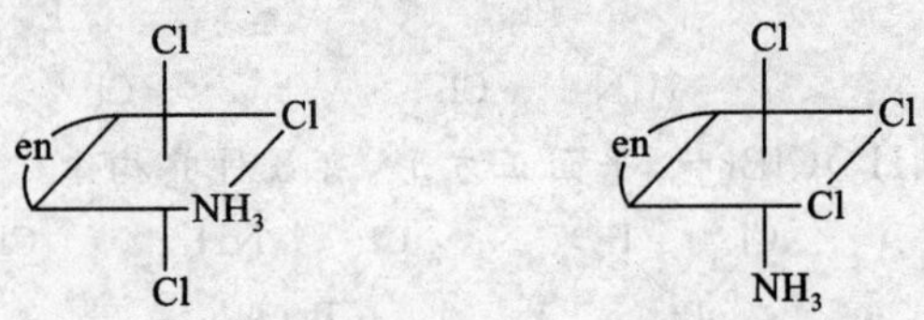

11.28

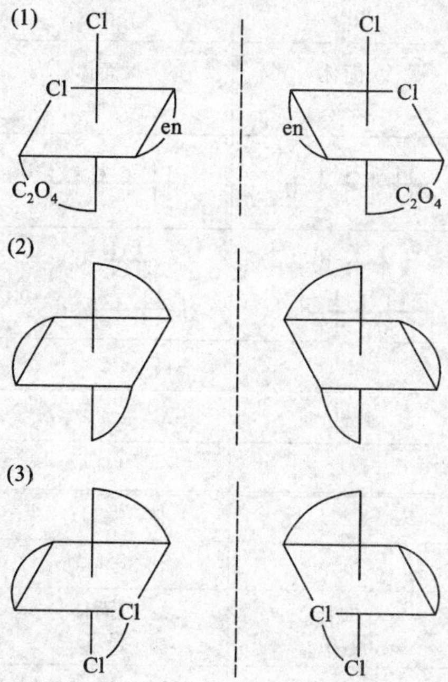

11.29 判断配位化合物是内轨型还是外轨型，实质是看中心内层 d 轨道是否与配体成键，即中心采取 $(n-1)\mathrm{d}\ n\mathrm{s}\ n\mathrm{p}$ 杂化还是 $n\mathrm{s}\ n\mathrm{p}\ n\mathrm{d}$ 杂化。中心采取的杂化方式与中心的价电子构型和配体强弱有关。判断结果如下：

题号	配位化合物	中心在球形场中的电子构型	配体类型	配位化合物中心的电子轨道式	中心的杂化方式	配位化合物类型
(1)	$[Cr(H_2O)_6]Cl_3$	$3d^3$	弱配体	↑ ↑ ↑ ○ ○	d^2sp^3	内轨型
(2)	$K_3[Cr(CN)_6]$	$3d^3$	强配体	↑ ↑ ↑ ○ ○	d^2sp^3	内轨型
(3)	$K_2(PtCl_4)$	$5d^8$	弱配体	↑↓ ↑↓ ↑↓ ↑↓ ○	dsp^2	内轨型
(4)	$K_2[Ni(CN)_4]$	$3d^8$	强配体	↑↓ ↑↓ ↑↓ ↑↓ ○	dsp^2	内轨型
(5)	$K_4[Mn(CN)_6]$	$3d^5$	强配体	↑↓ ↑↓ ↑ ○ ○	d^2sp^3	内轨型
(6)	$K_3[Fe(C_2O_4)_3]$	$3d^5$	弱配体	↑ ↑ ↑ ↑ ↑	sp^3d^2	外轨型
(7)	$[Fe(CO)_5]$	$3d^64s^2$	强配体	↑↓ ↑↓ ↑↓ ↑↓ ○	dsp^3	内轨型
(8)	$K_3[Fe(CN)_6]$	$3d^5$	强配体	↑↓ ↑↓ ↑ ○ ○	d^2sp^3	内轨型

11.30 结果见下表。

配位单元	$[CoF_6]^{3-}$	$[Fe(H_2O)_6]^{2+}$	$[Co(en)_3]^{2+}$
中心的电子构型	$3d^6$	$3d^6$	$3d^7$
晶体场类型	八面体 弱场	八面体 弱场	八面体 弱场
球形场中电子排布	↑↓ ↑ ↑ ↑ ↑	↑↓ ↑ ↑ ↑ ↑	↑↓ ↑↓ ↑ ↑ ↑
晶体场中电子排布	↑ ↑ d_γ ↑↓ ↑ ↑ d_ε	↑ ↑ d_γ ↑↓ ↑ ↑ d_ε	↑ ↑ d_γ ↑↓ ↑↓ ↑ d_ε
单电子数	4	4	3
磁矩/μ_B	4.90	4.90	3.87
CFSE	$4Dq$	$4Dq$	$8Dq$
配位单元	$[Fe(SCN)_6]^{3-}$	$[Ni(CO)_4]$	$[Mn(CN)_6]^{4-}$
中心的电子构型	$3d^5$	$3d^8 4s^2$	$3d^5$
晶体场类型	八面体 弱场	四面体 强场	八面体 强场
球形场中电子排布	↑ ↑ ↑ ↑ ↑	↑↓ ↑↓ ↑↓ ↑↓ ↑↓	↑ ↑ ↑ ↑ ↑
晶体场中电子排布	↑ ↑ d_γ ↑ ↑ ↑ d_ε	↑↓ ↑↓ d_γ ↑↓ ↑↓ ↑↓ d_ε	— — d_γ ↑↓ ↑↓ ↑ d_ε
单电子数	5	0	1
磁矩/μ_B	5.92	0	1.73
CFSE	$0Dq$	$0Dq$	$20Dq-2P$

11.31 能与 $AgNO_3$ 反应生成 AgCl 沉淀者，Cl^- 为外界，化学结构式为$[CoSO_4(NH_3)_5]Cl$
能与 $BaCl_2$ 反应生成 $BaSO_4$ 沉淀者外界为 SO_4^{2-}，化学结构式为$[CoCl(NH_3)_5]SO_4$
二个配合物之间属解离异构关系。

11.32 按照配位化合物价键理论，Co^{2+} 电子构型为 $3d^7$，没有空的价层 d 轨道；而 Cl^- 为弱配体，在形成$[CoCl_4]^{2-}$时不能使中心 d 轨道电子发生重排，Co^{2+} 只能采取 sp^3 杂化，如图(a)所示。

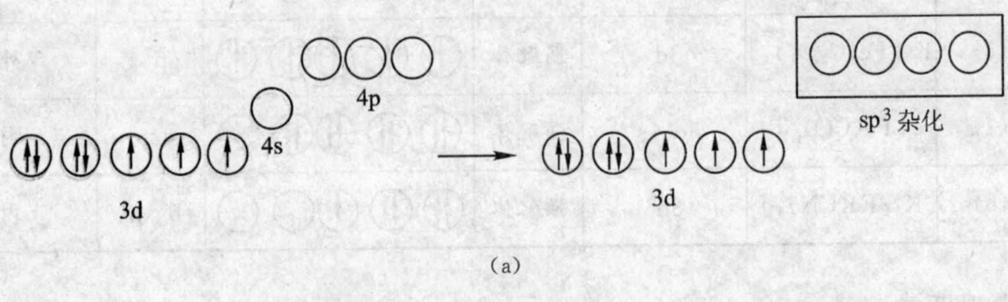

(a)

因此，$[CoCl_4]^{2-}$ 为四面体结构。

Ni^{2+} 电子构型为 $3d^8$，没有空的价层 d 轨道；而 Cl^- 为弱配体，在形成 $[NiCl_4]^{2-}$ 时不能使中心 d 轨道电子发生重排，Ni^{2+} 只能采取 sp^3 杂化，如图(b)所示。

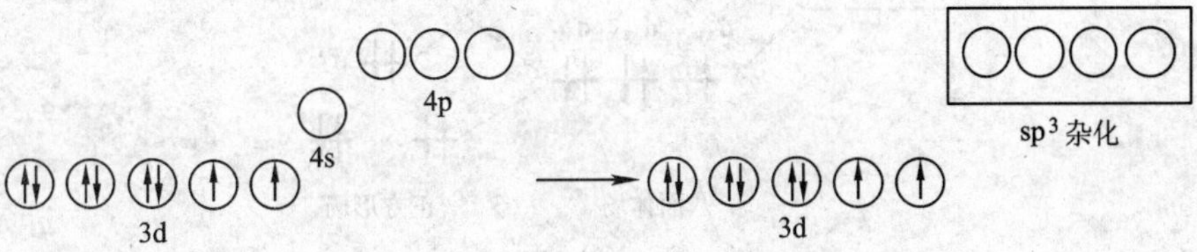

(b)

因此，$[NiCl_4]^{2-}$ 为四面体结构。

不能用价键理论讨论 Cu^{2+} 的四配位化合物的几何构型，而应由 Jahn－Teller 效应讨论其几何构型。按照晶体场理论，Cu^{2+} 的 $3d^9$ 电子构型在八面体场中的排布如图(c)所示。

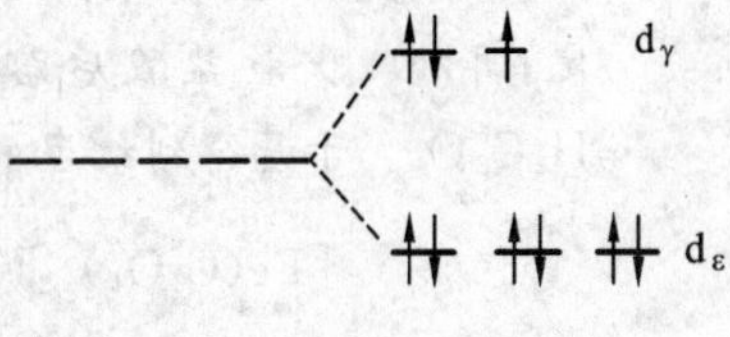

(c)

最后一个电子排布到 d_{z^2} 轨道，则 d_{z^2} 轴向上的 2 个配体受到的斥力大，距核较远，形成拉长的八面体。若轴向的 2 个配体拉得太远，则相当于失去轴向 2 个配体，变成正方形结构，这就是 Jahn－Teller 效应。故 $[CuCl_4]^{2-}$ 为正方形结构。

Pt^{2+} 电子构型为 $5d^8$，没有空的价层 d 轨道。但 Pt 为第六周期元素，5d 轨道较为扩展，即 5d 轨道与配体的斥力较大，使中心的分裂能 Δ 较大。Δ 较大可以看成 Cl^- 相当于强配体，能使 Pt^{2+} 的 5d 电子发生重排，空出 1 个 5d 轨道，采取 dsp^2 杂化，如图(d)所示。故 $[PtCl_4]^{2-}$ 为正方形结构。

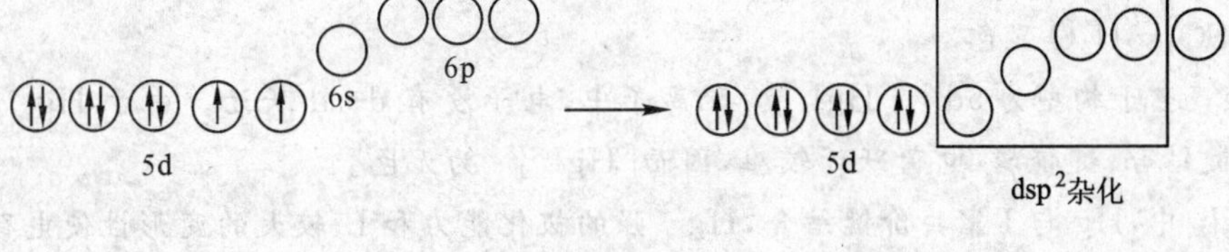

(d)

利用 Jahn－Teller 效应也能合理解释为什么 $[PtCl_4]^{2-}$ 为正方形结构而不是四面体结构。Pt^{2+} 为 d^8 电子构型，在八面体场中的排布为 $(d_\varepsilon)^6(d_\gamma)^2$，由于铂为高周期元素，配位化合物的分裂能较大，$d_{x^2-y^2}$ 和 d_{z^2} 轨道单电子的能量较高。八面体场经重排后转化成正方形场，在正方形场中最高能量轨道 $d_{x^2-y^2}$ 不填充电子，使正方形配位化合物有较大的晶体场稳定化能，如图(e)所示。

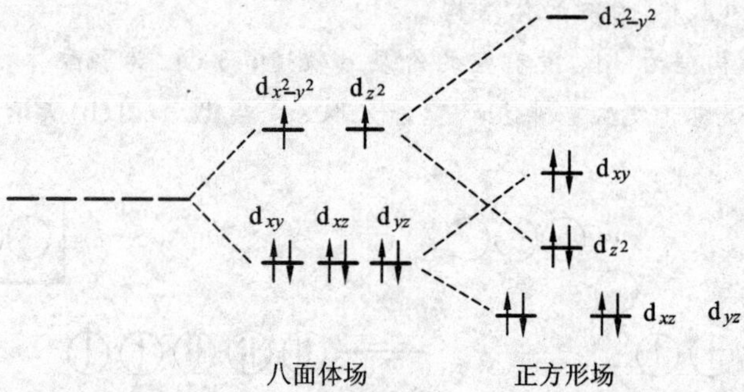

(e)

11.33 加入$(NH_4)_2C_2O_4$则溶液变黄绿色，是因为生成了$[Fe(C_2O_4)_3]^{3-}$：

$$Fe^{3+} + 3C_2O_4^{2-} = [Fe(C_2O_4)_3]^{3-}$$

再加入少量KSCN溶液，溶液颜色不变，是因为$[Fe(C_2O_4)_3]^{3-}$比$[Fe(SCN)_5]^{2-}$稳定；再加入少量盐酸后溶液变红，是因为加入强酸$[Fe(C_2O_4)_3]^{3-}$被破坏，生成弱酸$H_2C_2O_4$。于是得到红色的$[Fe(SCN)_5]^{2-}$：

$$[Fe(C_2O_4)_3]^{3-} + 6H^+ + 5SCN^- = [Fe(SCN)_5]^{2-} + 3H_2C_2O_4$$

最后加入NH_4F溶液，生成更稳定的$[FeF_5]^{2-}$，溶液变无色：

$$[Fe(SCN)_5]^{2-} + 5F^- = [FeF_5]^{2-} + 5SCN^-$$

11.34 $CuSO_4$：SO_4^{2-}场很弱，分裂能Δ很小，d电子在d—d跃迁时不吸收可见光而吸收红外光。因吸收的光不在可见光范围内，因而$CuSO_4$显白颜色。

$CuCl_2$：Cl^-晶体场使分裂能Δ大小恰好在可见光能量范围内，d—d跃迁时电子吸收可见光，因而$CuCl_2$显颜色。

$CuSO_4 \cdot 5H_2O$：配合物应写成$[Cu(H_2O)_4]SO_4 \cdot H_2O$，晶体场为$H_2O$而不是$SO_4^{2-}$。$Cu^{2+}$在$H_2O$场中分裂能Δ大小也恰好在可见光范围内，发生d—d电子跃迁而使$CuSO_4 \cdot 5H_2O$显色。

11.35 Hg^{2+}电子构型为$5d^{10}$，$[HgI_4]^{2-}$配离子中，电子没有d—d跃迁。由于Hg^{2+}与I^-靠配位键结合，键较弱，电荷跃迁较难，因而$[HgI_4]^{2-}$为无色。

HgI_2中，Hg与I靠共价键结合，Hg^{2+}强的极化能力和I^-较大的变形性使电荷跃迁很容易进行，因而HgI_2有较深的颜色。

11.36 (1) 稳定性$[Co(NH_3)_6]^{3+} > [Co(NH_3)_6]^{2+}$，因前者中心的正电荷高、离子半径小，对配体的引力大；

(2) 稳定性$[Zn(EDTA)]^{2-} > [Ca(EDTA)]^{2-}$，因$Zn^{2+}$的极化能力和变形性都比$Ca^{2+}$大；

(3) 稳定性$[Cu(CN)_4]^{3-} > [Zn(CN)_4]^{2-}$，$Cu^+$是软酸，$Zn^{2+}$为交界酸，$Cu^+$与软碱$CN^-$结合更稳定；

(4) 稳定性$[AlF_6]^{3-} > [AlCl_6]^{3-}$，$Al^{3+}$为硬酸，而碱的硬度为$F^- > Cl^-$，因而$Al^{3+}$与$F^-$结合更稳定；

(5) 稳定性$[Cu(H_2NCH_2CH_2NH_2)_2]^{2+}>[Cu(H_2NCH_2COO)_2]$，前者配体中配位原子都是N，后者配体中配位原子为N和O，N的配位能力比O强。

11.37 $pH=1.0, [H^+]=0.10\ mol\cdot dm^{-3}$，

$[Zn^{2+}]=0.010\ mol\cdot dm^{-3}$

$$K_{sp}^{\ominus}(ZnS)=[Zn^{2+}][S^{2-}]$$
$$=0.01\times\frac{K_1^{\ominus}\ K_2^{\ominus}[H_2S]}{[H^+]^2}$$
$$=K_1^{\ominus}\ K_2^{\ominus}[H_2S]$$

加入KCN后，设$[Zn^{2+}]=x\ mol\cdot dm^{-3}$则

$$Zn^{2+} \quad + \quad 4CN^- \quad \rightleftharpoons \quad [Zn(CN)_4]^{2-}$$

平衡浓度/$(mol\cdot dm^{-3})$ x $\quad 1.0-4(0.01-x) \quad 0.01-x$

$$K_{稳}^{\ominus}=\frac{0.01-x}{x[1.0-4(0.01-x)]^4}$$

得 $x=2.35\times10^{-19}$，

$[Zn^{2+}]=2.35\times10^{-19}\ mol\cdot dm^{-3}$

$$K_{sp}^{\ominus}(ZnS)=[Zn^{2+}][S^{2-}]=2.35\times10^{-19}\times\frac{K_1^{\ominus}\ K_2^{\ominus}[H_2S]}{[H^+]^2}$$

$$K_1^{\ominus}\ K_2^{\ominus}[H_2S]=2.35\times10^{-19}\times\frac{K_1^{\ominus}\ K_2^{\ominus}[H_2S]}{[H^+]^2}$$

得 $[H^+]=4.85\times10^{-10}\ mol\cdot dm^{-3}$，$pH=9.31$

11.38 $Au(CN)_2^-+e^- \rightleftharpoons Au+2CN^-$，标准状态时，

$[Au(CN)_2^-]=[CN^-]=1.0\ mol\cdot dm^{-3}$

则有 $$K_{稳}^{\ominus}[Au(CN)_2^-]=\frac{[Au(CN)_2^-]}{[Au^+][CN^-]^2}$$
$$=\frac{1}{[Au^+]}$$

$$E^{\ominus}[Au(CN)_2^-/Au]=E^{\ominus}(Au^+/Au)+0.059\ V\ lg\ [Au^+]$$
$$=1.69\ V+0.059\ V\ lg\ \frac{1}{K_{稳}^{\ominus}}$$
$$=-0.57\ V$$

11.39 (1) $$E^{\ominus}(FeF_6^{3-}/Fe^{2+})=E^{\ominus}(Fe^{3+}/Fe^{2+})+0.059\ V\ lg\ \{[Fe^{3+}]/[Fe^{2+}]\}$$
$$=0.77\ V+0.059\ V\ lg\ \{1/K_{稳}^{\ominus}(FeF_6^{3-})\}$$
$$=0.77\ V+0.059\ V\ lg\ \frac{1}{1.1\times10^{12}}=0.06\ V$$

$E^{\ominus}(FeF_6^{3-}/Fe^{2+})<E^{\ominus}(Sn^{4+}/Sn^{2+})$，无氧化还原反应发生。

(2) $$E^{\ominus}[Fe(SCN)_5^{2-}/Fe^{2+}]=E^{\ominus}(Fe^{3+}/Fe^{2+})+0.059\ V\ lg\ \frac{1}{K_{稳}^{\ominus}}$$
$$=0.77\ V+0.059\ V\ lg\ \frac{1}{2.6\times10^6}=0.39\ V$$

$E^{\ominus}[Fe(SCN)_5^{2-}/Fe^{2+}]>E^{\ominus}(Sn^{4+}/Sn^{2+})$，能发生氧化还原反应：

$2[Fe(SCN)_5]^{2-} + Sn^{2+} \longrightarrow 2Fe^{2+} + 10SCN^- + Sn^{4+}$

(3) $E^\ominus[Fe(SCN)_5^{2-}/Fe^{2+}] < E^\ominus(I_2/I^-)$，不发生氧化还原反应。

11.40 设 AgBr 在 $Na_2S_2O_3$ 溶液中的溶解度为 x mol·dm^{-3}

$$AgBr + 2S_2O_3^{2-} \longrightarrow [Ag(S_2O_3)_2]^{3-} + Br^-$$

$$1-2x \qquad\qquad x \qquad\qquad x$$

$$K^\ominus = \frac{[Ag(S_2O_3)_2^{3-}][Br^-]}{[S_2O_3^{2-}]^2}$$

$$= K_{sp}^\ominus(AgBr)\cdot K_{稳}^\ominus[Ag(S_2O_3)_2^{3-}] = 14$$

$$\frac{x^2}{(1-2x)^2} = 14 \quad 得\ x = 0.44$$

溶解 AgBr 的质量为

$0.44\ mol\cdot dm^{-3} \times 188\ g\cdot mol^{-1} \times 1.5\ dm^3 = 124.08\ g$

11.41 在水溶液中，$E^\ominus(Co^{3+}/Co^{2+}) > E^\ominus(O_2/H_2O)$，因此 Co^{3+} 能氧化水：

$$4Co^{3+} + 2H_2O \longrightarrow 4Co^{2+} + O_2 + 4H^+$$

当 Co^{3+} 生成$[Co(NH_3)_6]^{3+}$后

$$E^\ominus[Co(NH_3)_6^{3+}/Co(NH_3)_6^{2+}] = E^\ominus(Co^{3+}/Co^{2+}) + 0.059\ V\ \lg\frac{[Co^{3+}]}{[Co^{2+}]}$$

$$= E^\ominus(Co^{3+}/Co^{2+}) + 0.059\ V\ \lg\frac{K_{稳}^\ominus[Co(NH_3)_6^{2+}]}{K_{稳}^\ominus[Co(NH_3)_6^{3+}]}$$

$$= 1.81\ V + 0.059\ V\ \lg\frac{1.38\times10^5}{1.58\times10^{35}}$$

$$= 0.04\ V$$

在氨溶液中，设$[NH_3] = 1.0\ mol\cdot dm^{-3}$，则

$$[OH^-] = \sqrt{1.0\times1.8\times10^{-5}}\ mol\cdot dm^{-3} = 4.24\times10^{-3}\ mol\cdot dm^{-3}$$

$$O_2 + 4H_2O + 4e^- \longrightarrow 4OH^-$$

$$E(O_2/OH^-) = E^\ominus(O_2/OH^-) + \frac{0.059\ V}{4}\lg\frac{p(O_2)/p^\ominus}{[OH^-]^4}$$

$$= 0.40\ V + \frac{0.059\ V}{4}\lg\frac{1}{(4.24\times10^{-3})^4}$$

$$= 0.54\ V$$

$E^\ominus[Co(NH_3)_6^{3+}/Co(NH_3)_6^{2+}] < E(O_2/OH^-)$，故$[Co(NH_3)_6]^{3+}$不能氧化水。

11.42
$$Ag^+ + 2CN^- \rightleftharpoons [Ag(CN)_2]^-$$

平衡浓度/(mol·dm^{-3}) $\quad x \quad 2x \quad 0.1-x$

$$\frac{0.1-x}{x(2x)^2} = 1.25\times10^{21} \quad 得\ x = 2.7\times10^{-8}$$

$[Ag^+] = 2.7\times10^{-8}\ mol\cdot dm^{-3}$

溶液中加入 KCl 固体，使 Cl^- 的浓度为 0.10 mol·dm^{-3}

$Q = [Ag^+][Cl^-] = 2.7\times10^{-8}\times0.10 = 2.7\times10^{-9}$

$Q > K_{sp}^\ominus(AgCl)$，因而会有 AgCl 沉淀从溶液中析出。

11.43 电池的电动势

$$E^{\ominus}=E^{\ominus}[Cu(NH_3)_4^{2+}/Cu]-E^{\ominus}(Zn^{2+}/Zn)=0.712\ V$$

即 $$E^{\ominus}[Cu(NH_3)_4^{2+}/Cu]=E^{\ominus}+E^{\ominus}(Zn^{2+}/Zn)=0.712\ V+(-0.763\ V)=-0.051\ V$$

Nernst 方程 $$E^{\ominus}[Cu(NH_3)_4^{2+}/Cu]=E^{\ominus}(Cu^{2+}/Cu)+\frac{0.059\ V}{2}\lg[Cu^{2+}] \quad (1)$$

其中 $$Cu^{2+}+4\ NH_3 = [Cu(NH_3)_4]^{2+}$$

$$K^{\ominus}_{稳}=\frac{[Cu(NH_3)_4]^{2+}}{[Cu^{2+}][NH_3]^4}=\frac{1}{[Cu^{2+}]}$$

即 $$[Cu^{2+}]=\frac{1}{K^{\ominus}_{稳}}$$

代入(1)式 $$-0.051\ V=0.342\ V+\frac{0.059\ V}{2}\lg\frac{1}{K^{\ominus}_{稳}}$$

解得 $$K^{\ominus}_{稳}=2.1\times10^{13}$$

11.44 (1) 由配体(NO_2)的氮氧键不等长，说明(NO_2)不用 N 原子配位，两个 O 原子中只有 1 个配位，(NO_2)为氧配位的单基配体亚硝酸根 NO_2^-。

由$[MA_2(NO_2)_2]$为六配位单核配位化合物，则配体 A 为双基配体。

由配体 A 不含氧，且$[MA_2(NO_2)_2]$的组成分析结果中 N 含量较高，则 A 为含有 2 个 N 的双基配体，最有可能的是乙二胺 $NH_2CH_2CH_2NH_2$。

设 M 的相对原子质量为 A_r，则有

$21.68\%=A_r/(A_r+60\times2+46\times2)$

得 $A_r=58.7$

则 M 为 Ni。

在配位化合物中以稳定氧化数+2 价存在，所以题设配位化合物的化学式为$[Ni(en)_2(NO_2)_2]$。

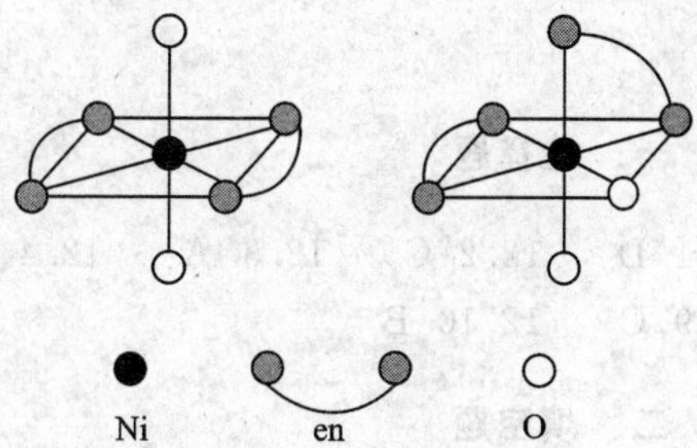

(2) $[Ni(en)_2(NO_2)_2]$为八面体结构，有两个几何异构体，如图所示。

11.45 设 Z 的化学式为 MCl_n，M 的相对原子质量为 A_r。

铜片溶解反应为 $$M^{n+}+\frac{n}{2}Cu = M+\frac{n}{2}Cu^{2+}$$

$$0.100\times\left(A_r-63.55\times\frac{n}{2}\right)=10.17$$

解得 $$A_r=31.775n+101.7$$

若 $n=1$ $A_r=133.5$ M 为 Cs(非惰性金属，不符合题意)

若 $n=2$ $A_r=165.3$ M 为 Ho(非惰性金属，不符合题意)

若 $n=3$ $A_r=197.0$ M 为 Au(惰性金属，符合题意)

若 $n=4$ $A_r=228.8$ 没有合适的金属，不符合题意

若 Z 为 $AuCl_3$，Au 在晶体 $AuCl_3$ 中的质量分数为

$$\frac{197}{197+3\times35.45}=0.6494$$

该数值大于晶体中M的质量分数0.4783，说明$AuCl_3$有结晶水。

设$AuCl_3$有n个结晶水：

$$\frac{197}{197+3\times35.45+18n}=0.4783$$

解得$n=6$，故Z的化学式为$AuCl_3\cdot6H_2O$。

若Z为配酸$H[AuCl_4]$，Au在晶体$H[AuCl_4]$中的质量分数为

$$\frac{197}{197+4\times35.45+1}=0.5798$$

该数值也大于晶体中M的质量分数0.4783，说明$H[AuCl_4]$有结晶水。

设$H[AuCl_4]$有m个结晶水：

$$\frac{197}{197+4\times35.45+1+18m}=0.4783$$

解得$m=4$，Z的化学式为$H[AuCl_4]\cdot4H_2O$。

组成为$AuCl_3\cdot6H_2O$的物质尚未见到，所以Z的化学式为$H[AuCl_4]\cdot4H_2O$。

第12章

一、选择题

12.1 D　12.2 C　12.3 A　12.4 D　12.5 B　12.6 C　12.7 B　12.8 D
12.9 C　12.10 B

二、填空题

12.11 液态石蜡，煤油。

12.12 Be，Cs；Li；Cs。

12.13 Be与Al，Li与Mg。

12.14 (1) CaF_2；(2) NaCl；(3) $CaSO_4\cdot2H_2O$；(4) $MgSO_4\cdot7H_2O$；(5) $Na_2SO_4\cdot10H_2O$；(6) $K_2SO_4\cdot Al_2(SO_4)_3\cdot24H_2O$；(7) $KCl\cdot MgCl_2\cdot6H_2O$；(8) $BaSO_4$；(9) $SrSO_4$；(10) $CaCO_3$；(11) $MgCO_3\cdot CaCO_3$；(12) Na_2SO_4。

12.15 $Be(OH)_2$具有两性，既溶于酸又溶于强碱；$Mg(OH)_2$为碱性，只溶于酸。

12.16 金属钙，电解时加入$CaCl_2$助熔剂而有少量的钙电解时析出。

12.17 降低盐的熔点；增加熔盐的导电性。

12.18 $BaCO_3$。

12.19 (1) $<$，(2) $>$，(3) $>$，(4) $<$，(5) $<$。

12.20 减小，减小，降低。

三、完成并配平下列反应方程式

12.21 $2Na_2O_2+2H_2O(热) = 4NaOH+O_2\uparrow$

12.22 $2Na_2O_2+2CO_2 = 2Na_2CO_3+O_2\uparrow$

12.23 $Mg_3N_2+6H_2O = 3Mg(OH)_2\downarrow+2NH_3\uparrow$

12.24 $3Li^++HPO_4^{2-} = Li_3PO_4\downarrow+H^+$

12.25 $MgCl_2\cdot 6H_2O \overset{\triangle}{=} Mg(OH)Cl+HCl\uparrow+5H_2O$

12.26 $Na(s)+KCl \overset{\triangle}{=} NaCl+K(g)$

12.27 $Be+2NaOH+2H_2O = Na_2[Be(OH)_4]+H_2\uparrow$

12.28 $TiCl_4+4NaH = Ti+2H_2\uparrow+4NaCl$

12.29 $4KO_3+2H_2O = 5O_2\uparrow+4KOH$

四、简答题

12.30 (1) $2Na+2H_2O = 2NaOH+H_2\uparrow$

(2) $2NH_3+2Na = 2NaNH_2+H_2\uparrow$

(3) $2C_2H_5OH+2Na = 2NaOC_2H_5+H_2\uparrow$

(4) $Na_2O_2+2Na = 2Na_2O$

(5) $MgO+2Na = Mg+Na_2O$

12.31 (1) 碱土金属有二个价电子，碱金属只有一个价电子，碱土金属的金属键比相应的碱金属的金属键强，所以碱土金属的熔点、硬度均比相应的碱金属高。

(2) 人们采用 Na_2O_2 作制氧剂，主要是基于以下优点：

① Na_2O_2 固体较稳定，便于携带；

② Na_2O_2 与水或 CO_2 反应都可放出氧气，使用更方便。

$$2Na_2O_2+2H_2O = 4NaOH+O_2\uparrow$$
$$2Na_2O_2+2CO_2 = 2Na_2CO_3+O_2\uparrow$$

③ Na_2O_2 放出氧后的产物溶解度大。

12.32 欲配制不含 Na_2CO_3 的 NaOH 溶液，可先配制饱和的 NaOH 溶液，Na_2CO_3 在饱和的 NaOH 溶液中溶解度极小而析出沉淀 。取上层清液，用煮沸除去 CO_2 后冷却的水稀释即可。

12.33 加入 $Ba(OH)_2$ 更好。$Ba(OH)_2$ 和 $BaCO_3$ 与 $FeCl_3$ 发生的反应分别为

$$2FeCl_3+3BaCO_3+3H_2O = 2Fe(OH)_3+3BaCl_2+3CO_2$$
$$2FeCl_3+3Ba(OH)_2 = 2Fe(OH)_3+3BaCl_2$$

由反应方程式可知，$BaCO_3$ 与 $FeCl_3$ 反应产物中有 CO_2，CO_2 不能完全脱离体系，有杂质存在。而 $Ba(OH)_2$ 与 $FeCl_3$ 反应没有杂质生成，若 $Ba(OH)_2$ 过量可以定量加入 HCl 转化为 $BaCl_2$。

12.34 碱金属中与水反应活性最低的是 Li，而同时 Li 的电极电势亦是同族元素中最低的

(−3.040 V)，但两者之间并不矛盾。电极电势反映的是热力学性质，即从热力学的角度上讨论物质的反应的可能性如何。但这里讨论的与水反应的活泼性主要指的是动力学上的活性，即反应速率的快慢。Li 与水发生反应，生成的产物 LiOH 溶解度小，它将覆盖在金属 Li 的表面阻碍 Li 与水的接触，从而减慢了 Li 和水的反应速率，所以观察到的是 Li 与水反应活性最低。

12.35 溶解度较小的碱金属盐主要有 LiF，Li_2CO_3，Li_3PO_4，$Na[Sb(OH)_6]$，$NaAc\cdot Zn(Ac)_2\cdot 3UO_2(Ac)_2\cdot 9H_2O$，$KClO_4$，$K[B(C_6H_5)_4]$，$K_2PtCl_6$，$KHC_4H_4O_6$，$K_2Na[Co(NO_2)_6]$，$Rb_2SnCl_6$，$CsClO_4$。

12.36 钾的沸点为 774 ℃，钠的沸点为 883 ℃，钾的沸点比钠低 109 ℃。控制温度在钠和钾沸点之间，则生成的钾从反应体系中挥发出来，有利于平衡向生成钾的方向移动。

由于反应是一个平衡过程，反应不够彻底。同时，钾易溶于熔融的氯化物中或易生成超氧化物等因素，使此方法并不切实可行。

12.37 由于 Li^+ 半径较小，极化能力较强，使锂与同族的钠、钾等元素及化合物有许多不同之处。

(1) 锂与水反应不如钠、钾与水反应激烈。主要原因是锂的熔点较高。LiOH 的溶解度较小。

(2) Li^+ 极化能力强，$LiNO_3$ 热分解产物与 $NaNO_3$ 等不同。

$$4LiNO_3 \xlongequal{\triangle} 2Li_2O + 4NO_2\uparrow + O_2\uparrow$$

$$2NaNO_3 \xlongequal{\triangle} 2NaNO_2 + O_2\uparrow$$

(3) 某些锂盐为难溶盐，而相应的钠盐、钾盐则为易溶盐。

难溶盐：LiF，Li_2CO_3，Li_3PO_4；

易溶盐：NaF，Na_2CO_3，Na_3PO_4，

KF，K_2CO_3，K_3PO_4。

(4) 锂在空气中燃烧产物与钠、钾不同。钠、钾在空气中燃烧的主要产物为过氧化物；而锂在空气中燃烧的产物为正常的氧化物。

(5) 锂与氮气在室温下即可缓慢化合，而钠和钾与氮的反应则应在高温下才能进行。主要原因是 Li^+ 半径小，Li_3N 较稳定。

(6) 与 NaCl，KCl 不同，LiCl 的水合物受热时发生水解。

(7) 锂的氯化物等为共价化合物，而钠、钾则形成离子化合物。

12.38 (1) 在空气中燃烧均生成正常的氧化物；

$$4Li + O_2 \xlongequal{} 2Li_2O$$

$$2Mg + O_2 \xlongequal{} 2MgO$$

(2) 与 N_2 化合能力较强，易生成 Li_3N 和 Mg_3N_2；

(3) 难溶盐：

LiF 与 MgF_2，Li_2CO_3 与 $MgCO_3$，Li_3PO_4 与 $Mg_3(PO_4)_2$ 等均为难溶盐；

(4) 氢氧化物溶解度较小，受热易脱水成氧化物；

$$2LiOH \xlongequal{\triangle} Li_2O + H_2O \qquad Mg(OH)_2 \xlongequal{\triangle} MgO + H_2O$$

(5) 硝酸盐热分解产物相似；

$$4LiNO_3 \xlongequal{\triangle} 2Li_2O + 4NO_2 + O_2$$
$$2Mg(NO_3)_2 \xlongequal{\triangle} 2MgO + 4NO_2 + O_2$$

(6) 水合氯化物受热易水解。

$$MgCl_2 \cdot 6H_2O \xlongequal{\triangle} Mg(OH)Cl + 5H_2O + HCl$$

12.39 Be 和 Al 单质及化合物性质有许多相似之处，可从以下几个方面来理解。

(1) Be 和 Al 都是两性金属，不仅能溶于酸，也都能溶于强碱放出氢气。

$$Be + 2NaOH + 2H_2O = Na_2[Be(OH)_4] + H_2\uparrow$$
$$2Al + 2NaOH + 6H_2O = 2Na[Al(OH)_4] + 3H_2\uparrow$$

(2) 铍和铝的氢氧化物都是两性化合物，易溶于强碱。

$$Be(OH)_2 + 2NaOH = Na_2[Be(OH)_4]$$
$$Al(OH)_3 + NaOH = Na[Al(OH)_4]$$

(3) $BeCl_2$ 和 $AlCl_3$ 都是共价化合物。易升华、聚合、易溶于有机溶剂。

(4) Be，Al 常温下不与水作用，与冷的浓硝酸接触时都发生钝化现象。

(5) 铍和铝的盐都易水解。

12.40 肯定存在：$MgCO_3$，Na_2SO_4。

肯定不存在：$Ba(NO_3)_2$，$AgNO_3$，$CuSO_4$。

混合物投入水中，得无色溶液和白色沉淀，则肯定不存在 $CuSO_4$。

溶液在焰色试验时，火焰呈黄色，则 Na_2SO_4 肯定存在。溶液中不存在 Ba^{2+}。

沉淀可溶于稀盐酸并放出气体，则肯定存在 $MgCO_3$，而 $Ba(NO_3)_2$ 则肯定不存在，因 Ba^{2+} 与 Na_2SO_4 生成 $BaSO_4$ 白色沉淀且不溶于强酸。$AgNO_3$ 也肯定不存在，因 $AgNO_3$ 遇 Na_2SO_4 将有些 Ag_2SO_4 白色沉淀生成，沉淀中 $MgCO_3$ 和 Ag_2SO_4 在稀盐酸中 $MgCO_3$ 溶解而 Ag_2SO_4 不溶。

12.41 不能用空气、氮气、二氧化碳代替氢气作制冷剂，因为电炉法炼镁时炉口馏出的镁蒸气温度很高，能和空气、氮气、二氧化碳发生反应：

$$2Mg + O_2 = 2MgO$$
$$3Mg + N_2 = Mg_3N_2$$
$$2Mg + CO_2 = 2MgO + C$$

第 13 章

一、选择题

13.1 D　13.2 C　13.3 D　13.4 A　13.5 A　13.6 B　13.7 C　13.8 D

13.9 B　13.10 D　13.11 A　13.12 B

二、填空题

13.13 Π_4^6，$BI_3 > BBr_3 > BCl_3 > BF_3$。

13.14 $B_3N_3H_6$，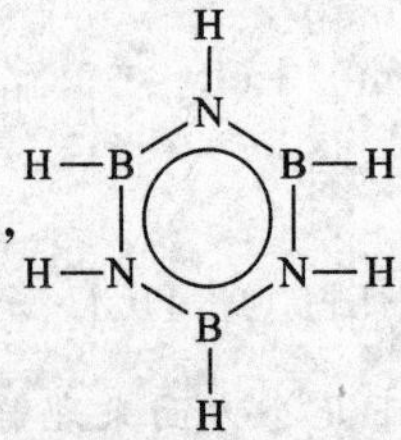，苯。

13.15 片，氢，分子间力，解理，润滑。

13.16 逆，$Ga[GaCl_4]$。

13.17 $Na_2B_4O_7 \cdot 10H_2O$，二。

13.18 (1)>，(2)>，(3)<。

13.19 小，AgCl；大，K(或 Rb)。

13.20 Cs 和 Ga。

13.21 $(C_2H_5O)_3B$，绿。

13.22 蓝，紫，绿，绿，黄。

三、完成并配平下列反应方程式

13.23 $Na_2B_4O_7 + 2HNO_3 + 5H_2O = 4H_3BO_3 + 2NaNO_3$

13.24 $Na_2CO_3 + Al_2O_3 \xlongequal{\triangle} 2NaAlO_2 + CO_2$

$NaAlO_2 + 2H_2O = Al(OH)_3 + NaOH$

13.25 $2Al + 2NaOH + 6H_2O = 2NaAl(OH)_4 + 3H_2$

13.26 $NaAlO_2 + NH_4Cl + H_2O = Al(OH)_3 + NH_3 + NaCl$

13.27 $TlOH + NaCl = TlCl + NaOH + 2H_2O$

13.28 $3\,Tl + 4\,HNO_3 = 3\,TlNO_3 + NO$

13.29 $TlCl_3 + 3\,KI = TlI + I_2 + 3\,KCl$

四、简答题和计算题

13.30 (1) OH^- 变形性小，与 Tl^+ 间极化作用差，TlOH 为离子化合物；Tl^+ 半径较大，与 OH^- 间的离子键不强；所以，TlOH 易溶。Cl^- 变形性比 OH^- 大，Cl^- 与半径大的 Tl^+ 间有相互极化作用，TlCl 中共价成分较大；所以，TlCl 难溶。

(2) 三氯化硼的共价性比三氯化铝强，而分子半径比三氯化铝小，因而三氯化硼的沸点应比三氯化铝低。

(3) $CuCl_2$ 中的 Cu^{2+} 电子构型为 $3d^9$，有 1 个单电子，因而 $CuCl_2$ 为顺磁性。$InCl_2$ 化合物是由 In^+ 和 In^{3+} 构成，即 $InCl_2$ 可以写成 $In[InCl_4]$，In^+ 和 In^{3+} 都无单电子，因而 $InCl_2$ 是反磁性的。

13.31　BCl_3 水解产物为 H_3BO_3 和 HCl

$$BCl_3 + 3\ H_2O = H_3BO_3 + 3\ HCl$$

BF_3 水解生成的 HF 能够与 BF_3 继续反应生成 BF_4^-

$$BF_3 + 3\ H_2O = H_3BO_3 + 3\ HF$$

$$BF_3 + HF = H^+ + BF_4^-$$

BF_3 水解产物中既有 H_3BO_3，也有 BF_4^-。

BCl_3 和 BF_3 水解产物不同的原因在于 F^- 半径小，与半径小的 B^{3+} 配位生成稳定的 BF_4^-；而 Cl^- 半径大，与 BCl_3 生成的 BCl_4^- 不稳定，因而不生成 BCl_4^-。

13.32　硼烷常见的五种键型分别为

(1) B—B 键

二中心二电子（正常 B—B 键）

(2) B—H 键

二中心二电子（正常 B—H 键）

(3) 氢桥键

三中心二电子键 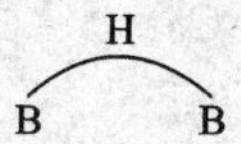

(4) 硼桥键

三中心二电子键 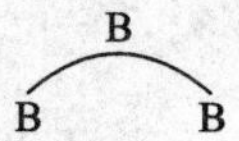

(5) 闭合式硼键

三中心二电子键 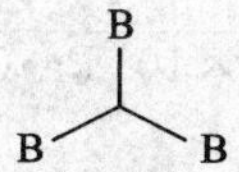

13.33　题中涉及的氧化物的 $\Delta_f G_m^\ominus$ 数据见下表。

Al_2O_3	Fe_2O_3	Cr_2O_3	MnO_2	CaO
−1 528.3	−742.2	−1 058.1	−465.1	−603.3

$$Fe_2O_3 + 2Al = Al_2O_3 + 2Fe$$

$$\Delta_r G_m^\ominus = \sum_i \nu_i \Delta_f G_m^\ominus(\text{生成物}) - \sum_i \nu_i \Delta_f G_m^\ominus(\text{反应物})$$

$$\begin{aligned}\Delta_r G_m^\ominus &= \Delta_f G_m^\ominus(Al_2O_3) - \Delta_f G_m^\ominus(Fe_2O_3)\\ &= (-1\,528.3\ \text{kJ}\cdot\text{mol}^{-1}) - (-742.2\ \text{kJ}\cdot\text{mol}^{-1})\\ &= -786.1\ \text{kJ}\cdot\text{mol}^{-1}\end{aligned}$$

$\Delta_r G_m^\ominus < 0$，可以利用铝热法从 Fe_2O_3 制取金属 Fe。

$$Cr_2O_3 + 2Al = Al_2O_3 + 2Cr$$

用铝热法制取金属 Cr 的反应，与制取金属 Fe 的反应类型相同。

$$\begin{aligned}\Delta_r G_m^\ominus &= \Delta_f G_m^\ominus(Al_2O_3) - \Delta_f G_m^\ominus(Cr_2O_3)\\ &= (-1\,528.3\ \text{kJ}\cdot\text{mol}^{-1}) - (-1\,058.1\ \text{kJ}\cdot\text{mol}^{-1})\\ &= -470.2\ \text{kJ}\cdot\text{mol}^{-1}\end{aligned}$$

计算结果表明 $\Delta_r G_m^\ominus < 0$，可以利用铝热法从 Cr_2O_3 制取金属 Cr。

$$3MnO_2 + 4Al \longrightarrow 2Al_2O_3 + 3Mn$$

$$\Delta_r G_m^\ominus = \sum_i \nu_i \Delta_f G_m^\ominus(\text{生成物}) - \sum_i \nu_i \Delta_f G_m^\ominus(\text{反应物})$$

$$\begin{aligned}\Delta_r G_m^\ominus &= 2\Delta_f G_m^\ominus(Al_2O_3) - 3\Delta_f G_m^\ominus(MnO_2)\\ &= 2\times(-1\,528.3\ \text{kJ}\cdot\text{mol}^{-1}) - 3\times(-465.1\ \text{kJ}\cdot\text{mol}^{-1})\\ &= -1\,661.3\ \text{kJ}\cdot\text{mol}^{-1}\end{aligned}$$

$\Delta_r G_m^\ominus < 0$，可以利用铝热法从 MnO_2 制取金属 Mn。

$$3CaO + 2Al \longrightarrow Al_2O_3 + 3Ca$$

$$\Delta_r G_m^\ominus = \sum_i \nu_i \Delta_f G_m^\ominus(\text{生成物}) - \sum_i \nu_i \Delta_f G_m^\ominus(\text{反应物})$$

$$\begin{aligned}\Delta_r G_m^\ominus &= \Delta_f G_m^\ominus(Al_2O_3) - 3\Delta_f G_m^\ominus(CaO)\\ &= (-1\,528.3\ \text{kJ}\cdot\text{mol}^{-1}) - 3\times(-603.3\ \text{kJ}\cdot\text{mol}^{-1})\\ &= 281.6\ \text{kJ}\cdot\text{mol}^{-1}\end{aligned}$$

$\Delta_r G_m^\ominus > 0$，不能利用铝热法从 CaO 制取金属 Ca。

13.34 由理想气体状态方程，得 A 的相对分子质量为

$$\begin{aligned}M &= \frac{RTm}{pV}\\ &= \frac{8.314\times10^3\ \text{dm}^3\cdot\text{Pa}\cdot\text{mol}^{-1}\cdot\text{K}^{-1}\times(69+273)\ \text{K}\times0.051\,6\ \text{g}}{2.96\times10^3\ \text{Pa}\cdot0.268\ \text{dm}^3}\\ &= 185.0\ \text{g}\cdot\text{mol}^{-1}\end{aligned}$$

A 中 B 与 Cl 原子数比为

$$M = \frac{23.4/10.81}{76.6/35.45} = 1$$

设 A 的化学式为 $(BCl)_a$，则 a 的值为

$$a = \frac{185.0}{10.81+35.45} = 4$$

所以，A 的化学式为 B_4Cl_4。

13.35 将明矾 $KAl(SO_4)_2\cdot12H_2O$ 溶于水，加入适量 KOH 溶液得到 $Al(OH)_3$ 沉淀

$$Al^{3+} + 3OH^- \longrightarrow Al(OH)_3\downarrow$$

过滤并洗涤即得到 $Al(OH)_3$。

将滤液蒸发浓缩即得到 K_2SO_4。

将 $Al(OH)_3$ 与 KOH 作用得无色溶液，蒸发浓缩后即得到 $KAlO_2$。

$$Al(OH)_3 + KOH \longrightarrow KAlO_2 + 2H_2O$$

13.36 H_3BO_3 为缺电子化合物，O—H 键不解离，而是接受水分子中的 OH^-，释放出 H^+：

$$H_3BO_3 + H_2O \longrightarrow [B(OH)_4]^- + H^+$$

因而为一元酸。

H_3PO_3 的结构式为

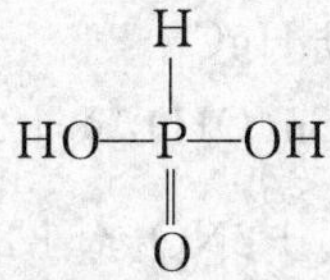

在水中,二个羟基(OH)氢可以电离或被置换,而与中心原子 P 以共价键相连的 H 不能解离或被置换,因而 H_3PO_3 为二元酸。

13.37 Ga 的电子构型为[Ar]$3d^{10}4s^24p^1$,显然形成 Ga(Ⅰ)和 Ga(Ⅲ)是容易的。若 $GaCl_2$ 中均为 2 价镓,则其应为顺磁性物质。既然在溶液中解离出简单阳离子和四氯阴离子,就可以推知简单阳离子中的 Ga 为+1 价,而配阴离子中的 Ga 为+3 价。即化合物的可能结构为 Ga[$GaCl_4$]。这种推断完全符合抗磁性的实验事实。

第 14 章

一、选择题

14.1 D　14.2 C　14.3 B　14.4 B　14.5 C　14.6 C　14.7 D　14.8 D
14.9 B　14.10 B　14.11 D　14.12 C

二、填空题

14.13 (1) $Cu_2S\cdot FeS\cdot GeS_2$;(2) SnO_2;(3) PbS;(4) C;(5) $NaHCO_3$;(6) SiO_2;(7) Na_2SiO_3;(8) Mg_2SiO_4;(9) $Sc_2Si_2O_7$;(10) PbO;(11) PbO;(12) Pb_3O_4。

14.14 $[Si_nO_{3n}]^{2n-}$,$[Si_nO_{2.5n}]^{n-}$,$[SiO_2]_n$。

14.15 气体通过 $Ca(OH)_2$ 溶液,气体通过酸性 $KMnO_4$ 溶液。

14.16 >,$NaHCO_3$ 在水中生成二聚的

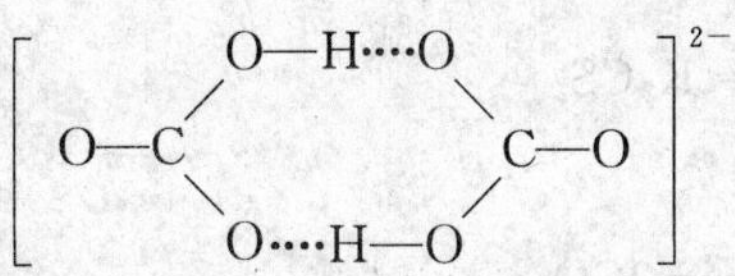
离子。

14.17 $Pb(PbO_3)$,$Pb_2(PbO_4)$,$Fe(FeO_2)_2$。

14.18 两,$[Pb(OH)_4]^{2-}$,醋,硝。

14.19 红,铅丹,1/3,PbO_2,2/3,$Pb(NO_3)_2$。

14.20 $HClO_4 > H_2SO_4 > H_3PO_4 > H_2SiO_3$。

14.21 白,黄,棕,黄,黑,白,黄,橙黄。

三、完成并配平下列反应方程式

14.22 $NH_3 + CO_2 + H_2O \Longrightarrow NH_4HCO_3\downarrow$

14.23 $SiO_3^{2-} + 2NH_4^+ \Longrightarrow H_2SiO_3\downarrow + 2NH_3$

14.24 $SnCl_2 + 4NaOH = Na_2[Sn(OH)_4] + 2NaCl$

$3Na_2[Sn(OH)_4] + 2Bi(NO_3)_3 + 6NaOH = 3Na_2Sn(OH)_6 + 2Bi\downarrow + 6NaNO_3$

14.25 $SnCl_2 + 2HgCl_2 = SnCl_4 + HgCl_2$

14.26 $[Sn(OH)_6]^{2-} + 2CO_2 = Sn(OH)_4\downarrow + 2HCO_3^-$

14.27 $Pb + 4HNO_3 \overset{\triangle}{=} Pb(NO_3)_2 + 2NO_2\uparrow + 2H_2O$

14.28 $Pb_3O_4 + 15I^- + 8H^+ = 3PbI_4^{2-} + I_3^- + 4H_2O$

14.29 $SnS + (NH_4)_2S_2 = (NH_4)_2SnS_3$

14.30 $Pb_3O_4 + 4HCl = Cl_2 + 3PbCl_2 + 4H_2O$

14.31 $2Mn^{2+} + 5PbO_2 + 5SO_4^{2-} + 4H^+ = 2MnO_4^- + 5PbSO_4 + 2H_2O$

14.32 $PbCrO_4 + 4NaOH = Na_2[Pb(OH)_4] + Na_2CrO_4$

14.33 $SiCl_4 + 2Zn = Si + 2ZnCl_2$

14.34 $SiO_2 + CaCO_3 \overset{高温}{=} CaSiO_3 + CO_2\uparrow$

14.35 $SiO_2 + 2C + 2Cl_2 \overset{加热}{=} SiCl_4 + 2CO\uparrow$

14.36 $SiO_2 + Na_2CO_3 \overset{熔融}{=} Na_2SiO_3 + CO_2\uparrow$

14.37 $SnO_2 + 2NaOH \overset{共熔}{=} Na_2SnO_3 + H_2O$

四、简答题和计算题

14.38 (1) CS_2 具有还原性而 CCl_4 没有明显的还原性：

$$5CS_2 + 4MnO_4^- + 12H^+ = 5CO_2 + 10S + 4Mn^{2+} + 6H_2O$$

CCl_4 有阻燃作用，可以做灭火剂，而 CS_2 易燃：

$$CS_2 + 3O_2 = CO_2 + 2SO_2$$

(2) CS_2 为酸性硫化物，与碱性物质反应，而 CCl_4 不与碱性物质反应：

$$CS_2 + K_2S = K_2CS_2$$

14.39 (1) C 和 CO 与 O_2 的反应有 3 个：

$$2C + O_2 = 2CO$$
$$C + O_2 = CO_2$$
$$2CO + O_2 = 2CO_2$$

由线段的斜率可以判断线段所代表的是哪一个反应。由 Gibbs 公式

$$\Delta_r G_m = \Delta_r H_m - T\Delta_r S_m$$

线段的斜率(k)等于反应的熵变 $\Delta_r S_m$ 的负值：

$$k = -\Delta_r S_m$$

即熵增加的反应，线段的斜率 $k>0$；熵减小的反应，线段的斜率 $k<0$，因此，各线段所表示的反应为

(a) $2CO+O_2 = 2CO_2$

(b) $C+O_2 = CO_2$

(c) $2C+O_2 = 2CO$

(2) (d)线在拐点之后斜率增大，即熵变减小；只有反应物的熵增大，才能使反应的熵变减小，由反应式 $2Mn+O_2 = 2MnO$ 可知，(d)线的拐点对应的温度是 Mn 的熔点。

(3) 由(1)的结果可知，(d)线先与(c)线相交，所以温度在 $T_y \sim T_z$ 之间由 MnO 得到 Mn 的反应为(c)－(d)，即

$$MnO+C = Mn+CO$$

(4) 在温度高于 T_z 后，C 和 CO 都能够将 MnO 还原为 Mn，即以下两个反应同时进行

$$MnO+C = Mn+CO$$
$$MnO+CO = Mn+CO_2$$

14.40 N_2 与 CO 有相同的分子轨道式，原子间都为三重键，互为等电子体。但两者成键情况不完全相同。N_2 分子结构为 :N≡N:，CO 分子结构 :C≒O:，由于 CO 分子中 O 向 C 有 π 配键，使 C 原子周围电子密度增大，另外，C 的电负性比 N 小得多，束缚电子能力弱，给电子对能力强，因此，CO 配位能力强。

14.41 实验室中制备 CO 气体的方法有两种。

一种是将甲酸滴加到热浓硫酸中，CO 气体的溶解度很小，从水中逸出：

$$HCOOH = CO\uparrow +H_2O$$

另一种方法是将草酸晶体与浓硫酸共热，使生成的混合气体通过固体 NaOH，吸收掉 CO_2 和少量的水汽得到纯净的 CO。

$$H_2C_2O_4 = CO_2\uparrow +CO\uparrow +H_2O$$

实验室中用碳酸盐，如 $CaCO_3$，和盐酸的作用来制备 CO_2：

$$CaCO_3+2HCl = 2CaCl+H_2O+CO_2\uparrow$$

经常使用一种称为启普发生器的装置，去完成上述反应。

14.42 (1) 先在空气中灼烧方铅矿粉：

$$2PbS+3O_2 = 2PbO+2SO_2$$

用过量的 NaOH 处理 PbO，则

$$PbO+2NaOH = Na_2PbO_2+H_2O$$

用 NaClO 氧化 Na_2PbO_2 得到 PbO_2：

$$Na_2PbO_2+NaClO+H_2O = PbO_2+NaCl+2NaOH$$

在高温下用碳还原 PbO，可得金属铅：

$$PbO+C = Pb+CO\uparrow$$

$$CO+PbO \xlongequal{\quad} Pb+CO_2\uparrow$$

(2) 在电炉中高温加热 SiO_2 和 C 的混合物，可得粗硅。反应为：

$$SiO_2+2C \xlongequal{\quad} Si+2CO\uparrow$$

提纯过程首先是将硅转化为 $SiCl_4$：

$$Si+2Cl_2 \xlongequal{\quad} SiCl_4(l)$$

蒸馏液态的 $SiCl_4$，得到纯的硅源。用 H_2 还原纯的 $SiCl_4$，可得纯硅：

$$SiCl_4+2H_2 \xlongequal{\quad} Si(纯)+4HCl$$

(3) 向偏硅酸钠(Na_2SiO_3)溶液中加盐酸：

$$Na_2SiO_3+2HCl \xlongequal{\quad} H_2SiO_3+2NaCl$$

当体系 pH 逐渐变小时，硅酸根发生聚合。pH7～8 时，形成胶体溶液。当胶体的相对分子质量大到一定程度时，析出凝胶。用热水洗涤凝胶去除体系中的 Na^+ 和 Cl^-，所得凝胶的组成是无序的 SiO_2，并含有结合的水，在硅氧骨架的空隙间也有水分子，需在 100 ℃条件下烘干，即可脱出这些水分子，得到多孔硅胶。再用 $CoCl_2$ 溶液浸泡，于 60～70 ℃下烘干至蓝色，并于 200 ℃下活化，即可得到多孔的变色硅胶。

14.43 如图所示的装置，可以用于锡直接氯化法制取 $SnCl_4$：

$$Sn+2Cl_2(g) \xlongequal{\quad} SnCl_4(l)$$

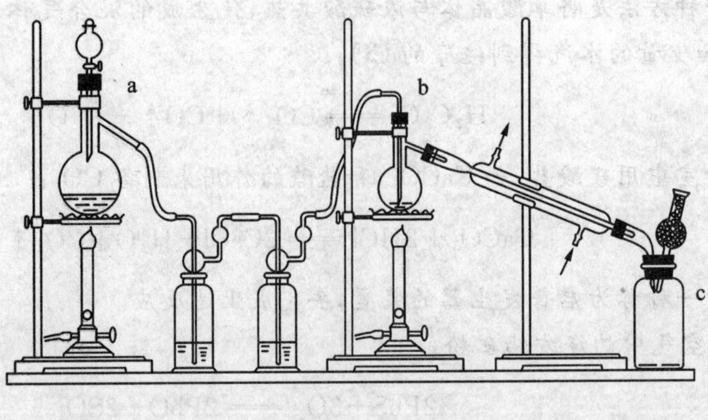

反应之前，可以将干燥的 CO_2 气体通过反应的气路，以赶尽反应装置中的潮湿空气；从烧瓶 a 出来的 Cl_2 要经过盛有浓硫酸的洗气瓶严格除水；反应在烧瓶 b 中进行，生成的气态 $SnCl_4$ 经冷凝后收集在插有干燥管的广口瓶 c 中，以防止外界的水汽与产物作用。

14.44 C 为第二周期元素只有 2s 2p 轨道可以成键，最大配位数为 4，CCl_4 无空轨道可以接受水的配位，因而不水解。

Si 为第三周期元素，形成 $SiCl_4$ 后还有空的 3d 轨道，d 轨道接受水分子中氧原子的孤电子对，形成配位键而发生水解。

BCl_3 分子中，B 虽无空的价层 d 轨道，但 B 有空的 p 轨道，可以接受电子对因而易水解。NCl_3 无空的 d 轨道或空的 p 轨道，但分子中 N 原子尚有孤对电子可以向水分子中氢配位而发生水解。

14.45 Si 和 C 单质都可采取 sp^3 杂化形成金刚石型结构，但 Si 的半径比 C 大得多，因此 Si—Si 键较弱，键能低，使单质硅的熔点、硬度比金刚石低得多。

14.46 硅与氟和氯形成的化合物 SiF_4，$SiCl_4$ 都是共价化合物，分子半径 $SiF_4 < SiCl_4$，色散力 $SiF_4 < SiCl_4$，因此熔点 $SiF_4 < SiCl_4$，常温下 SiF_4 为气态，$SiCl_4$ 为液态。

在锡的四卤化物中，氟的电负性较大，只有 SnF_4 为离子化合物（电负性差大）。而氯的电负性较小，与锡形成的 $SnCl_4$ 为共价化合物（电负性差 $\Delta\chi < 1.7$）。因而 SnF_4 熔点比 $SnCl_4$ 高，常温下 SnF_4 为固态，$SnCl_4$ 为液态。

14.47 将 $SnCl_2$ 加入一定量水中充分搅拌后，再边搅拌边滴加稀盐酸至沉淀消失后并稍过量。再加少许锡粒。

加入过量的盐酸是为抑制 $SnCl_2$ 的水解：

$$Sn(OH)Cl + HCl \rightleftharpoons SnCl_2 + H_2O$$

向配好的溶液中加少量 Sn 粒，防止 $SnCl_2$ 被氧化：

$$2Sn^{2+} + O_2 + 4H^+ = 2Sn^{4+} + 2H_2O$$

$$Sn^{4+} + Sn = 2Sn^{2+}$$

14.48 (1) 酸性条件下分别加入少量 $FeCl_3$ 溶液，充分反应后加入 KSCN 溶液，变红的未知液为 $SnCl_4$，另一为 $SnCl_2$。

$$2Fe^{3+} + Sn^{2+} = 2Fe^{2+} + Sn^{4+}$$

(2) 将少量溶液加入 $HgCl_2$ 溶液中，若产生白色沉淀，未知液为 $SnCl_2$，不产生沉淀的未知液为 $SnCl_4$。

$$2HgCl_2 + SnCl_2 = Hg_2Cl_2 \downarrow + SnCl_4$$

(3) 将未知液分别与 $(NH_4)_2S$ 溶液作用，产生黄色沉淀的为 $SnCl_4$，产生棕色沉淀的为 $SnCl_2$。

$$SnCl_4 + 2(NH_4)_2S = SnS_2 \downarrow + 4NH_4Cl$$

$$SnCl_2 + (NH_4)_2S = SnS \downarrow + 2NH_4Cl$$

(4) 向二未知液中加入过量 NaOH 溶液至生成的白色沉淀全部溶解，再加入 $BiCl_3$ 溶液，有黑色沉淀生成的为 $SnCl_2$，另一种为 $SnCl_4$。

$$SnCl_2 + 4NaOH = Na_2[Sn(OH)_4] + 2NaCl$$

$$3[Sn(OH)_4]^{2-} + 2Bi^{3+} + 6OH^- = 2Bi \downarrow + 3[Sn(OH)_6]^{2-}$$

14.49 Pb 与稀盐酸反应生成的 $PbCl_2$ 附在 Pb 的表面而阻止反应的进一步进行，因而 Pb 难溶于稀盐酸。但在浓盐酸中，$PbCl_2$ 与 HCl 生成配合物 H_2PbCl_4 而溶解，使反应能进行下去：

$$Pb + 4HCl \xlongequal{} H_2PbCl_4 + H_2\uparrow$$

Pb与稀硝酸反应生成可溶性$Pb(NO_3)_2$而使反应进行下去：

$$3Pb + 8HNO_3 \xlongequal{} 3Pb(NO_3)_2 + 2NO\uparrow + 4H_2O$$

但Pb与冷的浓硝酸反应生成致密的氧化膜使Pb钝化，从而使反应难以进行下去，因此，Pb易溶于稀硝酸而难溶于冷的浓硝酸。

14.50 烷烃、硅烷、硼烷的热稳定性依次减弱，且它们的分解方式也不同。如甲烷(CH_4)要在高温下才能分解：

$$2CH_4 \xlongequal{1\,500\ ℃} C_2H_2 + 3H_2$$

而甲硅烷(SiH_4)的分解温度比甲烷要低1 000 ℃左右：

$$SiH_4 \xlongequal{500\ ℃} Si + 2H_2$$

二硼烷(B_2H_2)不如甲烷和甲硅烷稳定，要在100℃以下保存，温度高时要分解放出H_2，并转变成其他高级硼烷：

$$2B_2H_6 \xlongequal{120\ ℃} B_4H_{10} + H_2$$

$$5B_4H_{10} \xlongequal{120\ ℃} 4B_5H_{11} + 3H_2$$

14.51 A—Si； B—Na_2SiO_3； C—H_2； D—Cu； E—SiO_2； F—SiF_4； G—H_4SiO_4； H—HF。

14.52 A—$SnCl_2$； B—Sn(OH)Cl； C—Sn^{2+},H^+,NO_3^-,Cl^-； D—AgCl； E—$[Ag(NH_3)_2]^+$,Cl^-； F—AgI； G—SnS； H—SnS_2； I—Hg_2Cl_2； J—Hg。

14.53 A—Pb_3O_4； B—PbO； C—$Pb(NO_3)_2$； D—$Pb(OH)_2$； E—$Na_2[Pb(OH)_4]$； F—PbO_2； G—MnO_4^-。

14.54 M—Sn； A—$SnCl_4$； B—$SnCl_2$； C—SnS_2； D—Na_2SnS_3； E—Hg_2Cl_2； F—$Sn(OH)_2$； G—$Na_2Sn(OH)_4$； H—Bi。

14.55 A—$Pb(NO_3)_2$； B—PbO； C—NO_2+O_2； D—PbO_2； E—$PbCl_2$； F—Cl_2； G—PbI_2。

14.56 A—$PbCO_3$； B—PbO； C—CO_2； D—$Pb(NO_3)_2$； E—$PbCrO_4$； F—$Pb(OH)_2$； G—$CaCO_3$。

第15章

一、选择题

15.1 D　15.2 A　15.3 D　15.4 C　15.5 B　15.6 B　15.7 A　15.8 B
15.9 C　15.10 B　15.11 A　15.12 C　15.13 B　15.14 B　15.15 A　15.16 D
15.17 D　15.18 B　15.19 D

二、填空题

15.20 (1) As_4S_4；(2) As_2S_3；(3) Sb_2S_3；(4) NiSbS；(5) Bi_2S_3；(6) As_2O_3；(7) Sb_2O_3；(8) Bi_2O_3。

15.21 取代，加合(配位)，氧化。

15.22 NH_3，HN_3，NH_3，HN_3，NH_3，NH_2OH。

15.23 三角锥，大，小，弱，强，差。

15.24 $<$，$>$，$<$，

15.25 H_3PO_2，H_3PO_3，H_3PO_4，HPO_3，$H_4P_2O_7$。

15.26 二，三，四；$H_3PO_3 > H_4P_2O_7 > H_3PO_4$。

15.27 $Ca(H_2PO_4)_2 > CaHPO_4 > Ca_3(PO_4)_2$。

15.28 SbOCl，$Cu(OH)NO_3 + HNO_3 + H_2O$，$CuO + HNO_3 + NO_2 + O_2 + H_2O$，$MnO_2 + NO_2 + O_2$。

15.29 As_2S_5，As_2S_3，Sb_2S_5，Sb_2S_3。

15.30 12，0。

15.31 Ag_3PO_4，黄。

15.32 AsH_3，亮黑色的砷镜。

15.33 Na_3AsO_3，Na_3AsO_4，NaI。

15.34 As_2S_3—黄色；As_2S_5—黄色；Sb_2S_3—橙色；Sb_2S_5—橙色；$AgNO_2$—黄色；$K_3[Co(NO_2)_6]$—黄色；$[Fe(NO)]^{2+}$—棕色；NO_2—棕色；N_2O_3—淡蓝；N_2O_4—无色。

三、完成并配平下列反应方程式

15.35 $NH_4Cl + HNO_2 = N_2 + 2H_2O + HCl$

15.36 $2NH_3 + 3CuO \xlongequal{\triangle} N_2 + 3Cu + 3H_2O$

15.37 $2NH_2OH + 2AgBr = N_2 + 2Ag + 2HBr + 2H_2O$

15.38 $2NO_2 + 2NaOH = NaNO_3 + NaNO_2 + H_2O$

15.39 $5HNO_2 + 2HIO_3 = 5HNO_3 + I_2 + H_2O$

15.40 $Pb(N_3)_2 \xlongequal{\triangle} Pb + 3N_2$

15.41 $HNO_3 + HNO_2 = 2NO_2 + H_2O$

15.42 $Au + HNO_3 + 4HCl = HAuCl_4 + NO + 2H_2O$

15.43 $3Pt + 4HNO_3 + 18HCl = 3H_2PtCl_6 + 4NO + 8H_2O$

15.44 $3Br_2 + 2P + 6H_2O = 6HBr + 2H_3PO_3$

15.45 $3P_4 + 20HNO_3 + 8H_2O = 12H_3PO_4 + 20NO$

15.46 $H_3PO_2 + 4AgNO_3 + 2H_2O = 4Ag\downarrow + H_3PO_4 + 4HNO_3$

15.47 $H_3PO_3 + 2NaOH = Na_2HPO_3 + 2H_2O$

15.48 $Zn_3P_2 + 6HCl(稀) = 2PH_3 + 6ZnCl_2$

15.49 $As_2S_3 + 3Na_2S = 2Na_3AsS_3$

15.50 $2Na_3AsS_4 + 6HCl \longequal As_2S_5\downarrow + 3H_2S + 6NaCl$

15.51 $4Sb_2S_5 + 24NaOH = 3Na_3SbO_4 + 5Na_3SbS_4 + 12H_2O$

15.52 $5NaBiO_3 + 2Mn^{2+} + 14H^+ = 5Bi^{3+} + 2MnO_4^- + 5Na^+ + 7H_2O$

四、简答题

15.53 硝酸盐受热分解的产物与阳离子的极化能力有关，按照阳离子的极化能力由弱至强，分别生成亚硝酸盐、金属氧化物、金属单质。若阳离子有还原性，则阳离子可被生成的氧氧化。

(1) $4LiNO_3 = 2Li_2O + 4NO_2\uparrow + O_2\uparrow$

(2) $2KNO_3 = 2KNO_2 + O_2\uparrow$

(3) $2AgNO_3 = 2Ag + 2NO_2\uparrow + O_2\uparrow$

(4) $4Bi(NO_3)_3 = 2Bi_2O_3 + 12NO_2\uparrow + 3O_2\uparrow$

(5) $2Pb(NO_3)_2 = 2PbO + 4NO_2\uparrow + O_2\uparrow$

(6) $4Fe(NO_3)_2 = 2Fe_2O_3 + 8NO_2\uparrow + O_2\uparrow$

(7) $NH_4NO_3 \xlongequal{>200\ ℃} N_2O\uparrow + 2H_2O$

$2NH_4NO_3 \xlongequal{300\ ℃} 2N_2\uparrow + O_2\uparrow + 4H_2O$

(8) $(NH_4)_2CO_3 = 2NH_3\uparrow + CO_2\uparrow + H_2O$

(9) $(NH_4)_2Cr_2O_7 = Cr_2O_3 + N_2\uparrow + 4H_2O$

(10) $NH_4Cl = NH_3\uparrow + HCl\uparrow$

(11) $2NaNH_2 = 2Na + N_2\uparrow + 2H_2\uparrow$

(12) $Pb(N_3)_2 = Pb + 3N_2\uparrow$

(13) $2NaNO_2 = Na_2O + NO_2\uparrow + NO\uparrow$

(14) $AgNO_2 = Ag + NO_2\uparrow$

15.54 (1) 将 $NaNO_3$ 加热分解，得到 $NaNO_2$ 固体：

$$2NaNO_3 \xlongequal{\triangle} 2NaNO_2 + O_2\uparrow$$

将 $NaNO_2$ 配制成饱和溶液，冰浴冷却至近 0 ℃，加入在冰浴中冷却至近0 ℃的稀硫酸：

$$NO_2^- + H^+ = HNO_2$$

(2) 向 $BiCl_3$ 溶液中加入过量 NaOH 溶液，滴加氯水或 NaClO 溶液，水浴加热，有土黄色 $NaBiO_3$ 沉淀生成：

$$BiCl_3 + 3NaOH = Bi(OH)_3\downarrow + 3NaCl$$
$$Bi(OH)_3 + Cl_2 + 3NaOH = NaBiO_3\downarrow + 3H_2O + 2NaCl$$

(3) 向 $SbCl_3$ 溶液中加入适量 NaOH 溶液和氯水，生成 $Sb(OH)_5$ 沉淀：

$$SbCl_3 + Cl_2 + 5NaOH = Sb(OH)_5\downarrow + 5NaCl$$

过滤、洗涤 $Sb(OH)_5$ 沉淀。加入过量 Na_2S 溶液，生成 Na_3SbS_4 溶液：

$$Sb(OH)_5 + 4Na_2S = Na_3SbS_4 + 5NaOH$$

向溶液中小心滴加稀盐酸，析出 Sb_2S_5 沉淀：

$$2Na_3SbS_4 + 6HCl \xlongequal{} Sb_2S_5\downarrow + 3H_2S\uparrow + 6NaCl$$

15.55 N为第二周期元素，电子构型 $2s^22p^3$，无价层d轨道，无法形成 sp^3d 杂化轨道，因而只能形成 NCl_3 而不存在 NCl_5。

Bi为第六周期元素，由于惰性电子对效应，6s轨道的二个电子难以参与成键，使Bi(V)氧化能力很强，$BiCl_5$ 不能稳定存在：

$$BiCl_5 \xlongequal{} BiCl_3 + Cl_2\uparrow$$

15.56 浓 HNO_3 与金属反应时，即使有NO生成，但由于在浓硝酸中下列平衡：

$$HNO_3 + NO \xlongequal{} NO_2 + H_2O$$

向右移动，因而产物主要是 NO_2。而稀硝酸与金属作用时上述平衡左移倾向较大，同时，NO_2 有较强的氧化性，即使有 NO_2 生成，NO_2 继续与金属作用而生成NO。

15.57 $SbCl_3$ 和 $Bi(NO_3)_3$ 都易水解生成沉淀：

$$SbCl_3 + H_2O \xlongequal{} SbOCl\downarrow + 2HCl$$

$$Bi(NO_3)_3 + H_2O \xlongequal{} BiONO_3\downarrow + 2HNO_3$$

为避免水解，在配制溶液时先将一定量的盐溶于酸中，再稀释到所需体积即可。配制 $SbCl_3$ 溶液时，先将 $SbCl_3$ 水合晶体溶于1：1盐酸中；配制 $Bi(NO_3)_3$ 溶液时，先将 $Bi(NO_3)_3$ 水合晶体溶于1：1硝酸中。

15.58 应选择稀硝酸，有两条理由。

(1) 选择稀硝酸更经济实用，Cu与稀硝酸反应主要还原产物为NO：

$$3Cu + 8HNO_3(\text{稀}) \xlongequal{} 3Cu(NO_3)_2 + 2NO + 4H_2O$$

Cu与浓硝酸反应，还原产物主要为 NO_2：

$$Cu + 4HNO_3(\text{浓}) \xlongequal{} Cu(NO_3)_2 + 2NO_2 + 2H_2O$$

可见，得到1 mol $Cu(NO_3)_2$，从理论上需稀硝酸8/3 mol，不足3 mol，而用浓硝酸，则需4 mol。

(2) 以浓硝酸与铜反应得到的硝酸铜浓度较大，易析出硝酸铜水合晶体而影响反应的继续进行。

15.59 (1) 向两种盐的溶液中分别加入 $AgNO_3$ 溶液，生成黑色沉淀的是 Na_3PO_3，生成黄色沉淀的是 Na_3PO_4；向两种盐的溶液中分别加入酸性 $KMnO_4$ 溶液，使 $KMnO_4$ 溶液褪色的是 Na_3PO_3，不能使 $KMnO_4$ 溶液褪色的是 Na_3PO_4。

(2) 试验两种盐溶液的pH，显弱酸性的是 NaH_2PO_4，显弱碱性的是 Na_2HPO_4；向两种盐的溶液中分别加入 $CaCl_2$ 溶液，有白色沉淀生成的是 Na_2HPO_4，没有白色沉淀生成的是 NaH_2PO_4。

(3) 将两种固体用煤气灯等加热，有棕色气体生成的是 $LiNO_3$，没有棕色气体生成的是 KNO_3；向两种盐的溶液中分别加入 NH_4F 溶液，有白色沉淀生成的是 $LiNO_3$，没有

沉淀生成的是 KNO_3。

(4) 将两种固体用煤气灯等加热，全部转化为气体的是 NH_4NO_3，另一种盐为 $NaNO_3$；试验两种盐溶液的 pH，显弱酸性的是 NH_4NO_3，显中性的是 $NaNO_3$。

15.60 (1) 在两支试管中分别加入待鉴定的盐，都加入 $FeSO_4$，加水溶解后沿试管壁缓慢加入浓硫酸，在水和浓硫酸界面生成棕色环的是 KNO_3，生成棕色溶液的是 KNO_2。

(2) 向两种盐的溶液中分别加入浓硫酸，有棕色气体生成的是 KNO_2，没有变化的是 KNO_3。

(3) 向两种盐的溶液中分别加入醋酸酸化，加入 KI 溶液，溶液变黄的是 KNO_2，没有变化的是 KNO_3（稀 HNO_3 不与 KI 溶液反应）。

(4) 向两种盐的溶液中分别加入 $CoCl_2$ 溶液，再加入醋酸酸化，微热，有黄色沉淀生成的是 KNO_2，没有黄色沉淀生成的是 KNO_3。

15.61 (1) 晶体在煤气灯上加热，KNO_3 转化为 KNO_2：

$$2KNO_3 \xlongequal{\triangle} 2KNO_2 + O_2$$

(2) 使气体通过 $FeSO_4$ 溶液除去 NO：

$$NO + FeSO_4 \xlongequal{} Fe(NO)SO_4$$

(3) 向溶液中加少量 $NaNO_2$ 后加热可除去 NH_4^+：

$$NH_4^+ + NO_2^- \xlongequal{\triangle} N_2 + 2H_2O$$

15.62 H_3PO_2 为一元酸，H_3PO_3 为二元酸。二者的结构为

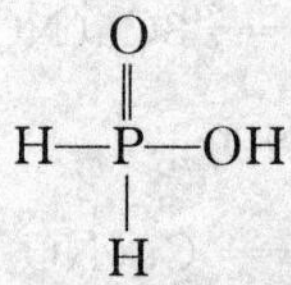

H_3PO_2 分子

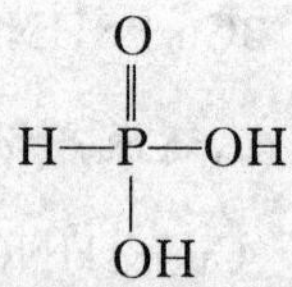

H_3PO_3 分子

在 H_3PO_2 分子结构中，有一个—OH 基团，因而为一元酸。在 H_3PO_3 分子结构中，有两个—OH基团，因而为二元酸。

15.63 $H_4P_2O_7$ 的结构式为

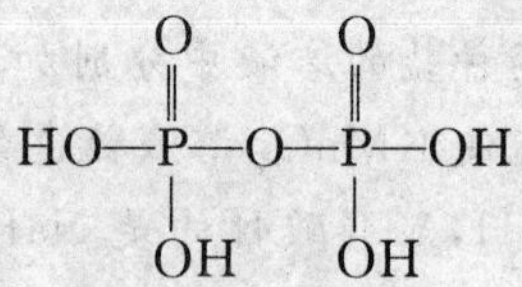

解离出第一个 H^+ 和第二个 H^+ 是从两个不同的磷氧四面体失去 H^+，二者解离时互相影响不大，因此，$K_1^\ominus$ 与 $K_2^\ominus$ 相差不大。但解离出第三个 H^+ 时，是从失去一个 H^+ 并带负电的四面体上再解离出第二个 H^+，显然困难得多。因而 $K_2^\ominus$ 与 $K_3^\ominus$ 相差极大。同

理，$K_3^{\ominus}$ 与 $K_4^{\ominus}$ 相近。

15.64 向 $SbCl_5$ 溶液中通入 H_2S 时，伴随 Sb_2S_5 的生成溶液的酸度提高，Sb^{5+} 氧化能力提高而与 H_2S 发生氧化还原反应，有 Sb_2S_3 和 S 沉淀生成。

$$2Sb^{5+} + 5H_2S \longrightarrow Sb_2S_5 \downarrow + 10H^+$$
$$2Sb^{5+} + 5H_2S \longrightarrow Sb_2S_3 \downarrow + 2S \downarrow + 10H^+$$

若制较纯的 Sb_2S_5，应在碱性条件先得到 SbS_4^{3-}，再小心加入稀酸即可。

$$2Sb^{5+} + 5S^{2-} \longrightarrow Sb_2S_5 \downarrow$$
$$Sb_2S_5 + 3S^{2-} \longrightarrow 2[SbS_4]^{3-}$$
$$2[SbS_4]^{3-} + 6H^+ \longrightarrow Sb_2S_5 \downarrow + 3H_2S$$

15.65 氧化能力：

$$BiO_3^- > NO_3^- > SbO_4^{3-} > AsO_4^{3-} > PO_4^{3-}$$

在氮族的五价化合物中，随周期数增加，元素 R 的半径增大，R—O 键强度减弱，则氧化能力增强。由于 Bi(Ⅴ)的惰性电子对效应，其氧化性最强且有一个突跃。而 N(Ⅴ)由于无空的价层 d 轨道，N—O 间不存在 d—pπ 配键使键强变弱，N—O 键易断而有明显的氧化性。

15.66 (1) 虽然 As 与 F 元素的电负性差较大，但由于 As^{3+} 半径小，极化能力强，因此在 AsF_3 中 As 与 F 之间形成共价键，即 AsX_3 都是共价化合物。随着卤素半径的增大，AsX_3 分子间色散力增大，因此化合物熔点顺序满足

$$AsF_3 < AsCl_3 < AsBr_3 < AsI_3$$

(2) Sb^{3+} 半径较大，极化能力较弱。在 SbF_3 分子中 Sb^{3+} 与 F 之间主要形成离子键，SbF_3 熔点较高。其他 SbX_3 分子中 Sb 与 X 间主要形成共价键，化合物的熔点随着卤素的半径增大而升高。

(3) PCl_3 为分子晶体，熔点低；PCl_5 为离子晶体，固态时以 $[PCl_5]^+[PCl_5]^-$ 形式存在。SbF_5 为共价化合物，分子的对称性高，非极性分子，分子间作用力小；而 SbF_3 为离子化合物，因此 SbF_3 熔点比 SbF_5。

15.67 As_2O_3 为酸性氧化物，在水中发生反应：

$$As_2O_3 + 3H_2O \longrightarrow 2H_3AsO_3$$

在盐酸浓度较低时，H^+ 抑制了 H_3AsO_3 的解离，因而随着盐酸浓度的增大，As_2O_3 溶解度降低。当盐酸浓度较大时，HCl 与 As_2O_3 或 H_3AsO_3 反应生成易溶的$[AsCl_4]^-$：

$$H_3AsO_3 + 3HCl \longrightarrow AsCl_3 + 3H_2O$$
$$AsCl_3 + Cl^- \longrightarrow [AsCl_4]^-$$

因而随盐酸浓度增大时，As_2O_3 的溶解度增大。

15.68 A—KH_2PO_4； B—Ag_3PO_4； C—$AgNO_3 + H_3PO_4$； D—$CaHPO_4$。

15.69 A—As_2O_3； B—$AsCl_3$； C—As_2S_3； D—Na_3AsS_3； E—Na_3AsS_4； F—AsO_4^{3-}。

15.70 A—$NaNO_2$； B—$AgNO_2$； C—Ag_2O； D—NO_2；E—$NaNO_2+NaNO_3$；F—O_2。

15.71 A—$AsCl_3$； B—AgCl； C—$[Ag(NH_3)_2]^+$； D—As_2S_3； E—$[AsS_3]^{3-}$；
F—AsO_4^{3-}； G—$MgNH_4AsO_4$； H—Ag_3AsO_4。

15.72 A—AgN_3； B—Ag； C—N_2； D—$AgNO_3$； E—NO； F—AgCl； G—Mg_3N_2；
H—$Mg(OH)_2$； I—NH_3； J—$MgSO_4$； K—Ag_2S； L—$(NH_4)_2S$； M—S。

15.73 A—$BiCl_3$； B—BiOCl； C—$BiCl_3$； D—Bi_2S_3； E—$Bi(OH)_3$； F—Bi； G—AgCl。

第 16 章

一、选择题

16.1 D　16.2 D　16.3 C　16.4 D　16.5 B　16.6 A　16.7 B　16.8 D
16.9 A　16.10 A　16.11 B　16.12 B　16.13 D　16.14 B　16.15 D　16.16 C
16.17 C　16.18 D　16.19 C　16.20 D

二、填空题

16.21 (1) $>$, $>$, $<$, $>$。
(2) $<$, $>$, $<$。

16.22 1.0,2.0,1.5。

16.23 sp^2,sp^3。

16.24 (1) $<$； (2) $>$； (3) $<$； (4) $>$； (5) $>$。

16.25 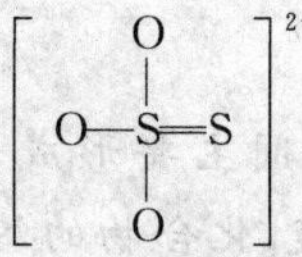； 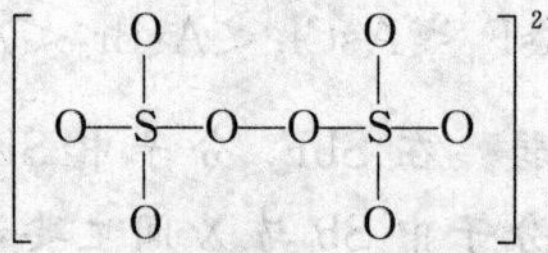；

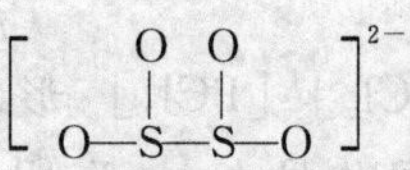　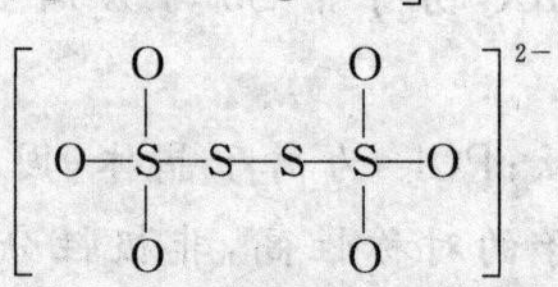。

16.26 Cu^{2+},Ag^+,Hg^{2+},Pb^{2+}。

16.27 NaOH,浓 H_2SO_4。

16.28 ZnS, MnS; SnS; CuS; HgS。

16.29 无,$[Ag(S_2O_3)_2]^{3-}$。白,$Ag_2S_2O_3$,黑,Ag_2S。

16.30 $Na_2S_2O_5+H_2O$, $Na_2SO_4+SO_3+O_2$；
$Na_2SO_4+Na_2S$。

16.31 H_2S被空气中的氧氧化。

16.32 $S_2O_3^{2-}$,$S^{2-}+SO_3^{2-}$,$S_2O_3^{2-}+S^{2-}$,$S_2O_3^{2-}+SO_3^{2-}$。

16.33 (1) PbS； (2) HgS； (3) ZnS； (4) $CuFeS_2$； (5) FeS_2； (6) $Na_2SO_4\cdot10H_2O$；
(7) $Na_2S_2O_3\cdot5H_2O$； (8) $Na_2S_2O_4\cdot2H_2O$。

16.34

$M_2S_2O_{(8)}$	(1)	(5)	(9)
$M_2S_2O_{(3)}$	(2)	(6)	(7)
$M_2S_2O_{(7)}$	(3)	(4)	(8)

16.35 ZnS—白色；MnS—粉红；CdS—黄色；SnS—棕褐色；As_2S_3—黄色；As_2S_5—黄色；Sb_2S_3—橙色；Sb_2S_5—橙色；$Ag_2S_2O_3$—白色；PbS_2O_3—白色。

三、完成并配平下列反应方程式

16.36 $H_2S+H_2O_2 = S\downarrow+2H_2O$

$H_2S+4H_2O_2 = H_2SO_4+4H_2O$

16.37 $3H_2S+ClO_3^- = 3S\downarrow+Cl^-+3H_2O$

$3H_2S+4ClO_3^- = 3SO_4^{2-}+4Cl^-+6H^+$

16.38 $2S^{2-}+SO_3^{2-}+6H^+ = 3S\downarrow+3H_2O$

16.39 $2Na_2S_2O_3+I_2 = Na_2S_4O_6+2NaI$

16.40 $SO_2+2H_2O+Cl_2 = H_2SO_4+2HCl$

16.41 $5H_2O_2+2MnO_4^-+6H^+ = 2Mn^{2+}+5O_2+8H_2O$

16.42 $4O_3+PbS = PbSO_4+4O_2$

16.43 $S_2O_3^{2-}+4Cl_2+5H_2O = 2SO_4^{2-}+8Cl^-+10H^+$

16.44 $4Br_2+H_2S+4H_2O = 8HBr+H_2SO_4$

16.45 $Na_2S_2+2HCl = 2NaCl+S\downarrow+H_2S$

16.46 $Cr_2S_3+6H_2O = 2Cr(OH)_3\downarrow+3H_2S$

16.47 $Na_2O_2+2H_2O$(冷) $= 2NaOH+H_2O_2$

$2Na_2O_2+2H_2O$(热) $= 2NaOH+O_2$

16.48 $O_3+2HI = O_2+I_2+H_2O$

$3O_3+HI = 3O_2+HIO_3$

16.49 $2[Ag(S_2O_3)_2]^{3-}+H_2S+6H^+ = Ag_2S\downarrow+4S\downarrow+4SO_2+4H_2O$

四、简答题

16.50 (1) O_2 的分子轨道式为

$$KK\ \sigma_{2s}^2\ \sigma_{2s}^{*2}\ \sigma_{2p_x}^2\ \pi_{2p_y}^2\ \pi_{2p_z}^2\ \pi_{2p_y}^{*1}\ \pi_{2p_z}^{*1}$$

可见 O_2 分子中有 2 个单电子，因而具有顺磁性。而 O_3 为反磁性，因 O_3 分子中无单电子。

O_3分子结构

O_3 分子中的 Π_3^4 能级图

(2) SO_2Cl_2 分子中，S—Cl 单键，键能小，易解离生成稳定的 S—O 键，因此，SO_2Cl_2 易发生水解反应：

$$SO_2Cl_2+2H_2O = H_2SO_4+2HCl$$

SF_6 分子为正八面体，分子的对称性高，不利于 H_2O 分子的进攻，因此，SF_6 分子不易水解。

(3) O_3 分子有 Π_3^4 离域键，O—O 键级为 1.5；而 O_2 分子结构O═O，O—O键级为 2.0。O_3 比 O_2 氧化能力强。原因有：① O_3 中 O—O 键级比 O_2 的小；② O_3 分子对称性比O_2 差。

16.51 O_2F_2 分子结构：

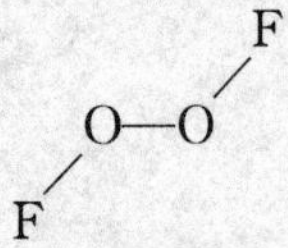

两个 O 为 sp^3 杂化

两个 O 与两个 F 不在同一平面

由于 F 的电负性大于 O，则 O 周围的电子密度降低使 O 有一定的正电性，两个 O 原子对共用电子对的引力变大，因而 O_2F_2 中 O—O 键变短。

16.52 (1) SO_2：Π_3^4 SO_3：Π_4^6 O_3：Π_3^4

(2) SO_3 为 H_2SO_4 的酸酐，SO_3 溶于水即得 H_2SO_4：

$$SO_3+H_2O = H_2SO_4$$

发烟硫酸是指浓硫酸吸收 SO_3 后，硫酸中有颜色，而且上部有烟雾。即硫酸中含有过量的 SO_3，则为发烟硫酸。

(3) $SOCl_2$ 分子的结构为

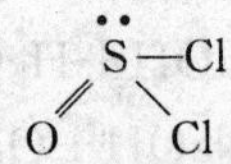

分子中的中心原子有孤对电子，能给出电子对，故可做 Lewis 碱。

分子的中心原子 S 有空的价层 d 轨道，又可以接受电子对，因此 $SOCl_2$ 又可做电子对接受体，为 Lewis 酸。

(4) 分子中 S—O 键强度：$SOF_2 > SOCl_2 > SOBr_2$

三个化合物的结构均为三角锥形，S 为中心原子，中心原子上有一孤对电子。

分子构型为

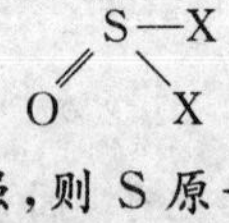

① X 电负性越大，吸引电子能力越强，则 S 原子周围的电子密度越低，硫的正电性高，S 对 O 的极化作用越强，S—O 键共价成分越大，键越短，故 S—O 键越强。

② S—O 间存在 d—p 反馈 π 键，S 周围电子密度小，吸引氧的反馈电子能力强，S—O 间键越强。

元素电负性 F>Cl>Br

分子中 S 周围电子密度 $SOF_2<SOCl_2<SOBr_2$

16.53 制备 H_2S 一般采用 FeS 或 Na_2S 与稀 H_2SO_4 或浓 H_3PO_4 反应，在通风橱中收集 H_2S 气体。由此可以判断 H_2S 有以下性质。

(1) 易挥发性和溶解度较小

H_2S 在水中溶解度较小且易挥发，因而用稀硫酸就可以放出 H_2S 气体。

(2) 强还原性

在制 H_2S 时不能用浓硫酸，因浓硫酸可将 H_2S 氧化：

$$H_2SO_4 + H_2S = S\downarrow + SO_2 + 2H_2O$$

(3) 毒性

H_2S 有毒，制备 H_2S 必须在通风橱内进行，并应对逸出的尾气进行吸收。

16.54 取少量试剂分别与稀盐酸作用。

(1) 无任何反应现象的是 Na_2SO_4；

(2) 有刺激性气体放出，但无沉淀生成的是 Na_2SO_3 或 $Na_2S_2O_6$：

$$SO_3^{2-} + 2H^+ = SO_2 + H_2O$$
$$S_2O_6^{2-} = SO_4^{2-} + SO_2$$

再滴加 $BaCl_2$，有白色沉淀生成的应是 $Na_2S_2O_6$，另一个为 Na_2SO_3；

(3) 有刺激性气体放出，同时有沉淀析出的是 $Na_2S_2O_3$。

$$S_2O_3^{2-} + 2H^+ = SO_2 + S\downarrow + H_2O$$

16.55 分别取少量溶液加入稀盐酸，产生的气体能使 $Pb(Ac)_2$ 试纸变黑的溶液为 Na_2S；产生有刺激性气体，但不使 $Pb(Ac)_2$ 试纸变黑的是 Na_2SO_3；产生刺激性气体同时有乳白色沉淀生成的溶液是 $Na_2S_2O_3$；无任何变化的则是 Na_2SO_4 和 $Na_2S_2O_8$，将这两种溶液酸化加入 KI 溶液，有 I_2 生成的是 $Na_2S_2O_8$ 溶液，另一溶液为 Na_2SO_4。

有关反应方程式：

$$S^{2-} + 2H^+ = H_2S\uparrow$$
$$H_2S + Pb^{2+} = PbS\downarrow(\text{黑}) + 2H^+$$
$$SO_3^{2-} + 2H^+ = SO_2 + H_2O$$
$$S_2O_3^{2-} + 2H^+ = SO_2 + S\downarrow + H_2O$$
$$S_2O_8^{2-} + 2I^- = 2SO_4^{2-} + I_2$$

16.56 将硫黄粉、石灰及水混合，煮沸制石硫合剂过程中发生如下反应：

$$CaO + H_2O = Ca(OH)_2$$
$$3S + 3Ca(OH)_2 = 2CaS + CaSO_3 + 3H_2O$$

过量的 S 粉与 CaS 进一步反应，生成多硫化物：

$$(x-1)S + CaS = CaS_x(\text{橙色})$$

CaS_x 为橙色，并随着 x 值升高显樱桃红色。

此外，过程中还发生以下反应：

$$S + CaSO_3 \xlongequal{\quad} CaS_2O_3$$

16.57 (1) 离子分离方案见图(a)或(b)。

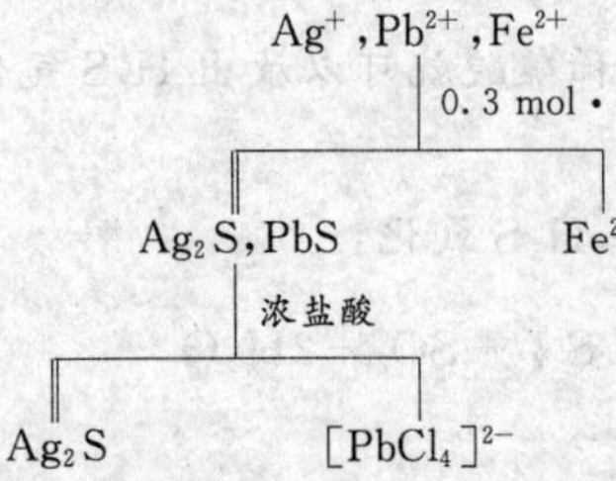

(a)

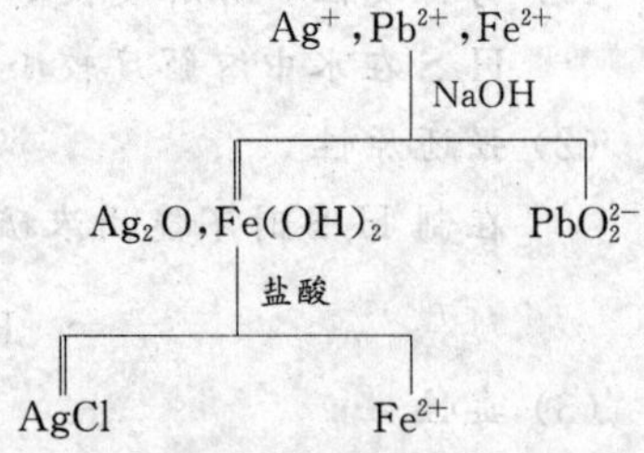

(b)

(2) 离子分离方案见图(c)。

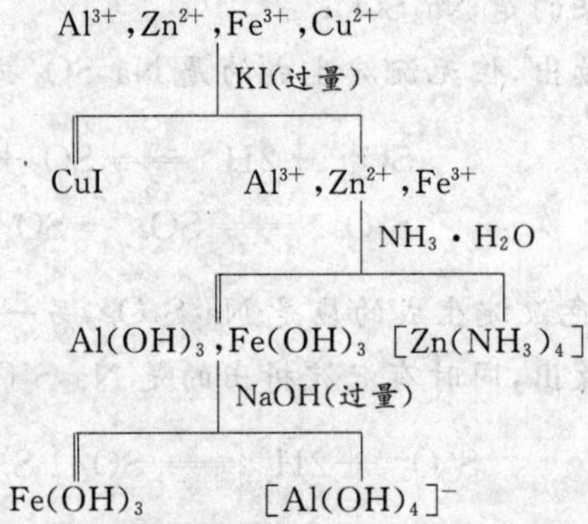

(c)

16.58 $NaHSO_3$ 受热，分子间脱水得焦亚硫酸钠：

$$2NaHSO_3 \xlongequal{\triangle} Na_2S_2O_5 + H_2O$$

由于 $NaHSO_3$ 受热易缩水，故不能用加热浓缩的方法制备亚硫酸氢钠。

16.59 根据价层电子对互斥理论：SOF_2 和 $SOCl_2$ 中

中心 S 原子：4 对电子，电子对构型：正四面体，配体数：3

所以，SOF_2 和 $SOCl_2$ 的空间构型为：三角锥形

SOF_2 和 $SOCl_2$ 分子中，中心 S 原子采取 sp^3 不等性杂化，如图。

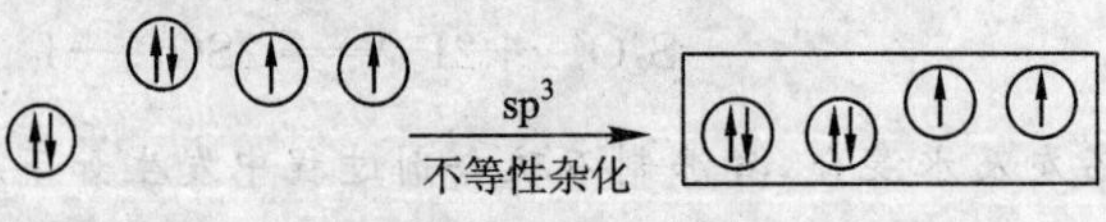

其中含有单电子的杂化轨道分别与两个卤素原子形成 σ 键。

端基配体中 O 原子的电子发生重排，由 $2p_x^2 2p_y^1 2p_z^1$ 变成 $2p_x^2 2p_y^2 2p_z^0$，即空出一条 2p 轨道，接受中心 Ssp^3 杂化轨道中的对电子，形成 σ 配键。同时中心 S 原子具有空的 3d 轨道，可以接受端基 O 原子的 p 轨道中的对电子，形成反馈 π 键。这个反馈键，就对称性而言属于 π 键，且是 d 轨道和 p 轨道的重叠，就电子对的来源属于配位键，故称为 d—pπ 配键。

在 SOF_2 和 $SOCl_2$ 分子中，F 原子的电负性比 Cl 原子的大，吸电子的能力强，使得

中心S原子更易于接受端基O原子中对电子的配入。故 SOF_2 分子中的 d—pπ 键比 $SOCl_2$ 分子中的强。

16.60　A—$CaO_2 \cdot 2H_2O$；　B—CaO_2；　C—CaO；　D—KI_3 或 I_2；　E—$I^- + IO_3^-$；　F—$CaIO_3$。

16.61　A—$(NH_4)_2S_2O_8$；　B—NH_3；　C—$[Ag(NH_3)_2]^+$；　D—AgCl；　E—$BaSO_4$。

16.62　A—KI；　B—H_2SO_4(浓)；　C—I_2；　D—H_2S；　E—KI_3；　F—$KIO_3 + KI$；　G—PbS；H—S。

16.63　A—$[Ag(S_2O_3)_2]^{3-}$；　B—SO_2；　C—AgI+S；　D—$[Ag(CN)_2]^-$；　E—Ag_2S；F—AgI。

16.64　A—Na_2SO_3；　B—SO_2；　C—SO_4^{2-}；　D—$Na_2SO_4 + Na_2S$；　E—CuS；F—$BaSO_4$。

第17章

一、选择题

17.1 C　17.2 D　17.3 D　17.4 C　17.5 B　17.6 A　17.7 B　17.8 C
17.9 B　17.10 B　17.11 C　17.12 C

二、填空题

17.13　Cl,F_2。

17.14　(1) CaF_2;(2) Na_3AlF_6;(3) $Ca_5F(PO_4)_3$;(4) $KCl \cdot MgCl_2 \cdot 6H_2O$;(5) $COCl_2$。

17.15　B,A,C,D。

17.16　$Ca(ClO_3)_2$ $CaCl_2$,NaBr $NaBrO_3$ CO_2,$NaIO_3$,NaI。

17.17　KCl,KF。

17.18　F原子半径,H—F键的解离能。

17.19　(1) $<$,(2) $<$,(3) $>$,(4) $<$。

17.20　增大。

17.21　$<$,$>$。

17.22　HClO,HIO_3。

17.23　Cl_2O_7,氧化,爆炸分解。

17.24　五,中强,正八面体,sp^3d^2,氧化。

17.25　V字形;短;ClO_2 分子中的 Cl—O 键级大于1,Cl_2O 分子中 Cl—O 键级等于1。

三、完成并配平反应方程式

17.26　$F_2 + BrO_3^- + 2OH^- = BrO_4^- + 2F^- + H_2O$

17.27　$ClO^- + Mn^{2+} + 2OH^- = MnO_2 \downarrow + Cl^- + H_2O$

17.28　$3Cl_2 + 3Na_2CO_3 \xlongequal{\triangle} NaClO_3 + 5NaCl + 3CO_2$

17.29　$I_2O_5 + 10I^- + 10H^+ = 6I_2 + 5H_2O$

17.30　$2FeI_2 + 3Cl_2 = 2FeCl_3 + 2I_2$

$I_2 + 5Cl_2 + 6H_2O \longrightarrow 2HIO_3 + 10HCl$

17.31 $2CrI_3 + 6ClO^- + 4OH^- \longrightarrow 2CrO_4^{2-} + 3I_2 + 6Cl^- + 2H_2O$

17.32 $2CuO + 4HI \longrightarrow 2CuI\downarrow + I_2 + 2H_2O$

17.33 $Cl_2 + KIO_3 + 2KOH \longrightarrow KIO_4 + 2KCl + H_2O$

17.34 KI 过量：

$$2I^- + ClO^- + H_2O \longrightarrow I_2 + Cl^- + 2OH^-$$

KClO 过量：

$$I_2 + 5ClO^- + 2OH^- \longrightarrow 2IO_3^- + 5Cl^- + H_2O$$

$$I_2 + 10ClO^- + 4H_2O \longrightarrow 2IO_3^- + 5Cl_2 + 8OH^-$$

17.35 $ClO^- + Cl^- + 2H^+ \longrightarrow Cl_2 + H_2O$

17.36 $ClO^- + Mn^{2+} + 2OH^- \longrightarrow Cl^- + MnO_2 + H_2O$

四、简答题

17.37 氟的半径特别的小，因而其 F^- 电子密度较大，生成氟离子时，放出的能量较少。

F_2 比 Cl_2 活泼，原因是 F 的半径小，氟原子非键电子对之间斥力较大而使 F_2 的解离能比 Cl_2 小，氟化物的晶格能比氯大，能量更低。其次，在水溶液中，F^- 的水合热比 Cl^- 大得多。

17.38 先有 I_2 生成，溶液由无色变黄、变橙、变棕直至析出紫黑色沉淀，最后紫黑色沉淀消失得无色溶液。

$$Cl_2 + 2KI \longrightarrow 2KCl + I_2$$

$$5Cl_2 + I_2 + 6H_2O \longrightarrow 2HIO_3 + 10HCl$$

17.39 (1) $BeCl_2\cdot 4H_2O \xlongequal{\triangle} BeO\downarrow + 2HCl\uparrow + 3H_2O$

(2) $MgCl_2\cdot 6H_2O \xlongequal{\triangle} Mg(OH)Cl\downarrow + HCl\downarrow + 5H_2O$

(3) $CaCl_2\cdot 6H_2O \xlongequal{\triangle} CaCl_2 + 6H_2O$

(4) $FeCl_3\cdot 6H_2O \xlongequal{\triangle} Fe(OH)Cl_2\downarrow + HCl\uparrow + 5H_2O$

17.40 室温下浓盐酸与 MnO_2 反应速率慢，制备 Cl_2 时需要加热，停止加热则反应速率很快降下来，因此该法优点是便于随制随停；另外，MnO_2 价格比 $KMnO_4$ 便宜，制备成本低。用浓盐酸与 $KMnO_4$ 反应制备 Cl_2 优点是不需要加热，但反应速率不易控制，不能随制随停；另外，$KMnO_4$ 价格比 MnO_2 贵，制备成本高。

17.41 (1) $4HCl(浓) + MnO_2 \xlongequal{\triangle} MnCl_2 + Cl_2 + 2H_2O$

$2Cl_2 + H_2O + CaCO_3 \longrightarrow CaCl_2 + CO_2 + 2HClO$

或 $2Cl_2 + H_2O + HgO \longrightarrow HgCl_2 + 2HClO$

(2) 电解 KCl 溶液，得到 KOH 和 Cl_2

$$2KCl + 2H_2O \xlongequal{电解} Cl_2 + 2KOH + H_2$$

电极不用隔膜，加热后 Cl_2 歧化得到 $KClO_3$

$$3Cl_2+6KOH \xlongequal{} 5KCl+KClO_3+3H_2O$$

用 MnO_2 做催化剂，加热分解 $KClO_3$ 得 O_2

$$2KClO_3 \xlongequal[\triangle]{MnO_2} 2KCl+3O_2$$

17.42 如果将红磷与 Br_2 混合，立即有易挥发的 PBr_3 生成，且反应放热而难以控制反应速率，不利于制备 HBr 气体。将红磷与 H_2O 混合后滴加 Br_2，可以通过滴加 Br_2 的速度控制反应；同时，生成的 PBr_3 立即水解生成 HBr，有利于制备 HBr 气体。

17.43 由于 I_2 在 KI 溶液中的浓度不同，溶液的颜色不同。按照浓度由低到高，溶液可以是黄色、橙色、红色、棕色。

17.44 (1) 向 KI 溶液中滴加 H_2O_2 溶液

溶液由无色变黄

$$H_2O_2+3I^-+2H^+ \xlongequal{} I_3^-+2H_2O$$

随着 H_2O_2 加入溶液颜色加深。

当 H_2O_2 过量时，有灰黑色沉淀生成，溶液变近无色

$$H_2O_2+2I_3^-+2H^- \xlongequal{} 3I_2+2H_2O$$

因 I^- 全部被 H_2O_2 氧化，I_2 在水中溶解度很小，生成 I_2 沉淀。

(2) 开始时 HIO_3 过量，生成的 I_2 不再反应，I_2 与淀粉作用显蓝色

$$2IO_3^-+5SO_3^{2-}+2H^+ \xlongequal{} I_2+5SO_4^{2-}+H_2O \quad 蓝色溶液$$

直至加入 Na_2SO_3 溶液过量时，溶液蓝色消失变无色

$$I_2+SO_3^{2-}+H_2O \xlongequal{} I^-+SO_4^{2-}+2H^+ \quad 无色溶液$$

(3) 开始时 Na_2SO_3 过量，HIO_3 还原产物为 I^-，溶液为无色

$$IO_3^-+3SO_3^{2-} \xlongequal{} I^-+3SO_4^{2-} \quad 无色溶液$$

直至加入 HIO_3 溶液过量时，溶液变蓝色

$$IO_3^-+5I^-+6H^+ \xlongequal{} 3I_2+3H_2O \quad 蓝色溶液$$

17.45 (1) 可将含有 ICl 和 IBr 的 I_2 与 KI 共热，发生如下反应：

$$ICl+KI \xlongequal{\triangle} KCl+I_2$$

$$IBr+KI \xlongequal{\triangle} KBr+I_2$$

这种反应进行的方向是生成晶格能大的物质，由于 KCl 和 KBr 的晶格能大于 KI，所以可以将 ICl 和 IBr 中的 I 元素游离出来。在加热的过程中 I_2 升华，与 KCl，KBr 分离得以纯化。

(2) 将样品溶于水，通少许 Cl_2 气，NaBr 将被 Cl_2 氧化：

$$NaBr+Cl_2 \xlongequal{} NaCl+Br_2$$

向溶液中加些许 CCl_4，振荡，过量的 Cl_2 和生成的 Br_2 溶解在 CCl_4 层。用分液漏斗进行分离。浓缩水相，结晶得纯净的 NaCl。

(3) 取三种粉末分别置于试管中，用 H_2O 溶解后滴加 $AgNO_3$ 溶液。根据生成的卤化银的颜色和溶解性可区别三种样品：

生成白色沉淀，且沉淀可溶于稀氨水，则为 NaCl。

生成浅黄色沉淀，且沉淀可溶于 $Na_2S_2O_3$ 溶液，则样品为 NaBr。

生成黄色沉淀，且沉淀不溶于 $Na_2S_2O_3$ 溶液，则样品为 NaI。

(4) 将固体样品溶于 H_2SO_4 中，并加入少许 $MnSO_4$ 稀溶液，微热，溶液显紫色的是 K_5IO_6，余下的为 $KClO_4$。K_5IO_6 氧化 Mn^{2+} 的方程式为：

$$2Mn^{2+} + 5H_5IO_6 \xlongequal{\triangle} 2MnO_4^- + 5IO_3^- + 11H^+ + 7H_2O$$

17.46 向四支试管中分别加入少许 CCl_4 和 $KMnO_4$，CCl_4 层变黄或橙色的是 HBr，CCl_4 层变紫的是 HI，CCl_4 层不变色，但 $KMnO_4$ 褪色或颜色变浅的是 HCl，无明显变化的是 H_2SO_4。本题也可由生成沉淀的实验加以鉴别。

17.47 漂白粉中的有效成分是 $Ca(ClO)_2$，在空气中易吸收 CO_2 生成 HClO

$$Ca(ClO)_2 + CO_2 + H_2O \xlongequal{} CaCO_3 + 2HClO$$

HClO 不稳定，易分解放出 O_2：

$$2HClO \xlongequal{} HCl + O_2$$

此外，生成的 HCl 与 $Ca(ClO)_2$ 作用产生 Cl_2 放出也消耗漂白粉的有效成分。

$$HCl + HClO \xlongequal{} H_2O + Cl_2$$

漂白粉中往往含有 $CaCl_2$ 杂质，吸收 CO_2 的 $Ca(ClO)_2$ 也与 $CaCl_2$ 作用：

$$Ca(ClO)_2 + 2CO_2 + CaCl_2 \xlongequal{} 2CaCO_3 + 2Cl_2$$

17.48 可用两种方法加以鉴别。

(1) 分别取少许固体加入干燥的试管中，再分别进行如下实验。

加入稀盐酸即有 Cl_2 气放出的是 KClO：

$$KClO + 2HCl \xlongequal{} KCl + Cl_2 + H_2O$$

加入浓盐酸有 Cl_2 放出且溶液变黄的是 $KClO_3$：

$$8KClO_3 + 24HCl(浓) \xlongequal{} 9Cl_2 + 8KCl + 6ClO_2(黄) + 12H_2O$$

另一种则为 $KClO_4$。

(2) 分别取少许固体加水溶解，几乎不溶于水的是 $KClO_4$。再进行如下实验。

加入 KI 溶液有 I_2 析出的是 KClO：

$$ClO^- + 2I^- + H_2O \xlongequal{} Cl^- + I_2 + 2OH^-$$

加入 KI 溶液不变，再加少许 H_2SO_4 酸化后有 I_2 生成的是 $KClO_3$：

$$ClO_3^- + 6I^- + 6H^+ \xlongequal{} 3I_2 + Cl^- + 3H_2O$$

17.49 稳定性 $KI_3 > KIBr_2 > KI_2Br$。阳离子相同，多卤阴离子的对称性越高，中心原子越大，则多卤阴离子越稳定。I_3^-，IBr_2^- 和 I_2Br^- 都是直线形结构，显然 $[I—I—Br]^-$ 对称性最低，稳定性最差；而$[I—I—I]^-$对称性比$[Br—I—Br]^-$高，因此I_3^-最稳定。

17.50 (1) 前者KI过量，生成的I_3不再反应，溶液显黄色；后者KClO过量，生成的I_2进一步被氧化为IO_3^-，溶液为无色。

(2) 前者H^+浓度低，$KClO_3$与HCl不反应；后者H^+浓度高，$KClO_3$与HCl反应生成黄色的ClO_2，所以溶液变黄：

$$8KClO_3+24HCl = 9Cl_2+8KCl+6ClO_2+12H_2O$$

(3) $E^\ominus(Fe^{3+}/Fe^{2+})=0.771\ V$，$E^\ominus(I_2/I^-)=0.535\ V$。由于$E^\ominus(I_2/I^-)<E^\ominus(Fe^{3+}/Fe^{2+})$，碘水不能氧化$Fe^{2+}$。因而向$FeSO_4$溶液中加入碘水时，碘水不褪色。加入$NH_4F$溶液后，$F^-$与$Fe^{3+}$生成稳定的配合物使$Fe^{2+}$的还原性增强，碘水褪色：

$$I_2+2Fe^{2+}+12F^- = 2I^-+2[FeF_6]^{3-}$$

17.51

	ClF_3	BrF_5	IBr	IF_7	$[ICl_4]^-$
中心价层电子对数	5	6	4	7	6
中心价层孤电子对数	2	1	3	0	2
中心原子杂化轨道	sp^3d	sp^3d^2	sp^3	sp^3d^3	sp^3d^2
分子或离子的空间结构	T字形	四角锥	直线形	五角双锥	正方形

17.52 A—NaCl； B—HCl； C—Cl_2； D—NaBr； E—Br_2； F—NaBr和$NaBrO_3$。

17.53 A—NaI； B—NaClO。

17.54 A为HIO_3，B为I_2O_5。

17.55 A为KBr。

第18章

一、选择题

18.1 A 18.2 C 18.3 C 18.4 B 18.5 D 18.6 B 18.7 C 18.8 C
18.9 B

二、填空题

18.10 H_3O^+。

18.11 氕，氘，氚，H，D，T。

18.12 水蒸气，炭层，水煤气，水蒸气，氧化铜，水，CO_2。

18.13 氦，氖，氩。

18.14 $XeOF_4$，XeO_3。

18.15 氩。

三、完成并配平下列反应方程式。

18.16 $KH+H_2O \longrightarrow KOH+H_2\uparrow$

18.17 $TiCl_4+4NaH \xrightarrow{高温} Ti+4NaCl+2H_2\uparrow$

18.18 $UO_2+CaH_2 \xrightarrow{高温} U+2Ca(OH)_2$

18.19 $2CO_2+BaH_2 \xrightarrow{高温} 2CO+Ba(OH)_2$

18.20 $LiAlH_4+4H_2O \longrightarrow Al(OH)_3+LiOH+4H_2\uparrow$

18.21 $5Na_4XeO_6+8MnSO_4+2H_2O \longrightarrow 5Xe+8NaMnO_4+6Na_2SO_4+2H_2SO_4$

18.22 $XeF_4+2ClO_3^-+2H_2O \longrightarrow Xe\uparrow+2ClO_4^-+4HF$

18.23 $XeF_2+IF_5 \longrightarrow IF_7+Xe\uparrow$

18.24 $XeF_4+2CF_3CF{=}CF_2 \longrightarrow 2CF_3CF_2CF_3+Xe\uparrow$

18.25 $XeF_4+2SF_4 \longrightarrow 2SF_6+Xe\uparrow$

18.26 $2XeF_6+SiO_2 \longrightarrow 2XeOF_4+SiF_4\uparrow$

四、简答题

18.27 稀有气体的第一电离能($I_1/kJ\cdot mol^{-1}$)分别为:He 2 372.3,Ne 2 080.7,Ar 1 520.6,Kr 1 350.7,Xe 1 170.3,Rn 1 037.1。由于He、Ne、Ar的电离能大,其化合物极难制得;而且化合物稳定性差,必须在低温下保存。Rn放射性强,半衰期很短。所以,对Xe以外的化合物研究较少。

18.28 氙的氟化物可以由两种单质直接化合生成。合成XeF_2的反应为

$$Xe(g)+F_2(g) \longrightarrow XeF_2(g)$$

要保证Xe大过量,避免XeF_4的生成,以确保XeF_2占主要地位。

合成XeF_4的反应为

$$Xe(g)+2F_2(g) \longrightarrow XeF_4(g)$$

要保证F_2过量,注意反应时间不要太长,避免XeF_6的生成,以确保XeF_4占主要地位。

合成XeF_6的反应为

$$Xe(g)+3F_2(g) \longrightarrow XeF_6(g)$$

要保证F_2大过量,且要保证反应时间长,这样可以保证XeF_6的大量生成。

18.29 (1) XeF_2 中心原子价层共5对电子对,Xe采用sp^3d杂化,电子对构型为三角双锥形。三对孤电子对占据在三角形上的位置,XeF_2分子构型为直线形,见下图(a)。

(2) XeF_4 中心原子价层中共有6对电子对,Xe采用sp^3d^2杂化,电子对构型为正八面体形。两个孤电子对占据两个相对的顶点,XeF_4分子构型为正方形,见下图(b)。

(3) XeF_6 XeF_6的结构很难用价层电子对理论预测。XeF_6中Xe采用sp^3d^3杂化,6个F原子位于八面体的6个顶点,而一个孤电子对伸向一个棱的中点,见下图(c)。

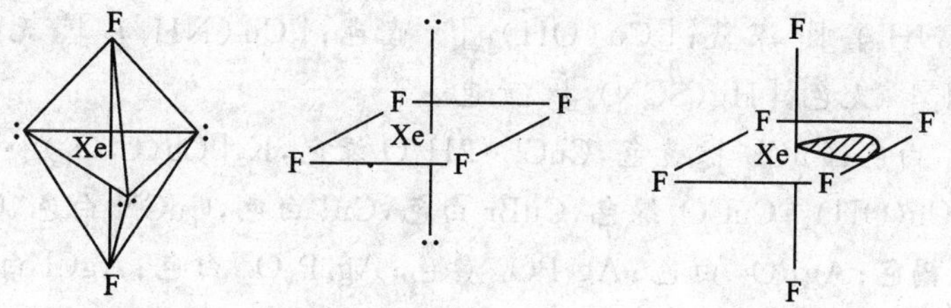

(a) XeF_2　　(b) XeF_4　　(c) XeF_6

(4) XeO_3　XeO_3 分子中有 4 对电子对，Xe 采用 sp^3 杂化，电子对构型为正四面体形。一个孤电子对占据一个四面体的顶点，XeO_3 分子构型为三角锥形。

(5) $XeOF_4$　$XeOF_4$ 分子中有 6 对电子对，Xe 采用 sp^3d^2 杂化，电子对构型为正八面体形。一个孤电子对占据一个八面体的顶点，$XeOF_4$ 分子构型为四角锥形。

第 19 章

一、选择题

19.1 C　19.2 C　19.3 B　19.4 D　19.5 A　19.6 B　19.7 C　19.8 B
19.9 B　19.10 B　19.11 A　19.12 C

二、填空题

19.13 (1) $CuFeS_2$；(2) Cu_2S；(3) Cu_2O；(4) CuO；(5) $CuCO_3 \cdot Cu(OH)_2$；(6) $CuSO_4 \cdot 5H_2O$；(7) ZnS；(8) $ZnCO_3$；(9) HgS；(10) ZnO；(11) $ZnS \cdot BaSO_4$；(12) CdS；(13) Hg_2Cl_2；(14) $HgCl_2$。

19.14 Cu—Zn，Cu—Zn—Sn，Cu—Ni。

19.15 Ag_3PO_4。

19.16 直线形，sp；$HgNH_2Cl + Hg$。

19.17 晶粒大小发生了变化；晶体出现了缺陷。

19.18 氨水。

19.19 歧化，$2Cu^+ \longrightarrow Cu^{2+} + Cu$。沉淀，配合物，CuI 和 Cu_2O，$[Cu(CN)_2]^-$ 或 $[CuCl_2]^-$。

19.20 歧化，沉淀剂，配合剂。$Hg_2(NO_3)_2$。

19.21 Hg_2Cl_2 见光分解为有毒的 $HgCl_2$ 和 Hg。

19.22

试液 / 产物与现象 / 试剂	NaCl	Na_2S	$K_2Cr_2O_7$	$Na_2S_2O_3$	K_2HPO_4
$AgNO_3$	$AgCl\downarrow$ 白色	$Ag_2S\downarrow$ 黑色	$Ag_2CrO_4\downarrow$ 砖红	$Ag_2S_2O_3\downarrow \rightarrow Ag_2S$ 白→黑	$Ag_3PO_4\downarrow$ 黄色

19.23 $[Cu(H_2O)_4]^{2+}$ 蓝色；$[CuCl_4]^{2-}$ 黄色；$[Cu(CN)_4]^{3-}$ 无色；$[CuCl_2]^-$ 无色；

$[Cu(NH_3)_4]^{2+}$深蓝；$[Cu(OH)_4]^{2-}$蓝色；$[Cu(NH_3)_2]^+$无色；$[CuCN_4]^{2-}$黄色，$[HgI_4]^{2-}$无色，$[Hg(SCN)_4]^{2-}$无色。

19.24 $CuSO_4$ 白色；$CuCl_2$ 棕黄色，$CuCl_2\cdot 2H_2O$ 绿色，$K_2[Cu(C_2O_4)]\cdot 2H_2O$ 蓝色，$Cu(OH)_2$ 淡蓝；$Cu(OH)_2\cdot CuCO_3$ 绿色，CuBr 白色，CuI 白色，CuCN 白色，CuO 棕黑；Cu_2O 红色；Ag_2O 褐色；$AgPO_3$ 白色；Ag_3PO_4 黄色；$Ag_4P_2O_7$ 白色；AgCl 白色，AgBr 浅黄色，AgI 黄色，$Ag_2S_2O_3$ 白色，$Zn[Hg(SCN)_4]$白色。ZnO 白色；ZnS 白色；CdO 暗棕；HgO 黄(或红)色；Hg_2Cl_2 白色，Hg_2I_2 黄色，HgI_2 红色。

19.25 (1) $>$,$>$；(2) $<$,$>$；(3) $>$,$>$。

三、完成并配平下列反应方程式

19.26 $2CuCl_2+NaHSO_3+H_2O = 2CuCl\downarrow+NaHSO_4+2HCl$

19.27 $2Cu^{2+}+4CN^- = 2CuCN\downarrow+(CN)_2$

$CuCN+CN^- = [Cu(CN)_2]^-$

19.28 $2Cu+O_2+CO_2+H_2O = Cu(OH)_2\cdot CuCO_3$

19.29 $4CuCl+O_2 = 2CuCl_2\cdot CuO$

19.30 $[Sn(OH)_4]^{2-}+2Ag^++2OH^- = [Sn(OH)_6]^{2-}+2Ag\downarrow$

19.31 $2AgNO_3+H_3PO_3+H_2O = 2Ag\downarrow+H_3PO_4+2HNO_3$

19.32 $[Ag(S_2O_3)_2]^{3-}+8Cl_2+10H_2O = AgCl\downarrow+15Cl^-+4SO_4^{2-}+20H^+$

19.33 $ZnCl_2+H_2O = H[ZnCl_2(OH)]$

$FeO+2H[ZnCl_2(OH)] = Fe[ZnCl_2(OH)]_2+H_2O$

19.34 $Zn+2OH^-+2H_2O = [Zn(OH)_4]^{2-}+H_2\uparrow$

19.35 $Hg(NO_3)_2+Hg = Hg_2(NO_3)_2$

$Hg_2(NO_3)_2+2HCl = Hg_2Cl_2\downarrow+2HNO_3$

19.36 $Hg_2Cl_2+2NH_3 = HgNH_2Cl\downarrow+Hg+NH_4Cl$

19.37 $HgO+2HI = HgI_2\downarrow+H_2O$

$HgI_2+2HI = H_2[HgI_4]$

19.38 $Ag_2O+2HCl = 2AgCl\downarrow+H_2O$

19.39 $3HgS+2Al+8OH^- = 3Hg\downarrow+2[Al(OH)_4]^-+3S^{2-}$

19.40 $Hg_2^{2+}+2OH^- = HgO\downarrow+Hg\downarrow+H_2O$

四、简答题和计算题

19.41 (1) Cu^{2+} 极化能力较强，而 HCl 为挥发性酸，$CuCl_2\cdot 2H_2O$ 受热时发生水解，因而得不到无水 $CuCl_2$。

$$CuCl_2\cdot 2H_2O \xlongequal{\triangle} Cu(OH)Cl+H_2O\uparrow+HCl\uparrow$$

$$Cu(OH)Cl \xlongequal{\triangle} CuO+HCl\uparrow$$

(2) 因 $H_2C_2O_4$ 酸性比 HCl 弱得多，而 Cl^- 与 Hg^{2+} 生成的配合物较稳定，因而 HgC_2O_4

溶于盐酸：

$$HgC_2O_4+4HCl \longrightarrow H_2[HgCl_4]+H_2C_2O_4$$

(3) NH_4NO_3 存在时，抑制了 NH_2^- 的生成，同时，$HgNH_2NO_3$ 溶解度较大，因而不能生成 $HgNH_2NO_3$ 沉淀，而生成了稳定的配合物$[Hg(NH_3)_4]^{2+}$：

$$Hg(NO_3)_2+4NH_3 \xlongequal{NH_4NO_3} [Hg(NH_3)_4]^{2+}+2NO_3^-$$

另外，向 $Hg(NO_3)_2$ 溶液中加入 NH_4Cl-NH_3 混合溶液时，仍能生成 $HgNH_2Cl$ 沉淀，这可能是 $HgNH_2Cl$ 溶解度小。

19.42 (1) $CuCl+HCl \longrightarrow HCuCl_2$

(2) $AgBr+2S_2O_3^{2-} \longrightarrow [Ag(S_2O_3)_2]^{3-}+Br^-$

(3) $2CuS+10CN^- \longrightarrow 2[Cu(CN)_4]^{3-}+2S^{2-}+(CN)_2$

(4) $HgI_2+2I^- \longrightarrow [HgI_4]^{2-}$

(5) $CuI+2S_2O_3^{2-} \longrightarrow [Cu(S_2O_3)_2]^{3-}+I^-$

(6) $HgNH_2Cl+4HCl \longrightarrow H_2[HgCl_4]+NH_4Cl$

19.43 (1) 生成的蓝色沉淀为 $Cu(OH)_2$：

$$CuSO_4+2NaOH \longrightarrow Cu(OH)_2\downarrow+Na_2SO_4$$

微热 $Cu(OH)_2$ 则转化为黑色的 CuO：

$$Cu(OH)_2 \longrightarrow CuO+H_2O$$

(2) Hg^{2+} 遇 NaOH 溶液生成黄色 HgO 沉淀：

$$Hg^{2+}+2OH^- \longrightarrow HgO\downarrow+H_2O$$

$HgCl_2$ 与氨水反应生成白色$[Hg(NH_2)]Cl$ 沉淀：

$$HgCl_2+2NH_3 \longrightarrow [Hg(NH_2)]Cl\downarrow+NH_4Cl$$

(3) $Hg(NO_3)_2$ 为离子化合物，$Hg(NO_3)_2$ 在水中水解析出黄色 $HgO\cdot Hg(NO_3)_2$ 沉淀：

$$2Hg(NO_3)_2+H_2O \longrightarrow HgO\cdot Hg(NO_3)_2\downarrow+2H^+$$

而 $HgCl_2$ 为共价化合物，溶于水主要以分子形式存在，虽有部分水解，但没有明显的沉淀析出。

(4) $Hg_2(NO_3)_2$ 与少量 KI 溶液作用，生成黄色 Hg_2I_2 沉淀：

$$Hg_2(NO_3)_2+2KI \longrightarrow Hg_2I_2\downarrow+2NO_3$$

KI 溶液过量，则 Hg_2I_2 歧化生成黑色的 Hg 沉淀和无色的$[HgI_4]^{2-}$ 溶液：

$$Hg_2I_2+2I^- \longrightarrow Hg+[HgI_4]^{2-}$$

19.44 (1) 加水，$HgCl_2$ 溶解而 Hg_2Cl_2 不溶。

(2) 将混合物溶于水后加入盐酸，使溶液中 HCl 浓度为 $1\ mol\cdot dm^{-3}$，再通入 H_2S，则

$$Cu^{2+}+H_2S \xrightarrow{1\ mol\cdot dm^{-3}\ HCl} CuS\downarrow+2H^+$$

$$Cd^{2+} + H_2S \xrightarrow{1\ mol\cdot dm^{-3}\ HCl} \text{不反应}$$

(3) 混合物溶于水后加入过量 NaOH 溶液，Hg^{2+} 生成沉淀而 Pb^{2+} 则溶解：

$$Hg^{2+} + 2OH^- \longrightarrow HgO\downarrow + H_2O$$
$$Pb^{2+} + 4OH^- \longrightarrow [Pb(OH)_4]^{2-}$$

(4) 加水使混合物溶解后加入盐酸，$AgNO_3$ 与 HCl 生成沉淀而 $Cu(NO_3)_2$ 则不能。

$$Ag^+ + Cl^- \longrightarrow AgCl\downarrow$$

过滤即可。

(5) 混合物溶于水后加入过量氨水，Sn^{2+} 生成沉淀而 Zn^{2+} 生成可溶性配合物：

$$Sn^{2+} + 2NH_3 + 2H_2O \longrightarrow Sn(OH)_2\downarrow + 2NH_4^+$$
$$Zn^{2+} + 4NH_3 \longrightarrow [Zn(NH_3)_4]^{2+}$$

19.45 (1) $CuSO_4 + Cu + 2KBr \xrightarrow{\triangle} 2CuBr\downarrow + K_2SO_4$

(2) $ZnS + 2HCl + nH_2O \longrightarrow ZnCl_2\cdot nH_2O + H_2S\uparrow$

$ZnCl_2\cdot nH_2O \xrightarrow[\triangle]{HCl\text{气}} ZnCl_2 + nH_2O$

(3) $3Hg + 8HNO_3 \longrightarrow 3Hg(NO_3)_2 + 2NO\uparrow + 4H_2O$

$Hg(NO_3)_2 + 4KI \longrightarrow K_2[HgI_4] + 2KNO_3$

(4) $ZnCO_3 + H_2SO_4 \longrightarrow ZnSO_4 + CO_2\uparrow + H_2O$

$2ZnSO_4 + 2H_2O \xrightarrow{\text{电解}} 2Zn + O_2\uparrow + 2H_2SO_4$

19.46 用久了的定影液中 $Na_2S_2O_3$ 大部分已与 AgBr 反应生成$[Ag(S_2O_3)_2]^{3-}$，$Na_2S_2O_3$ 浓度较低，溶解 AgBr 能力较差。胶片上有些部分的 AgBr 未被溶解而造成胶片“发花”。

19.47 (1) 向$[Cu(NH_3)_4]^{2+}$溶液中滴加盐酸，先有淡蓝色沉淀生成。

$$2[Cu(NH_3)_4]^{2+} + 2HCl + 2H_2O \longrightarrow Cu(OH)_2\cdot CuCl_2\downarrow + 4NH_4^+ + 4NH_3$$

盐酸过量时，沉淀溶解得蓝色溶液。

$$Cu(OH)_2\cdot CuCl_2 + 2HCl + 6H_2O \longrightarrow 2[Cu(H_2O)_4]^{2+} + 4Cl^-$$

若溶液浓度较大，盐酸也较浓，则最后溶液中$[CuCl_4]^{2-}$与$[Cu(H_2O)_4]^{2+}$浓度相当，溶液显绿色。

$$[Cu(H_2O)_4]^{2+}(\text{蓝}) + 4Cl^- \rightleftharpoons [CuCl_4]^{2-}(\text{黄}) + 4H_2O$$

(2) 将$[Cu(NH_3)_4]SO_4$溶液加热，先有淡蓝色沉淀生成，后沉淀转为黑色。

$$2[Cu(NH_3)_4]^{2+} + SO_4^{2-} + 2H_2O \xrightarrow{\triangle} Cu(OH)_2\cdot CuSO_4\downarrow + 2NH_4^+ + 6NH_3\uparrow$$

$$Cu(OH)_2\cdot CuSO_4 \xrightarrow{\triangle} CuO\downarrow + CuSO_4 + H_2O$$

(3) 生成的 CuI 与 I_2 混在一起，沉淀为黄色，当加入 Na_2SO_3 后，沉淀转为白色。

$$2[CuCl_4]^{2-} + 4I^- \longrightarrow 2CuI\downarrow + I_2\downarrow + 8Cl^-$$
$$I_2 + Na_2SO_3 + H_2O \longrightarrow 2HI + Na_2SO_4$$

19.48

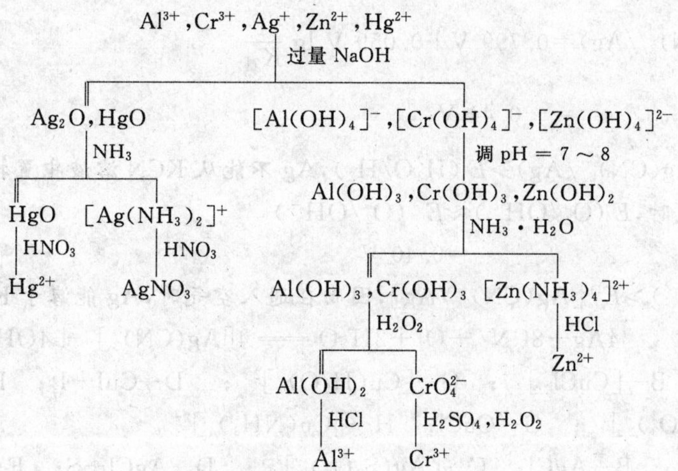

19.49

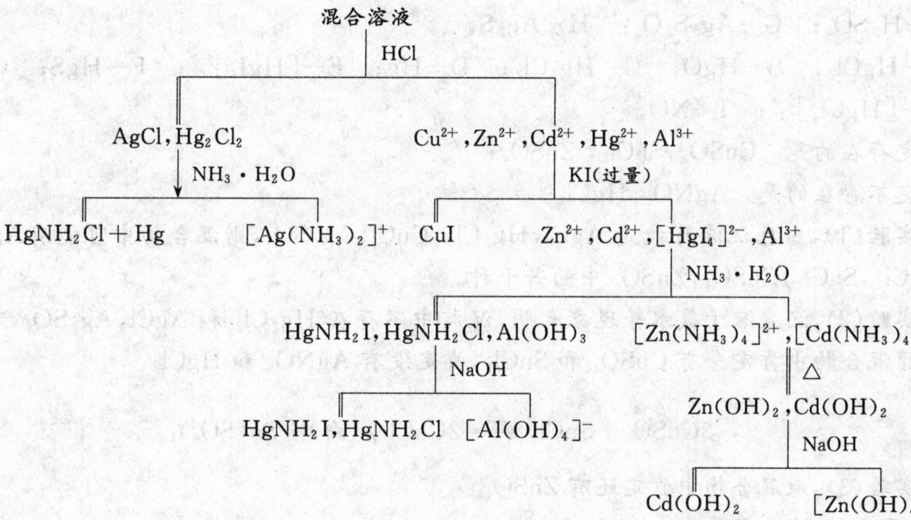

注意，在分离过程中不能用 NaOH 溶液分离 Zn^{2+} 和 Cu^{2+}，因 $Cu(OH)_2$ 有部分生成$[Cu(OH)_4]^{2-}$使分离不完全。

19.50 铜溶于 KCN 溶液，发生的反应为

$$2Cu+4CN^-+2H_2O = 2[Cu(CN)_2]^-+H_2\uparrow+2OH^-$$

对电极反应 $[Cu(CN)_2]^-+e^- = Cu+2CN^-$

$$E^\ominus(Cu(CN)_2^-/Cu)=0.52\ V+0.059V\lg\frac{1}{K^\ominus_{稳}}$$

$$=-0.90\ V$$

对于电极反应 $2H_2O+2e^- = H_2+2OH^-$

$E^\ominus(H_2O/H_2)=-0.83$ V，实际上，KCN 溶液的 OH^- 浓度低于 1 $mol\cdot dm^{-3}$，即

$E(H_2O/H_2)>E^\ominus(H_2O/H_2)=-0.83$ V

由于 $E(H_2O/H_2)>E^\ominus(Cu(CN)_2^-/Cu)$，所以 Cu 能溶于 KCN 溶液并置换出氢气。

对于电极反应 $[Ag(CN)_2]^-+e^- = Ag+2CN^-$

$$E^\ominus(Ag(CN)_2^-/Ag)=0.799\ V+0.059\ V\lg\frac{1}{K_{稳}}$$

$$=-0.44\ V$$

由于 $E^\ominus(Ag(CN)_2^-/Ag)>E(H_2O/H_2)$，Ag 不能从 KCN 溶液中置换出氢气。

在通入空气时，$E(O_2/OH^-)\approx E^\ominus(O_2/OH^-)$

$$=0.40\ V$$

$E(O_2/OH^-)>E^\ominus[Ag(CN)_2^-/Ag]$，因而在通入空气时，Ag 能溶于 KCN 溶液：

$$4Ag+8CN^-+O_2+2H_2O = 4[Ag(CN)_2]^-+4OH^-$$

19.51 A—CuO； B—$[CuCl_4]^{2-}$； C—$[Cu(H_2O)_4]^{2+}$； D—$CuI+I_2$； E—CuI； F—$[Cu(S_2O_3)_2]^{3-}$； G—CuCl； H—$[Cu(NH_3)_4]^{2+}$。

19.52 A—$AgNO_3$； B—AgCl； C—$[Ag(S_2O_3)_2]^{3-}$； D—AgCl+S； E—SO_2； F—H_2SO_4； G—$Ag_2S_2O_3$： H—Ag_2S。

19.53 A—$HgCl_2$； B—HgO； C—Hg_2Cl_2； D—Hg； E—$[HgI_4]^{2-}$； F—HgS； G—S； H—$[HgCl_4]^{2-}$； I—NO。

19.54 肯定存在的是 $CuSO_4$，$SnCl_2$，$ZnSO_4$；

肯定不存在的是 $AgNO_3$，$HgCl_2$。

由实验(1)，白色沉淀可能是 AgCl，Hg_2Cl_2，CuCl，Ag_2SO_4，则混合物中可能有 $AgNO_3$，$HgCl_2$，$SnCl_2$，$CuSO_4$，$ZnSO_4$ 中的若干种。

由实验(2)，沉淀溶于氨水等现象表明，沉淀中不存在 Hg_2Cl_2 和 AgCl，Ag_2SO_4，可以断定原混合物中肯定含有 $CuSO_4$ 和 $SnCl_2$，肯定没有 $AgNO_3$ 和 $HgCl_2$。

$$2CuSO_4+SnCl_2 \xlongequal{\triangle} 2CuCl\downarrow(白)+Sn(SO_4)_2$$

由实验(3)，原混合物中肯定还有 $ZnSO_4$。

19.55 (1) B—AgCl； E—NO_2； F—$BaSO_4$；

(2) 有 $[CuCl_4]^{2-}$ 生成，因 $[CuCl_4]^{2-}$ 为黄色；

(3) 还可能有 NH_4^+ 和 Ba^{2+}。

19.56 三种硝酸盐为 $AgNO_3$，$Pb(NO_3)_2$，$Hg_2(NO_3)_2$。

19.57 A—$CuCl_2$； B—$[CuCl_2]^-$； C—CuCl； D—$CuSO_4$； E—Cu； F—$Cu(OH)_2\cdot CuSO_4$； G—$[Cu(NH_3)_4]^{2+}$； H—SO_2。

19.58 A—$[Ag(S_2O_3)_2]^{3-}$； B—SO_2； C—Ag_2S； D—S； E—AgCl； F—Na_2SO_4； G—$BaSO_4$； H—AgI； I—$Na[Ag(CN)_2]$。

19.59 (1) A—$[Cu(H_2O)_4]^{2+}$ 蓝色； B—$[CuCl_4]^{2-}$ 黄色； C—CuCl 白色； D—$[Cu(NH_3)_2]^+$ 无色； E—$[Cu(NH_3)_4]^{2+}$ 蓝色。

(2) $4[Cu(NH_3)_2]^++O_2+2H_2O+8NH_3 = 4[Cu(NH_3)_4]^{2+}+4OH^-$

第 20 章

一、选择题

20.1 C　20.2 D　20.3 A　20.4 A　20.5 B　20.6 C　20.7 B　20.8 C
20.9 D　20.10 C　20.11 D　20.12 C

二、填空题

20.13 $TiCl_3$,$TiCl_4$,$VO(NO_3)_2$。

20.14 (1) TiO_2;　(2) $FeTiO_3$;　(3) $CaTiO_3$;　(4) $CaTiSiO_5$;
(5) $ZrSO_4$;　(6) ZrO_2;　(7) VS_4;　(8) $Pb_5(VO_4)_3Cl$。

20.15 TiO^{2+},VO^{2+}。

20.16 $Ti(OH)_4$,$Ti(CO_3)_4$。

20.17 V^{2+},VO^{2+}。

20.18 过氧链转移,$[V(O_2)]^{3+}$,$[VO_2(O_2)_2]^{3-}$。

20.19 Ti^{3+}紫红色,V^{2+}紫色,V^{3+}绿色,VO^{2+}蓝色,VO_2^+ 黄色,VO_4^{3-} 无色,$V_{10}O_{28}^{6-}$橙红色,$[TiO(H_2O_2)_2]^{2+}$橘黄色,$[V(O_2)]^{3+}$红棕色,$[VO_2(O_2)_2]^{3-}$黄色。

三、完成并配平下列反应方程式

20.20 $Ti+6HF = H_2TiF_6+2H_2\uparrow$

20.21 $3Ti^{3+}+NO_3^-+H_2O = 3TiO^{2+}+NO\uparrow+2H^+$ 或
$3TiCl_3+HNO_3+H_2O = 3TiOCl_2+NO\uparrow+3HCl$

20.22 $TiO_2+2C+2Cl_2 \xlongequal{\triangle} TiCl_4\uparrow+2CO\uparrow$

或 $TiO_2+CCl_4 \xlongequal{\triangle} TiCl_4\uparrow+CO_2\uparrow$

20.23 $TiO^{2+}+H_2O_2 = Ti(O_2)^{2+}+H_2O$

20.24 $TiCl_4+2NaH = Ti+2NaCl+2HCl$

20.25 $V_2O_5+H_2SO_4 = (VO_2)_2SO_4+H_2O$

20.26 $VO_2^++Fe^{2+}+2H^+ = VO^{2+}+Fe^{3+}+H_2O$

20.27 $5VO^{2+}+MnO_4^-+H_2O = 5VO_2^++Mn^{2+}+2H^+$

四、简答题和计算题

20.28 (1) $TiCl_3\cdot 6H_2O$有两种异构体:

$[Ti(H_2O)_6]Cl_3$ 为紫色　　$[Ti(H_2O)_5Cl]Cl_2\cdot H_2O$ 绿色

(2) Ti^{3+}还原能力比Sn^{2+}强,可以将Cu^{2+}还原为Cu^+而生成白色CuCl沉淀:

$$Ti^{3+}+Cu^{2+}+Cl^-+H_2O = TiO^{2+}+CuCl\downarrow+2H^+$$

(3) $MnO_4^-+5VO^{2+}+H_2O = Mn^{2+}+5VO_2^++2H^+$

20.29 (1) 溶液变为紫色,有 $TiCl_3$ 生成

$$2TiCl_4 + Zn \xlongequal{} 2TiCl_3 + ZnCl_2$$

(2) 有紫色沉淀生成

$$TiCl_3 + 3NaOH \xlongequal{} Ti(OH)_3\downarrow + 3NaCl$$

(3) 沉淀被 HNO_3 氧化后得到无色溶液

$$3Ti(OH)_3 + 7HNO_3 \xlongequal{} 3TiO(NO_3)_2 + NO\uparrow + 8H_2O$$

再加 NaOH 后得白色沉淀

$$TiO^{2+} + 2OH^- + H_2O \xlongequal{} Ti(OH)_4\downarrow$$

20.30 钛铁矿为 $FeTiO_3$。

$FeTiO_3 + 2H_2SO_4$(浓)$\xlongequal{} TiOSO_4 + FeSO_4 + 2H_2O$

$TiOSO_4 + 2H_2O \xlongequal{\triangle} H_2TiO_3 + H_2SO_4$

$H_2TiO_3 \xlongequal{\triangle} TiO_2 + H_2O$

$TiO_2 + 2Cl_2 + 2C \xlongequal{高温} TiCl_4 + 2CO$

$2TiCl_4 + H_2 \xlongequal{灼烧} 2TiCl_3 + 2HCl$

20.31 $2Ti + 6H^+ \xlongequal{} 2Ti^{3+} + 3H_2$

$5Ti^{3+} + MnO_4^- + H_2O \xlongequal{} 5TiO^{2+} + Mn^{2+} + 2H^+$

20.32 铅白 $Pb(OH)_2\cdot PbCO_3$，锌白(学名锌氧粉) ZnO，钛白(惰性颜料) TiO_2。

钛白作为染料的优点如下：

(1) 覆盖能力强，与铅白相似，比锌白强。

(2) 热稳定性高，属于惰性颜料。纯净的铅白非常稳定，若成分不纯则久后会发黄。同时铅白耐高温能力较差；锌白受热(阳光下直晒)会变成柠檬黄，但冷却时则又会恢复白色。

(3) 不变色，在空气中不与 H_2S 等气体作用。铅白易吸收空气中的 H_2S 气体而变黑。

(4) 无毒，与锌白相似，铅白有很强的毒性。

20.33 在酸性条件下，向 V^{3+} 溶液滴加 $KMnO_4$ 溶液，先后发生如下反应：

$$5V^{3+} + MnO_4^- + H_2O \xlongequal{} 5VO^{2+} + Mn^{2+} + 2H^+$$

$$5VO^{2+} + MnO_4^- + H_2O \xlongequal{} 5VO_2^+ + Mn^{2+} + 2H^+$$

产物 VO^{2+} 为蓝色，VO_2^+ 为黄色。当 VO^{2+} 的量与 VO_2^+ 的量相当时，溶液显二者的混合色——绿色。所以，向酸性的 V^{3+} 溶液中滴加 $KMnO_4$ 时，溶液先变蓝，继而又变为绿色。

20.34 向酸性的 V^{2+} 溶液中滴加 $KMnO_4$ 溶液，溶液的颜色变化及对应的钒的存在形式为：

紫色 ⟶ 绿色 ⟶ 蓝色 ⟶ 绿色 ⟶ 黄色

V^{2+}　　V^{3+}　　VO^{2+}　$VO^{2+} + VO_2^+$　　VO_2^+

20.35 由于 Ti^{4+} 的极化能力很强，因此 $TiCl_4$，$TiBr_4$，TiI_4 均为共价化合物，熔点较低。按 Cl^-，Br^-，I^- 的顺序，随着离子半径依次增大，即按 $TiCl_4$，$TiBr_4$，TiI_4 的顺序，分子半径依次增大，分子间范德华力增大，熔点依次升高。但 F^- 变形性很小，TiF_4 为离子化合物，故而熔点高。

20.36 化合物 $Ti(NO_3)_4$ 熔点明显偏低，说明该化合物分子之间的作用力小。NO_3^- 有时可作为双基配体，在 $Ti(NO_3)_4$ 中，NO_3^- 用两个 O 向 Ti^{4+} 配位，Ti^{4+} 周围有 8 个 O 配位，形成近球状的分子。$Ti(NO_3)_4$ 分子间靠范德华力结合，因而熔点偏低。

20.37 A—$TiCl_4$； B—AgCl； C—$TiCl_3$； D—$Ti(OH)_3$； E—$TiO(NO_3)_2$； F—TiO_2 或 H_2TiO_3

20.38 A—NH_4VO_3； B—V_2O_5； C—NH_3； D—$(VO_2)_2SO_4$； E—$NaVO_3$； F—$VOSO_4$； G—Ag_2O； H—$[Ag(NH_3)_2]^+$。

20.39 A—$TiCl_4$； B—TiO_2； C—$TiCl_3$； D—CuCl； E—$TiO(NO_3)_2$。

第 21 章

一、选择题

21.1 A　21.2 C　21.3 B　21.4 D　21.5 B　21.6 D　21.7 B　21.8 D
21.9 C　21.10 B　21.11 B　21.12 C　21.13 D　21.14 C　21.15 B

二、填空题

21.16 $CrCl_2$，$CrCl_3$。

21.17 Mn^{2+}；MnO_4^{2-}；MnO_2。

21.18 (1) $FeCr_2O_4$；　(2) $PbCrO_4$；　(3) Cr_2O_3；　(4) MoS_2；
(5) $PbMoO_4$；　(6) $CaWO_4$；　(7) MnO_2；　(8) Mn_3O_4；
(9) MnO；　(10) $MnCO_3$。

21.19 $[Cr(H_2O)_6]^{3+}$ 紫色，$[Cr(H_2O)_5Cl]^{2+}$ 浅绿色，$[Cr(NH_3)_6]^{3+}$ 黄色，$[Cr(OH)_4]^-$ 绿色，$[Cr(NH_3)_3(H_2O)_3]^{3+}$ 红色，CrO_4^{2-} 黄色，$Cr_2O_7^{2-}$ 橙色，$[Mn(H_2O)_6]^{2+}$ 浅红色，MnO_4^{2-} 绿色，MnO_4^- 紫色。

21.20 $Cr_2(SO_4)_3 \cdot 18H_2O$ 紫色，$Cr_2(SO_4)_3 \cdot 6H_2O$ 绿色，$Cr_2(SO_4)_3$ 红色，$CrCl_3 \cdot 6H_2O$ 绿色，Cr_2O_3 暗绿色，CrO_3 暗红色，CrO_5 蓝色，$Cr(OH)_3$ 灰蓝色，CrO_2Cl_2 深红色，$BaCrO_4$ 黄色，$PbCrO_4$ 黄色，Ag_2CrO_4 砖红色，$MnSO_4 \cdot 7H_2O$ 浅红色，K_2MnO_4 绿色，$KMnO_4$ 紫黑色，$Mn(OH)_2$ 白色，MnO_2 棕黑色。

21.21 PbO_2，$(NH_4)_2S_2O_8$，$NaBiO_3$，$(NH_4)_2S_2O_8$，$AgNO_3$（或 Ag^+）。

21.22 $Cr(OH)_3$，灰蓝。

21.23 H_2O_2，乙醚（或戊醇），蓝，CrO_5， 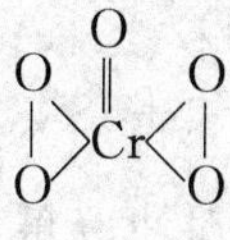 ，+6。

21.24 歧化，$KMnO_4$ 和 MnO_2。

21.25 MnO，Mn_2O_7。

21.26 $H_3[PW_{12}O_{40}]$。

三、完成并配平下列反应方程式

21.27 $10Cr^{3+} + 6MnO_4^- + 11H_2O \Longrightarrow 5Cr_2O_7^{2-} + 6Mn^{2+} + 22H^+$

21.28 $Cr_2O_3+2Al \xlongequal{\triangle} 2Cr+Al_2O_3$

21.29 $MnCO_3 \xlongequal{\triangle} MnO+CO_2\uparrow$

21.30 $4MnO_2+6H_2SO_4 \xlongequal{} 2Mn_2(SO_4)_3+O_2\uparrow+6H_2O$

$2Mn_2(SO_4)_3+2H_2O \xlongequal{} 4MnSO_4+O_2\uparrow+2H_2SO_4$

21.31 $2Mn^{2+}+5NaBiO_3+14H^+ \xlongequal{} 2MnO_4^-+5Bi^{3+}+5Na^++7H_2O$

21.32 $2MnO_4^-+3SO_3^{2-}+H_2O \xlongequal{} 2MnO_2+3SO_4^{2-}+2OH^-$

21.33 $2MnO_4^-+SO_3^{2-}+2OH^- \xlongequal{} 2MnO_4^{2-}+SO_4^{2-}+H_2O$

21.34 $Cr_2O_7^{2-}+3H_2O_2+8H^+ \xlongequal{} 2Cr^{3+}+3O_2\uparrow+7H_2O$

21.35 $Cr_2O_3+3K_2S_2O_7 \xlongequal{熔融} 3K_2SO_4+Cr_2(SO_4)_3$

21.36 $2CrI_3+21Cl_2+52OH^- \xlongequal{} 2CrO_4^{2-}+6IO_3^-+42Cl^-+26H_2O$

21.37 $2KMnO_4+2H_2SO_4$(浓) $\xlongequal{} Mn_2O_7+2KHSO_4+H_2O$

21.38 $MnO_2+4HCl \xlongequal{} MnCl_4+2H_2O$

21.39 $MnO_2+H_2O_2+H_2SO_4 \xlongequal{} MnSO_4+2H_2O+O_2\uparrow$

21.40 $K_2Cr_2O_7+4KCl+3H_2SO_4$(浓) $\xlongequal{} 2CrO_2Cl_2+3K_2SO_4+3H_2O$

21.41 $Cr_2O_3+3NaNO_3+4NaOH \xlongequal{} 2Na_2CrO_4+3NaNO_2+2H_2O$

21.42 $(NH_4)_2Cr_2O_7 \xlongequal{} Cr_2O_3+N_2\uparrow+4H_2O$

21.43 $2KMnO_4 \xlongequal{} K_2MnO_4+MnO_2+O_2\uparrow$

21.44 $MnSO_4 \xlongequal{} MnO_2+SO_2\uparrow$

四、简答题和计算题

21.45 (1) $Cr^{3+}+3OH^- \xlongequal{} Cr(OH)_3\downarrow$(灰蓝)

$Cr(OH)_3+OH^- \xlongequal{} [Cr(OH)_4]^-$(绿色)

$2[Cr(OH)_4]^-+3HO_2^- \xlongequal{} 2CrO_4^{2-}$(黄)$+OH^-+5H_2O$

(2) $Cr_2O_7^{2-}+3Zn+14H^+ \xlongequal{} 2Cr^{3+}+3Zn^{2+}+7H_2O$

$2Cr^{3+}+Zn \xlongequal{} 2Cr^{2+}+Zn^{2+}$

$4Cr^{2+}+O_2+4H^+ \xlongequal{} 4Cr^{3+}+2H_2O$

(3) $Cr_2O_7^{2-}+3SO_2+2H^+ \xlongequal{} 2Cr^{3+}+3SO_4^{2-}+H_2O$

(4) $Mn^{2+}+2OH^- \xlongequal{} Mn(OH)_2\downarrow$

$2Mn(OH)_2+O_2 \xlongequal{} 2MnO(OH)_2$

(5) $2MnO_4^-+5H_2S+6H^+ \xlongequal{} 2Mn^{2+}+5S\downarrow+8H_2O$

21.46 (1) 生成的 CrO_5 显蓝色。CrO_5 在乙醚中分解较慢，在水中分解却较快，因此乙醚层为蓝色；分解后生成的 Cr^{3+} 在水层，因而水层逐渐变绿。

$$Cr_2O_7^{2-}+4H_2O_2+2H^+ \xlongequal{} 2CrO_5+5H_2O$$

$$4CrO_5+12H^+ \xlongequal{} 4Cr^{3+}+6H_2O+7O_2\uparrow$$

(2) $BaCrO_4$ 与浓盐酸反应较慢；加热时反应速度较快，同时 Cr(Ⅵ)氧化能力增强。反应产物 $CrCl_3$ 为绿色。

$$2BaCrO_4 + 2H^+ \Longrightarrow Cr_2O_7^{2-} + 2Ba^{2+} + H_2O$$

$$Cr_2O_7^{2-} + 6Cl^- + 14H^+ \Longrightarrow 2Cr^{3+} + 3Cl_2\uparrow + 7H_2O$$

(3) $K_2Cr_2O_7$ 与 $AgNO_3$ 生成溶解度较小的 Ag_2CrO_4(砖红色)，加入 NaCl 后沉淀转化为溶解度更小的 AgCl。

$$Cr_2O_7^{2-} + 4Ag^+ + H_2O \Longrightarrow 2Ag_2CrO_4\downarrow + 2H^+$$

$$Ag_2CrO_4 + 2Cl^- \Longrightarrow 2AgCl\downarrow + CrO_4^{2-}$$

21.47 Cr^{3+} 与 $Cr(OH)_3$ 之间的转化：

$$Cr^{3+} + 3OH^- \Longrightarrow Cr(OH)_3\downarrow$$

$$Cr(OH)_3 + 3H^+ \Longrightarrow Cr^{3+} + 3H_2O$$

$Cr(OH)_3$ 与 CrO_2^- 之间的转化：

$$Cr(OH)_3 + OH^- \Longrightarrow CrO_2^- + 2H_2O$$

$$CrO_2^- + H^+(\text{适量}) + H_2O \Longrightarrow Cr(OH)_3\downarrow$$

CrO_2^- 与 CrO_4^{2-} 之间的转化：

$$2CrO_2^- + 3H_2O_2 + 2OH^- \Longrightarrow 2CrO_4^{2-} + 4H_2O$$

$$2CrO_4^{2-} + 3Zn + 4OH^- \Longrightarrow 2CrO_2^- + 3ZnO_2^{2-} + 2H_2O$$

CrO_4^{2-} 与 $Cr_2O_7^{2-}$ 之间的转化：

$$2CrO_4^{2-} + 2H^+ \Longrightarrow Cr_2O_7^{2-} + H_2O$$

$$Cr_2O_7^{2-} + 2OH^- \Longrightarrow 2CrO_4^{2-} + H_2O$$

Cr^{3+} 与 $Cr_2O_7^{2-}$ 之间的转化：

$$Cr_2O_7^{2-} + 3SO_3^{2-} + 8H^+ \Longrightarrow 2Cr^{3+} + 3SO_4^{2-} + 4H_2O$$

$$10Cr^{3+} + 6MnO_4^- + 11H_2O \Longrightarrow 6Mn^{2+} + 5Cr_2O_7^{2-} + 22H^+$$

MnO_4^- 与 Mn^{2+} 之间的转化：

$$2MnO_4^- + 6H^+ + 5SO_3^{2-} \Longrightarrow 2Mn^{2+} + 5SO_4^{2-} + 3H_2O$$

$$2Mn^{2+} + 5NaBiO_3 + 14H^+ \Longrightarrow 2MnO_4^- + 5Bi^{3+} + 7H_2O + 5Na^+$$

MnO_4^- 与 MnO_4^{2-} 之间的转化：

$$2MnO_4^- + 2OH^- + SO_3^{2-} \Longrightarrow 2MnO_4^{2-} + SO_4^{2-} + H_2O$$

$$2MnO_4^{2-} + Cl_2 \Longrightarrow 2MnO_4^- + 2Cl^-$$

MnO_4^- 与 MnO_2 之间的转化：

$$2MnO_4^- + H_2O + 3SO_3^{2-} \Longrightarrow 2MnO_2\downarrow + 3SO_4^{2-} + 2OH^-$$

$$3MnO_2 + 6KOH + KClO_3 \xlongequal{\text{熔融}} 3K_2MnO_4 + KCl + 3H_2O$$

$$2MnO_4^{2-} + Cl_2 \Longrightarrow 2MnO_4^- + 2Cl^-$$

MnO_4^{2-} 与 MnO_2 之间的转化：

$$MnO_4^{2-} + SO_3^{2-} + H_2O \xlongequal{} MnO_2 \downarrow + SO_4^{2-} + 2OH^-$$

$$2MnO_2 + 4KOH + O_2 \xlongequal{熔融} 2K_2MnO_4 + 2H_2O$$

MnO_2 与 Mn^{2+} 之间的转化：

$$MnO_2 + H_2O_2 + 2H^+ \xlongequal{} Mn^{2+} + 2H_2O + O_2 \uparrow$$

$$Mn^{2+} + 2OH^- + H_2O_2 \xlongequal{} MnO_2 \downarrow + 2H_2O$$

21.48 铬铁矿为 $Fe(CrO_2)_2$。

实验室中将氧化剂 KNO_3 和铬铁矿、K_2CO_3 按一定比例混合，用固相熔融法制备 K_2CrO_4：

$$2Fe(CrO_2)_2 + 4K_2CO_3 + 7KNO_3 \xlongequal{熔融} 4K_2CrO_4 + Fe_2O_3 + 7KNO_2 + 4CO_2 \uparrow$$

产物经水浸、过滤除去 Fe_2O_3，调 pH 至弱碱性除去 $Al(OH)_3$ 和 SiO_2 等杂质后，加酸调至溶液为酸性，得 $K_2Cr_2O_7$：

$$2K_2CrO_4 + 2H^+ \xlongequal{} K_2Cr_2O_7 + H_2O + 2K^+$$

工业上为降低成本，将铬铁矿和 Na_2CO_3 按一定比例混合后在空气中煅烧，得 Na_2CrO_4：

$$4Fe(CrO_2)_2 + 8Na_2CO_3 + 7O_2 \xlongequal{熔融} 8Na_2CrO_4 + 2Fe_2O_3 + 8CO_2 \uparrow$$

经除去杂质后，加酸调至溶液为酸性，得 $Na_2Cr_2O_7$：

$$2Na_2CrO_4 + 2H^+ \xlongequal{} Na_2Cr_2O_7 + H_2O + 2Na^+$$

向 $Na_2Cr_2O_7$ 溶液中加入 KCl，利用复分解反应生成 $K_2Cr_2O_7$：

$$Na_2Cr_2O_7 + 2KCl \xlongequal{} K_2Cr_2O_7 + H_2O + 2Na^+$$

$K_2Cr_2O_7$ 溶解度随温度变化较大，溶液蒸发浓缩后趁热过滤除去 NaCl 等，将滤液冷却后析出 $K_2Cr_2O_7$ 晶体。

21.49 离子分离方案如图所示：

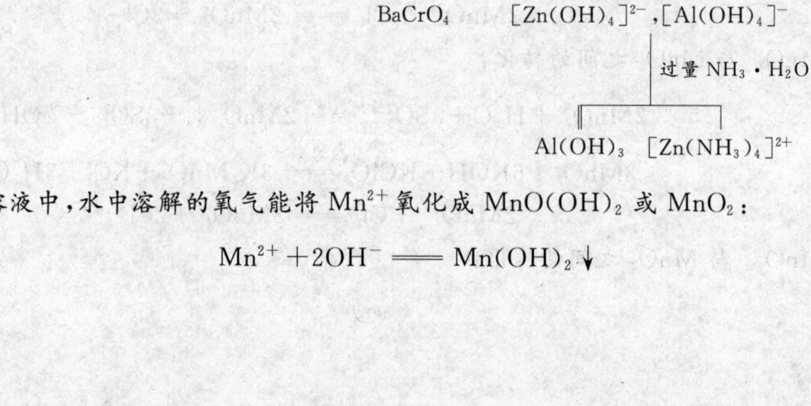

21.50 在碱性溶液中，水中溶解的氧气能将 Mn^{2+} 氧化成 $MnO(OH)_2$ 或 MnO_2：

$$Mn^{2+} + 2OH^- \xlongequal{} Mn(OH)_2 \downarrow$$

$$2Mn(OH)_2 + O_2 \xlongequal{\quad} 2MnO(OH)_2$$

在酸性溶液中，$MnO(OH)_2$ 能将 I^- 氧化成 I_2：

$$MnO(OH)_2 + 2I^- + 4H^+ \xlongequal{\quad} Mn^{2+} + I_2 + 3H_2O$$

通过测定 $S_2O_3^{2-}$ 可间接地测定水中溶氧量：

$$I_2 + 2S_2O_3^{2-} \xlongequal{\quad} S_4O_6^{2-} + 2I^-$$

根据上述反应式得各物质的计量关系：

$$O_2 \sim 2MnO(OH)_2 \sim 2I_2 \sim 4S_2O_3^{2-}$$

从而有 O_2 和 $Na_2S_2O_3$ 的定量关系为 $O_2 : S_2O_3^{2-} = 1:4$

21.51 $BaCrO_4$ 溶于硝酸而 $BaSO_4$ 不溶于硝酸，可从以下两方面来讨论。

第一，$HCrO_4^-$ 为弱酸($K_{a_2}^{\ominus} = 3.2\times10^{-7}$)而 HSO_4^- 却为中强酸($K_{a_2}^{\ominus} = 1.0\times10^{-2}$)，因而 $BaCrO_4$ 在酸性溶液中存在下列平衡：

$$BaCrO_4 + H^+ \rightleftharpoons Ba^{2+} + HCrO_4^-$$

在强酸溶液中，平衡右移，$BaCrO_4$ 溶解。

第二，酸中 CrO_4^{2-} 发生聚合反应：

$$2CrO_4^{2-} + 2H^+ \xlongequal{\quad} Cr_2O_7^{2-} + H_2O$$

$Cr_2O_7^{2-}$ 生成的 $BaCr_2O_7$ 溶解度较大，使 $BaCrO_4$ 能溶于强酸。

21.52 不矛盾。可从以下两方面考虑：

(1) 两个反应的电动势不同。

$2MnO_4^- + 3Mn^{2+} + 2H_2O \xlongequal{\quad} 5MnO_2 + 4H^+$

$E^{\ominus} = E^{\ominus}(MnO_4^-/MnO_2) - E^{\ominus}(MnO_2/Mn^{2+})$

$= 1.70\ V - 1.23\ V = 0.47\ V$

$MnO_4^- + 5Fe^{2+} + 8H^+ \xlongequal{\quad} Mn^{2+} + 5Fe^{3+} + 4H_2O$

$E^{\ominus} = 1.51\ V - 0.77\ V = 0.74\ V$

可见，MnO_4^- 更容易氧化 Fe^{2+}。

(2) MnO_4^- 与 Mn^{2+} 反应为慢反应，而 MnO_4^- 与 Fe^{2+} 反应为快反应。而且二者的反应速率相差悬殊。

21.53 A—$Cr(NO_3)_3$； B—$Cr(OH)_3$； C—$[Cr(OH)_4]^-$ 或 CrO_2^-； D—CrO_4^{2-}； E—$BaCrO_4$； F—$Cr_2(SO_4)_3$； G—NO。

21.54 A—K_2CrO_4； B—$Cr_2(SO_4)_3$； C—$[Cr(OH)_4]^-$ 或 CrO_2^-； D—CrO_4^{2-}； E—$PbCrO_4$； F—$Cr(OH)_3$。

21.55 混合溶液中的三种阴离子为：CrO_4^{2-}，MnO_4^-，Cl^-；沉淀 A 为 $AgCl + Ag_2CrO_4$。

21.56 A—K_2MnO_4； B—$MnSO_4$； C—$Mn(OH)_2$； D—MnO_2。

21.57 A—MnO_2； B—$MnSO_4$； C—$NaMnO_4$； D—Na_2MnO_4； E—$MnCl_4$； F—Cl_2； G—$MnCl_2$； H—$Mn(OH)_2$

第 22 章

一、选择题

22.1 B　22.2 A　22.3 B　22.4 C　22.5 C　22.6 B　22.7 B　22.8 D
22.9 C　22.10 D　22.11 A　22.12 B　22.13 C　22.14 B　22.15 D
22.16 B

二、填空题

22.17 血红，无，棕色 $Fe(OH)_3$ 沉淀。

22.18 $Mn^{2+}>Fe^{2+}>Cr^{3+}>V^{3+}$。

22.19 紫红；红棕，$BaFeO_4$。

22.20 (1) Fe_2O_3；(2) Fe_3O_4；(3) $2Fe_2O_3\cdot 3H_2O$；
(4) $FeCO_3$；(5) $CoAs_2$　(6) CoAsS
(7) Co_2S_4；(8) $K_3[Fe(CN)_6]$；(9) $K_4[Fe(CN)_6]\cdot 3H_2O$；
(10) $FeSO_4\cdot H_2O$；(11) $(NH_4)_2SO_4\cdot FeSO_4\cdot 6H_2O$；
(12) $NH_4Fe(SO_4)_2\cdot 12H_2O$；
(13) $Fe(C_5H_5)_2$；(14) $K[Pt(C_2H_4)Cl_3]$；
(15) *cis*-$Pt(NH_3)_2Cl_2$。

22.21 铁屑和硫酸，防止 Fe^{2+} 水解和被氧化。

22.22 双聚体 Fe_2Cl_6，$AlCl_3$；sp^3，$FeCl_3$ 中 Fe—Cl 键共价成分较多。

22.23 (1) Cu(Ⅱ)；(2) MnO_4^{2-}；(3) Cr(Ⅲ)；(4) Ni(Ⅱ)。

22.24 Co^{2+}，Ni^{2+}。

22.25 $[Co(CN)_6]^{4-}$，$[Co(CN)_6]^{3-}$。

22.26 $[Fe(H_2O)_6]^{2+}$ 绿色，$[Co(H_2O)_6]^{2+}$ 粉红色，$[Ni(H_2O)_6]^{2+}$ 绿色，$[Fe(H_2O)_6]^{3+}$ 淡紫色，$[FeCl_4]^-$ 黄色，$[Fe(SCN)_6]^{3-}$ 红色，$[FeF_5]^{2-}$ 无色，$[Fe(C_2O_4)_3]^{3-}$ 黄绿色，$[Fe(H_2O)_5OH]^{2+}$ 黄色，$[Co(NH_3)_6]^{2+}$ 棕黄色，$[CoCl_4]^{2-}$ 蓝色，$[Co(SCN)_4]^{2-}$ 蓝色，$[Ni(NH_3)_6]^{3+}$ 蓝色，$[Ni(CN)_4]^{2-}$ 黄色，$[PtCl_4]^{2-}$ 红色。

22.27 $FeSO_4\cdot 7H_2O$ 绿色，$FeSO_4$ 白色，$FeSO_4\cdot(NH_4)_2SO_4\cdot 6H_2O$ 浅蓝绿色，$Fe(OH)_2$ 白色，$K_4[Fe(CN)_6]\cdot 3H_2O$ 黄色，$Fe(C_5N_5)_2$ 橙黄色，$FeCl_3$ 棕黑色，$FeCl_3\cdot 6H_2O$ 黄色，$K_3[Fe(CN)_6]$ 红色，$K_3[Fe(C_2O_4)_3]\cdot 3H_2O$ 绿色，Fe_2O_3 红色，$Fe(OH)_3$ 棕色，$CoSO_4\cdot 7H_2O$ 粉红色，$CoCl_2\cdot 6H_2O$ 粉红色，$CoCl_2$ 蓝色，$Co(OH)_2$ 粉红色，$K_3[Co(NO_2)_6]$ 黄色，$Co[Hg(SCN)_4]$ 蓝色，$NiSO_4\cdot 7H_2O$ 绿色，$NiCl_2\cdot 6H_2O$ 绿色，$Ni(OH)_2$ 浅绿色，$Pt(NH_3)_2Cl_2$ 黄色，$K[Pt(C_2H_4)Cl_3]\cdot H_2O$ 橙黄色。

三、完成并配平下列反应方程式

22.28 $2Fe^{3+}+SO_2+2H_2O = 2Fe^{2+}+SO_4^{2-}+4H^+$

22.29 $V_2O_5 + 2Fe^{2+} + 6H^+ \longrightarrow 2Fe^{3+} + 2VO^{2+} + 3H_2O$

22.30 $Fe^{2+} + Fe(CN)_6^{3-} + K^+ \longrightarrow KFe[Fe(CN)_6]\downarrow$

22.31 $2Fe(OH)_3 + 3ClO^- + 4OH^- \longrightarrow 2FeO_4^{2-} + 3Cl^- + 5H_2O$

22.32 $2FeI_2 + 13Cl_2 + 12H_2O \longrightarrow 2FeCl_3 + 4HIO_3 + 20HCl$

22.33 $2FeSO_4 \xrightarrow{\triangle} Fe_2O_3 + SO_2\uparrow + SO_3\uparrow$

22.34 $Co_2O_3 + 6HCl \longrightarrow 2CoCl_2 + Cl_2\uparrow + 3H_2O$

22.35 $4Co(OH)_3 + 4H_2SO_4 \longrightarrow 4CoSO_4 + O_2\uparrow + 10H_2O$

22.36 $2CoCl_2 + Br_2 + 6NaOH \longrightarrow 2Co(OH)_3 + 4NaCl + 2NaBr$

22.37 $Co^{2+} + 7NO_2^- + 3K^+ + 2H^+ \longrightarrow K_3[Co(NO_2)_6]\downarrow + NO\uparrow + H_2O$

22.38 $Ni^{2+} + 2OH^- \longrightarrow Ni(OH)_2\downarrow$

$2Ni(OH)_2 + ClO^- + H_2O \longrightarrow 2Ni(OH)_3 + Cl^-$

22.39 $4Ni(OH)_3 \xrightarrow{\triangle} 4NiO + O_2\uparrow + 6H_2O$

22.40 $PdCl_2 + CO + H_2O \longrightarrow Pd\downarrow + CO_2\uparrow + 2HCl$

四、简答题和计算题

22.41 $Fe^{2+} + 2OH^- \longrightarrow Fe(OH)_2\downarrow$ 白色，遇 O_2 变蓝绿色

$4Fe(OH)_2 + O_2 + 2H_2O \longrightarrow 4Fe(OH)_3\downarrow$ 棕色

$Fe(OH)_3 + 3HCl \longrightarrow FeCl_3 + 3H_2O$ 黄色

$FeCl_3 + SCN^- \longrightarrow [Fe(SCN)]^{2+} + 3Cl^-$ 血红

$2[Fe(SCN)]^{2+} + SO_2 + 2H_2O \longrightarrow 2Fe^{2+} + SO_4^{2-} + 4H^+ + 2SCN^-$

$MnO_4^- + 5Fe^{2+} + 8H^+ \longrightarrow Mn^{2+} + 5Fe^{3+} + 4H_2O$

$Fe^{3+} + [Fe(CN)_6]^{4-} + K^+ \longrightarrow KFe[Fe(CN)_6]$

22.42 (1) $Fe^{3+} + nSCN^- \longrightarrow [Fe(SCN)_n]^{3-n}$ $n=1\sim6$ 血红色。

加入铁粉后，铁粉将$[Fe(SCN)_n]^{3-n}$还原，生成的 Fe^{2+} 不与 SCN^- 生成有色配合物，因而血红色消失。

$$2[Fe(SCN)_n]^{3-n} + Fe \longrightarrow 3Fe^{2+} + nSCN^-$$

(2) $FeCl_3$ 遇$(NH_4)_2C_2O_4$ 生成稳定的$[Fe(C_2O_4)_3]^{3-}$，其稳定性比$[Fe(SCN)]^{2+}$高，因而加入少量 KSCN 溶液时不变红。

$$Fe^{3+} + 3C_2O_4^{2-} \longrightarrow [Fe(C_2O_4)_3]^{3-}$$

$$[Fe(C_2O_4)_3]^{3-} + SCN^- \quad \text{不反应}$$

再加入盐酸时，$C_2O_4^{2-}$ 转化为 $HC_2O_4^-$ 弱酸或 $H_2C_2O_4$ 中强酸。而使$[Fe(C_2O_4)_3]^{3-}$破坏，再由 Fe^{3+} 与 SCN^- 结合使溶液变红。

$$[Fe(C_2O_4)_3]^{3-} + 3H^+ \longrightarrow Fe^{3+} + 3HC_2O_4^-$$

$$Fe^{3+} + SCN^- \longrightarrow [Fe(SCN)]^{2+}$$

(3) $E^\ominus(I_2/I^-) < E^\ominus(Fe^{3+}/Fe^{2+})$，$I_2$ 不能将 Fe^{2+} 氧化。在 KCN 存在时，Fe^{2+} 生成$[Fe(CN)_6]^{4-}$ 配离子，而 $E^\ominus(I_2/I^-) > E^\ominus[Fe(CN)_6^{3-}/Fe(CN)_6^{4-}]$，$I_2$ 能将

$[Fe(CN)_6]^{4-}$氧化。

$$2[Fe(CN)_6]^{4-}+I_2 = 2[Fe(CN)_6]^{3-}+2I^-$$

(4) 变色硅胶中含有吸湿指示剂($CoCl_2$)，随所含结晶水的数目不同，颜色不同。

$$\underset{\text{粉红色}}{CoCl_2\cdot 6H_2O} \rightleftharpoons \underset{\text{紫红色}}{CoCl_2\cdot 2H_2O} \rightleftharpoons \underset{\text{蓝紫色}}{CoCl_2\cdot H_2O} \rightleftharpoons \underset{\text{蓝色}}{CoCl_2}$$

所以，无水 $CoCl_2$ 显蓝色，$CoCl_2$ 结晶水较多时显粉红色。

22.43 (1) 鉴别 Fe^{3+}

Fe^{3+}遇 KSCN 立即变红。

$$Fe^{3+}+SCN^- = [Fe(SCN)]^{2+}$$

Fe^{3+}遇 $K_4[Fe(CN)_6]$变蓝。

$$Fe^{3+}+[Fe(CN)_6]^{4-}+K^+ = KFe[Fe(CN)_6]$$

(2) 鉴别 Fe^{2+}

Fe^{2+}遇 $K_3[Fe(CN)_6]$变蓝：

$$Fe^{2+}+[Fe(CN)_6]^{3-}+K^+ = KFe[Fe(CN)_6]$$

Fe^{2+}可使酸性高锰酸钾褪色。

$$5Fe^{2+}+MnO_4^-+8H^+ = 5Fe^{3+}+Mn^{2+}+4H_2O$$

(3) 鉴别 Co^{2+}

Co^{2+}与 KSCN 作用后用乙醚萃取，乙醚层为蓝色。

$$Co^{2+}+4SCN^- = [Co(SCN)_4]^{2-}\text{在乙醚中稳定}$$

Co^{2+}浓度较高时，加入浓盐酸生成蓝色$[CoCl_4]^{2-}$。

$$Co^{2+}+4Cl^- = [CoCl_4]^{2-}$$

Co^{2+}遇 NaOH 先有蓝色沉淀生成，沉淀逐渐转为粉红色(二者的组成相同)。

$$Co^{2+}+2OH^- = Co(OH)_2\downarrow$$

(4) 鉴定 Ni^{2+}

Ni^{2+}与少量氨水反应生成绿色沉淀，氨水过量时得蓝色溶液。

$$Ni^{2+}+6NH_3 = [Ni(NH_3)_6]^{2+}$$

Ni^{2+}与丁二酮肟在氨溶液中反应生成鲜红色沉淀。

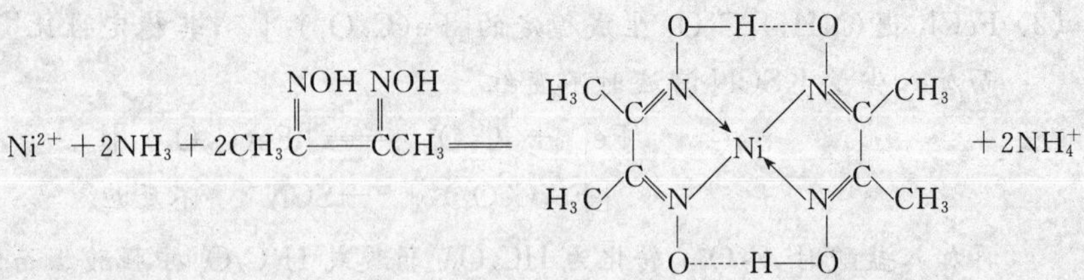

22.44 铂制容器中能进行有(1)，(5)，(6)中试剂参与的反应。因为 HF，Na_2CO_3，$NaHSO_4$ 均不单独与 Pt 反应。

铂制容器中不能进行有(2)，(3)，(4)，(7)中试剂参与的反应。因为 Pt 与王水、H_2O_2+HCl、Na_2O_2+NaOH、Na_2CO_3+S 均能发生反应。

$$3Pt+4HNO_3+18HCl = 3H_2PtCl_6+4NO\uparrow+8H_2O$$

$$Pt+2H_2O_2+6HCl \longrightarrow H_2PtCl_6+4H_2O$$

$$Pt+2Na_2O_2 \xlongequal{\triangle} PtO_2+2Na_2O$$

$$Pt+2S \xlongequal{\triangle} PtS_2$$

22.45 $K_4[Fe(CN)_6]$可由Fe^{2+}和KCN在水溶液中制备：

$$Fe^{2+}+6KCN \longrightarrow K_4[Fe(CN)_6]+2K^+$$

但$K_3[Fe(CN)_6]$不能由Fe^{3+}与KCN在溶液中直接制备，因Fe^{3+}能将CN^-氧化而有杂质$K_4[Fe(CN)_6]$生成：

$$2Fe^{3+}+2CN^- \longrightarrow 2Fe^{2+}+(CN)_2$$

$$Fe^{2+}+6CN^-+4K^+ \longrightarrow K_4[Fe(CN)_6]$$

正确的制备$K_3[Fe(CN)_6]$的方法是将$K_4[Fe(CN)_6]$氧化

$$2K_4[Fe(CN)_6]+H_2O_2 \longrightarrow 2K_3[Fe(CN)_6]+2KOH$$

22.46 (1) 向黄血盐溶液中滴加碘水，溶液由黄色变成红色。

$$2[Fe(CN)_6]^{4-}(\text{黄})+I_2 \longrightarrow 2[Fe(CN)_6]^{3-}(\text{红})+2I^-$$

(2) 将3 $mol\cdot dm^{-3}$ $CoCl_2$溶液加热，溶液由粉红变蓝。

$$[Co(H_2O)_6]^{2+}+4Cl^- \longrightarrow [CoCl_4]^{2-}+6H_2O$$

再加入$AgNO_3$溶液时，溶液由蓝变红，并有白色沉淀生成。

$$[CoCl_4]^{2-}+4Ag^++6H_2O \longrightarrow [Co(H_2O)_6]^{2+}+4AgCl\downarrow$$

(3) 水浴加热一段时间后，有绿色沉淀生成。

$$[Ni(NH_3)_6]^{2+}+2H_2O \xlongequal{\triangle} Ni(OH)_2\downarrow(\text{绿})+2NH_4^++4NH_3\uparrow$$

再加入氨水，沉淀又溶解，得蓝色溶液。

$$Ni(OH)_2+2NH_4^++4NH_3 \longrightarrow [Ni(NH_3)_6]^{2+}+2H_2O$$

(4) 用浓盐酸处理$Fe(OH)_3$时，棕色沉淀溶解，得黄色溶液。

$$Fe(OH)_3+3HCl \longrightarrow FeCl_3+3H_2O$$

用浓盐酸处理$Co(OH)_3$时，棕褐色$Co(OH)_3$溶解，得粉红色溶液，并有氯气放出。

$$2Co(OH)_3+2Cl^-+6H^++6H_2O \longrightarrow 2[Co(H_2O)_6]^{2+}(\text{粉红})+Cl_2\uparrow$$

浓盐酸过量时，溶液变蓝。

$$[Co(H_2O)_6]^{2+}+4Cl^- \longrightarrow [CoCl_4]^{2-}(\text{蓝})+6H_2O$$

用浓盐酸处理$Ni(OH)_3$时，黑色$Ni(OH)_3$溶解，得绿色溶液并有氯气放出。

$$2Ni(OH)_3+2Cl^-+6H^++6H_2O \longrightarrow 2[Ni(H_2O)_6]^{2+}+Cl_2\uparrow$$

22.47 (1) A—$[Co(H_2O)_6]Cl_2$； B—$H_2[CoCl_4]$； C—$[Co(NH_3)_6]Cl_3$。

(2) A—$[Co(H_2O)_6]^{2+}$，八面体；B—$[CoCl_4]^{2-}$，四面体。

22.48 (1) 取少许粉末加入$MnSO_4$溶液和H_2SO_4，微热，若溶液变红(有MnO_4^-生成)，则粉末为PbO_2。

$$5PbO_2+2Mn^{2+}+5SO_4^{2-}+4H^+ \longrightarrow 2MnO_4^-+5PbSO_4\downarrow+2H_2O$$

(2) 余下二种试剂分别加入浓盐酸，加热后放出Cl_2的是MnO_2粉末。

$$MnO_2+4HCl \xlongequal{\triangle} MnCl_2+Cl_2\uparrow+2H_2O$$

(3) 余下的一种为 Fe_3O_4。

22.49

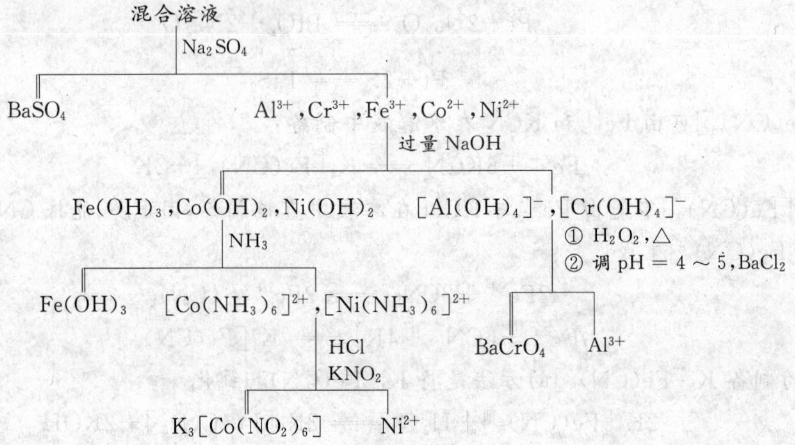

22.50 A—$(NH_4)_2SO_4 \cdot FeSO_4 \cdot 6H_2O$； B—$Fe(OH)_3$； C—$NH_3 \cdot H_2O$； D—$NH_3$； E—$[FeCl_4]^-$； F—$[Fe(SCN)]^{2+}$； G—$Fe^{2+}$； H—$KFe[Fe(CN)_6]$。

22.51 A—$Fe(OH)_2$； B—$Fe(OH)_3$； C—Fe_2O_3； D—$K_3[Fe(C_2O_4)_3] \cdot 3H_2O$； E—$FeCl_3$； F—$Na_2FeO_4$； G—$BaFeO_4$。

22.52 A—$CoCl_2$； B—$[Co(H_2O)_6]^{2+}$； C—$Co(OH)_2$； D—$Co(OH)_3$； E—$[CoCl_4]^{2-}$。

22.53 A—$MnO_4^- + Co^{2+}$； B—$[CoCl_4]^{2-}$， C—Cl_2； D—$Co(OH)_3$； E—MnO_4^{2-}； F—$Mn^{2+} + Co^{2+}$。

22.54 由(1)可知,$CuSO_4$ 和 KI 不可能同时存在。

由(2)可知,存在 $FeCl_3$,$SnCl_2$ 可能存在。蓝色溶液可能是 $[Cu(NH_3)_4]^{2+}$,$[Ni(NH_3)_6]^{2+}$,即 $CuSO_4$ 和 $NiSO_4$ 存在一种或两种。

由(3)可知,加 KSCN 无颜色变化,说明 $FeCl_3$ 与 $SnCl_2$ 共存。加入戊醇也无颜色变化,说明 $CoCl_2$ 肯定不存在。

由(4)可知,加入过量 NaOH 时溶液几乎无色,则肯定不存在 $CuSO_4$[$Cu^{2+} + 4OH^- \xlongequal{} [Cu(OH)_4]^{2-}$ 蓝色]。考虑到(2)的结果,$NiSO_4$ 肯定存在。加盐酸酸化时,有白色沉淀生成,说明存在 $ZnSO_4$,$SnCl_2$ 中的一种或两种[$Fe(OH)_3$ 已滤出]。

$$[Zn(OH)_4]^{2-} + 2H^+ \xlongequal{} Zn(OH)_2 \downarrow + 2H_2O$$

$$[Sn(OH)_4]^{2-} + 2H^+ \xlongequal{} Sn(OH)_2 \downarrow + 2H_2O$$

由(5)可知,混合物中肯定不存在 KI,因 AgI 为黄色沉淀。沉淀溶于氨水,说明沉淀为 AgCl或 Ag_2SO_4。

综合以上分析结果,混合物中肯定存在 $FeCl_3$ 和 $SnCl_2$,$NiSO_4$;肯定不存在 $CuSO_4$,$CoCl_2$ 和 KI;而 $ZnSO_4$ 是否存在还需经进一步实验才能肯定。

22.55 (1) $2MnO_4^- + 5C_2O_4^{2-} + 16H^+ \xlongequal{} 2Mn^{2+} + 5CO_2 + 8H_2O$

$MnO_4^- + 5Fe^{2+} + 8H^+ \xlongequal{} Mn^{2+} + 5Fe^{3+} + 4H_2O$

(2) 设混合物中有 x mol $K_3[Fe(C_2O_4)_3] \cdot 3H_2O$,$y$ mol FeC_2O_4

则有
$$(3x+y)\times 2/5+y\times 1/5=0.05\times 108/1\,000$$
$$(x+y)\times 1/5=0.05\times 20/1\,000$$

解得：$x=0.004$ mol

$y=0.001$ mol

产物组成为 $4K_3[Fe(C_2O_4)_3]\cdot 1FeC_2O_4$。

22.56 A—Fe；B—$FeCl_2$；C—$Fe(OH)_2$；
D—$Fe(OH)_3$；E—Fe_2O_3；F—Fe_3O_4；
G—$FeCl_3$(aq)；H—FeO_4^{2-}；I—$BaFeO_4$。

22.57 A—Fe；B—$CuSO_4$；C—Cu；
D—$FeSO_4+FeCl_2$；E—$CuSO_4$ 溶液；F—SO_2；
G—$Fe(OH)_3$；H—Fe_2O_3。

22.58 由题中给出的实验现象可作出如下判断：

肯定存在： $NaNO_2$； $AgNO_3$； NH_4Cl

肯定不存在：$CuCl_2$， $Ca(OH)_2$

可能存在： NaF， $FeCl_3$

理由如下：

(1) 混合物加水后，可得白色沉淀和无色溶液，说明混合物中不含带颜色的离子 Cu^{2+}，既不存在 $CuCl_2$。

(2) 无色溶液可使 MnO_4^- 褪色，说明混合物中有还原剂存在，即 $NaNO_2$ 存在：

$$5NaNO_2+2MnO_4^-+6H^+ = 2Mn^{2+}+5NaNO_3+3H_2O$$

(3) 加热溶液有气体放出，则混合物中存在 NH_4Cl，$NaNO_2$ 与 NH_4Cl 在一起加热则应有 N_2 生成：

$$NH_4Cl+NaNO_2 = NaCl+2H_2O+N_2\uparrow$$

(4) 加水后有白色沉淀，它又溶于 $NH_3\cdot H_2O$，说明混合物有 $AgNO_3$，与体系中的 NH_4Cl 作用生成 AgCl 沉淀，后溶于 $NH_3\cdot H_2O$：

$$Ag^+ +Cl^- = AgCl\downarrow$$
$$AgCl+2NH_3\cdot H_2O = [Ag(NH_3)_2]^+ +Cl^- +2H_2O$$

(5) 从以上反应中可以看出，溶液中不存在 $Ca(OH)_2$。因为溶液中含有 NH_4^+。若 $Ca(OH)_2$ 存在，则应有 NH_3 生成，实验中无 NH_3 气体生成。

(6) 混合物中可能含有 $FeCl_3$，NaF，但二者必须同时存在。因为若无 NaF 存在，则 $FeCl_3$ 会显颜色，并与 KSCN 作用生成血红色物质。但有 NaF 时 $FeCl_3$ 可能同时存在，它可形成$[FeF_6]^{3-}$ 配离子，无色且不易与 SCN^- 作用。

主要参考书目

[1] 宋天佑,程鹏,王杏乔,等.无机化学.2版.北京:高等教育出版社,2009.

[2] 格林伍德,厄恩肖.元素化学(上册).曹庭礼,王致勇,张弱非,等,译.北京:高等教育出版社,1996.

[3] 格林伍德,厄恩肖.元素化学(中册).李学同,孙玲,单辉,等,译.北京:高等教育出版社,1996.

[4] 格林伍德,厄恩肖.元素化学(下册).王曾隽,张庆芳,林蕴和,等,译.北京:高等教育出版社,1996

[5] 黄孟健,黄炜.无机化学考研攻略.北京:科学出版社,2004.

[6] 严宣申,王长富.普通无机化学.2版.北京:北京大学出版社,1999.

[7] 北京师范大学无机教研室.无机化学.4版.北京:高等教育出版社,2002.

[8] 北京大学化学系普通化学原理教学组.普通化学原理习题解答.北京:北京大学出版社,1996.

[9] 吉林大学,南开大学,广西大学,等.无机化学习题解答.长春:吉林教育出版社,1983.

[10] 杜尧国,马泰儒,王福元,等.无机化学习题集.2版.北京:高等教育出版社,1987.

[11] 黄孟健.无机化学答疑.北京:高等教育出版社,1989.

[12] 彭子莹,陈金兰.无机化学习题集.广州:华南理工大学出版社,1994.

[13] 孙天祥,曹晓峰.无机化学综合练习题及解答.太原:山西科学技术出版社,1993.

[14] 孙德坤,沈文霞,姚天扬,等.物理化学学习指导.北京:高等教育出版社,2007.